BEYOND INCLUSION AND EXCLUSION

BEYOND INCLUSION AND EXCLUSION

Jewish Experiences of the First World War
in Central Europe

Edited by Jason Crouthamel, Michael Geheran,
Tim Grady, and Julia Barbara Köhne

berghahn
NEW YORK • OXFORD
www.berghahnbooks.com

First published in 2019 by
Berghahn Books
www.berghahnbooks.com

© 2019, 2021 Jason Crouthamel, Michael Geheran, Tim Grady, and
Julia Barbara Köhne
First paperback edition published in 2021

All rights reserved. Except for the quotation of short passages
for the purposes of criticism and review, no part of this book
may be reproduced in any form or by any means, electronic or
mechanical, including photocopying, recording, or any information
storage and retrieval system now known or to be invented,
without written permission of the publisher.

Library of Congress Cataloging-in-Publication Data
Names: Crouthamel, Jason, editor. | Geheran, Michael, 1971– editor. | Grady, Tim (Timothy L.), editor. | Köhne, Julia, editor.
Title: Beyond inclusion and exclusion : Jewish experiences of the First World War in Central Europe / edited by Jason Crouthamel, Michael Geheran, Tim Grady, and Julia Barbara Köhne.
Description: First edition. | New York ; Oxford : Berghahn Books, 2019. | Includes bibliographical references and index.
Identifiers: LCCN 2018026306 (print) | LCCN 2018028774 (ebook) | ISBN 9781789200195 (ebook) | ISBN 9781789200188 (hardback : alk. paper)
Subjects: LCSH: World War, 1914-1918--Jews--Europe, Central. | World War, 1914–1918--Participation, Jewish. | Jews--Europe, Central--History--20th century. | World War, 1914-1918--Social aspects--Europe, Central. | Europe, Central--Ethnic relations--History--20th century.
Classification: LCC D639.J4 (ebook) | LCC D639.J4 B49 2019 (print) | DDC 940.3/143089924--dc23
LC record available at https://lccn.loc.gov/2018026306

British Library Cataloguing in Publication Data
A catalogue record for this book is available from the British Library

ISBN 978-1-78920-018-8 hardback
ISBN 978-1-80073-202-5 paperback
ISBN 978-1-78920-019-5 ebook

Contents

List of Figures and Tables   vii
Acknowledgments   x

        Introduction   1
        Jason Crouthamel, Michael Geheran, Tim Grady, and
        Julia Barbara Köhne

Part I. At the Margins: Minorities and the Military

Chapter 1   Hopes and Disappointments: German and French Jews during the Wars of 1870/71 and 1914–18   31
           Christine G. Krüger

Chapter 2   Habsburg Jews and the Imperial Army before and during the First World War   55
           Tamara Scheer

Chapter 3   The "Stepchildren" of the *Kaiserreich*: Alsatians in the German Army during the First World War   79
           Devlin M. Scofield

Part II. Relations: Contested Identities during the First World War

Chapter 4   Rethinking Jewish Front Experiences   111
           Michael Geheran

Chapter 5   "Being German" and "Being Jewish" during the First World War: An Ambivalent Transnational Relationship?   144
           Sarah Panter

Chapter 6   In the Shadow of Antisemitism: Jewish Women and the German Home Front during the First World War   170
           Andrea A. Sinn

Chapter 7	The Social Engagement of Jewish Women in Berlin during the First World War *Sabine Hank*	203
Chapter 8	"My Comrades Are for the Most Part on My Side": Comradeship between Non-Jewish and German Jewish Front Soldiers in the First World War *Jason Crouthamel*	228

Part III. Representation: The Culture of War

Chapter 9	Blind Spots and Jewish Heroines: Refashioning the Galician War Experience in 1920s Hollywood and Berlin *Philipp Stiasny*	257
Chapter 10	Agnon on the German Home Front in *In Mr Lublin's Store*: Hebrew Fiction of the First World War *Glenda Abramson*	286

Part IV. Contested Memories: Working through the Legacies of War

Chapter 11	Paper Psyches: On the Psychography of the Front Soldier According to Paul Plaut *Julia Barbara Köhne*	317
Chapter 12	Narrative Negotiations: Interpreting the Cultural Position of Jews in National(social)ist War Narratives from 1914 to 1945 *Florian Brückner*	362
Afterword	German Jewry and the First World War: Beyond Polemic and Apologetic *Derek Jonathan Penslar*	395

Index		401

Figures and Tables

Figures

2.1	Gravestone at Vienna Central Cemetery, example of Jewish losses in war service. Tamara Scheer, Private Archive.	70
2.2	Gravestone of Egon Goldschmied who fell during war service in officers' rank, Vienna Central Cemetery, Jewish section. Tamara Scheer, Private Archive.	71
3.1	"Beneath his german [sic] suit his heart remains French!"	83
3.2	"Alsatian soldiers recruited by the Germans rush to reach the French lines (14 August 1914)."	88
3.3	"Alsatian Comrades, War Year, 1914."	92
3.4	"War of 1914—Convoy of Alsacian-Lorrans [sic] prisonners [sic] in Gare de Juvisy."	94
7.1	Helene Meyer, painting, ca. 1915, privately owned by Andres Meyer.	205
7.2	Helene Meyer with her sons Walter Gerhard (left) and Kurt, ca. 1909, privately owned by Andres Meyer.	206
7.3	Instructions for use of cooking boxes and cooking bags. Courtesy of Centrum Judaicum Archive.	209
7.4	Concert announcement for a fundraiser, 1915. Courtesy of Centrum Judaicum Archive.	210
7.5	Train station attendant of the Jüdischer Volksverein at work, *Ost und West* 6, no. 7 (July 1906): 483–84.	212
7.6	A bedroom in the Jüdischer Volksverein hostel in Berlin, Auguststraße 20, Kriegsbericht 1914–16, o. O., o. J.	213
7.7	Food distribution in the Jüdischer Volksverein hostel in the exhibition halls at the zoo, Kriegsbericht 1914–16.	215
7.8	Hedwig Ehrenberg, first from the left and sitting, with nurses and the head doctor of the military hospital in the Jewish lodge on Kleiststraße, Berlin, ca. 1915, Jüdisches Museum Berlin, donated by Eva H. Ehrenberg.	217

7.9   Mothers' and children's home of the Frauenverein of the Berlin lodges, U. O. B. B. *Allgemeine Zeitung des Judentums* 79, no. 37 (8 September 1915): 439.   219

9.1   Rahel (Elizza la Porta) and Lieutenant Count Starhemberg (André Mattoni) fall in love but her father, Rabbi Süß (Albert Steinrück), strongly objects. Promotional still for *Leichte Kavallerie* from Deutsches Filminstitut, Frankfurt.   268

9.2   Russian soldiers invade the Jewish quarter in E. A. Dupont's *Zwei Welten*. Promotional still from Deutsches Filminstitut, Frankfurt.   274

11.1   Paul Plaut as a child in sailor jacket, around 1900; Jewish Museum Berlin, donated by Claire Allen.   325

11.2   Plaut in uniform with dagger, farewell postcard to Rudi Cassierer, dated 6 July 1915; Jewish Museum Berlin, donated by Claire Allen.   326

11.3   Plaut's *Militärpaß*; Jewish Museum Berlin, donated by Claire Allen.   327

11.4   Plaut's *Überweisungsnationale*; Jewish Museum Berlin, donated by Claire Allen.   328

11.5   Plaut in uniform with spiked helmet, dated 11 July 1916; Jewish Museum Berlin, donated by Claire Allen.   329

11.6   Group photo of Reserve-Infanterie-Regiment 237 (Plaut: top row, tenth from left), Roulers in Flanders, 1915; Jewish Museum Berlin, donated by Claire Allen.   330

11.7   Photograph of the destroyed school of Langemarck; Jewish Museum Berlin, donated by Claire Allen.   330

11.8   Plaut's copy of *Feldgebetbuch für die jüdischen Mannschaften des Heeres*; Jewish Museum Berlin, donated by Claire Allen.   331

11.9   Plaut's *Ehrenkreuz für Frontkämpfer*; Jewish Museum Berlin, donated by Claire Allen.   332

11.10   Plaut's *Österreichische Kriegserinnerungsmedaille mit den Schwertern*; Jewish Museum Berlin, donated by Claire Allen.   333

11.11   Title *Beihefte zur Zeitschrift für angewandte Psychologie*.   336

11.12   German soldier in the trenches of the First World War, Plaut's possession; Jewish Museum Berlin, donated by Claire Allen.   349

11.13   Memorial stone for the fallen soldiers of the Reserve-Infanterie-Regiment 237; Jewish Museum Berlin, donated by Claire Allen.   350

11.14 Plaut's photography of a destroyed farm with Christian
cemetery crosses in the background. 351

Tables

3.1 Number of Alsace-Lorrainers Killed, Wounded, Missing,
or Taken as Prisoners of War up to 1 January 1915. 86
3.2 Number of Alsace-Lorrainers Killed, Wounded, Missing,
or Taken as Prisoners of War up to June 1916. 86
5.1 Statistics on Jewish Communities in Germany, Austria,
Britain, and the United States. 145

Acknowledgments

This volume is the result of a sustained collaborative effort over several years. The inspiration originally came from a 2015 conference panel on Jewish soldiers during World War I, in which three of this volume's contributors participated. We are grateful to the participants, audience members, and commentator whose critical input inspired us to expand our project beyond German-Jewish soldiers and ex-servicemen, and to consider more broadly the diverse range of experiences of Central European Jewry during the Great War as a whole.

We owe a debt of gratitude to the authors of this volume, whose enthusiasm and abiding commitment to the project carried it over the finish line. Editing a book with authors from across Europe and the United States was a daunting enterprise, but our team of contributors have not only made our task intellectually rewarding, but also an unusually pleasant one.

We are also enormously grateful to our editorial team at Berghahn Books—notably Chris Chappell—for the enthusiasm with which they have seen the book through from conception to publication. Two anonymous reviewers provided critical input and we thank them for their helpful comments. In the end, we could not have hoped for a smoother review and production process.

Introduction

Jason Crouthamel, Michael Geheran, Tim Grady, and
Julia Barbara Köhne

On the eve of the First World War, the German Jewish Marcuse family gave the outward impression of leading a very comfortable middle-class existence. Thirty-eight-year-old Harry Marcuse—a medical doctor by profession—lived with his wife Mimi and two young daughters in Berlin. The start of armed hostilities in August 1914, however, tore their lives asunder. Harry departed for the Eastern Front, where his medical training was urgently needed. Meanwhile, his brother Josef headed in the opposite direction to serve with a cavalry battalion on the Western Front. Alone with two small children, Mimi moved to be near her parents in Teplice, then part of the Austro-Hungarian Empire. There, she managed to squeeze in time to help in a soup kitchen as well as with the Red Cross. Sadly, as it turned out, she was also well-positioned to provide her parents with emotional support. During the first winter of the war, Mimi's brother Paul vanished in the East, presumed captured, though he was never seen again. Another brother, Hans, failed to recover fully from typhoid fever and took his own life in 1917.[1]

The Marcuses' path through the First World War was remarkably varied. Family members were strewn across France, Germany, Austria-Hungary, and Russia, where their daily routines ranged from serving at the front lines, tending the wounded or—in the case of Mimi Marcuse—caring for the family and household. Irrespective of their own wartime role, loss and grief touched all in equal measure, the deaths of the two brothers, Hans and Paul, being most deeply felt. It is the sheer diversity of Jewish wartime experiences, as encapsulated by the Marcuse family, that lies at the very heart of this volume. Its central argument is that historians cannot interpret a singular Jewish war experience solely through the dynamics of antisemitism and Jewish identity, which could be a category of self-designation and self-perception ascribed from "within," or a category ascribed from "outside"—related to religion, heredity, or "race." "Jewishness" and "antisemitism" as such need to be understood as heterogenous, manifold, highly debated, and historically versatile categories. Central European Jewish experiences were diverse, and fragmented along gender, political, geographic, social, and subjective lines. In short, there was no single Jewish experience of the First World War that could be addressed as an empirical, epistemic, or theoretical entity.

The widest divergence surely occurred between those in the military and those at home, but even here the diversity of experience was wide. In total, some 100,000 Jews served in the German military, though of course not all were at the forward lines.[2] Some German Jews ended up in administrative roles, others in medical or garrison-based jobs. While most military-aged Jewish men were drafted into the army, it also needs to be stressed that German Jews served in the Imperial Navy and in the new German air force as well. The number of Jews fighting in the Austro-Hungarian army was much higher, with more than 300,000 men conscripted during the course of the First World War. The Habsburg Empire was also far more amenable to the idea of Jewish officers. By 1900, about 18 percent of the reserve officer corps consisted of Jews. In Germany, by stark contrast, the doors to the officer corps only started to slowly open during the war. Prior to the conflict, no more than a handful of Jewish officers had been commissioned, and these had all been in the Bavarian army.[3]

At home, Jews, whether in the German or the Austro-Hungarian Empire, or in other places in Central Europe, performed a wide variety of wartime roles. Like Mimi Marcuse, many middle-class women volunteered to run soup kitchens or to work at local railway stations, serving passing troop trains with supplies.[4] Elsewhere, Jewish women volunteered as nurses or threw themselves behind patriotic fundraising efforts. In Vienna, for example, middle-class Jewish women collected food and clothing for the thousands of refugees who had fled the fighting in Eastern Europe.[5] Jews also took on a prominent role in helping to shape the war economies of the two empires. Nowhere was this truer than with Walther Rathenau's establishment of the German War Ministry's War Raw Materials Department (Kriegsrohstoffabteilung des preußischen Kriegsministeriums), which coordinated economic planning and the distribution of essential industrial supplies.[6]

In many ways, the First World War should be seen as a history of traveling and journeys. Troops went in one direction, workers in another, while refugees, including large numbers of East European Jews, fled to the relative safety of Germany and Austria-Hungary. Mimi Marcuse herself traveled regularly from Berlin to Teplice during the war. This was not just a case of moving between home and family; it was also a journey between the metropole and the province, and between the German Empire and the Austro-Hungarian Empire. The way people experienced war in each of these settings was always very different. Most significantly, the Austro-Hungarian Empire split more quickly and deeply along regional and ethnic lines. As was the case in Germany, these divisions played out through strikes, protests, and social unrest.[7]

Regardless of the region, death was an all too common part of the conflict. It is estimated that some thirty thousand Jewish soldiers from the Austro-Hungarian army died in the war, while approximately twelve thousand German Jewish soldiers also lost their lives.[8] Mimi Marcuse's two brothers, Paul and Hans, were among this number. Mass death—for this is what it amounted to—may have occurred on the battlefield, but it shaped the lives of those at home too. People had to live with the constant fear that loved ones could be killed or maimed, while the Jewish communities in both Germany and Austria provided what comfort they could with a constant stream of remembrance services and elaborate funerals.[9]

One notable absence from the Marcuses' wartime diaries and memoirs is any mention of antisemitism. The reason why—at first glance—this is so surprising is that, eclipsing the "spirit of August 1914" and the *Burgfrieden* ("peace within the fortress"), in October 1916, the German military issued the infamous "Jew Count," the so-called *Judenzählung*, which was based on the questionnaire "Evidence of the Participation of Jewish Conscripts in the Army" (*Nachweisung der beim Heere befindlichen wehrpflichtigen Juden*) ordered by the Prussian War Ministry. It was a census of Jews serving in the army, based on flawed methods, which implied in effect that Jews had attempted to avoid frontline service.[10] However, while the census and the postwar "stab-in-the-back" myth (*Dolchstoßlegende*) reflected the hatred and prejudice imposed "from above," they did not necessarily dominate the narratives of Jewish soldiers and civilians who had extremely complex experiences and memories of the war. German Jewish experiences on the home and combat fronts were diverse and reflected different perceptions and interpretations of the war. Encounters with antisemitism in the daily interactions with frontline comrades or neighbors at home often made more of an impact than prejudice directed by military and political leaders. Wartime narratives by men and women are filled with anecdotes about positive and negative experiences with gentiles, often confusing feelings of acceptance mixed with anxieties over exclusion in everyday life, rather than reflections on the "Jew Count."

The central point on which this volume pivots, therefore, is less the Jewish census of 1916 and the wider history of Christian-based anti-Judaism or racial antisemitism. Instead, the chapters hinge far more on the exceedingly varied experiences of Jewish men and women during the war. By shifting the focus in this way, the volume broadens the way in which central European Jewish history is understood. Our approach is determinedly interdisciplinary, incorporating research perspectives from history, literature, cultural studies, Jewish studies, film studies, as well as gender studies. Only in this way is it possible to uncover new sites of inquiry and innovative methods that challenge existing assumptions about Jewish perceptions of identity, assimilation, and exclusion in the First World War. This volume addresses the following overlapping questions: How did the First World War impact Central European Jews, including men and women on the combat and home fronts? To what degree were German and Austrian Jewish experiences in the war distinct or universal? Which conclusions did Jewish men and women draw from their wartime experiences? How did they remember the war? To what extent did Jews share these memories with gentiles in a local context, and contextualize their own perceptions of the war? How did Jewish religious, ethnic, national, gender, and other identities intersect with and diverge from mainstream cultural identities?

The bifurcated historical debate over inclusion versus exclusion tends to obscure the complex, nuanced experiences of Jewish men and women who experienced often contradictory encounters that oscillated between signs of integration and acceptance and the perpetuation of negative stereotypes and prejudices. For most ordinary German Jewish men and women, the "Jew Count" was not necessarily a rupture in Jewish/non-Jewish relations. They had already experienced antisemitism before the war and it continued to exist after the "Jew Count." Therefore, the military's census could easily be shelved away as just another example of state-level prejudice. This volume seeks to highlight the complex responses to explicit, subtle, and latent forms of antisemitism as well as the diversity of experiences narrated by men and women in the Great War.

Historiographical Background and Methodologies

While recent scholarship on Jewish experiences in the First World War has emphasized the need for more international comparative approaches, there is still much to explore about the experiences of Central European Jews.[11] In particular, much of the existing narrative on German and Austrian Jews has been shaped by interwar memories of the war experience. Taking into consideration later National Socialist attacks and the Shoah, the existing narrative tends to highlight illusory hopes for integration that were shattered during the First World War. Interestingly, many of the first histories of German Jewish wartime participation to appear after the Second World War came not from Jewish scholars, but from non-Jewish German historians. Local and regional German histories of Jewish life, which gradually started to be published from the early 1960s onwards, often mentioned Jews in the First World War. However, these discussions touched on the war almost as a by-product of wider attempts to uncover the history of lost Jewish communities. In doing so, they tended to idealize particular facets of Jewish life in pre-Nazi Germany while downplaying other factors, such as chronic antisemitism.[12]

In the 1960s and 1970s, the first comprehensive body of scholarship began to emerge, beginning with Egmont Zechlin's work on German Jews and German politics during the First World War, and followed two years later by a collection of essays on German Jews in war and revolution edited by Werner Mosse and Arnold Paucker. Crucially, this volume included seminal contributions by Werner Jochmann, Saul Friedländer, and Eva Reichmann.[13] These histories were written in the context of destruction, as scholars sought to identify antecedents to the genocide of European Jewry put into operation by the Nazis. In general, they portrayed Jews as having been drawn to the liberal political spectrum, and thus in fundamental opposition to German nationalism, a view that continues to dominate histories of German Jewry to this day. In part, this may have been an attempt to explain why the war supposedly led to a hardening of divisions between Jews and non-Jews in German society. Werner Angress's meticulous study of the "Jew Count," followed by Ulrich Dunker's examination of the German Jewish war veterans' organization, the Reichsbund jüdischer Frontsoldaten (RjF), and its efforts to combat antisemitism during the Weimar period, cast further light on the institutionalized prejudice "from above," and the struggle of Jews to be recognized for their military sacrifices after the war.[14] Together, these histories fed the perception that for Jews, antisemitism was the enduring memory of the war and that the "Jew Count" had been the decisive moment when German Jewish relations unraveled.[15] "The *Judenzählung*," as Werner Jochmann concluded, "contributed to a decisive estrangement between Jews and their comrades."[16]

The work of the first generation of German Jewish historians set the foundations onto which others could build. During the late 1970s and into the 1980s, a handful of new histories appeared, but it was only in the 1990s that a second discernible trend in the historiography finally emerged.[17] This body of work placed the "Jew Count" of 1916 at the very center.[18] Studies by Peter Pulzer, Clemens Picht, and Christhard Hoffmann, to name a few, charted a trajectory of the First World War that began with Jewish enthusiasm in 1914, as Jews, along with other Germans, celebrated the war in the belief that it would obliterate antisemitic stereotypes and level any remaining barriers to social equality.[19] Despite volunteering to fight at the front lines in large numbers, it was argued, Jewish hopes for social acceptance ended disastrously amid increasing antisemitism, culminating in the military's census of October 1916. Further studies by Michael Brenner and Paul Mendes-Flohr on the history of German Jewry during the Weimar Republic similarly portrayed the First World War as having led to an irreparable rift between Jews and other Germans, and that these shattered hopes led to a strengthening of Jewish identity and intensified Jewish solidarity.[20]

As Derek Penslar has argued, however, much of the scholarship driving this interpretation is predicated on the contemporary writings of Jewish thinkers, activists, and prominent critics of assimilation, such as those of Reinhold Lewin and Ernst Simon.[21] Both men claimed afterwards that the "front experience" had been an alienating one for Jews, and that relationships between Jewish and Christian soldiers had been stifled by endemic antisemitism.[22] Another frequently quoted source in this narrative is the diary of Julius Marx, a Jewish officer who kept a meticulous journal describing his repeated confrontations with anti-Jewish prejudice at the front.[23] The diary's re-publication in 1964 strongly influenced another generation of scholarly work in this field, and is commonly cited as evidence of Jewish disillusionment during the war.[24] Nonetheless, much historical writing on the First World War continues to adhere rigidly to the original arguments of Lewin, Simon, and Marx. Without subjecting these sources to rigorous analysis, however, the well-worn narrative of Jewish exclusion established after 1918 is only sustained.[25]

While examples of antisemitism accurately reflected hatred and institutional prejudice imposed "from above," they did not necessarily dominate the narratives of ordinary men and women on the home front and those of the fighting troops in the field, who had much more complex experiences and memories of the war. Perhaps the most serious methodological problem in this corpus of literature is the tendency to view Jewish soldiers through the same analytical lens as civilians or the mainstream Jewish press.[26] To be sure, antisemitism drew considerable attention in Jewish newspapers, and it provoked fierce debates among Jewish writers and thinkers, as well as from religious and community leaders in Germany. But analyses of letters and diaries from the field, insofar as they had passed the random checks by military censorship (*Militärzensurkommissionen*), have provided little evidence that Jewish/non-Jewish relations at the front lines were in "crisis."[27]

In the last decade, scholars have searched for a more nuanced view of the First World War that moves beyond the assumption of permanent and omnipresent antisemitism. Greg Caplan, analyzing the writings of Jewish fraternity students during the war, concluded that the trauma of mass death and the horrors of trench warfare, not antisemitism, shaped the shared wartime experiences of both Jews and non-Jews involved in the fighting. These findings were supported by Ulrich Sieg's study of Jewish intellectuals during the war, which concurred that antisemitism was not the driving force between Jews and non-Jews in the front lines, as Jewish soldiers reacted to the "Jew Count" in often strikingly different ways than their civilian counterparts.[28] These studies have added considerable depth to this previously under-researched aspect of Jewish history, and challenged explanatory approaches focused on the "Jew Count" and narratives of Jewish disillusionment during the war.

Recent research has shown that particular aspects of Jewish military history during the First World War were integrated into a broader context of German history.[29] Tim Grady's work on the contested memory of Jewish war experiences argued that relations between Jews and other Germans did not end abruptly after 1918, but instead persisted throughout the Weimar era, even into the early years of the Third Reich.[30] Through the rubric of remembrance of the German Jewish war dead, Grady throws light on how Jews and other Germans created a shared memory culture of the First World War, which endured well beyond 1918. The agents of remembrance—memorial construction, local rituals of mourning and commemoration, and conservative narratives of national sacrifice—functioned as mechanisms of inclusion, ensuring that Jews remained actively engaged in Germany's interwar memory culture. David Fine in his monograph on Jews' integration in the German army went even further. He argued that levels of discrimination experienced by Jewish soldiers in the German military had in fact been overstated. Fine maintained that Jewish soldiers rarely mentioned antisemitism in their writings, nor were Jews denied promotions or battlefield decorations that their gentile counterparts received, a claim backed up by official statistics.[31] While Fine offered a welcome corrective to earlier studies that had solely focused on the development of antisemitism, there can be no denying that anti-Jewish discrimination was an unsavory feature of the war.

Over the last few years, a number of transnational histories have used comparative approaches to draw out the finer nuances of the German Jewish war experience. Works by Derek Penslar and Sarah Panter, as well as a collection of essays connected to an exhibition at the Jewish Museum in Munich, have led the field in this regard.[32] These studies attempt to integrate particular aspects of Jewish life into a wider German history of the First World War. Penslar's and Panter's books are emblematic of a recent trend in the scholarship, which sees antisemitism as crucial but not in all cases as the main aspect of the Central European Jewish war experience. These authors do not downplay the persistence of antisemitism in the German military: for many Jewish soldiers it was a feature of everyday life. But it did not lead to a breakdown in relations at the front, and there is little evidence that it irrevocably damaged Jewish morale or lessened their faith in the German cause. Over the last five years alone, the field has moved from a post-Mosse consensus on the "road to the final solution" to a more fragmented view, with many historians considering the 1914–18 experiences within their contemporary framework, rather than solely in hindsight from 1933.

Despite trends in recent scholarship, there are persisting debates about the significance of antisemitism in the context of a revaluation of German Jewish relationships during the First World War. Many historians continue to uphold older narratives, maintaining that antisemitism was the defining Jewish experience of the First World War. The premise of Jacob Rosenthal's detailed, well-received study of the "Jew Count" of 1916 and its consequences in the postwar years follows the trajectory of older studies, which hold that German Jewish relations both during and after the war were undermined by antisemitism. The war is depicted as an end point, the "crisis of the German Jewish symbiosis," as Rosenthal put it, in a long trajectory of failed integration.[34] Brian Crim's work on antisemitism in the German military community provides important insights into the RjF's campaign against antisemitism in Weimar Germany, and its tenuous relations with nationalist veterans' organizations. Yet it especially focuses on Jewish exclusion, embracing the notion that Jewish soldiers returned from the front lines in 1918 demoralized by the endemic antisemitism they encountered in the trenches.[35]

With the centenary of the First World War still reverberating, it is surely time to take stock of the historiographical eras discussed here and to move to a further stage. With this thought in mind, this volume emphasizes the diversity and complexity of Jewish war experiences in Central Europe as well as the multifaceted forms of antisemitism and responses to it. Relationships between Jews and gentiles, encounters with antisemitism, and memories of the war were complex. As Jay Winter reminds us, the diverse and often contradictory narratives of individuals who experienced "total war" elude categorization into collective memory paradigms.[36] Taken as single voices, they provide a much more subtle way of understanding history than the orchestral piece of grand history narratives. To uncover the varieties of Jewish experiences, this volume explores diverse narratives in their respective medial forms, including literature and film. This diversity of experience includes the erosion of fixed gender roles and the ensuing critique of the binary two-sex-model in European societies and academic reflections (e.g., in philosophy, sexology, criminology) around 1900.[37]

The impact of the war on conceptions of "masculinity" and "femininity" highlights the degree to which Jewish experiences converged and diverged with mainstream culture. Fulfilling prevailing gender ideals on the combat and home fronts reinforced Jewish men and women's conceptions of themselves as integrated and accepted members of society. On the one hand, German Jewish frontline soldiers, for example, saw "comradeship" as a universal masculine ideal. Just as gentile and Jewish men shared the traumatic experience of the trenches, they also shared ideals of manliness and comradeship that were fundamental to national identity.[38] The ideal of "hard" militarized masculinity that was ubiquitous in popular culture also had a "softer" side, as soldiers provided each other with emotional and psychological support in the traumatic environment of the front.[39] Despite a widespread "crisis in masculinity" in the face of industrialized violence, the image of the "good comrade," who provided friendship and love for their fellow front fighters, gave many men, including minorities who might have been considered social outsiders, the opportunity to assimilate into a male cultural ideal.[40]

Despite the antisemitic stereotypes that circulated on the home front and among military elites during the war, Jewish soldiers often felt a sense of "Germanness" in the front lines through their performance of manly ideals. The essentialist, racialized notion of comradeship and the "front community" later sanctified by the Nazis did not necessarily reflect the more inclusive notions of comradeship and masculinity embraced by not only German Jewish frontline fighters, but even gentile soldiers in 1914–18.[41] As historian Brian Feltman has demonstrated, even if the rise of National Socialism after 1933 caused German Jewish veterans to later revaluate their memories of the war, the experience of "comradeship" made them feel that at least between 1914 and 1918 they had been to some degree accepted.[42] In addition to pressuring men to conform to male gender ideals, the First World War can be seen as a test field for twisted gender roles and the transgression of traditional notions of "manliness" and "femaleness." This was not only due to the multiple role reversals in home front societies (at least as long as the war lasted), in which women with regard to their profession slipped into typical male roles,[43] but it is also the case for the phenomenon of cross-dressing within theatrical performances in the trenches and internment camps of the First World War, which occurred on all sides of the front.[44] The soldierly "prima donna" or "diva" of the front theatre—men taking on female roles in an illusionary sphere—were experimental figures providing alternative gender roles that undermined the dominant ideal of the steely combatant. As such they sent out ambiguous erotic signals, not necessarily with a homosexual undertone, substituting the absent "female element" in war and often reminding the soldiers and officers watching of their loved ones at home. These complex gender plays were common features in times of war. They simultaneously contradicted homogenous notions of virility and militarized masculinity and also reproduced hegemonic displays of gender.[45]

Though historians have placed greater attention on the experiences of German Jewish men in the war, Jewish women also felt greater acceptance through their performance of mainstream gender ideals.[46] Similar to men, women's experiences were much more diverse than previous scholarship would suggest, as diaries and letters by women on the home front reveal the ways in which, despite antisemitism, Jewish women, like their gentile counterparts, found new opportunities and spheres for exerting influence and agency while separated from husbands and fathers.[47] Similar to men, Jewish women were not simply objects of antisemitism. Women's particular experiences demonstrate the degree to which Jewish war experiences were gendered, as women's experiences, revealed through their letters and diaries, differed from men's. At the same time, though serving in a different sphere on the home front, women, like their male counterparts, also felt acceptance through their performance of wartime duties. Supporting their husbands, fathers, and sons, women experienced a sense of belonging as they contributed to the nation in its moment of crisis under the strains of total war.

This volume also contributes to recent scholarship that uses diverse media forms and regards them as comprehensive and valuable scientific sources in historical research. The idea that historical knowledge is always transmitted in the specific shape of a distinct medium gives some space for the "credo" that the mediality of a concrete historical source—its media-specific constitution—needs to be looked at more closely. Thus, medial forms—for example films—which, in the past, have not always been identified as fruitful sources for historiographical reconstructions and the epistemic revaluation of a particular discourse formation, need to be integrated into the broader dynamic of academic knowledge production. For this reason, this volume explores diverse medial narratives, including traditional research objects, written sources like journals, newspaper articles, and monographs, in addition to rather underexplored sites like ego-documents (diary entries, letters from the front, war memoirs) as well as fictional literature, photographs, and motion picture imagery after 1918. Feature films produced in the aftermath of the First World War in particular turn out to be a potent storage medium that communicates personal, psychological, as well as cultural and scientific knowledge,[48] referring to problems such as the defeated nation, the horrific effects of mass destruction, traumatic wounds and other mental injuries, dysfunctional postwar relationships, disrupted family values, and fragile gender identities in postwar societies, in a more or less disguised manner.[49] For example, Robert Reinert's 1919 *Nerven*, a black and white silent feature film that has just been restored by the Munich Film Museum, conveys not only a vivid picture of the "shattered nerves" and "twisted minds" of post-World War I conditions in political and social realms on an individual as well as a collective level; it also debates essential themes of contemporary scientific discourses including neuropsychiatry, psychoanalysis, psychopathology, mass psychology, and sexology, and it reflects on the 1918/19 revolution and the realm of contemporary political symbolism. Many of these fields, at this time, were dominated by renowned European Jewish scientists and researchers like Sigmund Freud, Hermann Oppenheim, and Magnus Hirschfeld[50]—to name just a few. Although European film cultures emerge as an important cultural player that highlight civilian populations' diverse war experiences, they remain relatively silent, with a few exceptions that are addressed in this volume, concerning explicit representations of Jewish war experiences. Nevertheless, this cultural void, gap, or silence in the postwar era points to psychological forces that apparently needed to be suppressed for some time after the war but left their mark in their own way, generating unique iconographies and aesthetics of cultural catastrophe.

Organization and Major Themes

The chapters in this volume focus on four interconnected themes, including the larger comparative context of minorities in the imperial German military, various forms of antisemitism in interrelations between Jews and gentiles, the cultural effects of the war on Jews through narrative and visual representation, and memories of war experiences. Part I examines the experiences of German Jews in the imperial army before and during the Great War. This section posits that German and Austrian Jewish experiences must be understood in the context of experiences of other minorities to uncover how they were perceived and how they perceived themselves in religious, ethnic, and nationalist terms. Part II analyzes antisemitism, Jewish-Christian relations, and identity formation during the war. This section concentrates on the experiences of "ordinary" German Jewish men and women who experienced war on the home and combat fronts. Utilizing letters, diaries, and memoirs, it complicates existing narratives about the effects of the "Jew Count" and state-sponsored antisemitism. Incorporating gender as a category of analysis, Part II also explores the ways in which men and women exerted agency in defining themselves as active members of front communities, and how these experiences convinced them that they were accepted into mainstream culture.

Cultural representations of the war in previously underexamined layers of literary and cinematic sources are the focus of Part III. Moving away from strictly soldiers' narratives of the war experience, this section sheds light on how German Jews in diverse communities imagined and narrated the effects of the war. This includes analysis of not only how the war affected Jewish life, but also how the lens of Jewish culture shaped perceptions of the war. Part IV builds on this with analysis of contested memories of the war. In addition to analyzing war remembrance through Jewish literature, this section also offers innovative approaches to how survivors defined and remembered the psychological and emotional effects of war trauma. Contributors place these memories within the context of both Jewish culture and the broader trends in political, medical, and cultural memory production.

Central European Jewish experiences in the First World War need to be analyzed in a broader international and comparative context.

To what degree were the experiences and treatment of German and Austrian Jews in the Great War similar or dissimilar to the experiences of minorities in different nations and chronological contexts? This is a question addressed by Christine Krüger in Chapter 1, who compares the experiences of German and French Jews in the 1870/71 war and in 1914–18. Compared to French Jews, Krüger argues, German Jews felt a greater sense of ambivalence about their participation in the Franco-Prussian War and the First World War. In France, a notion of citizenship based on voluntarism predominated, in contrast to an ethno-cultural conception of Jewish identity that governed the social and legal status of German Jews. These differences in defining the status of Jews would play an essential role in shaping Jewish war experiences.

This volume further expands this comparative national context by examining the experiences of Jewish soldiers in the Habsburg army during the Great War. As a multicultural, multiethnic force, consisting of Austrians, Hungarians, Czechs, and other groups, the Habsburg army offers a fascinating case study of how Jews, who served on all fronts and in diverse capacities, were perceived and perceived themselves.[51] The Habsburg army classified its soldiers by nationality rather than ethnicity, so Jewish soldiers were never given any official designation. Yet in her analysis of the everyday experiences of Jewish soldiers in Chapter 2, Tamara Scheer demonstrates that despite the lack of official recognition, soldiers were still unofficially recognized as Jewish. Especially as the war effort deteriorated, both the military and civilians blamed Jews, laying the groundwork for an imposed antisemitic stereotype that permeated culture on the home and combat fronts. Scheer emphasizes that this external identity formation of Jews as "scapegoats" shaped how "Jewishness" was understood in the Habsburg Empire.

In addition to comparative international contexts, this first section of the volume also compares the experiences of German Jews to other minorities within the German army. To what degree did prejudices against German Jews mirror prejudices against other groups? Devlin Scofield addresses this question in Chapter 3 by illuminating the experiences of Alsatian soldiers in the imperial army. He argues that German Alsatians' war experiences were very similar to those of German Jews, as both faced increased surveillance, exclusion from certain duties, and restrictions on leave, despite data collected by officials that proved pro-French sympathies among Alsatians were exaggerated. Scofield focuses on letters by Alsatian-German soldiers to reconstruct their attempts to prove their national loyalty. The experience of being treated as second class disillusioned otherwise loyal Alsatian-German soldiers in a way similar to the growing disillusionment felt by many German Jews who were treated as "outsiders" in their own nation.

The second section of the book shifts focus to the experiences of German Jewish men and women on the combat and home fronts. Their encounters with antisemitism, responses to war trauma, and feelings of belonging and "comradeship" reveal complex boundaries between exclusion and acceptance. In Chapter 4, Michael Geheran challenges the notion that Jewish experiences can be reduced to a singular Jewish *Kriegserlebnis* (wartime experience) by examining and contrasting the frontline experiences of acculturated, Zionist, and orthodox Jewish soldiers during the First World War. Geheran uses diaries, letters, and other contemporary primary sources by Jewish soldiers to argue that while antisemitism affected Jewish soldiers in their everyday relations with Christian comrades, these groups responded to it in often dramatically different ways. Geheran's chapter is important because, unlike prevailing scholarship, which has analyzed Jewish experiences primarily through the lens of acculturated Jewry, Jewish soldiers' cultural and religious identity—specifically whether they regarded themselves as "Germans of Jewish faith" or primarily as Jews—was crucial in shaping not only their expectations and perceptions during the war, but also how they remembered it afterwards. It governed why they fought, how they perceived and reacted to antisemitism, and it also influenced how they related to their gentile fellow soldiers, without which their memory of the First World War cannot be understood.

The ambivalent relationship between "being German" and "being Jewish" can also be examined in the transnational context beyond the trench experience. In Chapter 5, Sarah Panter compares the ambivalent relationship between "being German" and "being Jewish" to the experiences of German minorities in other parts of the world, including Britain and the United States. She identifies a number of similarities regarding classification of Jewish citizens and immigrants as "aliens" or "enemies."[52] Panter explores how "Jewishness" and "Germanness" were interpreted as compatible markers of their multiple and situational identities.[53] Paradoxically, where Jews in German-speaking countries had to fight for acceptance and inclusion into the German nation, Jews in English-speaking countries were stigmatized as "German" under the formula that "Jewishness" equaled "Germanness." Panter reveals just how fluid meanings of "Jewish" and "German" really were from different relational and cultural contexts, as Jews were ascribed multiple cultural identities.

Home front experiences of women are the focal point of Chapters 6 and 7. Andrea Sinn and Sabine Hank show that in contrast to much of the existing scholarship that often constructs German Jews as objects of antisemitism, a much more diverse picture of Jewish experiences and agency emerges through the lens of women's experiences. Sinn finds in Chapter 6 that despite continued antisemitism, the war created new opportunities for Jewish integration. Similar to Geheran, she utilizes letters, diaries, and other wartime sources from archives to offer new perspectives on the interplay of gender, politics, and war. In particular, she demonstrates that the infamous "Jew Count" was largely a gendered event that did not resonate in women's wartime autobiographical writings. In Chapter 7, Hank highlights the experiences of women who occupied positions of status and relative power in war relief organizations, where they played an influential role in welfare, education, and health care programs. As these programs expanded exponentially in the context of total war, so too did women's status as they volunteered in advisory positions in the Jewish community's efforts to contribute to the nation's victory.

In Chapter 8, Jason Crouthamel continues the volume's concentration on wartime letters and diaries to analyze gentile and Jewish soldiers' ideals of "comradeship" in the war.[54] This universal experience, Crouthamel argues, fueled German Jewish soldiers' sense of optimism about integration, which was rooted in a complex interchange between how they perceived themselves and how they were perceived by comrades. Like the chapters by Geheran and Sinn, Crouthamel's chapter complicates the history of antisemitism by showing that the "Jew Count" had little bearing on everyday life at the front. To illustrate the complex front experience for Jewish men, Crouthamel compares letters and diaries of Jewish soldiers to those of their gentile comrades, which reveal a wide range of philosemitic and antisemitic sentiments, suggesting that German Jewish soldiers' optimism about being accepted as "good comrades" was not entirely illusory.

Representations of the war experience in letters, diaries, and memoirs are only one dimension of narratives on the war experience. The war had a profound impact on virtually all layers of cultural production, including literature and cinema.[55] In the aftermath of mass violence, films became a site for debates over national memory, the meaning of loss, and competing interpretations of the war experience.[56] While some of the most familiar interwar films, like *Westfront 1918: Vier von der Infanterie* (*Western Front 1918*) and *All Quiet on the Western Front* (both 1930), illustrate the brutalizing effects of the front experience on soldiers, cinema also reflected the traumatic consequences of occupation and mass expulsion, including mass migrations of Jewish communities. Many of these relatively unknown films are lost, but remarkably, some rare examples of cinematic representations of Jewish civilians survive in archives. These are uncovered in Chapter 9 by Philipp Stiasny, who expands our focus to include the experiences of Eastern European Jewish civilians. Exploring feature films from the 1920s that deal with the Jewish population in Galicia, Stiasny poses several interrelated questions: What kinds of stories were told? How have these films been received by the public? How do they relate to other films about the war? He argues that these films gave space and voice to the perspective of civilians, in particular the Jewish population, engulfed in war. Thus, this chapter reveals another layer of Jewish voices in representing the effects of the war, as well as perceptions of that population through the relatively new medium of cinema.

Literary representations of Jewish war experiences are also underutilized by historians, yet these sources yield an important glimpse into the effects of the war on soldiers and civilian Jewish communities. In Chapter 10, Glenda Abramson dissects the boundaries between historical truth and fiction in her analysis of novels by Shmuel Yosef Agnon that deal with the social and psychological impact of the war. Abramson argues that in his reflections on the impact of the war on the home front in Leipzig, Agnon combines autobiography and imaginative constructions of memory, providing a kind of valediction of the old world of Jewish culture destroyed by the war. Exploring how these narratives fuse fiction with historical reality, Abramson sheds light on how the memory of the war was constructed through the lens of Jewish identity.

Some of the most important recent scholarship on the impact of the Great War has focused on the psychological dimensions of the modern war experience. Expanding our knowledge of the brutalizing effects of the war, historians have explored complex everyday coping mechanisms and emotional responses to violence.[57] The multifaceted psychological effects of the war also shook mental medicine and its capacity for diagnosing and treating "war neurosis."[58] In Chapter 11, Julia Barbara Köhne reveals the crucial role played by German Jewish scholars in studying the effects of the war on the psyches of front veterans.[59] She analyzes the illuminating case study of Paul Plaut, a Jewish front veteran and psychologist who investigated the effects of the war on the "soul of soldiers," including their emotional, religious, and psycho-sexual responses to the trench experience. Plaut's work was part of the military's larger aim to rationalize and economize the combat readiness of front soldiers.[60] At the same time, Köhne reveals that Plaut's 1920 work "Psychographie des Kriegers" ("Psychography of the Warrior") was exceptional in revealing the fragile inner life of soldiers with extraordinary frankness. Köhne's chapter thus puts Plaut's work in two overlapping contexts: both as an example of a German Jewish soldier's particular encounter with the psycho-traumatic effects of war and his intellectual sensitization for them, and as an example of an experimental psychologist who tried to transform the impact of mass violence and its preconditions into scientific knowledge.

Jewish survivors confronted and expressed their memories of the war through diverse media. On one hand, German Jewish memory construction can be placed in the larger context of interwar political fragmentation over the meaning of the war experience.[61] As many of the chapters in this volume attest, German Jews largely saw their own experiences as intertwined with broader experiences of "comradeship," nationalism, traumatic memory, and other social-psychological effects of war. At the same time, the war experiences of German Jews were treated as a separate sphere, distinct and excluded from the mainstream narratives that constructed "front communities" and "national communities." This is explored with new insight in Chapter 12 by Florian Brückner, who analyzes the place of Jews in the political debates over the war, with a focus on one of the most popular sites of memory construction, the war novel. War fiction provides an ideal site for analyzing how Jews were perceived within the larger narrative of a unified "front community" (*Frontgemeinschaft*), which later became the basis for the National Socialist conception of the "national community" (*Volksgemeinschaft*).[62] Brückner analyzes some of the most popular interwar right-wing nationalist literature to assess how Jews were portrayed and how Jews received these works. He argues that during the Weimar era, the war novel actually afforded German Jews an avenue to integrate themselves into the conservative-nationalist narrative of the "front community," and that it was not until the Nazis came to power in 1933 that literary depictions of the war experience became increasingly infused with antisemitic stereotypes. Thus, Brückner's chapter reveals how the memory of the trenches was not static, but an ever-evolving narrative from inclusive to more exclusive treatment of minorities who shared the "front experience." For the "coda" to the volume we invited Derek Penslar to share perspectives on the field, as his book *Jews and the Military: A History* influenced the approaches of many contributors to this study. Penslar points to key issues and new methodologies that still need to be explored, and he reflects on changing developments in the history of German Jewish men and women in the First World War.

Jason Crouthamel is a professor at Grand Valley State University in Michigan. He is the author of *An Intimate History of the Front: Masculinity, Sexuality and German Soldiers in the First World War* (Palgrave Macmillan, 2014) and *The Great War and German Memory: Society, Politics and Psychological Trauma, 1914–1945* (Liverpool University Press, 2009), and he co-edited, with Peter Leese, *Psychological Trauma and the Legacies of the First World War* and *Traumatic Memories of World War Two and After* (Palgrave Macmillan, 2016). He is completing a monograph titled *Trauma, Religion and Spirituality in Germany during the First World War*.

Michael Geheran is a Postdoctoral Fellow at the Center for Holocaust and Genocide Studies at the United States Military Academy. He is a graduate of Norwich University, Harvard University, and Clark University, where he earned his Ph.D. in 2016. He is currently working on a book based on his doctoral research, which examines the experiences of German Jewish First World War veterans during the Holocaust.

Tim Grady is a reader in modern history at the University of Chester and author of *A Deadly Legacy: German Jews and the Great War* (Yale University Press, 2017) and *The German-Jewish Soldiers of the First World War in History and Memory* (Liverpool University Press, 2011).

Julia Barbara Köhne is a visiting professor at the Institute for the History and Theory of Culture at Humboldt-Universität Berlin. Her publications include *Kriegshysteriker: Strategische Bilder und mediale Techniken militärpsychiatrischen Wissens, 1914–1920* (Matthiesen, 2009) and *Geniekult in Geisteswissenschaften und Literaturen um 1900 und seine filmischen Adaptionen* (Böhlau, 2014). Her current research project is titled "Trauma Translations: Stagings and Imaginations in Film and Theory."

Notes

1. Barbara Reisner, ed., *Kriegsbriefe 1914–1918: Dr. Harry & Mimi Marcuse* (London, 2013).
2. Tim Grady, *The German-Jewish Soldiers of the First World War in History and Memory* (Liverpool, 2011), 27.
3. Derek Penslar, *Jews and the Military: A History* (Princeton, 2013), 89–92. At the same time, some German Jewish men who converted to Christianity

had a better chance of being promoted into the officer corps, though discrimination persisted.
4. In general, see Adrian Gregory, "Railway Stations: Gateways and Termini," in *Capital Cities at War: Paris, London, Berlin 1914–1919*, vol. 2, *A Cultural History*, ed. Jay Winter and Jean-Louis Robert (Cambridge, 2007), 23–56.
5. Marsha Rozenblit, *Reconstructing a National Identity: The Jews of Habsburg Austria during World War I* (Oxford, 2001), 71.
6. Shulamit Volkov, *Walther Rathenau: Weimar's Fallen Statesman* (New Haven, 2012), 122–23; Christian Schölzel, *Walther Rathenau: Eine Biographie* (Paderborn, 2006), 176–79.
7. Alexander Watson, *Ring of Steel: Germany and Austria-Hungary at War, 1914–1918* (London, 2014), 368–74.
8. Erwin Schmidl, *Habsburgs jüdische Soldaten 1788–1918* (Vienna, 2014), 115.
9. Grady, *The German-Jewish Soldiers of the First World War*.
10. See Werner T. Angress, "The German Army's 'Judenzählung' of 1916: Genesis-Consequences-Significance," *Leo Baeck Institute Yearbook* 23 (1978): 117–37; see also Michael Geheran, "Judenzählung (Jewish Census)," in *1914–1918 Online: International Encyclopedia of the First World War*, ed. Ute Daniel et al. (Berlin, 2015), DOI: 10.15463/ie1418.10684.
11. Some of the leading influential scholarship on national and religious identities of Central European Jews in World War I includes Rozenblit, *Reconstructing a National Identity*; David Rechter, *The Jews of Vienna and the First World War* (Oxford, 2008). On prewar tensions between German/Austrian and Jewish identity, seminal works include Jehuda Reinharz, *Fatherland or Promised Land: The Dilemma of the German Jew, 1893–1914* (Ann Arbor, 1975); Marsha Rozenblit, *The Jews of Vienna, 1867–1914: Assimilation and Identity* (New York, 1984); Marsha Rozenblit and Jonathan Karp, eds., *World War I and the Jews: Conflict and Transformation in Europe, the Middle East, and America* (Oxford, 2017).
12. See, for example, Hans Franke, *Geschichte und Schicksal der Juden in Heilbronn vom Mittelalter bis zur Zeit der nationalsozialistischen Verfolgung 1050–1945* (Heilbronn, 1963).
13. Egmont Zechlin, *Die deutsche Politik und die Juden im Ersten Weltkrieg* (Göttingen, 1969); Werner E. Mosse and Arnold Paucker, eds., *Judentum in Krieg und Revolution 1916–1923* (Tübingen, 1971).
14. Angress, "The German Army's 'Judenzählung' of 1916," 117–37 (this is a translation of the original German-language version, which appeared in 1976); Ulrich Dunker, *Der Reichsbund jüdischer Frontsoldaten, 1919–1938: Geschichte eines jüdischen Abwehrvereins* (Düsseldorf, 1977).
15. George Mosse, *The Jews and the German War Experience, 1914–1918* (New York, 1977).
16. Werner Jochmann, "Ausbreitung des Antisemitismus," in Mosse and Paucker, *Judentum in Krieg und Revolution*, 426.
17. See, for example, Rolf Vogel, *Ein Stück von uns: Deutsche Juden in deutschen Armeen 1813–1976. Eine Dokumentation* (Mainz, 1977); and Militärgeschichtliches Forschungsamt, ed., *Deutsche jüdische Soldaten 1914–1945* (Freiburg, 1982).

18. This narrative has persisted in the major scholarship on Jewish service during the First World War. See Michael Brenner, "The German Army Orders a Census of Jewish Soldiers, and Jews Defend German Culture," in *Yale Companion to Jewish Writing and Thought in German Culture, 1096–1996*, ed. Sander L. Gilman and Jack Zipes (New Haven, 1996), 348–54.
19. Peter Pulzer, *Jews and the German State: The Political History of a Minority, 1848–1933* (Oxford, 1992); Clemens Picht, "Zwischen Vaterland und Volk: Das deutsche Judentum im Ersten Weltkrieg," in *Der Erste Weltkrieg: Wirkung, Wahrnehmung, Analyse*, ed. Wolfgang Michalka (Munich, 1994), 736–55; Christhard Hoffmann, "Between Integration and Rejection: The Jewish Community in Germany, 1914–1918," in *State, Society, and Mobilization in Europe during the First World War*, ed. John Horne (Cambridge, 1997), 89–104.
20. Michael Brenner, *The Renaissance of Jewish Culture in Weimar Germany* (New Haven, 1996); Paul Mendes-Flohr, "The *Kriegserlebnis* and Jewish Consciousness," in *Jüdisches Leben in der Weimarer Republik*, ed. Wolfgang Benz (Tübingen, 1998), 225–38.
21. Derek Penslar, "The German-Jewish Soldier: From Participant to Victim," *German History* 29 (2011): 445–69.
22. Reinhold Lewin, "Der Krieg als jüdisches Erlebnis," *Monatsschrift für die Geschichte und Wissenschaft des Judentums* 63 (1917): 1–14; Ernst Simon, "Unser Kriegserlebnis (1919)," in *Brücken: Gesammelte Aufsätze*, ed. Ernst Simon (Heidelberg, 1965), 17–23.
23. Julius Marx, *Kriegstagebuch eines Juden* (Frankfurt, 1964). Surprisingly, scholarship on German Jewry during the First World War has generally ignored the published diary of Herbert Sulzbach, which provides an interesting counterpoint to Marx. See Herbert A. Sulzbach, *Zwischen zwei Mauern: 50 Monate Westfront 1914–1918* (Berg am See, 1986); English translation: *With the German Guns: Four Years on the Western Front, 1914–1918* (London, 1973).
24. For a contemporary analysis of the diary and its impact on scholarship at that time, see Walther Huder, "Kriegs-Tagebuch eines Juden: Ein Beitrag zur Geschichte des deutschen Judentums," *Bulletin des Leo Baeck Instituts* 8 (1965): 240–49.
25. Recent proponents of this interpretation include Martina Steer, "Nation, Religion, Gender: The Triple Challenge of Middle-Class German-Jewish Women in World War I," *Central European History* 48 (2015): 176–98; Anna Ulrich, "'Nun sind wir gezeichnet': Jüdische Soldaten und die 'Judenzählung' im Ersten Weltkrieg," in *Krieg! Juden zwischen den Fronten 1914–1918*, ed. Ulrike Heikaus and Julia B. Köhne (Berlin, 2014), 215–38; Peter C. Appelbaum, *Loyalty Betrayed: Jewish Chaplains in the German Army during the First World War* (London, 2014); Michael Berger, "Erster Weltkrieg: 'Sie fielen fürs Vaterland!'" in *Jüdische Soldaten-Jüdischer Widerstand in Deutschland und Frankreich*, ed. Michael Berger and Gideon Römer-Hillebrecht (Paderborn, 2012), 89–111; and Jacob Rosenthal, *"Die Ehre des jüdischen Soldaten": Die Judenzählung im Ersten Weltkrieg und ihre Folgen* (Frankfurt, 2007).

26. See further Penslar, "The German-Jewish Soldier."
27. See, for example, Brenner, *The Renaissance of Jewish Culture*; Paul Mendes-Flohr, *German Jews: A Dual Identity* (New Haven, 1999); and Till van Rahden, *Jews and Other Germans: Civil Society, Religious Diversity, and Urban Politics in Breslau, 1860–1925* (Madison, 2008).
28. Gregory A. Caplan, "Wicked Sons, German Heroes: Jewish Soldiers, Veterans, and Memories of World War I in Germany," Ph.D. dissertation, Georgetown University, 2001; Ulrich Sieg, *Jüdische Intellektuelle im Ersten Weltkrieg: Kriegserfahrungen, weltanschauliche Debatten und kulturelle Neuentwürfe* (Berlin, 2001).
29. For a recent example of this approach, see Tim Grady, *A Deadly Legacy: German Jews and the Great War* (New Haven, 2017).
30. Grady, *The German-Jewish Soldiers of the First World War*.
31. David J. Fine, *Jewish Integration in the German Army in the First World War* (Berlin, 2012).
32. Penslar, *Jews and the Military*; Sarah Panter, *Jüdische Erfahrungen und Loyalitätskonflikte im Ersten Weltkrieg* (Göttingen, 2014); Ulrike Heikaus and Julia B. Köhne, eds., *Krieg! Juden zwischen den Fronten 1914–1918* (Berlin, 2014).
33. The war as a caesura in German-Christian relations is highlighted in George L. Mosse's chapter "On War and Revolution," in *Towards the Final Solution: A History of European Racism* (Madison, 1978).
34. Rosenthal, *Die Ehre des jüdischen Soldaten*, 193.
35. Brian E. Crim, *Antisemitism in the German Military Community and the Jewish Response, 1914–1938* (Lanham, 2014).
36. Jay Winter, *Remembering War: The Great War between Memory and History in the Twentieth Century* (New Haven, 2006), 18–22.
37. Sabine Mehlmann, *Unzuverlässige Körper: Zur Diskursgeschichte des Konzepts geschlechtlicher Identität* (Sulzbach/Taunus, 2006), 1–41.
38. German-Jews also "performed masculinity" in German university culture. See Lisa F. Zwicker, "Performing Masculinity: Jewish Students and the Honor Code at German Universities," in *Jewish Masculinities: German Jews, Gender and History*, ed. Benjamin Maria Baader, Sharon Gillerman, and Paul Lerner (Bloomington, 2012), 114–37.
39. Thomas Kühne, *The Rise and Fall of Comradeship: Hitler's Soldiers, Male Bonding and Mass Violence in the Twentieth Century* (Cambridge, 2017), esp. Chapter 1.
40. Monika Szcepaniak, *Militärische Männlichkeiten in Deutschland und Österreich im Umfeld des Großen Krieges* (Würzburg, 2011), 10. On the interwar "crisis in masculinity," see Birthe Kundrus, "Gender Wars: The First World War and the Construction of Gender Relations in the Weimar Republic," in *Home/Front: The Military, War and Gender in Twentieth-Century Germany*, ed. Karen Hagemann and Stefanie Schüler-Springorum (Oxford, 2002), 160. For comparative context on Jewish men seeking assimilation through military service, see Deborah Dash Moore, *GI Jews: How World War II Changed a Generation* (New York, 2006); for comparison to sexual minorities who embraced the mainstream masculine ideal of comradeship,

see Jason Crouthamel, *An Intimate History of the Front: Masculinity, Sexuality and German Soldiers in the First World War* (New York, 2014), esp. Chapter 5.
41. On National Socialist racial conceptions of comradeship and masculinity, see George L. Mosse's *The Image of Man: The Creation of Modern Masculinity* (Oxford, 1998), esp. Chapter 8.
42. Brian K. Feltman, "Conceptions of Comradeship: Hans H. Pinkus and the Nazification of the Reichsvereinigung ehemaliger Kriegsgefangener," *Leo Baeck Institute Yearbook* 61 (March 2016): 163–82. On assimilation through militarized masculinity, see Gregory A. Caplan, "Germanising the Jewish Male: Military Masculinity as the Last Stage of Acculturation," in *Towards Normality? Acculturation of Modern German Jewry*, ed. Rainer Liedtke and David Rechter (Tübingen, 2003), 159–84.
43. Kundrus, "Gender Wars," 159–79.
44. L. J. Collins, *Theatre at War, 1914–1918* (Basingstoke, 2004), 105–82.
45. Hermann Pörzgen, *Theater ohne Frau: Das Bühnenleben der kriegsgefangenen Deutschen 1914–1920* (Königsberg/Berlin, 1933); Martin Baumeister, *Kriegstheater: Großstadt, Front und Massenkultur 1914–1918* (Essen, 2005); Julia B. Köhne, Britta Lange, and Anke Vetter, eds., *MEIN KAMERAD – DIE DIVA: Theater an der Front und in Gefangenenlagern des Ersten Weltkriegs* (Munich, 2014).
46. On Jewish women's assimilation into middle-class culture, see Marion A. Kaplan, *The Making of the Jewish Middle Class: Women, Family, and Identity in Imperial Germany* (Oxford, 1994).
47. Ute Daniel, "Der Krieg der Frauen: Zur Innenansicht des Ersten Weltkriegs in Deutschland," in *"Keiner fühlt sich hier mehr als Mensch" … Erlebnis und Wirkung des Ersten Weltkriegs*, ed. Gerhard Hirschfeld et al. (Essen, 1993), 157–77.
48. Andreas Killen, *Homo Cinematicus: Science, Motion Pictures, and the Making of Modern Germany* (Pennsylvania, 2017).
49. Anton Kaes, *Shell Shock Cinema: Weimar Culture and the Wounds of War* (Princeton, 2010).
50. Christina von Braun, "Ist die Sexualwissenschaft eine 'jüdische Wissenschaft'? Säkularisierung und die Entstehung der Sexualwissenschaft," in *Preußens Himmel breitet seine Sterne …. Beiträge zur Kultur-, Politik- und Geistesgeschichte der Neuzeit*, vol. 2, ed. Willi Jasper and Joachim H. Knoll (Hildesheim, 2002), 697–714.
51. Rozenblit, *Reconstructing a National Identity*; see also Pieter M. Judson and Marsha L. Rozenblit, eds., *Constructing Nationalities in East Central Europe* (New York, 2005).
52. See, for example, Daniela L. Caglioti, ed., *Aliens and Internal Enemies during the First World War* (Munich, 2014).
53. On "situational ethnicity" to German Jewish identities, see Rahden, *Jews and Other Germans*.
54. On the sociological significance of "comradeship" in German society during the age of total war, see Kühne, *The Rise and Fall of Comradeship*.
55. Philipp Stiasny, *Das Kino und der Krieg: Deutschland 1914–1929* (Munich, 2009).

56. See, for example, Kaes, *Shell Shock Cinema*.
57. On the emotional effects of mass violence, see Alexander Watson, *Enduring the Great War: Combat, Morale and Collapse in the German and British Armies, 1914–1918* (Cambridge, 2008); on constructions of masculinity in response to emotional stress, see Crouthamel, *An Intimate History of the Front*, especially Chapter 4; on the history of emotions in shaping the war, see Ute Frevert, *Emotions and History: Lost and Found* (Budapest, 2011).
58. On the diagnosis of "war neurosis," see Paul Lerner, *Hysterical Men: History, Psychiatry and the Politics of Trauma in Germany, 1890–1930* (Ithaca, 2003); Hans-Georg Hofer, *Nervenschwäche und Krieg: Modernitätskritik und Kriegsbewältigung in der österreichischen Psychiatrie, 1880–1920* (Vienna, 2004); on medial representations of "war hysterics," see Julia Barbara Köhne, *Kriegshysteriker: Strategische Bilder und mediale Techniken militärpsychiatrischen Wissens, 1914–1920* (Husum, 2009); Julia Barbara Köhne, "Visualizing 'War Hysterics': Strategies of Feminization and Re-masculinization in Scientific Cinematography, 1916–1918," in *Gender and the First World War*, ed. Christa Hämmerle, Oswald Überegger, and Birgitta Bader Zaar (Basingstoke, 2014), 72–88; on the psychological impact of the war on soldiers and civilians, see Jason Crouthamel and Peter Leese, eds., *Psychological Trauma and the Legacies of the First World War* (New York, 2016).
59. On the central role of German Jewish psychiatrist Hermann Oppenheim in medical debates over the diagnosis and treatment of mental trauma, see Paul Lerner, "From Traumatic Neurosis to Male Hysteria: The Decline and Fall of Hermann Oppenheim, 1889–1919," in *Traumatic Pasts: History, Psychiatry and Trauma in the Modern Age, 1870–1930*, ed. Mark S. Micale and Paul Lerner (Cambridge, 2001), 140–71.
60. Lerner, *Hysterical Men*, 5.
61. One of the most important studies on the memory of the war is George L. Mosse, *Fallen Soldiers: Reshaping the Memory of the World Wars* (New York, 1991).
62. On constructions of the "national community" and its social-political significance, see Lisa Pine, *Hitler's "National Community": Society and Culture in Nazi Germany*, 2nd ed. (London, 2017).

Bibliography

Angress, Werner T. "The German Army's 'Judenzählung' of 1916: Genesis-Consequences-Significance." *Leo Baeck Institute Yearbook* 23 (1978): 117–37.

Appelbaum, Peter C. *Loyalty Betrayed: Jewish Chaplains in the German Army during the First World War*. London: Valentine Mitchell, 2014.

Baader, Benjamin Maria, Sharon Gillerman, and Paul Lerner, eds. *Jewish Masculinities: German Jews, Gender and History*. Bloomington: Indiana University Press, 2012.

Baumeister, Martin. *Kriegstheater: Großstadt, Front und Massenkultur 1914–1918*. Essen: Klartext-Verlag, 2005.

Berger, Michael. "Erster Weltkrieg: 'Sie fielen fürs Vaterland!'" In *Jüdische Soldaten-Jüdischer Widerstand in Deutschland und Frankreich*, edited by Michael Berger and Gideon Römer-Hillebrecht, 89-111. Paderborn: Verlag Ferdinand Schöningh, 2012.

Braun, Christina von. "Ist die Sexualwissenschaft eine 'jüdische Wissenschaft'? Säkularisierung und die Entstehung der Sexualwissenschaft." In *Preußens Himmel breitet seine Sterne.... Beiträge zur Kultur-, Politik- und Geistesgeschichte der Neuzeit*, vol. 2, edited by Willi Jasper and Joachim H. Knoll, 697-714. Hildesheim: Olms Verlag, 2002.

Brenner, Michael. "The German army orders a census of Jewish soldiers, and Jews defend German Culture." In *Yale Companion to Jewish Writing and Thought in German Culture, 1096–1996*, edited by Sander L. Gilman and Jack Zipes, 348-354. New Haven: Yale University Press, 1996.

——. *The Renaissance of Jewish Culture in Weimar Germany*. New Haven: Yale University Press, 1996.

Caglioti, Daniela L., ed. *Aliens and Internal Enemies during the First World War*. Munich: C.H. Beck Verlag, 2014.

Caplan, Gregory A. "Germanising the Jewish Male: Military Masculinity as the Last Stage of Acculturation." In *Towards Normality? Acculturation of Modern German Jewry*, edited by Rainer Liedtke and David Rechter, 159–84. Tübingen: Mohr Siebeck, 2003.

——. "Wicked Sons, German Heroes: Jewish Soldiers, Veterans, and Memories of World War I in Germany." Ph.D. dissertation, Georgetown University, 2001.

Collins, L. J. *Theatre at War, 1914–1918*. Basingstoke: Jade, 2004.

Crim, Brian E. *Antisemitism in the German Military Community and the Jewish Response, 1914–1938*. Lanham, MD: Lexington Books, 2014.

Crouthamel, Jason. *An Intimate History of the Front: Masculinity, Sexuality and German Soldiers in the First World War*. New York: Palgrave Macmillan, 2014.

Crouthamel, Jason, and Peter Leese, eds. *Psychological Trauma and the Legacies of the First World War*. New York: Palgrave Macmillan, 2016.

Daniel, Ute. "Der Krieg der Frauen: Zur Innenansicht des Ersten Weltkriegs in Deutschland." In *"Keiner fühlt sich hier mehr als Mensch" ... Erlebnis und Wirkung des Ersten Weltkriegs*, edited by Gerhard Hirschfeld et al., 157–77. Essen: Klartext Verlag, 1993.

Dunker, Ulrich. *Der Reichsbund jüdischer Frontsoldaten, 1919–1938: Geschichte eines jüdischen Abwehrvereins*. Düsseldorf: Droste Verlag, 1977.

Feltman, Brian K. "Conceptions of Comradeship: Hans H. Pinkus and the Nazification of the Reichsvereinigung ehemaliger Kriegsgefangener." *Leo Baeck Institute Yearbook* 61 (March 2016): 163–82.

Fine, David J. *Jewish Integration in the German Army in the First World War*. Berlin: De Gruyter, 2012.

Franke, Hans. *Geschichte und Schicksal der Juden in Heilbronn vom Mittelalter bis zur Zeit der nationalsozialistischen Verfolgung 1050–1945*. Heilbronn: Stadtarchiv, 1963.

Frevert, Ute. *Emotions and History: Lost and Found*. Budapest: Central European Press, 2011.

Geheran, Michael. "Judenzählung (Jewish Census)." In *1914–1918 Online: International Encyclopedia of the First World War*, edited by Ute Daniel et al. Berlin: Freie Universität Berlin, 2015. DOI: 10.15463/ie1418.10684. Retrieved 23 July 2018 from https://encyclopedia.1914-1918-online.net/article/judenzahlung_jewish_census.
Grady, Tim. *A Deadly Legacy: German Jews and the Great War*. New Haven, CT: Yale University Press: 2017.
———. *The German-Jewish Soldiers of the First World War in History and Memory*. Liverpool: Liverpool University Press, 2011.
Gregory, Adrian. "Railway Stations: Gateways and Termini." In *Capital Cities at War: Paris, London, Berlin 1914–1919*, vol. 2, edited by Jay Winter and Jean-Louis Robert, 23–56. Cambridge: Cambridge University Press, 2007.
Heikaus, Ulrike, and Julia B. Köhne, eds. *Krieg! Juden zwischen den Fronten 1914–1918*. Berlin: Hentrich und Hentrich Verlag, 2014.
Hofer, Hans-Georg. *Nervenschwäche und Krieg: Modernitätskritik und Kriegsbewältigung in der österreichischen Psychiatrie, 1880–1920*. Vienna: Boehlau Verlag, 2004.
Hoffmann, Christhard. "Between Integration and Rejection: The Jewish Community in Germany, 1914–1918." In *State, Society, and Mobilization in Europe during the First World War*, edited by John Horne, 89–104. Cambridge: Cambridge University Press, 1997.
Huder, Walther. "Kriegs-Tagebuch eines Juden: Ein Beitrag zur Geschichte des deutschen Judentums." *Bulletin des Leo Baeck Instituts* 8 (1965): 240–49.
Jochmann, Werner. "Ausbreitung des Antisemitismus." In *Judentum in Krieg und Revolution 1916–1923*, edited by Werner E. Mosse and Arnold Paucker, 409–510. Tübingen: Mohr Siebeck, 1971.
Judson, Pieter M., and Marsha L. Rozenblit, eds. *Constructing Nationalities in East Central Europe*. New York: Berghahn Books, 2005.
Kaes, Anton. *Shell Shock Cinema: Weimar Culture and the Wounds of War*. Princeton, NJ: Princeton University Press, 2010.
Kaplan, Marion A. *The Making of the Jewish Middle Class: Women, Family, and Identity in Imperial Germany*. Oxford: Oxford University Press, 1994.
Killen, Andreas. *Homo Cinematicus: Science, Motion Pictures, and the Making of Modern Germany*. Pennsylvania: University of Pennsylvania Press, 2017.
Köhne, Julia Barbara. *Kriegshysteriker: Strategische Bilder und mediale Techniken militärpsychiatrischen Wissens, 1914–1920*. Husum: Matthiesen, 2009.
———. "Visualizing 'War Hysterics': Strategies of Feminization and Re-masculinization in Scientific Cinematography, 1916–1918." In *Gender and the First World War*, edited by Christa Hämmerle, Oswald Überegger, and Birgitta Bader Zaar, 72–88. Basingstoke, UK: Palgrave Macmillan, 2014.
Köhne, Julia B., Britta Lange, and Anke Vetter, eds. *MEIN KAMERAD – DIE DIVA: Theater an der Front und in Gefangenenlagern des Ersten Weltkriegs*. Munich: edition text + kritik, 2014.
Kühne, Thomas. *The Rise and Fall of Comradeship: Hitler's Soldiers, Male Bonding and Mass Violence in the Twentieth Century*. Cambridge: Cambridge University Press, 2017.

Kundrus, Birthe. "Gender Wars: The First World War and the Construction of Gender Relations in the Weimar Republic." In *Home/Front: The Military, War and Gender in Twentieth-Century Germany*, edited by Karen Hagemann and Stefanie Schüler-Springorum, 159–179. Oxford: Berg, 2002.

Lerner, Paul. *Hysterical Men: History, Psychiatry and the Politics of Trauma in Germany, 1890–1930*. Ithaca, NY: Cornell University Press, 2003.

——. "From Traumatic Neurosis to Male Hysteria: The Decline and Fall of Hermann Oppenheim, 1889–1919." In *Traumatic Pasts: History, Psychiatry and Trauma in the Modern Age, 1870–1930*, edited by Mark S. Micale and Paul Lerner, 140–71. Cambridge: Cambridge University Press, 2001.

Lewin, Reinhold. "Der Krieg als jüdisches Erlebnis." *Monatsschrift für die Geschichte und Wissenschaft des Judentums* 63 (1917): 1–14.

Marx, Julius. *Kriegstagebuch eines Juden*. Frankfurt: Ner-Tamid-Verlag, 1964.

Mehlmann, Sabine. *Unzuverlässige Körper: Zur Diskursgeschichte des Konzepts geschlechtlicher Identität*. Sulzbach/Taunus: Helmer Verlag, 2006.

Mendes-Flohr, Paul. *German Jews: A Dual Identity*. New Haven, CT: Yale University Press, 1999.

——. "The *Kriegserlebnis* and Jewish Consciousness." In *Jüdisches Leben in der Weimarer Republik*, edited by Wolfgang Benz, 225–237. Tübingen: Mohr Siebeck, 1998.

Militärgeschichtliches Forschungsamt, ed. *Deutsche jüdische Soldaten 1914–1945*. Freiburg: Militärgeschichtliches Forschungsamt, 1982.

Moore, Deborah Dash. *GI Jews: How World War II Changed a Generation*. New York: Belknap, 2006.

Mosse, George L. *Fallen Soldiers: Reshaping the Memory of the World Wars*. New York: Oxford University Press, 1991.

——. *The Image of Man: The Creation of Modern Masculinity*. Oxford: Oxford University Press, 1998.

——. *The Jews and the German War Experience, 1914–1918*. New York: Leo Baeck Institute, 1977.

——. *Towards the Final Solution: A History of European Racism*. Madison: University of Wisconsin, 1978.

Mosse, Werner E., and Arnold Paucker, eds. *Judentum in Krieg und Revolution 1916–1923*. Tübingen: Mohr Siebeck, 1971.

Panter, Sarah. *Jüdische Erfahrungen und Loyalitätskonflikte im Ersten Weltkrieg*. Göttingen: Vandenhoeck & Ruprecht, 2014.

Penslar, Derek. "The German-Jewish Soldier: From Participant to Victim." *German History* 29 (2011): 445–69.

——. *Jews and the Military: A History*. Princeton, NJ: Princeton University Press, 2013.

Picht, Clemens. "Zwischen Vaterland und Volk: Das deutsche Judentum im Ersten Weltkrieg." In *Der Erste Weltkrieg: Wirkung, Wahrnehmung, Analyse*, edited by Wolfgang Michalka, 736–55. Munich: Piper Verlag, 1994.

Pine, Lisa. *Hitler's "National Community": Society and Culture in Nazi Germany*, 2nd ed. London: Bloomsbury, 2017.

Pörzgen, Hermann. *Theater ohne Frau: Das Bühnenleben der kriegsgefangenen Deutschen 1914–1920*. Königsberg/Berlin: Ost-Europa-Verlag, 1933.

Pulzer, Peter. *Jews and the German State: The Political History of a Minority, 1848–1933*. Oxford: Oxford University Press, 1992.
Rahden, Till van. *Jews and Other Germans: Civil Society, Religious Diversity, and Urban Politics in Breslau, 1860–1925*. Madison: University of Wisconsin Press, 2008.
Rechter, David. *The Jews of Vienna and the First World War*. Oxford: Littman Library of Jewish Civilization, 2008.
Reinharz, Jehuda. *Fatherland or Promised Land: The Dilemma of the German Jew, 1893–1914*. Ann Arbor: University of Michigan Press, 1975.
Reisner, Barbara, ed. *Kriegsbriefe 1914–1918: Dr. Harry & Mimi Marcuse*. London: Lulu, 2013.
Rosenthal, Jacob. *"Die Ehre des jüdischen Soldaten": Die Judenzählung im Ersten Weltkrieg und ihre Folgen*. Frankfurt: Campus Verlag, 2007.
Rozenblit, Marsha. *The Jews of Vienna, 1867–1914: Assimilation and Identity*. New York: State University of New York Press, 1984.
———. *Reconstructing a National Identity: The Jews of Habsburg Austria during World War I*. Oxford: Oxford University Press, 2001.
Rozenblit, Marsha, and Jonathan Karp, eds. *World War I and the Jews: Conflict and Transformation in Europe, the Middle East, and America*. Oxford: Berghahn Books, 2017.
Schmidl, Erwin. *Habsburgs jüdische Soldaten 1788–1918*. Vienna: Böhlau, 2014.
Schölzel, Christian. *Walther Rathenau: Eine Biographie*. Paderborn: Ferdinand Schöningh, 2006.
Sieg, Ulrich. *Jüdische Intellektuelle im Ersten Weltkrieg: Kriegserfahrungen, weltanschauliche Debatten und kulturelle Neuentwürfe*. Berlin: Akademie-Verlag, 2001.
Simon, Ernst. "Unser Kriegserlebnis (1919)." In *Brücken: Gesammelte Aufsätze*, edited by Ernst Simon, 17–23. Heidelberg: L. Schnieder. 1965.
Steer, Martina. "Nation, Religion, Gender: The Triple Challenge of Middle-Class German-Jewish Women in World War I." *Central European History* 48 (2015): 176–98.
Stiasny, Philipp. *Das Kino und der Krieg: Deutschland 1914–1929*. Munich: Edition Text, 2009.
Sulzbach, Herbert A. *Zwischen zwei Mauern: 50 Monate Westfront 1914–1918*. Berg am See: Kurt Vowinckel Verlag, 1986. English translation: *With the German Guns: Four Years on the Western Front, 1914–1918*. London: Leo Cooper, 1973.
Szczepaniak, Monika. *Militärische Männlichkeiten in Deutschland und Österreich im Umfeld des Großen Krieges*. Würzburg: Königshausen & Neumann, 2011.
Ulrich, Anna. "'Nun sind wir gezeichnet': Jüdische Soldaten und die 'Judenzählung' im Ersten Weltkrieg." In *Krieg! Juden zwischen den Fronten 1914–1918*, edited by Ulrike Heikaus and Julia B. Köhne, 215–238. Berlin: Hentrich und Hentrich Verlag, 2014.
Vogel, Rolf. *Ein Stück von uns: Deutsche Juden in deutschen Armeen 1813–1976. Eine Dokumentation*. Mainz: v. Hase & Koehler Verlag, 1977.
Volkov, Shulamit. *Walther Rathenau: Weimar's Fallen Statesman*. New Haven, CT: Yale University Press, 2012.

Watson, Alexander. *Enduring the Great War: Combat, Morale and Collapse in the German and British Armies, 1914–1918*. Cambridge: Cambridge University Press, 2008.

———. *Ring of Steel: Germany and Austria-Hungary at War, 1914–1918*. London: Allen Lane, 2014.

Winter, Jay. *Remembering War: The Great War between Memory and History in the Twentieth Century*. New Haven, CT: Yale University Press, 2006.

Zechlin, Egmont. *Die deutsche Politik und die Juden im Ersten Weltkrieg*. Göttingen: Vandenhoeck & Ruprecht, 1969.

Zwicker, Lisa F. "Performing Masculinity: Jewish Students and the Honor Code at German Universities." In *Jewish Masculinities: German Jews, Gender and History*, edited by Benjamin Maria Baader, Sharon Gillerman, and Paul Lerner, 114–137. Bloomington: Indiana University Press, 2012.

PART I

AT THE MARGINS

MINORITIES AND THE MILITARY

1

HOPES AND DISAPPOINTMENTS
German and French Jews during the Wars of 1870/71 and 1914–18

Christine G. Krüger

In August 1914, the German Jewish weekly newspaper *Der Israelit* released two articles that it had published for the first time forty-four years earlier, during the hottest phase of the Franco-Prussian War. One of these articles praised the patriotic commitment of the German Jews. It stressed that they participated in the war "voluntarily and joyfully." The article put a special emphasis on the fact that even if the Jews were still "the pariahs of society," this did not diminish their patriotism in any respect. As early as the German campaign against Napoleon I, their "fathers and grandfathers" had been "German patriots to the tips of their toes," although this had meant that they had to fight against the French, who "had come as liberators" for the German Jews still suffering "under a heavy and odious yoke."[1] Indeed, in many German territories the Jews had gained equal civic rights due to the legislation introduced under the Napoleonic occupation.

In the age of nationalism, the nation demanded the absolute commitment of its members. Nationalists claimed that patriotism should be superior to any other loyalty. Periods of war were the touchstone to prove this. For Jews the pressure to confirm their national loyalty was particularly high. Ever since discussions about their civic status had been sparked for the first time at the end of the eighteenth century, adversaries who opposed their emancipation had called into question whether the Jews, allegedly waiting for their return to Palestine, would regard their European nation as their fatherland. Thus, they concluded, as there could be no trust in the willingness of the Jews to fulfill their civic duties, and especially to defend their country in case of war, they could not attain civic rights either. Even if in the course of the nineteenth century and especially in its second half, Judeo-phobes complemented these allegations with ethnic or racial arguments, the mistrust towards the Jewish readiness to fight for their home country still remained a central element of antisemitic ideology. Doubts about Jewish patriotism were also common during the Franco-Prussian War of 1870/71—in Germany as well as France.[2] Certainly, in both countries, the war also put the patriotism of adherents of the respective Christian minority denomination to the test. French Protestants had to rebut allegations that they were sympathizing with the Germans, while German Catholics met doubts as to their patriotism because the head of their Church was the Roman Pope.[3] Yet the suspicions against Jews undoubtedly were stronger.

The Jews considered the war an opportunity to disprove such defamations. Many of them enthusiastically contributed to patriotic manifestations of all kinds. In both countries, they excelled in patriotic donations, in the nursing of the wounded, or in charitable organizations. In order to demonstrate their national belonging, Jewish publicists and preachers repeatedly pointed to their willingness to make sacrifices. Also, by pointing to their participation in every war of the nineteenth century, Jews in France and Germany tried to prove their patriotic reliability.[4] This had already been the goal of the cited article from 1870; the new publication of the article in 1914 again pursued the same aim, referring now to an even longer tradition of patriotic Jewish war effort.

In this chapter, I study in a synchronically and diachronically comparative perspective how French and German Jewish opinion leaders defined the relationship between Judaism and nationality and how these definitions developed between the Franco-Prussian War and the First World War. My thesis is that the patriotic participation in these wars engendered much more ambivalence for German Jews than for their French co-religionists. This can be attributed largely to the polarization of the two different definitions of the nation during the war of 1870/71. In the decades between the two wars as well as during the First World War itself, this ambivalence pluralized German Jewish self-definitions, whereas the Franco-Jewish self-understanding remained more stable and homogenous.

The reissue of the article in 1914 reveals the ambivalence German Jewish patriotism had to face during the Franco-Prussian War and the First World War alike. In 1914, the editors of *Der Israelit* added a footnote to the text, clarifying that the legal status of the German Jews had improved considerably since 1870. At the same time, however, this footnote deplored the fact that anti-Jewish discrimination was still very common in the German Empire. In November 1914, *Jeschurun*, another Jewish periodical, complained in an even sharper manner that the hopes of integration, which German Jews had cherished in respect to their commitment during the war of 1870, had been clearly disappointed. The author of the article stated: "The participation of Jews at war has not succeeded in permanently stifling the prejudices against them."[5]

On the French side, by contrast, Jewish authors did not feel challenged to justify their patriotism in the same manner. This might be surprising: between 1871 and 1914, antisemitism had also gained currency in France—the Dreyfus affair is only one example of this. Nevertheless, French Jews did not manifest any disappointment about their social status during the First World War. Indeed, Franco-Jewish expressions of patriotism had hardly changed. The difference between German and French Jewish self-definitions is the consequence mainly of the divergence of the two dominant definitions of the nation in the two countries, a divergence that the war of 1870/71 itself had sharpened to a considerable degree.

German Jewish as well as Franco-Jewish self-definitions have attracted a good deal of scholarly attention in recent decades. Early research often followed a Zionist interpretation, criticizing the numerous manifestations of Jewish commitment to their nation as "assimilationist" self-denial. This criticism was directed against French and German Jews alike, although its proponents explained it differently and in connection to the two divergent models of emancipation in the two countries: the revolutionary and the evolutionary models.[6] To the French Jews, emancipation was granted in the course of the French Revolution. Historians argued that the ideas of the Enlightenment and revolution went along with a strong pressure for homogenization and eventually led to a widespread abandonment of Jewishness.[7] Historiography on German Jews, by contrast, claimed that the German model of emancipation of the Jews particularly promoted assimilation, because it was widely considered a condition for gaining equal rights that Jews should first prove to be "worthy" citizens, and this meant that they were expected to cast off as much of their Jewishness as possible.[8]

The concept of Jewish assimilation did not remain undisputed, however. Historians have long highlighted that many Jews—in France as well as in Germany—upheld a strong attachment to their Jewishness and often tried to influence their non-Jewish environment as well as design their nation in a specific and self-confident way.[9] In recent years, studies in transnational or global history have confirmed this view from a new perspective. Their primary focus is on the increasing networks of Jewish internationalism in the nineteenth century, which they convincingly describe as an important trait of Jewish identity.[10] However, little attention has been paid to the question of how war between nations challenged the ideal of transnational Jewish solidarity. The aim of this chapter is to fill this gap. It can help us to gain a deeper understanding of the complex fabric of Jewish self-definitions, which can be explained neither by considering the national context alone nor by exclusively concentrating on transnational relations. Focusing on the Franco-Prussian War of 1870/71 first, and on the First World War second, it is possible to trace the relationship between nationalism, the ideal of Jewish solidarity, and Jewish self-definitions in a long-term perspective.

In the first part of this chapter, I analyze how French and German Jews defined the nation during the Franco-Prussian War of 1870/71 and particularly how they measured the relationship between religion and nation. In the second part, I will first focus on how the growing antisemitism in the last third of the nineteenth century and at the beginning of the twentieth century changed Jewish self-definitions and their understanding of nationhood and religion. Against this background, I will also compare the French and German Jewish public sphere of the First World War with that of the war in 1870/71.

A broad range of German Jewish and Franco-Jewish weekly periodicals, as well as rabbinical wartime sermons from both countries, give insight into the issues discussed here. These sources are not representative of the whole Jewry of both countries, but were intended mainly for an educated elite that felt attached to Judaism and was interested in Jewish matters. Yet these sources have a high analytical value, especially from a transnational perspective. From their beginnings in the first half of the nineteenth century, Jewish periodicals of both countries regularly interchanged information and ideas. They considered each other as partners cooperating in order to push forward the emancipation of the Jews in Europe and beyond.[11] This intensive transnational interchange distinguished Jewish periodicals from Catholic or Protestant ones, where news from abroad was rare, although not entirely absent.[12]

Jewish Self-Definitions in the Face of the National War of 1870/71

The Franco-Prussian War of 1870/71 was a crucial period for the polarization of French and German definitions of the nation. The main reason for this was the German annexation of Alsace-Lorraine after the French defeat. A wide majority of Germans justified the takeover of the two provinces as the legitimate recuperation of a region that France had once unlawfully incorporated. In their eyes, the fact that the mother tongue of many Alsatians was German proved that the region still belonged to Germany not only for historical but also for cultural reasons. In this line of argument, culture and language were the two main factors that determined nationality. The majority of the French, however, rejected this concept of a *Kulturnation*. They propagated instead the concept of voluntarism for the nation as *Staatsnation*, according to which the patriotic feeling of adherence alone defined nationality. Thus, in their eyes, the German annexation of Alsace and Lorraine was unlawful because it did not take into consideration the fact that most Alsatians were opposed to it.[13] For Jews, the question of how the nation in which they lived was defined was especially important, because it had direct consequences for their social and legal status. For this reason, the debate over these definitions fed into Jewish self-understanding. It is worthwhile to look more closely at the outcome of these debates in both countries.

French Jews unanimously agreed on how to define the nation. "*Ubi libertas, ibi patria*"—where there is freedom, there is the fatherland: this was the motto that Franco-Jewish authors repeatedly proclaimed during the war.[14] Again and again, they affirmed that the emancipation of the Jews in the course of the French Revolution explained the patriotic commitment they displayed. In September 1870, one journalist wrote: "For such a long time we have been bereaved of a fatherland! That is why we have devoted ourselves with all the forces of our soul and with our gratitude to this beloved France that has so generously opened her arms and has admitted us to the number of its children."[15] The importance of the French Revolution for Franco-Jews distinguished their patriotic confessions from those of representatives of the Christian Churches who normally considered the Revolution in a rather negative way as the starting point of secularization.[16]

Many Franco-Jewish authors interpreted the heavy protest that Alsatian Jews evinced against the annexation as proof of their gratefulness towards France.[17] One journalist argued that the attitude of the Alsatian Jews demonstrated that a "just fatherland" was going to "take advantage of having done justice."[18] More than half of the Franco-Jewish population lived in these two provinces. It was the Alsatian Jews themselves who grieved most heavily over the annexation. They feared that their social and legal status would worsen. In order to escape this fate, many of them left Alsace and Lorraine and moved to France or the United States.[19]

Tying patriotism to civic status, French Jews kept in line with the concept of voluntarism prevalent in France. Moreover, they expected their co-religionists on the other side of the Rhine to share the same understanding. They criticized the strong German Jewish patriotism as inadequate, because their social status left so much to be desired. Thus, in October 1870, a Franco-Jewish journalist addressed German Jewry, claiming: "The country where we are treated like strangers and excluded from the communal law is not a fatherland [mère-patrie] for us, but a stepmother that we ought to *fear* and not to *love*."[20] According to this logic, French Jews claimed that their German co-religionists should side with the French, and that they should disapprove of the annexation and protest against it in public.

For German Jews it was scarcely possible to fulfill such demands. This was primarily due to the fact that any form of criticism of the annexation was problematic, since the gain of Alsace-Lorraine was celebrated as a national victory by the German public. Whoever condemned the annexation—as some socialists or democrats did—was harshly attacked and denounced as unpatriotic. Secondly, and more important in our context, it was risky for German Jews to establish a link between patriotism and social or juridical status if they wanted to avoid reinforcing skepticism about their loyalty. Indeed, in fighting against France they had to fight against the first European nation that had emancipated the Jews, the example of which served to underline most of the claims German Jews were calling for in Germany. They could not deny that the civic and social status of their French co-religionists was much better than their own. A prominent example of this was Adolphe Crémieux, a Jewish lawyer who had already been the French minister of justice in 1848, and obtained this office again in the government of national defense formed after Napoleon III's surrender to the German army in September 1870. Such an appointment would have been inconceivable in Germany during that time.[21] Moreover, the war itself illustrated the French lead in the field of emancipation. For instance, France engaged Jewish military rabbis from the outset, whereas in Germany only at the end of the war could three rabbis join the troops. A further example was in military advancements. Hardly any Jews in Germany were able to become officers, whereas in France a military career was open to Jews. There were Jewish officers and, in 1871, even a Jewish general. This was all the more astonishing because the Jewish proportion of the population was only 0.25 percent in France, lower than in Germany where Jews accounted for 1.25 percent of the population.[22]

This difference in the status of Jews in the two countries, which was highlighted by the war, explains why an editorial in the *Allgemeine*

Zeitung des Judenthums from May 1871 explicitly rejected any connection between patriotism and the progress of emancipation: "The love of one's fatherland is a feeling that is too deep and too sacred to depend in any way on the rights one has already gained!"[23] However, in spite of such declarations, Jewish voices that commented on the war, patriotism, or nationality were much more heterogenous and ambiguous in Germany than in France. Although German Jews generally supported the definition of the nation as a *Kulturnation*, it is obvious that many of them considered this definition problematic and unsatisfactory. They did not want to dismiss the idea that the political consensus was also a constitutive element of the nation. This became manifest when they judged the patriotism of their French co-religionists and especially their attitude towards the annexation of Alsace and Lorraine. While German Jews vehemently denied any link between patriotism and social or legal status for their own patriotism, they definitively understood that their fellow Jews in the annexed regions had a different point of view.[24] In an article about the situation in the annexed provinces, a correspondent of the German Jewish weekly *Israelitische Wochenschrift*, for example, argued that every reasonable person had to admit that the fears of the Alsatian Jews—although they were excessive—nevertheless contained a "hint of truth." The editors of the journal added: "In our view, *far more* than a hint."[25] When German Jews defended the pro-French feelings of their Alsatian co-religionists, who after all accounted for 3 percent of the population in this region, they normally addressed it to the German government, urging it to care for the maintenance of their legal status. Furthermore, they claimed that the rights that Jews were enjoying in Alsace and Lorraine should serve as a yardstick for the future status of the Jews in the German Empire. The *Israelitische Wochenschrift* predicted: "If the denominational equality is allowed to become reality in the old parts of Germany, the mistrust that reigns in the new parts of Germany will quickly disappear!"[26] The sympathy that German Jews showed towards the pro-French feelings of their Alsatian co-religionists was a concession to understanding the nation on the basis of voluntarism.

With such concessions, German Jewish authors clearly distinguished themselves from the German public sphere in general as well as from the representatives of the Christian Churches. The Christian denominational press did not pay any interest to the situation in the annexed regions, nor did it publish or cite the opinions of French co-believers. The only exception was the occasional article citing French Christians who criticized the French policy.[27] German Protestants tried to present their Alsatian co-believers as well-disposed towards Germany. Similarly, the representatives of the German Catholic Church were convinced that the Catholics in Alsace and Lorraine were not particularly opposed to the annexation. Sometimes they noted with surprise that this image did not correspond to reality, but this did not mean that they would have admitted the strong patriotism of the Alsatians.[28]

The different definitions of the nation were also reflected in the divergent ways in which German and French Jews conceived of the relationship between religion and nation.[29] The impact of the annexation on transnational Jewish solidarity has already become obvious. Traditionally for the Jewish diaspora, the ideal of cross-border solidarity, being a commandment of the Talmud, had been a central element of their self-understanding.[30] Put into action, this ideal had, since the Middle Ages, often secured the survival of persecuted Jews in Europe. At the beginning of the nineteenth century, the communal efforts to advance the process of Jewish emancipation added a new quality to it.[31] National war, however, put this ideal to a harsh test. It rendered it necessary for Jews in both armies to take up arms against one another and even be forced to kill each other. Jewish authors in both countries regularly deplored this eventuality. An editorial in the *Allgemeine Zeitung des Judenthums* concluded that for the Jews every war was a "fraternal war."[32]

French Jews, however, frequently denied that the Jews of the two nations in war should feel any particular sympathy towards each other.[33] Thus, the *Univers israélite* observed that "since the beginning of the war, every intimacy, every friendship, every confraternity had necessarily disappeared between German and French Israelites. The Germans are strangers for us as we would be for them. Besides, I do not understand the desire to make the Israelites a special *caste*, nor do I understand that our German co-religionists suppose that we as Israelites should continue to esteem and to love them."[34] Another author even explicitly justified "the hatred" that French Jews would feel towards the Germans.[35]

In this respect, French and German attitudes differed to a considerable degree in 1870/71. In both countries, most Jews defined Judaism as a confession.[36] However, during the war, French Jews emphasized that a "complete divorce between nationality and religious faith" was impossible; their German co-religionists usually defined nationality and Judaism as two separate spheres, between which no cause for conflict existed.[37] For example, the rabbi Levi Herzfeld illustrated this understanding of the relationship between nation and Judaism, referring to other examples of harmonious togetherness of different loyalties: "We do not stop being fathers of a family when we have to represent professional interests [*Standesinteressen*] and the profession should not completely absorb us, because we belong to a family, etc."[38] According to this logic, German Jewish authors did not get tired of exhorting their readers not to transfer national hostility to inner-Jewish issues.[39] The *Allgemeine Zeitung des Judenthums*, for instance, admonished: "What we think and feel as Germans does not concern us as Jews."[40] In a similar way, many German Jewish authors tried to draw a clear line between Jewishness and nationality that made any conflict between the two impossible.

Such appeals to overcome enmity, even in times of war, were not necessarily restricted to the relationship between the Jews of the two countries. Numerous appeals against hatred and enmity appear in all of the German Jewish newspapers and in most of the rabbinical sermons. A headline article of the *Allgemeine Zeitung des Judenthums* from August 1870, with the title "On National Hatred," provides an example: "National hatred, the ingrained hatred between two peoples, is the most horrible of all passions of humankind. What means is there to disarm this national hatred, to disperse it little by little and finally to eradicate it? It is humanity. It is true civilization."[41]

For German Jews, there was one preferred way out of the quandary of having to reconcile the demands of nation and religion. All of the Jewish magazines, and many wartime sermons, agreed on one point: they assigned the task of counteracting national hatred, and fulfilling a mission of peace, to Judaism. They thought that the Jews were predestined for such a mission because of their difficult situation during the war and the conflict they faced between patriotism and religion. The *Allgemeine Zeitung des Judenthums* wrote:

> Being Germans or French, we are committed heart and soul to the interests and the policy of the German or the French nation. But because as Jews we are falling apart into so many different national fragments, because the different Jewish fragments are now clashing together in national combat, and because Jews are to be found in all armies and have to fight and to kill each other, because of all these reasons there is a noble political task for Jewry, a policy of rescuing it and all nations from those battles. This policy is the policy of humanism and religion.[42]

Generally, German Jewish periodicals showed less hostility towards France and the French than the German press in general or the Christian denominational press. Protestant newspapers and journals in particular interpreted the war as a religious campaign against a Catholic country. They did not hesitate to use very aggressive rhetoric towards France.[43] Catholic organs usually took a more moderate tone, but they too painted France in rather dark colors, since they associated the country with the French Revolution, and with laity and irreligiosity as its consequences.[44] In contrast, even orthodox Jewish authors, who likewise often criticized the progressing secularization in France, did not target the French Revolution, which, for them, remained a historic achievement having benefited Jews all over the world.

Certainly, German Jewish efforts to bring their patriotic enthusiasm into accord with their recognition of the merits that France had gained in the process of emancipation did not always succeed. Like most Germans—and maybe even more so because of their hopes for full equality in the future Empire—many Jews expected much from the war and the German unification following it. Nevertheless, all in all, Jewish commentators identified the dangers of war and nationalism more clearly than their compatriots did.

This was different in France. French Jews denied that a particular transnational Jewish solidarity should be maintained during times of war. Moreover, Jews in France hardly ever propagated the idea of a specific Jewish mission of peace. Nor did cosmopolitanism appeal to French Jews. Shortly after the war, a Franco-Jewish author asked: "Is it possible for the religious believer to be a patriot without contradiction, and is it possible for the cosmopolitan to be a good citizen?" His response was the following: "Our answer is that in the present state of the world, and maybe fatally under the conditions imposed on humanity, a man has first to love his family and his fatherland, before he loves the whole world. The universal feelings are an ideal, whereas the limited feelings are a necessity."[45]

In fact, the idea of a Jewish mission of peace or of cosmopolitanism, conciliating nation and religion, seemed to have been much less attractive to French Jews than to their German co-religionists. When French Jews reflected on the connection between nation and Judaism, other conclusions seemed more convincing. In their view, French goals were identical to Jewish goals. No conflict existed between them that needed to be abolished by cosmopolitanism. Accordingly, the wartime enemy Prussia, for French Jews, was not only the national enemy but also the enemy of Judaism. In one Franco-Jewish journal, we can even read the declaration that it was impossible to be a Prussian and a Jew at the same time.[46] Such a conviction was entirely opposed to an absolute divorce between nationality and belief, as targeted by German Jews, and the resulting suggestion that Jews in both countries should overcome enmity could not be shared by French Jews. With this suggestion German Jews were taking the easy way out, wrote a Franco-Jewish author. Especially in the face of "an enemy that was defeated, knocked to the ground and ruined," it would be "all too easy to be benevolent and generous and to say: 'As Jews let us remain brothers!'"[47]

Associating the French cause with the values of the French Revolution, Franco-Jewish opinion leaders distinguished themselves from the representatives of French Catholicism. They too were convinced that the war benefited the nation and religion at the same time, but they interpreted the conflict as an attack against Protestantism. They hoped that it would slow down or even reverse liberalization and secularization and that it would lead to a re-Christianization of French society.[48]

How German and French Jews defined the relationship between Judaism, nation, and nationalism differed considerably. Certainly, these differences increased because the French lost the war. The defeat and the resulting loss of Alsace-Lorraine were perceived as a national humiliation. The call for revenge became ever louder in the aftermath of the war. The plea for peace and international understanding found only a small number of supporters in Germany, but was definitively even less popular in France.

From 1871 to the First World War

In France and Germany alike, the period between the Franco-Prussian War and the First World War witnessed a substantial rise in aggressive nationalism that increasingly defined the nation in ethnic or racial terms excluding the Jews. In order to fight growing antisemitism, French and German Jews continued to emphasize their patriotism. When French Jews now evoked their participation in the Franco-Prussian War, their interpretation did not deviate from what it had been in 1870/71 and they kept to their republican definition of the nation. The French commemoration of the war focused primarily on the loss of Alsace and Lorraine and this no doubt favored the continuity of the Franco-Jewish interpretation of the war. Some French Jews, for example the writer Alexandre Weill with his *Lettres de vengeance d'un Alsacien* (An Alsatian's Letters of Revenge), vociferously supported the call for revenge that gained currency in France.[49]

In the German Jewish commemoration of the war, the weight shifted soon after 1871. German Jewish authors continued to stress equally the patriotic zeal of their co-religionists and they were reminded of the broad recognition they had received from non-Jews during the war itself. Yet other important parts of the German Jewish public discourse now receded into the background. The interpretation of the war became more homogenous, fractures were mended, and the ambivalence that many German Jewish authors had expressed in 1870/71 faded. In particular, the problems that arose from the war against the pioneer of Jewish emancipation, which German Jews had debated so hotly during the war, did not become part of the commemoration of the war. Only rarely did authors allude to these problems and the aim of such allusions now was to highlight the patriotism of German Jewish soldiers. An edition of the popular picture cycle by the German Jewish artist Moritz Oppenheimer, published in 1882, is an example here. The picture cycle included an engraving showing German Jewish soldiers in a French billet praying beneath the portrait of Napoleon I. The comment that accompanied the picture depicted the scene as follows:

> With a defiant eye the great Napoleon looks down. The spiked helmet that has brought disaster to him and to his nephew and that they have placed at his feet may annoy him, but he asks the Jews: "Why, you Jewish men, do you fight me, who has achieved such a great deal of good for you?"—For this, German Jews will be grateful towards him forever, without for that reason abandoning one iota of patriotic feeling, patriotic duty or spirit of sacrifice.[50]

In 1909, a historical report about the Franco-Prussian War by the former military rabbi Adolf Lewin argued in a similar vein. "Although France was the first of all states that has most comprehensively implemented the emancipation of the Jews," he wrote, "the Israelites have displayed the greatest enthusiasm and spirit of sacrifice for the German cause."[51] If German Jews paid less tribute to France's achievements in terms of equality, this can also be explained by the injury to her reputation as a model of emancipation in consequence of the Dreyfus affair. Even more important, however, seems to be the fact that the commemoration of the war in the first place served as a weapon to combat antisemitism and less as an argument for the advancement of emancipation.

There was another void in the commemoration of the war: the quandary that Jews had to fight each other in a war between nations was hardly ever problematized in this context. As in the case of the French lead in the emancipation of the Jews, German Jewish authors touched on this issue at best, when they wanted to illustrate Jewish patriotism. Lewin observed: "At that time, no Frenchman could be more chauvinistic than the Alsatian Jew towards the Jew from Baden with whom he normally had an amicable relationship and vice versa."[52] During the war, Lewin had noted with satisfaction that there had been many cases of ongoing friendly contacts between German and French Jews.[53] In 1909, he no longer mentioned such contacts. Other authors highlighted the fact that Jews had been fighting in both armies in order to nullify the suspicion of an international Jewish conspiracy. In 1895, for instance, an article in the *Israelit* asked: "And how will antisemites who combat the Jews not because of their religion, but because of their race, accept the fact that German Jews fought in the German army, and French Jews on the opposing side?"[54]

A final element of the German Jewish interpretation of the Franco-Prussian War that had been prominent in 1870/71 was missing in the commemorative discourse of the following decades. Just as the motif of the Jewish fraternal war was absent, the idea of a Jewish mission of peace had no place in historical accounts. It was not compatible with the fight against antisemitism that shaped the commemoration of the war. In their sermons celebrating the German victory on the Day of Sedan, some rabbis still warned of national hatred and of "too sharp an accentuation of one's own nationality," but such warnings were kept rather general in tone.[55] All in all, the commemoration of the war did not provide a forum for loud criticism of belligerent nationalism. This is not to say that Jewish anti-militarism vanished. A disproportionately high number of German Jews were actively involved in the peace movement. Likewise, they retained the idea of a specific Jewish mission of peace that was promoted among German Jewish authors, although it was not explicitly deduced from the experience of the war of 1870/71.[56] The commemorative discourse and the pacifist discourse followed different paths.

The growing antisemitism at the turn of the century had a significant impact on German Jewish self-definitions. Although the public commemoration homogenized German Jewish interpretations of the Franco-Prussian War, in general, the growing hostilities against Jews resulted in a clear pluralization of German Jewish identity constructions. The most obvious sign of this was the emergence of Zionism, the adherents of which also defined Judaism as an ethnic category. Other German Jews felt alienated from Judaism. Some of them followed the general trend and professed an increasingly aggressive German nationalism.

During the First World War, these divides were clearly visible.[57] At first glance, however, German Jewish reactions to the war appear similar to those in 1870/71—at least at its outset. The majority of German Jews once again placed strong emphasis on their patriotic commitment.[58] Even many Zionists initially supported the German cause. Two Zionist organizations declared: "We expect our youths to join the troops quickly with joyful hearts."[59] However, among Zionists other voices were also raised. The philosopher Gershom Scholem, for instance, criticized the patriotic zeal of his co-believers at the very beginning of the war. He was convinced that the Zionist movement would benefit if Great Britain and France were victorious.[60] Likewise, some socialists spoke out against the war because of their political convictions, joining their party comrades from other denominations.[61] Still, such antimilitaristic convictions were in the minority among German Jews at the commencement of the war.

A closer comparison between German Jewish interpretations of the Franco-Prussian War and the First World War, however, clearly reveals three crucial differences that also reflect the pluralization mentioned above. First, the idea of a transnational Jewish solidarity, which had been more or less uncontested in 1870/71, had lost ground in 1914. Some German Jews now rejected the idea that the relationship between Jews of different nationalities was in any way distinct from that of followers of the two Christian denominations.[62]

Second, ambivalence towards the wartime enemy had diminished in the First World War. Certainly, at this point, it has to be taken into consideration that Germany was not fighting against France alone but also against other adversaries. German Jews now argued that the German cause was congruent with the Jewish cause because Germany was fighting against the Czarist Empire, that is, also against its anti-Jewish policy.[63] Thus, the question of what it meant to fight against France as the pioneer of emancipation could be pushed into the background. It was easier, therefore, to suppress the ambivalence that had emerged from this question in 1870/71 and to join the mainstream nationalism. Some authors did not shrink away from chauvinistic tones, including Ernst Lissauer in his infamous "Song of Hate against England" from 1914.[64]

Third, the political truce that reigned in Germany at the very beginning of the war did not last long. Soon, a new wave of antisemitism hit the empire, disillusioning many Jews.[65] For instance, the so-called *Judenzählung* (Jewish census) that the German authorities arranged in order to measure Jewish participation in the army was a hard blow. Many German Jews felt deeply humiliated by this measure, which illustrated the harsh reality of continuing doubts about their loyalty.[66] Bitter feelings even intensified in the aftermath of the war, when an antisemitic version of the *Dolchstoßlegende* ("stab-in-the-back" myth) shifted the blame for the German defeat onto the Jews. In consequence, Zionism, although remaining a conviction of a minority group, gained appeal among German Jews—especially among youths.[67]

The German Jewish public discourse during the First World War differed from that of the 1870/71 war, particularly because of the rise of Zionism on the one hand and a more aggressive German nationalism among some German Jews on the other. Nevertheless, there are also obvious continuities. In comparison with the wider German public sphere, in general, German Jews still opposed aggressive nationalism more frequently and often tried to maintain cosmopolitan ideals instead.[68] Due to rigid censorship—another feature that distinguished the First World War from the Franco-Prussian War—it was hardly possible to express such critical opinions in public; they usually appear in unpublished private sources.[69]

In contrast to the growing differentiation in the German Jewish public sphere, Franco-Jewish self-definitions changed very little between 1870 and 1914. In general, they remained much more unanimous. The rise of antisemitism and its well-known manifestation in the Dreyfus affair did not shake the strong identification with France and her republican values to which they owed their emancipation. Zionism could not compete with this deeply ingrained conviction. It remained weak in France, attracting mainly immigrants from Eastern Europe—and not even all of them. Among some thirty thousand Eastern European Jews in France at the beginning of the First World War, many readily assumed Franco-Jewish values.[70] Even before naturalization was granted to them, they considered themselves French "with heart and soul."[71] One immigrant organization appealed to its members: "it is the moment to pay our tribute of gratitude to the country where we have found moral liberation and material welfare."[72] Indeed, many of the Eastern European immigrants volunteered for the French Foreign Legion.

Whereas fighting against the Czarist Empire helped the German Jews to interpret the war as conducive to the Jewish cause, the Franco-Russian alliance made it more difficult for French Jews to justify the war. Nevertheless, they claimed that the First World War promoted Jewish emancipation. In 1917, an author in the *Archives israélites* was convinced of the fact that "the Jewish emancipation that has begun in 1789 will be a *fait accompli* at the end of the present war ... The immortal glory of having been the initiator of the liberating movement will remain with France."[73] Instead of problematizing the alliance with Russia, French Jews preferred to emphasize once again that they were fighting against the antisemitic German Empire. Especially the Alsatian Jews—whether they had remained in Alsace or whether they had opted to move to France after 1871—were among the most passionate supporters of the French cause.[74] They depicted it as a victory for Judaism as well when France recuperated the two annexed provinces in 1918.

Conclusion

The differing self-definitions of French and German Jews were conditioned by the different social and legal status as well as by the divergent definitions of citizenship and nationhood in the two countries, which were a legacy of the Franco-Prussian War of 1870/71. The understanding of citizenship on the basis of voluntarism and the conception of a *Staatsnation* as it prevailed in France helped French Jews to claim their membership in the nation. They were backed by the fact that France was the country that pioneered the emancipation of the Jews. Consequently, they could bring their patriotism in line with their understanding of the ideals and aims of Judaism without any difficulty. Some even equated national and religious goals. Here, the attitude of Franco-Jewish writers was highly congruent with the discourse that dominated the French public sphere in general. French Jews kept to their republican convictions even in the face of the rise of antisemitism in the last third of the nineteenth century and at the beginning of the twentieth century. Therefore, there seemed to be no need to abandon these interpretative patterns in the First World War.

The situation was different in Germany. For German Jews, self-definition was much more problematic. The cultural understanding of the nation, which predominated in Germany, also offered them the possibility to claim membership in the nation. Difficulties arose, however, when they tried to harmonize this understanding of nationhood with the ideal of Jewish solidarity and especially with the transnational struggle for emancipation. The contradictions and ambivalence emerging here inevitably came to light during the national war of 1870/71, particularly in the annexation of Alsace and Lorraine. They grew in the aftermath of the conflict, when antisemitism spread and became more organized and aggressive. The result was an increasing pluralization of German Jewish self-definitions that also shaped the German Jewish war experience during 1914–18. The disappointments German Jews suffered during and in the aftermath of the First World War can be explained by this development, while at the same time they drove it forward themselves. Although some German Jews did not shy away from a fierce chauvinism, it cannot be argued that they represented the highly heterogenous German Jewish public. Even in its diversity, on the whole, German Jewish self-definitions still differed in many respects from mainstream German nationalism.

Christine G. Krüger is a researcher at the Collaborate Research Center "Dynamics of Security" at the University of Giessen. Her field of expertise is German and European history in the nineteenth and twentieth centuries, with special interests in Jewish history, antisemitism, nationalism, war experiences, and civil society. Her first monograph on German Jews during the Franco-Prussian War in 1870/71, *"Sind wir denn nicht Brüder?" Deutsche Juden im nationalen Krieg 1870/71* (Schöningh, 2006) won several prizes, including the Walter Witzmann Prize of the Heidelberg Academy of Sciences. Her most recent publication, *Dienstethos, Abenteuerlust, Bürgerpflicht: Jugendfreiwilligendienste in Deutschland und Großbritannien im 20. Jahrhundert* (Vandenhoeck & Ruprecht, 2016) is a comparative study on voluntary youth work in West Germany and Britain after 1945.

Notes

1. *Der Israelit*, no. 55, August 1914 (August 17, 1870/August 31, 1870).
2. On the German Jews during the war of 1870/71, see Christine G. Krüger, *"Sind wir denn nicht Brüder?" Deutsche Juden im nationalen Krieg 1870/71* (Paderborn, 2006).
3. Christian Rak, *Krieg, Nation und Konfession: Die Erfahrung des deutsch-französischen Krieges von 1870/71* (Paderborn, 2004).
4. For Jewish participation in the wars of the nineteenth and twentieth centuries in a transnational perspective, see Derek Penslar, *Jews and the Military: A History* (Princeton, NJ, 2013).
5. *Jeschurun*, no. 11, November 1914, 375–89, 377.
6. For comparative perspectives on both models, see Pierre Birnbaum and Ira Katznelson, eds., *Paths of Emancipation: Jews, States, and Citizenship* (Princeton, NJ, 1995); Michael Brenner, Vicki Caron, and Uri Kaufmann, eds., *Jewish Emancipation Reconsidered: The French and German Models* (Tübingen, 2003).
7. Arthur Hertzberg, *The French Enlightenment and the Jews* (New York, 1968).
8. Reinhard Rürup, "Jewish Emancipation and Bourgeois Society," *Leo Baeck Institute Yearbook* 14 (1969): 67–91. For a prominent example of the Zionist perspective, cf. Jacob Toury, *Soziale und politische Geschichte der Juden in Deutschland, 1847–1871: Zwischen Revolution, Reaktion und Emanzipation* (Düsseldorf, 1977).
9. For an early example of such a vision, see George L. Mosse, *German Jews beyond Judaism* (Bloomington, 1985). For a pronounced criticism of the concept of assimilation, cf. Simone Lässig, *Jüdische Wege ins Bürgertum: Kulturelles Kapital und sozialer Aufstieg im 19. Jahrhundert* (Göttingen, 2004).
10. See Eli Bar-Chen, *Weder Asiaten noch Orientalen: Internationale jüdische Organisationen und die Europäisierung "rückständiger" Juden* (Würzburg, 2005); Lisa Moses Leff, *Sacred Bonds of Solidarity: The Rise of Jewish Internationalism in Nineteenth-Century France*, Stanford Studies in Jewish History and Culture (Stanford, CA, 2006); Abigail Green, "Nationalism and the 'Jewish International': Religious Internationalism in Europe and the Middle East c. 1840–c. 1880," *Comparative Studies in Society and History* 50, no. 2 (2008): 535–58; Abigail Green, "Old Networks, New Connections: The Emergence of the Jewish International," in *Religious Internationals in*

the Modern World: Globalization and Faith Communities since 1750, ed. Abigail Green and Vincent Viaene (Palgrave Macmillan, 2012), 53–81.

11. Baruch Mevorah, "Effects of the Damascus Affair upon the Development of the Jewish Press 1840–1846" [Hebrew], *Zion* 23/4: 50/20 (1958/59); Johannes Valentin Schwarz, "Jüdische Presse," in *Handbuch zur Geschichte der Juden in Europa*, ed. Elke-Vera Kotowski, Julius Schoeps, and Hiltrud Wallenborn (Darmstadt, 2001), 285–95.
12. Christine G. Krüger, "Transnationale Öffentlichkeit—Nationale Feindschaft: Die deutsch-jüdische Presse und der Krieg von 1870/71," in *Deutsch-Jüdische Presse und jüdische Geschichte*, ed. Eleonore Lappin and Michael Nagel (Bremen, 2008), 33–45.
13. See Rogers Brubaker, *Citizenship and Nationhood in France and Germany* (Cambridge, MA, 1992).
14. *L'Univers israélite*, January 15, 1871, 212; *La Presse israélite*, February 1871, 582.
15. Zadoc Kahn, "Discours prononcé au service eligieux célébré en mémoire du Commandant Franchetti au Temple Israélite, le 6 décembre 1871," in *A la mémoire de Léon Franchetti*, ed. François Faverot de Kerbrech et al. (Paris, 1872), 13. See, for example, *Archives israélites*, no. 18, September 15, 1870, 554–55.
16. For Franco-Jewish republicanism, cf. Pierre Birnbaum, *Les fous de la république: Histoire politique des juifs d'État de Gambetta à Vichy* (Paris, 1994).
17. See, for example, Isaac Levy, *Echos patriotiques de la chaire israélite par Isaac Levy, ancien grand rabbin du Haut-Rhin, grand rabbin à Vesoul* (Colmar, 1873).
18. *Archives israélites*, no. 18, September 15, 1870, 551.
19. For the Alsatian Jews, see Vicki Caron, *Between France and Germany: The Jews of Alsace-Lorraine 1871–1918* (Stanford, CA, 1988).
20. *L'Univers israélite*, October 1, 1870, 80; emphasis in the original.
21. *Jüdische Presse*, no. 16, April 28, 1871, 334.
22. See for Germany Manfred Messerschmidt, "Juden im preußisch-deutschen Heer," in *Deutsche Jüdische Soldaten: Von der Epoche der Emanzipation bis zum Zeitalter der Weltkriege*, ed. Militärgeschichtliches Forschungsamt (Hamburg, 1996), 39–62. For France, Philippe Landau, "De l'Empire à la République: Les Juifs de France et la Guerre de 1870–1871," *Archives Juives* 37, no. 2 (2004): 111–26.
23. *Allgemeine Zeitung des Judenthums*, no. 20, May 16, 1871, 401.
24. For more on this, see Krüger, *"Sind wir denn nicht Brüder?"* 169–82.
25. *Israelitische Wochenschrift*, no. 5, January 31, 1872, 38; emphasis in the original.
26. *Israelitische Wochenschrift*, no. 44, November 1, 1871, 351.
27. For example, *Allgemeine Kirchenzeitung*, no. 32, August 10, 1870; *Allgemeine Evangelisch-Lutherische Kirchenzeitung*, no. 48, December 2, 1870, col. 900.
28. Rak, *Krieg, Nation und Konfession*, 157–62.
29. For more on this, see Christine G. Krüger, "'Der heilige Pakt, der unsere Kraft und unser Stolz...': Selbstpositionierungen deutscher und französischer Juden im Spannungsfeld von jüdischer Solidarität und Patriotismus, 1870/71," *Judaica* 63, no. 1/2 (2007): 76–102.

30. See Eli Bar-Chen, "Two Communities with a Sense of Mission: The Alliance Israélite Universelle and the Hilfsverein der Deutschen Juden," in *Jewish Emancipation Reconsidered: The French and German Models*, ed. Michael Brenner, Vicki Caron, and Uri Kaufmann (Tübingen, 2003), 111–21.
31. Green, "Nationalism and the 'Jewish International'"; Green, "Old Networks, New Connections."
32. *Allgemeine Zeitung des Judenthums*, no. 41, November 20, 1870, 800.
33. For the Franco-Jewish interpretation of the ideal of transnational solidarity in the middle of the nineteenth century in general, see Leff, *Sacred Bonds of Solidarity*. Leff interprets the transnational commitment of the French Jews as part of their effort to defend their own position within French society. She does not analyze how far national war put a challenge to the ideal.
34. *L'Univers israélite*, no. 6, November 15, 1871, 161.
35. *Revue israélite*, no. 14, March 15, 1872, 212.
36. See Ernst Schulin, "Doppel-Nationalität? Die Integration der Juden in die deutsche Kulturnation und die neue Konstruktion der jüdischen Geschichte," in *Die Konstruktion der Nation gegen die Juden*, ed. Peter Alter, Claus-Ekkehard Bärsch, and Peter Berghoff (Munich, 1999), 243–59; Michael A. Meyer, *The Origins of the Modern Jew: Jewish Identity and European Culture in Germany, 1749–1824* (Detroit, 1967); Simon Schwarzfuchs, *Du Juif à l'israélite: Histoire d'une mutation (1770–1870)* (Paris, 1989), especially 156.
37. See also Krüger, "Der heilige Pakt"; Krüger, *"Sind wir denn nicht Brüder?"* 229–36.
38. Levi Herzfeld, *Predigt, am ersten Tage des Peßachfestes gehalten von L. Herzfeld* (Braunschweig, 1871), 9.
39. *Archives israélites*, no. 18, September 15, 1871, 332; *Allgemeine Zeitung des Judenthums*, no. 49, December 5, 1871, 977. Cf. also *Israelitische Wochenschrift*, no. 36, September 14, 1870, 294; no. 29, July 19, 1871, 227; *Synodalblatt*, no. 9, October 4, 1871, 60.
40. *Allgemeine Zeitung des Judenthums*, no. 37, September 12, 1871, 741.
41. *Allgemeine Zeitung des Judenthums*, no. 35, August 30, 1870, 682. The author of this article was probably Ludwig Philippson.
42. *Allgemeine Zeitung des Judenthums*, no. 51, December 20, 1870, 993.
43. Rak, *Krieg, Nation und Konfession*, 216–26.
44. See, for example, *Der Katholik*, 1870, no. 29, 492; *Katholisches Sonntagsblatt*, no. 43, October 23, 1870, 358. See also Günter Brakelmann, "Der Krieg von 1870/71 und die Reichsgründung im Urteil des Protestantismus," in *Kirche zwischen Krieg und Frieden: Studien zur Geschichte des deutschen Protestantismus*, ed. Wolfgang Huber and Johannes Schwerdtfeger (Stuttgart, 1976), 307–8; Rak, *Krieg, Nation und Konfession*, 227–39.
45. *Archives israélites*, no. 20, October 15, 1872, 613.
46. *L'Univers israélite*, January 15, 1871, 204. The author spoke of the "incompatibilité qu'il y a entre Prussien et israélite."
47. *L'Univers israélite*, August 15, 1871, 487–88.
48. Daniel Mollenhauer, "Sinngebung in der Niederlage: Die französischen Katholiken und die 'Année Terrible' (1870/71)," in *"Gott mit uns!" Nation, Religion und Gewalt im 19. und frühen 20. Jahrhundert*, ed. Gerd Krumeich

and Hartmut Lehmann (Göttingen, 2000), 157–71; Michael Jeismann, *Das Vaterland der Feinde: Studien zum nationalen Feindbegriff und Selbstverständnis in Deutschland und Frankreich 1792–1918* (Stuttgart, 1992), 195.
49. Alexandre Weill, *Lettres de vengeance d'un Alsacien* (Paris, 1871).
50. Moritz Daniel Oppenheim, *Bilder aus dem altjüdischen Familien-Leben nach Original-Gemälden von Moritz Oppenheim: Mit Einführung und Erläuterungen von Dr. Leopold Stein* (Frankfurt am Main, 1882), n.p.
51. Adolf Lewin, *Geschichte der badischen Juden seit der Regierung Karl Friedrichs (1738–1909)* (Karlsruhe, 1909), 339.
52. Ibid.
53. *Israelitische Wochenschrift*, no. 7, February 15, 1871, 52.
54. *Israelit*, no. 68, August 1895, 1265.
55. Abraham Frank, *Die Schutzwehren des Deutschen Reiches: Festpredigt zur Erinnerung an den 2. September 1870 beim Festgottesdienst, Am Sonnabend, 31. August 1895 in der Synagoge zu Köln* (Cologne, [1895]). See also Benjamin Rippner, "Rede Zum 90. Geburtstag Kaiser Wilhelms I: Eine Religiöse Betrachtung," in *Eine Auswahl vaterländischer Reden des Herrn Rabbiner Dr. Rippner: Gesammelt und herausgegeben bei Gelegenheit der Feier seiner 25jährigen Amtstätigkeit in der Synagogen-Gemeinde zu Glogau* (Glogau, [1897]), 21–25, 21.
56. For the peace movement, cf. Karl Holl, "Der jüdische Beitrag zur Friedensbewegung," in *Begegnung und Erinnerung: Universitätssymposium Haifa—Bremen*, ed. Michael Nagel (Bremen, 1995), 69–84; Alan T. Levenson, "The German Peace Movement and the Jews: An Unexplored Nexus," *Leo Baeck Institute Yearbook* 46 (2001): 277–302; Jean Philippe Schreiber, "Judaisme et pacifisme," in *Le pacifisme est-il une valeur universelle? Acte du colloque de 25 et 26 Novembre 1999*, ed. Suzanne Lecocq and Jean-François Füeg (Mons, 2001), 11–28.
57. For the German Jews during the First World War, see Ulrich Sieg, *Jüdische Intellektuelle im Ersten Weltkrieg: Kriegserfahrungen, weltanschauliche Debatten und kulturelle Neuentwürfe* (Berlin, 2001); Eugen Tannenbaum, ed., *Kriegsbriefe deutscher und österreichischer Juden* (Berlin, 1915); Sabine Hank and Hermann Simon, *Feldpostbriefe jüdischer Soldaten 1914–1918: Briefe ehemaliger Zöglinge an Sigmund Feist, Direktor des Reichenheischen Waisenhauses in Berlin*, 2 vols., ed. Stiftung Neue Synagoge Berlin/Centrum Iudaicum (Teetz, 2002). With its main focus on the commemoration of the war, see also Tim Grady, *The German-Jewish Soldiers of the First World War in History and Memory* (Liverpool, 2011).
58. Sieg, *Jüdische Intellektuelle im Ersten Weltkrieg*, 53–86; Raymond Anthony Jonas, "Anxiety, Identity, and the Displacement of Violence during the Année Terrible: The Sacred Heart and the Diocese of Nantes, 1870–1871," *French Historical Studies* 21 (1998): 55–75.
59. *Jüdische Rundschau*, August 7, 1914, 343; see Peter Pulzer, "Der Erste Weltkrieg," in *Deutsch-jüdische Geschichte der Neuzeit*, ed. Michael A. Meyer, Michael Brenner, and Mordechai Breuer (Munich, 2000), 359.
60. Pulzer, "Der Erste Weltkrieg," 360; Sieg, *Jüdische Intellektuelle im Ersten Weltkrieg*, 59–60.

61. Pulzer, "Der Erste Weltkrieg," 360.
62. See "Umschau," *Im Deutschen Reich* 22, no. 9/10 (1916): 201.
63. See Sarah Panter, *Jüdische Erfahrungen und Loyalitätskonflikte im Ersten Weltkrieg* (Göttingen, 2014).
64. Ernst Lissauer, "Haßgesang gegen England," in *Der brennende Tag: Ausgewählte Gedichte*, ed. Ernst Lissauer (Berlin, 1916), 40. The poem was published in numerous other collections of war poems. Although German Jews also raised their voices against France, as far as I know, there is no testimony of any similar aggressiveness in tone directed against France. Perhaps this is due to ongoing respect paid to France by German Jews.
65. Pulzer, "Der Erste Weltkrieg," 366–74; Sieg, *Jüdische Intellektuelle im Ersten Weltkrieg*, 87–95.
66. German Jewish reactions to the Jewish census were not homogenous; some Jewish war letters or memoirs, for example, do not mention it at all. There are, however, numerous sources that display a deep disappointment. See Jacob Rosenthal, *"Die Ehre des jüdischen Soldaten": Die Judenzählung im Ersten Weltkrieg und ihre Folgen* (Frankfurt am Main, 2007). See also Penslar, *Jews and the Military*, 173.
67. Grady, *The German-Jewish Soldiers*, 60.
68. Eugen Fuchs, "Was nun?" *Neue jüdische Monatshefte* 7 (1919): 137–45. Cf. Sieg, *Jüdische Intellektuelle im Ersten Weltkrieg*, 151–62, 260–96.
69. Sieg, *Jüdische Intellektuelle im Ersten Weltkrieg*, 123.
70. Catherine Nicault, "La réceptivité au Sionisme, de la fin du XIXe siècle à l'aube de la Seconde Guerre Mondiale," in *Histoire politique des Juifs en France: Entre pluralisme et particularisme*, ed. Pierre Birnbaum (Paris, 1990); Philippe Landau, *L'opinion Juive et l'affaire Dreyfus* (Paris, 1995), 92–111.
71. Cited in Philippe Landau, *Les Juifs de France et la Grande Guerre: Un patriotisme républicain, 1914–1941* (Paris, 1999), 39.
72. Ibid.
73. "Passé et avenir," *Archives israélites*, April 19, 1917, cited in Philippe Landau, "'La patrie en danger': D'une guerre à l'autre," in Birnbaum, *Histoire politique des Juifs en France*, 81.
74. Caron, *Between France and Germany*, 178–86.

Bibliography

Bar-Chen, Eli. "Two Communities with a Sense of Mission: The Alliance Israélite Universelle and the Hilfsverein der Deutschen Juden." In *Jewish Emancipation Reconsidered: The French and German Models*, edited by Michael Brenner, Vicki Caron, and Uri Kaufmann, 111–21. Tübingen: Mohr Siebeck, 2003.

———. *Weder Asiaten noch Orientalen: Internationale jüdische Organisationen und die Europäisierung "rückständiger" Juden*. Würzburg: Ergon-Verlag, 2005.

Birnbaum, Pierre. *Les fous de la république: Histoire politique des juifs d'État de Gambetta à Vichy*. Paris: Fayard, 1994.

Birnbaum, Pierre, and Ira Katznelson, eds. *Paths of Emancipation: Jews, States, and Citizenship*. Princeton, NJ: Princeton University Press, 1995.

Brakelmann, Günter. "Der Krieg von 1870/71 und die Reichsgründung im Urteil des Protestantismus." In *Kirche zwischen Krieg und Frieden: Studien zur Geschichte des deutschen Protestantismus*, edited by Wolfgang Huber and Johannes Schwerdtfeger, 293–321. Stuttgart: Klett, 1976.

Brenner, Michael, Vicki Caron, and Uri Kaufmann, eds. *Jewish Emancipation Reconsidered: The French and German Models*. Tübingen: Mohr Siebeck, 2003.

Brubaker, Rogers. *Citizenship and Nationhood in France and Germany*. Cambridge, MA: Harvard University Press, 1992.

Caron, Vicki. *Between France and Germany: The Jews of Alsace-Lorraine 1871–1918*. Stanford, CA: Stanford University Press, 1988.

Frank, Abraham. *Die Schutzwehren des Deutschen Reiches: Festpredigt zur Erinnerung an den 2. September 1870 beim Festgottesdienst, Am Sonnabend, 31. August 1895 in der Synagoge zu Köln*. Cologne: Kohn, [1895].

Fuchs, Eugen. "Was nun?" *Neue jüdische Monatshefte* 7 (1919): 137–45.

Grady, Tim. *The German-Jewish Soldiers of the First World War in History and Memory*. Liverpool: Liverpool University Press, 2011.

Green, Abigail. "Nationalism and the 'Jewish International': Religious Internationalism in Europe and the Middle East c. 1840–c. 1880." *Comparative Studies in Society and History* 50, no. 2 (2008): 535–58.

———. "Old Networks, New Connections: The Emergence of the Jewish International." In *Religious Internationals in the Modern World: Globalization and Faith Communities since 1750*, edited by Abigail Green and Vincent Viaene, 53–81. Basingstoke: Palgrave Macmillan, 2012.

Hank, Sabine, and Hermann Simon. *Feldpostbriefe jüdischer Soldaten 1914–1918: Briefe ehemaliger Zöglinge an Sigmund Feist, Direktor des Reichenheischen Waisenhauses in Berlin*, 2 vols. Ed. Stiftung Neue Synagoge Berlin/Centrum Judaicum. Teetz: Hentrich und Hentrich, 2002.

Hertzberg, Arthur. *The French Enlightenment and the Jews*. New York: Columbia University Press, 1968.

Herzfeld, Levi. *Predigt, am ersten Tage des Peßachfestes gehalten von L. Herzfeld*. Braunschweig, 1871.

Holl, Karl. "Der jüdische Beitrag zur Friedensbewegung." In *Begegnung und Erinnerung:*
Universitätssymposium Haifa—Bremen, edited by Michael Nagel, 69–84. Bremen: Edition Temmen, 1995.

Jeismann, Michael. *Das Vaterland der Feinde: Studien zum nationalen Feindbegriff und Selbstverständnis in Deutschland und Frankreich 1792–1918*. Stuttgart: Klett-Cotta, 1992.

Jonas, Raymond Anthony. "Anxiety, Identity, and the Displacement of Violence during the Année Terrible: The Sacred Heart and the Diocese of Nantes, 1870–1871." *French Historical Studies* 21 (1998): 55–75.

Kahn, Zadoc. "Discours prononcé au service eligieux célébré en mémoire du Commandant Franchetti au Temple Israélite, le 6 décembre 1871." In *A la mémoire de Léon Franchetti*, edited by François Faverot de Kerbrech et al., 11–22. Paris: L'Imprimerie de la Claye, 1872.

Krüger, Christine G. "'Der heilige Pakt, der unsere Kraft und unser Stolz...': Selbstpositionierungen deutscher und französischer Juden im Spannungsfeld von jüdischer Solidarität und Patriotismus, 1870/71." *Judaica* 63, no. 1/2 (2007): 76–102.

———. *"Sind wir denn nicht Brüder?" Deutsche Juden im nationalen Krieg 1870/71*. Paderborn: Schöningh, 2006.

———. "Transnationale Öffentlichkeit—Nationale Feindschaft: Die deutschjüdische Presse und der Krieg von 1870/71." In *Deutsch-Jüdische Presse und jüdische Geschichte*, edited by Eleonore Lappin and Michael Nagel, 33–45. Bremen: Edition Lumière, 2008.

Landau, Philippe. "De l'Empire à la République: Les Juifs de France et la Guerre de 1870–1871." *Archives Juives* 37, no. 2 (2004): 111–26.

———. *Les Juifs de France et la Grande Guerre: Un patriotisme républicain, 1914–1941*. Paris: CNRS Editions, 1999.

———. *L'opinion Juive et l'affaire Dreyfus*. Paris: A. Michel, 1995.

———. "'La patrie en danger': D'une guerre à l'autre." In *Histoire politique des Juifs en France: Entre pluralisme et particularisme*, edited by Pierre Birnbaum, 74–91. Paris: Presses de la Fondation nationale des sciences politiques, 1990.

Lässig, Simone. *Jüdische Wege ins Bürgertum: Kulturelles Kapital und sozialer Aufstieg im 19. Jahrhundert*. Göttingen: Vandenhoeck & Ruprecht, 2004.

Leff, Lisa Moses. *Sacred Bonds of Solidarity: The Rise of Jewish Internationalism in Nineteenth-Century France*. Stanford Studies in Jewish History and Culture. Stanford, CA: Stanford University Press, 2006.

Levenson, Alan T. "The German Peace Movement and the Jews: An Unexplored Nexus." *Leo Baeck Institute Yearbook* 46 (2001): 277–302.

Levy, Isaac. *Echos patriotiques de la chaire israélite par Isaac Levy, ancien grand rabbin du Haut-Rhin, grand rabbin à Vesoul*. Colmar: Sandoz & Fischbacher, 1873.

Lewin, Adolf. *Geschichte der badischen Juden seit der Regierung Karl Friedrichs (1738–1909)*. Karlsruhe: Braun, 1909.

Lissauer, Ernst. "Haßgesang gegen England." In *Der brennende Tag: Ausgewählte Gedichte*, edited by Ernst Lissauer, 40. Berlin: Schuster & Loeffler, 1916.

Messerschmidt, Manfred. "Juden im preußisch-deutschen Heer." In *Deutsche Jüdische Soldaten: Von der Epoche der Emanzipation bis zum Zeitalter der Weltkriege*, edited by Militärgeschichtliches Forschungsamt, 39–62. Hamburg: Verlag E. S. Mittler & Sohn, 1996.

Mevorah, Baruch. "Effects of the Damascus Affair upon the Development of the Jewish Press 1840–1846" [Hebrew]. *Zion* 23/4: 50/20 (1958/59).

Meyer, Michael A. *The Origins of the Modern Jew: Jewish Identity and European Culture in Germany, 1749–1824*. Detroit: Wayne State University Press, 1967.

Mollenhauer, Daniel. "Sinngebung in der Niederlage: Die französischen Katholiken und die 'Année Terrible' (1870/71)." In *"Gott mit uns!" Nation, Religion und Gewalt im 19. und frühen 20. Jahrhundert*, edited by Gerd Krumeich and Hartmut Lehmann, 157–71. Göttingen: Vandenhoeck & Ruprecht, 2000.

Mosse, George L. *German Jews beyond Judaism*. Bloomington: Indiana University Press, 1985.

Nicault, Catherine. "La réceptivité au Sionisme, de la fin du XIXe siècle à l'aube de la Seconde Guerre Mondiale." In *Histoire politique des Juifs en France: Entre pluralisme et particularisme*, edited by Pierre Birnbaum, 92–111. Paris: Presses de la Fondation nationale des sciences politiques, 1990.

Oppenheim, Moritz Daniel. *Bilder aus dem altjüdischen Familien-Leben nach Original-Gemälden von Moritz Oppenheim: Mit Einführung und Erläuterungen von Dr. Leopold Stein*. Frankfurt am Main: Keller, 1882.

Panter, Sarah. *Jüdische Erfahrungen und Loyalitätskonflikte im Ersten Weltkrieg*. Göttingen: Vandenhoeck & Ruprecht, 2014.

Penslar, Derek. *Jews and the Military: A History*. Princeton, NJ: Princeton University Press, 2013.

Pulzer, Peter. "Der Erste Weltkrieg." In *Deutsch-jüdische Geschichte der Neuzeit*, edited by Michael A. Meyer, Michael Brenner, and Mordechai Breuer, 356–80. Munich: C. H. Beck, 2000.

Rak, Christian. *Krieg, Nation und Konfession: Die Erfahrung des deutsch-französischen Krieges von 1870/71*. Paderborn: Schöningh, 2004.

Rippner, Benjamin. "Rede Zum 90. Geburtstag Kaiser Wilhelms I: Eine Religiöse Betrachtung." In *Eine Auswahl vaterländischer Reden des Herrn Rabbiner Dr. Rippner: Gesammelt und herausgegeben bei Gelegenheit der Feier seiner 25jährigen Amtstätigkeit in der Synagogen-Gemeinde zu Glogau*, 21–25. Glogau: Flemming, [1897].

Rosenthal, Jacob. *"Die Ehre des jüdischen Soldaten": Die Judenzählung im Ersten Weltkrieg und ihre Folgen*. Frankfurt am Main: Campus Verlag, 2007.

Rürup, Reinhard. "Jewish Emancipation and Bourgeois Society." *Leo Baeck Institute Yearbook* 14 (1969): 67–91.

Schreiber, Jean Philippe. "Judaisme et pacifisme." In *Le pacifisme est-il une valeur universelle? Acte du colloque de 25 et 26 Novembre 1999*, edited by Suzanne Lecocq and Jean-François Füeg, 11–28. Mons: Édition Mundaneum, 2001.

Schulin, Ernst. "Doppel-Nationalität? Die Integration der Juden in die deutsche Kulturnation und die neue Konstruktion der jüdischen Geschichte." In *Die Konstruktion der Nation gegen die Juden*, edited by Peter Alter, Claus-Ekkehard Bärsch, and Peter Berghoff, 243–59. Munich: Wilhelm Fink, 1999.

Schwarz, Johannes Valentin. "Jüdische Presse." In *Handbuch zur Geschichte der Juden in Europa*, edited by Elke-Vera Kotowski, Julius Schoeps, and Hiltrud Wallenborn, 285–95. Darmstadt: Wissenschaftliche Buchgesellschaft, 2001.

Schwarzfuchs, Simon. *Du Juif à l'israélite: Histoire d'une mutation (1770–1870)*. Paris: Fayard, 1989.

Sieg, Ulrich. *Jüdische Intellektuelle im Ersten Weltkrieg: Kriegserfahrungen, weltanschauliche Debatten und kulturelle Neuentwürfe*. Berlin: De Gruyter, 2001.

Tannenbaum, Eugen, ed. *Kriegsbriefe deutscher und österreichischer Juden*. Berlin: Neuer Verlag, 1915.

Toury, Jacob. *Soziale und politische Geschichte der Juden in Deutschland, 1847–1871: Zwischen Revolution, Reaktion und Emanzipation*. Düsseldorf: Droste, 1977.

Weill, Alexandre. *Lettres de vengeance d'un Alsacien*. Paris: E. Dentu, 1871.

2

Habsburg Jews and the Imperial Army before and during the First World War

Tamara Scheer

One day in late August 1918, the Habsburg soldier Walter Herburger—a wounded veteran of the Italian front—was reading the local newspaper, the *Vorarlberger Wacht*. After catching up on the day's developments, he complained angrily in his diary about the Social Democratic press: "They shout 'down with war,' agitating for a civil war and insubordination," he wrote. But it was not just the thought of an uprising that so infuriated him; his anger also stemmed from the supposed background of the journalists. They "are not frontline soldiers," he claimed, "they are Jews who initiated this evil act with the help of paid Aryans ... aiming to poison the minds of the masses."[1] Herburger's personal views also found a dangerous echo in the workings of the state. In early 1918, the Austrian Ministry of Interior addressed a note to all governors: "The Hungarian ministry informed us that Socialists are financially supported by the Entente. We now know that the conspicuous financial support is made on behalf of them by using international networks. Imprisoned Jews should no longer be allowed to be set free. On the contrary, from now on the observation of Jews should be intensified."[2] This perception that there was a "Jewish conspiracy" at the heart of the revolution, underpinned by the fact that the intellectual leader of the Austrian Red Guards, Leo Rothziegel, and prominent members of the Social Democratic Party, such as Victor Adler and Otto Bauer, were Jewish, endured and even intensified after the dissolution of the empire in 1918.[3]

What is important in the context of this chapter is that Habsburg Jews, at the end of the war in particular, were exclusively portrayed as shirkers who not only refused to fight but also attempted to weaken the state and its political system. What Herburger did not mention throughout his war diary was that he almost certainly must have fought alongside Jewish soldiers and officers. Of course, he mentioned shirkers and disloyal behavior over the years, but usually where it concerned Italians and Czechs. The longer the war lasted, the more male citizens refused to be sent back to the front, deserted, or took active action against the state—regardless of their religious or ethnic background. Often certain nationalities were blamed, Jews too, but the diaries of the more supra-national state-loyal officers pointed to the fact "that among all nationalities" soldiers increasingly deserted or refused to return to the front after their leave.[4]

Starting with the Compromise between Austria and Hungary in 1867 and the constitutional era that followed up to the outbreak of the First World War, Jewish biographies are usually portrayed in literature and novels almost entirely as success stories. Habsburg Jews are described, and often described themselves, as having reached the goal of becoming an integral part of society.[5] As parliamentarians, scientists, journalists, business owners, and high-ranking civil servants and army officers, they actively contributed to, shaped, and modernized the Hungarian state as well as the Austrian half. Most of them are described as no longer standing outside society, with the exception of orthodox Jews. Nevertheless, due to the monarchy's ethnic diversity there was no common Habsburg society at all. There were plenty of different middle-class societies that usually identified themselves according to one of the Habsburg nationalities. There was a national Hungarian society, as well as a Czech and German national middle class. Jews often played an active part in nationalistic quarrels when they affiliated with one of these nationalities—for example, as Marsha L. Rozenblit calls it, "acculturated Jews who adopted German, Czech, or Polish cultures."[6] But many Jews tried to avoid showing any preference for national affiliation, and they emphasized their supra-national identities or attitude of indifference to nationalism by being loyal to the overall state and the emperor.

The Habsburg *fin de siècle*, to which Jews contributed to a major extent, ended in July 1914 when the First World War mobilized hundreds of thousands of men. At the same time, the home front civil society became more and more divided along national lines.[7] In their memoirs and diaries, Jewish writers after 1918 usually tended to highlight the positive sides of Habsburg rule, even though antisemitism was always present. Throughout the war, not only did antisemitic rhetoric grow, but there was also a change in how Jews were portrayed. The Habsburg army, as the main institution that covered the state as a whole, was and still is mostly perceived as standing separate from nationalism.[8]

This chapter analyzes the role of Jews in the army and in particular how they were evaluated by their non-Jewish comrades. Using published and unpublished autobiographical sources, the bulk written by members of the army, I examine the diversity of Jewish soldiers and officers before and during the war. Among army officers, German was the *lingua franca*. Therefore, even if many officers would not have identified themselves as being (Habsburg) Germans, they wrote their diaries and published their memoirs in this language.

In most cases, Jewish stories have to be compared to those of the members of other national and religious groups to discover similarities and particularities. I argue that antisemitism, in all of its various forms, played a role in generating tensions between Habsburg Jewish and non-Jewish soldiers and officers. Nevertheless, criticism was very often an outcome of other factors, such as general friction in the army or social prejudices distinct from antisemitism. It is also important to note where Jews served before and during the war, whether on the front lines or on the home front. In addition, it is necessary to locate incidents not only chronologically or geographically, but also in situational terms. Did a military operation fail, leading those involved to desperately look for someone to blame? As Jews—in contrast to other ethnic and religious groups—settled everywhere in the monarchy, they allow for greater insight into Habsburg nationalisms, loyalties, and identities as well as prejudices.

The Prewar Mindset: Habsburg Garrisons and Local Jewish Communities

In terms of the prejudices encountered by Jews as members of the army, it is important to analyze how Jewish civil communities in Habsburg army garrisons were described in autobiographical sources on the eve of the Great War. When the war started in July 1914 and many thousands of male inhabitants of these towns and villages—both Jews and non-Jews—became soldiers, the bulk of them looked back on prewar military training all over the monarchy. Officers, but also many enlisted men, usually served in parts of the monarchy that were not their home region. They experienced for a couple of months or even years a local culture that often totally differed from their own. It is therefore not a surprise that writers of diaries and memoirs emphasized local cultural features that appeared foreign to them. Interestingly, when it came to local Jewish cultures, in particular orthodox Jews in Galicia, the narratives of Jewish and non-Jewish writers did not differ from each other significantly. In particular, writers who held an officer's rank and usually came from a middle-class urban background assessed orthodox Jewry from a social and economic point of view rather than displaying only antisemitic prejudices.

It was therefore not only non-Jewish officers, but also their Jewish comrades, who when first entering Galicia highlighted and commented on the (orthodox) Jewish character of the towns and villages and the customs of locals. Usually this was mentioned in the first sentence, when the newcomer described his immediate impression on arrival. In addition, it has to be mentioned that being transferred to a Galician garrison was not what most officers hoped for. Instead, they hoped to be transferred to one of the main urban areas such as Prague, Vienna, Budapest, or even Sarajevo. Relocation to Galicia was very often used by the army authorities to punish an officer for misbehavior. The officer Julius Lustig von Preanfeld, for example, was unhappy when he was told that he had to transfer to the Galician town of Brody for two years—the monarchy's eastern-most garrison. He mentioned that he did not know any of the local languages, Ruthene and Polish. Brody, as he began his statement, was "a more than three quarters Jewish town."[9]

The Jewish officer Eugen Hoeflich quickly turned attention to the Jewish character of the garrison, but also to another trait: "The town Bogoria (today in Poland) [looked like] most of the other Polish towns, Jewish inhabitants mostly, but also in Jewish business sense [*Jüdischer Geschäftssinn*]."[10] The officer Karl Nowottny, who was sent to Przemyśl (today in Poland) also connected Jewishness to a certain behavior: "It is a characteristic for Galicia that small business is run by Jews exclusively."[11] Like his Jewish and non-Jewish fellow officers, he described a particular symbol of Galician Jewish business:

> For renting a flat in Galicia the *Faktor* was inevitable. These intrusive people who always looked like you have called them, Polish Jews, sold everything needed, but without their assistance we would have been totally helpless ... They were very helpful, but they were also dangerous as they exploited the young officers' money, and many who were inexperienced fell into usurers' hands afterwards.[12]

One of the most frequent reasons why Habsburg officers were dismissed from the army was because they had accumulated debts. Instead of blaming their own weakness or their comrades' foolishness, they more often accused the local Jews who lent them the money.

When reading memoirs and diaries it becomes obvious that "the others" living in Galicia, Poland, and Ruthenia, were marginalized. But Galician Jews were also comparable to another Habsburg religious group, namely Muslims. Narratives by officers regarding Bosnian-Herzegovinian garrisons mainly deal with Muslim culture and habits, while the customs of Croats and Serbs are marginalized. Presumably, this happened because orthodox Jewish and Muslim culture differed so much from the officers' own cultural backgrounds and they were therefore given a prominent place in autobiographical writings. In particular, when autobiographical stories were intended for publication, writers knew that stories about so-called backward orthodox Jews and exotic Muslims sold more than those about everyday Poles and Croats. "They were totally peregrine peoples whose sons we had to train," Franz Xaver Schubert wrote about his duty in the Carpathians as a young and inexperienced professional officer. He pointed to the fact that officers' training never dealt with how to interact with soldiers coming from "foreign" cultures: "I recognized that there was an interest on behalf of the officers, but no one explained it."[13] During his service in the Carpathian region, he developed a deep interest in observing church festivities of the Greek Orthodox, Greek Catholics, and the Jews.

The autobiographical notes quoted above can be interpreted as providing, to some degree, a kind of objective view of Jewish culture in Galicia. But it was usually in regard to the local business culture in Galicia, with the *Faktor* as its most prominent example and most often-discussed symbol, that army members tended to turn to antisemitic rhetoric. While soldiers lived in the barracks in the military camps, officers usually rented a flat or house from a landlord. This was the first challenge when arriving in a new garrison, so it was typical for men to discuss how to find a good place to live. What was exceptional was the role of Jews in this discussion. The officer Franz Xaver Schubert had to find a new temporary home in Kolomea (today Kolomyja in Ukraine):

> It was difficult finding a flat. A captain was transferred to Klagenfurt, who until then rented a flat with two rooms and a garden in the house of an attorney. I rushed to this place. On my way, a little sleazy Jew started following me and said, "You won't get the room rented without my support." He laughed.

In fact, the Jewish attorney refused to rent out the room, and commented:

> "I won't rent the room without *Faktor*. If I do so, they will all turn against me." Outside of the house the little Jew was waiting and laughing, sarcastically.[14]

Expressions like "a little sleazy Jew" and "laughing, sarcastically" in particular reflected typical Jewish stereotypes. A few months later, the same officer asked his commander to send him to Jewish festivities, specifically noting in his diary that he met very friendly and sympathetic people there.[15]

Closer, more private contact between officers (Jewish or non-Jewish) and local Galician Jews was the exception. What is obvious in most autobiographical sources is also mentioned by the officer Heinrich Wiedern: "We lived in harmony with the Christian civil middle class such as civil servants, physicians, engineers and their families (Brody had more than 70 percent Jews)."[16] Again, this focus on the local Christian middle class was similar to the descriptions of leisure activities and contacts with Muslim upper and middle class in Bosnia-Herzegovina. Although local officials, regardless of their religious background, were always invited to the garrison's festivities, such as the regimental day or the emperor's birthday, they did not invite each other to more informal events. The decisive factor therefore was not only antisemitism, but also the fact that cultural habits differed so much, from the issue of food and drink to the place of women in the public sphere.

When leaving Galicia and the eastern-most part of the monarchy with its orthodox Jewry, the question arises: what about middle-class Jews in other parts of the monarchy? How did Jewish and non-Jewish men in the army deal with secular Jewish civilians? The officer Adolf Stillfried von Rathenitz wrote about leisure activities in the Istrian multicultural international port town of Trieste. Besides spending his time among German-speaking upper-class families, not only for nationalistic reasons but also due to the German *lingua franca*, he drew attention to his favorite contact: "I have found the warmest hospitality in the house of the longstanding president of the Austro-Hungarian Lloyd, Baron Marco Morpurgo. He and his wife as well as their son were baptized Jews and in their *palais* the high society of Trieste gathered, with the exception of three or four Austrian noble families, who took offence at the Morpurgos' Jewish origin."[17] Laurence Cole describes the Morpurgo family as "being of national sentiment (they identified with Italianita) and loyalism with Habsburg" at the same time.[18] Although in those days "Triestine cosmopolitanism" was common, and the primacy of Italian culture and language was not exclusively interpreted from a nationalistic point of view, even wealthy, liberal, and influential Italian Jews somehow remained outsiders.[19] But this was not the case for the Habsburg officers who avoided being associated with nationalistic circles for the benefit of their careers. On the contrary, as they attempted to avoid nationalistic local middle-class society, they often ended up in Jewish salons. This stance often resulted in even closer contact.

When they wanted to marry, Habsburg professional officers had to pay a large amount of money. Therefore, if they did not come from a wealthy family background, they often sought wealthy spouses. The close proximity to wealthy Jewish families all over the monarchy's garrisons on the one hand, and on the other hand the desire of these Jewish families to assimilate even more or become real members of Habsburg society, created perfect win-win situations. Many Christian officers ended up in Jewish families. Jewish women therefore became an integral part of the officers' society all over the monarchy, and in all national circles.[20] This fact contributed to the tolerant stance towards Jews—at least in public—as the Jewish writer and reserve officer Otto Friedländer observed: "He did not feel antisemitism, as the army strongly and successfully ensured that no national or religious feeling was hurt. In particular, antisemitic rhetoric was avoided because many officers were married to Jewish women."[21]

Autobiographical sources also show that after the first contact with local Jewish communities, officers tended to write about Jews more negatively, but at a later point in their careers assessed them more positively. Certainly, one of the reasons for this was that most Jews stood outside nationalism, and spoke the army's *lingua franca*, German. Therefore, when writing about local civil Jews in memoirs and diaries, the word "but" is often used. Julius Lustig von Preanfeld, whose father had also been an officer, experienced garrison life as a schoolchild:

> Parents encountered great difficulties when it came to schooling. Me and my brothers are the best example. Karl attended Polish, Czech, and German [language] schools. Heinrich, when father was transferred to *Jungbunzlau* (today Mladá Boleslav is in the Czech Republic), had to be sent to a residential school in another town that had a German gymnasium, and I had to attend the Jewish school (*Judenschule*), because there was no other German primary school. ... I, for sure, cannot be called a Philosemite, but I have to admit that this school was an excellent one.[22]

This reference shows Preanfeld's antisemitic attitude and can in no way be taken as a positive evaluation of Jews in general. But it also indicates that Preanfeld's antisemitism did not go so far as to malign everything associated with Jews.

There are, of course, many examples of anti-Jewish riots in Habsburg lands that were expressed in public before the war. As in all cases of public unrest, it was not just the police but also the army that was sent to counter them.[23] Although they were seen as outsiders, it is important to mention that Jews—before the outbreak of the war—were usually not accused of disloyalty. On the contrary, it is clear that the authors of the diaries and memoirs discussed in this chapter perceived Jews as somehow representing the ideal supra-national Habsburg individual, as they lacked any officially recognized nationality of their own. They also shared this characteristic with Bosnian-Herzegovinian Muslims. Therefore, quotations such as the one by the officer Franz Putz were generally exceptions. After having served for a couple of years and meeting friendly comrades from all nationalities, he observed: "I can't help myself, I still deeply distrust Italians, Jews, and [ethnic] Hungarians."[24]

From Peace to War: Jews as Members of the Army

Unlike in other armies at that time[25] and the Habsburg civil service,[26] where Jews were not allowed to become members at all and met numerous restrictions or remained marginalized outsiders, Jews were an integral part of the Habsburg army. They were soldiers, non commissioned officers (NCOs), military civil servants, and officers serving in all branches of the army. For this reason, they are mentioned more frequently in autobiographical narratives than any other group. They lived everywhere in the empire and therefore almost every member of the army, whether an ordinary soldier or an officer, had a couple of comrades of Jewish faith or they had at least trained or fought alongside Jewish soldiers. It is no wonder, therefore, that Jews were always "part of the story," and there were plenty of opportunities for negative and positive moments. Often when those writing about the war mentioned a certain behavior that they assessed as being positive, the word "despite" is used. A Jew was a good comrade, "despite" being Jewish. This was not unique to Jews. The word was also used for all nationalities who were perceived to be disloyal towards the army, the emperor, or the state. For example, someone was a good comrade, "despite" being a Czech or an Italian. What is unique in the Jewish case is that when they were assessed negatively, the reason can often be traced back to general internal army frictions. Antisemitic rhetoric was then only added to increase a statement's value.

To the general public, the Habsburg officers' corps appeared as a homogenous group. From the inside, there were several layers of hierarchies resulting from a higher or lower rank, among other factors. One gap appeared between professional/career and reserve officers. The army reform in 1868 opened the possibility for young men who had graduated from high school to avoid serving for three years as ordinary rank and file. They served for a year with an option of being assigned a reserve officer's rank afterwards. As much more time and experience were required for professional officers to gain officer status, there was huge mistrust, envy, and anger on behalf of professional officers towards reserve officers.[27] Jews made up only a minority of professional officers, not reflecting their percentage within society. This was also the case for Romanians and Ruthenians who were usually portrayed as being the less educated peoples under the monarchy. In addition to mere numbers, István Deák concludes, "it would be good to know what prompted a Jew to become a professional officer, unfortunately memoirs usually recount only achievements, and not the motives."[28] By 1900, around 18 percent of the Austro-Hungarian reserve officers' corps were of "Mosaic confession" (not including the Jewish medical officers in the reserve), which was many times higher than the proportion of Jews in the monarchy (4.5 percent).[29] Regardless of the figures, the high number of Jewish reserve officers in autobiographical sources is often exaggerated. The officer Josef Leb noted: "It is true that in the school for one-year volunteers [that is, reserve officers] there had been up to 30 percent Jews."[30] Overall, all reserve officers, regardless of their religious and ethnic background, were portrayed in professional officers' autobiographical sources as outsiders, not as real officers. Because Jews made up around 15 to 20 percent, it is no wonder that in much of the general professional officers' criticism towards reserve officers, Jews played a major role or were targeted directly. This stance became even more evident after the first unsuccessful months of war with high casualties among professional officers of lower rank. The fallen were mainly replaced by reserve officers, therefore Jewish participation rose.[31]

Jews also made up a high number among military civil servants (*Militärbeamte*) and military physicians. Again, this group held the rank of officers but they were not perceived as real officers by professional officers and reserve officers alike. In particular, physicians usually served only for a couple of years before returning to their civil profession. The "Jewish military doctor" was among the typical stereotypes used by civilians as well as soldiers to portray pseudo-members of the army, wearing uniforms with golden stars but not knowing how to behave properly. It was not only Jewish military physicians but also Christian doctors who were targeted. Joseph Wittlin, for example, expressed the stereotype in a couple of lines in his novel *The Salt of the Earth* (*Das Salz der Erde*) by showing the doctor's difficult position between the army and civil society: "The army despised him, because he was a physician, and even more, because he was Jewish. His medical colleagues condemned him, because he served in the army ... Often he had to sit in the officers' club among the young officers, although according to his high rank he would have had the right to sit next to the major."[32] Rozenblit analyzes Jewish life in Vienna and refers to the novelist Arthur Schnitzler, who served in the army medical corps:

> It was not possible, especially not for a Jew in public life, to ignore the fact that he was a Jew ... Among the army medical students, as in almost every unit of those serving for one year only—and where not?— there was a clear cut division between Gentiles and Jews, or, since the national factor was being stressed more and more, between the Aryan and Semitic elements, and any private socializing was very narrowly circumscribed.[33]

There is another Habsburg army position in which Jews were overrepresented. The highest non-commissioned officer rank was called Paymaster (*Rechnungs-Unteroffizier*). The Paymaster was an important link between the sphere of the rank and file and the officers. It was a purely administrative role, and he was responsible for taking over soldiers' correspondence, applications for holidays, and payments. He was often blamed by soldiers when they felt badly treated by army bureaucracy. As there was no professional NCO corps in the Habsburg army until its dissolution in 1918, the *Rechnungs-Unteroffiziere* were usually taken from among the most intelligent rank and file, and therefore represented the local population. Good spoken and written German was obligatory, and a knowledge of other local languages highly desired. In some parts of the monarchy, such as in Galicia, most *Rechnungs-Unteroffiziere* were Jews. This is also often reflected in autobiographical sources. The officer Karl Nowottny wrote: "For the regiment's bureaucratic procedures, a captain was supported by a certified *Rechnungs-Unteroffizier*. If such a certified one was missing, then by a very literate soldier, who knew the German language (in [Habsburg] Polish regiments usually Jews)."[34] Even before the war, but particularly during the chaos of wartime, *Rechnungs-Unteroffiziere* were targeted by officers and rank and file alike when letters did not arrive, censorship was too harsh, and wages were not paid accordingly. Therefore, when this post-holder was blamed, it is no surprise that criticism was often accompanied by antisemitic rhetoric, simply because of the high number of Jews involved.

Jews were also overrepresented in some military branches. One artillery regiment was colloquially known as "Freiherr von Rothschild" as the officers' corps consisted of many Jews.[35] Army supply also consisted of a great number of Jews. Nevertheless, blaming the supply branch and Jewish contributions also revealed internal army frictions. Usually fighting units criticized the supply branch for serving safely far away from the front line, and for embezzling all kinds of food, tobacco, and drinks. As many Jews served in the supply branch, criticism of the supply branch therefore often included antisemitic rhetoric. The officer Josef Leb recalled: "People talked and mocked excessively about Jews in the supply branch."[36]

In addition to criticism of Jews that can be analyzed in a framework of general conflicts within the army, there are also comments in which Jews were blamed just for being Jewish. The officer Eduard Hentke von Hesshart can be quoted as a typical example of such a stance: "In the year 1889, I was transferred to the Infantry Regiment No 17. To my colonel's regret, I was replaced by a Jew, of which the regiment did not lack."[37] Many Habsburg army officers were afraid of being accused of being over-affiliated with any nationalism, and being too negative towards Jews could also harm a career. István Deák concludes that "anti-Semitism was rampant in middle class circles among all nationalities, but even the most rabid anti-Semite had to think twice in Austria-Hungary before insulting a Jew."[38] Although antisemitism was not welcome, and equal treatment in public of all nationalities and religious groups was expected, memoirs and diaries indicate that Jews were portrayed as the permanent other.

But what about the soldiers? Due to common conscription, all male Habsburg citizens regardless of their religion, ethnicity, and social background had to serve for three years (later two). Soldiers of the Habsburg army were not separately trained according to their faith, but along language lines, which was then interpreted as being a national affiliation. Eleven to twelve languages were officially used in the army. Since Yiddish and Hebrew were not among them, Jewish soldiers were usually assigned to one of the existing "national" training units. The Habsburg army therefore unintentionally not only established but also stabilized national categories.[39] Jews were often portrayed as being able to communicate in all local languages. The novelist Joseph Wittlin, born in 1896 in Galicia to a Jewish master collier, a volunteer in the war, dealt in his novel with the army experience of an ordinary soldier and the practice of assigning multilingual Galician inhabitants: "An NCO assigned the conscripts according to their language knowledge to certain groups. First, he separated the small German speaking group, which for the most part consisted of Jews, from the Polish and Ukrainian [Ruthenian] group."[40] Nevertheless, it also happened that Jewish soldiers were put into the Polish group.

Jews often tended to affiliate with German language and culture due to the language's high prestige. This caused additional anger on behalf of nationalists from the other groups. Rozenblit writes: "Bohemian and Moravian Jews might find themselves isolated as German speakers in Czech regiments."[41] In Croatia's capital Zagreb too, as Marija Vulesić argues, "with few exceptions, Jews constituted the strongest contingent of Germans in public and private life!" They were simply not accepted when claiming "to be good Croatians."[42] When being assigned to a certain national group in training, this meant that in army statistics they showed up as a percentage of nationalities.[43] Pieter M. Judson concludes that for the language frontiers—the ethnically and in particular linguistically mixed regions of the monarchy—"the local Jew [was] the quintessential man without a nation" or "the real danger" for nationalists as he was assignable to all local nationalities.[44]

Contemporary nationalists claimed that Jews were very often opportunistic in deciding which group they wished to be assigned to—or, to put it more bluntly, which nationality promised a higher social status or better business opportunities.[45] Something similar happened in the army when new recruits were enlisted and asked for their language skills. For Jews interested in an army career, it was certainly better to focus on German, while someone looking for a civil service career in Galicia, for example, might have been better off stressing Polish as their first language. Nevertheless, analysis of soldiers' personnel forms, and the language knowledge mentioned therein, indicates that something similar happened in language frontiers, and not only when Jews were involved. Bohemia and Moravia were known for their multilingual speakers. When analyzing the army personnel forms, only a minority mentioned German language knowledge, but this in no way reflected the linguistic reality. This indicates that many Czechs were well aware of the practice of being counted in statistics as Germans as soon as they mentioned their linguistic knowledge.[46]

What is of importance in the Jewish experience is that up until 1918, they never possessed their own national or ethnic box on these forms. As Pieter M. Judson observes, "Jewish nationalists in Galicia and Bukovina challenged the census, demanding the addition of a Jewish category." It was rejected by the courts.[47] Although never assigned their own national category, the memoirs and diaries indicate that in fact they had been an independent group standing separately from the recognized nationalities. When underscoring the diversity of their subordinates, officers always mentioned Jews as a separate group'. The professional officer August von Urbanski offers just one typical example: "As with the artillery in Görz [today divided between the Italian part, Gorizia, and the Slovene part, Nova Gorica] I had Hungarian, Croatian, and German recruits. In the brigade located in Transylvania, I witnessed that an officer had to train Germans, Hungarian, Romanians, Gypsies, and Jews at the same time ... There was somehow a similar situation in Lemberg, ... the bulk had been Ruthenes and Poles, sprinkled with Romanians, Gypsies, and Jews."[48] On his comrades during the war, he wrote: "The officers' corps of my battalion, almost exclusively reserve officers, was a mixture of nationalities. When I for the first time came for lunch in the officers' club, I found myself surrounded by German-Austrians, Czechs, and a couple of Jews, to which a Hungarian has to be added."[49] The Jewish reserve officer Otto Friedländer used this image in his novel: "In the army we do not care if someone is a Magyar [ethnic Hungarian], German, Czech or Jew—we only ask if this person is a good soldier or not."[50]

Jews and the Wartime Habsburg Army

István Deák observed: "World War I marked the apogee of Jewish participation in the life of Central Europeans. Jews were among the greatest enthusiasts in part as it was against antisemitic Russia, and in part because the outcome of the conflict promised to bring their final and complete acceptance."[51] According to Rozenblit, over 300,000 Jewish men served as soldiers in the Austro-Hungarian armed forces. About 25,000 educated middle-class Jews held commission as reserve officers. They fought alongside all other nationalities and commanded mixed national units too. She concludes that "in theory, Jewish participation in the army should have led to increased integration," but the reality was different.[52]

For Walter Herburger, an ordinary Christian soldier from Austria's western-most region, Vorarlberg, the character of the war changed with Italy's entry into it. For him, and all Tyrolians, Salzburgers, and Carinthians, the war turned into a defense of their homeland. With the war on their doorstep, the fighting on the Russian and Balkan fronts was no longer of such importance.[53] In a similar way, Jews also searched for their own vital interests and meaning in the war. As emphasized in Deák's quote, they were highly motivated in fighting against Russia. Rozenblit also argues that "like all Habsburg Jews, they focused on the war with Russia, the enemy of Austria and the Jewish people ... The war with Italy was not a Jewish war."[54] This analysis is also reflected in the journal *Jüdisches Archiv* (*Jewish Archive*), which tended to highlight Russian atrocities towards Jews.[55] Nevertheless, diaries and memoirs of non-Jewish army members do not indicate that their Jewish comrades in general tended to be less willing in fighting against Italians. In both cases, against Russia and Italy, they defended their Habsburg homeland.

Before the war, Jews were portrayed as permanent outsiders, but nevertheless loyal Habsburg citizens. However, their situation worsened during the war. One initial factor must be mentioned to explain this change. Due to misfortune on the Eastern Front, thousands of Jews found themselves as refugees in the first year of the war.[56] Around 200,000 Jewish refugees fled Galicia and Bukovina. As the bulk of them had been orthodox Jews from lower classes, this helped to reinforce perceptions that Jews were outsiders. The bulk settled in Vienna but many also settled in parts of Bohemia and Moravia. According to the Austrian Ministry of the Interior, by the end of 1915 some 386,000 refugees were living in Austria, two-fifths of them Jews. Others scraped by on Hungarian territory, some of them in designated refugee camps.[57] This refugee status of thousands of people in turn caused other problems, which in the end worsened Jewish lives. All inhabitants of territories bordering Russia became targeted as potential spies. As early as October 1914, the Viennese police reported to the War Surveillance Office on rumors that Galician Jews were spying for Russia. These inhabitants now worried that such suspicions might increase hostilities towards them.[58] The longer the war lasted, the more Jews became targets of denunciation all over the Habsburg home front. They were accused not only of being Russophile spies, but also of being usurers and shirkers.[59] The files of the Police Archive in Vienna contain not only regular reports on the general mood, but also a vast collection of letters of denunciation. Both show that Jews increasingly became the target of denunciations, but also that their Jewishness was emphasized by the denouncers. Accusations ranged from fraternization with the enemy, to political tendencies that threatened the Habsburg Empire, to usury and black market business.[60] With administrative reports on Jewish refugees, often called "Galicians," presumptions of disloyal behavior increased across the monarchy.[61]

At the same time, all business life was increasingly controlled by the state and the army. Factories were put under surveillance, and the free market soon evaporated. The black market flourished with its high prices. The small businesses often run by Jews in Galicia were not the central focus of authorities. This was one of the reasons why Jews were often denounced for participating in or even dominating the black market by selling desperately needed goods for exorbitant prices. The old Galician Jewish business symbol, the *Faktor*, changed, and this was experienced by thousands of soldiers serving at or near the frontline. The NCO Alfred Trendl noted in his war diary in July 1917: "A Jew arrived in the village. He asked for 6 crowns for one Hungarian cigarette. Usually, one hundred of them cost 1 crown. The well-known joke is therefore right: As long as not all Polish Jews are millionaires, the war won't be over."[62]

Another reason why Jews were increasingly blamed was the common conviction that they tried to avoid military service, especially at the front. "Jews, of course," Rozenblit argues, "were not the only soldiers to evade difficult military assignments."[63] War diaries are full of stories about soldiers—regardless of religious and ethnic background—and their ideas and techniques to avoid being sent to the most dangerous frontlines, or even being mobilized. Nevertheless, István Deák concludes that the proportion of Jews at the front was lower than in the population, and exemptions from military duty higher than those of the members of other confessional groups.[64] Even when serving at the front, they always felt like they were being observed by the others and that they had to continuously prove they were not cowards. For example, David Neumann from Vienna, who served in a Hungarian regiment with few Jews, observed "that I, as a Jew, had to prove that I was a good soldier." When Eric Fischer was drafted as a "one year volunteer" in 1916 after he graduated from the Wasa gymnasium in Vienna, he refused to tell the draft board about his heart condition because "I considered it my duty not to contribute to the often heard taunt of the Jews as cowards."[65] The Jewish case was again similar to other nationalities that were perceived as tending towards disloyalty. Italians, Czechs, and Serbs also reported that they had to be seen as braver than others.

Conversely, Jewish officers made up a great number in one particular field of war service that was characterized by its public visibility. In the Habsburg monarchy's main propaganda institution, the War Press Office (*Kriegspressequartier*), Jews made up a great number of the personnel. Journalists, novelists, poets, and painters, such as Roda Roda and Max Perutz, were among its members.[66] As this kind of war service usually meant successfully avoiding fighting at the front, all members, Christian and Jewish alike, were called "shirkers." As before 1914, Jewish soldiers continued to work in army offices due to their language skills and literacy. They were therefore often blamed for censorship, missing letters, and neglect of *Liebesgaben* (care packages) from the home front. Autobiographical writings highlight this repeatedly, as soldiers awaited messages from home with great anticipation. Miroslav Krleža referred to this in his prewar and wartime novel: "'What should

I do with this letter of this damned guy, should I forward it or not?' NCO Kohn, the head of the office, lamented after screwing up Honvéd Skomrak's letter. In civil life, Kohn sold luxurious goods *en gros*. He is 1.45 meters tall, 29 years old, has bow legs, wears a pince-nez. Thus he's a dwarf with tachycardia and cardiac neurosis."[67] In addition to being labeled as shirkers, Jewish soldiers and officers were often considered to be incompetent. Josef Leb's story is indicative of many of his comrades: "I was ordered to reconnoiter the Cordevola valley with all its neighboring valleys on horse—together with a second lieutenant, a little Jew, who was totally incompetent, a Czech veterinarian, who really hated Austria, and an Italian from South Tyrol."[68] While the other two, the Czech and the Italian, were called disloyal, the Jew was "only" blamed for incompetence. On the other hand, authors also underscored the positive qualities of Jewish soldiers, such as their perceived multilingualism. Wittlin mentioned that they were often called in to de-escalate tensions between the army and the local population.[69]

It was not only Jews who during the war years increasingly lost confidence in the state for which they were fighting. Rozenblit draws attention to the case of a Jewish author: "Mechner seemed eager to fight on the Isonzo front during the last year of the war. He (unsuccessfully)

Figure 2.1 Gravestone at Vienna Central Cemetery, example of Jewish losses in war service. Tamara Scheer, Private Archive.

Figure 2.2 Gravestone of Egon Goldschmied who fell during war service in officers' rank, Vienna Central Cemetery, Jewish section. Tamara Scheer, Private Archive.

begged to participate in the spring 1918 offensive after receiving a wound in his hand, and he was very proud of the medals he received in Italy; yet he did not view his service in Italy in patriotic terms, observing that by the summer of 1918, his patriotism was long gone, or at a low point."⁷⁰ Habsburg soldiers, regardless of their national and religious background, also experienced a dramatic decrease in their willingness to fight. Starving, Walter Herburger wrote in his diary what he felt in the moment when waiting for the order to attack the Italians, in the battle that later become known as the Karfreit/Caporetto Miracle in which the Central Powers were successful. Military obedience, the emperor's wish, comradeship, even war's final end and return to his home, were no longer important. The only thing he wished for was the full food stores of the Italian army.⁷¹

Conclusion

Why was it important to start this chapter with army members' positive experiences with prewar Jews? From early on, older rank and file and officers alike had spent many years in prewar garrisons, with Jewish comrades and Jewish communities. Criticism and even antisemitic rhetoric were often a result of personal experiences with unsympathetic soldiers or officers, or showed general frictions within the army. Nevertheless, following July 1914, the more positive image survived only for a while as war dragged on. With the war's end, only negative stereotypes regarding Jews remained, regardless of which nationality and culture they affiliated with, and what their role in the war had been, even after they had served four long years, been injured at the front line, or returned highly decorated.

The big difference between the prewar and wartime autobiographical image is that initially Jews were blamed for a certain incident or personal characteristic, and from time to time Jewishness was added to the criticism. During the war this antisemitism grew more and more intense. Jews were blamed in general, with criticism being based not solely on a certain personally experienced incident.⁷² István Deák also points this out: "Yet it appears that for the first time in the history of the monarchy, the valor of individual Jewish soldiers did not help to dampen antisemitism. As the situation worsened, the right-wing press increasingly attacked the Jews, despite censorship, for their alleged cowardice, war-profiteering, and treason."⁷³

On the whole, personal stories differ and mirror the exact moment in time and place when they were written—as was the case for most memoirs and novels after 1918 or even after the Second World War. It made a difference if the writer had lost family members or experienced violence and pogroms in Galicia, which experienced a civil war following the official end of the First World War, or if the writer had experienced the Holocaust.[74] In these cases, Habsburg rule is shown as much more harmonic, although this was not the case. The reason that antisemitism was only given minor importance, as Rozenblit argues, was that "censorship or self-censorship prevented Jewish newspapers from reporting antisemitic incidents in the army during the war."[75]

What is left out in most autobiographical sources of non-Jewish soldiers and officers are the thousands of nameless Jewish soldiers who were simply doing their duty, fighting and dying silently. The Jewish situation is similar to that of the ordinary Czech, Serbian, or Italian soldiers and officers who fought until the very end. They did not fit the new public image and were often excluded from the postwar state- and nation-building process'.

Tamara Scheer is a lecturer and research associate at the Institute for East European History at the University of Vienna. She specializes in nationalism and identity formation in the late Habsburg Empire, the history of Central and Southeastern Europe during the interwar period, as well as the First World War. Her publications include *Zwischen Front und Heimat: Österreich-Ungarns Militärverwaltungen im Ersten Weltkrieg* (Lang, 2009) and *"Minimale Kosten, absolut kein Blut": Österreich-Ungarns Präsenz im Sandžak von Novipazar, 1879–1908* (Lang, 2013). She is currently finishing a book on language diversity and loyalty in the Habsburg imperial army, 1868–1918.

Notes

For reading the manuscript and suggestions, I would like to thank in particular Simon Weyringer (Pontificio Istituto Biblico, Rome) and Erwin A. Schmidl (National Defence Academy, Vienna).

1. Stadtarchiv Dornbirn (StAD), Miszellen No. 806, Walter Herburger, *Sieg oder Tod im Alpenrot, Meine Kriegserlebnisse im Weltkrieg 1914–1918, Feldzug gegen Italien*, 20 August 1918, digitalized unpublished manuscript.
2. Note of the k.k. Ministry of Interior to the governors, No. 3619, 12 February 1918, Österreichisches Staatsarchiv (ÖStA)/Allgemeines Verwaltungsarchiv/Ministerium des Innern.
3. Robert Gerwarth, *The Vanquished: Why the First World War Failed to End* (London, 2016), 145–46.
4. Memoirs of August von Urbanski, Das Tornisterkind, No. 4, ÖStA/ Kriegsarchiv (KA)/Nachlasssammlung (NL), B/58, 283.
5. Most recently analyzed by Erwin A. Schmidl, *Habsburgs jüdische Soldaten: 1788–1918* (Vienna, 2014). As only one example of the memoirs of a

Jewish-background Viennese who served in the k.u.k. army before and during the war, see Siegfried Trebitsch, *Chronik eines Lebens* (Zürich, 1951).
6. Marsha L. Rozenblit, *Reconstructing a National Identity: The Jews of Habsburg Austria during World War I* (Oxford, 2001), 83.
7. See in particular Mark Cornwall, "Das Ringen um die Moral des Hinterlandes," in *Die Habsburgermonarchie 1848–1918, Band XI, 1. Teilband: Die Habsburgermonarchie und der Erste Weltkrieg*, ed. Helmut Rumpler (Vienna, 2016), 393–435, as well as Maureen Healy, *Vienna and the Fall of the Habsburg Empire: Total War and Everyday Life in World War I* (Cambridge, 2007).
8. See in particular István Deák, *Beyond Nationalism: A Social and Political History of the Habsburg Officer Corps, 1848–1918* (New York, 1990).
9. Memoirs of Julius Lustig-Prean von Preanfeld, Aus den Lebenserinnerungen eines alten k.u.k. Offiziers, unpublished manuscript, winter 1940/41, ÖStA/KA/NL, B/5:1, 6.
10. Eugen Hoeflich (Moshe Ya'akov Ben-Gavriel), *Tagebücher, 1915–1927*, ed. Armin A. Wallas (Vienna, 1999), 30 June 1915, 2.
11. Memoirs of Karl Nowottny, Erinnerungen aus meinem Leben während der Zeit von 1868–1918, vol. 1, ÖStA/KA/NL, B/417:13, 39.
12. Ibid., 38.
13. Diary of Franz Xaver Schubert, unpublished manuscript, edited and commented by him in 1943, ÖStA/KA/NL, B/833:2, 50.
14. Ibid., 42–43.
15. Ibid., 43.
16. Memoirs of Heinrich Wiedern Edler von Alpenbach, Lebensgeschichliche Skizze, unpublished, no pages, ÖStA/KA/NL, B/30:2.
17. Memoirs of Adolf Stillfried von Rathenitz, Erinnerungen aus meinem Leben, ÖStA/KA/NL, B/862:1, 17.
18. Laurence Cole, *Military Culture and Popular Patriotism in Late Imperial Austria* (Oxford, 2014), 227.
19. Ibid., 220.
20. Schmidl, *Habsburgs jüdische Soldaten*.
21. Otto Friedländer, *Maturajahrgang 1907* (Graz, 1963), 126.
22. Memoirs of Julius Lustig-Prean von Preanfeld, Aus den Lebenserinnerungen eines alten k.u.k. Offiziers, unpublished manuscript, winter 1940/41, ÖStA/KA/NL, B/5:1, 2.
23. See some of the chapters in Daniel L. Unowsky and Robert Nemes, eds., *Sites of European Antisemitism in the Age of Mass Politics 1880–1918* (Lebanon, NH, 2014).
24. Diary of Franz Putz, 31 January–31 March 1907, ÖStA/KA/NL, B/35:2, 18 February 1907.
25. For a comparison, see Sarah Panter, *Jüdische Erfahrungen und Loyalitätskonflikte im Ersten Weltkrieg* (Göttingen, 2014). On Tsarist Russia, see Semen M. Dubnov, *Geschichte eines jüdischen Soldaten: Bekenntnis eines von vielen* (Göttingen, 2012).
26. Waltraud Heindl, *Josephinische Mandarine: Bürokratie und Beamte in Österreich 1848–1907*, vol. 2 (Vienna, 2013), 260.

27. As just one example from a contemporary witness, see Liviu Rebreanu, *Der Wald der Gehenkten* (Berlin, 1966), 15. See also Deák, *Beyond Nationalism.*
28. Deák, *Beyond Nationalism,* 176.
29. Ibid., 133.
30. Memoirs of Josef Leb, Aus den Erinnerungen eines Trainoffiziers, written in autumn 1933 using diary and war letters, unpublished manuscript, ÖStA/KA/NL, B/580, 13.
31. Rozenblit, *Reconstructing a National Identity,* 86.
32. Joseph Wittlin, *Das Salz der Erde* (Frankfurt a.M., 1969), 85.
33. Marsha L. Rozenblit, *The Jews of Vienna, 1867–1914: Assimilation and Identity* (Albany,NY, 1983), 9.
34. Memoirs of Karl Nowottny, Erinnerungen aus meinem Leben während der Zeit von 1868–1918, vol. 1, ÖStA/KA/NL, B/417:13, 100.
35. Memoirs of Josef Leb, Aus den Erinnerungen eines Trainoffiziers, written in autumn 1933 using diary and war letters, unpublished manuscript, ÖStA/KA/NL, B/580, 13.
36. Ibid.
37. Memoirs of Eduard Hentke von Hesshart, Leben und Wirken, 1858–1919, unpublished manuscript, ÖStA/KA/NL, B/98:7, no pages.
38. Deák, *Beyond Nationalism,* 133.
39. Rok Stergar and Tamara Scheer, "Ethnic Boxes: The Unintended Consequences of Habsburg Bureaucratic Classification,"*Nationalities Papers: The Journal of Nationalism and Ethnicity* (2018), Special Issue: Nationalism and Classification, ed. Alexander Maxwell.
40. Wittlin, *Das Salz der Erde,* 100f.
41. Rozenblit, *Reconstructing a National Identity,* 92.
42. Marija Vulesić, "'An Antisemitic Aftertaste': Anti-Jewish Violence in Habsburg Croatia," in Unowsky and Nemes, *Sites of European Antisemitism,*115–36, here 127.
43. See the annually published army statistic, *Militär-Statistisches Jahrbuch,* edited by Über Anordnung des k.k. Reichskriegsministeriums bearbeitet und herausgegeben von der III. Section des Technischen und Administrativen Militär-Comite (Vienna).
44. Pieter M. Judson, *Guardians of the Nation: Activists on the Language Frontiers of Imperial Austria* (Cambridge, MA, 2006), 38.
45. Ibid., 31.
46. Sample of 10 boxes of soldiers' personnel files (1868–1914), Vojenský Ústředni Archiv (Prague), Kmenovy Listy.
47. Judson, *Guardians of the Nation,* 273.
48. Memoirs of August von Urbanski, Das Tornisterkind, No. 4, ÖStA/KA/NL, B/58, 95.
49. Ibid., 250.
50. Otto Friedländer, *Wolken drohen über Wien* (Vienna, 1949), 83–84.
51. Deák, *Beyond Nationalism,* 195.
52. Rozenblit, *Reconstructing a National Identity,* 82–83.
53. StAD, Miszellen No. 806, Herburger, *Sieg oder Tod im Alpenrot.*
54. Rozenblit, *Reconstructing a National Identity,* 83 and 86.

55. As just one example, see N.N., "Zur Lage der Juden in Österreich,"*Jüdisches Archiv. Mitteilungen des Komitees "Jüdisches Kriegsarchiv"* 1 (May 1915): 4–12.
56. Rebbekah Klein-Pejšová, "Beyond the 'Infamous Concentration Camps of the Old Monarchy': Jewish Refugee Policy from Wartime Austria-Hungary to Interwar Czechoslovakia,"*Austrian History Yearbook* (2014): 150–66, 154f.
57. Peter Gatrell, "Refugees," in *1914–1918-Online: International Encyclopedia of the First World War*, ed. Ute Daniel et al. (Berlin,2014).
58. Viennese Police to the War Surveillance Office, No. 6154, 1 October 1914, ÖStA/KA/Kriegsüberwachungsamt (KÜA).
59. Tamara Scheer, "Denunciation and the Decline of the Habsburg Home Front during the First World War," *European Review of History/Revue européenne d'histoire* 24, no. 2 (April 2017): 214–28, here 220.
60. Archiv der Bundespolizeidirektion Wien, Stimmungsberichte und Anzeigen, 1914–1918.
61. Letter of the Military Command in Leitmeritz to War Surveillance Office, 1 March 1915, Ústřední vojenský archiv, 9. Korpskommando, Präs, 52-1, 1915.
62. Alfred Trendl, Meine Erinnerungen vom September 1911 bis November 1916, unpublished diary, Manuscript in private possession of an heir.
63. Rozenblit, *Reconstructing a National Identity*, 90.
64. Deák, *Beyond Nationalism*, 196.
65. Rozenblit, *Reconstructing a National Identity*, 91.
66. Christoph Tepperberg, "War Press Office (Austria-Hungary)," in Daniel et al.,*1914–1918-Online*.
67. Miroslav Krleža, *Der kroatische Gott Mars: Kriegsnovellen* (Klagenfurt, 2009), 196.
68. Memoirs of Josef Leb, Aus den Erinnerungen eines Trainoffiziers, written in autumn 1933 using his diary and war letters, unpublished manuscript, ÖStA/KA/NL, B/580, 67.
69. Wittlin, *Das Salz der Erde*, 191.
70. Rozenblit, *Reconstructing a National Identity*, 89.
71. StAD, Miszellen No. 806, Herburger, *Sieg oder Tod im Alpenrot*, October 1917.
72. Also shown by Panter, *Jüdische Erfahrungen*, 203f.
73. Deák, *Beyond Nationalism*, 196.
74. Gerwarth, *The Vanquished*, 91.
75. Rozenblit, *Reconstructing a National Identity*, 93.

Bibliography

Cole, Laurence. *Military Culture and Popular Patriotism in Late Imperial Austria.* Oxford: Oxford University Press, 2014.

Cornwall, Mark. "Das Ringen um die Moral des Hinterlandes. "In *Die Habsburgermonarchie 1848–1918, Band XI, 1. Teilband: Die Habsburgermonarchie und der Erste Weltkrieg*, edited by Helmut Rumpler, 393–435. Vienna: Verlag Österreichischen Akademie der Wissenschaften, 2016.

Deák, István. *Beyond Nationalism: A Social and Political History of the Habsburg Officer Corps, 1848–1918*. New York: Oxford University Press, 1990.

Dubnov, Semen M. *Geschichte eines jüdischen Soldaten: Bekenntnis eines von vielen*. Göttingen: Vandenhoeck & Ruprecht, 2012.

Friedländer, Otto. *Maturajahrgang 1907*. Graz: Styria,1963.

———. *Wolken drohen über Wien: Lebens- und Sittenbilder aus den Jahren vor dem Ersten Weltkrieg*, Vienna: Ring Verl. 1949.

Gatrell, Peter. "Refugees." In *1914–1918-Online:International Encyclopedia of the First World War*, edited by Ute Daniel et al. Berlin: Freie Universität Berlin, 2014. https://encyclopedia.1914-1918-online.net/home.html.

Gerwarth, Robert. *The Vanquished: Why the First World War Failed to End*. London: Penguin, 2016.

Healy, Maureen. *Vienna and the Fall of the Habsburg Empire: Total War and Everyday Life in World War I*. Cambridge: Cambridge University Press, 2007.

Heindl, Waltraud. *Josephinische Mandarine: Bürokratie und Beamte in Österreich 1848–1907*, vol. 2. Vienna: Böhlau, 2013.

Hoeflich, Eugen (Moshe Ya'akov Ben-Gavriel). *Tagebücher, 1915–1927*. Edited by Armin A. Wallas. Vienna: Böhlau, 1999.

Judson, Pieter M. *Guardians of the Nation: Activists on the Language Frontiers of Imperial Austria*. Cambridge, MA: Harvard University Press, 2006.

Klein-Pejšová, Rebbekah. "Beyond the 'Infamous Concentration Camps of the Old Monarchy': Jewish Refugee Policy from Wartime Austria-Hungary to Interwar Czechoslovakia." *Austrian History Yearbook* 45 (2014): 150–66.

Krleža, Miroslav. *Der kroatische Gott Mars: Kriegsnovellen*. Klagenfurt: Wieser, 2009.

Militär-Statistisches Jahrbuch. Edited by k.k. Reichskriegsministeriumand III. Section des Technischen und Administrativen Militär-Comite. Vienna: k.u.k. Hof- und Staatsdruckerei, 1884.

Panter, Sarah. *Jüdische Erfahrungen und Loyalitätskonflikte im Ersten Weltkrieg*. Göttingen: Vandenhoeck & Ruprecht, 2014.

Rebreanu, Liviu. *Der Wald der Gehenkten*. Berlin: Verlag Volk und Welt, 1966.

Rozenblit, Marsha L. *The Jews of Vienna, 1867–1914: Assimilation and Identity*. Albany: State University of New York Press, 1983.

———. *Reconstructing a National Identity: The Jews of Habsburg Austria during World War I*. Oxford: Oxford University Press, 2001.

Scheer, Tamara. "Denunciation and the Decline of the Habsburg Home Front during the First World War." *European Review of History/Revue européenne d'histoire* 24, no. 2 (April 2017): 214–28.

Schmidl, Erwin A. *Habsburgs jüdische Soldaten: 1788–1918*. Vienna: Böhlau, 2014.

Stergar, Rok, and Tamara Scheer. "Ethnic Boxes: The Unintended Consequences of Habsburg Bureaucratic Classification." *Nationalities Papers: The Journal of Nationalism and Ethnicity* 46, no. 4 (2018): 575–591.

Tepperberg, Christoph. "War Press Office (Austria-Hungary)." In *1914–1918-Online: International Encyclopedia of the First World War*, edited by Ute Daniel et al. Berlin: Freie Universität Berlin, 2014. https://encyclopedia.1914-1918-online.net/home.html.

Trebitsch, Siegfried. *Chronik eines Lebens*. Zürich: Artemis Verlag, 1951.

Unowsky, Daniel L. and Robert Nemes, eds. *Sites of European Antisemitism in the Age of Mass Politics 1880–1918*. Lebanon, NH: Brandeis University Press, 2014.

Vulesica, Marija. "'An Antisemitic Aftertaste': Anti-Jewish Violence in Habsburg Croatia." In *Sites of European Antisemitism in the Age of Mass Politics 1880–1918*, edited by Daniel Unowsky and Robert Nemes, 115–136. Lebanon, NH: Brandeis University Press, 2014.

Wittlin, Joseph. *Das Salz der Erde*. Frankfurt a.M.: Buechergilde Gutenberg, 1969.

3

THE "STEPCHILDREN" OF THE *KAISERREICH*
Alsatians in the German Army during the First World War
Devlin M. Scofield

> Are you an Alsatian?
> —Imperial Mulhouse Military Tribunal Counsel to Defendant,
> cited in Joseph Rossé et al., *Das Elsass von 1870–1932*
>
> Are you German or Alsatian?
> —French Interrogator's Question to Captured German Alsatian
> Soldier, Bundesarchiv Berlin Lichterfelde, R 901 84132, 3
> November 1916
>
> At the beginning of the war we were *Wackes*, Frenchies, and spies and now the Alsatians are heroes and brave soldiers. But I don't want to be anything. The main thing is that we safely return home. Then we will see what we are.
> —Josef Kalbert to Johan Kalbert, 1 April 1918, Hauptstaatsarchiv-Stuttgart, M 30/1 107

Few contemporary observers could have predicted how the conflict that broke out in August 1914 would fundamentally reshape the political and demographic map of Europe. The rekindling of the Franco-German military rivalry was perceived as an opportunity and challenge by both the Central and Entente powers. Imperial authorities, such as Chancellor Theobold von Bethmann-Hollweg, believed that Alsatians' participation in a military victory against France would definitively draw the population of the *Reichsland*[1] into the German national fold.[2] For France, the war represented an opportunity to right the wrong of 1871 and a chance for Alsatians to prove their enduring French loyalties. The only guarantee for the population of Alsace was that the geographic location of their homes would likely bring the conflict to their doorsteps. Borderland residents' actions would be influenced by national allegiances throughout the next four years, but ultimately many would make decisions based upon regional loyalties and perceived self-interest. As mobilized Jean Lechner articulated in 1914, "I remain Alsatian in spite of my German uniform."[3]

The German government declared the *Reichsland* to be a defense zone under martial law on 31 July 1914. The war enthusiasm that gripped certain elements of German and French society was largely absent in Alsace. Despite the lack of "hurrah patriotism," German civilian and martial authorities like General Berthold von Deimling of the XV Army Corps praised the tranquility, order, and discipline of the mobilization in the province.[4] The military's assumption of power corresponded to restrictions being placed on peacetime freedoms. This included limiting freedom of movement, the evacuation of combat zones, and suspending articles of the Reich's constitution that guaranteed civil liberties. Authorities also targeted the French language as newspapers were closed, speaking French in public was forbidden, and French names were Germanized.[5] Violations were prosecutable offenses.[6] The overall effect on the *Reichsländer*'s relationship with Germany was catastrophic. On 7 June 1918, Social Democratic representative Hermann Wendel argued in the Reichstag that four-fifths of the population of Alsace and Lorraine would have voted to remain part of Germany before the war, but now the majority would undoubtedly choose France. He identified the causal factors as "... not out of love of the Tricolor, rather solely from exasperation, anger, and hate of what has been done to the Alsace-Lorrainers since 31 July 1914."[7] As this quote suggests, Alsatians' turn to France in both the civilian and martial realms was motivated by German actions rather than inherent French loyalties.

As with German Jews, there was no single war experience for soldiers from Alsace and Lorraine. The treatment Alsatians encountered in the German ranks, their response, and the seeming centrality of their regional identities varied significantly. Dominik Richert was in the midst of his required military service in August 1914. Richert and a number of his fellow Alsatians were removed from their units in the West and transferred to the Eastern Front. A reluctant soldier and increasingly resentful of the prejudice he faced as a *Reichsländer*, Richert deserted to French lines in July 1918.[8] Jean Lechner served in the German ranks on both the Eastern and Western Fronts for the entirety of the war despite possessing some Francophile sympathies. He was promoted to the rank of officer and decorated with the Iron Cross First and Second Class. In his journal he frequently reflected on his war experience, Alsatian identity, and occasionally on the future of the province.[9] Henri Levy served primarily on the Eastern Front as a cook and nurse. Never complaining about discrimination in his letters, Levy's only mention of issues related to his Alsatianness came in the spring of 1918, as he lamented the lack of leave for *Reichsländer*.[10] The authors' varying degree of focus on the discrimination they and their fellow Alsatians faced in the imperial ranks reflects a similar trend in German Jews' narratives of the First World War.[11] Yet the theme of unjustified differential treatment is consistently present, even if it does not dominate all Alsatians' recollections of the war years. At one level this variation may reflect the divergence in the postwar destinies of *Reichsland* soldiers and German Jews. The nature of the French national myth of Francophile Alsace made it in the self- and material interest of ex-German Alsatian soldiers to cultivate the negative memories of their time in the imperial ranks, while German Jews, facing an increasingly hostile government and society in Germany, perhaps found solace in recollections of the common purpose and community of the front. Regardless, despite the breadth of individual experiences, German authorities legislated towards both Alsatians and Jews categorically. A close study of official policies towards *Reichsländer* reveals the underpinning assumptions of both imperial and republican civilian and military leaders.

German and French authorities analyzed the *Reichsland*'s population and from their opposing perspectives differentiated between "good" and "bad" Alsatians. The force of the Entente's arms achieved the return of the "lost provinces" to France in 1918, but the French narrative of Alsace triumphed long before the guns were silenced. Ironically, the French owed the Germans a great deal of thanks for this victory. Throughout the war, imperial officials consistently treated Alsatians as nationally suspect. The fundamental fear that shaped German policies was that *Reichsland* soldiers secretly harbored Francophile sentiments. Such anxieties were often not based on real experiences with Alsace-Lorrainer combatants, but rather were directed at the preconceived image of the "disloyal" borderland soldier that imperial officials had constructed in their own minds. The Supreme High Command (OHL) and the upper echelons of the German officer corps repeatedly proved unable to overcome this stereotype and fundamentally alter their treatment of Alsatian soldiers.

German authorities enacted biased policies even though their own statistics demonstrated that fears of Alsatians' pro-French loyalties were exaggerated. The average Alsatian serving in the German army might not have been an ardent German nationalist, but was willing to loyally fulfill his military obligations.[12] This was true even of conscripts who possessed some French sympathies. Jean Lechner wrote in his journal shortly after being mobilized in August 1914, "I love France, I have always loved her."[13] Yet Lechner served with distinction in the field-gray uniform despite this ambiguity. The study of the relationship between imperial authorities and their Alsatian soldiers during the First World War demonstrates that in many cases "preventative" actions alienated *Reichsland* soldiers from Germany. Imperial officials' codified prejudice was responsible for turning Alsatians into the disloyal subjects that they were suspected of being.

Many mobilized Alsatians interpreted their treatment as "second-class soldiers" as evidence of their status as "second-class citizens" in the German Empire. A common familial metaphor that soldiers from Alsace utilized to express their relationship with Germany was that of a stepchild. In this construction, Alsatians saw themselves as related, but never fully accepted members of the German national "family." With little cause to hope for future change and witness to an array of discriminations in the imperial army, it was natural that many Alsatians redirected their aspirations to France. Alsatians' Francophile conversion did not reflect an innate pro-French predisposition or a preference for one model of the nation-state over another. Instead, Alsatians made an instrumental decision to cast their lot with an affirming and optimistic image of themselves and their future over the negative alternative in the present.[14]

For *Reichsländer* in field-gray uniforms, national cynicism, absence of longstanding relationships with fellow German soldiers, and lack of regimental loyalty combined to significantly weaken their ties to the imperial army. This internal institutional disillusionment was compounded by external factors. The close geographic proximity of a positive French alternative, a growing conviction in the futility of the German war effort, and a realization of the political ramifications of such a defeat encouraged resignation among imperial Alsatian soldiers rather than a redoubled effort to disprove official stereotypes. Moreover, it heightened the likelihood of their desertion to French lines or flight to Switzerland if the chance presented.

A well-established French nationalist narrative portrayed Alsatians as long-suffering patriots patiently waiting to reclaim their rightful place in the republic.[15] The construction of Alsatians as "reluctant Germans" was a common theme of prewar and wartime popular French literature and culture. One such articulation is Albert Bettannier's "Souvenir français," which depicts a young Alsatian about to depart for the imperial army. Surrounded by multiple generations of his family, the kneeling

Figure 3.1 "Beneath his german [sic] suit his heart remains French!" Albert Bettannier, "Souvenir français," prewar or wartime French postcard, author's collection.

young man accepts a tricolor cockade being pinned to his shirt over his heart and under his military uniform. The image's caption, "Beneath his german [sic] suit his heart remains French!" unambiguously conveyed the message that despite the Kaiser's uniform, Alsatian soldiers were loyal to France.

The French occupied an enviable position in relation to Alsace during the First World War. Officials merely had to offer up their lines as a safe haven for Alsatians, who were either reluctant Germans or unenthusiastic soldiers, and patiently wait as imperial authorities, floundering in their suspicions and efforts to curtail Alsatian desertion, enacted policies that promoted further disillusionment and defections. One propaganda pamphlet succinctly illustrated the positive alternative that France offered to the Alsatians in the German ranks:

> Why fight any longer for Germany? Come over to us and at the forward-most post call out "Alsatian" or "Lorrainer" and you will immediately be received as brothers. [...C]ome over to us, to France, where your forefathers, grandfathers, and fathers all felt happy, the country where you are not the slaves of the Prussian Junkers and military castes, but rather will be treated as respectable human beings.[16]

The positive image in combination with the vicissitudes of the conflict made the French narrative increasingly attractive. Each Alsatian who crossed to Allied lines became another shell in France's symbolic arsenal that supported their argument that Alsace had never ceased to be French and should be so again.

A number of scholars have stressed the longevity of borderland populations' "national indifference," local attachments, and instrumental nationality decisions in the face of state authorities' centralizing efforts.[17] The two institutions that states have traditionally called upon to align national identities and contemporary citizenship are schools and the military. For the latter, the spread of universal conscription reflected governments' identification of the military as an assimilatory organization.[18] Scholars have drawn a direct connection between political belonging and military service, as well as the establishment of an implicit reciprocal contract between combatants and the state. The state rewarded soldiers and their families with material security and prestige in return for their time in the ranks.[19] War was thus a potential proving ground for governments and combatants alike. The national emergency seemed to offer integrative opportunities for historically marginalized minorities. However, the euphoria surrounding the outbreak of war temporarily masked but did not destroy old prejudices in the summer of 1914. Prewar "suspect" groups' hopes for greater tolerance proved illusory.[20] National minorities' loyalties rapidly came under close scrutiny in multinational empires, as officials were divided on whether ethnic identities should be cultivated or suppressed.[21]

The study of Alsatians within the ranks of the imperial army during the First World War weaves together multiple historiographies. In the forty-three years since their annexation, imperial authorities had utilized both schools and the army to turn Alsatians into Germans. The 1914 conflict was the first major opportunity to gauge the success of these efforts and ultimately proved their failure. Imperial authorities demonstrated an extraordinary lack of faith in their Germanization program. The subsequent discriminatory policies that Alsatian soldiers experienced nullified one-half of the reciprocal relationship between state and combatant and proved ruinous for Alsatian–German relations. The critical difference between the residents of the *Reichsland* and most other minorities (such as Jews) was the presence of an alternative national destiny. Feeling rejected by Germany, Alsatians increasingly embraced their French portrayal as paradigms of patriotic virtue.

A Word on Statistics

Men from Alsace fought for both Germany and France during the First World War. The vast majority of Alsatians and Lorrainers (380,000) fought in the German army. Of this number, some 50,000 would fall in the field-gray uniform, an estimated 150,000 would be wounded, and 25,000 captured and interned in Entente prisoner-of-war camps.[22] Contemporaries almost immediately sought to mitigate these numbers with the observation that only 8,000 Alsatians and Lorrainers volunteered for war service.[23] A problematic aspect of this figure was that the interwar compilers utilized the official French definition of a "genuine" Alsatian, which was a status reserved for French citizens living in Alsace prior to 1871 or their descendants, so long as there was not a direct German paternal connection. Consequently, the sons of German immigrants living in Alsace were not included in the final figure. The low number of Alsatians serving in regiments that bore the "Alsatian" moniker is also highlighted as evidence of their reluctance to serve Germany.[24] Here, however, the lack of soldiers from Alsace reflected established imperial military tradition.[25] If the number of Alsatians serving in the German army has been downplayed, the opposite has been true for their compatriots who fought for France. Approximately 17,650 Alsatians and Lorrainers served in the French army.[26] The contributions that Alsatians made in the horizon-blue uniform were less important in real military terms than in their symbolic value. The actions of this minority of *Reichsländer* were interpreted by German and French authorities as representative of the psyches of *all* Alsatians.

Casualty statistics for Alsatians fighting in the German army fundamentally challenge a cornerstone of the pro-French narrative. In a March 1915 confidential report, the Statistical Office of the Federal State Alsace-Lorraine reported that, as of 1 January 1915, 1,525 Alsatian soldiers had been killed, 7,117 wounded, 2,337 reported missing, and 89 taken as prisoners of war while serving in imperial ranks. In all, 22.1 percent of the total casualties from Lower Alsace and 21.6 percent of casualties from Upper Alsace had either been reported missing or were confirmed POWs.[27] The statistics broke down as shown in Table 3.1.

The high percentage of casualties from Alsace-Lorraine identified as missing or captured was troubling to *Reichsland Statthalter* Hans von Dallwitz. Yet responding to the *Statthalter*'s subsequent enquiry in May 1915, Minister of War Franz von Wandel related that he did not consider the percentage extraordinary because the comparative figure for the entire German army was 18.44 percent.[28]

Table 3.1 Number of Alsace-Lorrainers Killed, Wounded, Missing, or Taken as Prisoners of War up to 1 January 1915.

	Dead	Wounded	Missing	Prisoners of War	Percentage of Total Casualties Missing or POW
Lower Alsace	886	4,308	1,402	75	22.1%
Upper Alsace	639	2,809	935	14	21.6%
Lorraine	641	3,030	1,033	19	22.3%
Total for Alsace-Lorraine	2,166	10,147	3,370	108	22.0%
Total for German Reich	90,000	400,000	140,000	Not Provided	Not Provided

Further studies by the Statistical Office in June 1916 demonstrated that the initial estimates of Alsatian and Lorrainer dead were well below the actual numbers.[29]

The figures in Table 3.2 are revealing in two ways, the first being that 91.8 percent of Alsatians and Lorrainers killed before 1 April 1916 had died outside of Alsace and Lorraine. This high percentage reveals the scope of German military operations in Europe, but it also reflects a reluctance to utilize Alsatians in the *Reichsland*. The table also suggests that many of the Alsatians and Lorrainers reported as wounded or missing in the 1915 report had either died of their injuries or been confirmed as killed. This alteration would likely have drawn the overall percentages of missing and captured *Reichsländer* even closer to those of the larger German army and concurrently decreased the overall number of Alsace-Lorrainers who may have intentionally fled imperial military service. The similarities in these figures during the first years of the war is important, for, as historian Christoph Jahr has demonstrated,

Table 3.2 Number of Alsace-Lorrainers Killed, Wounded, Missing, or Taken as Prisoners of War up to June 1916.

	Military Deaths in 1914	Military Deaths in 1915	Military Deaths up to 1 April 1916	Total Military Deaths	Number Died or Killed in Alsace-Lorraine	Number Died or Killed Outside of Alsace-Lorraine
Lower Alsace	2,585	3,038	150	5,773	538	5,235
Upper Alsace	1,343	1,975	61	3,379	226	3,153
Lorraine	2,184	3,594	138	5,916	460	5,456
Total	6,112	8,607	349	15,068	1,224	13,844

the desertion rates for Alsatians and Lorrainers were comparable to those of Germans from the rest of the Empire from December 1917 to September 1918.[30] Cumulatively the sources show that Alsatians were as likely to desert as any German soldier.

How are we to explain this discrepancy between the reality of *Reichsländer*'s contributions and German authorities' perception of their wartime service? Some authors from Alsace argued that a veritable "distrust psychosis" developed among imperial military leaders in relation to their Alsatian soldiers.[31] Jahr cements this impression by observing that one-third of all orders addressing themes of desertion and discipline in the German army focused on Alsatians and Lorrainers.[32] German officials' pre-existing suspicions regarding the national loyalties of their *Reichsland* subjects played an important role in the singularity of this focus. Authorities were predisposed to assume that any soldier from Alsace and Lorraine that was missing or taken prisoner had willingly gone over to the enemy.

The myth of mass Alsatian desertions in the summer of 1914 captured the official and popular imaginations in France and Germany. One legendary case of alleged Alsatian perfidy involved the Reserve Infantry Regiment 99 (RIR 99) in Upper Alsace. The RIR 99 was unique in that three-fifths of its soldiers originated in Alsace. French and German sources disagree on the timeline and course of subsequent events. French Lieutenant-Colonel Albert Carré gloatingly boasted that no Alsatians remained in the RIR 99 by 10 August 1914.[33] On that day, Carré claimed that some nine hundred *La Marseillaise* singing *Reichsländer* defected to French ranks.[34] German and Alsatian sources date the same event to 14 August and offer a different narrative. Karl Deuringer, author of the official history of the battle for the Bavarian army, described the RIR 99's position as "extraordinarily unfavorable."[35] Exposed from above and swept by flanking fire, several battalions took "considerable casualties" and were forced to withdraw. The Bavarian Reserve Infantry Regiment 15 was occupying a nearby position and that night reported the loss of some 231 soldiers missing in action, a number that was identical to RIR 99's losses.[36] Deuringer made no mention of Alsatian defections and concluded that defeat had been the result of "poorly chosen position and superior enemy forces."[37] The events of 14 August continued to be idealized in the postwar period. The French periodical *Le Pèlerin* cited the day in a postwar romanticized image that portrayed a scrum of handkerchief-wielding and *Pickelhaube*-clad *Reichsländer* rushing French lines to surrender. The perception of widespread desertions among their fellow landsmen had an immediate and lasting effect for Alsatians mobilized in the imperial ranks.

Figure 3.2 "Alsatian soldiers recruited by the Germans rush to reach the French lines (14 August 1914)." Eugène Damblins, "Des soldats alsaciens enrôlés par les Allemands s'empressent de gagner les lignes françaises (14 août 1914)," *Le Pèlerin: Revue Illustrée de la Semaine*, no. 2270 (26 September 1920): 8–9. Author's collection.

The Alsatian Experience within the German Ranks

Many Alsatians experienced differential treatment in the imperial army during the First World War because they were from the *Reichsland*. The alleged disloyalty of Alsace-Lorrainers in the early fighting in the West rapidly crystalized the image of the nationally suspect borderland soldier in the minds of the German military hierarchy. As early as October 1914, elements of the German occupation forces in Upper Alsace were requesting the replacement of Alsatian soldiers in their ranks.[38] In March 1915, von Wandel secretly ordered the separation and transfer of "politically suspect" *Reichsländer* from their units in the West to the Eastern Front.[39] To their credit, certain military authorities like General Deimling protested the order and retained the Alsatian and Lorrainer soldiers in his XV Army Corps.[40] The selective transfers did not last long, despite some resistance from below. Von Wandel amended his order in January 1916: "On account of multiple activities or manifestations of anti-German attitude it has been requested that *all Reichsland* military personnel regardless of their reputation, antecedents, and the witness of their superiors be transferred to the interior of Germany or the Eastern Front."[41] German military officials soon discovered that the wholesale transfer of Alsatian soldiers to the East was not a practical solution and in many cases created additional problems.

The removal of Alsatians from troop contingents on the Western Front was one of the most visible and resented actions taken against *Reichsländer* during the war. Sending Alsace-Lorrainer combatants to the East did not create "good" German soldiers. Instead, the discrimination only confirmed the French leanings of individuals who already possessed Francophile sentiments and alienated otherwise loyally serving soldiers. Compounding the entire issue was the fact that the transfers took potential individual malcontents, grouped them together, gave them additional (or real) cause for complaint, and then concentrated them in particular military formations, where they subsequently made up a significant proportion of the overall fighting force. In a classified memorandum from June 1917, Baron von Gall of the German War Ministry wrote: "The transfers [of *Reichsländer*] have permeated particular armies of the East with so many [unreliable] men ... who also represent a serious danger for the discipline and combat effectiveness of the force."[42] The situation was so alarming by December 1917 that General Erich Ludendorff warned all German army groups that sending more Alsace-Lorrainers to the Eastern Front threatened to create armies in which the majority of soldiers were from the *Reichsland*.[43]

Ludendorff also revealed an unintended consequence of the transfers in the same memorandum. He related: "It is to be kept in mind the chance of being released from the severe combat conditions of the West to the comparative calm and safety of the East puts a premium on unreliability. It is therefore to be feared that the urge of Alsace-Lorrainers to escape the dangers and strains of the West and the justifiable outrage of the 'old German' men over this apparent favoritism will cause unreliable elements to win further ground."[44] This observation illustrates an official belief that Alsatians were instrumentally using German military authorities' suspicions to escape the combat of the Western Front. The quote is also important because it reflects the larger twisted logic of the German High Command, which turned official discrimination into the fault of its victims, suggested that it constituted "preferential treatment," and that such handling justifiably outraged "German" soldiers.

Military authorities' suspicions regarding Alsatians increased in proportion to their distance from regular contact with ordinary soldiers. It was the disconnected highest martial policymakers that were responsible for the discriminatory policies. Their orders stemmed not from their own experience with Alsatians and Lorrainers, but rather from a preconceived image of the "disloyal" borderland soldier. This prejudice was transferred down the ranks. Richert related the "welcoming speech" by the battalion commander following his transfer to his fifth different unit:

> Up to that point there had not been any Alsatians in the regiment, so the Major was only familiar with hearsay. And after what he spoke, it seemed that he had heard little good about the Alsace-Lorrainers. First he walked among us, looking at each of our hats. "It's alright. I thought there would be more second class soldiers." This was the first sentence he spoke. (Second class soldiers, "felons," were not allowed to wear a cockade on their hats.) He continued, "What do I see? A few of you even wear the Iron Cross!" He seemed so astonished, as if he had discovered something completely impossible. I would have loved to punch the old scoundrel. He had earned it![45]

In this case, and throughout his memoir, Richert's anger and resentment was not directed at "Germany," but rather at those officers he perceived to be the authors of his mistreatment and others he deemed to be responsible for the war. The targeting of certain officers and war profiteers for hatred was a widespread source of discontent among German soldiers *as a whole*.[46] Nor did this antagonism prevent Richert from developing close relationships with other German soldiers in his units and even some officers.[47] After he successfully deserted to French lines, Richert refused to give his interrogators any information about the German trenches, explaining, "I had deserted to save my life and not to betray my former comrades."[48]

Differential handling did not define all Alsatian soldiers' experiences or every interaction with imperial authorities, despite its prevalence. Evidence shows that some lower-ranking German officers attempted to mitigate the effects of the discriminatory policies on *Reichsländer* in their units. The Third Reserve Division wrote to the Army High Command in 1917 that:

> […T]here were 445 Alsace-Lorrainers in the Division that were considered for the exchange. Among them were 105 who were decorated with the Iron Cross II Class (one with the Iron Cross I Class) and other individuals who had conducted themselves irreproachably and proved themselves before the enemy, so that their superiors, if possible, vouched for them. As a result, a transfer of only 173 unreliable men was requested, brought about, and approved by the High Command … at this time, 272 Alsace-Lorrainers are still in the Division.[49]

Unfortunately, not all retention efforts were as successful. Dominik Richert was ordered to remain behind on the Eastern Front when his regiment was transferred to France, despite having earned an Iron Cross II Class. He reported the general response among his *Reichsland*-originating comrades as "'Oh, still second-class soldiers. They're probably afraid we will desert' and so on." His German company leader took a more pragmatic approach and informed the Alsatians that "'I would have liked to keep you in the company. I was very satisfied with all of you ... You should actually see yourselves as fortunate to remain here because the danger on the Western Front is much greater.'"[50] The subsequent complaining against the Prussians that Richert recorded suggests that the Alsatians in his regiment found these words to be of little comfort.

These two sources raise an important cautionary flag for historians when discussing the treatment of Alsatians in the German army during the First World War. At one level, they prove that soldiers from the *Reichsland* were singled out to either remain or be transferred to the Eastern Front. Moreover, it is evident that being associated with the vaguely defined label of "unreliable" was sufficient cause for Alsatians to be removed from their existent troop contingents. The blurriness of this suspect category no doubt encompassed a range of Alsatians who were more aptly described as reluctant *soldiers* rather than as reluctant *Germans*. Jean Lechner wrote in 1917 that "I only want the war to end quickly. I want to save my skin and if later I must remain German or become French, what is that to me? For now, I just want to save my skin."[51] At another level, the memorandum demonstrates that Alsatians' experiences in the ranks ranged from discrimination to being recognized for their bravery. Many German military officials' first instincts may have been to suspect the loyalty of their *Reichsland* soldiers, but not all were irreconcilably prejudiced. This is evident in the statistic that nearly a quarter of Alsatians and Lorrainers in the Third Reserve Division had been decorated with the Iron Cross, but even more so by the fact that the recommendations of their superior officers enabled the majority of these soldiers to avoid the ordered transfer. However, Richert's case demonstrates the Janus-faced aspect of imperial policy towards Alsatians, extending an award for bravery with one hand and labeling them as suspect with the other.

Exile to the East was replaced by a number of different security measures after Russia's separate peace with Germany in March 1918. The increased number of Alsatians in the West did correspond to a rise in their desertions,[52] particularly in the latter half of the conflict.[53] Imperial officials found themselves caught in a classic Catch-22 in their relationship with their soldiers from Alsace. No single policy was sufficient to entirely eliminate desertions or return a single defector. It was the Alsatians who remained in the German ranks that would face the full retaliatory consequences of their compatriots' departure. In fact, by increasing their surveillance of *Reichsland* soldiers, limiting the positions they could occupy, and in some cases banishing them altogether to rear work details, officials risked alienating the remaining Alsatians. The end result was that an intensification of restrictions caused increased disillusionment among Alsatian soldiers that in turn led to more desertions, which corresponded to a tightening of constraints in an unending and vicious cycle.[54]

German military authorities feared that the close proximity to French troops would be an irresistible temptation for Alsatians to desert. This worry influenced the manner in which Alsatians were incorporated into various military formations and the activities they were allowed to undertake. Ludendorff circulated a confidential memorandum in March 1917 that ordered Alsatians and Lorrainers from the same district to be separated within their troop formations. He explained the order by saying, "… many untrustworthy [Alsace-Lorrainers] who have an inclination to desert will perhaps not find the courage to do so if their

Figure 3.3 "Alsatian Comrades, War Year, 1914." Alsatians (likely in Karlsruhe) at the beginning of the war. Fears of small group desertions caused German military authorities to break up such clusters in the later years of the conflict. "Elsässische Kammeraden Kriegsjahr 1914," wartime postcard, author's collection.

decision is not fortified by a like-minded comrade."⁵⁵ Experience had taught German military authorities that *Reichsländer* often only undertook the dangerous task of defecting in small groups.

It is impossible to ascertain how many potential Alsatian deserters were dissuaded by the enactment of Ludendorff's order. What is certain is that the dispersal of Alsatians had significant unintended ramifications. Military formations in the German army during the *Kaiserreich* were organized along regional lines. A soldier from Munich could expect to serve in a regiment surrounded by fellow Bavarians, a soldier from Berlin with fellow Prussians. Despite the variety of individual soldiers' social and political backgrounds, they shared a fundamental set of cultural references. These pre-existent connections served to cement ties of comradeship and helped maintain the cohesion of the unit around a regional identity, even in cases of disillusionment with imperial military service.

The dispersal of Alsatians prevented similar group-regional solidarity from taking root. Instead, soldiers from Alsace were brought together in large assemblies at moments when they had been identified as security liabilities by German military authorities. Richert described a train ride to Freiburg after he and fellow Alsatians were pulled from their units on the Western Front: "While underway the Alsatians gleefully railed against the Prussians and one heard expressions that could scarce be called patriotic."⁵⁶ Thus, the common regional experience that Alsatians shared was not necessarily the rigors and horrors of military service, but rather what they perceived to be their unwarranted victimization. Moreover, the continual rotation of regiments between fronts also meant that Alsatians could be incorporated and removed from their units more than once.⁵⁷ The lack of these critical nodes of fidelity became more significant as *Reichsland* soldiers increasingly felt rejected by the *Kaiserreich*. Alsatians' experiences of being targeted and labeled suspect for fears of what they might do, rather than their actual actions, created a self-understanding at odds with a larger German identity.

The official discrimination that Alsatian soldiers experienced negatively influenced their German national consciousness and provoked demonstrations of Francophile sentiment. A certain Eugen Eschmann from the 353rd Infantry Regiment wrote to his wife to describe Alsatians' reactions to being pulled from the front lines. Eschmann related that as they marched, the seventy men started singing *La Marseillaise*, wandered about, and took impromptu rests to spite the German lieutenant charged with accompanying them. He reported widespread approval when a "jokester" characterized their current state and hope for the future as, "Saw action in 1914/15/16/17, earned the Iron Cross, and

Figure 3.4 "War of 1914 — Convoy of Alsacian-Lorrans [sic] prisonners [sic] in Gare de Juvisy." J.C., "Guerre de 1914 — Convoi de prisonniers Alsaciens-Lorrains en Gare de Juvisy," wartime postcard, author's collection.

happily taken prisoner in 1918."[58] The desirability of French captivity for *Reichsländer* was not confined to disgruntled letters home. Some republican sources gave such rhetoric a concrete form. In the image shown in Figure 3.4, a trainload of seemingly unperturbed Alsatian prisoners of war share a bottle of alcohol with French soldiers in an unsubtle celebration of their capture and a seeming promotion of kinship with their captors. Even though the scene was likely deliberately staged to promote this message, it also precisely articulated imperial authorities' fears of the secret French loyalties of their Alsatian soldiers.

Eschmann would further describe the ordeal before concluding:

> After such treatment we can no longer feel German, as you yourself must concede. Hopefully, Alsace will not remain German, so that we finally know where we belong and will no longer be seen and treated as stepchildren because four years of wartime surveillance while German soldiers is already long enough.[59]

Several aspects regarding Alsatians' "pro-French" manifestations are evident in Eschmann's letter. The motivation to sing the French national anthem was clearly retaliation against their removal from their units and intended to shock their German chaperone. At another level, the deep offense that many Alsatians took to being singled out and suspected, despite their wartime accomplishments, is expressed in the rueful irony of the "jokester's" statement. Angry and disgusted after it became evident that loyal service appeared insufficient to earn the trust of German officials, Alsatians were willing to countenance an alternative. These manifestations of "pro-French" sentiment signaled a capitulation to official stereotypes. Alsatians were just living up to authorities' expectations.

Discriminatory policies confirmed an official sense of difference towards Alsatian soldiers serving in the German army. The orders that were directed against the imagined and undifferentiated disloyal *Reichsland* soldier articulated authorities' understanding that Alsatians and Lorrainers were not quite "German." After the Treaty of Brest-Litovsk necessitated the return of Alsatians to the Western Front, an internal note to the troop formations within the Argonne Army Group restricted the activities and movements of Alsatian soldiers by relating, "It is forbidden to allow Alsatians to take part in patrols. They are not to be allowed to hold posts in the foremost lines if they have not earned absolute confidence through a long period of service and even then, they are only allowed to stand a double post in tandem with a German."[60] The identification of Alsatians by their region of origin, while their comrade simply bore the moniker "German," articulates an important distinction made by the higher levels of the military hierarchy. National loyalties were naturalized among interior Germans but Alsatians remained suspect even in cases of longstanding service. Evidence suggests that the policy of keeping Alsatians out of the front lines was only partially realizable. Jean Lechner participated in reconnaissance missions, manned a frontline observation post, volunteered to repair telephone communications, and could have twice easily crossed to French lines.[61] Similarly, until his desertion, Dominik Richert regularly took part in patrols and occupied forward positions as the commander of a machine gun unit on the Western Front.[62]

The reasoning behind "mixed" postings was not always punitive. Ludendorff instructed, "Always use Alsace-Lorrainers together with 'old German' men. Boost the comradely sense of honor so that each feels himself bound to contribute to the honor and reputation of his formation and so avert desertion."[63] Here again a distinction was made between "old Germans" and soldiers from the *Reichsland*. The quote suggests that imperial military authorities promoted the development of immediate regimental ties because they believed that calls to defend the fatherland would have less traction among Alsace-Lorrainers. Thus, even in officials' efforts to include Alsatian soldiers, they were simultaneously imagined as different.

The indignation and humiliation felt by certain *Reichsland* soldiers after being singled out and removed from their frontline units was articulated in an Alsatian's letter to his family in May 1918. The account and official reaction warrant the text of the letter being quoted at length:

> My Dearest!
> I want to again tell you that I am once more in my old battery in the Regiment. As I told you in my last letter, we Alsatians were withdrawn from the Regiment and the front. We were taken back to a forest camp. The most beastly part was that escorts accompanied us and kept us under surveillance. It seemed to me as if I was in a prison camp.
> In the meantime, our regimental commander interceded for us and managed to secure our return to the regiment. It was very good of him, still, we would have all preferred if we could have left it behind, even if it was as prisoners, because of this *dishonor* and *disgrace* done to us! This is the thanks that one receives after nearly six years of soldiering and four years of faithfully fulfilling his duty.
> I declared to my battery leader that I did not want to, nor could I, occupy sensitive positions [*Vertrauensposten*]. I would not be able to take it anymore if I was once more treated as untrustworthy! My battery leader said he had the same trust in me as before and I should take up my old service, which I now have done. Still I can hardly bear it because this dishonor and humiliation that has been done to us still rankles me.
> ... My whole life I will never forget this time and dishonor that has unjustly been done to me. The lords above probably believe that we Alsatians have no spark of a sense of honor because otherwise they would not treat us so ....
> Many greetings to you all from your Eugen.[64]

Several aspects of Eugen's letter are revealing about his own experiences and the general policies of German authorities towards Alsatians. The differentiation in Eugen's attitude between the "lords above" and his own regimental commander and battery leader is striking. Rather than seeing all German officers as a single oppressive unit, he distinguished between his immediate superiors who demonstrated their trust in him and the higher anonymous staff officers who unjustly victimized him. The dislike of certain categories of officers was not a uniquely Alsatian phenomenon. Multiple scholars have demonstrated that tensions characterized relations between imperial officers and soldiers during the First World War and that in some cases resentment against the military hierarchy had a cohesive power among frontline soldiers.[65] Yet despite some similarities, the prejudice that Eugen and his fellow Alsatians faced was fundamentally rooted in perceived national rather than social differences. It marked *Reichsländer* as distinct even from their comparably ranked German comrades with whom they shared a close proximity and experience in the trenches. The sense of dissimilarity was only compounded by Alsatian soldiers' frequent transfers. At another level, Eugen's letter also articulates an expectation of reciprocity. He felt that the imperial government owed him a certain amount of respect and consideration in return for his six years of loyal soldiering. The fact that officials failed to recognize this service and treated him as suspect disillusioned Eugen and dampened his German national feelings.

To their credit, military authorities investigated the letter's allegations. The final report confirmed the basic facts of the narrative but disputed Eugen's interpretation.[66] The described events and the subsequent response from imperial officials clearly illustrates the lack of tact and self-defeating nature of German wartime policies towards Alsatians. These strategies were counterproductive. German military leaders may have prevented a few desertions by treating soldiers from Alsace as a nationally suspect mass, but in the process alienated many more like Eugen, who were loyally fulfilling their military duties. Perhaps, as Christoph Jahr has suggested, the desertion of Alsatians is not surprising. What really is astounding is that the majority chose not to.[67]

Not all German authorities believed that Alsatian defections were a problem. In fact, certain officials perceived the desertions and resulting denaturalizations as potentially positive. In one instance, the General Command of the XV Army Corps urged the Ministry of Alsace-Lorraine to continue to revoke the citizenship of deserters. He wrote: "The denaturalization procedures must be continued for political reasons. For one, on account of its deterrent effect, but also above all, so that by the conclusion of the peace the *Reichsland* will be cleansed of elements who are not inwardly committed to the German Reich."[68] From this point of view, the fires of war could be interpreted as a light that illuminated the darkest corners of *Reichsländer*'s hearts and revealed their "true" colors. As a result, and particularly for Alsace, German authorities postulated that those individuals who deserted had never been truly "German" and the Reich was well rid of them. This self-serving justification may have provided some measure of self-comfort, but it failed to fundamentally address the underlying issue that in many cases imperial officials themselves were responsible for the disillusionment and estrangement of their Alsatian soldiers.

Pensions and Support

The First World War confronted authorities with the daunting task of providing support to an unprecedented number of its citizens. The mobilization of all levels of German society removed millions of primary breadwinners from their households, while the carnage of the conflict left thousands of widows and disabled soldiers who needed to be kept on sound economic footing in the present and prepared for a productive future. Imperial authorities moved quickly to address the unique needs of these groups in Alsace. Germany's treatment of war-disabled Alsatian soldiers is an important counterpoint to the narrative of the victimization of *Reichsland* combatants. In stark contrast to the discrimination that Alsatian soldiers experienced in the ranks, German civil authorities went to extraordinary lengths to ensure the wellbeing and reintegration of ex-combatants whose lives had been permanently altered by the conflict. Around ten thousand Alsatians and Lorrainers had been granted a permanent or provisional pension by imperial officials by November 1918.[69] Thus, while Alsatian soldiers were handled as suspect at the front, their disabled comrades were treated as German at home.

The combination of a new industrial style of warfare and the mass armies of the First World War astronomically increased the number of debilitating wounds suffered by combatants. Already by 1916, some ten thousand soldiers with differing degrees of bodily mutilation or sickness had been discharged and returned to the provinces of Alsace and Lorraine.[70] German authorities acted quickly to address the requirements of the war disabled. The short-term intention of official aid was to provide immediate sustenance and lessen any direct emergency facing the applicant. The long-term goal of wartime support was to provide the requisite skills to return war invalids to contributing members of society. Taken together, the object of short- and long-term assistance measures was to minimize the conflict's disruption of the prewar economic and social order.

The most important assistance institution in the *Reichsland* was the State Welfare Office for the War Disabled and Surviving Dependents, which was signed into existence by *Statthalter* Hans von Dallwitz on 3 June 1915.[71] Approximately 2,984 war-disabled veterans had registered themselves with their local state welfare offices by March 1916. Imperial officials sought to establish uniformity by promulgating a general set of guidelines and goals for disability relief. The Institution's objectives were outlined thus:

> The goal of aid activities [for the disabled] is to secure the best possible curative treatment and make all combatants who have been damaged through injury, amputation, and physical or mental illness fully functional members of economic life in consideration of their personal and economic circumstances. The disabled should not become beggars, but rather taxpayers, they should not consume wealth, but rather create it. The war invalid organ grinder of the '70s must not re-emerge. It is not the role [of the aid activities] to secure a provisional livelihood. This is the responsibility of the Reich's welfare laws. Rather, medical knowledge and experiences plus all cultural and economic facilities and achievements should work together in order to effect an extensive compensation for the existent disability.[72]

A wide definition of infirmity was the foundation for the treatment of the war injured. Negative historical precedents were clearly in officials' minds, as evidenced by the emphasis on returning the disabled soldier to a civilian occupation rather than the dole. It is also evident that the responsibility for the rehabilitation of war disabled was perceived as a profoundly modern and collective responsibility.

Archival evidence demonstrates that local officials took their assignment to ease the transition of disabled Alsatian soldiers to civilian life seriously. Regular reports regarding the number of claimants and the success of their reintegration in an economic and occupational sense were submitted to the State Welfare Office from communities and districts such as Colmar and Mulhouse from 1916 to the end of the war. An even more exemplary case are the painstakingly detailed reports from the District Committee of Ribeauvillé that not only recorded the name of each returned war invalid in their jurisdiction, but also described their injuries and the efforts made to return them to the local workforce.

One exemplary case from the Ribeauvillé District Committee was that of August Berrel. Serving in the 52nd Reserve Field Artillery Regiment, Berrel suffered injuries that included a thigh wound, shell splinter to the chest, being gut shot, and a lame left arm. Unable to return to his prewar occupations of farmer and postal assistant, the Committee applied for and was granted support from the State Welfare Office to cover the costs of Berrel's vocational retraining and intermediate care. He was hired as a tax executory in Ribeauvillé upon completion of the course and achieved self-sufficiency.[73] The report also included similarly detailed descriptions of sixty other ongoing cases within the Committee's region.

Considering the scope of their assignment, limited resources, and continually burgeoning petitioner base, the efforts of the Ribeauvillé District Committee should be judged a success. Light manufacturing in Ribeauvillé, like many non-war essential industries across Alsace, suffered a significant downturn during the conflict. Members argued in 1916 that their continued accomplishments in the face of such obstacles was "proof that the District Committee and all of its liaison officers are fully conscious of their duty and who selflessly work in the care of our discharged war disabled and sick combatants."[74] Two more years of war would further challenge the Committee to meet the needs of local ex-soldiers. Nonetheless, on 15 October 1918, the Ribeauvillé District Committee's final communication reported that 466 of the 609 eligible applicants who had registered with their agency since its inception in 1915 had been returned to work. The factors that contributed to the incompletion of the remaining 143 cases were often the result of circumstances beyond the control of the Committee. A placement percentage of 76.5 percent of disabled and sick veterans during wartime was a significant accomplishment. The emphasis on providing care for returned disabled soldiers from the *Reichsland* suggests that having proved themselves through visible and permanent sacrifice for Germany, Alsatian war invalids were now judged to be worthy of receiving "the thanks of the fatherland."

Conclusion

Few other soldiers of the First World War experienced a homecoming quite like the Alsatians who had fought in the imperial army. These soldiers returned neither as victorious heroes nor lauded as former combatants who had valiantly defended their nation for four years against the combined might of much of the industrialized world. Instead, Alsatian soldiers who had fought for Germany returned home as veterans of an enemy army. Ex-combatants encountered a heady atmosphere and population that ceremonially celebrated the victory of their recent enemies, while rejoicing at their own defeat. Despite this seemingly paradoxical reception, Alsatians who had been treated as "second-class soldiers" for four years might have justifiably viewed the newly empowered French regime with a degree of optimism.[75] These hopes would quickly be dashed as it became evident that French administrators also viewed German Alsatian veterans as objects of suspicion.

Although they targeted different sections of the populace, republican authorities shared the basic assumption with their imperial colleagues that some elements of the population living in the borderland were not to be trusted. The French introduced an exclusionary model of citizenship to Alsace by distinguishing between "old Alsatians" and "old Germans." The subsequent *triage* program was the first official procedure that judged the desirability and awarded the right to remain in the province based on an individual's descent and an evaluation of their wartime actions.[76] French authorities were able to reconcile the majority of ex-soldiers they considered Alsatian to the established French nationalist narrative by characterizing them as unwilling conscripts in the German military. Acceptance into the French national fold came at a price for these Alsatians. It entailed their acquiescence to the status of victim and the subsummation of any wartime experiences that contradicted official accounts, causing some veterans like Jean Lechner to literally bury his Iron Crosses in the family garden.[77]

Devlin M. Scofield is Assistant Professor of History at Northwest Missouri State University. He completed his Ph.D. at Michigan State University in 2015 and is currently working on a monograph that examines Germany and France's treatment of former enemy soldiers in the borderland of Alsace from 1871 to 1953. His research was supported by the Berlin Program for Advanced German and European Studies, Michigan State University, the Central European History Society, and the German Historical Institute. He recently published a chapter entitled "Corpses of Atonement" in the edited volume *Human Remains in Society* (Manchester University Press, 2017).

Notes

1. After the German victory in the Franco-Prussian War, the annexed regions of Alsace and Lorraine were designated the *Reichsland Elsaß-Lothringen*. The administrative hyphenation elided significant regional and historical differences between the two provinces. Although this chapter focuses on the experience of Alsatians within the German ranks, many contemporary statistics did not make a distinction between the two populations. Consequently, I periodically utilize the terms *"Reichsland"* and "Alsace-Lorraine" when referring to the region, as well as *"Reichsländer"* and "Alsace-Lorrainer" when referring to the populace.
2. Alan Kramer, "*Wackes* at War: Alsace-Lorraine and the Failure of German National Mobilization, 1914–1918," in *State, Society and Mobilization in Europe during the First World War*, ed. John Horne (Cambridge, 1997), 106.
3. Catherine Lechner, *Alsace Lorraine: Histoires d'une Tragédie Oubliée* (Paris, 2004), 22. All translations are the author's unless stated otherwise.

4. Joseph Rossé et al., *Das Elsass von 1870–1932*, vol. 1 (Colmar, 1936), 187–88, 228, 232.
5. Ibid., 335–62.
6. German and French sources disagree on the exact figures. The *Reichsland* government reported that 1,640 individuals had been taken into "protective custody" as of 1 April 1918, while postwar French efforts identified some 4,820 cases. Ibid., 244.
7. Ibid., 339.
8. Dominik Richert, *Beste Gelegenheit zum Sterben*: *Meine Erlebnisse im Kriege 1914–1918*, ed. Angelika Tramitz and Bernd Ulrich (Munich, 1989).
9. See Lechner, *Alsace Lorraine*.
10. Karin Huser, *"Haltet gut Jontef und seid herzlichst geküsst"*: *Feldpostbriefe des Elsässer Juden Henri Levy von der Ostfront (1916–1918)* (Zürich, 2014). German authorities were reluctant to grant leave to soldiers from the *Reichsland* over fears that furloughed Alsatians might not return to their units.
11. See the introduction to this volume.
12. See Jean-Noël Grandhomme and Francis Grandhomme, eds., *Les Alsaciens-Lorrains dans la Grande Guerre* (Strasbourg, 2013), 83; Dan Silverman, *Reluctant Union: Alsace-Lorraine and Imperial Germany, 1871–1918* (University Park, 1972), 3; Rossé et al., *Das Elsass von 1870–1932*, 1: 183, 228.
13. Lechner, *Alsace Lorraine*, 22.
14. My argument reverses that of Alan Kramer in his chapter, "*Wackes* at War." Kramer contends that German authorities' discrimination reinvigorated an "underlying" anti-Reich mentality among Alsatians. See Kramer, "*Wackes* at War," 110.
15. Despite their idealized rhetoric, French authorities also worried about disloyalty among the borderland population. James A. Logan, chief of the US military mission with the French army, estimated in December 1914 that there were currently 8,000 Alsatians interned in various camps in France and another 13,700 who were free, but under police surveillance. See Hoover Institution Archives (hereafter cited as HIA), James Addison Logan Papers, Box No. 13, Letter from James A. Logan, 18 June 1915, 119–20.
16. "Elsass-Lothringer! Für wen kämpft und leidet Ihr? Für wen haben Tausende und abermals Tausende Elsass-Lothringer ihr junges Leben opfern müssen?" HIA, Great Britain, Director of Propaganda in Enemy Countries, Box No. 3.
17. See Kate Brown, *A Biography of No Place: From Ethnic Borderland to Soviet Heartland* (Cambridge, MA, 2005); Pieter M. Judson, *Guardians of the Nation: Activists on the Language Frontiers of Imperial Austria* (Cambridge, MA, 2006); Tara Zahra, *Kidnapped Souls: National Indifference and the Battle for Children in the Bohemian Lands, 1900–1948* (Ithaca, NY, 2011).
18. Ute Frevert problematizes the notion that "universal" conscription broke down pre-service barriers. Nonetheless, she argues that the army developed into an influential socialization institution. See Ute Frevert, *A Nation in the Barracks: Modern Germany, Military Conscription and Civil Society*, trans. Andrew Boreham with Daniel Brückenhaus (Oxford, 2004).

19. Josh Sanborn, *Drafting the Russian Nation: Military Conscription, Total War, and Mass Politics, 1905–1925* (Dekalb, IL, 2003) and Ronald R. Krebs, *Fighting for Rights: Military Service and the Politics of Citizenship* (Ithaca, NY, 2006).
20. The experience of German Jews has often been portrayed as a regression from determination to prove their unconditional patriotism to disillusionment, as the conflict provoked greater expressions of antisemitism. See Christhard Hoffmann, "Between Integration and Rejection: The Jewish Community in Germany, 1914–1918," in Horne, *State, Society and Mobilization*, 89–104; István Deák, *Beyond Nationalism: A Social and Political History of the Habsburg Officer Corps, 1848–1918* (Oxford, 1990), 196–97; Huser, *"Haltet gut Jontef und seid herzlichst geküsst"*, 65–80. Tim Grady has complicated this paradigm by arguing that the shared experience of mass bereavement brought Jews and Germans together in communities of mourning. See Tim Grady, *The German-Jewish Soldiers of the First World War in History and Memory* (Oxford, 2011).
21. See Erich Lohr, *Nationalizing the Russian Empire: The Campaign against Enemy Aliens during World War I* (Cambridge, MA, 2003) and Sanborn, *Drafting the Russian Nation*, 63–95.
22. Rossé et al., *Das Elsass von 1870–1932*, 1: 298–301.
23. In the XV Army Corps that was stationed in Strasbourg, only 3,153 out of 12,361 volunteers were "old Alsatians." The XIV Army Corps in Karlsruhe had an even smaller percentage, with 1,378 out of 27,225 and the XXI Army Corps in Saarbrücken only 3,500. Ibid., 1: 296.
24. Alan Kramer cites Rossé et al.'s figure as evidence of the failure of German mobilization efforts in Alsace-Lorraine. See Kramer, *"Wackes* at War," 107–8.
25. The low percentages of Alsace-Lorrainers in the ranks of "Alsatian" regiments like the 132nd Lower-Alsatian Infantry Regiment and the 143rd Lower-Alsatian Infantry Regiment that were both part of the XV Army Corps reflected a deliberate decision. *Reichsland* officials avoided filling locally garrisoned regiments with a majority of regional conscripts over worries of disloyalty and a belief that exposure to German culture and society outside Alsace would better facilitate the soldiers' integration into the Reich. Consequently, Alsatians were primarily incorporated into military formations in the Prussian army, a practice that continued into the war.
26. Lt. Colonel Albert Carré, *Les Engagés volontaires Alsaciens-Lorrains pendant la guerre* (Paris, 1923), 15. Unlike their German counterparts, Alsatians in the French army had the opportunity to choose the location of their posting. Most opted for service in the French colonies, particularly North Africa. Certain scholars have not recognized the element of personal initiative that Alsatians had in choosing their place of service. See Jean-Noël Grandhomme, "Introduction," in *Boches ou Tricolores: Les Alsaciens-Lorrains dans la Grande Guerre*, ed. Jean-Noël Grandhomme (Strasbourg, 2008), 29.
27. Archives Départementales du Bas-Rhin (hereafter cited as ADBR), 47 AL 90, "Die Verluste an aus Elsaß-Lothringen stammenden Militärpersonen, im

Kriege 1914, soweit sie in den bis 1. Januar 1915 erschienenen Verlustslisten veröffentlicht sind," 31 March 1915.
28. ADBR, 47 AL 90, Kriegsminister Franz von Wandel to Statthalter Hans von Dallwitz, 20 May 1915.
29. ADBR, 47 AL 92, "In Elsaß-Lothringen gezählte Militärsterbefälle 1914 bis 1. April 1916," 28 June 1916.
30. See Christoph Jahr, *Gewöhnliche Soldaten: Desertion und Deserteure im deutschen und britischen Heer, 1914–1918* (Göttingen, 1998), 278.
31. Rossé et al., *Das Elsass von 1870–1932*, 1: 318.
32. Jahr, *Gewöhnliche Soldaten*, 283.
33. Carré, *Les Engagés volontaires Alsaciens-Lorrains pendant la guerre*, 48. Carré was in charge of coordinating the screening and incorporation of *Reichsländer* into the French army.
34. Ibid., 52.
35. Karl Deuringer, *The First Battle of the First World War Alsace-Lorraine*, trans. and ed. Terence Zuber (Stroud, Gloucestershire, 2004), 51.
36. Rossé et al., *Das Elsass von 1870–1932*, 1: 204.
37. Deuringer, *The First Battle*, 53.
38. Rossé et al., *Das Elsass von 1870–1932*, 1: 302.
39. Ibid.
40. Ibid., 305.
41. Hauptstaatsarchiv-Stuttgart (hereafter cited as HStAS), M 30/1 107, Kriegsminister Franz Gustav von Wandel, 11 January 1916.
42. HStAS, M 33/2 681, Freiherr von Gall to the Armee Oberkommando, 2 June 1917.
43. HStAS, M 30/1 107, Erich Ludendorff to all Army Groups, 2 December 1917.
44. Ibid. The Ministry of War officially canceled the transfer of Alsace-Lorrainers to the East on 12 January 1918.
45. Richert, *Beste Gelegenheit zum Sterben*, 240–41.
46. See Bernd Ulrich and Benjamin Ziemann, eds., *German Soldiers in the Great War: Letters and Eyewitness Accounts*, trans. Christine Brooks (Barnsley, 2010). See also Thomas Kühne, *The Rise and Fall of Comradeship: Hitler's Soldiers, Male Bonding and Mass Violence in the Twentieth Century* (Cambridge, 2017), 17–44.
47. Richert, *Beste Gelegenheit zum Sterben*, 284–85, 364–66, 374.
48. Ibid., 387.
49. HStAS, M 33/2, 3 Reserve-Division gez. Rusche to Armee Oberkommando 4, 21 May 1917.
50. Richert, *Beste Gelegenheit zum Sterben*, 224.
51. Lechner, *Alsace Lorraine*, 125.
52. Elizabeth Vlossak, *Marianne or Germania? Nationalizing Women in Alsace, 1870–1946* (Oxford, 2010), 136–37.
53. The postal surveillance officer in Mulhouse put together an extended memorandum in which he sought to identify the primary causes of Alsatian desertion. He broke the motivations down into five broad categories that included an anti-German disposition, kinship with family members living

in France, the length of the war, and "special" treatment in the form of leave denials or poor handling by their direct superiors. See HStAS, M 30/1 107, Report from Mulhouse Überwachungsoffizier, 18 April 1918.
54. See Christopher J. Fischer, *Alsace to the Alsatians? Visions and Divisions of Alsatian Regionalism, 1870–1939* (Oxford, 2010), 110 and Kramer, "*Wackes* at War," 120–21.
55. HStAS, M 33/2 681, General Erich Ludendorff to the Armee Oberkommando, 8 March 1917.
56. Richert, *Beste Gelegenheit zum Sterben*, 87.
57. Dominik Richert reported that he had been forced to change regiments four times by 1917. Not only did this preclude the development of long-term relationships, but it also limited Richert's opportunities for promotions. See Richert, *Beste Gelegenheit zum Sterben*, 238. In contrast, the Grandhommes observe that a number of Alsatians were able to rise through the German ranks during the First World War. See Grandhomme and Grandhomme, *Les Alsaciens-Lorrains dans la Grande Guerre*, 99, 102.
58. HStAS, M 30/1 107, Mulhouse Überwachungsoffizier, "Auszüge aus Briefen elsäßischer Heeresangehöriger, welche Fahnenflucht beabsichtigen," 18 April 1918.
59. Ibid.
60. HStAS, M 30/1 330, St. Generalstab der Armee, Abteilung IIIb to the Oberkommando der Heeresgruppe Herzog Albrecht, 20 September 1918.
61. Lechner, *Alsace Lorraine*, 46, 87, 88.
62. See Richert, *Beste Gelegenheit zum Sterben*.
63. HStAS, M 30/1 107, Erich Ludendorff to all Army Groups, 2 December 1917.
64. HStAS, M 30/1 330, Eugen to his family, 25 May 1918. Emphasis in original.
65. Kühne, *The Rise and Fall of Comradeship*, 25–29.
66. HStAS, M 30/1 330, Report from the Feldartillerie Regiment 67, 6 August 1918.
67. Jahr, *Gewöhnliche Soldaten*, 282.
68. HStAS, M 30/1 107, Stellvertreter Generalkommando des XV. Armeekorps to the Ministerium Elsaß-Lothringen, 21 December 1917. The fact that imperial authorities only utilized policies of denaturalization and property confiscation against Alsace-Lorrainers and not the entirety of the German population was another source of discontent among *Reichsländer*. See Rossé et al., *Das Elsass von 1870–1932*, 1: 261.
69. Comité Alsacien d'Études et d'Informations, *L'Alsace depuis son Retour a la France, 1918–1932* (Strasbourg, 1932), 1: 79.
70. Archives Départementales du Haut-Rhin (hereafter cited as ADHR), 8 AL 1/1654, "Die Kriegsinvaliden- und Kriegshinterbliebenenfürsorge in Elsaß-Lothringen 1916," *Nachrichten* no. 12, 2.
71. ADHR, 8 AL 1/1658, "Kriegsinvalidenfürsorge in Elsaß-Lothringen," *Nachrichten der Landesfürsorgestelle für Kriegsinvalide* no. 16, 9.
72. ADHR, 8 AL 1/1655, "Kriegsinvalidenfürsorge," 3–4, 5 June 1915.
73. ADHR, 8 AL 1/1655, Landesfürsorgestelle für Kriegsinvalide und Kriegshinterbliebene Kreisausschuss-Rappoltsweiler to the Kaiserliche

Ministerium für Elsaß-Lothringen Landesfürsorgestelle für Kriegsinvalide und Kriegshinterbliebene, 8 January 1917.
74. ADHR, 8 AL 1/1655, Report from the Landesfürsorgestelle für Kriegsinvalide und Kriegshinterbliebene Kreisausschuss-Rappoltsweiler, 10 October 1916.
75. Fischer argues that the majority of Alsatians welcomed the French out of a sense of relief that the war was over and because they represented an alternative to the Germans. See Fischer, *Alsace to the Alsatians?* 121.
76. See Laird Boswell, "From Liberation to Purge Trials in the 'Mythic Provinces': Recasting French Identities in Alsace and Lorraine, 1918–1920," *French Historical Studies* 23, no. 1 (2000): 129–62.
77. Lechner, *Alsace Lorraine*, 165–66.

Bibliography

Boswell, Laird. "From Liberation to Purge Trials in the 'Mythic Provinces': Recasting French Identities in Alsace and Lorraine, 1918–1920." *French Historical Studies* 23, no. 1 (2000): 129–62.
Brown, Kate. *A Biography of No Place: From Ethnic Borderland to Soviet Heartland*. Cambridge, MA: Harvard University Press, 2005.
Carré, Lt. Colonel Albert. *Les Engagés volontaires Alsaciens-Lorrains pendant la guerre*. Paris: Ernest Flammarion, 1923.
Comité Alsacien d'Études et d'Informations. *L'Alsace depuis son Retour a la France, 1918–1932*. Strasbourg: Comité Alsacien d'Études et d'Informations, 1932.
Deák, István. *Beyond Nationalism: A Social and Political History of the Habsburg Officer Corps, 1848–1918*. Oxford: Oxford University Press, 1990.
Deuringer, Karl. *The First Battle of the First World War Alsace-Lorraine*. Translated and edited by Terence Zuber. Stroud, Gloucestershire: The History Press, 2004.
Fischer, Christopher J. *Alsace to the Alsatians? Visions and Divisions of Alsatian Regionalism, 1870–1939*. Oxford: Berghahn Books, 2010.
Frevert, Ute. *A Nation in the Barracks: Modern Germany, Military Conscription and Civil Society*. Translated by Andrew Boreham with Daniel Brückenhaus. Oxford: Berg, 2004.
Grady, Tim. *The German-Jewish Soldiers of the First World War in History and Memory*. Oxford: Oxford University Press, 2011.
Grandhomme, Jean-Noël. "Introduction." In *Boches ou Tricolores: Les Alsaciens-Lorrains dans la Grande Guerre*, edited by Jean-Noël Grandhomme, 19–33. Strasbourg: La Nuée Bleue, 2008.
Grandhomme, Jean-Noël, and Francis Grandhomme, eds. *Les Alsaciens-Lorrains dans la Grande Guerre*. Strasbourg: La Nuée Bleue, 2013.
Hoffmann, Christhard. "Between Integration and Rejection: The Jewish Community in Germany, 1914–1918." In *State, Society and Mobilization in Europe during the First World War*, edited by John Horne, 89–104. Cambridge: Cambridge University Press, 1997.

Huser, Karin. *"Haltet gut Jontef und seid herzlichst geküsst": Feldpostbriefe des Elsässer Juden Henri Levy von der Ostfront (1916–1918)*. Zürich: Chronos Verlag, 2014.

Jahr, Christoph. *Gewöhnliche Soldaten: Desertion und Deserteure im deutschen und britischen Heer, 1914–1918*. Göttingen: Vandenhoeck & Ruprecht, 1998.

Judson, Pieter M. *Guardians of the Nation: Activists on the Language Frontiers of Imperial Austria*. Cambridge, MA: Harvard University Press, 2006.

Kramer, Alan. "*Wackes* at War: Alsace-Lorraine and the Failure of German National Mobilization, 1914–1918." In *State, Society and Mobilization in Europe during the First World War*, edited by John Horne, 105–122. Cambridge: Cambridge University Press, 1997.

Krebs, Ronald R. *Fighting for Rights: Military Service and the Politics of Citizenship*. Ithaca, NY: Cornell University Press, 2006.

Kühne, Thomas. *The Rise and Fall of Comradeship: Hitler's Soldiers, Male Bonding and Mass Violence in the Twentieth Century*. Cambridge: Cambridge University Press, 2017.

Lechner, Catherine. *Alsace Lorraine: Histoires d'une Tragédie Oubliée*. Paris: Séguier, 2004.

Lohr, Erich. *Nationalizing the Russian Empire: The Campaign against Enemy Aliens during World War I*. Cambridge, MA: Harvard University Press, 2003.

Richert, Dominik. *Beste Gelegenheit zum Sterben: Meine Erlebnisse im Kriege 1914–1918*. Edited by Angelika Tramitz and Bernd Ulrich. Munich: Knesebeck & Schuler, 1989.

Rossé, Joseph, et al. *Das Elsass von 1870–1932*. 4 Vols. Colmar: Verlag Alsatian, 1936–38.

Sanborn, Josh. *Drafting the Russian Nation: Military Conscription, Total War, and Mass Politics, 1905–1925*. Dekalb, IL: Northern Illinois University Press, 2003.

Silverman, Dan P. *Reluctant Union: Alsace-Lorraine and Imperial Germany, 1871–1918*. University Park: The Pennsylvania State University Press, 1972.

Ulrich, Bernd, and Benjamin Ziemann, eds. *German Soldiers in the Great War: Letters and Eyewitness Accounts*. Translated by Christine Brooks. Barnsley: Pen & Sword, 2010.

Vlossak, Elizabeth. *Marianne or Germania? Nationalizing Women in Alsace, 1870–1946*. Oxford: Oxford University Press, 2010.

Zahra, Tara. *Kidnapped Souls: National Indifference and the Battle for Children in the Bohemian Lands, 1900–1948*. Ithaca, NY: Cornell University Press, 2011.

PART II

RELATIONS

CONTESTED IDENTITIES DURING THE FIRST WORLD WAR

4

RETHINKING JEWISH FRONT EXPERIENCES
Michael Geheran

Twenty years after the end of the First World War, Hermann Klugmann reflected on the meaning of his wartime experiences as a soldier in the German army as he composed his memoirs. A self-described "assimilated" German Jew, Klugmann served in an infantry regiment on the Western Front from 1917 to 1918 and recalled how his experience fighting alongside other Germans in the trenches had solidified his faith in assimilation, for "common destiny," he wrote, "proved to be a bond that would endure over the years."[1]

> The war experience and the experience of becoming a soldier have left me with many unforgettable impressions. The social distinctions of bourgeois life ended; when in uniform, one was a soldier only and left behind one's civilian profession. At the front, the experience of comradeship came into the foreground: religious, social, and any other distinctions vanished; everyone shared each other's burdens.[2]

Klugmann wrote these passages in Allston, Massachusetts in 1940, as a refugee from the Nazis, having fled Germany the year before in the wake of the Pogrom of November 1938, and out of fear for his family's safety. Despite the trauma and hardships of two years of war and his ordeals under National Socialism, Klugmann believed then, as he did in November 1918, that Jewish sacrifices for the fatherland had not been in vain. He wrote at length about his feeling of belonging in the army and the bonds he forged with other Germans at the front, insisting he had never experienced antisemitism as a soldier. Only after the war, in the wake of Imperial Germany's collapse, did he describe his first significant encounters with hatred towards Jews.

Klugmann's testimony defies the well-worn narrative that describes Jewish soldiers as having been excluded from the officer corps, shunned by their gentile comrades, and depressed due to lack of recognition for their sacrifices, conditions which, the memoir suggests, were far from common. Such sources have led historians to re-evaluate Jewish encounters with antisemitism during the First World War, and question whether Jew hatred actually precipitated a "crisis" in German–Jewish relations at the front, as had been claimed by several prominent intellectuals writing after the war. Recent arguments tend to suggest that many of those Jewish soldiers who did not mention antisemitism at the front lines did not experience it. Significantly, these arguments are used to reinforce the idea that most Jewish soldiers were well integrated in the German army and regarded as equals by their gentile comrades, that the spiritual "break" described by Jewish activists such as Reinhold Lewin and Ernst Simon after 1918 was a postwar construction.[3] Yet many of these studies rely heavily on sources by acculturated Jewry in order to draw general conclusions about Jewish experiences in the First World War, notably using memoirs written by individuals like Klugmann, published diaries,[4] or the edited letter collections of the Reichsbund jüdischer Frontsoldaten (RjF).[5] Most Jews who belonged to this group were members of the liberal Reform Community, who, like Klugmann, had not practiced orthodox Judaism, in terms of either religion or culture, for several generations. They were German nationals with a long history in the country. They spoke German, identified themselves first and foremost as natives of Germany rather than as Jews, had adopted German names, customs, and manners of dress, and would not have been easily recognizable as Jewish.[6]

Although Klugmann's testimony seems quite adequate to characterize middle-class, assimilated German Jewry, the picture becomes more complex when including the more traditional, non-assimilated Jewish population, and their responses to the war. For in addition to non-religious Jews and members of the Reform Community, there was a more conservative Jewish population in Germany, who practiced the Jewish faith, whether with reformist or orthodox affiliations, and cultivated strong cultural and religious ties to Judaism. Another prominent group was the Zionists, many of whom came from acculturated, middle-class families, but professed a distinct Jewish national, cultural, and racial identity, and saw themselves not as "German" Jews, but as Jewish citizens of Germany. Such distinctions are often overlooked, with the result that assimilated Jews' reactions to certain wartime developments, such as the so-called *Judenzählung*, for example, are held to be universal. The impact of the bias in the scholarship has been a tendency to promote a universal Jewish war experience, rather than examining the diversity of Jewish responses to the war.

In what follows, this chapter examines and contrasts the experiences of assimilated and Zionist German Jews, as well as those of a more conservative religious persuasion, during the First World War, paying close attention to the tensions between Jewish soldiers' expectations, perceptions, and their actual experiences. It will consider how these two dominant groups responded to antisemitism, how they dealt with discrimination and antisemitic superiors, which coping mechanisms they developed, and how they perceived relations with other Germans, and other Jews, at the front lines. A study of Jewish war experiences raises a series of overarching questions: How did Jewish soldiers perceive antisemitic discrimination at the front? What conclusions did they draw from these encounters, and how were they embedded in their wartime experiences? Was comradeship able to bridge religious, class, and social distinctions at the front? Can the enthusiasm and disappointments German Jews experienced during and in the aftermath of the First World War be explained by their cultural, national, or religious identity? This chapter argues that Jewish soldiers interpreted and reacted to wartime developments in often dramatically different ways, and that these experiences were heavily influenced by soldiers' cultural and ideological backgrounds. Their rationales for fighting, and their support for Germany's war, reactions to discrimination, and perceptions of in-group belonging, were contingent not only on actual circumstances, but also on their self-identification as Germans or as Jews.

Crucially, the chapter will try to determine whether wartime experiences constituted a fundamental departure from combatants' previously held values, assumptions, and beliefs. Reducing the scope to Zionist, conservative religious, and assimilated Jews is both broad enough to arrive at some useful conclusions about the diverse ways in which Jews of different backgrounds perceived intergroup relations at the front and responded to antisemitism, and limited enough in scope for a manageable analysis that complicates Jewish war experiences, which until now have been portrayed primarily through the lens of acculturated Jewry.

In an effort to analyze the subjective nature of Jewish *Kriegserlebnisse* (war experiences), this study relies on largely unpublished, contemporary writings of Jewish soldiers, such as private letters and war diaries.

These sources present a number of methodological challenges, as most wartime combatants were dispassionate recorders and interpreters of dates, events, and other historical information.[7] Letters and diaries from the forward lines typically lacked introspection and analysis, and rarely divulged detailed biographical information about the authors, so we are left knowing relatively little about a writer's prewar attitudes, religious identity, or previous encounters with antisemitism.[8] The greatest challenge for any historian, perhaps, is to derive objective impressions of antisemitism, or abstract concepts such as comradeship, in the writings of frontline soldiers. No soldier's encounters with antisemitism can tell us anything definite about the experiences and reactions of others, so as sources they often amount to little more than a set of discrete, subjective results. This study therefore relies on the "critical mass" approach used by Christopher Browning, in which he addresses the subjective nature of ego-documents by looking for corroboration, so that they are relevant beyond the individual case.[9] Thus, if several Zionist writers mention the same thing, for example, equating the "Jew Count" with the existence of deep-seated, pervasive hatred of Jews in German society, it is taken to suggest that the statement may be significant beyond the individual case. To be sure, there will be exceptions to nearly every socially conceived notion of comradeship and identity, or perceived discrimination. Yet this approach presents a viable means of evaluating multiple individual sources and enables us to draw some general conclusions about how Jews experienced the Great War, and the spiritual condition in which the survivors returned to Germany in 1918.

Jewish *Kriegserlebnisse*

Individual wartime experiences were contingent on a range of social and situational factors, central to which were a soldier's expectations in August 1914 and to what degree they were being fulfilled. The gap between these expectations and the extent to which they were realized undergirded Jewish expressions of enthusiasm, hope, ambivalence, and disappointment. In addition to age, education, profession, and temperament, Jewish soldiers' cultural and religious identity, and their sense of integration into German society, largely determined how they perceived and reacted to wartime events, and how these events were later transfigured into memory.[10]

Acculturated German Jewry overwhelmingly saw the war as a catalyst for social change; it represented the long-awaited moment for them to publicly demonstrate their loyalty to the fatherland and overcome the last hurdles towards complete integration in German society. Kaiser Wilhelm's famous declaration before a delegation of Reichstag deputies, in which he vowed to no longer recognize political parties or religious confessions, but "only Germans," emboldened Germany's assimilated Jewish population, leading to calls that "the common baptism of blood on the battle will forge a brotherhood that is everlasting."[11] These aims were dramatically different than those of Zionist Jews, who were far less enthusiastic about integrating themselves into gentile society. A powerful impetus for Zionists was that the war was being fought against Russia, a regime widely regarded as the greatest oppressor of the Jews. Standing shoulder to shoulder with their Jewish brethren in Russia, they saw a victorious German campaign against the Tsar—"the archenemy of all Jews"—as an opportunity to free millions of East European Jews from oppressive, autocratic rule.[12]

A second decisive factor in determining soldiers' wartime experiences was the capacity in which they served, that is, whether they fought as part of combat units at the front or performed a support function behind the lines. For soldiers engaged in the actual fighting, the encounter with extreme violence comprised a central element of their wartime experiences. They underwent face-to-face encounters with the enemy and were thrust into situations that those who had not been "there" would find hard to imagine. Combat created unparalleled levels of fear and duress, putting soldiers in sometimes daily confrontations with life-or-death situations. Enduring prolonged shelling by artillery, the deafening noise of grenades and small arms fire, days, even weeks, living in the mud and rain, without opportunities to bathe or change one's clothes, amid rats and the corpses of soldiers torn apart by shells, were realities that distinguished the experiences of the fighting troops from the soldiers stationed in the so-called *Etappe*, or rear areas.[13]

Despite the horrific realities of protracted, industrial-style warfare, there was a "constructive" side to military violence. Combat was an exercise in community building; it established social bonds. Mortal danger created a powerful sense of community among the soldiers who endured it. Confrontations with death, mourning fallen comrades, fear of wounds and dismemberment, and killing, were experiences that transgressed the norms of civilian society. Confronting them together fed the experience of community.[14] Amid the constant dread of being killed or severely wounded, Edwin Halle, an artilleryman on the Western Front, recorded in his diary the sense of reassurance he felt in the forward trenches, among comrades:

> Between us chaps here up front, the inner comradeship is more pronounced than ever. The proximity to the enemy welds people even closer together. Here in the earth, where one can glimpse only a sliver of sky, in the mud through which one wades, one realizes that we are little more than the worms that root around underneath us. Life can be extinguished in an instant: that was made clear to us by Schlitte's sudden death. Yet here, we felt especially safe.[15]

What Halle described was a solidarity born of survival; this central, overriding emotion engendered cooperation and mutual dependence between members of a military primary group.[16] This dynamic enabled soldiers to survive; they fought together under extreme conditions, and continued to do so even after their initial enthusiasm had faded.[17] Jews forged powerful bonds with their Christian comrades under fire, bonds that withstood social and ideological rifts, including antisemitism. An oft-repeated claim in letters written home was how proximity to danger erased distinctions of class, religion, and social background in the field, as inner tensions, prejudices, and personal rivalries were displaced by solidarity in what George Simmel called the "extreme environment" of war.[18] "That I am at the front smoothes over a lot of things that would normally provide fodder for constant conflict, as everyone is afraid and is committed to each other," wrote Alfred Koch, a war volunteer from Offenbach am Main who served with the Field Artillery Regiment No. 21 in Flanders. "Hopefully things will stay that way."[19] Joachim Beutler, an infantryman also stationed in Flanders, was even more explicit in a letter to his parents:

> We receive several attacks daily from Frenchmen and Negroes, accompanied by volleys of hand-grenades, the crackling of machine-gun bullets overhead, to the point where one believes hell on earth has finally come. One consolation for us in these dark hours is our comradeship ... I never experienced anything in the way of antisemitism here, times are too serious for that.[20]

Such "extreme experiences," to be sure, did not characterize the routines of everyday life at the front. The great material battles on the Western Front such as Verdun and the Somme continue to shape popular perceptions of the First World War, but there were prolonged lulls in the fighting, and combat deployments were punctuated by extended periods of rest and refitting behind the trenches.[21] Yet studies have shown that comradeship encompassed far more than "hard" masculinity of the type that inspired acts of bravery and resilience among soldiers engaged in combat. It incorporated elements of a "softer," altruistic side, bringing relief and psychological sustenance to soldiers confronted by daily violence, and providing emotional and social support to men far removed from home, and often confronted by loneliness, deprivation, and the omnipresence of death.[22]

In many cases, comradeship offered a refuge, a space for Jewish soldiers to cope under the brutality of antisemitic superiors. In his diary, Edwin Halle praises his fellow soldiers for sustaining him through the rigors of basic training, especially after it was revealed that his battery commander, Lieutenant Schröder, was an unapologetic Jew hater. The man "had a grudge against us Jews from the very beginning: Adler, Telheimer, Rosenthal and me," Halle wrote. "He makes no secret about being an antisemite."[23] A few days after writing these lines, the lieutenant falsely accused Halle of committing a minor infraction. He was punished and arbitrarily sentenced to a short period of confinement to the barracks, an incident which left Halle shaken and deeply disillusioned about his prospects in the army.

> I am without question a patriot in body in soul and have done everything within my power to serve the fatherland. I learned—I wanted to excel! But with such treatment one loses it, the commitment to becoming a soldier. If one's honor is besmirched in this way, it is like suffering a moral death. And here I lodge my complaint: if from now on I am no longer able to do what is required of me, that man who now leads our battery and despises me for no reason—because I am a Jew—is responsible! God forgive me! There are limits, at which even the best man loses his bearing![24]

Halle felt shame for allegedly discrediting the reputation of the battery and leaving his comrades "in the lurch." As he returned to his outfit to await the judgment of his comrades, he was "afraid to look at anyone" and "unable to overcome the feeling of having been dishonored." To Halle's surprise, he was enthusiastically welcomed back. "When I reported back to the battery this afternoon, the sense of elation was enormous," he wrote. "It felt good, to experience this heartfelt joy shown to me by not only my comrades, but also my superiors, from privates all the way up to the staff sergeant."[25] Such incidents suggest that amid the helplessness of soldiers subjected to a system of hierarchy and obedience, comradeship provided comfort, reassurance, and a sense of empowerment. Halle was outraged over the injustice, yet it was quickly forgotten. His dignity was rehabilitated by the devotion of his comrades, and the confrontation did not fundamentally change Halle's commitment to the German cause.

Like Halle, Otto Meyer also became the target of antisemitic slurs from a non-commissioned officer during basic training. The 29-year-old small business owner from Rheda, Westphalia, was drafted into a

Prussian foot artillery regiment in 1915 and immediately singled out by a racist sergeant. "As a Jew, I was particularly berated," he wrote to his wife in April 1915. "Yet I don't complain about this, my sweetheart. You cannot imagine the inner peace I have achieved. And my patriotism is not affected by these things, for what can the fatherland do about it?"[26] Meyer related few details about what happened, yet his reaction says something significant about how acculturated Jewish soldiers responded to antisemitism. Despite this setback, he continued to view his military experience as generally positive. The behavior of the antisemitic NCO did not undermine his self-understanding as a German of Jewish faith. Meyer encountered prejudice in different forms throughout the war. His diary is punctuated with expressions of resignation, bitterness, and disbelief. Yet amid such disappointments, the dominant thread in his writings is not antisemitism, but the sense of community among his fellow soldiers. "Comradeship," Meyer wrote on 28 April 1915, "makes it possible for me to remember the spiritual amid the overwhelming physical experiences and exertions."[27] He formed deep attachments to the other men in his unit, and when he was promoted to sergeant, his feelings were conflicted as it meant transferring to a different unit and leaving behind his comrades.

> I have waited for this day with longing. My military adolescence is now completed, the time of manhood now begins; I realize that I have to take leave of other things as well, the carefree camaraderie and the wonderful cohabitation with the others, the commoners and really shabby ones alike. Whether I shall be able to live together with my old comrades as before, the one-yearers who will also become non-coms, is not yet certain....[28]

It would be a mistake to imagine that comradeship hinged on the presence of enduring personal relationships or friendships. As Thomas Kühne and Benjamin Ziemann have shown, the bonds forged between soldiers, thrust into roles from which they could not escape, were characterized foremost by contingency. The micro-level solidarity forged under fire was situational, immediate, and ad hoc, arising from a common mission and a psychological instinct to survive life-threatening dangers. In his war diary, Fritz Frank described good relations with his comrades throughout the entire conflict, insisting time and again that "common crisis and work weld us together," yet not once does he ever mention anything resembling a deep personal connection or friendship.[29] Alfred Koch maintained a regular correspondence with his mother and brother, Richard, that lasted through almost four years of war. In general, the army was no place for expressions of misery, self-doubt, or vulnerability, and as the war dragged on, Koch's letters began to assume the quality of a private confessional. His letters, stitched together and preserved by his mother after he was killed at Soissons in April 1918, reveal the frustration of a young man from a privileged bourgeois background forced to live in close quarters with rural peasants and "shit farmers" who, in Koch's eyes, behaved like animals.

> If you knew what that means: when one lives 14 hours a day, side-by-side with people you would otherwise not even spit in the face. These people are built to completely different specifications than we are. 90% animal ... I regard my fate, which has brought me into ongoing association with these people, foremost as my contribution to the great sacrifice.[30]

Confronted with lower-class male behavior for the first time, Koch struggled to reconcile being forced to live with people to whom under normal circumstances he would have never got close enough to "spit in their faces." "One has to take the position," he complained to his mother in October 1914, "that the majority of people stand on a much, much lower cultural level than even the most degenerate Jewish scrounger ... one can only regard them as a different species of people who cannot be compared to us."[31] Koch's inability to "fit in" was a recurring preoccupation throughout his wartime writings, as his letters conveyed a persistent sense of aloneness: "how rarely one meets another person with whom one can talk about something else besides the usual battery gossip. Since I've been here in the regiment, I haven't found anyone."[32] But despite his personal feelings of distance, Koch acknowledged the bravery and competence of his fellow soldiers under fire. "Despite everything, I am quite lucky to stand among my comrades," he wrote on 17 March 1917, "they are primitive chaps, but also skillful and full of love."[33]

It is striking that Halle, Meyer, and Koch described comradeship in fundamentally different ways. While they experienced (and acknowledged) the mutual cooperation of soldiers under fire, for Koch this solidarity was functional, extemporaneous, and impersonal. His letters conveyed nothing of the sort of emotional attachment or group identification described by acculturated Jews like Halle or Meyer. These findings suggest that comradeship encompassed far more than human behavior *in extremis*. Very often it articulated itself as something intangible, as an organizing discourse, an abstract means of self-identification and expression of group consciousness.[34] In Jewish writings from the field, comradeship becomes a mechanism of self-definition, a sign of inclusion, and a category through which Jews interpreted their sense of belonging with other Germans.

Like many of his assimilated co-religionists, Albrecht Mugdan described the outbreak of war in 1914 as an exhilarating, empowering experience, invoking the classic bourgeois tropes of national unity, love of fatherland, and the righteousness of Germany's cause. The son of upper middle-class parents in Breslau, Mugdan saw the war as a kind of adventure, a masculine rite of passage, and a means to escape the predictable routines of civilian life. The handwritten, hastily scrawled letters and postcards from the field exhibited an immense pride at serving in the front lines and obtaining an officer's commission in an elite alpine regiment. An "unforgettable" moment occurred just two months before Mugdan was killed at Verdun, when the Iron Cross was pinned on him by Kaiser Wilhelm II personally.[35] The decidedly nationalistic tone of his writings, which remained a constant until his death, was not the result of actual wartime experiences, however. His attitude and the style and tenor of his writings did not change from the beginning of the war until he was killed. This finding suggests that Mugdan's outlook was not shaped exclusively by the "positive" experiences he described in his letters, but also by the values and expectations of his social milieu. It should be remembered that the Centralverein (CV) saw the conflict as an opportunity to create "a brotherhood that is everlasting," and in general, this is how Mugdan portrays his war experience. Life at the front is invariably described as "good" and "very nice," even during those times his unit was engaged in combat and suffering casualties. Mugdan repeatedly praised the solidarity of his platoon; relations with his fellow soldiers are "unconstrained and cozy," and "better than I could wish for."[36] He felt at home among comrades, emphasized the sense of oneness between officers and men, and saw himself as part of a community of fate bound by a common mission and purpose, where race and background were seemingly irrelevant. Exposure to danger invigorated this sense of belonging. After an engagement with enemy soldiers, he wrote:

> The comradeship among us members of the first platoon becomes ever stronger. We all understand each other very well and are inseparable. It is truly wonderful, and I believe this solidarity is a reflection of everything we experience together...[37]

To Mugdan, this fraternal bond became a self-affirming war experience, an expression of self- and group identity driven by a desire for community with other Germans. According to Robert Nelson, comradeship was not only a psychological reaction, but also "pre-war socialization followed by the wartime search for self-justification."[38] It does not come as a great surprise, then, that frontline solidarity emerged as a leitmotif in the writings of acculturated Jews, for it seemed to affirm Jewish hopes for social acceptance and equality after the war. For soldiers like Mugdan, who did not identify themselves as Jewish, whether in a religious or a cultural sense, the military primary group was their own, and the acceptance of Jews as "comrades" by the gentile frontline community strengthened their identities as German Jews. The authors' Jewish faith often remained in the background, seemingly eclipsed by the exigencies of the war. At no point in his letters did Albrecht Mugdan mention being a Jew.[39] While such cases are the exception, most contemporary diarists made only veiled or situational references to Jewish identity; rather, they tended to elevate the "we" of the primary group, that is, the sameness and commonality with other Germans.

The orientation to comradeship and the "fatherland" were central political-moral values for the assimilated Mugdan and held far greater importance than for religious Jews like Franz Rosenzweig. Rosenzweig self-identified neither as orthodox nor as a Zionist, but nevertheless embraced a distinct Jewish national and cultural identity. His wartime letters described the "front experience" with a sense of disappointment, claiming that the experience living and fighting alongside other Germans merely intensified the sense of separateness between Germans and Jews. The feeling of otherness, he wrote, "is never switched off except when one happens to meet someone else who is also 'different,'" meaning Jewish. Comradeship, in Rosenzweig's eyes, did not bridge differences or bring Germans closer together, it was merely "enforced togetherness in spite of otherness."[40] His letters contrast the deepening sense of alienation between Jewish and Christian Germans in the field to the comfort and sense of community derived from meeting other Jewish soldiers at field religious services or when they were fortunate enough to be assigned to the same unit. The idea that Jews should sacrifice self for the "we" of the German *Volk* was anathema to Rosenzweig. To a far greater extent, he saw "solidarity" as an expression of Jewish distinctiveness, and a means to assert the honor of Jewish soldiers who fought not as Germans, but as Jews who were citizens of the German nation.

Despite months of enduring hardships and dangers together in battle, Alfred Koch's comrades—the members of his artillery battery—whom he invariably described as "dependable," "trustworthy," "efficient," and "skilled," remain obscure and more or less anonymous. At no point are they ever mentioned by name, nor do we ever learn much about their backgrounds, values, or personalities. The only other soldiers

Koch described in detail were *Glaubensgenossen* (comrades in faith), a more affective, symbolically laden term that frequently appears in the writings of Jewish nationalist or religious Jews and gave expression to a sense of shared identity. To Koch's mind, this solidarity was exclusive, restricted to fellow Zionists, as he considered "assimilationists" and "inferior Jews" (converts to Christianity) outsiders.[41] Crucially, this solidarity did not hinge on the actual presence of Jewish comrades or on face-to-face relationships; far more it revealed itself as identification with a more abstract, Jewish consciousness. As the only Jewish soldier in his battery, Koch's sense of detachment from his "comrades" was assuaged by the joy derived from learning about other Jews, whether through letters from home or in the division newspaper, who had been promoted or had received the Iron Cross, occasions that brought him such joy, "as if it were my own."[42] At the heart of his writings was a moral imperative, a devotion not to his gentile comrades or to the fatherland, but to his *Glaubensgenossen*: "What is always closest to my heart," Koch related to his brother just two weeks before he was killed, "is to do my share to strengthen and honor the Jewish name."[43]

Perhaps the most frequently cited Jewish autobiographical source from the First World War is the diary of Julius Marx.[44] As a source that is frequently used to support claims that antisemitism was the defining Jewish wartime experience, Marx's diary requires closer examination. The author portrays himself as an acculturated German Jew whose run-ins with antisemitism eventually led him to embrace a newfound sense of Jewish identity. Yet historians must take into account that Marx published his diary in Switzerland in 1939, as a protest against the *Novemberpogrom* and the policies of the Nazi government, and reconsider its value as a contemporary source.[45] From what is known about Marx, he came from a devout orthodox family and was himself deeply religious.[46] This may explain why, in terms of language and semantic tone, his writings bear a striking resemblance to postwar Zionist narratives. It is quite clear, for example, that Marx was already skeptical about Jewish prospects for emancipation at the war's outbreak. In October 1914, an NCO, under the pretense of humor, mocked him as a "cowardly Jew," an incident that caused Marx to request a transfer to a different unit and declare that the solidarity of August 1914 was a farce, one that concealed divisions that had already existed before the war. "At war's outbreak every prejudice seemed to have vanished, there were only Germans then," he wrote, "now one hears that old, slanderous talk *again*."[47] The proposition that fighting alongside other Germans would be rewarded with social acceptance was, at best, illusory, if not naive. His writings conveyed an increasing disenchantment about the prospects of Jewish assimilation, as he painstakingly chronicled how anti-Jewish hostility intensified as the likelihood of a German victory diminished.

A notable feature in the writings of Zionists or "Jewish" Jews is the mention of prewar antisemitic incidents. The authors tend to portray anti-Jewish hostility as a regular feature of life in Germany before 1914, and Marx, too, suggested that the deteriorating relations between Jews and gentiles he witnessed at the front had a precedent. After the incident involving the antisemitic joke, he wrote, "*once again*, we are Christians and Jews, rightists and leftists, officers and conscripts, and no longer just soldiers."[48] Repeated confrontations with antisemitic superiors, as well as jokes and taunting from fellow soldiers, led him to see the much-exalted comradeship as a facade, one that camouflaged prejudices that had already existed prior to the war. Only when "shells come crashing down," he wrote, did these tensions subside. "All of a sudden there aren't Christians and Jews anymore—only people, strained to the utmost to overcome their fear of death so they can perform their damn duty and do their part—and then you have it: community—a stream of altruism—comradeship—humanity."[49] Marx went on to describe a growing sense of estrangement from his gentile fellow soldiers, as the front experience merely reinforced an insurmountable feeling of otherness, of "being alone among comrades."[50]

For those soldiers who oriented themselves towards a specifically Jewish identity, discrimination had a very different impact than it did for acculturated Jews, central to which, the sources suggest, was a heightened sense of unity and belonging to the Jewish community. The point is alluded to by Alfred Koch, who noted the importance of field religious services in strengthening the sense of togetherness among Jews, and meeting people "who fully understand me."[51] Marx, too, attached great meaning to regularly attending religious services:

> Jewish religious services in the church at Miraumont. Some twenty men, who had just been resting, took part in the devotional. Intelligent faces. Which makes the experiences of the past few months all the clearer in their faces. Branch of service. Rank—who bothers to ask about this? Fellow sufferers they were, content to fulfill their difficult duty out of love for homeland—yet lonely. The service did me a lot of good.[52]

The fact that such events are as well detailed as they are shows their clear significance to those involved. Such reactions can only be understood within the context of a Jewish minority in Germany that rejected the premise of assimilation and advocated Jewish separateness. For these writers, the experience fighting alongside other Germans reinforced a distinct sense of Jewish particularity and served to strengthen their solidarity with their co-religionists. Crucially—and here is the important point—soldiers' perceptions of comradeship and their reactions to discrimination were rarely indicative of a wartime re-evaluation of preexisting beliefs and values. Rosenzweig, Koch, and arguably Marx did not undergo a profound spiritual or political transformation between 1914 and 1918. Rather, these experiences were used to legitimize existing attitudes that individuals had brought with them into the war. Far from manifesting itself as objective reality, these examples suggest that comradeship's integrative power was fed by soldiers' belief in, and sense of belonging to, "their" group.

Contrasting Responses to Antisemitism

When Joachim Beutler wrote that amid "volleys of hand grenades, the cracking of machine-gun bullets overhead" times were "too serious" for antisemitism, he lauded the one thing that the inhumanity of war could never taint: comradeship.[53] In doing so, he gave voice to the hopes and expectations of acculturated German Jewry, who believed that the exigencies of frontline combat left no room for antisemitism, that the micro-level solidarity forged under fire would bridge differences of class, religion, and background.

Beutler was not alone in foregrounding the "positive" elements of the war experience in his letters home. What is remarkable about this account, however, is that the topic of antisemitism is broached, even when it was not present. It suggests that Jews remained ever vigilant in the front lines, continually interrogating their surroundings, and that the writers had probably encountered some form of prejudice previously, whether before or sometime during the war. Beutler's letters tell us little about why or in what context antisemitism was brought up, whether in response to a question, a statement to allay the concerns of family, or an affirmation of the writer's ideological stance. Yet they suggest that antisemitism, even *in absentia*, exerted a significant influence on Jewish thinking and behavior during the war.

What frequently arises in Jewish writings from the field, for example, is the image of the Jewish *Drückeberger*, or shirker. Even in the absence of direct confrontations with these stereotypes, many Jewish soldiers expressed concern about being associated with the "cowardly Jew," the weak, second-rate soldier, who purportedly dodged his obligation to serve in combat. Ever conscious of such stereotypes, many Jewish soldiers reacted like Ernst Löwenberg, who turned down an offer by his platoon leader to work behind the lines as the company clerk. "I have spoken as my inner conscience demands," he wrote to his parents, "as a Jew, I have no right to sit behind a desk."⁵⁴ Löwenberg had been an enthusiastic soldier throughout the war. He described close relations with his comrades and "never felt antisemitism," except from certain officers. He made no mention of personal encounters with anti-Jewish prejudice, yet the prospect of being a shirker in the eyes of gentiles was deeply troubling to Löwenberg, one that undoubtedly had a precedent.

The need to counter antisemitic stereotypes through acts of bravery is a recurring theme in the letters of Alfred Koch. When he volunteered for the army in August 1914, Koch was dismayed to discover that he had been assigned to the baggage train, not to the fighting troops as he had wanted. He found serving in a supply unit boring, tedious, and humiliating—an "infamy" (*Infamie*), as he put it.⁵⁵ So when the opportunity arose to volunteer for an artillery unit, Koch took it, describing the decision as his "duty" (*Pflicht*). "If I hadn't taken the first opportunity to get away from here, the accusation that I was suited only for the [baggage] train would have been completely justified," he wrote. "For it would have meant that I chose to stay despite having the chance to leave."⁵⁶ Koch did not mention from whom such an "accusation" might have come. Yet such utterances reveal that it mattered immensely to him to be regarded as a brave soldier, especially in the eyes of gentile society. In a letter to his brother written just before his death, he again justified his decision to leave the safety of the baggage train in order to serve in combat:

> It was an unbearable thought to stand there as the archetype of the Jewish rear-area soldier, a luxury which has commanded a price, one that I am now prepared to pay in full awareness of the consequences. I would have deserved more pity had I declined and remained a sutler. Furthermore, I had the gratification of winning the respect of my superiors and soldiers. In the battery, I have the reputation as being one of the "coldest" ones, and for me this has always been a most worthwhile goal, not for my personal vanity, but as seen from a higher perspective.⁵⁷

Koch's behavior was calculated; he felt compelled to prove his competence and courage under fire to his non-Jewish comrades, and by doing so, obviate any suspicions that he might be a coward. The Jewish rear-area soldier was tainted with the stain of unmanliness, and Koch deemed it essential to demonstrate that he was not afraid to risk his life in battle. His letters make no mention of actual, face-to-face encounters with this stereotype. But the image of the unmanly Jew haunted him; it was a foil through which he evaluated his behavior, compelling him time and again to disassociate from stereotypical "Jewish" traits.

This kind of implicit antisemitism exerted a powerful influence on Jewish behavior in the front lines: it governed the way Jewish soldiers acted, how they interpreted and reacted to certain situations, and it determined how they carried themselves in the presence of gentile comrades. As Jason Crouthamel's chapter on comradeship between Jews and gentiles argues, the majority of Jewish men who fought in the First World War entered the conflict believing that rigorous demonstrations of bravery and conformity could succeed in changing German perceptions of Jewry.[58] Their behaviors were shaped by specific performances intended to earn the respect of gentiles and shatter antisemitic stereotypes. In the trenches it mattered immensely to be regarded as a tough fighter and a reliable comrade, and Jews in particular felt compelled to prove their mettle under fire, to achieve fraternal respect. Jews, to be sure, had this in common with other Germans. What distinguished the Jewish combatants, however, was that these behaviors were intended to counter stereotypes of Jewish cowardice and weakness; they were a counterweight to the image of the *Drückeberger*.

Antisemitism manifested itself in more tangible ways, however, from jokes, teasing, and gossip, to outright hostility and exclusion. It did not distinguish between Zionist, orthodox, or acculturated Jews, yet Jewish soldiers interpreted and reacted to it in often dramatically different ways. In general, the letters and diaries of assimilated Jews rarely recorded incidents involving taunting or anti-Jewish jokes by comrades, and when they did, most responded like Fritz Goldberg, who brushed them off as "very general and never directed against the individual," attributing them to the same kind of teasing that went on between the Protestants and Catholics he grew up with.[59] Others attributed racism to the officer corps or the War Ministry, but only rarely to comrades. Yet one wonders how many soldiers consciously obviated such confrontations by concealing their Jewishness, like Hermann Berel Barsqueaux, who attributed the "good camaraderie" in his unit to the fact that "the others don't know which religion I belong to."[60]

A persistent setback encountered by the majority of the Jewish soldiers examined in this study was exclusion from the officers' corps. Not untypical is the experience of Bernhard Bing, a middle-aged factory owner from Nuremberg who served in an artillery resupply train of the 6th Bavarian Reserve Division on the Western Front. The 41-year-old Bing was repeatedly commended by his superiors for his performance. He had already been promoted to sergeant when, at the urging of his company commander, he submitted his application for an officer's commission, easily passing both the written and oral examinations.[61] His nomination was rejected, however, after it was put to the obligatory vote before the board of regimental officers, because the commander of the regiment "did not want to promote any Jews to the officer ranks."[62] This is the first and only time in his diary where Bing mentions anti-Jewish discrimination. It is also the only point where he refers to himself as a Jew. The setback did not deter him, however; he was eventually promoted to lieutenant rank after transferring to another unit.[63] Bing's diary indicates that the injustice left him bitter and outraged, but it did not shake his strong identification with Germany or visibly weaken his faith in the prospects of Jewish assimilation. His resolve did not diminish; Bing remained a loyal soldier and a good comrade. At least this is how he presented himself in his diary.[64]

Bing's response to discrimination can be extended beyond the individual case, for it says something important about how many acculturated Jews acted in the face of adversity. He attributed the setback to a single antisemitic actor; at no point did he conflate the injustice with the presence of a broader, endemic Jew hatred in the military. Moreover, Bing drew a clear distinction in his diary between his comrades and the racist officer who derailed his promotion. His belief that fulfilling his duty as a soldier and fighting side by side with other Germans would be rewarded with social recognition after the war remained unshaken. This was a recurring message in his diary: despite reversals and disappointments, Bing never questioned his identity as a "German of Jewish faith," and remained convinced that the example he set would help change the status of Jews in Germany. These beliefs did not abruptly end as a result of discrimination. We can conclude, therefore, that silence regarding antisemitism should not be understood as proof that it was absent, but that their self-understanding as Germans and Jews was not severely challenged because of it.

The letters of Alfred Koch reveal that he, too, was no stranger to antisemitism in the German military, yet from the outset he interpreted such incidents in a very different way. Exclusion from the officer corps left Koch resentful and disenfranchised; it also strengthened his belief that Jews would never be accepted as equals by German society. Writing before the war, as Koch fulfilled his one-year military service obligation, he lamented that, as a Jew, the opportunities for advancement were all but closed to him. "Despite all my acceptance, it offends me that the prospects for promotion are so bad. It makes one lose all enthusiasm for this whole business. I can do everything at least as well, and many things even better than the *Gojims*," he wrote. "As a result, my somewhat slumbering Zionism has been reawakened."[65] It is at this time that Koch mentioned Bernhard Bing, who had served in the same unit before the war.

A non-commissioned officer told me: "we know, our Captain simply does not promote Jews like everyone else." The year before there was a Nuremberg Jew here, Bing, who had supposedly been very competent, from a good family, and he never even made it to officer candidate. A very nice chap, he is now away participating in a field exercise.[66]

It cannot be determined whether Koch and Bernhard Bing encountered each other before the war, or if Koch was merely relaying what he heard from others. It is striking, however, that the incident negatively impacted Koch, while Bing himself never mentioned it. In fact, even though neither ever described face-to-face encounters with antisemitism during their time in the army, on 30 September 1916 Koch confided to his mother that he had been keeping his Jewish identity a secret because he was certain that "everyone from the General to the stable boy was a *Judenfresser* [Jew hater]."[67] This implicit antisemitism was a recurring thread in his war letters. The picture that emerges is of a pervasive divide separating Koch from his Christian fellow soldiers; he insisted that the war would never overcome deep-seated prejudice, and rejected the premise that the communal experience of combat would erase the sense of "otherness" of Jews and gentiles. If antisemitism was ignored or suppressed by many assimilated Jews, for conservative or Zionist Jews like Koch it reinforced an innate Jewish distinctiveness, something that public avowals of solidarity or shared suffering could not erase.

Much has been made of the *Judenzählung*, the infamous census of Jewish soldiers implemented by the Prussian War Ministry on 11 October 1916.[68] The "Jew Count," as it became known, was carried out on the premise of unfounded accusations that Jews were shirking frontline military service, and its purpose was to ascertain the number of Jewish soldiers in combat units in proportion to those serving in support roles behind the lines. Many historians portrayed the measure as a watershed in German–Jewish relations, and despite recent studies that make a strong case for the contrary, it is a view accepted by many scholars to this day. What is most remarkable about the Jew Count, however, is how seldom it is mentioned in Jewish writings from the front. The census does not come up in any of the more than eight hundred letters written by Jewish soldiers to the director of their former Jewish community orphanage in Berlin.[69] Bernhard Bing does not mention it in his diary, nor does the census arise anywhere in the war letters of Alfred Koch or Franz Rosenzweig, all the more surprising as both were astute commentators on politics and Jewish affairs throughout the entire war.[70] The silence is confounding. It suggests that many Jews were not even aware of the census as it was being carried out, or that it was simply dismissed as another example of harassment "from above," that is, by the officers' corps.[71] Those Jewish soldiers who wrote about the census in their diaries and letters expressed outrage, shock, and disbelief; their testimonies leave no doubt that the news came as a blow. Yet with very few exceptions, anger over the incident tended to subside rather quickly, and there is little evidence to suggest that it led to a fundamental break with prewar values and beliefs.[72]

In general, it can be said that confrontations with antisemitism did not result, as Derek Penslar put it, in "a Nietzschean reevaluation of values."[73] While, of course, examples exist of acculturated Jews turning their backs on integration, this, the sources suggest, was a relatively rare occurrence. Far more common were men who, although extremely disappointed, continued to embrace assimilation and, in doing so, sustained a key element of their identities as German Jews. These findings corroborate recent studies, which have put to rest the notion that the Jew Count precipitated a breakdown in German–Jewish relations at the front.[74] Jewish diaries and letters from the field show little sign of long-term demoralization after the *Judenzählung*; the tone and discursive style of their writings remained the same before, during, and after the census was carried out. During the final months of 1918, Jewish soldiers placed a far greater emphasis on the worsening military situation and the collapse of the political order, indicating that German defeat and the revolutionary upheavals at home preoccupied Jewish thinking far more than antisemitism. Jewish soldiers had experienced discrimination long before October 1916. They encountered it before the war, at school and universities, in the workplace, even amid the euphoria of July and August 1914, and they continued to do so after the Prussian War Ministry's infamous order. It did not intensify or diminish over time but persisted unabated throughout the war. Antisemitism was ever present, it was the *Normalzustand* at the front.

The Legacies of Antisemitism, the Front Experience, and the *Judenzählung*

Although the Jew Count was not a caesura in German–Jewish relations during the First World War, and did not lead to a sweeping re-evaluation of values and beliefs among the Jewish wartime combatants, an altogether different issue is how the census was interpreted after the war. Because the results of the *Judenzählung* were never disclosed to the German public, the mere fact that it had been carried out was enough to fuel speculation and wild rumors about the Jewish war record.⁷⁵ Even though the Prussian War Minister, General Hermann von Stein, had assured Reichstag deputy Oskar Cassel in a letter on 20 January 1917 that any charges leveled against the Jewish war record were unfounded, this meek acknowledgment did little to stifle the controversy. The census became a rhetorical weapon for the political far right, which used it to undermine Jewish claims for equality and recognition for having risked their lives in the front lines. The accusations that Jews had collectively dodged their duty to serve in combat would form the core element of the *Dolchstoßlegende* (stab-in-the-back myth), and was repeated not only by antisemitic interest groups like the Alldeutscher Verband (Pan-German League), but also by former officers such as Erich Ludendorff and Max Bauer, who, eager to deflect blame for their own military failures, claimed that a conspiracy of socialists, pacifists, and Jews had undermined the fighting power of the German army.⁷⁶

These views were not confined to the extreme fringes of the nationalist right, but also entered mainstream conservative discourses after the First World War.⁷⁷ It became an article of faith among the conservative middle classes that Jews had not sacrificed in equal numbers as other Germans, and had been overrepresented in the left-wing revolutionary movements that had brought about the demise of the monarchy.⁷⁸ Many organizations of the nationalist right—the Stahlhelm being the most prominent example—justified their antisemitic stance as a defensive measure, a necessary response to guard against the unfettered power of Jewry.⁷⁹ To be sure, many conservative Germans made distinctions between "Jewry" and former comrades, some even publicly praised nationally-minded Jewish organizations such as the Reichsbund jüdischer Frontsoldaten (RjF).⁸⁰ But these relations did not weaken the dominant antisemitic position held by the nationalist right, as contemporary sources reveal a verifiable tendency approaching an outright consensus among conservatives that saw "Jewry" as having been complicit in Germany's defeat. Of course, such views were not confined exclusively to the political right. One needs to looks no further than Remarque's antiwar novel, *The Road Back*, for evidence that by the early 1930s these stereotypes had also penetrated left-wing discourses on the war.⁸¹ Although allegations of Jewish cowardice and indifference to the fatherland had been prevalent before the First World War, they were given new life after 1918. The Jew Count gave these accusations a veneer of credibility. It generated ambivalence, uncertainty, and reasonable doubt. The fog of ambiguity hanging over the Jewish war record fed suspicions of Jewish disloyalty, and compelled Jewish veterans of the First World War to form the RjF.

A more difficult question to answer, and the more important one for this study, is how Jewish former soldiers themselves interpreted these developments after the war, and whether—or to what degree— the legacy of the Jew Count impacted upon German–Jewish relations in the postwar years. Accusations of shirking—that Jews had collectively sought refuge in comfortable, rear-area postings while "real" Germans had died facing the enemy—represented a serious humiliation for Jewish veterans, the impact of which can hardly be overstated. Antisemites well recognized the power of the discursive link between military service, gender identity, and national belonging. By attacking Jews' loyalty and performance under fire, the extreme right sought to undermine Jewish claims for recognition and equal rights based on military sacrifice. The term *Drückeberger* evoked powerful images of cowardice and treachery.[82] Shirkers were men without honor, bad comrades, and weak soldiers. They survived by hiding behind the forward ranks, manipulating the comradeship and bravery of the "real" soldiers to their personal advantage, and to secure their own safety. To Jewish ex-servicemen, these allegations came as a blow. Writing in 1920, Samuel Jacobs, an orthodox Jew from a small town outside Hannover, was adamant that he had never encountered antisemitic prejudice during the war. Jacobs had been an enthusiastic soldier, referred to himself as a "loyal German warrior" in his memoirs, revealing that his time in the army had left a deep impression. But now, in the wake of Germany's defeat, the fact that his bravery was being questioned left him disillusioned. "A bitter feeling comes over me now, when I see today how we Jews are marked as second-class citizens," he wrote, "one tries to deprive us of our most sacred possession: our honor."[83]

Jewish war veterans were therefore thrust into the unenviable position of having to prove their war record. Jewish organizations, led by the CV and RjF, expended enormous energy and resources countering this antisemitic campaign with statistics on Jewish war service, painstakingly compiled by activists and local communities across Germany.[84] While the impact of these efforts upon everyday Germans is difficult to quantify, there is little doubt that from 1918 onward, Jews were engaged in an unrelenting fight to convince gentile society about the extent of Jewish sacrifices.

Conclusion

This chapter has argued that Jewish soldiers' reactions to antisemitism, and their perceptions of comradeship and inclusion, were heavily influenced by their cultural and ideological background, that is, whether they self-identified as "Germans of Jewish faith" or primarily as Jews. It determined why they fought, how they reacted to discrimination, how they related to their gentile fellow soldiers, and it also governed how they interpreted their wartime experiences after the fighting was over. In 1940, Harvard University collected more than 230 testimonies on "life in Germany before and after January 30th 1933" as part of a project to analyze "the social and psychological effects of National Socialism on German society and on the German people."[85] Most of the authors had fled the Third Reich shortly after the *Novemberpogrom*. Thus, the writers were not subject to the same kind of reflective analysis that shaped memoirs written after 1945 to a much greater degree. The manuscripts, many of which are accompanied by letters, photographs, diary fragments, newspaper clippings, and other personal documents, describe the steady unraveling of German–Jewish relations in the years after Hitler's "seizure" of power.[86] Crucially, the diversity of the submissions—forty were written by Jewish frontline veterans of the First World War, and at least nine by non-combat veterans—allows us to get some sense of how the writers reappraised their war experiences in light of new developments, and whether or not they believed their sacrifices had borne any positive results some twenty years later.

A close reading of these texts not only highlights the centrality of soldiers' social, religious, and cultural backgrounds in shaping war experiences, it also provides little evidence that wartime encounters with antisemitism led to an abandonment of prewar attitudes and beliefs. Zionist writers, for example, described racism as prevalent in German society before the war and as something they had encountered throughout most of their adult lives in Germany. The *Judenzählung* did not come as a shock in this regard. To many Zionists it merely confirmed what they had already known: that Jews constituted their own nationality and would never be accepted as equals in German society. The census, wrote Max Moses Polke, "was the culmination of anti-Jewish hostility that had been simmering in the army and at home throughout the entire war."[87] As he struggled to overcome the "betrayal" and "dishonor" inflicted by Germany, Polke, like other Zionists, drew spiritual strength from turning inward and immersing himself in his Judaism. The war experience had invigorated his sense of Jewishness, and for men in this group the greatest legacy of the First World War was that it reminded them "how necessary it was that Jews became a living nation again."[88]

If the strengthening of Jewish identity emerges as a leitmotif in Zionist writings, for acculturated Jewry the main feature of these seemingly ritualized postwar narratives was comradeship. They tended to frame their wartime experiences in more positive terms, echoing the CV's claim that during the war that prejudice had been displaced by the commonality of the "front experience." "The cooperation between Christian and Jewish soldiers was excellent," Hugo Moses wrote, "for the soldier, who saw death before him at every moment, who fought together shoulder to shoulder, religious beliefs were secondary."[89] Narratives on comradeship varied from one soldier to another, yet acculturated Jews described it in a remarkably similar way. Considered a symbol of belonging and social acceptance that is clear in the sources, it is striking that many works both by contemporary diarists and by writers writing decades after the war rely on the same terminology to describe their wartime experiences. These statements were intended, in part, to preserve a key element of their German identity during the Nazi years, for by delineating their comrades, and by extension ordinary Germans more generally, from the Nazis, the Third Reich becomes an aberration of the real Germany. It enabled them to maintain a semblance of their former identity and, with it, faith in assimilation, for conceding that would have meant that four bloody years of fighting would have been in vain.

Michael Geheran is a Postdoctoral Fellow at the Center for Holocaust and Genocide Studies at the United States Military Academy. He is a graduate of Norwich University, Harvard University, and Clark University, where he earned his Ph.D. in 2016. He is currently working on a book based on his doctoral research, which examines the experiences of German Jewish First World War veterans during the Holocaust.

Notes

1. Hermann Klugmann, "Mein Leben in Deutschland vor und nach dem 30. Januar 1933," Houghton Library, Harvard University, bMS 91 (113).
2. Ibid.
3. Reinhold Lewin, "Der Krieg als jüdisches Erlebnis," *Monatsschrift für die Geschichte und Wissenschaft des Judentums* 63 (1917): 1–14; Ernst Simon, "Unser Kriegserlebnis (1919)," in *Brücken: Gesammelte Aufsätze* (Heidelberg: Verlag Lambert Schneider, 1965), 17–23. For a critique of historians' reliance on Lewin and Simon as primary sources, see Derek Penslar, "The German-Jewish Soldier: From Participant to Victim," *German History* 29 (2011): 445–69.

4. Among the frequently cited contemporary autobiographical sources are Herbert Sulzbach, *Zwischen zwei Mauern: 50 Monate Westfront 1914–1918* (Berg am See, 1986); translated into English as *With the German Guns: Four Years on the Western Front, 1914–1918* (London, 1973); and Victor Klemperer's memoir of the war years, *Curriculum Vitae: Erinnerungen, 1881–1918*, 2 vols. (Berlin, 1996).
5. David J. Fine, *Jewish Integration in the German Army in the First World War* (Berlin, 2012). See also Derek J. Penslar, *Jews and the Military: A History* (Princeton, NJ, 2013); Michal Grünwald, "Antisemitismus im Deutschen Heer und Judenzählung," in *Jüdische Soldaten-Jüdischer Widerstand in Deutschland und Frankreich*, ed. Michael Berger and Gideon Römer-Hillebrecht (Paderborn, 2012), 129–44; and Tim Grady, *A Deadly Legacy: German Jews and the Great War* (New Haven, CT, 2017).
6. Mosche Zimmermann, *Die Deutschen Juden 1914–1945* (Munich, 1997), 2–7, 32–34, 80–89; and Stephen Poppel, *Zionism in Germany 1897–1933: The Shaping of Jewish Identity* (Philadelphia, 1976).
7. See, for example, Richard Herzstein, "Meine Kriegszeit. 15 Juli 1916–30 November 1918," Leo Baeck Institute New York (hereafter LBINY) ME 245; and Curt Heymann, "Kriegstagebuch," LBINY AR 4259.
8. Regarding the potential methodological pitfalls posed by wartime letter correspondence, see Bernd Ulrich, *Die Augenzeugen: Deutsche Feldpostbriefe in Kriegs- und Nachkriegszeit, 1914–1933* (Essen, 1997), 40–52; Klaus Latzel, *Deutsche Soldaten-nationalsozialistischer Krieg? Kriegserlebnis-Kriegserfahrung 1939–1945* (Paderborn, 1998), 103–32; and Dieter Langewiesche, "Nation, Imperium und Kriegserfahrungen," in *Kriegserfahrungen. Krieg und Gesellschaft in der Neuzeit: Neue Horizonte der Forschung*, ed. Georg Schild and Anton Schilling (Paderborn, 2009), 213–30.
9. Christopher R. Browning, *Collected Memories: Holocaust History and Postwar Testimony* (Madison, 2003), 37–59; and Browning, *Remembering Survival: Inside a Nazi Slave Labor Camp* (New York, 2010), 5–12.
10. Langewiesche, "Nation, Imperium und Kriegserfahrungen"; Benjamin Ziemann, "Das 'Fronterlebnis' des Ersten Weltkrieges: eine sozial historische Zäsur? Deutungen und Wirkungen in Deutschland und Frankreich," in *Der Erste Weltkrieg und die europäische Nachkriegsordnung: Sozialer Wandel und Formveränderung der Politik*, ed. Hans Mommsen (Cologne, 2000), 43–82.
11. *Im deutschen Reich*, no. 1–2, January 1915, 6.
12. Quoted from Heinrich Loewe, "Feinde Ringsum," *Jüdische Rundschau*, August 1914. See also Penslar, *Jews and the Military*, 169–70.
13. For an overview on the conditions of trench warfare, see Alexander Watson, *Enduring the Great War: Combat, Morale and Collapse in the German and British Armies, 1914–1918* (Cambridge, 2008); and Peter Hart, *The Great War: A Combat History of World War I* (Oxford, 2013).
14. On the dynamics of community building through military violence, see Thomas Kühne, *The Rise and Fall of Comradeship: Hitler's Soldiers, Male Bonding and Mass Violence in the Twentieth Century* (Cambridge, 2017), 17–44; and Michael Geyer, "How the Germans Learned to Wage War: On the Question of Killing in the First and Second World Wars," in *Between*

Mass Death and Individual Loss: The Place of the Dead in Twentieth Century Germany, ed. Paul Betts, Alon Confino, and Dirk Schumann (New York, 2008), 25–50.
15. Edwin Halle, diary entry for 24 August 1915, "Kriegserinnerungen mit Auszügen aus meinem Tagebuch, 1914–1916," LBINY MM 31.
16. The "primary group," a term conceived by the American sociologist Charles Horton Cooley, is defined as a group of people with whom an individual comes into regular contact in intimate, face-to-face association and cooperation. In the form of family, school, and personal acquaintances, the group was an individual's major source of social influence through adulthood. See Charles Horton Cooley, *Social Organization: A Study of the Larger Mind* (New York, 1909), 25–31. For the importance of the primary group in contemporary military sociology, see Christian Stachelbeck, *Militärische Effektivität im Ersten Weltkrieg: Die 11. Bayerische Infanteriedivision 1915 bis 1918* (Paderborn, 2010), 340–44; and Siniša Malešević, *The Sociology of War and Violence* (Cambridge, 2010), 221–31.
17. US sociologists wrote extensively about the primary group after the Second World War, recognizing small-group cohesion as the backbone of modern military organizations. See Edward A. Shils and Morris Janowitz, "Cohesion and Disintegration in the Wehrmacht in World War II," *The Public Opinion Quarterly* 12 (1948): 280–315.
18. Anthony Kellet, "The Soldier in Battle: Motivational and Behavioral Aspects of the Combat Experience," in *Psychological Dimensions of War*, ed. Betty Glad (Newbury Park, CA, 1990), 226; Simmel quoted from Langewiesche, "Nation, Imperium und Kriegserfahrungen," 214.
19. Alfred Koch, letter to parents, 23 June 1917, "Alfred Koch Briefe: Briefe und Gedichte unseres Alfred an Eltern, Geschwister und seine Kindheitsgefaehrtin und einzelne andere 1910–1920," LBINY ME 1568.
20. Joachim Friedrich Beutler, letters from 21 September 1916 and 8 January 1917, quoted from Reichsbund jüdischer Frontsoldaten, ed., *Kriegsbriefe gefallener Deutscher Juden* (Berlin, 1935), 12, 16.
21. Ziemann, "Das 'Fronterlebnis' des Ersten Weltkrieges," 51–52. On average, infantry regiments were withdrawn from the lines for a period of nine days for each eighteen-day deployment to the front. See Stachelbeck, *Militärische Effektivität im Ersten Weltkrieg*, 263–79.
22. Kühne, *The Rise and Fall of Comradeship*, esp. Chapter 1.
23. Edwin Halle, entry for 5 May 1915, "Kriegserinnerungen mit Auszügen aus meinem Tagebuch, 1914–1916," LBINY MM 31.
24. Ibid., entry for 7 May 1915.
25. Ibid., entry for 20 May 1915.
26. Otto Meyer, letter dated 2 April 1915, in Otto Meyer, *Als deutscher Jude im Ersten Weltkrieg: Der Fabrikant und Offizier Otto Meyer*, ed. Andreas Meyer (Berlin, 2014), 66.
27. Ibid., letter dated 28 April 1915, 71–72.
28. Ibid., undated letter to wife (probably August or September 1915), 78–80.
29. Fritz Frank, entry for 29 January 1915, "Das Stahlbad. Aufzeichnungen eines Arztes 1914–1918," LBINY ME 133.

30. Alfred Koch, letter to parents, 10 October 1914, "Alfred Koch Briefe: Briefe und Gedichte unseres Alfred an Eltern, Geschwister und seine Kindheitsgefaehrtin und einzelne andere 1910–1920," LBINY ME 1568.
31. Ibid., letter to parents, 9 October 1914.
32. Ibid., letter to brother, 23 November 1917.
33. Ibid., letter to brother, 13 March 1917.
34. Kühne, *The Rise and Fall of Comradeship*, 45–69, 290–96; Robert L. Nelson, *German Soldier Newspapers of the First World War* (Cambridge, 2011), 89–92; Aribert Reimann, *Der große Krieg der Sprachen: Untersuchungen zur historischen Semantik in Deutschland und England zur Zeit des Ersten Weltkriegs* (Essen, 2000), 120–24.
35. Albrecht Mugdan, letter to mother, 5 April 1916, "Kriegstagebuecher 1914–1916," LBINY ME 455.
36. Ibid., letter to mother, 10 April 1915.
37. Ibid., letter to mother, 3 March 1915.
38. Nelson, *German Soldier Newspapers*, 90.
39. This is also the case in Herbert Sulzbach's published diary, *Zwischen zwei Mauern*.
40. Letter to parents dated 9 March 1918, in Franz Rosenzweig, *Feldpostbriefe: Die Korrespondenz mit den Eltern (1914–1917)* (Freiburg, 2013), 594. See also Franz Rosenzweig Collection 1832–1999, LBINY AR 3001.
41. Alfred Koch, letter to parents, 18 June 1917, "Alfred Koch Briefe: Briefe und Gedichte unseres Alfred an Eltern, Geschwister und seine Kindheitsgefaehrtin und einzelne andere 1910–1920," LBINY ME 1568.
42. Ibid., letter to parents, 9 April 1915.
43. Ibid., letter to brother, 27 March 1917.
44. Julius Marx, *Kriegstagebuch eines Juden* (Frankfurt am Main, 1964), "Vorwort." For an insightful analysis of Marx's diary, see Ulrich Sieg, *Jüdische Intellektuelle im Ersten Weltkrieg: Kriegserfahrungen, weltanschauliche Debatten und kulturelle Neuentwürfe* (Berlin, 2001), 124.
45. In his memoirs, which he published in 1970, Marx claimed that his diary was based on notes he had taken during the war. Julius Marx, *Georg Kaiser, ich und die anderen. Alles in einem Leben: Ein Bericht in Tagebuchform* (Gütersloh, 1970), 37.
46. Ibid., 12–14. See also Walther Huder, "Kriegs-Tagebuch eines Juden: Ein Beitrag zur Geschichte des deutschen Judentums," *Bulletin des Leo Baeck Instituts* 8 (1965): 240–49.
47. Marx, *Kriegstagebuch eines Juden*, entry for 5 October 1914, 32. Author's emphasis.
48. Ibid., entry for 8 September 1916, 118. Author's emphasis.
49. Ibid., entry for 24 September 1916, 128–31.
50. Ibid., entry for 5 October 1914, 32.
51. Alfred Koch, letter to brother on 23 November 1917, "Alfred Koch Briefe: Briefe und Gedichte unseres Alfred an Eltern, Geschwister und seine Kindheitsgefaehrtin und einzelne andere 1910–1920," LBINY ME 1568.
52. Marx, *Kriegstagebuch eines Juden*, entry for 21 January 1915, 50.

53. Beutler, letters from 21 September 1916 and 8 January 1917, quoted from Reichsbund jüdischer Frontsoldaten, ed. *Kriegsbriefe*, 12, 16.
54. Ernst Löwenberg, letter to parents, 15 May 1917, "Mein Leben in Deutschland vor und nach dem 30. Januar 1933," Houghton Library, Harvard University, bMS 91 (145).
55. Koch, letter to parents, 25 November 1914, "Alfred Koch Briefe: Briefe und Gedichte unseres Alfred an Eltern, Geschwister und seine Kindheitsgefaehrtin und einzelne andere 1910–1920," LBINY ME 1568.
56. Ibid.
57. Ibid., letter to brother, 18 April 1918.
58. See Jason Crouthamel's chapter in this volume, "'My Comrades Are for the Most Part on My Side': Comradeship between Non-Jewish and German Jewish Front Soldiers in the First World War."
59. Fritz Goldberg (John Hay), "Mein Leben in Deutschland vor und nach dem 30. Januar 1933," Houghton Library, Harvard University, bMS 91 (89).
60. Hermann Berel Barsqueaux, letter from 19 January 1918, in Sabine Hank and Hermann Simon, eds. *Feldpostbriefe jüdischer Soldaten, 1914–1918* (Potsdam, 2002), 105–6.
61. Bernhard Bing, diary entry for 4 December 1916, "Kriegstagebuch von Bernhard Hugo Bing," Deutsches Tagebucharchiv (hereafter DTA) 1920/1,2,3.
62. Ibid., entry for 3 February 1917.
63. Ibid., entry for 14 March 1917.
64. Bing was awarded the Iron Cross Second Class after the battles at the Somme, a moment that brought him great "joy." See ibid., entry for 13 October 1916.
65. Koch, letter to parents, 2 March 1913, "Alfred Koch Briefe: Briefe und Gedichte unseres Alfred an Eltern, Geschwister und seine Kindheitsgefaehrtin und einzelne andere 1910–1920," LBINY ME 1568.
66. Ibid.
67. Ibid., letter to parents, 30 September 1916.
68. Order from Adolf Wild von Hohenborn on 11 October 1916, Kriegsministerium: Abteilung für allgemeine Armeeangelegenheiten, Hauptstaatsarchiv Stuttgart (Hereafter HStAS), M 1/4, Bü 1271; Nachweisung der beim Heere befindlichen (einschl. der noch vorhandenen vertraglich angenommenen Ärzte) wehrpflichtigen Juden," 11 October 1916, Kriegsministerium: Abteilung für allgemeine Armeeangelegenheiten, HStAS, M 1/4, Bü 1271; see further: "Maßnahmen gegen angebliche 'Drückeberger' unter der wehrpflichtigen jüdischen Bevölkerung im 1. Weltkrieg," Sammlung zur Militärgeschichte, HStAS, M 738, Bü 46. Although nearly forty years old, the most comprehensive work on the *Judenzählung* remains Werner T. Angress, "Das deutsche Militär und die Juden im Ersten Weltkrieg," *Militärgeschichtliche Mitteilungen* 19 (1976): 77–146. See also Grünwald, "Antisemitismus im Deutschen Heer und Judenzählung."
69. These letters are reproduced in their entirety in Hank and Simon, eds. *Feldpostbriefe jüdischer Soldaten, 1914–1918*.

70. "Feldpostbriefe der Brüder Walther und Victor Strauss an ihre Eltern," Militärischer Nachlass Victor Strauss (1894–1966), HStAS, M 660/325, Bü 1; and "Kriegstagebuch," HStAS, M 660/325, Bü 3.
71. Friedrich Solon, a lieutenant serving in the Prussian 56th Field Artillery Regiment, reported learning "absolutely nothing" about the census during the war. Friedrich Solon, "Mein Leben in Deutschland vor und nach dem 30. Januar 1933," LBINY ME 607.
72. An example of such a reaction can be found in the diary of Paul Josephtal, an officer who had been transferred out of frontline service due to a wound suffered during the initial advance into France in October 1914. The census came as a particular shock, because Josephtal was considered a rear-area soldier, despite having served in combat. The census is not mentioned again throughout the rest of the diary. Paul Josephtal, entry for 24 November 1916, Kriegstagebuch, LBINY AR 4179.
73. Penslar, *Jews and the Military*, 172–73.
74. See further Gregory A. Caplan, "Wicked Sons, German Heroes: Jewish Soldiers, Veterans, and Memories of World War I in Germany" (Ph.D. dissertation, Georgetown University, 2001); Sieg, *Jüdische Intellektuelle im Ersten Weltkrieg*; Grady, *A Deadly Legacy*; Fine, *Jewish Integration in the German Army*; and Penslar, *Jews and the Military*.
75. Max Bauer, *Der große Krieg in Feld und Heimat: Erinnerungen und Betrachtungen* (Tübingen, 1921); and Erich Ludendorff, *Kriegführung und Politik* (Berlin, 1922), 108–55. Surprisingly, in the first edition of his memoirs that were published in 1919, Ludendorff neither mentions the Jew Count nor denounces the Jewish war record. See Erich Ludendorff, *Meine Kriegserinnerungen 1914–1918* (Berlin, 1919). See also the memoirs of Ernst von Wrisberg, deputy to Wild von Hohenborn, the initiator of the Jew Count in October 1916: Ernst von Wrisberg, *Heer und Heimat 1914–1918* (Leipzig, 1921), esp. 93–95.
76. The most popular of these political pamphlets was Otto Armin, *Die Juden im Heere: Eine statistische Untersuchung nach amtlichen Quellen* (Munich, 1919). This "analysis" was actually written by Alfred Roth, a one-time chairman of the Reichshammerbund, who wrote under the pseudonym Otto Armin. In 1922, Jacob Segall and Franz Oppenheimer published detailed statistical analyses on the number of Jews who had served in the German military during the war, decisively refuting Roth's (and others') claims. See Franz Oppenheimer, *Die Judenstatistik des preußischen Kriegsministeriums* (Munich, 1922); and Jacob Segall, *Die deutschen Juden als Soldaten im Kriege 1914–1918* (Berlin, 1922).
77. See Florian Brückner's chapter in this volume, "Narrative Negotiations: Interpreting the Cultural Position of Jews in National(social)ist War Narratives from 1914 to 1945."
78. On the attitudes of the postwar conservative-nationalist political milieu, see Shelley Baranowski, *The Sanctity of Rural Life: Nobility, Protestantism, and Nazism in Weimar Prussia* (New York, 1995), 39–50; and Thomas Rohkrämer, *A Single Communal Faith? The German Right from Conservatism to National Socialism* (New York, 2007), 9–17, 52–54.

79. On the Stahlhelm and the "Jewish Question," see Peter Fritzsche, *Rehearsals for Fascism: Populism and Political Mobilization in Weimar Germany* (New York, 1990), 166–89; and Brian E. Crim, *Antisemitism in the German Military Community and the Jewish Response, 1914–1938* (Lanham, MD, 2014), 33–64.
80. See, for example, Walter Bloem's remarks at the RjF's ten-year anniversary gathering in Hamburg in 1929: "Nachklänge zu Hamburgs Zehn-Jahr-Feier," *Der Schild*, 1 January 1930; and "Der deutschen Zwietracht mitten ins Herz!" *Der Schild*, 22 November 1929.
81. Erich Maria Remarque, *Der Weg Zurück* (Cologne, 2014). Max Weil, the lone Jewish protagonist in Remarque's 1931 novel, is chided by the other soldiers for shirking and later becomes the leader of a Marxist soldiers' council (*Soldatenrat*).
82. On the concept of shirking and stereotypes of the Jewish *Drückeberger*, see Volker Ullrich, "Fünfzehntes Bild: Drückeberger," in *Bilder der Judenfeindschaft: Antisemitismus, Vorurteile und Mythen*, ed. Julius H. Schoeps and J. Schlör (Augsburg, 1999), 210–17. For a more general use of the term in military circles, see Ralph Winkle, *Der Dank des Vaterlandes: Eine Symbolgeschichte des Eisernen Kreuzes* (Essen: Klartext Verlag, 2007), 263–65.
83. Samuel Jacobs, "Gedanken und Erinnerungen aus dem Weltkriege 1914–1918," LBINY ME 328.
84. These efforts culminated in Jacob Segall's extensive report, which concluded that approximately 100,000 Jews had served in the wartime German military from 1914 to 1918. Of these, 80,000 Jewish soldiers had been stationed at the front lines, 35,000 received decorations, 23,000 were promoted—2,000 to the officers' ranks—and 12,000 had been killed in action. Segall further calculated that 17.3 percent of German Jews had served in armed forces during the war, and 12 percent of the Jewish wartime combatants had been killed in action. Segall, *Die deutschen Juden als Soldaten*. Other works that challenged antisemites' manipulation of the Jew Count are Walter Leiser, *Die Juden im Heer: Eine Kriegsstatisktik* (Berlin, 1919); Oppenheimer, *Judenstatistik*; and Adolf Eckstein, *Haben die Juden in Bayern ein Heimatrecht? Eine geschichtswissenschaftliche Untersuchung mit kriegsstatistischen Beilagen* (Berlin, 1928).
85. G. W. Allport, J. S. Bruner, and E. M. Jandorf, "Personality under Social Catastrophe: Ninety Life-Histories of the Nazi Revolution," *Character and Personality* 10 (1941): 1–22.
86. Surprisingly, only limited use has been made of these sources. See, for example, Jürgen Matthäus and Mark Roseman, *Jewish Responses to Persecution, Volume I, 1933–1938* (Lanham, MD, 2010), 331–32; Margarete Limberg and Hubert Rübsaat, eds., *Germans No More: Accounts of Jewish Everyday Life, 1933–1938* (New York, 2006); and Trude Maurer, "Customers, Patients, Neighbors and Friends: Relations between Jews and non-Jews in Germany, 1933–1938," in *Nazi Europe and the Final Solution*, ed. David Bankier and Israel Gutman (Jerusalem, 2003), 73–92.
87. Max Moses Polke, "Mein Leben in Deutschland vor und nach dem 30. Januar 1933," Houghton Library, Harvard University, bMS 91 (178).
88. Ibid.

89. Hugo Moses, "Mein Leben in Deutschland vor und nach dem 30. Januar 1933," Houghton Library, Harvard University, bMS 91 (159).

Bibliography

Allport, G. W., J. S. Bruner, and E. M. Jandorf. "Personality under Social Catastrophe: Ninety Life-Histories of the Nazi Revolution." *Character and Personality* 10 (1941): 1–22.

Angress, Werner T. "Das deutsche Militär und die Juden im Ersten Weltkrieg." *Militärgeschichtliche Mitteilungen* 19 (1976): 77–146.

Armin, Otto. *Die Juden im Heere: Eine statistische Untersuchung nach amtlichen Quellen.* Munich: Deutscher Volks-Verlag, 1919.

Baranowski, Shelley. *The Sanctity of Rural Life: Nobility, Protestantism, and Nazism in Weimar Prussia.* New York: Oxford University Press, 1995.

Bauer, Max. *Der große Krieg in Feld und Heimat: Erinnerungen und Betrachtungen.* Tübingen: Osiander, 1921.

Browning, Christopher R. *Collected Memories: Holocaust History and Postwar Testimony.* Madison: University of Wisconsin Press, 2003.

———. *Remembering Survival: Inside a Nazi Slave Labor Camp.* New York: W. W. Norton, 2010.

Caplan, Gregory. "Wicked Sons, German Heroes: Jewish Soldiers, Veterans, and Memories of World War I in Germany." Ph.D. dissertation, Georgetown University, 2001.

Cooley, Charles Horton. *Social Organization: A Study of the Larger Mind.* New York: Charles Scribner's Sons, 1909.

Crim, Brian E. *Antisemitism in the German Military Community and the Jewish Response, 1914–1938.* Lanham, MD: Lexington Books, 2014.

Eckstein, Adolf. *Haben die Juden in Bayern ein Heimatrecht? Eine geschichtswissenschaftliche Untersuchung mit kriegsstatistischen Beilagen.* Berlin: Philo Verlag, 1928.

Fine, David J. *Jewish Integration in the German Army in the First World War.* Berlin: De Gruyter, 2012.

Fritzsche, Peter. *Rehearsals for Fascism: Populism and Political Mobilization in Weimar Germany.* New York: Oxford University Press, 1990.

Geyer, Michael. "How the Germans Learned to Wage War: On the Question of Killing in the First and Second World Wars." In *Between Mass Death and Individual Loss: The Place of the Dead in Twentieth Century Germany,* edited by Paul Betts, Alon Confino, and Dirk Schumann, 25–50. New York: Berghahn Books, 2008.

Grady, Tim. *A Deadly Legacy: German Jews and the Great War.* New Haven, CT: Yale University Press, 2017.

Grünwald, Michal. "Antisemitismus im Deutschen Heer und Judenzählung." In *Jüdische Soldaten-Jüdischer Widerstand in Deutschland und Frankreich,* edited by Michael Berger and Gideon Römer-Hillebrecht, 129–44. Paderborn: Ferdinand Schöningh, 2012.

Hank, Sabine, and Hermann Simon, eds. *Feldpostbriefe jüdischer Soldaten, 1914–1918*. Potsdam: Hentrich & Hentrich, 2002.
Hart, Peter. *The Great War: A Combat History of World War I*. Oxford: Oxford University Press, 2013.
Heikaus, Ulrike, and Julia B. Köhne, eds. *Krieg! Juden zwischen den Fronten 1914–1918*. Berlin: Hentrich und Hentrich Verlag, 2014.
Hoffmann, Christhard. "Between Integration and Rejection: The Jewish Community in Germany, 1914–1918." In *State, Society, and Mobilization in Europe during the First World War*, edited by John Horne, 89–104. Cambridge: Cambridge University Press, 1997.
Huder, Walther. "Kriegs-Tagebuch eines Juden: Ein Beitrag zur Geschichte des deutschen Judentums." *Bulletin des Leo Baeck Instituts* 8 (1965): 240–49.
Kellet, Anthony. "The Soldier in Battle: Motivational and Behavioral Aspects of the Combat Experience." In *Psychological Dimensions of War*, edited by Betty Glad, 215–35. Newbury Park, CA: Sage Publications, 1990.
Klemperer, Victor. *Curriculum Vitae: Erinnerungen, 1881–1918*. 2 vols. Berlin: Aufbau-Verlag, 1996.
Kühne, Thomas. *The Rise and Fall of Comradeship: Hitler's Soldiers, Male Bonding and Mass Violence in the Twentieth Century*. Cambridge: Cambridge University Press, 2017.
Langewiesche, Dieter. "Nation, Imperium und Kriegserfahrungen." In *Kriegserfahrungen. Krieg und Gesellschaft in der Neuzeit: Neue Horizonte der Forschung*, edited by Georg Schild and Anton Schilling, 213–30. Paderborn: Ferdinand Schöningh, 2009.
Latzel, Klaus. *Deutsche Soldaten-nationalsozialistischer Krieg? Kriegserlebnis-Kriegserfahrung 1939–1945*. Paderborn: Ferdinand Schöningh, 1998.
Leiser, Walter. *Die Juden im Heer: Eine Kriegsstatisktik*. Berlin: Philo Verlag, 1919.
Lewin, Reinhold. "Der Krieg als jüdisches Erlebnis." *Monatsschrift für die Geschichte und Wissenschaft des Judentums* 63 (1917): 1–14.
Limberg, Margarete, and Hubert Rübsaat, eds. *Germans No More: Accounts of Jewish Everyday Life, 1933–1938*. New York: Berghahn Books, 2006.
Ludendorff, Erich. *Kriegführung und Politik*. Berlin: E. S. Mittler & Sohn, 1922.
———. *Meine Kriegserinnerungen 1914–1918*. Berlin: E. S. Mittler & Sohn, 1919.
Malešević, Siniša. *The Sociology of War and Violence*. Cambridge: Cambridge University Press, 2010.
Marx, Julius. *Georg Kaiser, ich und die anderen. Alles in einem Leben: Ein Bericht in Tagebuchform*. Gütersloh: C. Bertelsmann Verlag, 1970.
———. *Kriegstagebuch eines Juden*. Frankfurt am Main: ner-tamid-verlag, 1964.
Matthaus, Jurgen, and Mark Roseman. *Jewish Responses to Persecution, Volume I, 1933–1938*. Lanham, MD: AltaMira Press, 2010.
Maurer, Trude. "Customers, Patients, Neighbors and Friends: Relations between Jews and Non-Jews in Germany, 1933–1938." In *Nazi Europe and the Final Solution*, edited by David Bankier and Israel Gutman, 73–92. Jerusalem: Yad Vashem, 2003.
Meyer, Otto. *Als deutscher Jude im Ersten Weltkrieg: Der Fabrikant und Offizier Otto Meyer*. Edited by Andreas Meyer. Berlin: be.bra Wissenschaft Verlag, 2014.

Nelson, Robert L. *German Soldier Newspapers of the First World War*. Cambridge: Cambridge University Press, 2011.
Oppenheimer, Franz. *Die Judenstatistik des preußischen Kriegsministeriums*. Munich: Verlag für Kulturpolitik, 1922.
Penslar, Derek. "The German-Jewish Soldier: From Participant to Victim." *German History* 29 (2011): 445–69.
——. *Jews and the Military: A History*. Princeton, NJ: Princeton University Press, 2013.
Poppel, Stephen. *Zionism in Germany 1897–1933: The Shaping of Jewish Identity*. Philadelphia: Jewish Publication Society of America, 1976.
Reichsbund jüdischer Frontsoldaten, ed. *Kriegsbriefe gefallener Deutscher Juden*. Berlin: Vortrupp, 1935.
Reimann, Aribert. *Der große Krieg der Sprachen: Untersuchungen zur historischen Semantik in Deutschland und England zur Zeit des Ersten Weltkriegs*. Essen: Klartext Verlag, 2000.
Remarque, Erich Maria. *Der Weg Zurück*. Cologne: Kiepenheuer & Witsch, 2014.
Rohkrämer, Thomas. *A Single Communal Faith? The German Right from Conservatism to National Socialism*. New York: Berghahn Books, 2007.
Rosenthal, Jacob. *"Die Ehre des jüdischen Soldaten": Die Judenzählung im Ersten Weltkrieg und ihre Folgen*. Frankfurt: Campus Verlag, 2007.
Rosenzweig, Franz. *Feldpostbriefe: Die Korrespondenz mit den Eltern (1914–1917)*. Freiburg: Verlag Karl Alber, 2013.
Segall, Jacob. *Die deutschen Juden als Soldaten im Kriege 1914–1918*. Berlin: Philo-Verlag, 1922.
Shils, Edward A., and Morris Janowitz. "Cohesion and Disintegration in the Wehrmacht in World War II." *The Public Opinion Quarterly* 12 (1948): 280–315.
Sieg, Ulrich. *Jüdische Intellektuelle im Ersten Weltkrieg: Kriegserfahrungen, weltanschauliche Debatten und kulturelle Neuentwürfe*. Berlin: Akademie-Verlag, 2001.
Simon, Ernst. "Unser Kriegserlebnis (1919)." In *Brücken: Gesammelte Aufsätze*, 17–23. Heidelberg: Verlag Lambert Schneider, 1965.
Stachelbeck, Christian. *Militärische Effektivität im Ersten Weltkrieg: Die 11. Bayerische Infanteriedivision 1915 bis 1918*. Paderborn: Ferdinand Schöningh, 2010.
Sulzbach, Herbert. *Zwischen zwei Mauern: 50 Monate Westfront 1914–1918*. Berg am See: Kurt Vowinckel Verlag, 1986.
Ulrich, Bernd. *Die Augenzeugen: Deutsche Feldpostbriefe in Kriegs- und Nachkriegszeit, 1914–1933*. Essen: Klartext Verlag, 1997.
Ullrich, Volker. "Fünfzehntes Bild: Drückeberger." In *Bilder der Judenfeindschaft: Antisemitismus, Vorurteile und Mythen*, edited by Julius H. Schoeps and J. Schlör, 210–17. Augsburg: Weltbild, 1999.
Watson, Alexander. *Enduring the Great War: Combat, Morale and Collapse in the German and British Armies, 1914–1918*. Cambridge: Cambridge University Press, 2008.
Winkle, Ralph. *Der Dank des Vaterlandes: Eine Symbolgeschichte des Eisernen Kreuzes*. Essen: Klartext Verlag, 2007.
Wrisberg, Ernst von. *Heer und Heimat 1914–1918*. Leipzig: Koehler, 1921.

Ziemann, Benjamin. "Das 'Fronterlebnis' des Ersten Weltkrieges: eine sozial historische Zäsur? Deutungen und Wirkungen in Deutschland und Frankreich." In *Der Erste Weltkrieg und die europäische Nachkriegsordnung: Sozialer Wandel und Formveränderung der Politik*, edited by Hans Mommsen, 43–82. Cologne: Böhlau Verlag, 2000.

Zimmermann, Mosche. *Die Deutschen Juden 1914–1945*. Munich: Oldenbourg Verlag, 1997.

5

"BEING GERMAN" AND "BEING JEWISH" DURING THE FIRST WORLD WAR

An Ambivalent Transnational Relationship?

Sarah Panter

On 15 August 1914, only eleven days after Britain had declared war on Germany and entered an alliance with the Russian Empire and France, Leopold Greenberg, the editor of Anglo-Jewry's most influential newspaper, the *Jewish Chronicle*, issued a note of protest in the *London Times*.[1] Disturbed by the many charges of Jewish disloyalty and pro-German leanings in Britain in the first days of the war, and in particular in Jewish strongholds such as London, Leeds, or Manchester, he pointed to a complex dilemma:

> Instance after instance has come to my knowledge of the ignorant assumption up and down the country that every Jew is necessarily a German and is hence being made an object of hatred as an enemy of this country. In Germany I learn that our Jews are in a somewhat similar case. But there they are not called "German" Jews, but "Russian" Jews. The fact is, of course, that Jews are by their tradition and, indeed, by absolute Jewish law, bound in loyalty to the country of which they are citizens. The Jew in Germany is no more German than the German, and the Jew in England is no less English than the English.[2]

Embedding these dynamics into a larger transnational context, Greenberg, in an almost far-sighted fashion, pointed to a pivotal challenge that Jewish communities around the globe faced during the war: how to balance their bonds of Jewish solidarity with the obligations stemming from their loyalties as citizens of a particular nation-state or empire.[3] A broader question emerges when looking at this issue in an international context: How did religious, ethnic, or national minorities experience the war and were thus impacted by their constant need to negotiate difference on a local and international scale?[4] This chapter addresses this question by focusing on the ambivalent relationship between "being German" and "being Jewish" from a comparative and transnational perspective.

During the war, debates concerning the "Germanness" of minorities arose not only in German-speaking countries, but also in those English-speaking parts of the world that contained "Germans as minorities."[5] More recent scholarship focusing in particular on the long nineteenth century has tried to grasp this transnational space analytically with the concepts "German diaspora" and "Germans abroad,"[6] without taking explicitly into account the very illustrative case of the German Jewish diaspora so far. The wartime debates in Germany, Austria, Britain, and the United States reveal quite paradoxical similarities regarding these societies' underlying classifications of their Jewish citizens and immigrants as "aliens" or "enemies"[7] and their entanglement with the issue of whether Jewishness and Germanness were interpreted as compatible markers of their multiple and situational identities.[8] Having said this, however, one should keep in mind that the Jewish communities in question had quite different starting positions, strengths of Jewish populations, and social compositions, such as the ratio between native and foreign Jews (see Table 5.1).

Table 5.1 Statistics on Jewish Communities in Germany, Austria, Britain, and the United States.

Country	Year	Jewish Population (total)
Austria	1910	**1,313,687** (including 871,906 Jews in Galicia and 102,929 in Bukovina)
Germany	1910	**615,021** (including 70,000 Jewish immigrants from Eastern Europe)
United Kingdom	1915	**257,000** (including 150,000 to 200,000 Jewish immigrants from Eastern Europe)
United States	1917	**3,012,141** (including 2.5m Jewish immigrants from Eastern Europe)

Sources: "Statistics of Jews, A. Jewish Population of the World," *American Jewish Year Book* 19 (1917–18): 409–13; Hasia R. Diner, *The Jews of the United States: 1654 to 2000* (Berkeley, 2004), 88; Todd M. Endelman, *The Jews of Britain: 1656 to 2000* (Berkeley, 2000), 127; Jack Wertheimer, "'The Unwanted Element': East European Jews in Imperial Germany," *Leo Baeck Institute Year Book* 26 (1981): 32; Theodor Haas, "Die Ergebnisse der Volkszählung vom 31. Dezember 1910 und die jüdische Bevölkerung in Oesterreich," *Zeitschrift für Demographie und Statistik der Juden* 12 (1912): 149.

Looking at the complex transnational relationship of "being Jewish" and "being German" not only serves as a mirror to analyze the specific Jewish struggles to come to terms with this dilemma during the war, but also gives some more general insights into how the four societies at war negotiated the difference of social, religious, ethnic, or political minorities in their midst. Seen from this perspective, important shifts in the relationship between inclusive (universalistic) or exclusionary (particularistic) concepts of citizenship become particularly visible, given that since the Enlightenment Jews had been both "insiders" and "outsiders" in society at large.[9]

On one hand, Jews could define themselves (positively) as being Germans while non-Jewish circles claimed the opposite and tried to exclude them from their community of the nation. In this context, for example, German and Austrian Jews vividly evoked their belonging to German culture and actively defended their Germanness, often quite regardless of whether they adhered to Jewish nationalism or not. On the other hand, Jews could be identified (negatively) as being German, that is, as being sympathetic to the German cause. In this sense, perceptions of being German in the Anglo-American context were mainly driven by external pressure and forced Jews on many occasions to distance themselves from an assumed Germanness. The corresponding charges of disloyalty against Jews in English-speaking countries that arose within the non-Jewish sphere (and sometimes also within the Jewish sphere) did not necessarily take into account how intense the Germanness of Jews actually was, or whether claiming some kind of Germanness was at all a relevant part of their identity as British and North American Jews, and hence a matter of choice. In this context, one has to stress here that not all Jews in these two English-speaking countries accused of sharing a sentiment of "being German" during the war were actually born in German-speaking Europe. It was also often attributed to Yiddish-speaking Jewish immigrants with family roots in Eastern Europe, who had voiced their anti-Russian feeling openly since August 1914. This, however, makes this transnational approach even more important, for it shows how fluid and complex ethnic markers of difference in terms of "being Jewish" and "being German" actually were during the war. Depending on the context, they could take on different forms and shapes, overlap, or even contradict each other.

Whereas Jewishness and Germanness refer to a concept rather than an actual practice, I also employ the analytical terms of "being Jewish" and "being German," in particular when pointing to the processual dynamics of such markers of identity and difference.[10] De-centralizing the perspective on "being German" and "being Jewish" from a narrow framework of German (Jewish) historiography thus promises to make visible the ambivalent transnational dynamics of these ethnic ascriptions, which would otherwise remain hidden.

In this chapter, I will first focus on the challenges British and North American Jews faced when repudiating the narrative of a strong German sentiment among Jews in the Anglo-American sphere, looking primarily at examples from Jews with roots in German-speaking countries whose families had usually emigrated to the US in the mid nineteenth century, as part of the larger phenomenon of Central European immigration. Hence, by the time of the First World War they were usually naturalized or even native-born British and American citizens; their pro-German sentiment stemmed therefore as much from the hopes set in Germany's war against Russia as from their cultural affiliations to Germany.[11] The second part of this chapter will then contrast this with the struggle of Jews in Germany and Austria to have their self-assertions that "Germanness" and "Jewishness" are mutually inclusive markers of identity accepted within their own societies but also within their own local Jewish communities. Because my argumentation is focusing in particular on conceptual aspects, only some facets of the diverse Jewish experiences at these four home fronts can be touched on here in more detail. Finally, I will draw some overarching conclusions and give a brief outlook on how a transnational approach to the intertwined meanings of "being Jewish" and "being German" during the war might enable us to analyze the ambiguity, fluidity, and multi-sidedness of both ethnic ascriptions.

Taking a Stance against Charges of "Being German": The Repudiating Narrative of Jews in Britain and the United States

The Assumed Identity of Germans and Jews in Britain in the Summer of 1914

Since Britain had entered the war on 4 August 1914 on the side of Russia—the archenemy of Jews around the globe—its Jewish residents experienced heightened pressure to demonstrate that their Jewish and civic loyalties were not standing in conflict with each other. Accordingly, Anglo-Jewry publicly voiced its undivided loyalties in times of war towards the British nation.[12] Yet compared to expressions of war enthusiasm among, for instance, Jews in the German-speaking countries, who had legitimized the war by pointing to its possible liberating effects on Jews in Russia, Anglo-Jewish spokesmen referred not so much to their willingness to sacrifice their lives for king and country but rather to their gratitude towards Britain's past hospitality to Jews:

> We are one and undivided as a nation, and of that nation there is no section which, from end to end of the country, indeed from end to end of the Empire, has more reason ... to stand by her wholeheartedly ... than has the Jews. England has been all she could be to Jews; Jews will be all they can be to England.[13]

Given the large number of Jews from Eastern Europe in their midst, through whose home towns (or *shtetls*) the war raged now on the Eastern Front, such patriotic expressions were accompanied from the start by warnings to avoid positions subverting "official" declarations of Anglo-Jewish loyalty.[14] This was especially triggered by the Anglo-Russian alliance that caused a multi-sided dilemma for many Jews in Britain. As a response to these pressures of conformity, Anglo-Jewish representatives attempted to strategically reframe their negatively connoted prewar image of Russia by arguing, for example, that antisemitism in Russia was basically a German ideology, transplanted there from Germany. From this perspective, then, "a defeat of Germany, involving as it must a crushing of Prussian militarism," as one comment in the *Jewish World* hoped, was supposed to "destroy the best support which antisemitism has had in the home of its very cradle."[15] Hence, Anglo-Jewry's attempts to demonstrate its undivided loyalty more often than not required walking a tightrope and soon reached their limits.[16]

Someone who would constantly warn of the long-term consequences of such an overstretched adjustment strategy was the already mentioned Leopold Greenberg, who published many critical comments on the local and international Jewish situation during the war under the pseudonym of Mentor. On 21 August 1914, for example, after anti-German sentiment had seen a first strong wave in Britain in the context of the internment of enemy aliens, he issued an article titled "A Voice in the Wilderness" that addressed the dangerous xenophobic dynamics across the country. In doing so, he heavily criticized the Germanophobia in the realm of everyday culture, as expressed, for example, in cancellations of classical concerts that were supposed to include pieces from German composers. In his view, such measures did not represent acts of "true" patriotism but rather pointed to a major dilemma of all wars: that each belligerent party claims its cause to be "just" and "righteous."[17]

Such xenophobic attitudes were by no means restricted to Britain; its counterpart, Anglophobia, was also prevalent in Germany, as Matthew Stibbe has demonstrated in more detail.[18] What this entailed in the realm of everyday experiences becomes visible in the diary entries of German-born American rabbi William Rosenau, who was visiting Berlin in the summer of 1914. From there he reported that the US embassy had advised all its citizens to refrain from speaking English in the public sphere in order not to be mistaken for Englishmen.[19] Even though manifestations of Germanophobia equally challenged non-Jewish Germans living in Britain or those British citizens with cultural and familial bonds with Germany, the situation of Jews in Britain was even more complicated because of the multiple options of defining Jewishness *vis-à-vis* the concepts of nation, citizenship, and ethnicity. The Jewish community in Britain (if defined in a broad sense) included not only native-born Jews and "naturalized" Jews but also "enemy alien" Jews from the German-speaking lands and so-called "friendly alien" Jews who were still subjects of the Russian Empire. This pluralistic make-up of the Jewish community in Britain seemed now to be outright problematic; in times of national crisis, societies at war searched for clear-cut loyalties to sketch out "friends" and "enemies" at home and abroad alike.

In this context, then, the war catalyzed already existing stereotypes about Germans and Jews in Britain, meaning not only that the terms "alien," "Jew," and "German" were used interchangeably but also that the corresponding practice to this phenomenon itself could lead to local conflicts, such as in Wales in 1914, and later in the war in other places, such as Leeds and London.[20] Thereby, the boundaries were blurred between such external ascriptions of disloyalty, the individual self-identifications, as well as the legal positions of Jews (citizen vs. alien; friend vs. enemy). Despite all the protests Jews voiced against such superfluous equations of Jewishness and Germanness that after 1917 became intermingled with the emerging stereotype of "bolshevism,"[21] they would permeate British society further throughout the war, causing many Jews with roots in the German-speaking lands to change their names.[22] Hence, the negative meaning of being German left a deep mark on the positive self-assertion regarding the German cultural heritage of some members of the Anglo-Jewish elite, even though it had already been prevalent underneath the surface since the turn of the century. Here, then, the First World War marked a deep cultural watershed.[23]

Changing Constellations and the German Dilemma of North American Jews

Although North American Jews had not been directly involved in the war before April 1917, they were nevertheless affected by the events in Europe from the start, due to their transnational ties to almost all belligerent countries. Complicated further by the constellation of American neutrality in the initial stages of this global armed conflict, North American Jews started to renegotiate what being Jewish was supposed to mean in reference to their current and past homelands. Torn between neutrality and their transatlantic connections, they were therefore faced with a dilemma leaving them far from being merely neutral spectators of the European theatre of the war before 1917.[24]

Whereas the Yiddish-language immigrant press, with its stronghold in New York, sided with Germany openly because, paralleling the expectations of Jews in German-speaking lands,[25] they hoped for a liberation of Russian Jews from Czarist rule, the American Jewish press voiced a more cautious interpretation of the events in Europe. This was, in part, because it represented the voices of persons such as, to mention a few prominent names, Jacob Schiff, Louis Marshall, Judah L. Magnes, Richard Gottheil, or Louis Brandeis, who had different agendas with regard to the course American Jewry as a whole should follow amidst the circumstances of neutrality. Many among these actors were also deeply involved in German American affairs, so their positions also give evidence to the fact that German Americans—whether Jewish or not—shared some of their experiences during the war.[26]

Immediately after the war broke out in Europe, Jews in the US tried to evade the dilemma of conflicting loyalties by distinguishing between the politics and the culture of the belligerents. Accordingly, the *American Hebrew* wrote on 7 August, when reflecting on the situation of Germany, that "the ideals of the [German] army" were "not the ideals of the people."[27] During the first months of the war, North American Jews, and in particular those of Central European descent, quite often pointed out that not all prewar ideals associated with Germany should be completely abandoned. At the same time, this leitmotif served a strategic purpose as well, for it could legitimize personal (and sometimes business) entanglements with Germany and the sympathies that went along with them.[28] Yet conflicting assumptions about American Jewish loyalties in times of war polarized further as the war dragged on, especially after the turn of the year 1914/15. At that point it had become clear to many contemporary observers that the war would not be over by Christmas. As a consequence, the pressures of conformity within the American public grew stronger on a local and national level. This general pattern was reflected, for example, in the mutual accusations from different camps within American Jewry of having breached "neutrality."[29]

It was against this background that Richard Gottheil, Professor of Semitic Languages at Columbia University and leading member of the American Jewish community as well as the Federation of American Zionists, attempted to promote a pro-Allies counter-image. Gottheil's positioning is particularly interesting, firstly because it shows how superfluous assumptions about Jewish sympathies were often made and secondly because it exemplifies the different shades of the American Jewish dilemma during the war. Born in Manchester in 1862, Gottheil had family roots in the German-speaking lands as well. His father, the well-known rabbi Gustave Gottheil, had emigrated from Prussia to England before settling with his family in the US when Richard was eleven years old.[30] In a letter addressed to the famous philosopher Horace Kallen—one of the main thinkers behind the concept of "cultural pluralism"[31]—dated 19 October 1914, Gottheil warned of the "dangerous and delicate [position]" of Jews in the US. From Gottheil's perspective, this constellation resulted from a crucial misperception, in particular among ambassadors from France, Britain, and Russia, regarding the "apparent German leanings of the Jewish masses and leaders."[32] Gottheil was, however, not the only one equating being Jewish with being German or, in this case, with a pro-German stance during the war. Hence, it could also be interpreted as a decisive factor in winning over sympathies among the (German) Jewish diaspora in the US—a construct that was in itself not easy to define given that being (pro-)German was frequently also ascribed to Jewish immigrants from Russia, in particular those who spoke Yiddish, and that this marker furthermore included Jews born within the boundaries of either the German or the Habsburg Empire.

When the United States finally declared war on Germany on 6 April 1917, not all of its Jewish citizens and residents, particularly those of socialist and pacifist leanings, joined their country's call to arms overenthusiastically. As Louis Marshall phrased his fears: "I find that there is a strong undercurrent of indifference, as well as a decided and affirmative opposition in some quarters."[33] Yet compared to the situation confronting Jewish communities in Europe in the summer of 1914, and in particular Anglo-Jewry, one major obstacle—the system of Czarist oppression—had been erased by the February Revolution in Russia in 1917. Hence, the American entry into the war coincided with the emancipation of Russian Jews. Even the official journal of the Federation of American Zionists, the *Maccabaean*, which had before promoted a strict course of neutrality, now wholly embraced Woodrow Wilson's decision, for, as it argued, even "the extreme of pacifists" had to recognize that there was no alternative and that the "cause of America is ours."[34]

American Jewish manifestations of patriotism were not always immune to the hysteria at the American home front. And despite all rhetorical efforts to stress their undivided patriotism, the loyalties of American Jewry remained heavily contested. This was particularly challenging because claims for "100 percent" Americanism were no longer only applicable to more recent immigrants from Eastern Europe, as in the prewar period, but also to those native-born, acculturated North American Jews with family roots in the German-speaking lands. Many prominent German Americans chose therefore to publicly declare their loyalty towards the US by joining, for example, the so-called League of American Citizenship. Its members were supposed to act in the way of "missionaries" of Americanization among immigrants from the German-speaking lands. This idea, however, remained contested. In particular, Felix Warburg, who was equally engaged in German American as well as American Jewish causes, criticized the methods underlying such a pro-active (and slightly forced) endeavor. In his view, it would be more effective to increase the loyalty of German Americans not by adding more pressures to conform but by showing them the advantages of the model of American democracy and society.[35]

In many instances, public proclamations of patriotism could indeed counter accusations of disloyalty. Yet from time to time, name and recognition could not spare Jews in the US with familial bonds or cultural sympathies towards Germany from becoming the subject of anti-German hysteria—as the case of Gotthard Deutsch exemplifies. Deutsch had been born in 1859 in Dolní Kounice (Kanitz), a small town in Moravia that belonged to the Habsburg Empire. Trained at the famous Jewish Theological Seminary of Breslau, he had come to the US in 1891 after being appointed as a professor at the Hebrew Union College in Cincinnati. One reason for his marginal situation in 1917 was that he had not abandoned his "pacifist" stance after the US had entered the war. Another, more concrete reason was his statement at a local court in Cincinnati on 21 November, where he was questioned during the naturalization hearing for Hyman David Sway. In this context, Deutsch had refused to answer the judge's question, whether he would hope for a German or an American victory, because it seemed to him irrelevant to the subject matter.[36]

The refusal of Deutsch to answer this question—which he felt questioned his loyalty *a priori*—turned into a public affair amidst the general climate of anti-German hysteria, bringing claims that he should resign from his faculty position at the Hebrew Union College. That Deutsch was able to keep his position was finally due to the supporting statements he received from many prominent North American Jews who did not deny that he was wrong to refuse to answer the judge but who acquitted him at least of charges of disloyalty. On a more general level, the affair in regard to Deutsch's loyalties symbolized how deeply American Jewry had been sucked into the wartime hysteria of the American home front, of whose long-term consequences Louis Marshall, civil rights activist and leading member of the American Jewish Committee, had warned Edward Heinsheimer, the president of the Board of Governors of the Hebrew Union College, on 7 December:

> Dr. Deutsch … has given expression to his loyalty as an American citizen. … He has given the most eloquent evidence of his Americanism, by giving his children to the cause of the country. … Let us not become the victims of hysteria or lose our sense of proportion in a desire to give evidence of our loyalty, which should be taken for granted and which should not require proof of our own assertions or corroboration by the endorsement of our fellow-citizens.[37]

More often than not, such suspicions could turn into outright accusations of espionage that permeated the sphere of everyday experiences. This becomes visible, for example, in an article in the orthodox-leaning New York newspaper *Hebrew Standard* that was reprinted in London's *Jewish World* and told the story of Adolph Schwabacher, a German-born, naturalized American Jew. Prior to the outbreak of the war, he had been sent to study at the Politechnicum in Karlsruhe (Germany) with the goal of becoming a "wireless telegraphist." As soon as he foresaw the entry of the United States into the war, he had set sail for his adopted homeland. On his transatlantic voyage, as the story continued, he became a "spy suspect" when other passengers on board, unaccustomed to Judaism, saw him praying according to the orthodox rite, and reported him wearing "little boxes and straps." The charges were only dropped in the end by chance, when one of his co-passengers, the last to be questioned, pointed to the possibility that Adolph Schwabacher was merely an observant, praying Jew.[38]

As strategically motivated as the publication of this story might have been in the minds of the *Hebrew Standard*'s editors, it points, nonetheless, to an important wartime dynamic in the Anglo-American sphere: ignorance and fear of something "alien" as a catalyst for suspicions of disloyalty that mixed markers of being German with being Jewish. Hence, it was the interplay of a no longer tolerated self-identification with Germany on the one hand, and external ascriptions of a pro-German attitude among Jews on the other, that troubled Jews on the American home front as much as it had their British counterparts.

Together with other aspects, in particular the empowerment of Jewish immigrants from Eastern Europe in communal affairs during the war, the war's impact would be a "de-Germanization" of American Jewry on a cultural and institutional level.

Defending the Compatibility of "Being German" and "Being Jewish": The Symbiotic Narrative of Jews in Germany and Austria

The Contested German Jewish Symbiosis and Exclusionary Wartime Dynamics in Germany

After Germany had entered the war in the summer of 1914, German Jews, like many other religious, ethnic, and social minorities, hoped to further their integration by displaying an undivided patriotism towards the German nation. In this context, Jewish currents across the bench—whether liberal-integrationist,[39] orthodox,[40] or Zionist[41]—emphasized that each of their notions of Jewishness were mutually inclusive and hence compatible with a mainly ethnic or culturally coined concept of Germanness. This was reflected, for example, in the self-assertion of German Zionists whose notion of Jewishness was based mainly on an ethnic-national understanding: "We have not stopped being Jews during the war ... Germanness and Jewishness are not supposed to amalgamate but rather constitute *two* souls, two souls that fructify and enrich each other."[42] During the first months of the war, the persuasiveness of this rhetoric that "being Jewish" and "being German" were compatible was particularly aided by the fact that, concerning the situation of the approximately six million Jews on the Eastern Front, Jews and non-Jews alike interpreted Germany's struggle not only as a war of self-defense but also as one of liberation, that is, a war to bring German culture to the East.[43]

As the war progressed and antisemitic propaganda increased again on the German home front, this positive-fashioned relationship between Germanness and Jewishness became more and more contested, picking up fissures that went back to the 1880s. Not only was the patriotism and willingness of Jews to serve their country contested, as reflected in the infamous "Jew count" (*Judenzählung*) issued in October 1916, but even more importantly for the following argument, questions about Jewish belonging to the German nation became further entangled with fears of heightened Eastern European Jewish immigration after the war. The relationship between "being German" and "being Jewish" thus became more contested the more the general wartime disappointment at the

German home front grew, regardless of the fact that the majority of German Jews felt deeply rooted within German culture.[44] Hence, it was no coincidence that German Zionists, and in particular the younger, more radical generation of its leaders, who before the war had already questioned the liberal-integrationist narrative of a German Jewish symbiosis, now pointed to the fact that this ideal clearly clashed with antisemitic attempts to push Jews to the margins of German society.[45] From their perspective, striving for complete integration into German society based primarily on civic loyalty towards the German state and nation had failed, and it was not compatible with their goal to create a self-confident and visible Jewish ethnic identity:

> If only no Eastern European Jews arrive … then the Jewish question in *Germany* will sort itself out … If there are no Jews, then no Jewish question can exist. This is how the Eastern Jewish question that has transformed into a Western Jewish question [during the war] presents itself.[46]

These exclusionary dynamics that fully unfolded in 1916 led to an intense search for reorientation at home, particularly among intellectual circles within Germany Jewry in 1917–18. In this context, all camps within German Jewry renegotiated what a compatibility of Jewishness and Germanness was supposed to mean in the future. The journal of the Central Association of German Citizens of Jewish Faith (Centralverein deutscher Staatsbürger jüdischen Glaubens) remained, however, very much focused on finding an answer that was suitable for their dialogue with and acceptance within a non-Jewish space. Yet even among liberal-integrationist proponents of the classical German Jewish symbiosis narrative, the lines became semantically blurred between the two notions of a community of faith (*Glaubensgemeinschaft*) and a community of common descent (*Abstammungsgemeinschaft*).[47] As Michael Brenner has emphasized, this can be argued even in light of the fact that they officially continued to reject the "concept of a Jewish nation"[48] after the war. Whereas the notion of a tribe (*Stamm*) that had become fashionable within German Jewry since 1900 pointed to the fact that the relationship between "being German" and "being Jewish" acknowledged at least some ethnic components,[49] Jews did not necessarily perceive this concept as exclusionary in its implications. By contrast, they instead pointed to the fact that German Jews, like the Swabs or Bavarians, constituted one of the many German tribes that differed only by "birth, tradition and education." According to such a notion of Germanness, "civil rights" were rooted only "in citizenship acquired by birth" and thus considered "independent from belief or descent."[50] Whereas such a concept seems pluralistic on the surface, when it comes to writing German Jews into the concept of German citizenship, it does not say much about how it was supposed to handle the situation of Jewish immigrants.

Liberal-integrationist Jews in Germany therefore held onto their image and belief in a profound symbiosis of Germanness and Jewishness, even amidst and despite their disillusionment. This is reflected, for example, in an advertisement from the spring of 1917 regarding Hermann Cohen's seminal work on Germanness and Jewishness.[51] In the mind of its reviewer, Felix Goldmann, a well-known reform rabbi from Leipzig, Cohen resembled the personified unification of both concepts: his "consciousness, to be a religious, good Jew strengthens his German power, and his German sentiment through and through provides permanently a new nourishment for his Jewishness." Therefore, Goldmann continued further, Cohen was "not German, *despite* being Jewish, but *because* of his being Jewish."[52]

This emphasis on the exceptional compatibility of both self-assertions can, on the one hand, be interpreted as giving voice to an unshattered belief in the consolidated position of German Jews. On the other hand, it can also be read as an attempt to cover up disorientation and distress experienced by many Jews on a daily basis during the war. At the same time, the strong emphasis by many liberal-integrationist Jews on their culturally as well as nationally inspired Germanness points paradoxically to their inner dilemma during the war. For despite the fact that their self-identification was rooted in a strong identification with German culture, a growing part of German society—but also of Jewish nationalists—denied this to be true.

One of the most emotional statements of such a strong identification with Germanness during the war was made by the chairman of the Central Association (Centralverein), Eugen Fuchs, in August 1917, openly attacking Zionist notions of Jewishness:

> For us, Palestine is not our country of birth, the cradle of our childhood, not the gravesite of our parents; I don't know it and it is far from being the country of my longing, not the homeland [*Heimat*] I strive for, not *ille angulus, qui mihi praeter omnes ridet*. I speak German, feel German; German culture and German spirit fulfil me more than Hebrew literature and Jewish culture. When I'm away from home, it is Germany, German nature, fellow Germans that are the objects of my desire; I neither want to live in the Orient nor die there. As once my parents and ancestors turned into German dust, so shall I do one day.[53]

German Zionists, of course, took a very different perspective during the last two years of the war. As their hopes from the beginning of the war—that is, to help German authorities in the occupational zone to "Germanize" Eastern Europe by pointing to the image of Yiddish-speaking Eastern European Jews as brokers of "Germanness"—became dashed, their point of reference had shifted more and more to the dynamics of Jewish life in Poland and Russia and its future for the Jewish people itself. Here, then, local and transnational developments at home and abroad during the war started to influence each other. On the one hand, Zionists in 1917–18 were thus well aware that their power as a movement had largely increased in Europe as well as around the globe, something that was particularly fostered by the Balfour Declaration of the British government in November 1917.[54] Yet this perception of Zionism that reflected a particularistic take on the compatibility of Germanness and Jewishness did not necessarily match the notions of Jewish nationalism and Zionism in the German-occupied zones of Eastern Europe.[55] And while still clinging to this message of uncontested German Jewish loyalties from their specific perspective as Western Zionists, they had also come to acknowledge that Eastern European Jews themselves had played a major part in the transformation of German Zionism. They had finally rebutted all theories about the "non-existence of the Jewish nation."[56]

Citizens, but Aliens? The Refugee Question as a Catalyst for an Austrian Jewish Reorientation

After Emperor Franz Joseph had called on his loyal subjects on 29 July 1914 to support his decision to declare war on Serbia, Austrian Jews in all parts of the multiethnic Habsburg Empire invoked their dynastically fashioned loyalty.[57] Whereas the Jewish community of Vienna (*Israelitische Kultusgemeinde Wien*) had emphasized its civic loyalties by pointing to its uncontested willingness to "sacrifice goods and blood for emperor and fatherland,"[58] Austrian Zionists were no less enthusiastic and called on all its members to display the "courage of the Maccabees."[59] Compared to the case of German Jews, the discourse among Austrian Jews about the compatibility of "being German" and "being Jewish" was, however, influenced by a specific structural trajectory: their rootedness in a multiethnic empire. As Marsha Rozenblit has argued, Austrian Jews had adapted to these peculiarities since the second half of the nineteenth century by adopting a tripartite identity: an ethnic one (Jewish), a cultural one (German or Czech), and a national one (Austrian).[60] Though this description seems quite adequate to characterize the Jews in Vienna, Bohemia, and Moravia who resembled many features of middle-class, acculturated Jews in Germany, the picture becomes more complex when including the large number of Yiddish-speaking, strictly orthodox, and often Jewish nationalist-leaning Jews in the empire's Eastern provinces, Galicia and Bukovina. For, among other things, they strongly fostered the concept of Jewish autonomy within the boundaries of the empire.[61]

Immediately after the outbreak of the war, Jews from Galicia and Bukovina were faced with Russian troops occupying their homes and hence had to flee inwards. During the war, 70,000 out of approximately 350,000 Jewish refugees arrived in Vienna (and respective numbers in other cities as well, such as Prague).[62] In this context, the loyalties and self-assertions of Austrian Jews became heavily contested, showing remarkable psychological parallels to the "Eastern Jewish question" in Germany, yet with the striking exception that they were not aliens in a legal sense but citizens of the empire. Hence, it was against this background that the compatibility of a culturally and dynastically defined marker of being German and Austrian, on the one hand, and a religiously and ethnically defined marker of being Jewish, on the other, was questioned.[63] Whereas liberal-integrationist Jews, as mainly represented in the Jewish communities of Prague and Vienna, called upon the state and the whole empire to help the Jewish refugees as citizens in need, Austrian Zionists voiced concerns about this course of action and called upon them to increase Jewish self-help and strengthen their own welfare institutions. As the *Jüdische Zeitung* wrote as early as October 1914, "when Jews have become destitute, ultimately it have always and frequently been only Jews that have helped them!"[64] Yet many well-rooted Jews in Vienna and Prague were more concerned with reducing the public visibility of refugees, or, as one report to the Jewish community of Vienna wrote, "of those groups of the poorest among the poor, wandering around in every street,"[65] because they feared antisemitic outbursts. Thus, there was a decisive cultural difference between the empire's "Eastern" and "Western" Jews. Despite this, there also existed public proclamations of truce and unity within Austrian Jewry at the outbreak of the war.

One field of conflict, as in other belligerent states as well, was the catalyzed power struggle over whose definition of Jewishness should dominate Austrian Jewish power hierarchies in the future. Because being Austrian pointed more or less to the dynastic component of the empire, being German was thus the cultural marker of identity against whose background this clash became obvious. It was particularly in the sphere of the military, which had been known for its integrative effects and included therefore a historically unprecedented number of Jewish officers, that the conflicts of the declining multiethnic state appeared magnified since 1917.[66] Including a large number of Yiddish-speaking, orthodox Jews in its ranks as soldiers, many acculturated Austrian Jewish soldiers felt increasingly alienated by the emphasis on the soldier's Jewishness in discourse and practice. It was in this context that forty non-commissioned Jewish officers and one-year volunteers addressed a letter of complaint to the "leaders of Austrian Jewry."[67] By referring to the situation of German Jews as a positive counterexample, the signatories pointed to the fact that specific Jewish interests, such as providing soldiers with German prayer books or Jewish literature, were not taken care of sufficiently:

> We are at the front and fight first of all for emperor and fatherland. Yet at the same time we fight for the honor of Judaism. This is something our Jewish leaders in Vienna really need to consider. ... Does Austrian Jewry feel no sense of *obligations* towards its sons at the front?[68]

At first it might seem rather vague how exactly this letter connected the question of Jewishness and Germanness with a general sense of cultural difference. Yet if one looks at the specific claims of the signatories, a more concrete picture emerges. They not only explicitly demanded to be provided with "a German prayer book for field service" but also specified its intellectual content further. It was supposed to be "wisely drafted in order to satisfy the sentiments of the well-educated"[69] soldiers, and hence, one could add, less so the sentiments of those Jewish soldiers whom chaplain Majer Tauber had described in contrast as "bearded reserve fighters,"[70] that is, more religiously traditional, Yiddish-speaking soldiers from the empire's Eastern provinces.

Almost nothing is known about the self-assertions and reactions of Galician Jews, and the sparse accounts we have, offering a glimpse into their experiences, are mainly based on reports by Jewish chaplains. They functioned, on the one hand, as mediators between "tradition" and "modernity"[71] but, on the other, they adhered to different concepts of Jewishness themselves, stretching, as another Jewish chaplain, R. Faerber, pointed out, from "non-denominationals, to conservatives and orthodox."[72] Additionally, this lack of first-hand accounts is also due to some particular circumstances of the war. First, the families of Jewish soldiers from Austria's Eastern provinces had to flee westwards, that is inwards within the empire. This meant, apart from the huge emotional distress they had to face, that it was, for example, no longer possible to reach them by letters sent back home. Second, as is indicated in the minutes of Austria's Imperial Assembly (*Reichsrat*), Jewish soldiers from these regions—as well as their families and relatives at home or in exile—were either not allowed to write letters in their Yiddish mother tongue, that is in Hebrew script, or if they were allowed to do so, these often fell under military censorship. Altogether, then, this posed a major structural obstacle for communication during the war.[73]

The compatibility of being Jewish, German, and Austrian at once was even more intensely questioned at the moment of the empire's dissolution. Not only were most of the Jewish refugees turned into stateless aliens in November 1918, adding therefore to the already existing cultural difference a legal and political one. Rather, in 1918–19 the concept of (German) Austrian citizenship became increasingly defined in terms of categories of racial exclusion. Hence, under these new circumstances there was no longer much space for convincing the non-Jewish public that being Jewish and being Austrian were compatible markers of identity, neither for Jews from the former Eastern provinces of the dissolved empire nor for the middle-class, highly acculturated Jews rooted in Vienna. As a result, both groups' Austrianness that had before overlapped at least in part with their actual or assumed Germanness was now challenged like never before. Though trying to adapt their tripartite identity to the new circumstances of the German-Austrian rump state, and then from 1919 onwards to the First Austrian Republic, Jews were thus now no longer able to find protection under the multiethnic umbrella of the Habsburg Empire.[74]

The Implications of "Germanness" and "Jewishness" during the First World War: Some Concluding Thoughts

This chapter has addressed the ambivalent relationship between Germanness and Jewishness as markers of cultural difference and sensors for conflicting loyalties during the war in the respective societies in which Jewish communities played an integral role. As has been shown, charges of disloyalty were voiced against Jews whether they lived in German-speaking or English-speaking countries. Yet the dynamics and reasons behind this negative entanglement of "being German" and "being Jewish" showed varieties that were influenced both by the situational dynamics of the war and the peculiar historical trajectories of Jews in Germany, Austria, Britain, and the United States.

Depending on the local context, cultural and political markers of difference in terms of what being German was supposed to mean took on different shapes in the case of Jews as minorities. On the one hand, many middle-class, native-born Jews in Britain and the US had strong familial and cultural ties to the German-speaking lands, which in their opinion did not conflict with their loyalties as British or American citizens. On the other hand, Jews in the German diaspora were often (regardless of the complexity of Jewish self-identifications) regarded by others (negatively) as pro-German, that is, as friendly or sympathetic to the German cause. Paradoxically, this also included on many occasions Yiddish-speaking, working-class Jewish immigrants from Eastern Europe. Thus, ascriptions and self-assertions of "Jewishness/being Jewish" and "Germanness/being German" were marked by a high degree of relationality during the war, functioning as markers both for loyalty and disloyalty.

Whereas this categorization of Jews into "friends" and "enemies" in the English-speaking countries was constructed along the lines of the formula "Jewishness" equals "Germanness," Jews in the German-speaking countries had to fight for the acceptance of their positive self-identification as Germans and Jews, and hence for their inclusion into a German nation—a concept that had become more exclusive during the war. From this perspective, it seems therefore quite paradoxical that Jews in Britain and the US were identified at different levels as mediators of Germanness abroad. From a transnational perspective, being German and being Jewish as well as their intertwined meanings were thus complex constructs that included elements of self-identification and external ascriptions. Depending on the perspective, the image of a "German Jewish symbiosis" could either take on the shape of an ideal, a myth, or function as an accusation and was hence much more Janus-faced than is often assumed when the historical analysis remains merely within the framework of German (Jewish) historiography.

That we can find such diverse manifestations and meanings of Jewishness and Germanness during the First World War on both sides of the conflict points also to another important aspect: that despite all homogenizing pressures on ethnic groups or minorities during the war, the markers of "being German" and "being Jewish" were more fluid than often assumed in hindsight. Hence, in contrast to viewing the Jewish experiences of the First World War merely as a first step on the road to the Second World War, as is particularly done in the German and European context, such a transnational perspective brings to light that Jewishness was just one—and not always the most decisive—ethnic marker ascribed to Jews at this historical juncture.

Hence, whereas the war itself left an ambivalent legacy for Jews concerning the relationship between Germanness and Jewishness, it meant that German Jews abroad could be made part of a larger concept of the German nation, while at the same time Jews within the German Empire and the German-speaking parts of Austria were pushed to the margins of an increasingly racially drafted concept of the German nation. The Jewish case is therefore also highly illustrative for identifying changes in the universalistic and particularistic elements of the four societies' concepts of citizenship that have never been as clear-cut as the long historiographical prevalence of the models of ethnic and civic nationalism have drafted in the past.[75]

Sarah Panter is research associate at the Leibniz Institute of European History in Mainz. She studied Modern History and Political Science at the University of Freiburg and the University of Michigan, Ann Arbor. In 2013, she received her Ph.D. from the University of Freiburg. Her publications include her first book, *Jüdische Erfahrungen und Loyalitätskonflikte im Ersten Weltkrieg*, which was published by Vandenhoeck & Ruprecht in 2014, and, as guest editor, *European History Yearbook: Mobility and Biography* (vol. 16, 2015). Her research interests focus on modern Jewish history in Europe and the United States, and, more recently, on the transnational lives of exiles from the revolutions of 1848–49.

Notes

1. On Greenberg, who had been born into an orthodox family in Birmingham in 1861, but later started to sympathize with Zionist aspirations, see "Greenberg, Leopold Jacob," in *The Palgrave Dictionary of Anglo-Jewish History*, ed. William D. Rubinstein, Michael A. Jolles, and Hillary L. Rubinstein (Basingstoke, 2011), 372.
2. "Jew and German: A Protest against Unfair Suspicion," *The Times*, 15 August 1914, 3.
3. For an in-depth analysis of this dilemma, see Sarah Panter, *Jüdische Erfahrungen und Loyalitätskonflikte im Ersten Weltkrieg* (Göttingen, 2014).
4. The experiences of minorities during the First World War have just recently gained more interest. See Santanu Das, ed., *Race, Empire and First World War Writing* (Cambridge, 2011); Hannah Ewence and Tim Grady, eds., *Minorities during the First World War: From War to Peace* (Basingstoke, 2017).
5. Panikos Panayi, ed., *Germans as Minorities during the First World War: A Global Comparative Perspective* (Farnham, 2014).
6. Stefan Manz, *Constructing a German Diaspora: The Greater German Empire, 1871–1914* (New York, 2014); H. Glenn Penny and Stefan Rinke, eds., *Germans Abroad: Respatializing Historical Narrative* (Göttingen, 2015).
7. Daniela L. Caglioti, ed., *Aliens and Internal Enemies during the First World War* (Munich, 2014).
8. On the concept of situational ethnicity and its application to German Jewish identities, see Till van Rahden, *Jews and Other Germans: Civil Society, Religious Diversity, and Urban Politics in Breslau, 1860–1925* (Madison, 2008).
9. David Biale, Michael Galchinsky, and Susannah Heschel, "Introduction: The Dialectic of Jewish Enlightenment," in *Insider/Outsider: American Jews*

and Multiculturalism, ed. David Biale, Michael Galchinsky, and Susannah Heschel (Berkeley, 1998), 1–16; Pierre Birnbaum and Ira Katznelson, eds., *Paths of Emancipation: Jews, States, and Citizenship* (Princeton, 1995). For an intense discussion on the issue of which parameters are apt for a comparison between Europe and the US, see David Sorkin, "Is American Jewry Exceptional? Comparing Jewish Emancipation in Europe and America," *American Jewish History* 96, no. 3 (2010): 175–200.
10. On the relationship between identity and difference, see Rogers Brubaker, *Grounds for Difference* (Cambridge, MA, 2015).
11. On the different immigration waves to the US, see Hasia R. Diner, *The Jews of the United States: 1654 to 2000* (Berkeley, 2004), 78–83; and more recently, Tobias Brinkmann, "'German Jews'? Reassessing the History of Nineteenth-Century Jewish Immigrants in the United States," in *Transnational Traditions: New Perspectives on American Jewry*, ed. Ava F. Kahn and Adam D. Mendelsohn (Detroit, 2014), 144–64.
12. David Cesarani, "An Embattled Minority: The Jews in Britain during the First World War," *Immigrants & Minorities* 8 (1989): 61–81; Sam Johnson, *Pogroms, Peasants, Jews: Britain and Eastern Europe's "Jewish Question", 1867–1925* (Basingstoke, 2011), 1–15.
13. "The War," *Jewish Chronicle*, 7 August 1914, 5.
14. "The War: A Warning to the Public," *Jewish Chronicle*, 7 August 1914, 6.
15. "Wider Aspects," *Jewish World*, 30 September 1914, 4.
16. For further discussion of Anglo-Jewry's ambivalent relationship to Russia during the war, see Panter, *Jüdische Erfahrungen*, 66–70, 131–39, and 213–26.
17. "In the Communal Armchair. The Goal of War. A Voice in the Wilderness," *Jewish Chronicle*, 21 August 1914, 7. On the intensity of anti-German sentiment during the first weeks of the war in Britain, see Panikos Panayi, *The Enemy in Our Midst: Germans in Britain during the First World War* (London, 1991), 70–74.
18. Matthew Stibbe, *German Anglophobia and the Great War, 1914–1918* (Cambridge, 2001).
19. Diary, Summer 1914, pp. 28–30, Box 12, Fol. 7, MS-41, American Jewish Archives (AJA). Rosenau was born in 1865 in Prussian Wollstein (today Wolsztyn in Poland) and emigrated with his family to the US in 1876, where he became a famous Reform rabbi later in his life.
20. "Jews in England Charged with German Sympathies," *American Hebrew*, 21 August 1914, 430; "Jews Mistaken for Germans," *American Israelite*, 27 August 1914, 3; "South Wales: Germans and Jews Again," *Jewish World*, 21 October 1914, 3. For a general overview, including the situation of Eastern European Jews, see Severin Adam Hochberg, "The Jewish Community and the Aliens Question in Great Britain, 1881–1917" (Ph.D. dissertation, New York University, 1989), 263–319.
21. Sharman Kadish, *Bolsheviks and British Jews: The Anglo-Jewish Community, Britain, and the Russian Revolution* (London, 1992).
22. Eugene C. Black, *The Social Politics of Anglo-Jewry, 1880–1920* (Oxford, 1988), 322.

23. Colin Holmes, "Immigrants and Refugees in Britain," in *Second Chance: Two Centuries of German-Speaking Jews in the United Kingdom*, ed. Werner E. Mosse and Julius Carlebach (Tübingen, 1991), 26–27.
24. Panter, *Jüdische Erfahrungen*, 77–81.
25. Joseph Rappaport, *Hands across the Sea: Jewish Immigrants and World War I* (Lanham, MD, 2005); Gennady Estraikh, "American Yiddish Socialists at the Wartime Crossroads: Patriotism and Nationalism versus Proletarian Internationalism," in *World War I and the Jews: Conflict and Transformation in Europe, the Middle East, and America*, ed. Marsha L. Rozenblit and Jonathan Karp (New York, 2017), 279–302.
26. On the situation of German Americans during the war, see Tammy M. Proctor, "'Patriotic Enemies': Germans in the Americas, 1914–1920," in Panayi, *Germans as Minorities*, 213–34.
27. "The War in Europe," *American Hebrew*, 7 August 1914, 388.
28. For such an argumentation, see "The Teuton against the Slav," *American Hebrew*, 14 August 1914, 403; "The Feeling against Germany," *American Hebrew*, 14 August 1914, 412.
29. "Neutrality," *Jewish Criterion*, 23 October 1914, 3; L. Marshall to J. Schiff, 30 December 1914, p. 2, Box 439, Fol. 1, MS-456, AJA; J. L. Magnes to L. Brandeis, 7 December 1914, A138, Fol. 16, Central Zionist Archives Jerusalem (CZA); Confidential Letter by Louis Lipsky (undated), Box 1, Fol. 10, MS-127, AJA.
30. "Gottheil, Gustave" and "Gottheil, Richard James Horatio," in *The Concise Dictionary of American Jewish Biography*, ed. Jacob Rader Marcus and Judith M. Daniels (Brooklyn, NY, 1994), 224.
31. Daniel Greene, *The Jewish Origins of Cultural Pluralism: The Menorah Association and American Diversity* (Bloomington, 2011).
32. R. Gottheil to H. Kallen, 19 October 1914, Box 12, Fol. 1, MS-1, AJA.
33. L. Marshall to J. Schiff, 20 April 1917, p. 2, Box 454, Fol. 2, MS-456, AJA. This pertained mainly, however, to Eastern European Jewish immigrants, whose public statements were much more critical. See "Censorship of Yiddish Press," *American Hebrew*, 19 October 1917, 663; Alexander Trachtenberg, ed., *The American Socialists and the War: A Documentary History of the Attitude of the Socialist Party toward War and Militarism since the Outbreak of the Great War* (New York, 1917), 45.
34. "The Month: America Declares Itself," *Maccabaean*, April 1917, 193. The same enthusiasm was voiced by liberal-integrationist as well as orthodox Jews. See "The Response of the Orthodox Jew to the Call of the President," *Jewish Criterion*, 27 April 1917, 10–11; "The War for Peace," *American Hebrew*, 6 April 1917, 726.
35. W. E. Mosher to F. Warburg, 1 February 1918, "League of American Citizenship. The Purpose," Box 176, Fol. 8, MS-457, AJA; F. Warburg to W. E. Mosher, 6 February 1918, p. 2, Box 176, Fol. 8, MS-457, AJA.
36. See "biographical sketch" in American Jews Archives, ed., *A Finding Aid to the Gotthard Deutsch Papers (1881–1921). Manuscript Collection No. 123*, http://collections.americanjewisharchives.org/ms/ms0123/ms0123.html (accessed 28 June 2018).

37. L. Marshall to E. Heinsheimer, 7 December 1917, p. 6, Box 454, Fol. 2, MS-456, AJA.
38. "The Spy Suspect," *Jewish World*, 17 April 1918, 11 [Reprinted from the *Hebrew Standard*].
39. "Als Deutsche und als Juden," *Allgemeine Zeitung des Judentums*, 28 August 1914, 409–10.
40. "Die Weile des Zornes und das große Erbarmen," *Israelit*, 13 August 1914, 1; "Der gesetzestreue Jude und der Krieg," *Jeschurun*, November 1914, 388.
41. "Reichstreue und Volkstreue," *Jüdische Rundschau*, 16 October 1914, 387.
42. "Krieg und Kultur," *Ost und West*, September–December 1914, 663–64. The author has translated all German quotes in this chapter. Emphasis in the original.
43. For the importance of Eastern Europe as a mental map of German Jewry, see Sarah Panter, "Zwischen Nationalstaat und multiethnischem Empire: Die Aushandlung jüdischer Selbstverortungen während des Ersten Weltkriegs," in *Kulturelle Souveränität: Politische Deutungs- und Handlungsmacht jenseits des Staates im 20. Jahrhundert*, ed. Gregor Feindt, Bernhard Gißibl, and Johannes Paulmann (Göttingen, 2017), 85–93.
44. On the overlapping of these two aspects, see Sarah Panter, "Between Friends and Enemies: The Dilemma of Jews in the Final Stages of the War," in Ewence and Grady, *Minorities during the First World War*, 63–87.
45. On this generational shift within German Zionism during the war, see Stefan Vogt, *Subalterne Positionierungen: Der deutsche Zionismus im Feld des Nationalismus in Deutschland, 1890–1933* (Göttingen, 2016), 197–252.
46. "Die Ostjudenfrage I," *Ost und West*, February–March, 1916, 83. Emphasis in the original.
47. "Neuorientierung in der Judenfrage?," *Im deutschen Reich*, March 1917, 110.
48. Michael Brenner, *The Renaissance of Jewish Culture in Weimar Germany* (New Haven, CT, 1996), 37.
49. Franz Oppenheimer, "Stammesbewusstsein und Volksbewusstsein," *Die Welt*, 18 February 1910, 139–43. This has been discussed in more detail by Till van Rahden, "Germans of the Jewish Stamm: Visions of Community between Nationalism and Particularism, 1850 to 1933," in *German History from the Margins*, ed. Neil Gregor, Nils Roemer, and Mark Roseman (Bloomington, 2006), 27–48.
50. "Die Rassen-Legende," *Im deutschen Reich*, April 1917, 149.
51. Hermann Cohen, "Deutschtum und Judentum," in *Hermann Cohen: Kleinere Schriften*, Vol. 6, ed. Hartwig Wiedebach and Helmut Holzhey (Hildesheim, 2002), 109–32.
52. "Deutschtum und Judentum," *Im deutschen Reich*, April 1917, 168. Emphasis in the original. Two years earlier, Felix Goldmann had published a critical comment on the recurring discourse of a discriminatory, anti-Jewish immigration policy. See "Deutschland und die Ostjudenfrage," *Im deutschen Reich*, October–November 1915, 200.
53. "Glaube und Heimat," *Neue Jüdische Monatshefte*, 25 August 1917, 632.

54. For one of the most nuanced accounts on the empowerment of Zionism during the war to date, see Michael Berkowitz, *Western Jewry and the Zionist Project, 1914–1933* (Cambridge, 1997), 7–25.
55. On the clash between German Jews and Eastern European Jews regarding the future collective self-assertion of Jews in Poland that concerned not only Zionists but also orthodox Jews, see Tobias Grill, "The Politicisation of Traditional Polish Jewry: Orthodox German Rabbis and the Founding of Agudas Ho-Ortodoksim and Dos Yidishe Vort in Gouvernement-General Warsaw, 1916–18," *East European Jewish Affairs* 39 (2009): 227–47.
56. "Die Erstarkung des Zionismus," *Jüdische Rundschau*, 22 June 1917, 206.
57. "Der Kaiser ruft!," *Österreichische Wochenschrift*, 31 July 1914 [no page number]; "An Meine Völker!," *Wiener Zeitung*, 29 July 1914, 1. On the general importance of dynastic loyalty for Austrian Jews, see David Rechter, "Kaisertreu: The Dynastic Loyalty of Austrian Jewry," in *Jüdische Identitäten: Einblicke in die Bewußtseinslandschaft des österreichischen Judentums*, ed. Klaus Hödl (Innsbruck, 2000), 189–208.
58. "Aufruf der IKG Wien zum Kriegsausbruch," 29 July 1914, p. 1, A/W 357, 2, Central Archives for the History of the Jewish People (CAHJP), Jerusalem.
59. "Krieg!," *Jüdische Volksstimme*, 30 July 1914, 1.
60. Marsha L. Rozenblit, *Reconstructing a National Identity: The Jews of Habsburg Austria during World War I* (Oxford, 2001), 3.
61. See David Rechter, *The Jews of Vienna and the First World War* (London, 2001).
62. Evelyn Adunka, "Der ostjüdische Einfluss auf Wien," in *Ist jetzt hier die "wahre Heimat"? Ostjüdische Einwanderung nach Wien*, ed. Peter Bettelheim and Michael Ley (Vienna, 1993), 78.
63. Panter, *Jüdische Erfahrungen*, 171–77.
64. "Die galizischen Flüchtlinge und die Wiener Kultusgemeinde," *Jüdische Zeitung*, 9 October 1914, 1.
65. "Schreiben an die IKG Wien," 9 September 1914, A/W 357, 1, CAHJP.
66. For a thorough transnational contextualization of the relationship between Jews and the military since 1800 that opens up the perspective for similarities and differences around the globe, see Derek Penslar, *Jews and the Military: A History* (Princeton, NJ, 2013).
67. "Korrespondenzen. Offenes Schreiben an die Führer der österreichischen Judenschaft in Wien," *Österreichische Wochenschrift*, 9 November 1917, 708.
68. Ibid. Emphasis in the original.
69. Ibid.
70. "Feldpostbrief eines jüdischen Militärseelsorgers," *Österreichische Wochenschrift*, 16 April 1915, 289.
71. Rozenblit, *Reconstructing a National Identity*, 98–101.
72. R. Faerber, "Unsere israelitische Militärseelsorge," *Hickls jüdischer Volkskalender für das Jahr 5678* (1917–18): 46.
73. "Stenographisches Protokoll. Haus der Abgeordneten, 21. Sitzung," 15 July 1917, p. 1151, http://alex.onb.ac.at/cgi-content/alex?aid=spa&datum=0022&size=54&page=2109 (accessed 6 December 2016); "Die Zensur

der mit hebräischen Schriftcharakteren geschriebenen Schriftstücke," *Österreichische Wochenschrift*, 11 January 1918, 20–21.
74. On the changing concept of citizenship in 1918–19, see Ulrike von Hirschhausen, "From Imperial Inclusion to National Exclusion: Citizenship in the Habsburg Monarchy and in Austria, 1867–1923," *European Review of History* 16 (2009): 560–62.
75. See, for such a critical perspective from a general point of view, in particular, Rogers Brubaker, *Ethnicity without Groups* (Cambridge, MA, 2004), 132–46.

Bibliography

Adunka, Evelyn. "Der ostjüdische Einfluss auf Wien." In *Ist jetzt hier die "wahre Heimat"? Ostjüdische Einwanderung nach Wien*, edited by Peter Bettelheim and Michael Ley, 77–88. Vienna: Picus Verlag, 1993.
Berkowitz, Michael. *Western Jewry and the Zionist Project, 1914–1933*. Cambridge: Cambridge University Press, 1997.
Biale, David, Michael Galchinsky, and Susannah Heschel. "Introduction: The Dialectic of Jewish Enlightenment." In *Insider/Outsider: American Jews and Multiculturalism*, edited by David Biale, Michael Galchinsky, and Susannah Heschel, 1–16. Berkeley: University of California Press, 1998.
Birnbaum, Pierre, and Ira Katznelson, eds. *Paths of Emancipation: Jews, States, and Citizenship*. Princeton, NJ: Princeton University Press, 1995.
Black, Eugene C. *The Social Politics of Anglo-Jewry, 1880–1920*. Oxford: Basil Blackwell, 1988.
Brenner, Michael. *The Renaissance of Jewish Culture in Weimar Germany*. New Haven, CT: Yale University Press, 1996.
Brinkmann, Tobias. "'German Jews'? Reassessing the History of Nineteenth-Century Jewish Immigrants in the United States." In *Transnational Traditions: New Perspectives on American Jewry*, edited by Ava F. Kahn and Adam D. Mendelsohn, 144–64. Detroit: Wayne State University Press, 2014.
Brubaker, Rogers. *Ethnicity without Groups*. Cambridge, MA: Harvard University Press, 2004.
———. *Grounds for Difference*. Cambridge, MA: Harvard University Press, 2015.
Caglioti, Daniela L., ed. *Aliens and Internal Enemies during the First World War*. Munich: C. H. Beck Verlag, 2014.
Cesarani, David. "An Embattled Minority: The Jews in Britain during the First World War." *Immigrants & Minorities* 8 (1989): 61–81.
Cohen, Hermann. "Deutschtum und Judentum." In *Hermann Cohen: Kleinere Schriften*, Vol. 6, edited by Hartwig Wiedebach and Helmut Holzhey, 109–32. Hildesheim: Georg Olms, 2002.
Das, Santanu, ed. *Race, Empire and First World War Writing*. Cambridge: Cambridge University Press, 2011.
Diner, Hasia R. *The Jews of the United States: 1654 to 2000*. Berkeley: University of California Press, 2004.

Endelman, Todd M. *The Jews of Britain: 1656 to 2000*. Berkeley: University of California Press, 2000.

Estraikh, Gennady. "American Yiddish Socialists at the Wartime Crossroads: Patriotism and Nationalism versus Proletarian Internationalism." In *World War I and the Jews: Conflict and Transformation in Europe, the Middle East, and America*, edited by Marsha L. Rozenblit and Jonathan Karp, 279–302. New York: Berghahn Books, 2017.

Ewence, Hannah, and Tim Grady, eds. *Minorities during the First World War: From War to Peace*. Basingstoke: Palgrave Macmillan, 2017.

"Gottheil, Gustave" and "Gottheil, Richard James Horatio." In *The Concise Dictionary of American Jewish Biography*, edited by Jacob Rader Marcus and Judith M. Daniels, 224. Brooklyn, NY: Carlson Publishers, 1994.

"Greenberg, Leopold Jacob." In *The Palgrave Dictionary of Anglo-Jewish History*, edited by William D. Rubinstein, Michael A. Jolles, and Hillary L. Rubinstein, 372. Basingstoke: Palgrave Macmillan, 2011.

Greene, Daniel. *The Jewish Origins of Cultural Pluralism: The Menorah Association and American Diversity*. Bloomington: Indiana University Press, 2011.

Grill, Tobias. "The Politicisation of Traditional Polish Jewry: Orthodox German Rabbis and the Founding of Agudas Ho-Ortodoksim and Dos Yidishe Vort in Gouvernement-General Warsaw, 1916–18." *East European Jewish Affairs* 39 (2009): 227–47.

Haas, Theodor. "Die Ergebnisse der Volkszählung vom 31. Dezember 1910 und die jüdische Bevölkerung in Oesterreich." *Zeitschrift für Demographie und Statistik der Juden* 12 (1912): 143–149.

Hirschhausen, Ulrike von. "From Imperial Inclusion to National Exclusion: Citizenship in the Habsburg Monarchy and in Austria, 1867–1923." *European Review of History* 16 (2009): 551–73.

Hochberg, Severin Adam. "The Jewish Community and the Aliens Question in Great Britain, 1881–1917." Ph.D. dissertation, New York University, 1989.

Holmes, Colin. "Immigrants and Refugees in Britain." In *Second Chance: Two Centuries of German-Speaking Jews in the United Kingdom*, edited by Werner E. Mosse and Julius Carlebach, 11–30. Tübingen: Mohr Siebeck, 1991.

Johnson, Sam. *Pogroms, Peasants, Jews: Britain and Eastern Europe's "Jewish Question", 1867–1925*. Basingstoke: Palgrave Macmillan, 2011.

Kadish, Sharman. *Bolsheviks and British Jews: The Anglo-Jewish Community, Britain, and the Russian Revolution*. London: Routledge, 1992.

Manz, Stefan. *Constructing a German Diaspora: The Greater German Empire, 1871–1914*. New York: Routledge, 2014.

Panayi, Panikos. *The Enemy in Our Midst: Germans in Britain during the First World War*. London: Bloomsbury, 1991.

——— , ed. *Germans as Minorities during the First World War: A Global Comparative Perspective*. Farnham: Ashgate, 2014.

Panter, Sarah. *Jüdische Erfahrungen und Loyalitätskonflikte im Ersten Weltkrieg*. Göttingen: Vandenhoeck & Ruprecht, 2014.

——— . "Zwischen Nationalstaat und multiethnischem Empire: Die Aushandlung jüdischer Selbstverortungen während des Ersten Weltkriegs." In *Kulturelle Souveränität: Politische Deutungs- und Handlungsmacht jenseits des*

Staates im 20. Jahrhundert, edited by Gregor Feindt, Bernhard Gißibl, and Johannes Paulmann, 79–106. Göttingen: Vandenhoeck & Ruprecht, 2017.

———. "Between Friends and Enemies: The Dilemma of Jews in the Final Stages of the War." In *Minorities during the First World War: From War to Peace*, edited by Hannah Ewence and Tim Grady, 63–87. Basingstoke: Palgrave Macmillan, 2017.

Penny, Glenn H., and Stefan Rinke, eds. *Germans Abroad: Respatializing Historical Narrative*. Göttingen: Vandenhoeck & Ruprecht, 2015.

Penslar, Derek. *Jews and the Military: A History*. Princeton, NJ: Princeton University Press, 2013.

Proctor, Tammy M. "'Patriotic Enemies': Germans in the Americas, 1914–1920." In *Germans as Minorities during the First World War: A Global Comparative Perspective*, edited by Panikos Panayi, 213–34. Farnham: Ashgate, 2014.

Rahden, Till van. "Germans of the Jewish Stamm: Visions of Community between Nationalism and Particularism, 1850 to 1933." In *German History from the Margins*, edited by Neil Gregor, Nils Roemer, and Mark Roseman, 27–48. Bloomington: Indiana University Press, 2006.

———. *Jews and Other Germans: Civil Society, Religious Diversity, and Urban Politics in Breslau, 1860–1925*. Madison: University of Wisconsin Press, 2008.

Rappaport, Joseph. *Hands across the Sea: Jewish Immigrants and World War I*. Lanham, MD: Hamilton Books, 2005.

Rechter, David. "Kaisertreu: The Dynastic Loyalty of Austrian Jewry." In *Jüdische Identitäten: Einblicke in die Bewußtseinslandschaft des österreichischen Judentums*, edited by Klaus Hödl, 189–208. Innsbruck: Studien Verlag, 2000.

———. *The Jews of Vienna and the First World War*. London: Littman Library of Jewish Civilization, 2001.

Rozenblit, Marsha L. *Reconstructing a National Identity: The Jews of Habsburg Austria during World War I*. Oxford: Oxford University Press, 2001.

Sorkin, David. "Is American Jewry Exceptional? Comparing Jewish Emancipation in Europe and America." *American Jewish History* 96, no. 3 (2010): 175–200.

Stibbe, Matthew. *German Anglophobia and the Great War, 1914–1918*. Cambridge: Cambridge University Press, 2001.

Trachtenberg, Alexander, ed. *The American Socialists and the War: A Documentary History of the Attitude of the Socialist Party toward War and Militarism since the Outbreak of the Great War*. New York: Leopold, 1917.

Vogt, Stefan. *Subalterne Positionierungen: Der deutsche Zionismus im Feld des Nationalismus in Deutschland, 1890–1933*. Göttingen: Vandenhoeck & Ruprecht, 2016.

Wertheimer, Jack. "'The Unwanted Element': East European Jews in Imperial Germany." *Leo Baeck Institute Year Book* 26 (1981): 32–46.

6

IN THE SHADOW OF ANTISEMITISM
Jewish Women and the German Home Front during the First World War

Andrea A. Sinn

The memory of the First World War, though hazy for many, still concerns families as well as nations as a whole. Family history searches turn up great-grandfathers who died very young in some corner of a foreign field; wartime poetry has embedded itself in our collective consciousness; and if nothing else, the centenary of the outbreak of the Great War returns our attention to this bloody conflict of unprecedented scale. Until the 1960s, scholarly research on the First World War tended to focus on questions regarding the conflict's political dimensions. These studies were followed by social and later cultural histories, which examined diverse facets of this war that completely transformed the map, cultures, politics, and mentalities of Europe. Traditionally, the history of the Great War is told from the vantage point of men, and despite the increase in scholarship on this topic, the number of studies highlighting female and minority perspectives within the German context is still surprisingly small.[1] In fact, it is only fairly recently that scholars writing about the First World War have shifted from discussing German Jews mainly as objects of policy to exploring male Jewish experiences. And only within the field of women's and gender history can one find a small number of pioneering studies that offer some insights into the experience of Jewish women and families in Germany between 1914 and 1918.[2]

To further advance our understanding of this chapter of German Jewish history, this chapter provides an introduction to the historiography of the several past decades and stresses the gendered nature of

German Jewish wartime experiences. Underlying the analysis here is the assumption that the war created an atmosphere of change that not only affected (Jewish) men but also impelled (Jewish) women to act. Some women decided to accept roles that directly aided the military.[3] However, the great majority of Jewish women, just like their gentile counterparts, made significant contributions to their home societies. They maintained their domestic and familial roles while also taking on "a variety of challenging tasks that made them a vital, active part of the wartime nations."[4] It is therefore crucial that we include women's perspectives in our analyses, in order to more comprehensively portray the complex wartime realities of the German people.

In support of the argument that the wartime experience can only be fully understood if the men who sacrificed their lives as soldiers and the many women who fought on the home front are both included, this chapter introduces a small sample of Jewish women's perspectives which have not become an integral part of the (Jewish) memory of the First World War. Additionally, the well-known linear narrative that portrays the German Jewish wartime experience as one that was dominated by antisemitism,[5] most notably symbolized by the infamous *Judenzählung* or "Jew Count" of 1916, is challenged. As will be shown below, a close reading of Jewish women's autobiographical texts suggests that the war created, at times, new opportunities for Jewish integration—with women as the notable instigators. This discussion also reveals that the way in which the war is remembered often does not reflect the gendered nature of the war experience. On the contrary, existing scholarship largely promotes a culture of memory that was formed alongside religious lines, and considers gender differences only secondarily. Presenting a sample of Jewish women's autobiographical writings, this chapter provides an example of how gendering existing narratives may offer new and more inclusive perspectives on often overlooked issues concerning the interplay of gender, religion, ethnicity, politics, and war.

More than Objects of German Policy

For a long time, scholars discussing the position that Jews occupied within Germany during the First World War focused on three particular critical moments for the Jews within Germany: the emperor's *Burgfrieden* of 1914 (known as the "civil truce"); the Military High Command's "Jew Count" of 1916; and the Prussian government's *Grenzsperre* or barrier of Germany's eastern border for Jewish immigration in 1918.[6] It is only fairly recently that scholars writing about the First World War have shifted away from discussing German Jews mainly as objects of policy. Studies published after the late 1980s reflect a new trend. They introduce German Jews as participants in the war effort and focus particularly on Jewish organizations, Jews who served in the military, and male Jewish intellectuals who tried to incorporate the new situation into their worldview.[7]

The great wave of patriotism that engulfed the nation when war broke out in August 1914 is legendary and was nostalgically recalled during the Weimar Republic. While a range of political, religious, ethnic, and social tensions affected Germany and its party politics at the beginning of the twentieth century, the "spirit of 1914"—the alleged jubilation at the outbreak of the First World War—was a powerful emotion that temporarily helped to hide the bitter divisions in German society.[8] Most notably, the German Emperor Wilhelm II's speech of 1 August 1914, in which he declared, "I no longer recognize any parties or any confessions; today we are all German brothers and only German brothers," received high publicity and supposedly put an end to internal divisions.[9] Certainly, not all Germans were convinced by such announcements. Many, however, particularly in the middle class, believed that Germany had ended its decades of bitter domestic political conflict. After the proclamation of the *Burgfrieden*, much of the preceding discrimination against Jews, especially pertaining to restrictions on positions in state service, disappeared, at least for the moment. Jewish businessmen, scientists, and academics were invited to serve their country in positions of responsibility and trust, within a number of governmental offices and agencies. Jews serving in the military were finally able to rise to the rank of officer.[10]

Historians like Peter Pulzer and Paul Mendes-Flohr agree that Germany's Jews—who had been excluded and discriminated against for many centuries—greeted the war with euphoria, and saw it as their first real opportunity since emancipation in 1871 to prove their loyalty and make the ultimate sacrifice for their country.[11] As part of their argument, they refer to the main pillars of German Jewish institutional life, which—as historian Tim Grady has put it—"willingly aligned themselves in support of the war, not out of some misplaced sense of obligation but because they were actually patriots."[12] The Centralverein deutscher Staatsbürger jüdischen Glaubens (CV), the most significant Jewish organization in Imperial Germany, founded in 1893, and the Zionistische Vereinigung für Deutschland (ZVfD), which up to that point had focused on attacking the non-Zionist establishment for their policy of assimilation, both supported the statement "that every German Jew is ready to sacrifice property and blood as duty demands."[13] They each called on their supporters "to give yourself ... to serve the fatherland."[14] Powerful declarations of support were also published by German rabbis.[15]

This conviction was shared by another organization, the Jüdischer Frauenbund (League of Jewish Women), which had been founded by Jewish suffragette Bertha Pappenheim (1859–1936)[16] in 1904 and joined the Bund Deutscher Frauenvereine (Union of German Women's Organizations, or BDF) in 1907. As historians Marion Kaplan and Martina Steer discussed in their studies addressing this association and the organization's founder, the Jüdischer Frauenbund absorbed some traditional Jewish women's charities, as well as programs that Jewish women's groups had pioneered; they also offered a feminist approach to social welfare.[17] When the war broke out, its thirty-two thousand members reflected the overwhelmingly middle-class position of German Jews. Most were housewives engaged in volunteer activities.[18] However, in 1914, many Jewish women expressed their support for the war for reasons aside from the aforementioned patriotic sentiments circulating among the Jewish minority. These Jewish women had another motivation for their willingness to make sacrifices. Together with non-Jewish emancipated women, they saw their participation as a chance to "earn" equal gender rights in German society. Thus, many Jewish women were actually fighting on two fronts. They wanted to prove to German antisemites that they were fully integrated in the society, and at the same time they sought to demonstrate their capabilities in that male-dominated world. Accordingly, the first declaration of the League of Jewish women stated: "We want to be a united nation of sisters, not dreading any hardship and danger!"[19]

Because of the war, the Jüdischer Frauenbund suspended its advocacy work and its members utilized their experiences, particularly in the fields of social work and manpower, to promote the economic survival, social cohesion, and national defense of the country. In fact, just like the other members of the BDF, women in the Jüdischer Frauenbund actively participated in the Nationaler Frauendienst (National Women's Service), founded by the head of the BDF and active participant in the German civil rights feminist movement, Gertrud Bäumer (1873–1954), on 31 July 1914. This organization comprised not only the members of the BDF (and thus both the Jüdischer Frauenbund and the Deutsch-Evangelischer Frauenbund or League of Protestant Women) but also the Katholischer Frauenbund (Catholic Women's League), trade unions, and social democratic women's organizations. These bodies were not normally associated with the Jewish and bourgeois women's movement. In this moment of national ferment, these women from diverse backgrounds expressed solidarity and set for themselves four main tasks, namely: maintaining a consistent food supply; placing jobless women in employment; offering social counselling; and providing welfare to "men-less" or destitute families.[20] Jewish women vigorously engaged in these aforementioned organizations; in addition, individuals and some groups of women participated in activities organized in accordance with local or national initiatives, and they cooperated with gentile women's groups and state institutions. One example of this is the activities of the Israelitisch-humanitärer Frauenverein (Jewish Humanitarian Women's Association) in Hamburg, founded in 1893. The roughly one thousand members of this organization established a "soup kitchen" in the so-called Logenheim at Hartungstrasse, which supported up to six hundred people in need per day, irrespective of their religious or ethnic identification.[21] Under the leadership of Sidonie Werner (1860–1932)—a dedicated teacher, feminist, co-founder of the Jüdischer Frauenbund, and member of the city's Frauenkomitee der allgemeinen Kriegshilfe (Women's Committee of War Relief)—the association increased its contributions during the war years, engaging in numerous activities to benefit children, adolescents, and women. These included the creation of a kitchen used for preserving fruit and vegetables, in which unemployed women and girls were given the opportunity to work; the creation of a sewing workshop, in which forty women produced all kinds of needlework; and the creation of a daycare center for children between the ages of eighteen months and six years.[22] Yet despite all of this activity, modern scholarship has stressed that the (alleged) social truce during the period following the outbreak of the First World War either did not actually exist, or if it was acknowledged, that it did not last very long.

Indeed, by the autumn of 1914, Jewish newspapers had begun to complain about antisemitic slanders. Denunciations then increased and grew more violent by 1916, by which time they targeted Jewish men and women alike. The reasons for this mounting antisemitic campaign are complex. One of the basic preconditions and most significant causes of the revival of intense antisemitism was undoubtedly the general deterioration of living conditions for the majority of the civilian population. Food shortages and other privations increased from month to month, causing growing segments of the German people who had ignored antisemitic propaganda before the war to become more susceptible to it. As the war dragged on, non-Jewish Germans also began to demand explanations for why the quick victory they had been promised had not materialized. Accusations emerged from antisemitic quarters (the traditional right-wing enemies of the Jews) that German military efforts had been compromised because Jews were dodging the draft and avoiding service at the front.[23] The Military High Command's "Jew Count" in October 1916 seems to have further challenged the Jewish hope that non-Jewish Germans would accept the process of Jewish acculturation and social integration.[24] Most likely, the War Ministry could not find any evidence to corroborate the accusation that Jews were shirking frontline combat. In any case, those in charge decided against publishing the results and considered the issue of the Jewish census closed in January 1917.[25]

The "Jew Count" and its aftermath created uneasiness, indignation, and deep resentment among certain groups within German Jewry.[26] According to reliable calculations, roughly 100,000 Jews wore the German military uniform; 30,000 of these were decorated; and almost 12,000 Jewish men were killed in the fighting. The number of those who fought at the front represents roughly 18 percent of the total Jewish population, which at that time was estimated at about 550,000. Given these statistics presented by the Ausschuss für Kriegsstatistik (Committee on War Statistics),[27] the Verband der deutschen Juden and also individuals such as the Hamburg banker Max Warburg tried hard to arrange a formal announcement about Jewish soldiers who were doing their duty just as faithfully as non-Jews.[28] In contrast, the League of Jewish Women remained silent, despite the fact that the "Jew Count" was a clear violation of the emperor's proclaimed *Burgfrieden*. Likewise, the Centralverein and the Zionist Organization for Germany refrained from calling for a revocation of the decree, and instead narrowed their protest to written appeals and published objections.[29]

Interestingly, for a long time scholarly researchers paid very little attention to Jewish soldiers' individual responses to the "Jew Count" of 1916. These responses actually varied greatly. Some army rabbis, for instance, reported deep despair among the Jewish troops, while others did not mention the census at all.[30] Given these findings, historian Tim Grady concludes that "in many ways the daily hardship of an ongoing war gradually superseded the controversy over the military's Jew count" and "does not suggest that the relationship between Jews and non-Jews changed significantly in late 1916."[31] This interpretation is supported by scholars such as historian Derek Penslar, who convincingly demonstrated in his most recent study on Jews and the military that the census gained significance only retroactively.[32]

A third critical moment for Jews in Germany was the decision of the Prussian government in April 1918 to impose a "border barrier" against Polish Jews.[33] The decision to restrict or prohibit Jewish immigration into Germany had been repeatedly discussed since Jewish immigration from Eastern Europe to the West had intensified during the second half of the nineteenth century. It is within the context of the antisemitic pogroms in Czarist Russia, the increasing pauperization of Jews living in regions such as Galicia, and the temptations of prosperous Western Europe that one must seek reasons that Jews were willing to leave their homes in Eastern Europe at that time. When the war broke out in 1914, Jewish migration from the East to the West certainly was nothing new; by then, it had been ongoing for more than half a century.[34] The war, which enlarged the Austrian-German controlled territory far to the east but also devastated regions with significant Jewish population centers, further increased this migration and also brought some thirty-five thousand Polish war workers and the same number of prisoners of war into the country.[35] It is within this context that nationalistic circles pushed during the war for action to be taken to prevent an alleged mass immigration of Polish Jews into Germany. The unilateral closing of the border to Jews from Eastern Europe in 1918 can be considered a result of the nationalists' efforts, following a shift in the political power balance in their favor. The distinctly antisemitic motives of this measure are clearly expressed in the wording of the order. According to the decree, "Polish-Jewish day-laborers were unwilling to work, filthy, morally unreliable ... in large part lice-infested ... particularly suitable as source of typhus and other infectious diseases."[36]

As in the past, German Jewry did not remain motionless when the Prussian government was discussing and later introduced their plans to restrict or prohibit Jewish immigration into Germany. On the contrary, they established the Vereinigung jüdischer Organizationen Deutschlands zur Wahrung der Rechte der Juden des Ostens (VjOD), or Union of German Jewish Organizations for Protecting the Rights of the Jews in the East,[37] which lodged a formal protest with the German chancellor, Count Hertling. Despite this action, in the dying days of the war the opinions and sensitivities of even the most patriotic Jews were no longer of any importance. It took the government three and a half months to reply that the measures taken "had to do with medical controls" only, which represented another indication of the unwillingness of the Central Powers to pay attention to fundamental Jewish demands. By that point, perspectives had turned full circle since the government's assumption in 1914 that Jews, inside or outside Germany, represented an interest group to be treated with respect and conciliation. According to this storyline, the Jews were disillusioned and isolated, or as Professor Franz Oppenheimer put it when commemorating the Jewish Social Democrat Ludwig Frank (who had been the first member of the Reichstag to die on the front in 1914): "Don't entertain false hopes, you are and will remain Germany's Pariah."[38]

More than Just Objects of German Antisemitism

There is no question that scholarly writing on the First World War has broadened over the course of the last several decades. In particular, analyses of Jewish male intellectuals' and Jewish soldiers' experiences, as discussed for example by historians Ulrich Sieg, Sarah Panter, Jason Crouthamel, and Gerald Lamprecht, provide a more nuanced picture of the German Jewish experience, stress the diversity of Jewish perspectives, and offer new explanations for the community's positioning.[39] These studies raise our awareness of the unique (physical, emotional, social, intellectual, and spiritual) challenges that Jewish men faced, while also demonstrating that Jewish soldiers shared a number of similar experiences with gentile Germans during the first "total war."[40] Among the three historic occasions discussed — the emperor's *Burgfrieden* policy of 1914, the Military High Command's *Judenzählung* of 1916, and the Prussian government's *Grenzsperre* of Germany's eastern border for Jewish immigration in 1918 — most scholars single out the "Jew Count" as the critical turning point in German–Jewish relations. In their view, this census was both a temporary peak in a growing wave of antisemitic attacks and an expression of a newly intensified form of racial antisemitism that set the tone for future developments and perhaps marked the beginning of the end of German-Jewish cooperation.[41]

These historians' line of argument is largely based on a first analysis of newspapers, bulletins, and military letters, and it supports the grand narrative that portrays the German Jewish wartime experience as one that was dominated by antisemitism. Moving forward, it is important to pay closer attention to the context in which these documents were created and to extend the source base of projects addressing this time period. For example, can we assume that Jewish soldiers' letters sent home from the front actually reflect wartime realities? Or should we consider these testimonies expressions of loyalty that reflect the pressure Jews felt to prove their patriotism and commitment to the fatherland? Could they be documents that tell us more about expectations and aspirations than wartime realities? A more holistic and inclusive approach to portraying German Jewish wartime experiences should also recognize women as participatory actors in the war. By examining the themes and topics addressed in female authors' writings, we may gain valuable insights into the situation on the home front and open a new line of discussion regarding the interplay of gender, politics, religion, ethnicity, and war.[42]

Ever since the debate between historians Marion Kaplan and Miriam Gebhardt regarding the scope and limitations of autobiographical source materials, scholars in the fields of German Jewish and women's and gender history have become more aware of the challenges attached to this unique body of sources. The fact that most Jewish female diarists were members of the more assimilated middle class is only one of the difficulties.[43] Currently, there seems to be a broad consensus that "the historical interpretation of ego-documents as media of subjective knowledge and truth requires sensitivity to context, awareness of human psychology, and the skill of literary analysis. Nothing in the text can be taken merely at face value; analysis must sound out the omissions, ambiguities, contradictions, and indeterminacies inherent to both the written word and ways of speaking of self and experience."[44] As studies of autobiographies have significantly increased since the year 2000, it is now even more important to pay attention to the complexities and contradictions within people's experiential histories. The many popular genres of contemporary life narrative include online presentations and graphic memoirs, film and video records, and even installation art. In this context, it is crucial to understand "autobiographical occasions as dynamic sites for the performance of identities that are constructive of subjectivity"; these must be analyzed, as gender theorist Judith Butler has stressed, with consideration for the subject's "embeddedness in social conditions, its engagement with others, and its recourse to cultural norms of narration in telling the story of itself."[45] Despite plausible reservations about the use of ego-documents—not least because of the genre's mixture of "fact" and "fiction" and the autobiographical subject's tendency to reflect norms of life narration while externalizing themselves—both contemporary and retrospective sources present authentic voices and reveal psychological facts that can be used to offer important contributions to social history generally, and to gender-specific studies particularly. With regard to the First World War, they can provide insights into what dilemmas Jewish women faced during the years of the war and remembered later on. Do the reports and descriptions of these predominantly middle-class writers support the large Jewish associations' positions, or existing scholarly interpretations of the period that are based mainly on male writings? What are the themes that Jewish women address in their writings? And do their individual accounts differ from those of their male counterparts, and if so, in what ways?

When she was thirty-eight years old, Jenny Hirsch (born 1876) used the back pages of a booklet in which her affluent family's silver possessions had been cataloged over the centuries to address developments that took place between 1 August 1914 and the 1918/19 revolutions in Germany.[46] A number of very impersonal, general sentences describing the sequence of events leading to the German involvement in the First World War mark the beginning of the handwritten German-language journal. This mother of two goes on to describe at length the mobilization in her hometown, Frankfurt am Main, and how the local women went to the train stations to support those who were leaving for the front by handing out charitable donations. She later reported that as the war went on, women like her started knitting for those serving on the front, and at the same time they set up soup kitchens and other support systems for those whose providers were fighting far away from home.[47] These introductory remarks mirror patriotic sentiments that were supposedly prevalent within the broader German population at the outbreak of the war. The *Burgfrieden* policy of the German emperor seems to have molded not only her political discourse, but also this writer's autobiographical work. A majority of the thirty-nine pages in her journal are, however, dedicated to detailed explanations regarding the rising food prices and decreasing food rations. Interestingly, the positive and negative changes that she mentioned are often linked to German military successes or losses—as when she stated in December of 1916 that, "We Germans conquered lots of territory and consequently also a lot of crops."[48] The author's Jewish upbringing, religion, and heritage are not mentioned in any part of the journal, which above all emphasizes the themes of patriotism, social diversity, and wartime solidarity. These thematic priorities may serve as an initial indicator of the impact that the declaration of war and the establishment of a political and social *Burgfrieden* had on bourgeois women. These seem to have shaped their consciousness, just as they affected men's perceptions. Yet it is important to emphasize that detailed descriptions of women's wartime efforts at home, which can be found in many contemporary narratives and resemble each other in some ways (like their male counterparts' reflections about everyday life for a soldier on the front), are (despite being central) only one component of these personal reflections. Aside from that, many female authors dedicated a large portion of their writing to reflections about their personal situations, love lives, grave concerns about the fate of loved ones fighting at the front,[49] and raising children; occasionally they also included questioning of their religion.

Another example of this type of autobiographical writing is the diary of the feminist Jenny Wieruszowski (1866–1919), whom Marion Kaplan labeled a promoter of a modern concept of motherhood.[50] She kept a diary between the years 1894 and 1918, in which she provided many details of the domestic life of her family; offered portraits of her young daughters Marie, Helene, Clara, Lilli, and Ruth, and her son who had died at the age of three months in 1892; and reflected—within this context—on her child-rearing practices. From 1884, she was married to Judge Alfred Ludwig Wieruszowski (1857–1945). The couple lived in Cologne and raised their children in the Protestant faith. Both advocated for the establishment of a girl's high school in their home city, which was realized in 1903. In addition, Jenny Wieruszowski was actively involved in the board of the Allgemeiner Deutscher Frauenverein (General German Women's Association, or ADF), an organization that was seriously committed to the promotion of education in support of women as well as to equality in study opportunities,[51] and at the outbreak of the First World War, she headed the youth group of this organization in Cologne.[52]

Aside from descriptions of birthdays, Christmas celebrations, outings, and vacations, she reflected in detail on her children's reactions to the war. Her children grew up with soldiers around them, Jenny Wieruszowski reported, and soon even her youngest daughter Ruth (1910–1993) seemed to have adapted to the new situation.

> Every soldier was her friend. ... Her patriotism is unlimited. She is aware of everything, when it comes to the "enemies"; [she] knows all flags, the pictures of counts and generals—in short, she lives and moves completely in the spirit .... After I had taken Ruth to the military hospital one day, she wanted to come along every time I went. Even the sickest was delighted to see her, and she ran from one to the other, handed out cigarettes, did not forget anyone, and knew exactly to whom she had given his share already. ... Whether all of these impressions and the feelings of hatred against England will live on in her heart—who knows.[53]

Due to the war, the youngest daughter grew up in an environment that differed significantly from the one her sisters remembered as part of their childhood. According to Wieruszowski, the deprivations of the ongoing war and ill health presented serious challenges for the family and forced the youngest to become independent at a very young age.[54] Her mother worried that being surrounded by "sad faces" could impact Ruth's happy character in a negative way. This concern might explain why she paid close attention to her behavior and noticed that Ruth adopted faith as a coping mechanism, particularly towards the end of the war, when the situation had taken a turn for the worse.

> Rarely am I in the mood to continue writing in this notebook; these are terrible and sad times. And yet it is a shame that Ruth's development is

not portrayed here comparably to the growth of the other children. ... She read and listened to Biblical stories with great enthusiasm; she was consumed by it and asked her sister Leni to tell her everything about Egypt. She is religious in some strangely silent and discrete way that is quite odd for such a young and otherwise very childish girl. For some time now, she wished to pray by herself—she does it half-loud, so that no one can understand anything. If one happens to disturb her, by chance, she loses all control of herself.[55]

Baptized as a child, Ruth returned to Judaism in 1936, just two years before she emigrated to Palestine in 1938. Regardless of whether they thought of themselves as Jews or not, she and her sisters (of whom one became Catholic, another one atheist, and only the fourth remained Protestant) had been considered Jews in accordance with the Nuremberg Laws, which the Nazi regime passed in 1935. This legislation, which provided a legal definition identifying Jews not by religious affiliation but according to racial antisemitism, officially excluded Jews from German citizenship while at the same time limited their rights as members of society. The experience of being persecuted not for what they believed, but for who they—or their parents—were by birth caused many, including Ruth and her sisters, to re-examine both their ideas about religion and the balance between their own identity and the question of belonging.

Not surprisingly, Jewish women's diaries differ significantly in length and style, but their tone overall is informal and the content often contains raw expressions of emotion. During the First World War and during the later years of the war in particular, the importance of religion in general and belief in particular appears to surface in these contemporary accounts mainly when the authors discuss the celebration of holidays, or describe events like weddings and funerals, or when they reflect about their personal searches for meaning in life. The latter pursuit seems to have been a particularly important motivation for German Jewish female authors who were born at the turn of the century and decided to write a memoir following their experiences of discrimination, exclusion, and persecution in Nazi Germany. In the years following the Holocaust, German Jewish emigrants and survivors of the concentration and extermination camps were surrounded by, and at times actively involved in, discussions concerning the reconstruction and re-establishment of Jewish life and culture. In addition, they faced the daunting task of making sense of what had happened and redefining their own identities in the wake of the Holocaust.

One example of this rather comprehensive interpretive approach can be found in the memoir of Mally Dienemann (1883–1963), the daughter of a well-to-do merchant. She decided to type her personal recollections after arriving with her family in Palestine in 1939.[56] She described in detail her childhood, the family's assimilation in Gollub, West Prussia (on the border of the Polish-Russian town Dobrzyn) where she was enrolled in a *Höhere Töchternschule* (girls' secondary school), and her first encounter with and later marriage to Rabbi Dr Max Dienemann (1904), who was a leading figure in progressive Judaism. During the First World War, the couple lived in the city of Ratibor, Upper Silesia. There, Mally Dienemann became involved in war relief work organized by the Nationaler Frauendienst, the officially recognized, patriotic German women's organization that understood its work as the female equivalent to serving at the front. For the first time in her life, this task introduced her to the plight of workers' families and allowed her to feel a profound connection to those around her:

> [In] 1914 the war broke out. One awakened from one's peaceful life and realized that everything had been as wonderful as previously thought.... By distributing assistance, which I delivered to the homes of soldiers' wives, I was given the opportunity to see the inside of the apartments of working-class families for the very first time. In many cases, I felt appalled by the sights that met me there. I wouldn't have thought that in rich Upper Silesia workers would live like that... . The war continued, and life got harder day by day. We had many losses in the Jewish community, and my husband and I had the impression that these difficult, shared experiences linked us with these people much more closely and intimately.[57]

Besides her observations about both home-front activities and class differences among those living in Ratibor, Dienemann explicitly wrote about the Jewish experience at the time and expressed her sentiments concerning the war. Though she did not doubt the emperor's desire for peace in 1914 (something that the other nations were reluctant to believe), she reported being disgusted by the invasion of Belgium.[58] Moreover, she recalled "standing rather alone in our outrage," but admitted that "even during the third and fourth year of the war, despite being opposed to the unrestricted submarine warfare, we were unable to imagine Germany's defeat." However, after witnessing the rise of the Nazi Party in Offenbach, where her family of five had settled in 1919, she seems rather critical of her strong identification with Germany's cause during the First World War. She explained retrospectively: "We were so extremely patriotic and blind, as only Germans can be ...."[59]

The autobiographical account of 35-year-old Elsa Steinitz (1879–1997) represents a similar approach. She was born and raised in Posen and wrote her recollections of the First World War as part of her memoirs in

1981. At that point, she lived in New York City, where she had arrived as a refugee from Nazi Germany in 1940.[60] Similar to Mally Dienemann, Steinitz—a physician's daughter—demonstrated a much more pronounced awareness of political contexts than either Jenny Hirsch or Jenny Wieruszowski. Steinitz's insights most likely were acquired after the end of the war.[61] However, other points of focus seem rather similar. For example, the descriptions of her assigned tasks during the war are presented as part of the female war effort:

> Even very young, unskilled girls were needed in the war effort. Every morning at sunrise, I went to the railway station to distribute hot coffee to soldiers who were on their way to the front. They were not allowed to leave the train stations. Trains that came from the front were carefully hidden from the public view. At noon, I handed out food in the kitchen to the poor: 6 prunes into every canteen that was handed to me by the people that stood in line. I remember I had an uneasy, embarrassed feeling. In the afternoon, I worked in a uniform factory, or taught arts and crafts in public schools. Classes were open all day for children of working mothers.[62]

In contrast to Hirsch, who portrayed herself as German and at times as a very nationalistic participant in the German war effort, Steinitz closed her reflections on the First World War with a comment in which she characterized herself as a rather critical middle-class opponent of war:

> We young people of my middle-class background expressed our rebellion against the war by reading and discussing the speeches of Karl Liebknecht and poems of Rosa Luxemburg. But none of us, either then or later, had any connection with the working class. Our interest in political and social questions was theoretical, idealistic, and half-baked. But at least we were searching for a tool to measure the terrible facts of the present, and for words that called them by their proper names, instead of the double-talk and concealing language of the government and press. Inflation and hunger made an end to the war.[63]

By making references to Liebknecht and Luxemburg, two opponents of Germany's participation in the First World War and co-founders of the Spartacist League and the Communist Party of Germany, Steinitz clearly rejected any identification with the war. Moreover, her remarks suggest that with hindsight—affected by the exclusion and persecution that she experienced after the Nazi takeover of power—she evaluated her own behavior, the Jews' identification with the German cause during the war years, and the degree of integration before 1933 highly critically.

These select examples demonstrate how authors who wrote their memoirs long after the recalled events not only captured their memories, but—in contrast to diarists—also offered their personal, retrospective interpretations of the events they had experienced. Yet, as Michael Mascuch, Rudolf Dekker, and Arianne Baggermann have pointed out, we must remember when working with autobiographical writing that

> a diary is never a simple transcript of its writer's thoughts: Its inventory of subjective knowledge is always partial. Diaries record traces of thought, not thinking or knowledge itself. "Knowledge" is after all an abstraction no less problematic than "truth"; it is the referent of an unspecifiable process in which knowing, not knowing, denying and not wanting to know, or even not wanting to believe, is mediated.[64]

Despite the differences arising from the fact that these reflections were written at different points in time (contemporary vs. retrospective), it is interesting that these women's autobiographical writings share strikingly similar characteristics and a number of common thematic focal points (such as patriotism, home-front activities, food prices, family affairs, and political awareness). Obviously, these sources are highly individualized accounts and cannot be considered representative of German Jewish women's attitudes and experiences during the First World War in general. But they are certainly important sources that have not been sufficiently considered in historical examinations of this period to date. It is striking that a majority of these German Jewish bourgeois women who reported their experiences at home during the "Great War" in diaries or memoirs, in different languages and at different stages of their lives, stressed the existence of a female wartime solidarity that bridged religious spheres that up to 1914 had defined home life. Some of their narratives even show characteristics of an alternative social structure based on traditional feminine values. It is also noteworthy that by 1917, many diaries would reflect, at least between the lines, some sense of war-weariness and longing for peace, rather than documentation of the people's "war fever" and wartime solidarity. Whether this was a change of mindset or a more accurate reflection of emotions that were present throughout the war (but not voiced at its outbreak) is difficult if not impossible to answer.

Strangely enough, one of the events that none of these examples of female diarists addressed in their personal wartime writings was the "Jewish census" of 1916. This glaring omission of the moment that modern scholarship tends to identify as the key turning point for German Jewish history seems quite astonishing. Self-censorship could possibly provide an explanation, but this seems rather unlikely when one considers that Jewish women did not generally hesitate to comment critically on other developments or explicitly criticize the German government's decisions when discussing the First World War. The fact that women did not mention the Jewish census of 1916, even in passing, thus may indicate that at the time it simply did not define Jewish women's experiences. Indeed, if we interpret the Jewish census as an example of a gender-specific form of modern antisemitism, this omission may be far less surprising. As is well known, the "Jew Count" of 1916 did not call for all Jews living in Germany at the time to be registered. Instead, it exclusively targeted Jewish men serving at the front, and there is little evidence that those who were directly affected by this legislation addressed the topic in their communications with those at home. In this context, historian Derek Penslar's findings are particularly illuminating. Using a sizable sample of German Jewish front soldiers' letters, he determined that, "The census is not mentioned in any of the more than seven hundred wartime letters that were written by former residents of the Berlin Jewish community orphanage and sent from the field to the institutions director."[65] While women undoubtedly cared tremendously for their loved ones who fought at the front and were very keen to find out exactly how they were doing, they obviously faced their own set of challenges and had to confront waves of antisemitism and other forms of discrimination at home.[66] These issues affected them in their daily lives and did find their way into their autobiographical writings. This notable distinction is an additional support for the argument that female perspectives should be included in future scholarly writing.

As a final point, we should note that one striking discrepancy between contemporary and retrospective German Jewish autobiographical accounts results in two conflicting pictures of women's wartime experiences. The manner in which Jewish female authors of memoirs written after 1933 describe their experiences during the First World War does not always align with the known and complex wartime realities and the nature of its gendered experiences discussed in contemporary accounts. On the contrary, the culture of memory as it is expressed in the aforementioned memoirs was firstly formed alongside religious lines, and took gender differences into account only secondarily. An explanation for this cannot be found by turning to the First World War. It seems rather that this difference is rooted in the experiences of revolution and defeat, the widespread "stab-in-the-back" myth, and after 1945, more importantly, the Holocaust. These events led to re-evaluations of the First World War and reassessments of German antisemitism, which resulted in retrospective rewriting of this chapter in German Jewish relations—first at the individual level (this can be traced in memoirs of Holocaust survivors) and later in narratives produced by Jewish historians.

Conclusion

When comparing the situation of German Jews between 1914 and 1918, not much seems to have changed. Antisemitism had been virulent in Germany before the First World War, and Germany's subsequent defeat only served to exacerbate it. Contrary to former scholarly interpretations, I argue in accordance with scholars such as Tim Grady and Derek Penslar that the four years of the war should be understood as a period in which German Jews had briefly been eager participants in Germany's national conflict. Alongside their Christian fellow-citizens, Jewish men joined the military as volunteers in large numbers to fight for the fatherland. Among them were Zionists, orthodox, and liberal Jews. However, extending beyond earlier interpretations, I argue that the war created an atmosphere of change that not only affected Jewish men but inspired Jewish women to action in equal measure.[67] They engaged in cooperations across religious boundaries and offered support for those suffering the most, regardless of their class. Beyond that, a close reading of contemporary sources shows that women's narratives and experiences differed in certain ways significantly from those of their husbands, fathers, sons, and other men who fought as soldiers in the war.

Moreover, Jewish women's autobiographical accounts provide unique insights to enhance our understanding of German Jewish experiences and thoughts about participation in the First World War, as well as of their contributions to that war's literature. The intriguing diversity of Jewish female perspectives clearly underscores Penslar's critical observation that up to this point "historians of German Jewry have all too often mapped the sensibilities of the articulate elites, and particularly of a few representative intellectuals and activists, onto the community as a whole."[68]

Women's sources may lead to historical revisions that will expand current interpretations, mainly for two reasons. First, it seems that many studies in the field of German Jewish history still promote a story of the German Jewish wartime experience that is largely or solely based on information that reflects the male perspective alone. This approach—rooted as it is in a time in which "knowledge, truth, and reality have been constructed as if men's experiences were normative, as if being human meant being male"[69]—produces narratives that tend to be one-sided, in that they mostly omit the spectrum of female efforts and suffering that is related in numerous personal accounts authored by women.

Secondly, the ways in which Jewish women, particularly those fighting at home, described the everyday realities of war and communicated their views in ego-documents suggest to the reader that, in the shadow of antisemitism, the war forced women not only to confront a great number of practical, economic, social, cultural, and emotional challenges that differed from those of men fighting at the front, but also allowed (or forced) them to explore new spheres of influence. Additionally, it created, at times, new opportunities for Jewish integration—with women as the notable instigators. The preliminary findings presented in this chapter (similar to the most recent interpretations of Jewish soldiers' responses to the "Jew Count") strongly suggest that a more thorough examination of the German Jewish wartime experience should be conducted. This expanded research could challenge the established scholarly narrative that portrays the war as a period dominated by antisemitism most notably symbolized by the "Jew Count." However that may be, ultimately I pose that deeper consideration of women's writings will help to highlight both the gendered and often distinct nature of wartime experiences, and also will change the way we think and write about the Jewish experience, antisemitism, and religion in Germany during the First World War. Additionally, that expanded perspective may alter how we commemorate the war and depict its impacts on German society.

Andrea A. Sinn is Assistant Professor of History and Director of the Jewish Studies Program at Elon University. Previously, she served as DAAD Visiting Professor at the University of California, Berkeley. Her recent publications include *Jüdische Politik und Presse in der frühen Bundesrepublik* (V&R, 2014) and *Die Erfahrung des Exils: Vertreibung, Emigration und Neuanfang—Ein Münchner Lesebuch*, with Andreas Heusler (Walter de Gruyter, 2015).

Notes

1. An early study examining working women in Germany during wartime is Ute Daniel's *Arbeiterfrauen in der Kriegsgesellschaft: Beruf, Familie, und Politik im Ersten Weltkrieg* (Göttingen, 1989). For an overview discussing the impact of the First World War on women's emancipation, see Ute

Frevert, "World War I: The Father of 'Women's Emancipation'," in *Women in German History: From Bourgeois Emancipation to Sexual Liberation*, ed. Ute Frevert (Oxford, 1989), 151–67. More recent studies paint a more complex picture of (gendered) experiences, and also of those at home; see Belinda Davis, *Home Fires Burning: Food, Politics, and Everyday Life in World War I* (Chapel Hill, 2000); Karen Hagemann and Stefanie Schüler-Springorum, eds., *Heimat-Front: Militär und Geschlechterverhältnisse im Zeitalter der Weltkriege* (Frankfurt/Main, 2002); and Christa Hämmerle, Oswald Überegger, and Birgitta Bader Zaar, eds., *Gender and the First World War* (Basingstoke, Hampshire, 2014). For a useful discussion of the difficult beginnings and challenges of gendering German military history, see Karen Hagemann, "Military, War, and the Mainstreams: Gendering Modern German Military History," in *Gendering Modern German History: Rewriting Historiography*, ed. Karen Hagemann and Jean H. Quataert (New York, 2007), 63–85.

2. See Marion Kaplan, *The Making of the Jewish Middle Class: Women, Family, and Identity in Imperial Germany* (New York, 1991), esp. 219–27; Martina Steer, "Nation, Religion, Gender: The Triple Challenge of Middle-Class German-Jewish Women in World War I," *Central European History* 48, no. 2 (2015): 176–98; Michaela Raggam-Blesch, "Jüdische Frauen im Krieg," in *Weltuntergang: Jüdisches Leben und Sterben im Ersten Weltkrieg*, ed. Marcus G. Patka (Vienna, 2014), 159–67; and Sabine Hank and Uwe Hank, *Jüdische Frauen im Ersten Weltkrieg: Paula Glück, Juliane Herrmann, Helene Meyer, Johanna Nathan* (Berlin, 2017).

3. This chapter deals exclusively with the vital contributions of Jewish women who joined the war effort on the home front. For a discussion of exceptional roles that (Jewish) women occupied (such as military nursing), see Birgit Seemann, "'Wir wollen sein ein einig Volk von Schwestern': Jüdische Krankenpflege und der Erste Weltkrieg," *Nurinst* 7 (2014): 87–101.

4. Susanne Grayzel, "Women at Home in a World at War," British Library, retrieved 25 June 2017 from https://www.bl.uk/world-war-one/articles/women-at-home.

5. At the beginning of the twentieth century, antisemitism was a "widespread social norm." It was driven by racial assumptions and constructions rather than prejudice against Judaism as a religion. For the Jewish community—since their emancipation in 1871—religious difference was the key question when considering or discussing integration and/or their role in German society. See Hermann Greive, *Geschichte des modernen Antisemitismus in Deutschland* (Darmstadt, 1983), 72. Many books and articles about German antisemitism have been written and cannot all be discussed here. An introduction to the special character of nineteenth-century German antisemitism and the most important literature is offered, for example, in Oded Heilbronner, "From Antisemitic Peripheries to Antisemitic Centres: The Place of Antisemitism in Modern German History," *Journal of Contemporary History* 35, no. 4 (2000): 559–76.

6. See Hans-Ulrich Wehler, *Deutsche Gesellschaftsgeschichte*, vol. 4 (Munich, 2003), 128–34.

7. Recently published examples, many around the centennial, are David J. Fine, *Jewish Integration in the German Army in the First World War* (Berlin, 2012); Peter C. Appelbaum, *Loyalty Betrayed: Jewish Chaplains in the German Army during the First World War* (London, 2014); Michael Berger, *Für Kaiser, Reich und Vaterland: Jüdische Soldaten. Eine Geschichte vom 19. Jahrhundert bis heute* (Zurich, 2015); and Julius H. Schoeps, "Kriegsbegeisterung und Ernüchterung," *Zeitschrift für Religions- und Geistesgeschichte* 66, no. 1 (2014): 76–89.
8. Roger Chickering, "'War Enthusiasm?' Public Opinion and the Outbreak of War in 1914," in *An Improbable War: The Outbreak of World War I and European Political Culture before 1914*, ed. Holger Afflerbach and David Stevensohn (New York, 2007), 200–12; and Jeffrey Verhey, *The Spirit of 1914: Militarism, Myth, and Mobilization in Germany* (Cambridge, 2000).
9. "Zweite Balkonrede Wilhelm II. (1.8.1914)," in *Deutsche Quellen zur Geschichte des Ersten Weltkriegs*, ed. Wolfdieter Bihl (Darmstadt, 1991), 49.
10. Peter Pulzer, "Der Erste Weltkrieg," in *Deutsch-Jüdische Geschichte in der Neuzeit, Vol. 3: Umstrittene Integration, 1871–1918*, ed. Steven M. Lowenstein (Munich, 1997), 356–79; Berger, *Für Kaiser, Reich und Vaterland*, 47; Fine, *Jewish Integration*, 10–14.
11. This attitude was nothing new; it had already been expressed by German Jews during the French-German war of 1870/71. See Christine G. Krüger, *"Sind wir denn nicht Brüder?" Deutsche Juden im nationalen Krieg 1870/71* (Paderborn, 2006). At the outbreak of the war, only very few German Jewish intellectuals like Franz Rosenzweig, Joseph Carlebach, and Gershom Sholem expressed a critical attitude towards the war. See Rivka Horwitz, "Voices of Opposition to the First World War among Jewish Thinkers," *Leo Baeck Institute Year Book* 33 (1988): 233–59. For a discussion of the impact of the war in Zionist circles, see Christian Wiese, "Martin Buber und die Wirkung des Ersten Weltkriegs auf die Prager Zionisten Hugo Bergmann, Robert Weltsch und Hans Kohn," *Tel Aviver Jahrbuch für deutsche Geschichte* 43 (2015): 181–222.
12. Tim Grady, *The German-Jewish Soldiers of the First World War in History and Memory* (Liverpool, 2011), 24.
13. "An die deutschen Juden!" *Im deutschen Reich*, September 1914, 339; "An die deutschen Juden" *Frankfurter Zeitung*, 3 August 1914, 2. For a useful overview of the transformation of German Zionism (which cannot be discussed in this chapter), see Stefan Vogt, "The First World War, German Nationalism, and the Transformation of German Zionism," *Leo Baeck Institute Year Book* 57 (2012): 267–91. A discussion of German expectations with respect to censorship of the press during the first year of the war can be found in Letter, Oberzensurstelle Berlin an das Oberkommando in den Marken, Presse-Abteilung, 27 August 1915, Bay. HStA /Abt. IV, Stellv. GenKdo I. A.K. 1727.
14. "Deutsche Juden," *Jüdische Rundschau*, 7 August 1914, 343. For a discussion of the two organizations' standpoints and the positioning of the Jewish press, see Jürgen Matthäus, "Deutschtum and Judentum under Fire: The Impact of the First World War on the Strategies of the Centralverein and

the Zionistische Vereinigung," *Leo Baeck Institute Year Book* 33 (1988): 129–47; Johann Nicolai, "'Unsere Fohnen brengen eich Recht un Freiheit' — Das deutsche Judentum zwischen Patriotismus, Antisemitismus, und 'Ostjudenfrage'," *Nordost-Archiv: Zeitschrift für Regionalgeschichte* 24 (2015): 143–57; and Nathanael Riemer, "'So kam es, daß wir in den Krieg zogen, weil wir Zionisten waren, nicht aber, obwohl wir Juden sind.' Nationaljüdischer Deutsch-Patriotismus zu Beginn des Ersten Weltkriegs im Spiegel der Jüdischen Rundschau," *Historisches Jahrbuch* 135 (2015): 412–52.

15. See Berger, *Für Kaiser, Reich und Vaterland*, 46 et seq. and 50–62. For details concerning the role of religion and the tasks of German rabbis who served in the field, see David J. Fine, "Jüdische Soldaten und Religion an der Front," in *Krieg! Juden zwischen den Fronten 1914–1918*, ed. Ulrike Heikaus and Julia B. Köhne (Berlin, 2014), 133–54; Sabine Hank, Hermann Simon, and Uwe Hank, "Einleitung," in *Feldrabbiner in den deutschen Streitkräften des Ersten Weltkrieges: Gemeinsam herausgegeben von der Stiftung Neue Synagoge Berlin — Centrum Judaicum und dem Zentrum für Militärgeschichte und Sozialwissenschaften der Bundeswehr*, ed. Sabine Hank, Hermann Simon, and Uwe Hank (Berlin, 2013), 7–15; and Appelbaum, *Loyalty Betrayed*, esp. Chapter 5 and 6.

16. The Austrian Jewish feminist Bertha Pappenheim, who came from a family that had roots in orthodox Judaism, became heavily involved in social and political activities after arriving in Frankfurt am Main in 1888. Before moving to Germany, she had been treated for a variety of nervous symptoms and was diagnosed with hysteria by her attending physician, Dr Josef Breuer, who published her case study under the pseudonym Anna O. in his book *Studies on Hysteria* (1895), written in collaboration with Sigmund Freud. See Josef Breuer and Sigmund Freud, *Studies on Hysteria* (New York, 1957).

17. The organization's bylaws (1904) further explained the specific aims of the association: strengthening community consciousness among Jews, furthering the ideals of the bourgeois women's movement, expanding women's roles in the Jewish community, providing women with career training, and fighting the traffic in women. The League's large membership and support for these goals of the German bourgeois women's movement distinguished it from other Jewish women's organizations at the time. Kaplan, *The Making of the Jewish Middle Class*, esp. 219–27; Marion Kaplan, *The Jewish Feminist Movement in Germany: The Campaigns of the Jüdischer Frauenbund, 1904–1938* (Westport, CT, 1979); Martina Steer, "'Wir wollen sein ein einig Volk von Schwesten, vor keiner Not uns fürchten und Gefahr!' Der Jüdische Frauenbund im Ersten Weltkrieg," in *Geschlecht, Religion und Engagement: Die jüdischen Frauenbewegungen im deutschsprachigen Raum, 19. und frühes 20. Jahrhundert*, ed. Margarete Grandner and Edith Saurer (Vienna, 2005), 103–21; and Martina Steer, "Patriotismus, Frauensolidarität und jüdische Identität: Der jüdische Frauenbund im Ersten Weltkrieg," *Nurinst* 7 (2014): 59–72.

18. Martina Steer outlines the unique characteristics of different Jewish women's organizations in Steer, "Nation, Religion, Gender."

19. Quoted from Steer, "'Wir wollen sein ein einig Volk von Schwesten," 110.
20. Andrea Süchting-Hänger, "Nationaler Frauendienst," in *Enzyklopädie Erster Weltkrieg*, 2nd ed., ed. Gerhard Hirschfeld, Gerd Krumeich, and Irina Renz (Paderborn, 2014), 731 et seq.; Angelika Schaser, *Helene Lange und Gertrud Bäumer: Eine politische Lebensgemeinschaft* (Cologne, 2010), esp. 158 et seq.
21. The only difference between the Israelitisch-humanitärer Frauenverein's kitchen and the ones run by non-Jewish organizations was that it was set up in compliance with the Jewish community's ritual rules. "Hamburgische Kriegshilfe," in Staatsarchiv Hamburg (StAHH), 731-8, A 320, *Hamburger Fremdenblatt* No. 230 B, 22 September 1914.
22. Ibid.; and Kirsten Heinsohn, "Israelitisch-humanitärer Frauenverein," *Das Jüdische Hamburg*, retrieved 14 July 2017 from http://www.dasjuedischehamburg.de/node/212.
23. The deterioration in the climate of public opinion is discussed in so-called "Stimmungsberichte," in Bay. HStA /Abt. IV, Stellv. GenKdo I.A.K. 1942. For further discussion of the rise of antisemitism among the German population, see Saul Friedländer, "Die politischen Veränderungen der Kriegszeit und ihre Auswirkungen auf die Judenfrage," in Werner E. Mosse, ed., *Deutsches Judentum in Krieg und Revolution 1916–1923*, ed. Werner E. Mosse (Tübingen, 1971), 27–65; Werner Jochmann, "Die Ausbreitung des Antisemitismus," in Mosse, ed., *Deutsches Judentum*, 409–510; Björn Hofmeister, "Weltanschauung, Mobilisierungsstrukturen und Kriegserfahrungen: Antisemitische Radikalisierung des Alldeutschen Verbandes als Prozess 1912–1920," *Jahrbuch für Antisemitismusforschung* 24 (2015): 119–54; and Berger, *Für Kaiser, Reich und Vaterland*, 47 et seq.
24. Letter, Kriegsministerium Nr 247/8 16 C 1 b an sämtl. Armee-Oberkommandos usw. gez. Wild von Hohenborn, Berlin, 11 October 1916, Bay. HStA /Abt. IV, Stellv. GenKdo I. A.K. 594. Questionnaires and completed reports providing the required statistical information can be found in Bay. HStA /Abt. IV, Infanteriedivisionen (WK) 8683; and Bay. HStA / Abt. IV, Stellv. GenKdo I. A.K. 594.
25. For more details, see Marion Kaplan, ed., *Jewish Daily Life in Germany, 1618–1945* (Oxford, 2005), "Part III: As Germans and as Jews in Imperial Germany," 173–270, esp. 267–69; and Jacob Rosenthal, *Die Ehre des jüdischen Soldaten: Die Judenzählung im Ersten Weltkrieg und ihre Folgen* (Frankfurt/Main, 2007), 207. Rosenthal compares the Jew Count to the boycott of Jewish stores on 1 April 1933 and suggests that there was a connection between the census and the events that took place during the Third Reich.
26. Many scholars have written about the *Judenzählung*. See, for example, Michael Brenner, "The German Army Orders a Census of Jewish Soldiers, and Jews Defend German Culture," in *Yale Companion to Jewish Writing and Thought in German Culture, 1096–1996*, ed. Sander L. Gilman and Jack Zipes (New Haven, CT, 1996), 348–54; Ulrich Sieg, *Jüdische Intellektuelle im Ersten Weltkrieg: Kriegserfahrungen, weltanschauliche Debatten und kulturelle Neuentwürfe* (Berlin, 2001), 87–96; Egmont Zechlin, *Die deutsche Politik und die Juden im Ersten Weltkrieg* (Göttingen, 1969), 516–67; Rosenthal, *Die Ehre*

des jüdischen Soldaten; Anna Ullrich, "'Nun sind wir gezeichnet': Jüdische Soldaten und die 'Judenzählung' im Ersten Weltkrieg," in Heikaus and Köhne, *Krieg!*, 215–38; and Pulzer, "Der Erste Weltkrieg."
27. Based on former experiences, the Verband der deutschen Juden had started to collect the names of Jewish soldiers in 1915. In 1916, they founded the Committee on War Statistics (Ausschuss für Kriegsstatistik) that collected any material providing information about the involvement of German Jews in the war effort. The results were published by Jacob Segall, *Die deutschen Juden als Soldaten im Kriege 1914–1918: Eine statistische Studie. Mit einem Vorwort von Heinrich Silbergleit* (Berlin, 1921). See also Franz Oppenheimer, *Die Judenstatistik des preußischen Kriegsministeriums* (Munich, 1922).
28. See, for example, the detailed correspondence available in Bundesarchiv Berlin-Lichterfelde (BArch Berlin), R43/908.
29. See the article "Judenzählung," *Jüdische Rundschau*, 27 October 1916, 351 (published by the ZVfD). The CV wrote many letters, even long after the census occurred; see Letter, Centralverein an das stellvertretende General-Kommando des I. Kgl. Bayer. Armee, München, 8 April 1918, Bay. HStA / Abt. IV, Stellv. GenKdo I. A.K.
30. See the archival documents of German rabbis during the First World War published in Hank, Simon, and Hank, *Feldrabbiner in den deutschen Streitkräften*, 218 et seq.
31. Grady, *The German-Jewish Soldiers*, 34.
32. Derek Penslar, *Jews and the Military: A History* (Princeton, NJ, 2013), 173. See also Derek Penslar, "The German-Jewish Soldier: From Participant to Victim," *German History* 29, no. 3 (2011): 423–44, esp. 428. Fine, *Jewish Integration*, 14, points out that the Jewish census does not appear as a dominant theme in the sources consulted for his study. In fact, "most do not mention the census order at all," which is why he agrees that the judgment that it was a passing episode remains compelling. In this, he follows the argument of Werner T. Angress in "The German Army's 'Judenzählung' of 1916: Genesis—Consequences—Significance," *Leo Baeck Institute Year Book* 23 (1978): 117–37, who concludes that the Jew Count in itself was "a mere episode."
33. For more details, see Trude Maurer, "Medizinalpolizei und Antisemitismus: Die deutsche Politik der Grenzsperre gegen Ostjuden im Ersten Weltkrieg," *Jahrbücher für Geschichte Osteuropas. Neue Folge* 33 (1985): 205–30; Zechlin, *Die deutsche Politik*, esp. 260–77; and Friedländer, "Die politischen Veränderungen," 34 et seq.
34. Steven J. Zipperstein provides an overview on Jewish refugees in "The Politics of Relief: The Transformation of Russian Jewish Communal Life during the First World War," in *The Jews and the European Crisis, 1914–1921*, ed. Jonathan Frankel (New York, 1988), 22–40. See also Peter Gatrell, *A Whole Empire Walking: Refugees in Russia during World War I* (Bloomington, 1999); Peter Gatrell, "Refugees and Forced Migrants during the First World War," *Immigrants and Minorities* 26, no. 1 (2008): 82–110; and Jochen Oltmer, "'Verbotswidrige Einwanderung nach Deutschland': Osteuropäische

Juden im Kaiserreich und in der Weimarer Republik," *Aschkenas* 17, no. 1 (2009): 97–121. Aspects of the pogroms are discussed in John D. Klier and Shlomo Lambrosa, eds., *Pogroms: Anti-Jewish Violence in Modern Russian History* (Cambridge, 1992); and Heinz-Dietrich Löwe, *The Tsar and the Jews: Reform, Reaction and Anti-Semitism in Imperial Russia 1772–1917* (Chur, 1993).

35. Between 1914 and 1921, approximately 100,000 Jews from Eastern Europe arrived in Germany; by 1921, at least 40 percent had moved on and emigrated to another country, such as Belgium or France, or by their preference the USA. Concerning the situation of the so-called "Ostjuden," see Steven E. Ascheim, *Brothers and Strangers: The East European Jew in German and German Jewish Consciousness, 1800–1923* (Madison, 1982); Trude Maurer, *Ostjuden in Deutschland 1918–1933* (Hamburg, 1986); and Lutger Heid, *Maloche—nicht Mildtätigkeit: Ostjüdische Arbeiter in Deutschland 1914–1923* (Hildesheim, 1993). The history of Jews in Eastern Europe, particularly in Habsburg Austria, is discussed in Frank M. Schuster, *Zwischen allen Fronten: Osteuropäische Juden während des Ersten Weltkrieges (1914–1919)* (Cologne, 2004); and Marsha L. Rozenblit, *Reconstructing a National Identity: The Jews of Habsburg Austria during World War I* (Oxford, 2001).

36. Pulzer, "Der Erste Weltkrieg," 376.

37. See Maurer, "Medizinalpolizei"; and Sarah Panter, *Jüdische Erfahrungen und Loyalitätskonflikte im Ersten Weltkrieg* (Göttingen, 2014), 283 et seq.

38. "Macht Euch keine Hoffnung, Ihr seid und bleibt die Parias Deutschlands." Quoted from Heinrich August Winkler, *Der lange Weg nach Westen, Vol. 1: Deutsche Geschichte vom Ende des Alten Reiches bis zum Untergang der Weimarer Republik*, 6th ed. (Munich, 2005), 344. A brief overview of the ways in which the First World War influenced Jewish identity can be found in Moshe Zimmermann, *Die deutschen Juden 1914–1945* (Munich, 1997), 4–9.

39. Sieg, *Jüdische Intellektuelle*, esp. 53 et seq. and 85; Panter, *Jüdische Erfahrungen*, 41 et seq.; Jason Crouthamel, "Paul Lebrechts Kriegstagebuch," in Heikaus and Köhne, *Krieg!*, 107–32; and Gerald Lamprecht, "Juden in Zentraleuropa und die Transformationen des Antisemitismus im und nach dem Ersten Weltkrieg," *Jahrbuch für Antisemitismusforschung* 24 (2015): 63–88.

40. For a discussion of the term "total war," see Roger Chickering, "Total War: The Use and Abuse of a Concept," in *Anticipating Total War: The German and American Experiences 1871–1914*, ed. Manfred Boemeke et al. (Cambridge, 1999), 13–28. For a discussion of frontline soldiers' experiences and the myth of the war experience, see George L. Mosse, "Two World Wars and the Myth of the War Experience," *Journal of Contemporary History* 21, no. 4 (1986): 491–513.

41. See the essays in Mosse, *Deutsches Judentum* (Tübingen, 1971); Stephen Magill, "Defense and Introspection: The First World War as a Pivotal Crisis in the German Jewish Experience" (Phil. dissertation, Los Angeles, 1977); Clemens Picht, "Zwischen Vaterland und Volk: Das deutsche Judentum im Ersten Weltkrieg," in *Der Erste Weltkrieg: Wirkung, Wahrnehmung, Analyse*, ed. Wolfgang Michalka (Weyarn, 1997), 736 and 746 et seq.; Zimmermann, *Die deutschen Juden*, 3–9; Christhard Hoffmann, "Between Integration

and Rejection: The Jewish Community in Germany 1914–1918," in *State, Society and Mobilization in Europe during the First World War*, ed. John Horne (Cambridge, 1997), 89–104, and particularly 98; and Berger, *Für Kaiser, Reich und Vaterland*, esp. 47. A different interpretation that considers the Jew Count as another antisemitic episode but not a new phenomenon was expressed by Angress, "The German Army's 'Judenzählung' of 1916"; see also Fine, *Jewish Integration*, 14; and Christoph Jahr, "Episode oder Wasserscheide? Der Deutsche Antisemitismus im Ersten Weltkrieg," in *"Hoffet mit daheim auf fröhlichere Zeit" — Juden und Christen im Ersten Weltkrieg. Laupheimer Gespräche (2014)*, ed. Haus der Geschichte Baden-Württemberg (Heidelberg, 2014), 59–62.

42. The importance of autobiographical sources and women's perspectives to be able to achieve an important reinterpretation of older historical arguments is also stressed by Sigurður Gylfi Magnússon, "Gender: A Useful Category in the Analysis of Ego-Documents? Memory, Historical Sources and Microhistory," *Scandinavian Journal of History* 38, no. 2 (2013): 202–22; Hank and Hank, *Jüdische Frauen*, 7 et seq.

43. Kaplan, *The Making of the Jewish Middle Class*; Marion Kaplan, "Weaving Women's Worlds: Zur Bedeutung von Memoiren für die deutsch-jüdische Frauengeschichte," in *Deutsch-jüdische Geschichte als Geschlechtergeschichte: Studien zum 19. und 20. Jahrhundert*, ed. Stefanie Schüler-Springorum and Kirsten Heinsohn (Göttingen, 2005), 250 et seq.; Miriam Gebhardt, *Das Familiengedächtis: Erinnerungen im deutsch-jüdischen Bürgertum 1890 bis 1932* (Stuttgart, 1999); and Miriam Gebhardt, "Der Fall Clara Geißmar, oder von der Verführungskunst weiblicher Autobiographik," in Schüler-Springorum and Heinsohn, *Deutsch-jüdische Geschichte*, 233–49. See also Tzvi Howard Adelman, "Self, Other, and Community: Jewish Women's Autobiography," *Nashim: A Journal of Jewish Women's Studies and Gender Issues* 7 (2004): 116–27.

44. Michael Mascuch, Rudolf Dekker, and Arianne Baggermann, "Ego-documents and History: A Short Account of the Longue Durée," *The Historian* 78, no. 1 (2016): 11–56, here 39 et seq. Winfried Schulze introduced the term "egodocuments" (*Selbstzeugnis* or *Ego-Dokument*), coined by the Dutch academic historian Jacques Presser (1899–1970), to German scholarship in 1992. It is currently used to identify a broad category comprising several forms of autobiographical texts, including autobiographies, memoirs, diaries, travel journals, and personal letters. These texts are not only historical sources but also works of literary writing. Mascuch, Dekker, and Baggermann, "Egodocuments and History," 11 et seq.

45. Judith Butler's approach offered in *Giving an Account of Oneself* (New York: Fordham UP, 2005), is discussed and quoted from Sidonie Smith and Julia Watson, "New Genres, New Subjects: Women, Gender, and Autobiography after 2000," *Revista Canaria de Estudios Ingleses* 58 (2009): 13–40, esp. 14 et seq.

46. Jenny Hirsch, "Diary," Private Ownership. English translations have been provided by the author.

47. Ibid., 6 et seq.

48. Ibid., 28.
49. Cf. Margarete Schratter, née Schall (1899–1926), "Mein Tagebuch," LBINY, LBI Archives, Digital Collection, ME 1181, MM II 37, retrieved 25 June 2017 from http://www.lbi.org/digibaeck/results/?qtype=pid&term=410423.
50. Jenny Wieruszowski, née Landsberg, "Mutters Kindertagebücher," LBINY, LBI Archives, Digital Collection, ME 930, MM II 18, retrieved 25 June 2017 from http://www.lbi.org/digibaeck/results/?qtype=pid&term=592790. The English translation has been provided by the author. For more biographical information, see Kaplan, *Jewish Daily Life in Germany*, Part III, 189 et seq.
51. The founding of the ADF by Louise Otto-Peters and Auguste Schmidt in 1865 constituted the beginning of the organized women's movement in Germany. For more information, see Irene Stoehr, *Emanzipation zum Staat? Der Allgemeine Deutsche Frauenverein—Deutscher Staatsbürgerinnenverband, 1893–1933* (Pfaffenweiler, 1990).
52. Susan Richter, ed., *Wissenschaft als weiblicher Beruf? Die ersten Frauen in Forschung und Lehre an der Universität Heidelberg* (Heidelberg, 2008).
53. Wieruszowski, "Mutters Kindertagebücher," 233 et seq. (29 January 1915).
54. Ibid., 236 et seq. (18 July 1917).
55. Ibid., 241 (31 January 1918), and 243 (31 January 1918).
56. Mally Dienemann, "Aufzeichnungen, 1883–1939," LBINY, LBI Archive, Digital Collection, ME 112, MF 96, MM 18, retrieved 25 June 2017 from http://www.lbi.org/digibaeck/results/?qtype=pid&term=939510. Since 1919, the couple and their three children—Dora, Paula, and Gabriele—had lived in Offenbach on the Main from where they emigrated via England to Palestine in 1938. Dr Max Dienemann died in December 1938; in 1949, Mally Dienemann emigrated to the United States. She died in Chicago in 1963. See "Mally Dienemann," in *Germans No More: Accounts of Jewish Everyday Life, 1933–1938*, ed. Margarete Limberg and Hubert Rübsaal (New York, 2006), 183; and Marion Kaplan, *Between Dignity and Despair: Jewish Life in Nazi Germany* (New York, 1999).
57. Dienemann, "Aufzeichnungen, 1883–1939," 3. The English translation has been provided by the author.
58. Ibid.
59. Ibid.
60. Elsa Steinitz, "My Memoirs," LBINY, LBI Archive, Digital Collection, ME 1105, MM II 31, retrieved 25 June 2017 from http://www.lbi.org/digibaeck/results/?qtype=pid&term=397718.
61. Ibid., 7.
62. Ibid.
63. Ibid.
64. Mascuch, Dekker, and Baggermann, "Egodocuments and History," 40 et seq.
65. Penslar, *Jews and the Military*, 173. See also Penslar, "The German-Jewish Soldier," 428.
66. The conflict scenario in the Bund Deutscher Frauenvereine from the years 1915/16—most often addressed as a disagreement between Bertha Pappenheim and Helene Lange—can serve as an example of a situation in

which exclusively Jewish women were confronted with antisemitism in the bourgeois women's movement. For more detail, see Mechthild Bereswill and Leonie Wagner, "Public or Private? Antisemitism and Politics in the Federation of German Women's Association," *Journal of Genocide Research* 1, no. 2 (1999): 157–68.
67. That historical changes may affect men and women differently, and thus may provide perspectives in any particular epoch that differ from men's views, is an important insight. See Joan Kelly, "The Social Relation of the Sexes," reprinted in Joan Kelley, *Women, History, and Theory: The Essays of Joan Kelly* (Chicago, 1984), 3; and Judith R. Baskin, "Integrating Gender Studies into Jewish Studies," *Shofar* 9, no. 4 (1991): 92–97.
68. Penslar, "The German-Jewish Soldier," 428.
69. Mary Jo Maynes, *Interpreting Women's Lives: Feminist Theory and Personal Narratives* (Indianapolis, 1989), 3.

Bibliography

Primary Sources

"An die deutschen Juden!" *Im deutschen Reich*, September 1914, 339.
"An die deutschen Juden!" *Frankfurter Zeitung*, 3 August 1914, 2.
"Deutsche Juden." *Jüdische Rundschau*, 7 August 1914, 343.
Dienemann, Mally. "Aufzeichnungen, 1883–1939." Leo Baeck Institute New York (LBINY), LBI Archive, Digital Collection, ME 112, MF 96, MM 18. Retrieved 25 June 2017 from http://www.lbi.org/digibaeck/results/?qtype=pid&term=939510.
"Hamburgische Kriegshilfe." Staatsarchiv Hamburg (StAHH), 731-8, A 320, *Hamburger Fremdenblatt* No. 230 B, 22 September 1914.
Hirsch, Jenny. "Diary." Private ownership. English translations have been provided by the author.
Letter, Centralverein an das stellvertretende General-Kommando des I. Kgl. Bayer. Armee, München, 8 April 1918. Bayerisches Hauptstaatsarchiv (Bay. HStA) /Abt. IV, Stellv. GenKdo I. A.K.
Letter, Kriegsministerium Nr 247/8 16 C l b an sämtl. Armee-Oberkommandos usw. gez. Wild von Hohenborn, Berlin, 11 October 1916. Bay. HStA /Abt. IV, Stellv. GenKdo I. A.K. 594.
Letter, Oberzensurstelle Berlin an das Oberkommando in den Marken, Presse-Abteilung, 27 August 1915. Bay. HStA /Abt. IV, Stellv. GenKdo I. A.K. 1727.
Schratter, Margarete (née Schall) (1899–1926). "Mein Tagebuch." LBINY, LBI Archives, Digital Collection, ME 1181, MM II 37. Retrieved 25 June 2017 from http://www.lbi.org/digibaeck/results/?qtype=pid&term=410423.
Steinitz, Elsa. "My Memoirs." LBINY, LBI Archive, Digital Collection, ME 1105, MM II 31. Retrieved 25 June 2017 from http://www.lbi.org/digibaeck/results/?qtype=pid&term=397718.
"Stimmungsberichte." Bay. HStA /Abt. IV, Stellv. GenKdo I. A.K. 1942.

Wieruszowski, Jenny (née Landsberg). "Mutters Kindertagebücher." LBINY, LBI Archives, Digital Collection, ME 930, MM II 18. Retrieved 25 June 2017 from http://www.lbi.org/digibaeck/results/?qtype=pid&term=592790.
"Zweite Balkonrede Wilhelm II. (1.8.1914)." In *Deutsche Quellen zur Geschichte des Ersten Weltkriegs*, edited by Wolfdieter Bihl (Darmstadt: Wiss. Buchges., 1991), 49.

Secondary Sources

Adelman, Tzvi Howard. "Self, Other, and Community: Jewish Women's Autobiography." *Nashim: A Journal of Jewish Women's Studies and Gender Issues* 7 (2004): 116–27.
Angress, Werner T. "The German Army's 'Judenzählung' of 1916: Genesis—Consequences—Significance." *Leo Baeck Institute Year Book* 23 (1978): 117–37.
Appelbaum, Peter C. *Loyalty Betrayed: Jewish Chaplains in the German Army during the First World War*. London: Mitchell, 2014.
Ascheim, Steven E. *Brothers and Strangers: The East European Jew in German and German Jewish Consciousness, 1800–1923*. Madison: University of Wisconsin Press, 1982.
Baskin, Judith R. "Integrating Gender Studies into Jewish Studies." *Shofar* 9, no. 4 (1991): 92–97.
Bereswill, Mechthild, and Leonie Wagner. "Public or Private? Antisemitism and Politics in the Federation of German Women's Association." *Journal of Genocide Research* 1, no. 2 (1999): 157–68.
Berger, Michael. *Für Kaiser, Reich und Vaterland: Jüdische Soldaten. Eine Geschichte vom 19. Jahrhundert bis heute*. Zurich: Orell Füssli Verlag, 2015.
Brenner, Michael. "The German Army Orders a Census of Jewish Soldiers, and Jews Defend German Culture." In *Yale Companion to Jewish Writing and Thought in German Culture, 1096–1996*, edited by Sander L. Gilman and Jack Zipes, 348–54. New Haven, CT: Yale University Press, 1996.
Breuer, Josef, and Sigmund Freud. *Studies on Hysteria*. New York: Basic Books, 1957.
Chickering, Roger. "Total War: The Use and Abuse of a Concept." In *Anticipating Total War: The German and American Experiences 1871–1914*, edited by Manfred Boemeke et al., 13–28. Cambridge: Cambridge University Press, 1999.
———. "'War Enthusiasm?': Public Opinion and the Outbreak of War in 1914." In *An Improbable War: The Outbreak of World War I and European Political Culture before 1914*, edited by Holger Afflerbach and David Stevensohn, 200–12. New York: Berghahn Books, 2007.
Crouthamel, Jason. "Paul Lebrechts Kriegstagebuch." In *Krieg! Juden zwischen den Fronten 1914–1918*, edited by Ulrike Heikaus and Julia B. Köhne, 107–32. Berlin: Hentrich & Hentrich, 2014.
Daniel, Ute. *Arbeiterfrauen in der Kriegsgesellschaft: Beruf, Familie, und Politik im Ersten Weltkrieg*. Göttingen: Vandenhoeck & Ruprecht, 1989.
Davis, Belinda. *Home Fires Burning: Food, Politics, and Everyday Life in World War I*. Chapel Hill: University of North Carolina Press, 2000.

Fine, David J. *Jewish Integration in the German Army in the First World War.* Berlin: de Gruyter, 2012.

———. "Jüdische Soldaten und Religion an der Front." In *Krieg! Juden zwischen den Fronten 1914–1918,* edited by Ulrike Heikaus and Julia B. Köhne, 133–54. Berlin: Hentrich & Hentrich, 2014.

Frevert, Ute. "World War I: The Father of 'Women's Emancipation'." In *Women in German History: From Bourgeois Emancipation to Sexual Liberation,* edited by Ute Frevert, 151–67. Oxford: Berg, 1989.

Friedländer, Saul. "Die politischen Veränderungen der Kriegszeit und ihre Auswirkungen auf die Judenfrage." In *Deutsches Judentum in Krieg und Revolution 1916–1923,* edited by Werner E. Mosse, 27–65. Tübingen: J. C. B. Mohr, 1971.

Gatrell, Peter. "Refugees and Forced Migrants during the First World War." *Immigrants and Minorities* 26, no. 1 (2008): 82–110.

———. *A Whole Empire Walking: Refugees in Russia during World War I.* Bloomington: Indiana University Press, 1999.

Gebhardt, Miriam. "Der Fall Clara Geißmar, oder von der Verführungskunst weiblicher Autobiographik." In *Deutsch-jüdische Geschichte als Geschlechtergeschichte: Studien zum 19. und 20. Jahrhundert,* edited by Stefanie Schüler-Springorum and Kirsten Heinsohn, 233–49. Göttingen: Wallstein, 2005.

———. *Das Familiengedächtis: Erinnerungen im deutsch-jüdischen Bürgertum 1890 bis 1932.* Stuttgart: Steiner, 1999.

Grady, Tim. *The German-Jewish Soldiers of the First World War in History and Memory.* Liverpool: Liverpool University Press, 2011.

Grayzel, Susanne. "Women at Home in a World at War." British Library. Retrieved 25 June 2017 from https://www.bl.uk/world-war-one/articles/women-at-home.

Greive, Hermann. *Geschichte des modernen Antisemitismus in Deutschland.* Darmstadt: Wissenschaftliche Buchgesellschaft, 1983.

Hagemann, Karen. "Military, War, and the Mainstreams: Gendering Modern German Military History." In *Gendering Modern German History: Rewriting Historiography,* edited by Karen Hagemann and Jean H. Quataert, 63–85. New York: Berghahn Books, 2007.

Hagemann, Karen, and Stefanie Schüler-Springorum, eds. *Heimat-Front: Militär und Geschlechterverhältnisse im Zeitalter der Weltkriege.* Frankfurt/Main: Campus Verlag, 2002.

Hämmerle, Christa, Oswald Überegger, and Birgitta Bader Zaar, eds. *Gender and the First World War.* Basingstoke, Hampshire: Palgrave Macmillan, 2014.

Hank, Sabine, and Uwe Hank. *Jüdische Frauen im Ersten Weltkrieg: Paula Glück, Juliane Herrmann, Helene Meyer, Johanna Nathan.* Berlin: Hentrich und Hentrich, 2017.

Hank, Sabine, Hermann Simon, and Uwe Hank, "Einleitung." In *Feldrabbiner in den deutschen Streitkräften des Ersten Weltkrieges: Gemeinsam herausgegeben von der Stiftung Neue Synagoge Berlin—Centrum Judaicum und dem Zentrum für Militärgeschichte und Sozialwissenschaften der Bundeswehr,* edited by Sabine

Hank, Hermann Simon, and Uwe Hank, 7–15. Berlin: Hentrich & Hentrich, 2013.
Heid, Lutger. *Maloche—nicht Mildtätigkeit: Ostjüdische Arbeiter in Deutschland 1914–1923*. Hildesheim: Georg Olms Verlag, 1993.
Heilbronner, Oded. "From Antisemitic Peripheries to Antisemitic Centres: The Place of Antisemitism in Modern German History." *Journal of Contemporary History* 35, no. 4 (2000): 559–76.
Heinsohn, Kirsten. "Israelitisch-humanitärer Frauenverein." *Das Jüdische Hamburg*. Retrieved 14 July 2017 from http://www.dasjuedischehamburg.de/node/212.
Hoffmann, Christhard. "Between Integration and Rejection: The Jewish Community in Germany 1914–1918." In *State, Society and Mobilization in Europe during the First World War*, edited by John Horne, 89–104. Cambridge: Cambridge University Press, 1997.
Hofmeister, Björn. "Weltanschauung, Mobilisierungsstrukturen und Kriegserfahrungen: Antisemitische Radikalisierung des Alldeutschen Verbandes als Prozess 1912–1920." *Jahrbuch für Antisemitismusforschung* 24 (2015): 119–54.
Horwitz, Rivka. "Voices of Opposition to the First World War among Jewish Thinkers." *Leo Baeck Institute Year Book* 33 (1988): 233–59.
Jahr, Christoph. "Episode oder Wasserscheide? Der Deutsche Antisemitismus im Ersten Weltkrieg." In *"Hoffet mit daheim auf fröhlichere Zeit"—Juden und Christen im Ersten Weltkrieg. Laupheimer Gespräche (2014)*, edited by Haus der Geschichte Baden-Württemberg, 59–62. Heidelberg: Universitätsverlag Winter, 2014.
Jochmann, Werner. "Die Ausbreitung des Antisemitismus." In *Deutsches Judentum in Krieg und Revolution 1916–1923*, edited by Werner T. Mosse, 409–510. Tübingen: Mohr, 1971.
Kaplan, Marion. *Between Dignity and Despair: Jewish Life in Nazi Germany*. New York: Oxford University Press, 1999.
———. *The Jewish Feminist Movement in Germany: The Campaigns of the Jüdischer Frauenbund, 1904–1938*. Westport, CT: Greenwood Press, 1979.
———. *The Making of the Jewish Middle Class: Women, Family, and Identity in Imperial Germany*. New York: Oxford University Press, 1991.
———. "Weaving Women's Worlds: Zur Bedeutung von Memoiren für die deutsch-jüdische Frauengeschichte." In *Deutsch-jüdische Geschichte als Geschlechtergeschichte: Studien zum 19. und 20. Jahrhundert*, edited by Stefanie Schüler-Springorum and Kirsten Heinsohn, 250–74. Göttingen: Wallstein, 2005.
Kaplan, Marion, ed. *Jewish Daily Life in Germany, 1618–1945*. Oxford: Oxford University Press, 2005.
Kelly, Joan. *Women, History, and Theory: The Essays of Joan Kelly*. Chicago: University of Chicago, 1984.
Klier, John D., and Shlomo Lambrosa, eds. *Pogroms: Anti-Jewish Violence in Modern Russian History*. Cambridge: Cambridge University Press, 1992.
Krüger, Christine G. *"Sind wir denn nicht Brüder?" Deutsche Juden im nationalen Krieg 1870/71*. Paderborn: Schöningh, 2006.

Lamprecht, Gerald. "Juden in Zentraleuropa und die Transformationen des Antisemitismus im und nach dem Ersten Weltkrieg." *Jahrbuch für Antisemitismusforschung* 24 (2015): 63–88.

Löwe, Heinz-Dietrich. *The Tsar and the Jews: Reform, Reaction and Anti-Semitism in Imperial Russia 1772–1917*. Chur: Harwood Academic Publishers, 1993.

Magill, Stephen. "Defense and Introspection: The First World War as a Pivotal Crisis in the German Jewish Experience." Phil. dissertation, Los Angeles, 1977.

Magnússon, Sigurður Gylfi. "Gender: A Useful Category in the Analysis of Ego-Documents? Memory, Historical Sources and Microhistory." *Scandinavian Journal of History* 38, no. 2 (2013): 202–22.

"Mally Dienemann." In *Germans No More: Accounts of Jewish Everyday Life, 1933–1938*, edited by Margarete Limberg and Hubert Rübsaal, 183. New York: Berghahn Books, 2006.

Mascuch, Michael, Rudolf Dekker, and Arianne Baggermann. "Egodocuments and History: A Short Account of the Longue Durée." *The Historian* 78, no. 1 (2016): 11–56.

Matthäus, Jürgen. "Deutschtum and Judentum under Fire: The Impact of the First World War on the Strategies of the Centralverein and the Zionistische Vereinigung." *Leo Baeck Institute Year Book* 33 (1988): 129–47.

Maurer, Trude. "Medizinalpolizei und Antisemitismus: Die deutsche Politik der Grenzsperre gegen Ostjuden im Ersten Weltkrieg." *Jahrbücher für Geschichte Osteuropas. Neue Folge* 33 (1985): 205–30.

———. *Ostjuden in Deutschland 1918–1933*. Hamburg: Christians, 1986.

Maynes, Mary Jo. *Interpreting Women's Lives: Feminist Theory and Personal Narratives*. Indianapolis: Indiana University Press, 1989.

Mosse, George L. "Two World Wars and the Myth of the War Experience." *Journal of Contemporary History* 21, no. 4 (1986): 491–513.

Mosse, Werner E. *Deutsches Judentum in Krieg und Revolution 1916–1923*. Tübingen: Mohr, 1971.

Nicolai, Johann. "'Unsere Fohnen brengen eich Recht un Freiheit' — Das deutsche Judentum zwischen Patriotismus, Antisemitismus, und 'Ostjudenfrage'." *Nordost-Archiv: Zeitschrift für Regionalgeschichte* 24 (2015): 143–57.

Oltmer, Jochen. "'Verbotswidrige Einwanderung nach Deutschland': Osteuropäische Juden im Kaiserreich und in der Weimarer Republik." *Aschkenas* 17, no. 1 (2009): 97–121.

Oppenheimer, Franz. *Die Judenstatistik des preußischen Kriegsministeriums*. Munich: Verlag für Kulturpolitik, 1922.

Panter, Sarah. *Jüdische Erfahrungen und Loyalitätskonflikte im Ersten Weltkrieg*. Göttingen: Vandenhoeck & Ruprecht, 2014.

Penslar, Derek. "The German-Jewish Soldier: From Participant to Victim." *German History* 29, no. 3 (2011): 423–44.

———. *Jews and the Military: A History*. Princeton, NJ: Princeton University Press, 2013.

Picht, Clemens. "Zwischen Vaterland und Volk: Das deutsche Judentum im Ersten Weltkrieg." In *Der Erste Weltkrieg: Wirkung, Wahrnehmung, Analyse*, edited by Wolfgang Michalka, 736–58. Weyarn: Seehamer, 1997.

Pulzer, Peter. "Der Erste Weltkrieg." In *Deutsch-Jüdische Geschichte in der Neuzeit, Vol. 3: Umstrittene Integration, 1871–1918*, edited by Steven M. Lowenstein, 356–79. Munich: C. H. Beck, 1997.
Raggam-Blesch, Michaela. "Jüdische Frauen im Krieg." In *Weltuntergang: Jüdisches Leben und Sterben im Ersten Weltkrieg*, edited by Marcus G. Patka, 159–67. Vienna: Styria, 2014.
Richter, Susan, ed. *Wissenschaft als weiblicher Beruf? Die ersten Frauen in Forschung und Lehre an der Universität Heidelberg*. Heidelberg: Universitätsmuseum, 2008.
Riemer, Nathanael. "'So kam es, daß wir in den Krieg zogen, weil wir Zionisten waren, nicht aber, obwohl wir Juden sind.' Nationaljüdischer Deutsch-Patriotismus zu Beginn des Ersten Weltkriegs im Spiegel der Jüdischen Rundschau." *Historisches Jahrbuch* 135 (2015): 412–52.
Rosenthal, Jacob. *Die Ehre des jüdischen Soldaten: Die Judenzählung im Ersten Weltkrieg und ihre Folgen*. Frankfurt/Main: Campus-Verlag, 2007.
Rozenblit, Marsha L. *Reconstructing a National Identity: The Jews of Habsburg Austria during World War I*. Oxford: Oxford University Press, 2001.
Schaser, Angelika. *Helene Lange und Gertrud Bäumer: Eine politische Lebensgemeinschaft*. Cologne: Böhlau, 2010.
Schoeps, Julius H. "Kriegsbegeisterung und Ernüchterung." *Zeitschrift für Religions- und Geistesgeschichte* 66, no. 1 (2014): 76–89.
Schuster, Frank M. *Zwischen allen Fronten: Osteuropäische Juden während des Ersten Weltkrieges (1914–1919)*. Cologne: Böhlau, 2004.
Seemann, Birgit. "'Wir wollen sein ein einig Volk von Schwestern': Jüdische Krankenpflege und der Erste Weltkrieg." *Nurinst* 7 (2014): 87–101.
Segall, Jacob. *Die deutschen Juden als Soldaten im Kriege 1914–1918: Eine statistische Studie. Mit einem Vorwort von Heinrich Silbergleit*. Berlin: Philo-Verlag, 1921.
Sieg, Ulrich. *Jüdische Intellektuelle im Ersten Weltkrieg: Kriegserfahrungen, weltanschauliche Debatten und kulturelle Neuentwürfe*. Berlin: Akademie Verlag, 2001.
Smith, Sidonie, and Julia Watson. "New Genres, New Subjects: Women, Gender, and Autobiography after 2000." *Revista Canaria de Estudios Ingleses* 58 (2009): 13–40.
Steer, Martina. "Nation, Religion, Gender: The Triple Challenge of Middle-Class German-Jewish Women in World War I." *Central European History* 48, no. 2 (2015): 176–98.
———. "Patriotismus, Frauensolidarität und jüdische Identität: Der jüdische Frauenbund im Ersten Weltkrieg." *Nurinst* 7 (2014): 59–72.
———. "'Wir wollen sein ein einig Volk von Schwestern, vor keiner Not uns fürchten und Gefahr!' Der Jüdische Frauenbund im Ersten Weltkrieg." In *Geschlecht, Religion und Engagement: Die jüdischen Frauenbewegungen im deutschsprachigen Raum, 19. und frühes 20. Jahrhundert*, edited by Margarete Grandner and Edith Saurer, 103–21. Vienna: Böhlau, 2005.
Stoehr, Irene. *Emanzipation zum Staat? Der Allgemeine Deutsche Frauenverein—Deutscher Staatsbürgerinnenverband, 1893–1933*. Pfaffenweiler: Centaurus, 1990.

Süchting-Hänger, Andrea. "Nationaler Frauendienst." In *Enzyklopädie Erster Weltkrieg*, 2nd ed., edited by Gerhard Hirschfeld, Gerd Krumeich, and Irina Renz, 731 et seq. Paderborn: Schöningh, 2014.

Ullrich, Anna. "'Nun sind wir gezeichnet': Jüdische Soldaten und die 'Judenzählung' im Ersten Weltkrieg." in *Krieg! Juden zwischen den Fronten 1914–1918*, edited by Ulrike Heikaus and Julia B. Köhne, 215–38. Berlin: Hentrich & Hentrich, 2014.

Verhey, Jeffrey. *The Spirit of 1914: Militarism, Myth, and Mobilization in Germany*. Cambridge: Cambridge University Press, 2000.

Vogt, Stefan. "The First World War, German Nationalism, and the Transformation of German Zionism." *Leo Baeck Institute Year Book* 57 (2012): 267–91.

Wehler, Hans-Ulrich. *Deutsche Gesellschaftsgeschichte*, vol. 4. Munich: C. H. Beck, 2003.

Wiese, Christian. "Martin Buber und die Wirkung des Ersten Weltkriegs auf die Prager Zionisten Hugo Bergmann, Robert Weltsch und Hans Kohn." *Tel Aviver Jahrbuch für deutsche Geschichte* 43 (2015): 181–222.

Winkler, Heinrich August. *Der lange Weg nach Westen, Vol. 1: Deutsche Geschichte vom Ende des Alten Reiches bis zum Untergang der Weimarer Republik*, 6th ed. Munich: C. H. Beck, 2005.

Zechlin, Egmont. *Die deutsche Politik und die Juden im Ersten Weltkrieg*. Göttingen: Vandenhoeck & Ruprecht, 1969.

Zimmermann, Moshe. *Die deutschen Juden 1914–1945*. Munich: Oldenbourg, 1997.

Zipperstein, Steven J. "The Politics of Relief: The Transformation of Russian Jewish Communal Life during the First World War." In *The Jews and the European Crisis, 1914–1921*, edited by Jonathan Frankel, 22–40. New York: Oxford University Press, 1988.

7

The Social Engagement of Jewish Women in Berlin during the First World War

Sabine Hank

Women's social engagement, that is to say, actions that are directed towards a community for the purpose of providing help and commitment to others, has a long tradition. The social commitment of women during the First World War was based on this tradition and, in particular, on the structures developed over several decades in the form of social welfare for the purpose of charity. Jewish welfare gradually became established in the last third of the nineteenth century. It originated from traditional Jewish charities (*Zedaka*) and bourgeois private charities, which supported the needy of all kinds (the poor, the sick, the elderly, the disabled, the desperate, people in crisis) and especially provided help for families and children. During this same period, a new approach to social work emerged that focused on sustainability, education through self-help and preventative health care, employment, and social reform.[1] These reforms required the break-up of traditional professional career patterns and the unilateral professional structure. The concentration of Jewish workers in the trade sector had to be dismantled. In particular, an expansion of the range of activities in agricultural and craft trades was sought. This happened not only as a means to defend against antisemitism, but also in response to a rapidly changing economy and resulting demands and opportunities. It was for this reason that by the turn of the century, Jewish organizations, such as the League of Jewish Women (Jüdischer Frauenbund, JFB) founded in 1904 and the B'nai B'rith lodges, created facilities for professional counseling and employment. During the First World War this process intensified due to the influx of Eastern European Jewish workers and refugees.[2]

Jewish social engagement was extremely diverse. This is not just a question of the different kinds of social assistance, but also of the institutions that operated. A survey of Jewish welfare institutions in Berlin and its suburbs of 1906 shows a total of 376 institutions, foundations, legacies, or similar institutions for welfare needs.[3] Women worked in all of these institutions, but primarily in those that took care of women and children. This included care for women who had recently given birth, widows, unmarried women, and brides; for children there were pediatric centers, holiday retreats, and welfare institutions for orphans.

In this chapter, I will use published literature as well as archival records to explore the social commitment of Jewish women during the First World War. The focus here is on women who lived in Berlin and who were free to work as volunteers, especially to help other women, both Jews and other Germans. Their activities can be placed into two main categories: first, activities within the Jewish Community and its institutions; and second, activities outside the community, in associations and foundations as well as local organizations. This chapter will focus on three institutions, which will allow for a detailed investigation into women's social engagement: the War Relief Commission (Kriegshilfskommission), the Jewish People's Association (Jüdischer Volksverein), and the Women's Association (Frauenverein) of Berlin's B'nai B'rith Lodges. These institutions have been chosen as case studies because this chapter focuses on middle-class Jewish women, rather than women who were active in working-class movements, such as the Social Democratic Party. The latter represents an area where further research needs to be undertaken.[4]

I would first like to make a few basic remarks about the Jewish Community of Berlin, its welfare work, and the corresponding institutions.[5] Around 1900, approximately 100,000 Jews lived in Berlin and the surrounding countryside. The number had almost tripled within three decades. Most Jews had moved from the Prussian province of Posen. In 1910, about 24 percent of German Jews and 35 percent of Jews registered in Prussia lived in the greater Berlin area. These included the entire Jewish community in Berlin, without distinction of religious orientations within Judaism, except for those who belonged to the Orthodox congregation Adass Jisroel after 1885. At the beginning of the imperial period, there were four synagogues (the Old Synagogue on Heidereutergasse since 1714, the synagogue on Johannisstraße since 1853, the New Synagogue on Oranienburger Straße since 1866, and the synagogue in the Kaiserstraße since 1869), but their number had actually grown to ten by 1916. In addition, there were numerous private synagogues.[6] Altogether, there were about forty-four thousand seats in synagogues in Berlin.

As everywhere else, the Jewish community in Berlin was not only a religious center, but also a provider of education and welfare. Thus, the community saw it as a duty to look after its needy and distressed

Figure 7.1 Helene Meyer, painting, ca. 1915, privately owned by Andres Meyer. Published with permission.

members.[7] Early measures like a donation fund for the poor led to the establishment of the Commission for the Poor (Armenkommission) in 1837. Gradually a network of modern welfare institutions emerged, with their central tasks including provisions for children, work, and health. In order to oversee their activities, the religious community set up various commissions, including commissions for donations, orphans, and welfare, and support for transients. Shortly before the war, in 1913, a further commission began work for collective guardianship of illegitimate, orphaned, and endangered children, providing for their legal and personal concerns.

For Jewish women at this time, helping in welfare organizations offered the only opportunity to work within the framework of the Jewish Community, and thus also gave them the chance to promote their emancipation. During the administration of the chairman of the Commission for the Poor, Wilhelm Feilchenfeld (1905–13), women were able to work on this commission for the first time, whereas previously they had worked only as caretakers in the welfare commission. As "distinguished" or "honorable" women (so called *Ehrendamen*), they were now occupying positions of status and relative power in these organizations, in which they played honored advisory roles. They often did the same work as their male counterparts, but had no right to vote. Nevertheless, *Ehrendamen* played an influential role during the war

Figure 7.2 Helene Meyer with her sons Walter Gerhard (left) and Kurt, ca. 1909, privately owned by Andres Meyer. Published with permission.

in organizing welfare, education, and health care programs. As these programs expanded exponentially in the context of total war, so too did women's status as they volunteered in advisory positions to administer war relief in the Jewish community.

The War Relief Commission (Kriegshilfskommission) of the Berlin Jewish Community and Its Department of Women's and Youth Welfare (Abteilung Frauen- und Jugendfürsorge), Chaired by Helene Meyer

Helene Meyer (née Herzfeld) was born on 21 September 1873 in Grätz (Posen). She came from a middle-class Jewish family and was married to lawyer Samuel Meyer (1859–1916). She was first active in the local Jewish Women's Association (Israelitischer Frauenverein) at an early phase of her life in Stargard, Pomerania, where she was the director of the organization for several years. She also took over the leadership of the League of Jewish Women (JFB). In these positions, she took part in various important functions. Job placement and career counseling were the main focus of Helene Meyer's activities for many years. In 1913, she moved to Charlottenburg near Berlin with her husband, the head of the poor and orphanage administration in the Jewish community of Berlin. Meyer successfully continued her engagement in the Berlin community. The mother of two sons and widowed in 1916, she remained active in social policies for women until her emigration to Argentina in August 1933. Helene Meyer died in February 1953 in Buenos Aires.[8]

At the very beginning of the war, the War Relief Commission (Kriegshilfskommission) was formed as another welfare organization to be administered by the Jewish community in Berlin.[9] The families of war veterans could not be, and did not want to be, provided for by the Commission for the Poor.[10] The task of the new commission was to support "those members of the community who were in crisis due to their war service or from other effects of the war."[11] Their work was to be carried out when local or state aid was not sufficient. The War Relief Commission had a total of thirty-one members (fourteen women and seventeen men); Bernhard Breslauer, the municipal councilor, supervised it.[12] It was divided into a main department as well as two subdivisions: Department M for men's care and Department F for women's and youth care.

Samuel Meyer and his wife Helene belonged to the main department of the War Relief Commission, where they worked on and approved applications and granted cash grants to needy individuals. The main responsibility of their department was the care of the wounded and sick in the hospitals, as well as help for refugees, a considerable number of whom were women. In addition to rabbis providing care in the hospitals and in the prison camps of Berlin, the War Relief Commission assigned a male or female assistant for regular visits to each hospital.[13] In 1916, their total came to thirty-eight. According to current research, twenty-seven female helpers are known by name. They all came from the Jewish middle class and were generally married to men who played a leading role in the Jewish community.[14] Benas Levy, for example, was responsible for the provision of men's welfare.[15] One of the community's goals was to open up new employment opportunities for men who were out of work. This was done in close cooperation with the Association for Work Certification (Verein für Arbeitsnachweis, which was part of the Work Placement Agency, or Arbeitsvermittlung). If this did not happen, the association also offered the opportunity to earn income through the sale of its own newspapers and postcards.

The range of tasks carried out by the Department of Women's and Youth Welfare (Abteilung Frauen- und Jugendfürsorge), whose chairmanship was occupied by Helene Meyer throughout the war,[16] was much more complex than projects undertaken by organizations for men.[17] This was mainly due to the fact that many women could not be placed straight into employment. They had to be brought into the workforce by means of training courses. For this reason, courses in sewing were of great importance, and thus a sewing school was established. In addition, the War Relief Commission provided women with their own sewing and knitting jobs, which could be done in sewing schools or as home work. Sewing and embroidery work could also be carried out in the evenings, for which only a small amount of donated food was available. In the context of training for employment, provisions were also made for the care of children by accommodating them in kindergartens, as well as in recreation programs in the countryside. Another major task was the procurement and distribution of food, clothing, and fuel. The needy received food and fuel ration cards and were supplied with clothes from a clothing house and warm meals from a civic kitchen until January 1916. All these activities allowed the development, enlightenment, and mentorship of women in the most broad and narrow sense. In the girls' school of the Jewish community and in the Toynbee Hall[18] of the Berlin Lodge, for example, lectures were given on medical and domestic topics, including how to better use food and save fuel.[19]

In order to deal with all these different tasks, the Department of Women's and Youth Welfare, which was composed of fourteen

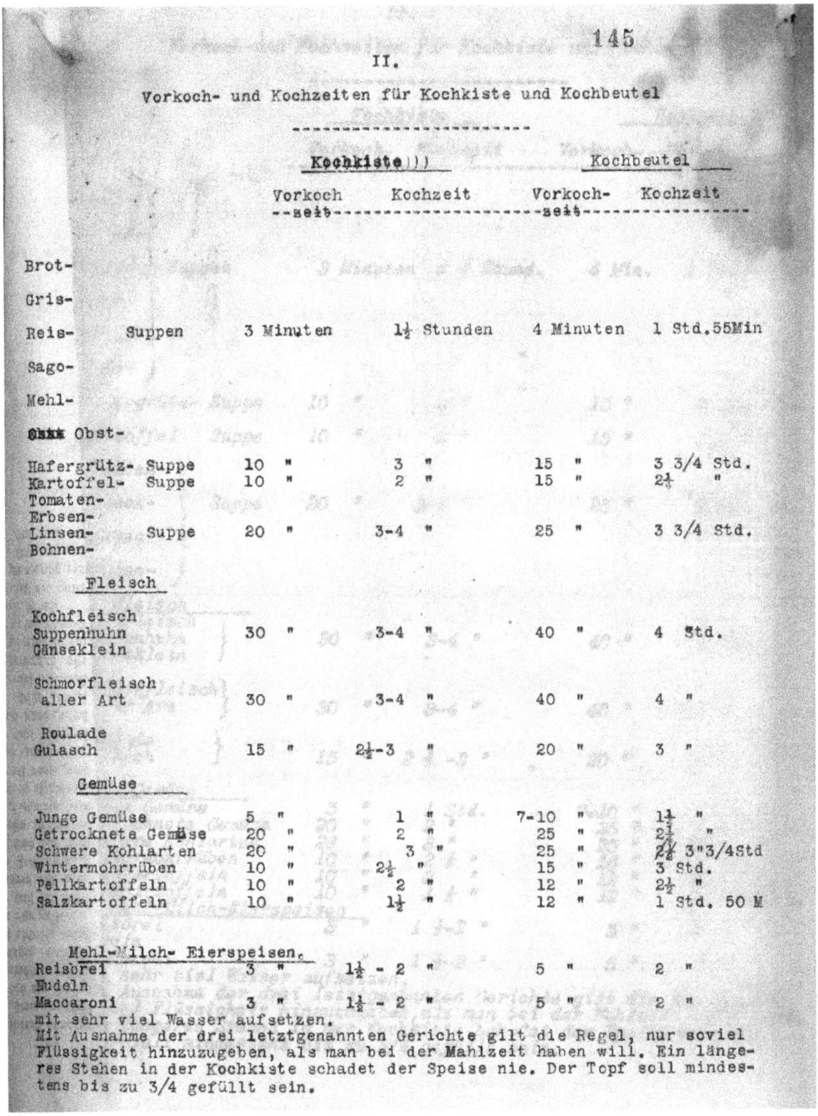

II.
Vorkoch- und Kochzeiten für Kochkiste und Kochbeutel

		Kochkiste		Kochbeutel	
		Vorkoch-zeit	Kochzeit	Vorkoch-zeit	Kochzeit
Brot- Gris- Reis- Sago- Mehl-	Suppen	3 Minuten	1½ Stunden	4 Minuten	1 Std.55Min
Obst-					
Hafergrütz- Suppe Kartoffel- Suppe		10 " 10 "	3 " 2 "	15 " 15 "	3 3/4 Std. 2¼ "
Tomaten- Erbsen- Linsen- Bohnen-	Suppe	20 "	3-4 "	25 "	3 3/4 Std.
Fleisch					
Kochfleisch Suppenhuhn Gänseklein		30 "	3-4 "	40 "	4 Std.
Schmorfleisch aller Art		30 "	3-4 "	40 "	4 "
Roulade Gulasch		15 "	2½-3 "	20 "	3 "
Gemüse					
Junge Gemüse		5 "	1 "	7-10 "	1½ "
Getrocknete Gemüse		20 "	2 "	25 "	2¼ "
Schwere Kohlarten		20 "	3 "	25 "	2¼ " 3"3/4Std
Wintermohrrüben		10 "	2½ "	15 "	3 Std.
Pellkartoffeln		10 "	2 "	12 "	2½ "
Salzkartoffeln		10 "	1½ "	12 "	1 Std. 50 M
Mehl-Milch- Eierspeisen					
Reisbrei Nudeln Maccaroni		3 " 3 "	1½ - 2 " 1½ - 2 "	5 " 5 "	2 " 2 "

mit sehr viel Wasser aufsetzen.
Mit Ausnahme der drei letztgenannten Gerichte gilt die Regel, nur soviel Flüssigkeit hinzuzugeben, als man bei der Mahlzeit haben will. Ein längeres Stehen in der Kochkiste schadet der Speise nie. Der Topf soll mindestens bis zu 3/4 gefüllt sein.

Figure 7.3 Instructions for use of cooking boxes and cooking bags. Courtesy of Centrum Judaicum Archive.

women and three men, created twelve further subcommittees in Berlin with 140 female assistants. The foundation for the work of the War Relief Commission came, on the one hand, from funds approved by the *Gemeinde*, and on the other hand, from donations of goods and money. The latter provided the bulk of the revenue. The acquisition of

Figure 7.4 Concert announcement for a fundraiser, 1915. Courtesy of Centrum Judaicum Archive.

donations was therefore enormously important. All possibilities had to be explored for this. In addition to making calls and a targeted approach to finding donors, other paths were also taken. In February 1915, the Jewish Community organized a concert at the Philharmonic, the proceeds of which were to be used primarily to support the vocational training of Jewish women and girls.

The chair for collecting donations was Helene Meyer, supported by her representative Rosa Lilienthal,[20] and they were responsible for the organization and coordination of work in her department and for all assistants in the subcommittees. The Department of Women's and Youth Welfare published a detailed monthly report on the activity and provided statistics on their work, which intermittently appeared in the Jewish press, including in the *Berliner Jüdisches Gemeindeblatt* and the *Allgemeine Zeitung des Judentums*.

The Jewish People's Association (Jüdischer Volksverein)

The Jewish People's Association[21] was founded in 1905 in Berlin as an auxiliary association to support Jewish immigrants. The first chairmen were Hans Mühsam and Ilja Ber.[22] The association initially consisted of a train station attendant (*Bahnhofswache*), an information office, and a few sleeping rooms. In the wake of the 1904–06 Russian pogroms against Jews, the Volksverein was able to help refugees. The inflow of funds decreased somewhat, and financial support was also reduced. Thus, emigrants and also returnees had to stay in Berlin longer than planned. There was therefore a need to set up a larger hostel. This was done in 1908 with the approval of the board of the Jewish community. Implementation and a reorganization of the association took place a year later. On Auguststraße 20 in central Berlin, the first rooms for a hostel were made available in 1910. After gaining the approval of the Jewish community's commission on refugees, those concerned were transferred to the hostel of the Jewish People's Association. The community paid for them.[23] The German Association for Assistance of German Jews (Hilfsverein der Deutschen Juden), the Universal Jewish Alliance (Alliance Israélite Universelle), and the Berlin lodges of the B'nai B'rith Order also supported the Jewish People's Association. In a 1913 list of welfare institutions, Salli Kirschstein[24] is mentioned as the chairman of the following institutions within the Jewish People's Association: (1) the center for Jews who are travelling, located on Auguststraße 20 (which provided free hostel and boarding); (2) train station attendants for the accommodation and transportation of Jews; (3) a body providing information on matters of scholarship, law, and welfare institutions; and (4) patient care for hospitals.[25]

A contemporary publication provides an interesting picture of the daily activities of the Jewish People's Association.[26] The train station

Figure 7.5 Train station attendant of the Jüdischer Volksverein at work, *Ost und West* 6, no. 7 (July 1906): col. 483–84. Public domain image.

attendants were allowed to enter the platform free of charge. They were recognizable to the conductor by wearing a white metal plate with the Star of David on their clothes. In addition to receiving information and assistance, the needy were also given light refreshments in tea houses created at the train stations.

The office also provided booklets in Yiddish and German, with relevant questions answered for emigrants; much of this information had already been distributed at the borders. Only women worked in the health care unit. They visited emigrants in the hospitals and took care of them (helping them with correspondence, providing distraction, going on walks and errands, assisting in exchanges with doctors and medical staff, taking care of their discharge). The way in which the association developed contact with emigrants is particularly interesting. Red posters were placed in hospitals and hostels, which, in Yiddish and German, called on emigrants to sign up if they needed care in the hospital or better accommodation. In a department for making clothing, women also knitted and crocheted new garments for those who needed them. In January 1914, in a letter to the board of the Jewish Community, the Volksverein asked to lease a community building on

Auguststraße 14–16 (until then the old city Jewish hospital had been located there), in order to be able to create more hostel rooms. With the start of hostilities, the church provided rooms there as well as in other parts of the neighborhood.[27]

What kind of work did the Jewish People's community undertake in the war, especially with regard to the work of women, including *Ehrendamen*, who were women of high social status serving in advisory roles?[28] As the situation for refugees, immigrants, and migrants changed and intensified during the war, women increasingly played a greater role in supporting this growing population. With the war's outbreak, many travelers, predominantly from Russia but also from the then Russian-occupied areas, could not return to their homeland. They had been on vacation, on convalescence, or carrying out business, and were taken by surprise by the war, which essentially made them refugees. In many cases, they did not have enough money or contacts to help themselves in the new situation. Therefore, they had to quickly get help and support.[29] Working with the Volksverein, the Jewish Community (*Jüdische Gemeinde*), and the Berlin lodges, the municipal administration and private persons provided accommodation that could be used by the association. The military authorities approved the establishment of eight such hostels, which were open to people beyond the needy in

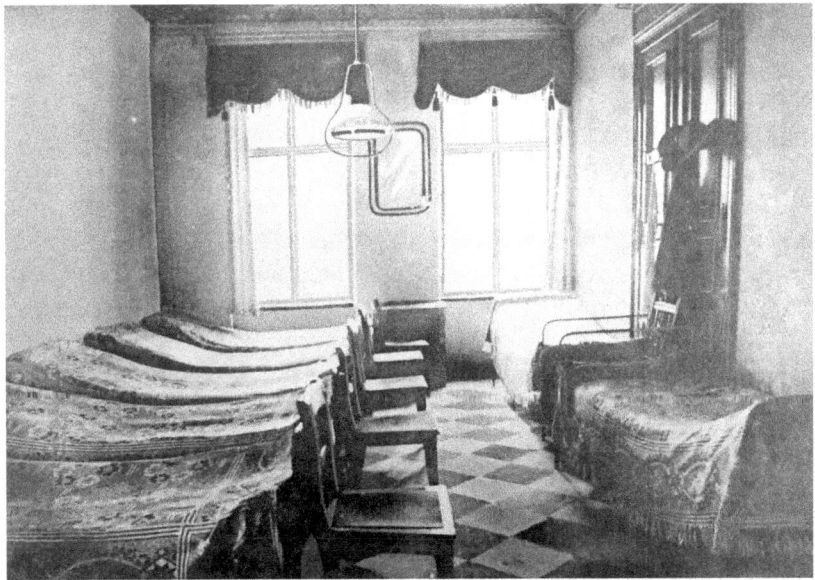

Figure 7.6 A bedroom in the Jüdischer Volksverein hostel in Berlin, Auguststraße 20, Kriegsbericht 1914–16, o. O., o. J. Public domain image.

the Jewish community.[30] In these, up to one thousand persons each day could find accommodation and care.

In the hostels, women supervised the kitchens, distributed food, and provided the needy with the essentials (clothes, blankets, and bedding). They listened to their troubles and sorrows and tried to provide consolation and hope. Women also helped people with correspondence, including writing to authorities. Apart from the first chairman Salli Kirschstein and thirteen other men, the board of the Jüdischer Volksverein also included three *Ehrendamen* from 1914 to 1916.

One of these *Ehrendamen* was Paula Kirschstein (née Fabian), the mother of Salli Kirschstein.[31] Born on 26 February 1848 in Tuchel (West Prussia), she lived with her husband, the merchant Abraham Kirschstein, in Chodzies (Kolmar in Posen) and Thorn (West Prussia). Shortly after his death in 1901 she moved to Berlin. Due to the obscurity of existing source material, it is not entirely clear when Paula Kirschstein began her commitment to the Volksverein. Because of her already advanced age, however, it might be assumed that she took a role as an *Ehrendame* and worked with her son, as he also held an administrative position with the association. *Ehrendamen* in the Volksverein acted as directors of the internal administration of the hostels, which included disseminating information and helping people find employment. Together with the executive committee, they also handled communication with the authorities, including acquiring residence permits from the Royal Prussian Command Headquarters (Königlich-Preußische Kommandantur) in Berlin. Paula Kirschstein died in Berlin on 5 November 1936. She was buried at the Jewish cemetery in Berlin-Weißensee.[32]

There were a few lists issued in August and September 1914 of previous inhabitants of Russian villages, as well as residence permits for persons of Russian nationality, who were regarded as hostile foreigners. On these documents it was noted that the persons concerned were allowed to stay in Berlin until further notice (they had to give their address) and they had to report to the police station every three days. For this reason, their residence could not be changed without permission. They were also prohibited from spreading news of "the war effort or war preparations," which meant that the correspondence had to be sent openly.[33]

An August 1914 memorandum from the War Relief Commission makes it clear that there was also a direct collaboration between the Jewish People's Association and the War Relief Commission for the creation of accommodation facilities by the Jewish community. This

Figure 7.7 Food distribution in the Jüdischer Volksverein hostel in the exhibition halls at the zoo, Kriegsbericht 1914–16. Public domain image.

is suggested in the request of Frau "Herrmann" Aron for clothes for Russian Jews who were housed in the exhibition halls of Berlin Zoo. The commission arranged the distribution of the desired clothes from her wardrobe.[34]

It is interesting to note that Frau Aron is also mentioned in *Gemeinde* publications as a helper (*Helferin*) in the War Relief Commission, and she is specifically named as an honorary woman (*Ehrendame*) who lived in a retirement home of the Jewish Community (on Schönhauser Allee).[35] Her first name was Sara (née Silberstein).[36] In October and November 1914, most of the hostels were disbanded, except for those on Auguststraße 17 and 20 and on Spandauer Straße 31. Shortly thereafter, the Jewish People's Association became the main point of entry for the growing migrant population of Eastern European Jews. After the war, they eventually operated only one hostel on Auguststraße 17. It served once again as a shelter for foreign travelers. The Jewish People's Association probably existed until 1920; there is no evidence for its existence after that.

The Berlin B'nai B'rith Lodge and Its Women's Association (Frauenverein)

B'nai B'rith International was founded in 1843 in New York by German Jewish immigrants as a men's fraternity, in the tradition of the Free Masons, and saw itself as committed to the humanistic ideals of tolerance, humanity, and welfare. For this reason, it dedicated itself to awakening and strengthening identity through education about Jewry. Social work became one of the primary activities of B'nai B'rith. Beginning in 1882, it also expanded throughout Germany. Lodges were established in Berlin and several other cities, and by the beginning of the First World War there were eighty lodges in total. From 1912, the main Lodge House of the four Berlin lodges that existed at the time was located at Kleiststraße 10 in Schöneberg.[37]

At the outbreak of the First World War, the Berlin lodges established a permanent War Relief Committee (Kriegshilfsausschuß),[38] whose responsibilities were both varied and extensive. Training courses on wartime medical care as well as a general information and consultation office were created, providing welfare for families of soldiers as well as the needy. In Toynbee Hall at Gipsstraße 12a in central Berlin, for example, a regular wartime welfare dinner was held.[39] In cooperation with its own employment office, the committee also announced employment opportunities, assumed responsibility for welfare and curatorship for the families of lodge members, and maintained a statistical record of their service. A significant activity of the lodges was the conversion of the lodge house into the organization's military hospital in August 1914, a facility that remained in operation for the duration of the war.[40]

In addition, the War Relief Committee supported other wartime welfare initiatives, not least those of the Jewish Community in Berlin and those of the Jewish People's Association, through financial contributions. The latter included, as has been mentioned, practical assistance by making hostel rooms available (as was the case at Kleiststraße 12, which belonged to the building complex of the lodge).

To a significant degree, the efforts of the War Relief Committee were defined by the engagement of women, especially lodge "sisters." Thus, for example, in the aforementioned hospital of the Berlin lodges, nine women served as *Ehrendamen*. In the case of Minna Schwarz, we know for a fact that she had been a lodge "sister."[41] For the other women involved, this assumption is also valid, and it meant that members of a lodge were engaged in an honorary capacity in their organization.

Figure 7.8 Hedwig Ehrenberg, first from the left and sitting, with nurses and the head doctor of the military hospital in the Jewish lodge on Kleiststraße, Berlin, ca. 1915, Jüdisches Museum Berlin, donated by Eva H. Ehrenberg. Published with permission.

Another of the known *Ehrendamen* was Hedwig Ehrenberg (née Schachian). Born on 27 July 1875 in Driesen (Neumark), she had been married to the insurance director and member of the Montefiore Lodge, Albert Ehrenberg (1857–1925) since 1897.[42] The couple had three children. Hedwig Ehrenberg emigrated to Great Britain in 1939. She most likely died there, in Wembley, in 1945.[43]

The responsibilities of the *Ehrendamen* in the organization's military hospitals were varied. Among other tasks, they were charged with caring for the sick and wounded, organizing events and presentations, field trips, and visits to the theatre. They acquired reading material and ensured that patients had contact with their family members. Apparently, they also collected donations for the military hospital. In what follows, the Frauenverein of the Berlin Lodges and their founder and first chairwoman, Minna Schwarz,[44] will be examined.

Minna Schwarz, née Rosenau, was born on 25 November 1859 in Pyritz, Pomerania. In 1882 she married the businessman Meyer Schwarz (1853–1929) and the couple lived together in Berlin. Together with relatives, her husband managed several clothing and textile businesses and was a member of the Berthold-Auerbach Lodge.[45] They remained childless. Meyer Schwarz's financial potential and social standing ensured that his wife would receive the support necessary for her to play an active role in the lodge's social outreach. Minna Schwarz did not commit herself exclusively to the Frauenverein of the Berlin lodges, but also worked actively in the management of the League of Jewish Women (JFB) in the Berlin Jewish Community, and in the Central Association of German Citizens of Jewish Faith (CV). She also belonged to numerous other organizations and committees. During the war she was on the War Relief Committee of the Jewish Community and, as mentioned, an *Ehrendame* in the military hospital of the Berlin lodges.[46] From 1934, Minna Schwarz lived at Brunnenstraße 41 in central Berlin, where a section of her mother's home and nursery functioned as an old age home. She lived there until her death on 27 December 1936. Minna Schwarz was buried in the Jewish cemetery at Berlin-Weißensee.[47]

The Women's Association of the Berlin lodges was established in 1888, and Minna Schwarz was among its principle co-founders and long-time members. In addition to the Frauenverein, there were several other sister leagues, specifically organizations in Berlin that were affiliated with the individual lodges.[48] These lodges distinguished themselves from other Jewish women's organizations by the fact that only wives of lodge "brothers" were allowed to become members, and that "sisters" were also required to pay initial member dues. Women and children in particular were cause for attention in the social welfare program. Work communities were also established, which dealt with a variety of subjects, such as Jewish culture, modern social work, and education, including pedagogy and psychology.[49]

From its inception, the Frauenverein saw as its primary role the legal protection of mothers and infants. Initially members provided care for poor Jewish women who had recently given birth, including single unwed mothers. Primary caregivers were sent into households in order to guide and accompany the women. In addition, from 1908 priority was given to creating space for expectant mothers in receiving assistance, and in 1910 a maternity home was established. During the war, the need to protect mothers and their infants grew in importance, so these efforts were expanded even further. Originally established in 1913, a new wing was added to the mothers' and children's home in the Brunnenstraße at the end of 1914, once the existing space no longer sufficed.[50]

The war left many women and mothers in great distress, as their finances were increasingly restricted due to the absence of the male breadwinner and the lack of day-to-day support from partners. The home even accepted female refugees from East Prussia, Galicia, and Belgium. In June 1917, the mothers' and children's home opened an

Figure 7.9 Mother's and children's home of the Frauenverein of the Berlin lodges, U. O. B. B. (United Orders of B'nai B'rith) *Allgemeine Zeitung des Judentums* 79, no. 37 (8 September 1915): 439. Public domain image.

affiliated information center for mothers. Beyond that, it became necessary, given the widespread shortage of foodstuffs, to ensure that unrestricted access to infant nutrition and medicine was maintained. In October of that year, the association established regular childcare training courses and weekly caregivers.[51] In 1926, the mothers' and children's courses were recognized by the state as an official Infant's Care School.[52]

In addition to these primary tasks, the Frauenverein was active in other areas as well. For example, the aforementioned wartime soup kitchen (*Kriegsspeiseanstalt*) in the Toynbee Hall was run exclusively by association members. The association further supported the staff of the Department of Women's and Youth Welfare of the War Relief Commission. Even in the soup kitchens of the Berlin Jewish Community, the Frauenverein was active.

Conclusion

While the Jewish Community in Berlin and its social welfare committee, the Jewish People's Association, as well as the Berlin lodges of B'nai B'rith and their women's association, worked independently before and during the war, they remained connected and supported each other in a variety of ways. The People's Association, as the smallest entity, received practical and financial assistance from the two larger associations, and especially from the community. It in turn represented, through its engagement with the community and the lodges, supplementary support and relief. It is apparent when examining all three organizations that they adapted to the new demands imposed upon them by the war. The community reacted to these developments by creating the War Relief Commission. Likewise, they strove to combine their resources in ever more effective ways. This found expression in, among other things, the work undertaken by women.[53]

The women who had been active in this field, as far as the sources reveal, belonged almost without exception to the Jewish bourgeoisie. This was the case for Helene Meyer, Paula Kirschstein, Minna Schwarz, and Hedwig Ehrenberg. Not a small number of women were active in different capacities and were members of multiple organizations. In this way, their efforts were not relegated to Berlin or to serving exclusively Jewish special interests. Helene Meyer and Minna Schwarz, for example, played leading roles in the League of Jewish Women (JFB); they were also active throughout the war in the National Women's Service (Nationaler Frauendienst). Through this voluntary work, many of the mentioned and unnamed women met and knew each other.

Such engagement became possible for women only because their spouses provided important material support and offered free space. Like other family members, the husbands of many women held positions in the Jewish community, and it was not uncommon for them to have been involved in welfare activities. This was the case with Samuel Meyer, husband of Helene Meyer, and with Salli Kirschstein, the son of Paula Kirschstein. The men presided over crucial relationships. Through them, connections were forged with the lodges. Salli Kirschstein, Meyer Schwarz, and Albert Ehrenberg belonged to this group in Berlin. In this way, Minna Schwarz was accepted into a lodge and was able to act in the same capacity as a lodge "sister." By interpreting such circumstances, one could arrive at the conclusion that it was fashionable in many Jewish middle-class marriages for both partners to adhere to socially prescribed—in other words unequal—gender roles.

The motivations of individual women to become socially active were of course diverse. For some, the primary motive was humanitarian engagement. Especially during the war, with its particular demands on individual initiative, patriotism was an important motivating factor. Even if we have no testimonies that explicitly articulate this motive, it is clear that, despite all the differences in their German Jewish self-image, they clearly belonged to the assimilated Jewish middle class and thus were integrated into German society. This, in turn, influenced their activities. Another important factor was the quest for emancipation, which varied according to the location and perspective of the individual actors.

Further studies are required to investigate these aspects in greater detail. For this reason, the chapter will end with an observation by Helene Meyer on the eve of the First World War, which conveys her attitude towards female participation in the war effort quite clearly. Invoking the deployment of women in community care, she called for a stronger involvement of female members in community life and pointed to the need for not only voluntary but also professional activity. Meyer reached the following conclusion: "For the attainment ... of these goals in their entirety, however, the first basic requirement must be suffrage for the female commission members and eventually demand for voting rights for the women in the community; for only suffrage will guarantee that women have adequate influence on the implementation of all desired social measures."[54]

Sabine Hank is an archivist at the New Synagogue Berlin, Centrum Judaicum Foundation. She has co-authored and edited numerous volumes on German Jews during the First World War, including *Feldpostbriefe jüdischer Soldaten 1914–1918* (Hentrich & Hentrich, 2002), *"Bis der Krieg uns lehrt, was der Friede bedeutet": Das Ehrenfeld für die jüdischen Gefallenen des Weltkrieges auf dem Friedhof der Berliner Jüdischen Gemeinde* (Hentrich & Hentrich, 2004), *Feldrabbiner in den deutschen Streitkräften des Ersten Weltkrieges* (Hentrich & Hentrich, 2013), and *Jüdische Frauen im Ersten Weltkrieg: Paula Glück, Juliane Herrmann, Helene Meyer, Johanna Nathan* (Hentrich & Hentrich, 2017).

Notes

This chapter is based on a lecture given at the 27th International Summer Academy of the Institut für jüdische Geschichte Österreichs, which took place from 5 to 7 July 2017 in Vienna under the theme "For Emperor and Fatherland: Jewish and Non-Jewish Experiences in the First World War." I would like to thank Hermann Simon (Berlin) for the professional exchanges and critical review of the manuscript, and I would like to especially thank my husband, Uwe Hank, for his comprehensive support in the preparation of the lecture and this chapter. I would also like to thank Daniela Müller (Berlin) and Stephan

Kummer (Centrum Judaicum Foundation, Berlin) for supporting and editing the English translation of my article.

1. See Claudia Prestel, "Weibliche Rollenzuweisung in jüdischen Organisationen: Das Beispiel des Bnei Briss", in *Bulletin des Leo Baeck Instituts* 85 (1990): 51–79, here 51.
2. See Angelika Kipp, *Jüdische Arbeits- und Berufsfürsorge in Deutschland 1900–1933 (Dokumente—Texte—Materialien)*, Zentrum für Antisemitismusforschung der Technischen Universität Berlin, 31 (Berlin, 1999), 38 et seq.
3. *Die Wohlfahrtseinrichtungen für Jüdische Hilfsbedürftige in Berlin und Vororten*, ed. by der Armenkommission der Jüdischen Gemeinde zu Berlin (Berlin, 1906).
4. For this approach, see Michaela Raggam-Blesch, "Frauen zwischen den Fronten: Jüdinnen in feministischen, politischen und philanthropischen Bewegungen in Wien an der Wende des 19. zum 20. Jahrhundert," in *Geschlecht, Religion und Engagement: Die jüdischen Frauenbewegungen im deutschsprachigen Raum, 19. und frühes 20. Jahrhundert* (L'Homme. Europäische Zeitschrift für Feministische Geschichtswissenschaft, Schriften, 9), ed. Margarete Grandner and Edith Sauer (Vienna, 2005), 25–55, here 47 ff.
5. See Chana Schütz, "Die Kaiserzeit (1871–1918)," in *Juden in Berlin*, ed. Andreas Nachama, Julius H. Schoeps, and Hermann Simon (Berlin, 2001), 89–136, here 94 et seq.
6. See Max M. Sinasohn, *Die Berliner Privatsynagogen und ihre Rabbiner 1671–1971: Zur Erinnerung an das 300 jährige Bestehen der Jüdischen Gemeinde zu Berlin* (Jerusalem, 1971).
7. An overview of the development of Jewish welfare is provided in Fritz Lamm "1833–1933: Hundert Jahre Gemeindewohlfahrtspflege," in *Gemeindeblatt der Jüdischen Gemeinde zu Berlin* 23, no. 10 (October 1933): 326–329.
8. See also Sabine Hank and Uwe Hank, *Jüdische Frauen im Ersten Weltkrieg: Paula Glück, Juliane Herrmann, Helene Meyer, Johanna Nathan*. Jüdische Miniaturen 192 (Berlin, 2017), 33–53.
9. On the origins and work of the commission, see the description in *Gemeindeblatt der Jüdischen Gemeinde zu Berlin* 4, no. 9 (11 September 1914): 113; and no. 12 (11 December 1914): 154–155; *Mitteilungen über die Verwaltung der jüdischen Gemeinde zu Berlin*, ed. Vorstand des Liberalen Vereins für die Angelegenheiten der jüdischen Gemeinde zu Berlin (Berlin, 1916), 32–38; Ernestine Eschelbacher, "Die Arbeit der jüdischen Frauen in Deutschland während des Krieges," *Ost und West. Illustrierte Monatsschrift für das gesamte Judentum* 19, no. 5/6 (May/June 1919): col. 137-150, here 138 et seq.
10. See Lamm, "1833–1933," 328.
11. Verwaltungsbericht des Vorstandes der jüdischen Gemeinde zu Berlin für die Zeit vom 1. April 1913 bis 31. März 1916, Berlin 1916, Centrum Judaicum Archiv (hereafter CJA), (CJA, 1 A Be 2, No. 3, #226, folio 167-167 vr), 9–10, here 9.

12. Dr. Bernhard Breslauer (born 16 November 1851, Posen; died 11 February 1928, Berlin) worked from 1880 as a lawyer and notary in Berlin. He was the co-founder of the Verband der deutschen Juden in 1904 and the Vereinigung für das liberale Judentum in Deutschland in 1908. He was the head of the latter until 1917.
13. *Gemeindeblatt der Jüdischen Gemeinde zu Berlin* 5, no. 8 (13 August 1915): 99–100; and 6, no. 8 (11 August 1916): 93–95.
14. I would like to thank Frau Uta Drews (Fehrbellin-Brunne) for uncovering these names.
15. Benas Levy (born 9 September 1856, Krotoschin, Posen; died 20 November 1931, Berlin) founded a wholesale enterprise of cotton goods in Berlin. He was a member of the assembly of representatives in the Jewish Community for many years. Levy launched the first Jewish Reading Room in Berlin and became a member and sponsor of the Library Commission and the art collection of the *Gemeinde*. He also worked in the *Kuratorium* of the second orphanage of the Jewish Community in Berlin-Pankow.
16. See Eschelbacher, "Die Arbeit der jüdischen Frauen," col. 141 (Image).
17. In the archives of the Centrum Judaicum there is only a single file (CJA, 1 C Ge 1, No. 956, #10846) that documents the activities of the Department of Women and Youth Care in the time from August 1914 to July 1916, and this source is thus the basis for the following statements.
18. On the Toynbee Hall, see the excerpt *Die Berliner Bne-Briss-Logen und deren Frauenverein* (anonymous).
19. *Gemeindeblatt der Jüdischen Gemeinde zu Berlin* 5, no. 11 (12 November 1915): 144–145; CJA, 1 C Ge 1, No. 956, #10846,. fol. 144–146 (*Anleitung zur Verwendung von Kochkisten und Kochbeuteln*).
20. Rosa Lilienthal, née Bab (born 25 November 1873, Berlin; died 8 December 1933, Berlin) was the wife of Justice Council Dr Leo Lilienthal, who was a member of the board of the Jewish Community of Berlin and its longstanding syndicate. Like Helene Meyer, Rosa Lilienthal held an honorary office as a second chairperson of the War Relief Commission.
21. On the history and activities of the Verein, see Hans Mühsam, "Der Dornenweg des jüdischen Wanderers," *Ost und West. Illustrierte Monatsschrift für das gesamte Judentum* 6, no. 7 (July 1906): col. 479–488; "Jüdischer Volksverein (Saumeich Nauflim)," *Ost und West* 11, no. 6 (June 1911): col. 569-578.
22. Dr Hans Günther Mühsam (born 15 July 1876, Berlin; died 1957, Haifa), brother of the well-known publicist, writer, and political activist Erich Mühsam, worked as a doctor in Berlin. He emigrated in 1938 to Palestine. Ilja Ber (born 12 January 1848, Wirballen, Ostpreußen; died 20 December 1911, Berlin) was a stock producer from Berlin.
23. In September 1914, the municipality supported the association with an extraordinary ongoing subsidy of 4,000 Marks. See the *Gemeindeblatt der Jüdischen Gemeinde zu Berlin* 4, no. 9 (11 September 1914): 113.
24. Salli Kirschstein, born in Chodziesen (Kolmar, in Posen) on 26 July 1869, was a merchant and owner of a clothing company. He volunteered for a long period of time in Berlin's Jewish community. For example,

he volunteered in the Armenkommission and in the Commission for Welfare of travelling Jews in need of help (Kommission zur Unterstützung hilfsbedürftiger durchreisender Juden). Kirschstein was also a member of the German Reichsloge. He appeared as a successful collector of Jewish artifacts and founded a private museum. Salli Kirschstein died in Berlin on 11 January 1935. He was buried at the Jewish cemetery in Berlin-Weißensee. See Hermann Simon, "Ein leidenschaftlicher Judaica-Sammler," in *Gerhard Hentrich, Der Verleger: Festschrift zum 70. Geburtstag für Gerhard Hentrich*, ed. Werner Buchwald and Hermann Simon (Berlin, 1994), 223–232.

25. *Die Wohlfahrtseinrichtungen von Groß-Berlin*, Nachtrag April 1913, ed. by the Zentrale für private Fürsorge, Berlin, 1913, 14.
26. See Noëmi Banéth, *Soziale Hilfsarbeit der modernen Jüdin: Ein Vortrag* (Berlin, 1907). Note on the author: Noëmi (Naomi) Baneth (born 1883) was the daughter of Rabbi Prof. Dr Eduard Baneth, lecturer at the Lehranstalt für die Wissenschaft des Judentums in Berlin.
27. CJA, Sammlung Benas Levy, not registered, letter from 1 January 1914.
28. See here the Jüdischer Volksverein, Herberge, Auguststrasse 20, E. V., Kriegsbericht 1914-1916, Berlin [1916] (The National Library of Israel, Sign.: 2008 B 4350), 24 pp. I would like to thank Lea Simon (Berlin) for making this publication available. See also Eschelbacher, "Die Arbeit der jüdischen Frauen," col. 143–144.
29. In November 1914, the Volksverein asked the municipal authorities of Berlin for 3,000 Marks in financial support, in order to be able to continue the operation of the hostel in Auguststraße 17. The magistrate granted the request in the same month. See Landesarchiv Berlin, A Rep 001-02, No. 1964, fol. 17–18 and 23.
30. This includes the following hostels: Auguststraße 20 u. 17 (Jüdischer Volksverein), Spandauer Straße 31 (Jüdische Gemeinde), Ausstellungshallen am Zoo (Direktor Freudenberg), Sanatorium Niederschönhausen (Dr. Josselewski), Krausnickstraße 11 (Malermeister Löwenstein), Molkenmarkt 1 (Königliches Polizeipräsidium), Kleiststraße 12 (Berliner Logen), and Auguststraße 14–16 (Jüdische Gemeinde).
31. Regarding Eschelbacher, "Die Arbeit der jüdischen Frauen," col. 142, Paula Kirschstein was erroneously identified as chair of the Verein.
32. Jüdischer Friedhof Berlin-Weißensee, Beisetzungsregister (meaning the Registry of Funerals), No. 94827.
33. CJA, Sammlung Benas Levy, not registered.
34. CJA, 1 C Ge 1, No. 956, #10846, Sitzungsprotokoll 28 August 1914, fol. 22–25 and 27, here fol. 24.
35. Monatsbericht der Kriegshilfskommission, Abteilung Frauen- und Jugendfürsorge, December 1914, in CJA, 1 C Ge 1, No. 956, #10846, fol. 157–158, here fol. 158 (including a list for the women working in the war relief commission); *Mitteilungen über die Verwaltung der jüdischen Gemeinde zu Berlin*, 53.
36. Sara Aron, née Silberstein (born 1 July 1855, Serteggen, Ostpreußen; died 8 January 1935, Berlin). Her husband Hermann Aron (1855–1934) was the

leader of the Jüdischen Volksverein as well as a member of the Armen- and the Durchreisendenkommission (commission for travelling through) in the Jewish community.
37. These was the Deutsche Reichsloge, the Berthold-Auerbach-Loge, the Montefiore-Loge, and the Spinoza-Loge. See CJA, 1 C Ve 1, No. 136, #12759, fol. 229.
38. See the report of the Großloge für Deutschland VIII U. O. B. B., No. 8, September 1914, 115–117 and 118–122; ibid., No. 10, December 1914, 154–156. (online source: http://sammlungen.ub.uni-frankfurt.de/cm/search?op eration=searchRetrieve&query=vl.corporation%3D%22Independent%20 Order%20of%20B%27nai%20B%27rith%20%2F%20Gro%C3%9Floge%20 f%C3%BCr%20Deutschland%22%20and%20vl.domain%3Ddomain%20 sortBy%20dc.title%2Fasc, 09.07.2018)
39. The Toynbee Halls of the B'nai-B'rith Lodges, originating from the United Kingdom, were set up in various places following the examples established by the economist and social reformer Arnold Toynbee (1852–1883). Their purpose was to provide access to culture and education for poorer Jewish social classes through free lectures and entertainment. The Toynbee Hall of the Berlin Lodges was opened in Kaiserstraße 10 in Charlottenburg in 1904. In November 1909, it moved to central Berlin in the Gipsstraße. In 1937 they were dissolved.
40. See Josef Hirsch, "Das Vereinslazarett der Berliner Logen U. O. B. B.," Kleiststraße 10, Berlin 1919.
41. See reference to Minna Schwarz below.
42. Mitglieder-Verzeichnis der Berliner Logen U. O. B. B., 1922/23, Berlin [1923], 55. I thank Aubrey Pomerance (Jewish Museum Berlin) for the references to the family Ehrenberg/Schachian. The cooperation on the board of the association in providing work certification can be confirmed by Albert Ehrenberg.
43. Landesarchiv Berlin, Heiratsurkunde, No. 718, 8 July 1897; *Biographisches Handbuch der deutschsprachigen Emigration nach 1933*, ed. Werner Röder and Herbert A. Strauss, vol. 2, *The Arts, Sciences, and Literature*, ed. Hannah Caplan and Belinda Rosenblatt, part 1 (Munich, 1983) (unchanged reprint 1999), 238 (Ehrenberg, Werner); Hirsch, *Vereinslazarett*, 32.
44. See Sabine Krusen, "Das Minna-Schwarz-Heim in der Brunnenstraße 41: Eine Wirkungsstätte des Frauenvereins der Berliner Logen Bne Briss," in *Juden in Berlin-Mitte: Biografien—Orte—Begegnungen*, ed. Horst Helas (Berlin, 2000), 151–157. I would like to thank Renate Rosenau (Alzey) for the information on her great aunt. See also the report of the Großloge für Deutschland VIII U. O. B. B., No. 3, March/April 1916, 47–48; "Jubiläum des Frauenvereins der Berliner Logen U. O. B. B. (Mütter- und Säuglingsheim)," in *Nachrichtendienst*, ed. der Zentralwohlfahrtsstelle der deutschen Juden (April/May 1928), 8–9; "Nachruf Minna Schwarz," in *Die Bne Briss, Jüdischer Orden. Mitteilungen der Großloge für Deutschland* VIII U. O. B. B., No. 1/2, January/February 1937, 13.
45. U. O. B. B. Adressbuch 1928/29, Kassel [1929], 38. Work cited can be found in German libraries or Israel.

46. Monatsbericht der Kriegshilfskommission, Abteilung Frauen- und Jugendfürsorge, December 1914, in CJA, 1 C Ge 1, No. 956, #10846, fol. 157–158, here fol. 158 (mit einer Auflistung der für die Kriegshilfskommission tätigen Frauen); Hirsch, *Vereinslazarett*, 32.
47. Jüdischer Friedhof Berlin-Weißensee, Beisetzungsregister, No. 95182.
48. In 1923 there was the Schwesternbund der Montefiore-Loge, the Schwesternbund der Deutschen Reichsloge, the Schwesternbund der Berthold-Auerbach-Loge, the Schwesternvereinigung der Timendorfer-Jubiläumsloge, the Schwesternbund der Spinoza-Loge, and the Schwesternbund der Akiba-Eger-Loge. See Alfred Goldschmidt, *Der deutsche Distrikt des Ordens Bne Briss U. O. B. B.* (Berlin, 1923), 85.
49. See Prestel, "Weibliche Rollenzuweisung," 52–58.
50. *Allgemeine Zeitung des Judentums* 79, no. 37 (8 September 1915): 439.
51. Report of the Großloge für Deutschland VIII U. O. B. B., No. 7, August 1917, 107-108.
52. *Monatsschrift der Berliner Logen U. O. B. B.* 6, no. 4 (July 1926): 70.
53. This can be compared to similar developments in Jewish welfare organizations in Vienna. See Raggam-Blesch, "Frauen zwischen den Fronten," 26 ff.
54. "Teilnahme der Frauen am Gemeindeleben: Eine Umfrage," in *Gemeindeblatt der Jüdischen Gemeinde zu Berlin* 4, no. 2 (15 February 1914): 16–17, here 17.

Bibliography

Banéth, Noëmi. *Soziale Hilfsarbeit der modernen Jüdin: Ein Vortrag*. Berlin: Louis Lamm, 1907.

Eschelbacher, Ernestine. "Die Arbeit der jüdischen Frauen in Deutschland während des Krieges." *Ost und West. Illustrierte Monatsschrift für das gesamte Judentum* 19, no. 5/6 (May/June 1919): col. 137–50.

Goldschmidt, Alfred. *Der deutsche Distrikt des Ordens Bne Briss U. O. B. B.* Verlag der Großloge, Berlin, 1923.

Hank, Sabine, and Uwe Hank. *Jüdische Frauen im Ersten Weltkrieg: Paula Glück, Juliane Herrmann, Helene Meyer, Johanna Nathan*. Jüdische Miniaturen, 192. Berlin: Hentrich & Hentrich, 2017.

Kipp, Angelika. *Jüdische Arbeits- und Berufsfürsorge in Deutschland 1900–1933 (Dokumente—Texte—Materialien)*. Zentrum für Antisemitismusforschung der Technischen Universität Berlin, 31. Berlin: Metropol, 1999.

Krusen, Sabine. "Das Minna-Schwarz-Heim in der Brunnenstraße 41: Eine Wirkungsstätte des Frauenvereins der Berliner Logen Bne Briss." In *Juden in Berlin-Mitte: Biografien—Orte—Begegnungen*, edited by Horst Helas, 151-157. Berlin: Trafo, 2000.

Lamm, Fritz. "1833–1933: Hundert Jahre Gemeindewohlfahrtspflege." *Gemeindeblatt der Jüdischen Gemeinde zu Berlin* 23, no. 10 (October 1933): 326–29.

Mühsam, Hans. "Der Dornenweg des jüdischen Wanderers." *Ost und West. Illustrierte Monatsschrift für das gesamte Judentum* 6, no. 7 (July 1906): col. 479–88.

Prestel, Claudia. "Weibliche Rollenzuweisung in jüdischen Organisationen: Das Beispiel des Bnei Briss." *Bulletin des Leo Baeck Instituts* 85 (1990): 51–79.

Raggam-Blesch, Michaela. "Frauen zwischen den Fronten: Jüdinnen in feministischen, politischen und philanthropischen Bewegungen in Wien an der Wende des 19. zum 20. Jahrhundert." In *Geschlecht, Religion und Engagement: Die jüdischen Frauenbewegungen im deutschsprachigen Raum, 19. und frühes 20. Jahrhundert* (L'Homme. Europäische Zeitschrift für Feministische Geschichtswissenschaft, Schriften, 9), edited by Margarete Grandner and Edith Sauer, 25–55. Vienna: Böhlau, 2005.

Schütz, Chana. "Die Kaiserzeit (1871–1918)." In *Juden in Berlin*, edited by Andreas Nachama, Julius H. Schoeps, and Hermann Simon, 89–136. Berlin: Hentrich & Hentrich, 2001.

Simon, Hermann. "Ein leidenschaftlicher Judaica-Sammler." In *Gerhard Hentrich, Der Verleger: Festschrift zum 70. Geburtstag für Gerhard Hentrich*, edited by Werner Buchwald and Hermann Simon, 223–32. Berlin: Hentrich & Hentrich, 1994.

Sinasohn, Max M. *Die Berliner Privatsynagogen und ihre Rabbiner 1671–1971: Zur Erinnerung an das 300 jährige Bestehen der Jüdischen Gemeinde zu Berlin*. Jerusalem, 1971.

8

"My Comrades Are for the Most Part on My Side"

Comradeship between Non-Jewish and German Jewish Front Soldiers in the First World War

Jason Crouthamel

In late 1917, Willy Rosenstein, a German Jewish fighter pilot in fighter squadron 27 (*Jagdstaffel* 27), requested a transfer to another squadron. His commander in *Jagdstaffel* 27 provided him with a recommendation, which said: "[Rosenstein] has won the confidence of his squadron commander due to his aggressiveness in air combat and the affection of his squadron-mates because of his fine comradeship."[1] The author of the recommendation letter was future *Reichsmarschall* and Gestapo chief Hermann Göring. This concept of "comradeship" played a decisive role in how German Jewish soldiers perceived themselves, and how they were perceived by their fellow non-Jewish soldiers at the front. After the war, many German Jewish veterans sanctified a memory of the war experience in which they felt accepted through a path of sacrifice and comradeship. This chapter investigates whether or not that memory of comradeship was just an illusion or whether it accurately reflected experiences in 1914–18. How did German Jewish and non-Jewish soldiers at the front perceive each other and how did the war experience influence social relations between Jews and non-Jews? To what degree did antisemitism in Germany's imperial political culture reflect broader attitudes in the German army?

While Jewish soldiers encountered antisemitism at the front, many felt accepted by their comrades and integrated into German society as a result of their war service.[2] I argue that German Jewish soldiers' optimism was rooted in their conception of inclusive comradeship, a result of how they saw themselves and how they believed they were seen by their comrades. It is important to also reconstruct non-Jewish soldiers' perspectives. Their letters about their Jewish comrades reveal different layers of overlapping, sometimes contradictory, sentiments. These ranged from antisemitic prejudices to philosemitic revelations as some gentile soldiers discovered that their ingrained prejudices did not reflect their actual experiences with Jewish comrades.

"Comradeship" was a centerpiece of the early twentieth-century masculine ideal, which fused self-sacrifice and self-control with emotions of nurturing and familial love that many men found necessary for survival in the stress of frontline combat.[3] Jewish front soldiers perceived positive relations between themselves and non-Jewish soldiers in the close units at the front where they could prove themselves as "good comrades," while antisemitism, they believed, emanated primarily from ignorant officers and civilians unaware of life at the front. When non-Jewish soldiers expressed admiration for the "comradeship" performed by Jewish fellow soldiers, it bolstered Jewish soldiers' self-perception of integration and acceptance. The ideal of "comradeship" gave German Jewish veterans a kind of refuge, or space that made them feel insulated against institutional prejudices.

Analyzing the complex relationships between non-Jewish and Jewish soldiers in the trenches complicates the history of wartime and postwar antisemitism. Much of the scholarship on antisemitism in the war has focused on hatred disseminated by the military and political leadership (in particular the notorious 1916 *Judenzählung*, the "Jewish census" or "Jew Count"), and reactions from cultural and intellectual elites.[4] Antisemitism "from above" did not necessarily reflect the more complex relationships between Christian and Jewish comrades. The "Jew Count" was rarely mentioned in the letters or diaries of German Jewish front veterans.[5] Historians have characterized 1916 as a break in Jewish–Christian relations, and a key step on the road to the Holocaust.[6] However, evidence suggests that the "Jew Count" played a more decisive role in political battles on the home front than it did for ordinary Jewish soldiers, whose everyday relationships with their non-Jewish comrades did not alter decisively. Instead, defeat and revolution in 1918–19, and the "stab-in-the-back" legend (*Dolchstoßlegende*), which blamed Jews and other "social outsiders" for betraying the nation and causing defeat, had a greater impact on Jewish veterans who fought after the war for recognition for their sacrifices and loyalty to the German nation.

Focusing on relationships between non-Jewish and Jewish soldiers in the trenches reflects a general shift in scholarship on the Great War, which has expanded analysis to include complex perceptions and values of ordinary men who coped with the traumatic effects of the front experience.[7] As historian Derek Penslar has observed, the history of German Jews in the war has focused primarily on intellectual elites and activists, which resulted in the problem of conflating the experiences and perceptions of elites and ordinary Jews. Meanwhile, Penslar argues, the actual war experience of ordinary Jewish soldiers at the front has remained largely unexplored by historians.[8] Similar to other social groups, experiences and memories of the war were complex and sometimes contradictory.[9] The challenge that faces us is reconstructing these individual experiences and memories of war.

By looking at interactions between ordinary Jewish and non-Jewish soldiers, historians have complicated the history of antisemitism in German society. Historian Tim Grady argues that instead of viewing the First World War as a disastrous turning point for Jewish life in Germany, there were actually "considerably positive interactions between Jews and other Germans" during and even after the war. Grady calls on historians to move away from institutional approaches to a "broader analysis" sensitive to more complex interactions between ordinary Christian and Jewish German soldiers.[10] Antisemitic discourse had become particularly virulent in Germany from the late nineteenth century, as bestselling works by Otto Weininger and mass political movements like Adolf Stoecker's Christian Social Party disseminated and mainstreamed racism.[11] But letters and diaries from the trenches reveal that when German Jewish soldiers encountered antisemitism from comrades at the front, they saw it as exceptional, the rantings of unpopular, marginalized men who could be easily quashed with reason and evidence of positive relations in the front experience.

The war experiences of German Jewish soldiers, as revealed in their war-time letters and diaries, can be placed in a broader context of traumatic experiences, nationalism, and disillusionment with or reinvigoration of heroic ideals felt by other soldiers in the Great War. The experience of comradeship reveals how the experiences of non-Jewish and Jewish soldiers converged. Just as non-Jewish and Jewish front soldiers shared the traumatic experience of the trenches, they also shared ideals of manliness and comradeship that were fundamental to male national identity.

Ideals of "Comradeship" in the Imperial German Army

The ideal of "comradeship" was a key elementof the masculine image in Germany. Popular culture portrayed Germany as a nation of comrades. War was widely seen as the "school for masculinity" in imperial Germany, and it provided the opportunity for men to prove their individual worth through the collective act of defending the nation.[12] As soldiers, men could demonstrate their commitment to "manly valor" and "national sacrifice" that German poets and the cultural elite celebrated as essentially "German" male characteristics.[13]

"Comradeship" gave men a sense of meaning and self-actualization in the age of total war. The ideal of a *Männerbund* in the army and in youth movements like the *Wandervogel* provided a sense of belonging and emotional support outside traditional social structures. Millions of German men were drawn to this experience.[14] The ideal of comradeship appealed to men who sought acceptance as patriotic, masculine reflections of the "warrior image." For soldiers in the First World War, comradeship was also essential for surviving psychological stress. It provided an acceptable way for men to express emotional support and compassion, and it gave them a sense of familial bonds that were crucial for survival as men felt both isolated and distant from their traditional social structures.[15]

Ideals of comradeship were not homogenous. Despite the celebration of comradeship as a cornerstone of masculinity and postwar memory-building of the front experience, it was a contested concept, and postwar constructions did not always reflect wartime experiences. The heroic image, sanctified and celebrated by many soldiers, especially early in the war, was a universal masculine ideal that permeated soldiers' letters, diaries, and front newspapers.[16] However, narratives by front soldiers reveal different conceptions of heroism and comradeship, which prove to be much more complex than what is reflected in ideals and memories constructed and sanctified, especially by right-wing groups, in the interwar years.[17] For the Nazis, racism governed their perception of whether or not one could be included in the "front community" or "national community." However, for many groups marginalized as social outsiders (including sexual minorities, in particular homosexual men), the essential definition of the "good comrade" was not based on essentialist notions of "who you are," but rather one's performance and experience at the front.[18] "Comradeship" became an umbrella concept under which men from different backgrounds felt they could achieve status as "real men." As wartime letters by soldiers attest, later Nazi conceptions of "comradeship" as essentialist did not necessarily reflect how non-Jewish soldiers perceived the comradely ideal. In fact, Jewish soldiers' perceptions that they were accepted because of their performance as "good comrades" are reinforced in sources by their non-Jewish comrades who also believed that it was one's behavior, rather than "essential" identity, that determined whether one was a loyal comrade, member of the front community, and thus a "good German."

German Jewish Soldiers' Perceptions of Comradeship

As Michael Geheran demonstrates in his chapter for this volume, Jewish soldiers responded to antisemitism and the front experience in different ways, depending on their social and cultural backgrounds and the degree to which they felt integrated into German society. At the same time, like gentile soldiers at the front, German Jewish men were profoundly affected by the feeling of comradeship with fellow fighting men.[19] The wartime diaries and letters written by German Jewish soldiers at the front reveal that they had to negotiate relationships with both supportive and prejudiced comrades, and their attempts to make sense of these friendships and conflicts led them to draw conclusions about the degree to which they were accepted or excluded in the "front community." An interesting case study of this is Paul Lebrecht, who volunteered as a corporal (*Gefreiter*) and served on the Western and Eastern Fronts between 1916 and 1918. Lebrecht kept a diary in which he made entries virtually every day for over two and a half years. Born in Nuremberg in 1882 (aged thirty-four when he first went to the front in 1916), Paul Lebrecht was older than most of his comrades. From a middle-class German Jewish family, he co-owned a tin wholesale business (*Blechgrosshandlung*) with his father before the war. He married Hedwig—whom he affectionately called "Hedi" in his diaries—in 1913, and they had a daughter, Ilse, born at the end of that year. As a member of the reserve home guard (*Landsturmmann*), Lebrecht was called up as an infantryman in the summer of 1916 to serve with the 28th Bavarian Infantry Regiment. His unit was first sent to fight in the Vosges mountainous region in Alsace-Lorraine. In October 1916, he was sent to the Romanian front, and then he was brought back to France in the spring of 1918 to fight in the war's final decisive battles, where he witnessed the ultimate defeat of the German army in November 1918.

As a relatively older man, Lebrecht saw himself as a fatherly figure who could provide encouragement to younger men terrified by the war experience. For Lebrecht, comradeship had a paternalistic quality. He portrayed himself in his diary as an "optimistic" comrade who tried to ease fears with his humor and positive outlook. He wrote that under shell fire he would calm his fellow soldiers and help ease their anxiety: "I myself was totally cool and didn't get nervous at all. I even made a few jokes."[20] For many men, macabre humor and fatalism were the norm, but Lebrecht enthusiastically played a role as the unit's good-natured comedian.[21] Finding his place as a "good comrade" was a source of great pride to Lebrecht, and it gave him a sense of belonging and acceptance. In his diary, he included a photograph of himself wearing his steel helmet, uniform, and a brilliant smile, with the caption: "Based on the poster motif: buy war bonds."[22] This was a reference to a famous popular poster image of the steel-helmeted ordinary soldier (*Feldgrauer*) that promoted the signing of war bonds, and Lebrecht, with a bit of humor, identified with this symbol of patriotism, solidarity, comradeship, and masculinity.

Lebrecht saw himself as a popular, well-liked, optimistic fellow soldier, and he wrote that he wanted to simply "do my duty as a good comrade" at the front, and not be treated as different because he was Jewish.[23] At the same time, he also tried to maintain his Jewish cultural identity. From a liberal reform background, he wrote that he endeavored to remain pious, but he was not particularly strict, and his diary does not offer much reflection on God or spirituality.[24] He did not maintain a kosher diet—pork was one of his favorite meals—and he sometimes attended Christian church services, especially when he was invited by Christian comrades. He did not find the Christian services particularly interesting, and actually fell asleep during sermons.[25] Lebrecht sometimes complained that the synagogue services he went to while in Romania were also "boring."[26] He once left synagogue early to pursue his hobby, buying postcards for his collection, including Christmas postcards, which he pasted into his diary. Lebrecht admitted that he sometimes went to synagogue only for the food after the service, and he enjoyed Christmas because of the better food rations, care packages, and the good mood of his Christian comrades.[27]

Lebrecht's interactions with Eastern European Jewish civilians caused him to reflect on his identity both as a German and as a Jew. The large Romanian Jewish population, many of whom spoke German, made him and other Jewish soldiers feel welcome at their synagogue and at Jewish-owned businesses and restaurants.[28] But their reaction to him also made him feel like he identified more with his German comrades than with the Jewish community.[29] Romanian Jews interested him, but he observed them more as an anthropologist who was interested in how they dressed and behaved differently from Germans.[30] He also wrote that Romanian civilians were suspicious of German soldiers. They could not believe that there could be a Jewish soldier in the supposedly cruel German army, and they were surprised to find that he was quite civilized. Lebrecht expressed pride that he gave a civilized face to German culture.[31]

Although Lebrecht did not see himself as particularly spiritually pious, he was still made to feel different from his comrades when he tried to observe Jewish holidays, particularly Rosh Hashanah.[32] When he requested leave for the Jewish New Year on 16 September 1917, his commanding officer accused him of seeking favoritism. Lebrecht argued that he was due for leave anyway, regardless of the Jewish holiday. The officer made Lebrecht feel guilty by telling him that he should make the same sacrifices as his Christian comrades, and that other Jewish soldiers did not ask for leave.[33] When Christmas Eve arrived, Lebrecht noted that while his Christian comrades observed the "holy night," and got lighter work duty, it was the usual grind for him.[34] The next year, in September 1918, his sergeant (*Feldwebel*) was more sympathetic and let Lebrecht take a few days off, though this got canceled when desperate defenses against Allied advances did not permit a break.[35] Like many other Jewish soldiers, Lebrecht had to negotiate between his Jewish cultural identity and his duties as regulated by a Christian culture that expected him to assimilate on mainstream culture's terms.

Despite his frustration with officers who would not make concessions for Jewish holidays, according to his diary Lebrecht rarely encountered antisemitism from men in his unit, and when he did, he noted that it was unusual. In fact, antisemitic comments came from only one of his comrades, a fellow soldier named Friedl. His first confrontation occurred when Friedl complained that Jews did not serve in "high military positions," and he said that this was probably because Jews would be easily bribable and would probably betray the army. Lebrecht brushed off Friedl's comments: "Now I'd had enough. I declared he was ripe for the lunatic asylum and ended the conversation. My comrades are for the most part on my side."[36] Lebrecht believed that with his good humor and reason he had begun to win over Friedl, and that his other comrades were sympathetic, making Friedl feel isolated in his prejudice. When Friedl suggested they all sing some patriotic songs, Lebrecht reminded him that the German Jewish poet, Heinrich Heine, wrote the text for one of Germany's most famous traditional songs, the "Loreley."[37] By June 1917, he wrote that he and Friedl actually got along well and cooperated in their work.[38] Though he felt he was winning the battle for comrades' respect, he had more difficulties with his military superiors. He suspected that he was being passed over for promotions because he was Jewish, and he commented on another Jewish comrade who had the same problem.[39]

Despite the occasional slights, Lebrecht wrote in his diary that he actually felt more comfortable at the front than he did at home. Spending a few weeks' leave at home in summer 1917, he expressed disappointment and fatigue with the routine of visitors and parties.⁴⁰ Food shortages on the home front made him feel a little guilty that he had better provisions in the trenches. By the time his leave was over, he felt alienated and anxious. He could not wait to get back to his friends in his battalion, and in fact called the front "home": "Now it's time to go back *home* [underlined in text] to the front!" Although the ideal of an unchanged domestic oasis still soothed his imagination while at the front, like many other front soldiers, home felt strange in reality.⁴¹

Even though the front started to feel like "home" to Lebrecht, in late 1917 he endured a humiliation that shattered him. On the Eastern Front, after the Russian Revolution and the Russian army's failed Kerensky offensive that summer, he was confident that the war would soon be over. In November, however, he was arrested for spying. Lebrecht was an obsessive collector of newspaper clippings and postcards, and he was a devoted diarist whose personal writings were sometimes written in a shorthand that only he could understand. This brought him under suspicion of delivering sensitive military information to the enemy. In his diary, he characterized the arrest as a "ridiculous" misunderstanding about his "harmless collection," which was personal and not of military relevance. Amazingly, he kept up his sense of humor about it and was convinced that the truth would come out. He pointed to the irony of his arrest in light of the fact that he had earned the Iron Cross Second Class and, just two weeks before his arrest, the Military Service Cross (*Militärverdienstkreuz*).⁴² Confined to a filthy jail cell, he became increasingly bitter that he should be imprisoned for a crime he did not commit after loyally serving the fatherland.⁴³ Spending Christmas in jail, he included a postcard of a Christmas tree surrounded by comrades in his diary, with his handwritten caption, "How it could have been."⁴⁴ By New Year's Day, he confessed that he had become depressed. When he was finally released at the end of January, and later cleared of criminal charges, he wrote that his comrades had welcomed him back. But he was profoundly changed by the experience. Writing in the third person to his former idealistic self, he reflected: "Paul, Paul, what has become of you? Where is your enthusiasm and love of fatherland? I have to wonder about myself!"⁴⁵

Lebrecht wrote in his diary that compared to other soldiers he was actually the least bitter, despite having been unjustly arrested. He distinguished love of fatherland from his disappointment with what he called "the idiocy of militarism," the pig-headed bureaucracy that he blamed for his arrest the previous year. While he insisted that he was still patriotic, his diary revealed a deepening cynicism about the military and its propaganda machine. It was not the "Jew Count," but military bureaucracy that caused his disillusionment. By August 1918, with British and American counterattacks that broke through the German lines on "the black day of the German army," the contrast between military propaganda and the reality of a shattered army struck him as absurd. He wrote it was a "good joke" to read an official newspaper that characterized the army's crumbling front as a "mobile defensive battle."[46] Lebrecht lamented that the German army's morale had reached such a low point that men were refusing to risk their lives when the war was clearly lost by September 1918. Despite the popular postwar legend that the German army was "stabbed in the back" by "enemies" on the home front, including Jews, socialists, and "war weary" civilians, Lebrecht emphasized in his diary that in reality the military was defeated and German soldiers were exhausted and mutinous. He expressed disapproval when he saw his comrades avoid fighting when they knew the war was nearly at an end.[47] In October 1918, he blamed low morale on the generals and blind "militarism," under which he saw himself as a victim. He was not a radical leftist. He did not approve of the revolutionary soldiers' and workers' councils who, he wrote, brought disorder and disrespect, but rather he said most men just wanted peace. "Everybody just wants the war to end," he wrote, and though he lamented defeat, it was better than the futile killing: "Indeed the peace will not be brilliant for us, but it's certainly better than this *never-ending, useless* [underlined in text] blood-letting."[48]

After the war, Lebrecht joined the Association of Jewish War Veterans (Reichsbund jüdischer Frontsoldaten) in Nuremberg. Like millions of other men who were brutalized by the war, he grew cynical about what he perceived as a dehumanizing military system. At the same time, he was proud of his war service, which to him symbolized his loyal devotion to the nation and proved that his Jewish identity was inconsequential when it came to defining his German identity. However, the front experience, sacrifice, and ideals of "comradeship" could not save him from racial hatred. Lebrecht died on 11 November 1938, a few days after he was attacked on *Reichspogromnacht*, 9–10 November. His wife Hedi fled to Mexico shortly thereafter. Regardless of Jewish soldiers' military service between 1914 and 1918 and their sense of acceptance into the "front community," the Nazis annihilated Jewish veterans as inherent enemies of the "national community."

Lebrecht's diary reveals just how multilayered the front experience was for German Jewish soldiers who faced both antisemitic and sympathetic comrades. It also reveals his agency in shaping his comrades' attitudes, his belief that he was winning over antisemitic soldiers, and his struggle to redefine his own political values and identity in the face of brutalization under war, militarism, and separation from home. For Lebrecht, the primary threat that he faced was not antisemitic prejudices at the front, but rather what he characterized as petty militarism and bureaucracy, which eroded the comradeship and spirit of men in the trenches.

Lebrecht's feeling of acceptance within his circle of comrades was not universally experienced by German Jewish soldiers. For some men, constant antisemitic attacks made "comradeship" seem remote. For example, Julius Marx experienced chronic harassment from his fellow infantrymen. From the small town of Freudental in Baden-Württemberg, he served all four years of the war and fought at Arras, Verdun, and the Somme. Marx was from a middle-class background, and when the war broke out he volunteered as a non-commissioned officer (*Unteroffizier*). He kept a diary during the war, which he published in 1939 while in exile in Switzerland (he left Germany in 1935 after losing his automobile company under the Nuremberg Laws). In the excitement of August 1914, he at first did not detect hatred: "At the beginning of the war, it seemed like every prejudice disappeared. There were only Germans." But only a few months after the outbreak of the war, he wrote in his diary, "one now hears the old, hateful expressions again."[49] Marx could not endure the verbal abuse, and he reported to his commanding officer: "Captain, I cannot remain at this post. They're always scolding me behind my back about the 'cowardly Jews.'"[50]

His captain was sympathetic and invited Marx to the officers' quarters. They treated him to dinner and assured him that not all men in the unit were antisemitic, and that his friends valued his comradeship and dedication. This promise seemed genuine to Marx, as he gradually rose through the ranks, was promoted to *Leutnant*, and earned an Iron Cross for his bravery. But he continued to face antisemitic stereotypes. In August 1917, he encountered a psychologically traumatized soldier named Lewenherz who broke down under fire and complained that "the war was already lost." Men who heard of the soldier's breakdown speculated that Lewenherz must be a "cowardly Jew." Marx pointed out that Lewenherz was actually not Jewish, but his comrades continued to spew their anti-Jewish stereotypes. Two other men, embarrassed by their hate-filled comrades, later apologized to Marx, but the insults still stung, and Marx felt it was impossible to prove to antisemites in his unit that he was a loyal, courageous soldier.[51]

The "Jew Count" was rarely mentioned in most wartime writings, but it comes up in Marx's diary. Since his diary was published in 1939, and he characterizes its publication as a protest against the *Reichspogromnacht*, it is difficult to determine how much was originally written in the trenches versus how much was edited postwar. In his entry for 2 November 1916, however, in the midst of intense fighting and enormous casualties during the Battle of the Somme, Marx recounts being summoned by his company commander. He recorded that his CO, gesturing to a survey form on his desk, stuttered with embarrassment:

> [Company CO]: Yes—the War Ministry—we have been encouraged by the War Ministry—well, it must be firmly established, how many Jews are to be counted at the front—
> [Marx]: And how many behind the lines? What is this nonsense?! Do they want to degrade us into second-class soldiers, make us a joke in front of the entire army? They bully us, don't promote us, but they then get outraged if … some of us would rather watch the war play itself out from the rear [*Etappe*]—!
> [CO]: You are completely right, but I can't do anything to change it. When were you born?[52]

Marx then concludes this dialogue with the thought: "To hell with this! For this one risks his skull for his country!"[53] This passage is interesting on several levels. He portrays his company commander as ultimately in complete agreement that the "Jew Count" is unjust and "nonsense," yet his commanding officer is powerless in making policy and ultimately follows orders and goes through the motions of filling out the census. Marx suggested the CO only carried out the census but did not actually believe its premise. In this way, Marx separates the War Ministry's racist project from the attitudes of men within the unit. His CO recognizes Marx's bravery and sacrifice, even if the War Ministry does not. Unfortunately, the empathetic comradeship Marx receives from his company commander did not stretch further up the military ladder. In the next diary entry, Marx complains that "a recognized brave soldier" named Nathan, despite his accomplishments, got passed over for selection as an officer because he was a Jew. Marx noted that "the old officers of the regiments are not antisemites," but the new regiment commander at the higher level, who did not reflect the view of the officers within the company, was responsible for overlooking Nathan's promotion due to antisemitism.[54]

This picture of the close unit of comrades as a relatively insular entity, separate from the antisemitism disseminated from above, permeates German Jewish soldiers' narratives. Jewish front soldiers tended to characterize comrades who actually knew them, and witnessed their bravery, as friendly and sympathetic, while it was higher-ups or home front politicians, ignorant of the actual performance of Jewish men in the trenches, who perpetuated stereotypes. An example of this can be seen in the letters of Hermann Lehrer, a German Jewish infantryman who corresponded regularly from the Eastern Front with the director of his old school and orphanage in Berlin. Lehrer wrote extensively about how "the war has made an entirely new person out of me."[55] On one hand, this is because of the traumatic violence he encountered. But he also wrote about what he described as the "positive" elements of his experience, including his self-reliance for survival and the sense of confidence that came with military discipline, which he believed would make his old teacher proud. But it was the experience of "comradeship" that he cherished most. The shared experience of survival, he wrote, meant that the front universe was essentially free of division and prejudice between men. He was happy to return to the combat front after a period of leave in 1918, when he felt nothing but disappointment and alienation on the home front:

> It was on the fifth or sixth day of my leave and I had come there straight from the front, when I realized that on the front while at my post I felt no class difference [*Standesunterschied*]. First of all there were really no antisemites and the one antisemitic lieutenant, who had been antisemitic at home, is now a great friend of the Jews [*ist jetzt ein großer Judenfreund*] and has become a good friend of mine.[56]

The front experience, according to Lehrer, "cured" antisemitism—at least on a superficial level—and even turned a once antisemitic lieutenant, whose hatred seemed to be derived from life at home, into a "good friend." For Lehrer, there was a clear division between combat and home fronts, with the former a kind of separate universe immune to the conflicts that characterized civilian life.

While some German Jewish front soldiers perceived the front lines and comradeship as a haven from home front divisions and politics, others saw comradeship as precarious and conditional. There were cases of men who were not certain that they were really accepted as Jewish, but only accepted as comrades as long as their non-Jewish fellow soldiers did not know they were Jewish. This tentative comradeship can be seen in the case of Hermann Berel Barsqueaux, a student of the same school and orphanage as Hermann Lehrer, who also wrote regularly to his old teacher. Barsqueaux joined an observation balloon battalion, where he relished the feeling of belonging. He wrote that "good comradeship dominates" his experience on the front. He included a flyer called "An Evening of Comradeship," which detailed a night of musical entertainment.[57] However, this comradeship only existed, he wrote, because he did not reveal he was Jewish. During training in 1917, he noted that a fellow Jewish soldier was treated well "despite differences of confession" but "just couldn't make it" when his superior officers singled him out for strenuous drills.[58] While at the front, he wrote: "I am the only Jew in the unit. But we all get along well with each other because the others don't know what religion I belong to."[59] Thus Barsqueaux endeavored to be a good comrade, which held the promise of acceptance, but only at the cost of concealing his religious identity. By May 1918, he wrote enthusiastically about a Jewish Soldiers' Home (*Jüdisches Soldatenheim*) that he found while deployed in Straßburg. "It's the first one I've seen up until now," he commented. "In Berlin or even Frankfurt am Main there was no such place." There he found snacks and what he described as Jewish magazines (*Jüdische Zeitschriften*) and books.[60] Hermann Barsqueaux oscillated between two worlds. At the front, he could emulate comradeship as long as he hid who he was. But when he found a *Jüdisches Soldatenheim*, he savored the safe place where he did not have to hide his Jewish identity.

Although letters from the front offer a candid glimpse into daily life at the front, one must consider letters as potentially problematic due to censorship. Military censorship imposed on *Feldpostbriefe* would suggest that men were limited in describing experiences that may have contradicted traditional ideals or the "civil truce" (*Burgfrieden*) proclaimed by Kaiser Wilhelm II in 1914. However, the Supreme Army Command (OHL, Oberste Heeresleitung) had to deal with on average 6.8 million letters sent every day from soldiers to the home front.[61] The eight thousand officials assigned to censor this massive amount of mail could only monitor it superficially, and disillusionment and criticism of the war, officers, and the home front often got through.[62] At the same time, men often anticipated censorship and censored themselves. This can be seen in the case of Herbert Czapski, a sergeant and medical orderly who wrote extensively in 1917 about his "frayed nerves" and exhaustion in dealing with overcrowded field hospitals and the avalanche of war wounds on the Eastern Front. But he feared that he could not be frank about the antisemitism he witnessed:

> There are occurrences that I would like to report on, but cannot talk about it in a letter, about the experiences of Jewish soldiers and the behavior of our captain, which contradicts the Kaiser's proclamation: "I no longer recognize any parties." For now this may be enough said. Perhaps when I'm eventually on leave I can talk more about this. I have plenty of things to talk about, as long as it doesn't have any personal repercussions for me.[63]

Though Czapski says he "cannot talk about" the specific antisemitic incident, his implicit criticism of his captain suggests he could not have been too fearful of censorship. Further, he turned the tables on the "Jew Count," undertaken several months before this letter, as he accused his non-Jewish officer of being disloyal to the Kaiser's call for civil truce.

For many, comradeship still transcended the petty hatreds they blamed on the military hierarchy, which they saw as separate from their friendships at the front. For example, Joseph Kurt, who served in an observation balloon unit in the German air force, wrote in his memoir about the effects of antisemitism. While he experienced comradeship between his fellow enlisted men at the front, his goal of earning an Iron Cross and gaining promotion by volunteering for the most dangerous missions was quashed as he was consistently overlooked by officers who favored Christian soldiers. Without bitterness towards his fellow enlisted men, he reflected: "I felt it was futile for me to become a good German soldier and had in mind only to remain a good comrade to my fellow soldiers without taking an active part in the affairs and duties of war."[64] Kurt was pessimistic that assimilation in the antisemitic military culture was even possible, but he perceived "comradeship" as still desirable and untainted by the "duties of war," which were plagued by hatred and prejudice. His friendships with fellow soldiers at the front trumped his ambition or belief in military discipline. Interestingly, Kurt argued that while "antisemitic people say that a Jew tries to escape his duties," it was the antisemitic culture that made him, an otherwise patriotic and enthusiastic soldier, feel apathetic about military duty.[65] Kurt survived the war but shortly after the Nazis came to power he was imprisoned in Sachsenhausen concentration camp. He emigrated to Britain just before the Second World War broke out and wrote his memoir in the hope that "never again in times to come will human beings be persecuted or killed because of their race, religion or their nationality."[66]

German Christian Soldiers' Perceptions of their Jewish Comrades

While racism existed within the ranks of comrades at the front, Jewish soldiers' perception that they won over the respect of fellow front fighters had a basis in reality. Despite escalating antisemitism generated by the military high command, which culminated in accusations that Jews were not making their share of sacrifices in the war, not all non-Jewish soldiers and officers were susceptible to racist beliefs. In fact, letters home from the front reveal that based on their experiences some Christian front soldiers reconsidered antisemitic prejudices.

Many discovered that their Jewish comrades did not fit the familiar stereotypes. An interesting case study of a non-Jewish soldier finding comradeship with Jewish men is *Leutnant* Rudolf Veek, a middle-class Christian who volunteered for service at the outbreak of the war. For two years Veek wrote to his wife, Julie, every day. Veek was emotionally very close to her and he told her in graphic detail about the violence that he witnessed at the front. His letters convey how he was traumatized by the war experience, but also how he discovered friendship and even a sense of humanity as a way to cope with the shattering effects of war.

Veek saw the close bond of comradeship as essential to survival and the most emotionally important element of the front experience. He was wounded in September 1914, and he wrote to Julie about how he was haunted by the moment in which a bullet struck him in the lung and he believed he would die.[67] He wrote extensively about the deaths of comrades and detailed their last moments, as well as the different injuries suffered by men in the hospital beds around him. He included in one of his letters a handwritten, autobiographical pamphlet, "Rudolf Veek, My Life, After my Wounding on September 25, 1914," and a poem called "My Dead Comrades from Chilly," about a mass grave of German soldiers and his "tears that streamed into my hands" when he reflected on the terrible wounds they suffered.[68] Veek's close encounters with death profoundly changed him. He told his wife that it was not the soldierly image or skill at killing that made men real men, but rather the expressions of love between comrades at the front. He wrote: "Is it possible for men who are still capable of love to become brutalized? I've never seen more examples of selfless love than there at the front, where in blood and desperation we fight through the most difficult days."[69] Comradeship provided Veek with a sense of love and intimacy that counterbalanced and helped him survive the brutality of the trenches.

Rudolf Veek told his wife that the antisemitic stereotypes that he had been taught before the war did not make sense at the front. The front experience caused him to criticize the stereotype that Jews were selfish, unmanly cowards. Veek intimated to his wife that his Jewish comrades actually took every opportunity to show their courage. He wrote in October 1914 about three friends in the unit who were Jewish, and how they constantly volunteered to go back to the front, even when they were on leave. When one of his Jewish comrades, Schumacher, lost a brother at the front, Veek told his wife how impressed he was by Schumacher's courage. He wrote that though Schumacher was given the opportunity to go on leave to mourn his dead brother, he chose to stay with his comrades at the front. Schumacher eventually invited Veek to a synagogue for a Sabbath worship service, where a *Synagogenvorstand* made him feel welcome. He told his wife that the synagogue service was "beautiful and relaxing."[70]

Similar to Paul Lebrecht's experience in going to a Christian worship service, Veek's visit to a synagogue made him realize that his Jewish comrades were not so different. But even more so than Lebrecht, Veek's experience in visiting a different place of worship gave him a glimpse into the community of "the other" that he had not really considered before. Critical of stereotypes about Jews as unmanly shirkers, he intimated to Julie: "Jews really do give all their courage to fulfill their duty."[71] For the next two years at the front, Rudolf Veek continued to rely on his comrades for emotional support until his death on 2 July 1916, at the Battle of the Somme.

The ideal of comradeship was not always universally felt. Resentments, divisions, and old prejudices still persisted in the front lines. Antisemitic remarks in the *Feldpostbriefe* and diaries of German Christian front soldiers indicate that institutionalized prejudices disseminated in the *Judenzählung* also reflected the sentiments of some ordinary front soldiers. German Christian soldiers saw Eastern European Jews in particular as a cultural and racial "other." For example, when evangelical Lutheran lieutenant Georg G. was stationed on the Eastern Front, he wrote extensively to his parents about what he saw as "unbelievably dirty little Jewish towns" in Galicia. He told his parents that the local communities should "thank God that the Germans are occupying Russia" and bringing civilization to the region.[72]

Non-Jewish front soldiers also expressed antisemitism towards German Jewish comrades in their own military units. For example, *Leutnant* Hermann B., who volunteered in 1916, frequently criticized his Jewish comrades, and the war experience only seemed to reinforce his hatred of Jews. Hermann B. told his parents that he felt alienated from his fellow soldiers. Within a few weeks of arriving in the trenches, he described "comradeship" as an illusion. Drunken fellow officers who visited the brothels behind the lines repulsed him, and he wrote to his parents that in the trenches he did his duty, but he felt completely isolated:

> In the future I want to completely cut myself off from the society of comrades [*Gesellschaft der Kameraden*], where I'm a machine gun specialist. In fact it's really easy for me to start hating other people here in ways that wouldn't be natural in peacetime … [O]ne has to carry on with everything undertaken by comrades, but just out of duty. There is very little freedom here.[73]

Rather than unify men in a common struggle for survival, the trench experience actually intensified Hermann B.'s hatreds. "Comradeship" seemed a facade that had no appeal.

Hermann B. had chronic problems with his fellow officers, and his resentments quickly devolved into antisemitic rhetoric. He wrote to his parents that he did not like working with Austrian officers who visited his unit, because "every tenth Austrian officer looks Jewish."[74] In an August 1917 letter to his father, he complained: "I'm having a real difficult time with a technical officer in the 3rd Machine Gun Company. This guy Karl is causing me a lot of problems—he's a certain kind of Jew [*ein ganz gewisser Jude*]."[75] He characterized Jews in his unit as imposters who put on a show of comradeship but were actually conniving to betray him:

> It's amazing how these Jews try to flatter us all the time, and we let ourselves be fooled by them. But every word they say is hollow and their only aim is to gain an advantage. I don't think our Major sees this at all, but I recognize this one guy for exactly what he is … The interesting thing about war is that one has to get to know different kinds of people. Or at least one is forced to, because one has to always be around them.[76]

Hermann B. resented Jews "pretending" to be comrades, and he was full of bitterness when another lieutenant who was Jewish beat him to a promotion.

Hermann B.'s letters were characterized by incessant anger. Even when he took leave in Berlin, he avoided his comrades and preferred to explore the streets, museums, opera house, and restaurants on his own. He wrote to his mother: "I seem to feel nothing but irritation with life."[77] His festering hatred caused chronic stress.[78] In August 1918, Hermann B. told his parents that "all of my anger makes me feel really nervous," and he admitted the war left him isolated, lonely and exhausted. His parents suggested that he seek help from a doctor, but he feared being ridiculed by other men if he complained that his nerves were shattered. The symptoms of "war neurosis" would have stigmatized him as an unmanly coward and malingerer.[79]

Case studies of both supportive and hateful Christian comrades are important to analyze because Jewish front soldiers had to negotiate these two extremes in their daily experiences. To return to the Jewish fighter pilot, Willy Rosenstein, mentioned at the opening of this chapter, this dichotomy between "good" Christian comrades and antisemitic comrades created considerable confusion. When his squadron commander Hermann Göring expressed admiration for Rosenstein's "fine comradeship" in 1917, Rosenstein later wrote in his memoirs that he suspected Göring actually gave the favorable recommendation only to cover up his antisemitism. In fact, just a few weeks before the "fine comradeship" recommendation, Göring had made an anti-Jewish remark in front of other officers in the squadron mess hall, which led the humiliated Rosenstein to apply for a squadron transfer.[80]

When he got his transfer to *Jagdstaffel* 40, Rosenstein felt much more accepted by his comrades and his new squadron commander, Carl Degelow. In his memoir published just after the war, Degelow expressed admiration for Rosenstein as an essential member of the squadron and his most "able colleague," whom he frequently chose to accompany him on dangerous missions. Degelow wrote: "[Rosenstein] was our 'patron saint,' performing for us the essential duty of keeping our squadron formation free of enemies, as he flew last and highest in our formation."[81] In choosing a wingman for missions over enemy lines, Degelow regularly chose Rosenstein to fly with him, and the squadron commander wrote a letter to his superiors recommending his comrade for a Knight's Cross of the Royal Order of Hohenzollern with Swords medal for bravery.

Degelow's respect for Rosenstein was mutual, and Rosenstein developed a lifelong friendship with him. After the war, Rosenstein and his former squadron mates remained close: "Every few years we met in Berlin to spend a few hours with old friends." This circle of friends was important to Rosenstein, whose life in the interwar years was disastrous. He suffered the death of his first wife, Hede, in 1926 from kidney disease. Deeply depressed and alone raising their young son Ernst, he struggled with morphine addiction, which he says intensified "when the catastrophic event of Hitler's advent to power took place. The state of my nerves was such these days that I myself felt it could not go on like this. More or less I lived exclusively on drugs."[82] When the Nazis came to power, Degelow came to Rosenstein's assistance. According to Rosenstein, Degelow "quite publicly never concealed his anti-Nazi attitude," and Degelow was even briefly imprisoned by the Nazis in 1933, for reasons not given by Rosenstein in his 1940 self-published memoir. However, Rosenstein notes that due to Degelow's war record, namely his status as a recipient of the *Pour le Merité*, the highest medal for bravery in imperial Germany, Degelow was released from prison.[83]

After Rosenstein lost his right to earn a living under the Nuremberg Laws in 1936 and was unable to emigrate due to bureaucratic and financial problems, help came from an unexpected source. A chance meeting in a Berlin café with a sympathetic old comrade from the squadron where he served under Hermann Göring saved him. The mutual friend offered to meet with Göring on Rosenstein's behalf and solicited a letter that cut through bureaucratic obstacles and expedited Rosenstein's emigration to South Africa without incident. Rosenstein had not met Göring since the antisemitic incident in their squadron in 1917, but he wrote bemusedly: "I must admit that Göring's letter made things easier in some ways."[84] In South Africa, Rosenstein trained a new generation of pilots who would soon fly against Nazi Germany. By the time the war broke out, he had trained over fifty pilots, including his own son, who served in the South African Air Force and the British Royal Air Force. Despite this, he was detained at Internment Camp Nr. 2 near Rostenberg, South Africa, in 1940, where he suffered a nervous breakdown. He also dealt with an ever-growing addiction to morphine: "The cure for everything ... my old friend M." It was in the internment camp where he typed a memoir for British government authorities who suspected him of subversion because he was a German immigrant.[85]

One of Rosenstein's most ironic, but lifelong, experiences with comradeship was solidified with another comrade in *Jagdstaffel* 40 after an incident of mistaken Jewish identity. When Rosenstein initially arrived at the *Jagdstaffel* in July 1918, he felt particularly welcome because one of his flying comrades, Adolf Auer, had a Star of David symbol painted on the side of his new Fokker fighter aircraft. Thinking this was a fellow Jewish pilot, Rosenstein suggested a "special toast of comradeship," but Auer, who was Christian, was slightly embarrassed, and intimated that he had no idea it was a Jewish symbol. He thought it was just "an emblem from his favorite beer brewer" from his home town.[86] The honest mistake resulted in a long-lasting squadron joke that cemented a lifelong friendship between Auer and Rosenstein. After the Second World War, Rosenstein provided a letter of support for Auer's de-Nazification file, in which he testified that Auer was not a war criminal.[87] Interestingly, Rosenstein's son flew for the British Royal Air Force and was killed flying a Spitfire in a strafing run over Italy in April 1945. Rosenstein died in a plane crash on his farm in South Africa, where he gave flying lessons, in 1949.

Conclusion

Rosenstein's experience, which ranged from humiliation under the antisemitism of Hermann Göring to feeling genuine lifelong acceptance from his new comrades, highlights the contradictions German Jewish soldiers faced. Letters and diaries by Jewish soldiers suggest that they were quite realistic about the persistence of what *Leutnant* Julius Marx called "those old hateful expressions," but they also recognized that many of their Christian comrades were critical of antisemitic stereotypes and accepted Jewish soldiers as "brothers in comradeship."[88] From the perspective of many German Jewish front soldiers, ideals of comradeship were accessible to all men who performed their duties of self-sacrifice, heroism, and friendship. At the same time, German Jewish men often saw themselves as facing another challenge that tested their optimism about integration: the fight against antisemitism. They were engaged in a struggle for recognition in their own ranks among comrades with whom they shared the traumatic experience of war. But for a large number of Jewish front fighters, hatred from comrades was rare. They generally ascribed prejudice to those behind the lines who were ignorant of sacrifices at the front, and they latched on to what they felt was sincere comradeship from the majority of men who fought with them side by side.

These complex interactions reveal that historians need to consider the 1914–18 experience within its own context. From the perspectives of ordinary men, there was not a straight line from the 1916 "Jew Count" to 1933. Looking at this history in hindsight from 1933 distorts the more complex experiences of the war. Instead of representing a caesura in Jewish–Christian relations and a key step on the road to the Holocaust, from the perspective of many Jewish soldiers the war experience sparked tremendous optimism that they had earned respect as "good comrades." After the defeat, the optimism that they had expressed in diaries and letters seemed less tangible, and the experiences with antisemitism in the trenches, which had once felt marginal, loomed larger.

In postwar memoirs, Jewish veterans tried to make sense of the mixed, confusing memories of both inclusion and exclusion that they experienced in the war. German Jewish soldiers' perceptions that they had gained respect were confirmed by their memories of comradeship and accounts by at least some of their non-Jewish comrades. Historian Peter Gay famously observed in his memoir that the rise of Nazism proved that "Jews loved Germany but Germany did not love the Jews."[89] While "those old hateful expressions" still persisted, many ordinary Jewish soldiers remembered that love from fellow German comrades was not entirely an illusion.

Jason Crouthamel is a professor at Grand Valley State University in Michigan. He is the author of *An Intimate History of the Front: Masculinity, Sexuality and German Soldiers in the First World War* (Palgrave Macmillan, 2014) and *The Great War and German Memory: Society, Politics and Psychological Trauma, 1914–1945* (Liverpool University Press, 2009), and he co-edited, with Peter Leese, *Psychological Trauma and the Legacies of the First World War* and *Traumatic Memories of World War Two and After* (Palgrave Macmillan, 2016). He is completing a monograph titled *Trauma, Religion and Spirituality in Germany during the First World War*.

Notes

1. Willy Rosenstein memoir, written in 1940, ME 527.MM64, Leo Baeck Institute, New York (LBINY), 2. Rosenstein composed this unpublished narrative while imprisoned in a South African internment camp in 1940; on Rosenstein's background as a flying instructor before 1914 and as a volunteer for the Luftstreitkräfte after the war broke out, see Michael Berger, *Für Kaiser, Reich und Vaterland: Jüdische Soldaten, eine Geschichte vom 19. Jahrhundert bis heute* (Zürich, 2015), 92–94.
2. Recent scholarship on the complex experiences of German Jewish soldiers in the trenches includes Derek Penslar, *Jews and the Military: A History* (Princeton, NJ, 2013), see esp. chapter 5; Brian Crim, *Antisemitism in the German Military Community and the Jewish Response, 1914–1938* (Lanham, MD, 2014); Ulrike Heikaus and Julia B. Köhne, eds., *Krieg! Juden zwischen den Fronten, 1914–1918* (Berlin, 2014).
3. Thomas Kühne, *The Rise and Fall of Comradeship* (Cambridge, 2017), 30–31; see also Kühne's essay, "Comradeship: Gender Confusion and the Gender Order in the German Military, 1918–1945," in *Home/Front: The Military, War and Gender in Twentieth-Century Germany*, ed. Karen Hagemann and Stefanie Schüler-Springorum (Oxford, 2002), 233–54.
4. On the impact of the *Judenzählung* as a precursor to Nazi antisemitism, see Jacob Rosenthal, *"Die Ehre des jüdischen Soldaten": Die Judenzählung im Ersten Weltkrieg und ihre Folgen* (Frankfurt, 2007); Anna Ullrich, "'Nun sind wir gezeichnet': Jüdische Soldaten und die 'Judenzählung' im Ersten Weltkrieg," in Heikaus and Köhne, *Krieg! Juden zwischen den Fronten*, 215–38. See also George L. Mosse, *Toward the Final Solution* (New York, 1997); William Brustein, *Roots of Hate: Anti-Semitism in Europe before the Holocaust* (Cambridge, 2003).
5. Derek Penslar emphasizes this in *Jews and the Military: A History*, 173. He cites the more than seven hundred letters by Jewish soldiers, who never mentioned the *Judenzählung*, found in Sabine Hank and Hermann Simon, eds., *Feldpostbriefe Jüdischer Soldaten, 1914–1918: Briefe ehemaliger Zöglinge an Sigmund Feist, Direktor des Reichenheimschen Waisenhauses in Berlin*, vols 1 and 2 (Berlin, 2002).
6. Mosse, *Toward the Final Solution*, chapter 11; Egmont Zechlin and Hans Joachim Bieber, *Die deutsche Politik und die Juden im Ersten Weltkrieg* (Göttingen, 1969), 516–25.
7. See, for example, Alexander Watson, *Enduring the Great War: Combat, Morale and Collapse in the German and British Armies, 1914–1918* (Cambridge, 2008).

8. Penslar, *Jews and the Military*, 172–73.
9. Jay Winter, *Remembering War: The Great War between Memory and History in the Twentieth Century* (New Haven, CT, 2006), 18–22.
10. Tim Grady, *German-Jewish Soldiers of the First World War in History and Memory* (Liverpool, 2011), 9–10.
11. See George Mosse's seminal work on the particularities of German antisemitism in *Toward the Final Solution* and *The Crisis of German Ideology* (New York, 1999).
12. Karen Hagemann, "Of 'Manly Valor' and 'German Honor': Nation, War and Masculinity in the Age of the Prussian Uprising against Napoleon," *Central European History* 30, no. 2 (1997): 187–220.
13. Ibid., 201–2.
14. Bernd Widdig, *Männerbünde und Massen: Zur Krise männlicher Identität in der Literatur der Moderne* (Wiesbaden, 1992), 11–32.
15. Kühne, *The Rise and Fall of Comradeship*, 34–35.
16. Jessica Meyer, *Men of War: Masculinity and the First World War in Britain* (New York, 2009), 2–4.
17. Thomas Kühne, "'…aus diesem Krieg werden nicht nur harte Männer heimkehren': Kriegskameradschaft und Männlichkeit im 20. Jahrhundert," in *Männergeschichte—Geschlechtergeschichte: Männlichkeit im Wandel der Moderne*, ed. Thomas Kühne (Frankfurt, 1996), 174–91.
18. Jason Crouthamel, *An Intimate History of the Front: Masculinity, Sexuality and German Soldiers in the First World War* (New York, 2014), chapter 5.
19. On the experience of combat for German Jewish soldiers, see Gregory Caplan, "Wicked Sons, German Heroes: Jewish Soldiers, Veterans and Memories of World War I in Germany," PhD dissertation, Georgetown University, 2001.
20. Paul Lebrecht Kriegstagebuch, 27 August 1916, Bayerisches Armeemuseum, made available by the Jüdisches Museum, Munich, thanks to Ulrike Heikaus and Julia B. Köhne. More analysis of Lebrecht's diary appears in my chapter in their collected volume: Jason Crouthamel, "Paul Lebrechts Tagebuch," in Heikaus and Köhne, *Krieg! Juden zwischen den Fronten*, 105–32.
21. On soldiers' psychological coping mechanisms for violence, see Watson, *Enduring the Great War*, chapter 3.
22. Paul Lebrecht Kriegstagebuch, 6 June 1917, Image 2739. Original: "Frei nach dem Plakatmotiv: Zeichnet Kriegsanleihe."
23. Paul Lebrecht Kriegstagebuch, 24 September 1916.
24. Paul Lebrecht Kriegstagebuch, 19 September 1917.
25. Paul Lebrecht Kriegstagebuch, 16–17 September 1917.
26. Paul Lebrecht Kriegstagebuch, 16–17 September 1917.
27. Paul Lebrecht Kriegstagebuch, 3 December 1916.
28. Paul Lebrecht Kriegstagebuch, 28 September and 3 December 1916.
29. This perception of Eastern European Jews as different and difficult to identify with can be seen in numerous letters by German Jewish soldiers. See, for example, Otto Köhler, who refers to Eastern European Jews as "Glaubensgenossen" but otherwise socially and culturally distinct in a

letter to Sigmund Feist, 15 January 1915, letter 352a-h, in Sabine Hank and Hermann Simon, eds, *Feldpostbriefe Jüdischer Soldaten, 1914–1918*, 356–58.
30. Paul Lebrecht Kriegstagebuch, 17 September 1917.
31. Paul Lebrecht Kriegstagebuch, 3 December 1916 and 18 January 1917.
32. On the tensions between integration and antisemitism, see Christhard Hoffmann, "Between Integration and Rejection: The Jewish Community in Germany, 1914–1918," in *State, Society and Mobilization during the First World War*, ed. John Horne (Cambridge, 1997), 89–104.
33. Paul Lebrecht Kriegstagebuch, 3 October 1917.
34. Paul Lebrecht Kriegstagebuch, 21 December 1917.
35. Paul Lebrecht Kriegstagebuch, 2–6 September 1918.
36. Paul Lebrecht Kriegstagebuch, 3 March 1917. Original: "Jetzt hatte ich genug, erklärte ihn reif für's Irrenhaus und brach das Gespräch ab. Die Kameraden sind größtenteils auf meiner Seite."
37. Paul Lebrecht Kriegstagebuch, 9 April 1917.
38. Paul Lebrecht Kriegstagebuch, 15 June 1917.
39. Paul Lebrecht Kriegstagebuch, 2 October 1917.
40. Paul Lebrecht Kriegstagebuch, 15–16 March 1917.
41. On soldiers' anxieties about changes on the home front, see Robert L. Nelson, *German Soldier Newspapers of the First World War* (Cambridge, 2011), 186–91.
42. Paul Lebrecht Kriegstagebuch, 21 November 1917.
43. Paul Lebrecht Kriegstagebuch, 27 December 1917.
44. Paul Lebrecht Kriegstagebuch, 25 December 1917.
45. Paul Lebrecht Kriegstagebuch, 24 February 1918.
46. Paul Lebrecht Kriegstagebuch, 22 August 1918.
47. On the widespread mutinies at the front, see Wilhelm Deist, "Verdeckter Militärstreik im Kriegsjahr 1918," in *Der Krieg des kleines Mannes*, ed. Wolfram Wette (Munich, 1997), 146–67.
48. Paul Lebrecht Kriegstagebuch, 10 October and 14 October 1918.
49. Julius Marx, *Kriegstagebuch eines Juden* (Frankfurt am Main, 1964), 5 October 1914 diary entry, 32.
50. Ibid., 1 December 1914 diary entry, 41.
51. Ibid., 29 August 1917 diary entry, 181.
52. Ibid., 2 November 1916 diary entry, 138.
53. Ibid.
54. Ibid., 3 November 1916 entry, 139.
55. Hermann Lehrer, letter to Sigmund Feist, 24 April 1918, letter 398a–398d, in Hank and Simon, *Feldpostbriefe jüdischer Soldaten*, vol. 2, 400. Hank and Simon note that the biographical background on Lehrer's age and fate is not clear, but he was a student of Dr Feist at the Reichenheimisches Waisenhaus in Berlin before 1914.
56. Ibid.
57. Hermann Berel Barsqueaux, letter to Sigmund Feist, 25 March 1918, letter 91a-b, and letter from 4 April 1918, letter 92a-ab, in Hank and Simon, *Feldpostbriefe jüdischer Soldaten*, vol. 1, 115–16.

58. Hermann Berel Barsqueaux, letter to Sigmund Feist, 29 September 1917, letter 72RS, in Hank and Simon, *Feldpostbriefe jüdischer Soldaten*, vol. 1, 94.
59. Hermann Berel Barsqueaux, letter to Sigmund Feist, 19 January 1918, letter 84, in Hank and Simon, *Feldpostbriefe jüdischer Soldaten*, vol. 1, 105–6.
60. Hermann Berel Barsqueaux, letter to Sigmund Feist, 28 May 1918, letter 98a-b, in Hank and Simon, *Feldpostbriefe jüdischer Soldaten*, vol. 1, 120–21.
61. Bernd Ulrich, *Die Augenzeugen: Deutsche Feldpostbriefe in Kriegs- und Nachkriegszeit, 1914–1933* (Essen, 1997), 40.
62. Ibid., 40, 78.
63. Herbert Czapski, letter to Sigmund Feist, 4 March 1917, letter 144a-b, in Hank and Simon, *Feldpostbriefe jüdischer Soldaten*, vol. 1, 163–64.
64. Joseph Kurt, memoir, "No Homesickness" (undated, written while Kurt was in Great Britain in the 1940s), ME 338.MM 42, LBINY, 6–7.
65. Ibid., 8.
66. Ibid., 1.
67. Letter from Rudolf Veek to his wife, Julie, 17 October 1914, MsG 2/2901, Bundesarchiv-Militärarchiv, Freiburg (BAMF).
68. Letter from Rudolf Veek to his wife, Julie; the handwritten pamphlets were included in the letter of 28 October 1914, MsG 2/2901, BAMF.
69. Ibid.
70. Rudolf Veek, letter to his wife, 30 August 1914, MsG 2/2901, BAMF.
71. Ibid.
72. Georg G., letters to his parents, 23 and 29 May 1915, MsG 2/3600, BAMF.
73. Hermann B., letter to his parents, 30 May 1916, MsG 2/18075, BAMF.
74. Hermann B., letter to his parents, 3 February 1917, MsG 2/18075, BAMF. Original: "Jeder 10 österr. Offizier sieht jüdisch aus."
75. Hermann B., letter to his parents, 22 August 1917, MsG 2/18075, BAMF.
76. Hermann B., letter to his parents, 12 September 1917, MsG 2/18075, BAMF.
77. Letter from Hermann B. to his parents, 29 November 1917, MsG 2/18075, BAMF.
78. Letter from Hermann B. to his parents, 9 August 1918, MsG 2/18075, BAMF.
79. Letter from Hermann B. to his parents, 16 July and 8 August 1917, MSG 2/18075, BAMF. On the stigma associated with "war neurosis," see Jason Crouthamel, *The Great War and German Memory: Society, Politics and Psychological Trauma, 1914–45* (Liverpool, 2009), esp. chapter 1.
80. Willy Rosenstein memoir, written in 1940, ME 527.MM64, LBINY, 2. An account of Rosenstein's service record is also given in Felix Theilhaber's *Jüdische Flieger im Weltkrieg* (Berlin, 1924), 76–78.
81. Carl Degelow, *Mit dem weissen Hirsch durch Dick und Dünn: Erlebnisse und Betrachtungen eines Kampffliegers* (Altona-Ottensen, 1920), 38.
82. Willy Rosenstein memoir, written in 1940, ME 527.MM64, LBINY, 6–8.
83. Ibid., 3
84. Ibid., 15.
85. Ibid., 15.
86. Adolf Auer, Personal-Bogen, cited in Peter Kilduff, *Black Fokker Leader: The First World War's Last Airfighter Knight* (London, 2009), 132.
87. Ibid.

88. Marx, *Kriegstagebuch eines Juden*, 97.
89. Peter Gay, *My German Question: Growing Up in Nazi Berlin* (New Haven, CT, 1999), 111.

Bibliography

Berger, Michael. *Für Kaiser, Reich und Vaterland: Jüdische Soldaten, eine Geschichte vom 19. Jahrhundert bis heute*. Zürich: Orell Füssli, 2015.

Brustein, William. *Roots of Hate: Anti-Semitism in Europe before the Holocaust*. Cambridge: Cambridge University Press, 2003.

Caplan, Gregory. "Wicked Sons, German Heroes: Jewish Soldiers, Veterans and Memories of World War I in Germany." Ph.D. dissertation, Georgetown University, 2001.

Crim, Brian. *Antisemitism in the German Military Community and the Jewish Response, 1914–1938*. Lanham, MD: Lexington Books, 2014.

Crouthamel, Jason. *The Great War and German Memory: Society, Politics and Psychological Trauma, 1914–45*. Liverpool: Liverpool University Press, 2009.

———. *An Intimate History of the Front: Masculinity, Sexuality and German Soldiers in the First World War*. New York: Palgrave Macmillan, 2014.

———. "Paul Lebrechts Tagebuch." In *Krieg! Juden zwischen den Fronten, 1914–1918*, edited by Ulrike Heikaus and Julia B. Köhne, 105–32. Berlin: Hentrich und Hentrich Verlag, 2014.

Degelow, Carl. *Mit dem weissen Hirsch durch Dick und Dünn: Erlebnisse und Betrachtungen eines Kampffliegers*. Altona-Ottensen: Adolff, 1920.

Deist, Wilhelm. "Verdeckter Militärstreik im Kriegsjahr 1918." In *Der Krieg des kleines Mannes*, edited by Wolfram Wette, 146–167. Munich: Piper, 1997.

Gay, Peter. *My German Question: Growing Up in Nazi Berlin*. New Haven, CT: Yale University Press, 1999.

Grady, Tim. *German-Jewish Soldiers of the First World War in History and Memory*. Liverpool: Liverpool University Press, 2011.

Hagemann, Karen. "Of 'Manly Valor' and 'German Honor': Nation, War and Masculinity in the Age of the Prussian Uprising against Napoleon." *Central European History* 30, no. 2 (1997): 187–220.

Hank, Sabine, and Hermann Simon, eds. *Feldpostbriefe Jüdischer Soldaten, 1914–1918: Briefe ehemalige Zöglinge an Sigmund Feist, Direktor des Reichenheimschen Waisenhauses in Berlin*, vols 1 and 2. Berlin: Hentrich & Hentrich, 2002.

Heikaus, Ulrike, and Julia B. Köhne, eds. *Krieg! Juden zwischen den Fronten, 1914–1918*. Berlin: Hentrich und Hentrich Verlag, 2014.

Hoffmann, Christhard. "Between Integration and Rejection: The Jewish Community in Germany, 1914–1918." In *State, Society and Mobilization during the First World War*, edited by John Horne, 89–104. Cambridge: Cambridge University Press, 1997.

Kilduff, Peter. *Black Fokker Leader: The First World War's Last Airfighter Knight*. London: Grub Street, 2009.

Kühne, Thomas. "'…aus diesem Krieg werden nicht nur harte Männer heimkehren': Kriegskameradschaft und Männlichkeit im 20. Jahrhundert."

In *Männergeschichte—Geschlechtergeschichte: Männlichkeit im Wandel der Moderne*, edited by Thomas Kühne, 174–91. Frankfurt: Campus Verlag, 1996.

———. "Comradeship: Gender Confusion and the Gender Order in the German Military, 1918–1945." In *Home/Front: The Military, War and Gender in Twentieth-Century Germany*, edited by Karen Hagemann and Stefanie Schüler-Springorum, 233–54. Oxford: Berg, 2002.

———. *The Rise and Fall of Comradeship*. Cambridge: Cambridge University Press, 2017.

Marx, Julius. *Kriegstagebuch eines Juden*. Frankfurt am Main: ner-tamid-verlag, 1964.

Meyer, Jessica. *Men of War: Masculinity and the First World War in Britain*. New York: Palgrave Macmillan, 2009.

Mosse, George L. *The Crisis of German Ideology*. New York: Howard Fertig, 1999.

———. *Toward the Final Solution*. New York: Howard Fertig, 1997.

Nelson, Robert L. *German Soldier Newspapers of the First World War*. Cambridge: Cambridge University Press, 2011.

Penslar, Derek. *Jews and the Military: A History*. Princeton, NJ: Princeton University Press, 2013.

Rosenthal, Jacob. *"Die Ehre des jüdischen Soldaten": Die Judenzählung im Ersten Weltkrieg und ihre Folgen*. Frankfurt: Campus Verlag, 2007.

Theilhaber, Felix. *Jüdische Flieger im Weltkrieg*. Berlin: Verlag der Reichsbund jüdischer Frontsoldaten, 1924.

Ullrich, Anna. "'Nun sind wir gezeichnet': Jüdische Soldaten und die 'Judenzählung' im Ersten Weltkrieg." In *Krieg! Juden zwischen den Fronten, 1914–1918*, edited by Ulrike Heikaus and Julia B. Köhne, 215–38. Berlin: Hentrich und Hentrich Verlag, 2014.

Ulrich, Bernd. *Die Augenzeugen: Deutsche Feldpostbriefe in Kriegs- und Nachkriegszeit, 1914–1933*. Essen: Klartext Verlag, 1997.

Watson, Alexander. *Enduring the Great War: Combat, Morale and Collapse in the German and British Armies, 1914–1918*. Cambridge: Cambridge University Press, 2008.

Widdig, Bernd. *Männerbünde und Massen: Zur Krise männlicher Identität in der Literatur der Moderne*. Wiesbaden: Vs Verlag für Sozialwissenschaften, 1992.

Winter, Jay. *Remembering War: The Great War between Memory and History in the Twentieth Century*. New Haven, CT: Yale University Press, 2006.

Zechlin, Egmont, and Hans Joachim Bieber. *Die deutsche Politik und die Juden im Ersten Weltkrieg*. Göttingen: Vandenhoeck & Ruprecht, 1969.

PART III

REPRESENTATION

THE CULTURE OF WAR

9

BLIND SPOTS AND JEWISH HEROINES
Refashioning the Galician War Experience in 1920s Hollywood and Berlin

Philipp Stiasny

To Mellie for listening

It came as a shock to the Jewish population of Galicia when Russian troops invaded the Austrian province in the autumn of 1914. Known to be loyal to Emperor Franz Joseph, the Jews suffered outbursts of antisemitic violence during the first weeks of the First World War. The Russian army leadership collectively suspected them of espionage and ambushes, and there were many pogroms.[1] Although they resulted from rampant prejudice and the troops' poor discipline rather than official orders, the consequences were catastrophic: Jews became victims of humiliation, depredation, pillaging, rape, and murder. In Lemberg (Ukrainian: L'viv; Polish: Lwów), the capital of the province, Cossacks rode through the Jewish quarter shooting and killing fifty people on 27 September, three weeks into the occupation. News of such atrocities led half of the Galician Jews, approximately 400,000 people, to flee west to Hungary, Moravia, and Austria. Those who stayed behind, together with other Jews from Eastern Europe, ended up caught between the fronts of what historians call a largely "forgotten war."[2]

Accounts of the Russian occupation of Galicia and the miserable predicament of the Jews and its other inhabitants appeared early on in the press, particularly in the wake of the Battle of Gorlice-Tarnów in May 1915 and the subsequent recapture of the province by Austro-Hungarian and German troops. A few months later, Sándor (Alexander) Bródy (1863–1924) presented the first theatrical adaptation of the events in his tragedy *Lea Lyon*. It premiered at the Hungarian Theatre in Budapest on 4 September 1915. Labeled a "Jewish war drama," the story is set in the early days of the war on the Russian-Austrian border, where Russian Cossacks invade a village of orthodox Jews. Their commander, the young Russian prince Konstantin, falls in love with Lea, the rabbi's daughter, who initially resists his advances and romantic overtures. Running out of patience, Konstantin threatens to burn down the village if Lea does not submit to his wishes voluntarily. Torn between individual and societal constraints, between the desire to live and love and her father's strict demand to prefer a martyr's death, the young woman visits Konstantin. Willfully ignoring that Austro-Hungarian troops are approaching, he spends the night with her and then commits suicide to escape captivity. After she has admitted her affair with the enemy, Lea is killed by her father.[3]

While the play did address the war and its effects, the Jewish Hungarian author of *Lea Lyon* was primarily interested in the ancient ethnic enmity between Russians and Jews.[4] His play was banned in Vienna but enjoyed considerable success in Budapest, where the Jewish community constituted almost a quarter of the city's population. A film adaptation under the direction of Sándor (Alexander) Korda premiered in Budapest on 1 November 1915 and was later released in Austria and Germany as well. In the film version of the story, Konstantin tries to escape with Lea and they are chased by her fiancé, Joshua, who aims at his rival but accidentally kills Lea. Konstantin then shoots himself, so that, as one reviewer notes, "the rabbi's daughter and the Russian officer would be reunited in death."[5]

In 1916, about a year after Galicia was recaptured, another widely distributed fictional account of the Russian occupation appeared, *Hotel Imperial*, by the Jewish Hungarian author Lajos (Ludwig) Bíró (1880–1948), a war correspondent at the time who tackled Jewish topics more than once in his oeuvre.[6] The German translation of his novel, *Hotel Stadt Lemberg* (*Hotel City of Lemberg*), released by the Berlin-based publisher Ullstein, became an immediate bestseller.[7] While the location is not explicitly identified in the novel, it is evident that the story takes place in the city of Tarnów (some eighty kilometers east of Kraków). The events unfold between November 1914, when the Russians advanced to the Dunajec River in Western Galicia after defeating the Austro-Hungarian army in the Battle of Lemberg, and May 1915, when the Central Powers gained the upper hand in the Galician campaign following the Battle of Gorlice-Tarnów.

In his novel, Bíró follows the aristocratic Austro-Hungarian Hussar lieutenant Paul Almasy, who is caught behind enemy lines. Pursued by the Russians, he flees into an almost deserted hotel and is hidden by the parlor maid Anna, the real hero. When the Russians move into town, their general chooses the hotel as his headquarters. Immediately attracted to Anna, he makes her the lady of the house and outfits her with fashionable clothes and jewelry. Meanwhile, Almasy masquerades as the head waiter and is protected by Anna. When a Russian spy returns on a secret mission with decisive information about the deployment of Austro-Hungarian troops, Almasy, with Anna's help, murders the spy in cold blood. Soon after, the town is liberated.

Although none of the main protagonists in *Hotel Imperial* are Jewish, the themes of antisemitism and Polish-Jewish conflict are prominent. The heroine Anna, a Czech national, sides with the Jewish hotel porter Elias who—like the whole pro-Austrian Jewish community of the town—is severely threatened and bullied, not so much by the Russian military but by collaborationist Poles who denounce the Jews and want to profit from their discrimination.

A year after its publication, Bíró's novel was successfully adapted for the theatre in 1917. Jenő Janovics then also produced a film version of *Hotel Imperial* in Hungary, where the film industry had grown significantly during the war. When the film was finally released in late 1918, the First World War was over, the Austro-Hungarian Empire had collapsed, and Galicia would become the contested territory in another war between the newly founded states of Poland and Ukraine. In this situation, *Hotel Imperial* could be promoted as an antiwar statement for in the end the male hero Almasy (played by Mihály Várkonyi, later known as Victor Varconi) feels ashamed for having killed a defenseless enemy spy. "The murder has left him disillusioned; never again will he be a soldier."[8] Today both Hungarian films, Korda's *Lea Lyon* (1915) and Janovics's *Hotel Imperial* (1918), are lost. Only a few photographs, posters, and reviews survive.

The life of Eastern European Jews, especially in Russia under the Czar, their misery, legal discrimination, and experience of antisemitic violence were not uncommon themes in the cinema during and after the First World War. In Germany, topics like these were addressed, for instance, in *Der gelbe Schein* (*The Yellow Passport*, GER 1918, dir. Victor Janson, Eugen Illés), *Die Geächteten*, aka *Der Ritualmord* (*The Outlawed* aka *Ritual Murder*, GER 1919, dir. Joseph Delmont), and *Pogrom* (GER 1919, dir. Alfred Halm). The most prominent German pogrom film from the 1920s that has survived is *Die Gezeichneten* (*The Stigmatized* aka *Love One Another*, GER 1922, dir. Carl Theodor Dreyer), a work that depicts, with great precision, prejudice, hate propaganda, mob violence, murder, and expulsion. It may have been a response to the new wave of pogroms—many in Galicia—during the Polish-Ukrainian war of 1918/19, the arrival of refugees in the West, and rising antisemitic sentiment in Germany.

Yet at a time when film more than ever before developed into a medium of global reach and distribution, Galicia and the war experience of its Jewish population were only rarely addressed in the cinema. It took ten years until two major film productions depicted the period of the Russian occupation: Mauritz Stiller's new adaptation of Bíró's *Hotel Imperial* and Edward Sloman's new adaptation of Bródy's *Lea Lyon* (now titled *Surrender*), both released in 1927. These two films refashioned the Galician experience for a worldwide audience—now from Hollywood's point of view.

Hollywood's main competitor, Germany, contributed two more films on the subject, *Leichte Kavallerie* (*Light Cavalry*, GER 1927, dir. Rolf Randolf) and *Zwei Welten* (*Two Worlds*, GER/UK 1930, dir. E. A. Dupont). Thematically and topographically these films stand out as the only German films on the Jews in wartime Galicia. At the same time, they are part of a wave of First World War movies running in the cinemas from the mid 1920s. In this context, Stiller's Hollywood version of *Hotel Imperial* occupies a special place. It paved the way for thematically related films.

This chapter focuses on these later re-appropriations whose production took place under entirely different historical, national, political, and commercial circumstances than the films from the 1910s. What kind of narratives were woven around the events in Galicia? What kind of Jewish war experience was reconstructed? How did the films relate to each other? As it turns out, none of the films discussed in this chapter deal with the Jewish war experience in the form of a combat movie focusing on the depiction of military violence and the perspectives of soldiers. Instead, these films are melodramas whose stories are concerned with the love between Jews and non-Jews and with conflicts within the Jewish family. The films are also characterized by their Jewish heroines, that is, the activity of emancipated female protagonists who struggle at the same time with the regime of occupation and the patriarchal order. Regarding the developments within the Jewish community, we are presented with allegories of a generational divide. Again and again, the films center on the relation between father and daughter, ancient and well-founded skepticism, and an interreligious optimism that wants to overcome mutual prejudice and barriers. Viewed from a distance, it seems that all these films do not merely answer to the discourses of their times but that they are in dialogue with each other. It is as if they were constantly returning to the same constellation, the same anxieties, and the same utopian vision.

Tarnów on the Pacific

In 1926, the Hotel Imperial lay in Madrid and the former Galicia was a dream built out of Californian plywood. In fact, the American film of the same title was shot on the sets of the Hollywood production *The Spanish Dancer* (USA 1923, dir. Herbert Brenon), which were still on the Famous Players Lasky (Paramount) lot.[9] Both *The Spanish Dancer* and *Hotel Imperial* (1926/27) starred Pola Negri, the most celebrated and eccentric European import of that era. Therefore, *Hotel Imperial* is arguably a Pola Negri film, first of all. The role of Anna, the strong-willed parlor maid, allowed Negri, born in Poland under Russian rule and brought to fame in the films by Ernst Lubitsch, to add a new facet to her profile as the beautiful and somewhat "exotic" woman who, with charm and cunning, ascends the social ladder (is it a coincidence that in *Hotel Imperial* she is first seen cleaning the stairs?).[10]

Secondly, *Hotel Imperial* is an Erich Pommer film. If things had gone according to Pommer, the famous producer, the film would have been made in Germany—before Pommer's short 1926/27 Hollywood *intermezzo*. However, Ufa, the largest German production company and Pommer's employer, rejected Bíró's 1916 bestseller.[11] The film's international success in 1927 proved them wrong.[12] In 1939 and 1943, two more Hollywood films adapted Bíró's story for the cinema, the latter made by Galician-born Billy Wilder.[13]

Not least, in its visual style and mannerisms *Hotel Imperial* is very much a Mauritz Stiller film. According to Arne Lunde, the director Stiller, who had earned himself an enormous artistic reputation with his Swedish films, had difficulties adjusting to Hollywood and saw himself as an outsider—being a European, a Jew, and a homosexual. In *Hotel Imperial*, he "ultimately managed to appropriate for himself a stylistic mode of protest and critique—inside a narrative of deceptive identity masquerades set in highly destabilized, claustrophobic, and anxiety-filled border spaces. In *Hotel Imperial* (1927), Stiller forged an exilic narrative of vertiginous displacement, alienation, identity confusion, and dislocation …."[14] In contrast to the film's original American title, the German title of both the novel and the 1927 film release was *Hotel Stadt Lemberg*, alluding to specifically located memories and expectations. Lemberg—then part of the Republic of Poland—was known as the former capital of Galicia and part of the Habsburg Empire until 1918. Stressing the topographical aspect even more with direct reference to the victorious Battle of Gorlice-Tarnów, the version released in Germany also bore the subtitle, "The Heroine of Tarnow."[15]

Unlike Bíró's novel, which covers several months of the Russian occupation, most of the screen time is devoted to the events of the last two days.[16] When the Russian spy Petroff (Michael Vavitch) returns during a rambunctious Russian festival covered in mud, but apparently successful, the disguised Austro-Hungarian officer and now head waiter Almasy (James Hall) senses danger.[17] In order to keep the Russian general (George Siegmann) from receiving the spy, Anna (Pola Negri) gets him drunk in his room and ensures that Petroff is not allowed in. Instead of waiting, Petroff takes a hot bath during which he is shot by Almasy. He had to do it, Almasy explains to Anna, to save the lives of thousands. Anna then takes the initiative, burns Petroff's notebooks, and makes it look like a suicide. When suspicion falls on Almasy and he is threatened with execution, Anna provides an alibi saying that they spent the time in question together. In a jealous rage, the general rips off Anna's expensive clothes and casts her out. Almasy escapes the same night and makes his way back to his regiment.

The big offensive of the Austro-Hungarian army begins the next day, taking the Russians completely off guard. The troops have to pull out in a hurry and abandon the hotel. Shortly thereafter, Almasy enters the city on horseback in his dress uniform alongside the victorious troops, who are greeted enthusiastically by the townsfolk. The soldiers take part in a Mass in front of the church, after which Almasy is supposed to be honored with a medal for his bravery. He calls the unsuspecting Anna forward and introduces her to the commandant, who greets her like a noblewoman, thanking her for her great service to her country. He then grants Almasy a short leave to get his personal affairs in order—that is, to marry Anna. Thus, while at the end of Bíró's 1916 novel Almasy condemns murder as a man's patriotic duty and therefore resigns from military service ten years later, at the end of the American film patriotism and national glory prevail, cold-blooded murder notwithstanding.

Transformations and Transgressions

In *Hotel Imperial*, Galicia is represented primarily by the not particularly elegant and dusty hotel, a place cut off from the outside world. The wall around the building and the heavy venetian blinds covering the windows only allow glimpses through narrow slits and bars onto the threatening world outside, and not many good things make it through the doors. Most of the action takes place at night in small, cramped rooms. Only the hotel's big staircase introduces a rare diagonal, drawing attention to the symbolic passage between above and below. Russians, Austrians, Hungarians, and other unspecified ethnic groups, (female) civilians and (male) soldiers encounter each other in this space.

Here also the different social classes come into contact (with fluid camera work that stresses and duplicates the movement). Next to the male personnel, the porter Elias (Max Davidson) and the sullen cook Anton (Otto Fries), who is in love with Anna, we first meet Anna as a hotel maid scrubbing the stairs. Later, though not yet a countess, she is outfitted like a rich mistress and, finally, in a simple dress, she finds her prince. Anna always brings out the sexuality of the belligerent men. As she explains to the general, men only make war because their wives have begun to bore them; in search of sexual adventure in war, they exert violence on women.

We meet a noble officer who loses his troops and military rank, has to disguise himself, suffers in fear of discovery, and undergoes a demotion in social class by masquerading as a waiter; a general who first demonstrates independence and a certain masculine strength, and in the end jealousy and overconfidence; a spy who appears in a diverse array of disguises and then, when he tries to climb naked into a bathtub, is shot by another man in disguise. As if to discover his true identity, the first thing the murderer Almasy does after the crime is to wipe the steam off the mirror and stare in horror at his own reflection; we already had occasion to imagine the nightmares about war that wake him at night covered in sweat. Compulsion and this game of hide-and-seek characterize Almasy as much as the rest of the film.

The Hotel Imperial is thus a place of transformations, of both the crossing and the blurring of borders, where occupier and occupied live under one roof, and camouflage and masquerade are essential for survival. Not even the hotel's name remains untainted by a loss of meaning and oscillation, because the Habsburg Empire, which the hotel's name obviously points to, fails to protect its subjects from the imperial might of the Czar. It seems an especially bitter irony that the film equates the invasion of various armies—first Russian, then Austro-Hungarian—into the civilian world of the city. It was all the same to the viewer who saw the film in 1927, the year it was released: both empires, the Austro-Hungarian as well as the Russian, had long since passed into history, just like the former province of Galicia.

Only a few days after *Hotel Imperial* premiered in New York on 1 January 1927, the film came to Germany, too. There critics raved about its engrossing drama, the elegant cinematography, and the performance of the actors, especially Pola Negri. At the same time, they noted a commercial mixture of romance, adventure, and war.[18] Others saw an exciting spy movie laden with special effects.[19] Opinion was divided over aesthetic and political sensibilities as to whether or not to criticize *Hotel Imperial* or even flatly dismiss it as a "fairly regular hero film"[20] and a "typically German, Austro-Hungarian film for American palates."[21] "The miracle has happened: the Americans, who were still making anti-German war movies two years ago, have created a counter-example here; a more German-friendly version could hardly be thought of," praised the right-wing, conservative *Börsen-Zeitung*.[22] Meanwhile the liberal *Berliner Tageblatt* condemned the manner in which "bloody and lewd situations in the guise of a freshly experienced war are exploited for excitement, emotion, and enthusiasm."[23] Clearest is the condemnation from the communist press:

> This film about 1915 is filmed in such a way as to give 1915 all honors. Imperial and royal through thick and thin. Exactly as it is, it could have cropped up in Austro-Hungary and Germany in those days as cheap propaganda. Nothing's missing. Avowals: "we are good Austrians." Dream-images of God, Emperor and fatherland. ... One hardly believes one's eyes. More than ten years have passed since then—and yet people still dare to bring out such a "timely" piece of trash that rekindles the hopeless Austro-Hungarian militarism![24]

On the audience reaction after the withdrawal of the Russians, Willy Haas writes in the *Film-Kurier*: "At the entrance of the Austrian troops thunderous applause rang out and lasted for minutes. But it was no war fever, no nationalism. It was because it achieved a *Bildmusik*, like sunshine blazing forth, exultant and radiant. It's a very particular film: it is, in a sense, without precedent."[25]

The Blind Spot

Neither in contemporary reviews nor in the plot of the film *Hotel Imperial* is it clear that Galicia, where the story takes place, was, among other ethnic groups, home to a large Jewish population. Cities like Tarnów and Lemberg were centers of urban Jewish culture. In 1910, Jews constituted 41 percent of the population of Tarnów and 28 percent of the population of Lemberg. That the film almost entirely ignores this important historical connection seems a curious omission. This happened even despite the fact that (or because) most of the responsible people involved in the production of *Hotel Imperial* were European Jews and American Jews with immigrant backgrounds. That goes for the producer and the actual driving force, the German Erich Pommer, the Hungarian novelist Lajos Bíró, and the director Mauritz (Moshe) Stiller, who was born in the then Czarist province of Finland (his parents had emigrated out of Russia and Poland). On the American side, the Hungarian emigrant Adolph Zukor, head of Paramount Studios, his business partner Jesse L. Lasky, and the author of the screenplay, Jules Furthman, were also Jewish. Certainly, all of them were aware of the history of the Jews in Galicia and their fate of emigration and expulsion.

Looked at more closely, in one short scene an older man with a beard and fur cap is visible, who—as in Bíró's novel—represents a rabbi. He is part of a delegation of city notables who pay their respects to the Russian general. The hotel porter, Elias, is played by Max Davidson, whose face would have been familiar to American audiences (and, potentially, many German audiences as well). While the film contains no explicit clue that the character of Elias should be identified as a Jew, the available information, knowledge of the context, the role, the appearance, and the facial expressions must have been sufficient to evoke that particular association for the viewer. In any event, in his 1927 review, the cultural critic and sociologist Siegfried Kracauer describes Davidson, that is, Elias, as a "small, touching, little Jewish man, who is so human and who throws up his hands so fearfully in despair."[26]

As a matter of fact, since the 1910s, Max Davidson, a Jew of German origin, portrayed almost exclusively Jewish characters in Hollywood. As a stock character, he also appeared prominently in the mid 1920s in various comedies that caricatured cultural and ethnic stereotypes of Jewish and Irish immigrants. In the Metro-Goldwyn-Mayer (MGM) productions *Old Clothes* (USA 1925, dir. Edward F. Cline) and *The Ragman* (USA 1925, dir. Edward F. Cline) he appeared alongside the world-famous child star Jackie Coogan. Coogan played the role of the young Irishman, Tim Kelly, and Davidson the role of his fatherly friend, the Jewish ragman Ginsberg. In 1926/27, Davidson was the main character in a series of short comedies set in the Jewish immigrant milieu in America, produced by Hal Roach first for Pathé and then MGM. The series was partially distributed in Germany, too. Despite its success, it was canceled in 1928. The decisive factor was apparently the unease felt by the two heads of MGM, Louis B. Mayer and Nicholas Schenck, both of Russian Jewish descent. They both began turning against films that perpetuated the stereotype of the unassimilated Jewish immigrant.[27]

In 1920s Hollywood (and Germany), the reasons to avoid or even suppress the dramatization of Judaism and Jewish subject matter and milieus were numerous. Jewish immigrants had manifold aspirations and a great number put Judaism aside in favor of a secular "Americanness." Also, there existed different opinions within the American Jewish community between established, often assimilated,

Western European Jews and Eastern European Jews who had immigrated later. The most important reason to avoid Jewish subject matter in the movies was, however, antisemitism in certain parts of American society that expressed itself in prejudice and discrimination—especially in the campaign supported by the industrialist Henry Ford against the alleged prevalence of Jews in Hollywood.[28]

Even after this campaign, Hollywood films with Jewish themes appeared on the screen, including the outstandingly successful *The Jazz Singer* (USA 1927, dir. Alan Crosland).[29] Nevertheless, in order to not give a big production like *Hotel Imperial* a particular ethnic and cultural bias, it may have seemed expedient to suppress overt references to the strong presence of Jews in Galicia as well as the displacement of refugees caused by the war.

Certain narrative elements are always compressed or even dropped when novels are adapted into films. Still, when comparing the film to Bíró's novel, it is impossible to overlook how important it was for the author from the outset to show the threat faced by the Jewish community, not only as a result of the Russian invasion. Antipathy towards Jews is evident in the Polish population of the city. Anna's admirer, the Czech cook Anton, also proves himself an aggressive antisemite, when he scares the Jewish porter Elias Buttermann "with the air of a victor" by telling him: "The Russians are here, they're letting all the Jews hang, and I can beat you up too, if I want."[30] When the Polish city mayor presents the Russian general with the delegation of citizens, he separates them into Jews and non-Jews without prompting. Afterwards a Jewish doctor accuses him of "delivering" and "betraying" the Jews in a headlong rush of obsequiousness.[31] The same city mayor uses his position of power during the Russian occupation to allow Jewish businessmen to be punished under a pretext in order to give their property to his friends. Anna, who is Czech, becomes an advocate for the oppressed Jews, and she helps them. In Bíró's novel, the Jews prove themselves loyal followers of Emperor Franz Joseph, risking their lives to hide Austro-Hungarian soldiers who remained in the city.[32]

The Russian invaders do not, however, appear as brutes. On the contrary, Bíró accentuates their kind-heartedness, and, in contrast to the film, Anna's relationship to the much older general, who pampers and indulges her, seems fairly ambiguous. On the one hand, the beautiful Anna's relationship to the amorously devoted general recalls—in the book more strongly than in the film—the Old Testament story of the brave Jewess Judith, often portrayed in Western art, who gets the Assyrian commander Holofernes drunk, beheads him, and thereby rescues the people of Israel (the star profile of Pola Negri was characterized by vamps whose unfettered sexuality pushes men to perdition). On the other hand, Anna answers the question of whether she was the general's lover after the Russians' withdrawal with "yes." The boundaries between friend and enemy become increasingly blurred in the novel. Almasy—tired, emotionally insecure, and perpetually in doubt—becomes morally conflicted about whether he can kill the Russian spy, who is not entirely unlikeable. He cannot hate him. And after the murder he is in such doubt over the justice of his act that he does not want to receive any decoration after the city is retaken, and—because he can no longer kill—quits the army. Almasy's murder of the spy, like all killing in war, is explicitly compared to Cain's fratricide of Abel. Finally, Bíró brings to the fore that the Russian and Austro-Hungarian troops resemble one another in the treatment of the—also explicitly Jewish—civilian population. Similarities and parallels abound. At the end, once again, the Russians are barely gone before the Austrian general adopts the hotel for his headquarters. By contrast, the film definitively restores the military power and legitimacy of the Austro-Hungarian Dual Monarchy at the end without question. The now socially elevated lady Anna—standard-bearer of patriotism and loyal servant of the old system—is also metaphorically adopted into the masculine sphere of the army and decorated like a soldier.

The Hussar and the Beautiful Jewess in *Light Cavalry* (1927)

Within twelve months of the German premiere of *Hotel Imperial*, *Leichte Kavallerie* (*Light Cavalry*, GER 1927) and *Surrender* (USA 1927), a new adaptation of Bródy's *Lea Lyon*, were released in Germany. Both are set in wartime Galicia, and in contrast to the earlier American film, the Jewish population plays a central role.[33] As no copy of the German film has survived, all information has to be drawn from censorship and press materials. Nevertheless, the relationship of *Light Cavalry* to *Hotel Imperial*, remarked on by many contemporary critics, is obvious, to such an extent that one could employ an expression from the period and call it a *Neuauflage*, a rehash or new edition.[34] The story takes place in Galicia in October 1914 near the Russian border, where in this case not Russian troops, but a squadron from the Austro-Hungarian Hussar Regiment Nr. 9 stops in a small village during their advance. The first lieutenant (Alfons Fryland) finds quarters in the estate of the countess Komaröff (Vivian Gibson), lieutenant count Starhemberg (André Mattoni) is lodged in the house of Rabbi Süß (Albert Steinrück), and the Hungarian sergeant Farkas (Fritz Kampers) with the general store

Figure 9.1 Rahel (Elizza la Porta) and Lieutenant Count Starhemberg (André Mattoni) fall in love but her father, Rabbi Süß (Albert Steinrück), strongly objects. Promotional still for *Leichte Kavallerie* from Deutsches Filminstitut, Frankfurt. Public domain image.

owner Moritz Wasserstrahl (Siegfried Arno), an apparently orthodox Jew with *payot* (sidelocks).[35] According to one reviewer, the Jewish milieu was "depicted lovingly and with obvious expertise."[36]

As in *Hotel Imperial*, the encounter between the civilians and the soldiers, who are not entirely welcome, is intertwined with struggles over love, jealousy, and espionage. The countess Komarôff, who makes a secret pact with the Russians, manages to seduce the first lieutenant and pump him for information that she sends to the Russian army leadership through her husband (Jack Mylong-Münz), who is in hiding (and often appears in disguise). At the same time, Starhemberg and Rahel (Elizza la Porta), the rabbi's charming daughter, fall in love. But the rabbi cannot accept Rahel's relationship with someone of a different creed and wants to send her as quickly as possible out of the combat zone. He wants her to live with relatives in Vienna and protect her (sexual) integrity. Starhemberg, on the other hand, confesses his love for her and tells the rabbi that he feels strongly enough to "overcome outmoded prejudices."[37]

The melodramatic entanglements of the officers are contrasted with a comic male duo, played by Fritz Kampers as Farkas and Siegfried Arno as Wasserstrahl.[38] Farkas teases Wasserstrahl by constantly mispronouncing his name (Wasservogel, Wasserkopf, Wasserkrug). In addition, the Hungarian Farkas is a lady's man; he constantly repeats the verse of the song that gives the film its title: "Today it's her—tomorrow she, / Thus kisses the light cavalry!"[39]

In the last third of the film, events follow in rapid succession. Farkas, Wasserstrahl, and the rabbi learn that the countess Komarôff has betrayed an important order to the Russians, who now plan to attack the town. The lieutenant is informed, but the Russians have already cut the telephone lines to the next unit. Though the squadron is surrounded and about to be defeated, at the last moment Rahel manages to sneak through the enemy lines and bring German soldiers to the rescue; the Russians are forced to retreat, and the victors enter the city to the tune of a march (at this point, the premiere audience applauded loudly).[40] The commandant thanks Rahel in grand style for her "decisive and self-sacrificing actions."[41] While she devotes herself to caring for Starhemberg, who was wounded in the battle, Wasserstrahl reports to Farkas to volunteer for military service. While Wasserstrahl wore the clothing of an orthodox Jew at the beginning of the film, at the end he wears an Austro-Hungarian uniform. One can only presume that this should be read as a renunciation of tradition-conscious Judaism (that Rahel's father, the rabbi, stands for) and a pointed identification with the (Roman Catholic) Austrian Empire—even, perhaps, as an act of conversion.

The commonalities between *Light Cavalry* and *Hotel Imperial* in terms of plot are striking. They include the love between officers and civilians, a love rendered more complex because of social, religious, and ethnic differences; the seduction of an officer; the betrayal of a secret; the decisive assistance of a woman with the defeat of the enemy and the official recognition of her services at the end. Whereas the Jewish dimension of Bíró's novel comes through only cryptically, if at all, in Stiller's film version of *Hotel Imperial*, it is immediately present in the screenplay for *Light Cavalry*, written by the Bucharest-born Jewish author Emanuel Alfieri. Military success in this latter film depends directly on the loyalty of Jewish civilians, which is motivated in turn by a historically conditioned fear of persecution by the Russian army as well as by romantic relationships that are able to transcend differences between Jews and Christians. However, since the surviving information about the film is limited, it remains an open question whether the transformations and the crossing and blurring of borders were portrayed in *Light Cavalry* as they are in *Hotel Imperial*. Most critics saw *Light Cavalry* as a conventional production that showed none of the artistic and moral ambition of the American precursor. While some objected,[42] others found the "mixture of sentimental, serious, and humorous [aspects]" to be "skillful" and a recipe for a good box office in provincial cinemas.[43]

The Prince and the Beautiful Jewess: *Lea Lyon* becomes *Surrender* (1927)

Like *Light Cavalry*, *Surrender* (USA 1927, dir. Edward Sloman) avoided the realistic depictions of war that first became central, if not dominant, modes of the cinematic portrayal of war in the wake of *The Big Parade*

(USA 1925, dir. King Vidor), and in a major way only after *All Quiet on the Western Front* (USA 1930, dir. Lewis Milestone). As in *Hotel Imperial*, in Sloman's *Lea Lyon* adaptation a young woman occupies the focal point. Once again, the audience encounters romantic entanglements with allegorical significance between Jews and non-Jews as in *Light Cavalry*. Critics also pointed to the close connection between *Surrender* and *Hotel Imperial*.[44]

The story is set at the beginning of the war in a small town with a mainly Jewish population in the Austrian part of Galicia close to the Russian border.[45] Here, Rabbi Mendel Lyon (Nigel de Brulier) is the unquestioned authority in every respect, representing the justice and wisdom of the ancient laws. From the start, he is the one to reconcile disputes among members of the orthodox community, depicted first in the image of two brothers who quarrel over business—bearded men with sidelocks, caftans, dark hats, and heavily exaggerated gestures. At the river that marks the border between the two empires, Lea (Mary Philbin), the rabbi's daughter, meets a Russian named Konstantin (Ivan Mosjukin). When Lea's father finds them holding hands, he attacks Konstantin and accuses him of being an oppressor of the Jews. He demands that the Russian leave Austrian soil. Konstantin replies dismissively that he is not used to taking orders from Jews. When a delegation of Russian officers arrives on the scene, to the surprise of both Lea and her father, it is revealed that Konstantin is the commander of a Cossack regiment and a member of Russian high aristocracy.

The party splits up, but shortly afterwards, when the war breaks out, Konstantin's regiment occupies the town where Lea lives. He wants to see her again and orders all houses searched. Eventually he finds her hidden in the Torah Ark, where the rabbi has locked her away out of concern for her safety. That very moment the beginning of the Sabbath is announced, and Konstantin, the uninvited visitor, joins in the Jewish family's celebration. His violent intrusion and ignorance of Jewish ritual stand in stark contrast to the rabbi's dignity. The situation darkens when the Russian guards bring in a young man who wears the habit of an orthodox Jew. Joshua (Otto Matieson) has been engaged to Lea for many years, but it is quite obvious that no mutual bond of love exists between the two. Konstantin asks Lea whether she loves Joshua. As she hesitates to answer, her father replies that it is her duty to do so. Joshua agrees. Coldly, Konstantin puts the party to a test. He gives orders that the guards execute Joshua on the spot unless Lea was willing to ask for mercy on Joshua's behalf and give him, Konstantin, a kiss. She refuses. Konstantin, now enraged, issues an ultimatum that the town with all inhabitants will be burnt to the ground if Lea does not visit him in his hotel room that very evening. Quickly the whole community gathers in front of the rabbi's house and begs Lea to fulfill Konstantin's demand, following the example of the biblical Esther who sacrificed herself for the sake of her people. But the rabbi answers the crowd that, according to the law of Moses, one is not allowed to commit a sin, even if this were to save one from death. Thus, it becomes a question of what is more important: biblical-ethical values or life itself.

The Russian soldiers board up the houses and wait with burning torches for Konstantin's order to expire. Only then Lea walks down the street to see Konstantin who—as if he were another person—now welcomes her in a sweet and gentle way. He tries his best to make her forget the night atmosphere full of fear and threat. Finally, the two kiss, confessing their mutual affection and exchanging a ring as a token of their love. As at the beginning of the film, the couple are interrupted. This time Konstantin receives the message that the Austrians are approaching and his regiment has to retreat immediately. He remains with Lea until the town is taken by the Austrians and they are surprised by Joshua. When Joshua shoots at Konstantin, Lea takes his gun away and thus enables Konstantin to flee.

In the liberated town, the Jewish community—agitated by Joshua—gathers into a mob and accuses Lea of treachery. Even her father abandons her. He only changes his mind when people start to throw stones at her. As the rabbi tries to save his daughter, he himself is killed by a stone. Years later, after the end of the war and the revolution, Konstantin, no longer a prince and dressed in the costume of a simple peasant, returns to the small town where Lea is taking care of her father's grave. The couple meet on a bridge and are finally reunited. Compared to the 1915 theatrical version of *Lea Lyon*, the beginning and the end have been changed. Now, Lea and Konstantin have met (and, it seems, fallen in love) prior to the outbreak of war without knowing their respective nationalities and social position. Also, both lovers survive and finally offer an image of reconciliation between Jew and Russian.

Contemporary audiences in Germany would probably have been inclined to notice the similarities between *Surrender*, *Hotel Imperial*, and *Light Cavalry*. As in Stiller's film, the heroine is a young woman who arouses the desire of an enemy officer. Also, there is a stark social imbalance between the Jew and the Russian prince. From this relationship arises a conflict within the Jewish family that resembles the one in *Light Cavalry*. The rabbi's daughter is enthralled by Konstantin, to whom her father clearly objects. In *Surrender*, as in the earlier films, the young heroine is ultimately responsible for saving her community from its enemies.

Made by the Hollywood studio Universal Pictures, *Surrender* was shot under the presidency of Carl Laemmle, himself a German immigrant. Austro-Hungarian-born Paul Kohner led the production. Like Laemmle and Kohner, the director Edward Sloman, born in England, was Jewish. He cast inhabitants of the Los Angeles Jewish quarter as extras and took great care that Jewish rituals were presented accurately.[46] The main roles were given to Irish-American Mary Philbin and the newest European import, Ivan Mosjukin, in his first and only Hollywood film. Philbin's Lea Lyon, in a sense, echoed her role in the *Beauty and the Beast* scenario that made her famous in *The Phantom of the Opera* (USA 1925, dir. Rupert Julian). The Russian star Mosjukin, on the other hand, was heralded as the successor of the recently deceased sex symbol Rudolph Valentino.[47] Like Valentino, Mosjukin was able to appear brutal, passionate, and courtly in the same film. Moreover, he often displayed a certain ironic detachment and arrogance.

In German cinemas, *Surrender* started its run in January 1928. Most reviewers disliked the film and criticized the implausible narrative, weak directing, and poor casting, particularly with regard to the heroine Lea played by Mary Philbin.[48] They conceded that the film had a certain box office appeal because of the popularity of Ivan Mosjukin. They also lauded the accurate portrayal of the Jewish milieu.[49] Still, critics found the film's conflicts trivial, overly romanticized, and thereby too easily consumable (in a stab at Hollywood and Americanism in general). The review from *Film-Kurier* put it this way:

> It is an old fairy tale: the blond-haired knight falls in love with the beautiful Jewish mademoiselle. Esther saved the Jews by dispossessing Haman. Judith was an even more hysterical heroine. And Lea Lyon from Alexander Brody's play, on which this film was modeled, belongs in the same line of heroic Jewish women. However, here she acts in the film's spirit like a child of her Americanized time: She protects her Russian Holofernes instead of killing him, and she marries him after the war. Circa 1924.[50]

Prior to the release of *Surrender* in Germany, the board of censorship, the Film-Prüfstelle, decided that the original German release title *Hingabe*—one of the possible translations of the title concept of "surrender"—had to be changed, because it connoted sexual submission to which the board imputed a corrupting influence.[51] This raises a few questions. While the original title *Surrender* can be understood both as emotional release and, in a military sense, as capitulation, the new German title *Opfer* (which means both victim/s and sacrifice) leaves everything open to interpretation. Who or what is meant to be understood as a "victim" or a "sacrifice"? Is the viewer invited to regard Lea's involuntary extradition to the enemy as a "sacrifice"? Or should we see the civilians, that is, the Jews in occupied Galicia as "victims" of war and violence?[52] The question is further complicated by the fact that "victims" turn into perpetrators in the course of events. Lea sacrifices herself for her community but is eventually made a victim of this very community, when she is expelled and stoned by a fanatical crowd. Indeed, Sloman depicts the upheaval at the end like a pogrom. The erotic relationship between a Jewish woman and Russian man that is suggested from their first, accidental encounter at the river is a mortal sin to the Jewish community, a sin for which the woman has to pay with her life. By this logic, the woman can only be a savior or a sinner. And there is no mercy for the heroine who saved the community once she is declared a sinner. The film clearly criticizes this moralistic rigor by ending with an image of the new couple and the reconciliation of apparent opposites.

Neither *Hotel Imperial* nor *Light Cavalry* were so clear and unmistakable about the brutality directed against the Jews during the war, or the taking of civilian hostages and the menace the Jewish population faced. *Surrender* also shows that the regime of occupation went hand in hand with the imminent threat of rape. The actual raping of Lea does not happen, but the way Konstantin, the rabbi, and the crowd manipulate and force her to publicly act against her free will is as close to rape as it can get in a Hollywood film in 1927. One only has to observe the social pressure put on Lea, the shutting away of the people in their houses, and the burning torches ready to set the town on fire.

The Lieutenant and the Beautiful Jewess in *Two Worlds* (1930)

Violence against Jewish civilians is also of great importance in the last film set in Galicia shown in German cinemas before the National Socialist Party came to power in January 1933. The British-German coproduction *Zwei Welten* (*Two Worlds*), the only sound film in the corpus of films discussed in this chapter, was directed by E. A. Dupont and shot in three different language versions (English, German, French) with different casts at Elstree Studios in England.[53] The German version premiered on 16 September 1930 in Berlin, only two days after the Nazi Party made substantial gains in the national elections and became the second largest faction in parliament. The political earthquake that followed had its roots not least in the politicization of the war experience, in contradictory ideas about the First World War and its effects,

Figure 9.2 Russian soldiers invade the Jewish quarter in E. A. Dupont's *Zwei Welten*. Promotional still from Deutsches Filminstitut, Frankfurt. Public domain image.

and attitudes towards Jews and antisemitism, that is, issues very much present in *Two Worlds* and its contemporary reception.

In this case, too, critics pointed to the proximity between *Two Worlds* and the 1926/27 film *Hotel Imperial*.⁵⁴ The story takes place in 1917 in a Galician town occupied by the Austro-Hungarian army.⁵⁵ After the Easter service in church, a pogrom occurs in the Jewish quarter. There is shooting on the streets and offenders break into houses (the film leaves it open who the offenders really are). The Austrian commander Oberst von Kaminsky (Friedrich Kayßler) orders his son, Lieutenant Stanislaus von Kaminsky (Peter Voß) to take his soldiers and end the upheaval in the Jewish quarter. During street fights that ensue, the completely uninvolved young man Nathan is killed and the house of his father, the elderly watchmaker Simon Goldscheider (Hermann Vallentin), is attacked. When one of the attackers tries to rape Goldscheider's daughter, Esther (Helene Sieburg), the Austrian lieutenant shows up just in time to save her. Nevertheless, Goldscheider, upon learning of Nathan's death, accuses the officer of not having protected the Jews effectively, grabbing Kaminsky by the collar. For this assault against military personnel, the old man is humiliated and jailed for five days, making it impossible to say the Kaddish for his son.⁵⁶

Charmed by a Viennese soubrette who performs for the soldiers in a front theatre, Lieutenant Kaminsky leaves his post and spends the night in a hotel with the woman. He does not notice his army's retreat, waking up the next morning just as the Russians occupy the town. When he attempts to flee and collapses in front of Goldscheider's house, he is injured. Now it is Esther's turn to save him: she carries him inside and, when the Russians conduct a search of the house, makes her father lie and tell them that Kaminsky is his son. Weeks pass. Esther has nursed the lieutenant back to health and they have fallen in love, knowing that Esther's father opposes their relationship. Desperate to end this love affair, Goldscheider writes a letter to the Russian commander denouncing Kaminsky. But his letter finds the wrong addressee. As the town has been recaptured by the Austrians, Oberst von Kaminsky, once again in command, receives it. When his son confronts him with the intention to marry Esther and, if necessary, quit the army, the father gives him an impossible choice. Either the lieutenant ends his relationship with Esther or Goldscheider will be shot for denunciation. At the end, Esther suffers a breakdown as her beloved leaves Goldscheider's house without saying goodbye.

Two Worlds presents us with several confrontations and contrasts, as Siegbert Prawer has shown in his analysis of the film. There is the confrontation of Christian and Jewish religion and rites; of power and powerlessness; of the generation of the sons and daughters and their fathers who are unwilling to accept the new ways of their children.[57] Confrontations and contrasts can be found on various levels of the film: in the narrative construction, camera work and lighting, in casting, clothing, and make-up, as well as the use of parallel editing and songs.[58]

Like *Hotel Imperial*, *Two Worlds* is a film with a telling *mise-en-scène*. Again and again, the protagonist's movements and the viewer's gaze are blocked and framed through doors, window frames, and furniture, thus offering insights into the character's feeling of entrapment and their inability to move about. With its low ceilings, big staircase, narrow spaces, and meaningful shadows, the watchmaker's house that serves as the lieutenant's hide-out resembles an ancient castle and a prison at the same time. The proximity of *Hotel Imperial* and *Two Worlds* in terms of aesthetic choices is particularly apparent where events are shown in an almost identical fashion. This is especially evident in the scene where Kaminsky wakes up in an unfamiliar bed, in a room whose windows are covered with blinds, and suddenly realizes that the Russian troops are invading the town to the sound of marching music.

Some early sound films are full of experimentation with dialogue, music, ambient sound, and noise. One of the boldest films in this regard was Georg Wilhelm Pabst's *Westfront 1918* (*Westfront 1918*), the first big German First World War movie in sound, which premiered in May 1930. Together with the American production of *All Quiet on the Western Front* (1930), Pabst's film begins a completely new chapter in the cinematic depiction and analysis of war.

Compared with these modern classics, *Two Worlds* marks the end of an earlier chapter. Here the war experience is still narrated in the genre of heavy melodrama, complete with individual suffering, tragic mistakes, hide-and-seek, and elements of a spy thriller. In no way does this film engage the history of the anonymous mass killing of a whole generation as it is portrayed in *Westfront 1918*. Quite aptly, Ernst Jäger notes a "philosemitic essence of the story" in his review and mentions the great distance between the two films, "Ostfront 1917" (as he calls *Two Worlds*) and *Westfront 1918*. For him, the script of *Two Worlds* is mainly characterized by an appeal to the broad audience and its taste for novels. Thus, the viewer will detect "an air of Austro-Schnitzlerian flirtation," "Hungarian sensations," and "the strong tradition of Jewish theater." Yet the script completely ignores the present: "The curtain has fallen over these fairy tale worlds. We are standing in front of an entirely different set of still smoking ruins. Six million Hitler voters—we cannot ignore them (and with epic adventure movies this German labyrinth will not be pacified)." Finally, the weakness of *Two Worlds* according to Jäger is that it enters the battle of public opinion without a clear political stand: "Whoever fights for two worlds must step in in favor of *one* world. From the bird's-eye view of a neutral bystander it is impossible to give shape to confessions and passions in a film."[59]

The Nazis, on the other hand, attacked *Two Worlds* for its supposed partisanship as soon as the film entered cinemas. Two weeks after the premiere, the Interior Ministry in the State of Thüringen, headed by the National Socialist Wilhelm Frick, demanded that approval by the Board of Censorship should be annulled for this "incendiary film" (*Hetzfilm*), which gave the impression that, compared with the officers, the Jews were better human beings. Depicting the Austrian officers as negligent and lacking discipline might be understood "in Germany and abroad as hateful defamation of the officer corps of a former German ally, the Austrian army, and thus an affront to the German army and German reputation in general."[60] This attack was accompanied by a campaign in the Nazi press claiming that *Two Worlds* presented "the most evil hate propaganda against the old German army" created by "the Jews" to spread their "poison" in a new fashion.[61] While the Board of Censorship did not annul this film's approval, a few weeks later the Nazis succeeded elsewhere when the approval of *All Quiet on the Western Front* was withdrawn due to a massive Nazi campaign.

For the Nazis, the depiction of Jews in *Two Worlds* was too positive and the depiction of the Austrian officers too unsympathetic. Reviewers in liberal and left-wing newspapers criticized the film for different reasons. For them, the story was too convoluted and full of cheap showmanship, the direction poor, the acting weak. The *Berliner Tageblatt* lamented a "pogrom story set in an operetta world war."[62] At least the Eastern Jewish milieu found some praise, as did the actors who played the Jews in the film's "atmospheric ghetto images."[63]

What and Which Galicia?

If we want to sum up the observations in this chapter, we have to begin with a paradox. None of the films presented here could be properly described as a modern war movie. Few of the motifs, themes, and elements that characterized the genre at that time are present: the display of weapons and the machinery of war, the military hierarchies and often depicted friction between simple soldiers and the higher ranks, the miserable food supply, the sleeplessness, the lice, the mud, the noise, and, of course, the combat scenes on the battlefield, the killing and dying.

Instead, these films set in Galicia are melodramas or, to an extent, spy films located in the border region of Galicia near Russia during the First World War. However, Galicia is not depicted as a space that is recognizable because of its geographical features, its landscape, or urban topography. In fact, the Galicia presented on screen could be anywhere because it is largely studio-made (and when, in one of the few exceptions, a nature setting is used in *Surrender*, the squirrel that catches the protagonist's attention is quite clearly not of Eastern European but Californian origin). This studio-made space offers a few street scenes from a small country town that otherwise mainly consists of indoor scenes in old, dark, narrow houses, almost fortresses, stressing the difference between the inside and outside worlds.

The defining feature of Galicia—according to *Light Calvary*, *Surrender*, and *Two Worlds*—is a Jewish population divided into competing generations of old fathers and young daughters. The father—religious, bearded, strong in his beliefs and judgments, troubled and shaken by disruptions of the new era—appears as the embodiment of an orthodox lifestyle presented as exotic and archaic with a past marked by discrimination and murderous antisemitic violence as dramatized in *Surrender*. By contrast, the daughter embodies an open-minded generation that seeks to overcome the burden of trauma. Active and courageous, it is she who heroically saves the Jewish community and the non-Jewish Austro-Hungarian soldiers too. The new generation, raised in ancient beliefs, challenges prejudice as well as authoritarian and patriarchal rule. In a sense, the daughter represents the post-religious citizens of Austria-Hungary, or, in more historically embedded terminology, she seeks assimilation—a concept that was hotly debated in and outside the Jewish discourse at the time of the films' production and public exhibition. With the possible exception of *Two Worlds*, these Galicia films paint an affirmative, at times nostalgic and idealized picture of the lost Habsburg Empire.[64] In the heroine's attempt to withdraw from the old, male, religiously defined order, she plays the mythical role of the savior who makes a sacrifice and becomes a victim herself.

This scenario is riddled with stereotypes and utopian longings. *Light Cavalry*, *Surrender*, and *Two Worlds* all focus on the romance between an aristocratic Christian officer and the legendary beautiful Jewish commoner. The films suggest that there is mutual attraction and that it is not only the man who saves the woman in distress, but in fact much more the woman who saves and heals the man. In this way, the Galicia films consistently present a counter-image to other contemporary war films that focus on a male war experience, thought to be incompatible with female civilians. Here, on the contrary, instead of separating them, war unites them as a couple.

Jewish Galicia appears as a multidimensional space of erotic and religious encounters, of gender and age conflicts, contrasts and confrontations, and attempted albeit not always successful reconciliation. The films discussed in this chapter lie at the margin of Weimar cinema that touches on the First World War. They give space and voice to the perspective of a civilian population confronted with military occupation. They pay special attention to the trials of the Jewish population in the eastern Habsburg Empire, and in doing so, they tell of a chapter in history that was otherwise ignored by films of the era.

Acknowledgments

Many thanks to James Straub (University of California, Davis) for translating most of the text and commenting on it. I am extremely thankful to Mila Ganeva (Miami University), Christian Rogowski (Amherst College), Cynthia Walk (University of California, San Diego), and Joel Westerdale (Smith College) for their comments and support. I also owe many thanks to André Mieles and the Deutsches Filminstitut (Frankfurt) for kindly supplying me with film photographs and to R. Peter Stens (Conrad Veidt Society) for making available a copy of *Two Worlds*. An earlier version of this chapter was written for the Austrian Science Fund Project *Moving Images of Habsburg's Final War* directed by Hannes Leidinger (University of Vienna) and appeared in *Habsburg's Last War: The Filmic Memory (1918 to the Present)*, edited by Hannes Leidinger (University of New Orleans Press, 2018).

Philipp Stiasny teaches film history at Film University Babelsberg *Konrad Wolf* and works at the Film Museum Potsdam, Germany. He is researcher in the Franco-German ERC project "The Healthy Self as Body Capital" at Max Planck Institute for Human Development, editor of the film historical journal *Filmblatt*, an associate at the research center CineGraph Babelsberg, and a curator of film series. In spring 2016 he was Visiting Professor at the University of California at Davis. His publications include *Das Kino und der Krieg: Deutschland 1914–1929* (edition text und kritik, 2009) as well as numerous articles that have appeared in edited collections and journals.

Notes

1. For this and the following, see Alexander Watson, *Ring of Steel: Germany and Austria-Hungary in World War I* (New York, 2014), 181–88; and John R. Schindler, *Fall of the Double Eagle: The Battle for Galicia and the Demise of Austria-Hungary* (Lincoln, 2015).
2. See Frank M. Schuster, *Zwischen allen Fronten: Osteuropäische Juden während des Ersten Weltkriegs (1914–1919)* (Cologne, 2004).
3. For a review, see Elsa Stephani, "Lea Lyon," *Pester Lloyd*, 5 September 1915.
4. See Alexander Bródy, "Premiere in Budapest, 'Lea Lyon'," *Wiener Journal*, 7 September 1915. In the same year, Bródy also published an essay, "Zsidókról" [On Jews], about orthodox Galician Jews seeking refuge in Budapest during the First World War. See Ivan Sanders, "Bródy, Sándor," in *The Yivo Encyclopedia of Jews in Eastern Europe*, http://www.yivoencyclopedia.org/article.aspx/Brody_Sandor.
5. "Lyon Lea," *Kinematographische Rundschau*, no. 406, 19 December 1915. See review of the film's premiere in Budapest: "Lyon Lea," *Kinematographische Rundschau*, no. 400, 7 November 1915. Reviews from several Viennese newspapers are reprinted in *Kinematographische Rundschau*, no. 409, 9 January 1916. *Lea Lyon* was first banned in Germany but then released under the title *Kosaken* (Cossacks) in March 1917. The film featured Amália Jákó as Lea, Sándor Virányi as Konstantin, and Emil Fenyvessi as Rabbi Lyon.
6. One of Bíró's works that depict antisemitism is the historical novel *A bazinizsidók* (*The Jews of Bazin*, 1921), published in German as *Die Juden von Bazin* (Berlin, 1921). See János Kőbányai, "Bíró, Lajos," in *The Yivo Encyclopedia of Jews in Eastern Europe*, http://www.yivoencyclopedia.org/article.aspx/Biro_Lajos.
7. See Ludwig Bíró, *Hotel Stadt Lemberg*, trans. Eduard Kadossa (Berlin, 1916). The novel underwent numerous editions; by 1928, 281,000 copies were published. See also Lajos Bíró: *Hotel Imperial. Szinmü négy felvonásban* (Budapest, 1917).

8. "Hotel Stadt Lemberg," *Neue Kino-Rundschau*, no. 95, 28 December 1918. The film's antiwar message is stressed in *Neue Kino-Rundschau*, no. 92, 7 December 1918. In Austria, the film's title was *Hotel Stadt Lemberg*.
9. See Kevin Brownlow, *The Parade's Gone By...* (New York, 1968), 243.
10. On Negri, see Diane Negra, "Immigrant Stardom in Imperial America: Pola Negri and the Problem of Typology," in *Off-White Hollywood: American Culture and Ethnic Female Stardom* (London and New York, 2001), 55–83, on *Hotel Imperial*, 60–61. Contrary to Negra's remarks on Negri's decreasing popularity, Koszarski notes Negri's growing salary and the fact that *Hotel Imperial* was a "tremendous hit." See Richard Koszarski, *An Evening's Entertainment: The Age of the Silent Feature Picture 1915–1928* (History of the American Cinema 3) (Berkeley, 1990), 298. According to Rob Edelman, *Hotel Imperial* was "one of Paramount's biggest moneymakers." See "Hotel Imperial," in *Magill's Survey of Cinema: Silent Films*, vol. 2, ed. Frank N. Magill (Englewood Cliffs, NJ, 1982), 558–61, quote from 559.
11. See Roland Schacht, "Das Problem der deutschen Filmproduktion," *Kunstwart* 40, no. 6 (March 1927): 416. On Erich Pommer and the production of *Hotel Imperial*, see Wolfgang Jacobsen, *Erich Pommer: Ein Produzent macht Filmgeschichte* (Berlin, 1989), 79–82.
12. In Germany in 1929, the subject matter had enough popular appeal for Jean Gilbert and Ernst Neubach, who adapted *Hotel Stadt Lemberg* for an operetta in Berlin.
13. See *Hotel Imperial* (USA 1939, dir. Robert Florey) and *Five Graves to Cairo* (USA 1943, dir. Billy Wilder). Wilder was born in Galicia in 1906 and his family migrated to Vienna during the war. For some time, Wilder's father was the owner of a hotel.
14. Arne Lunde, "Hotel Imperial: The Border Crossings of Mauritz Stiller," in *Nordic Exposures: Scandinavian Identities in Classical Hollywood Cinema* (Seattle: University of Washington Press, 2010), 63–90, quote from 65–66.
15. Apparently, the city of Tarnów was directly mentioned in the German version as critics referred to Tarnów in their reviews. See F.D.-S. [Fränze Dyck-Schnitzer], "Hotel Stadt Lemberg," *Berliner Volks-Zeitung*, no. 9, 6 January 1927 and Willy Haas, "Hotel Stadt Lemberg," *Film-Kurier*, no. 5, 6 January 1927, reprinted in Haas, *Der Kritiker als Mitproduzent: Texte zum Film 1920–1933*, ed. Wolfgang Jacobsen et al. (Berlin, 1991), 192–95.
16. Neither the German version of *Hotel Imperial* nor the censorship card with the German intertitles have survived. Therefore, my analysis refers to the American version of which a 35 mm print (2.160 m) is held in the Library of Congress (Washington). The film has been released on DVD by Grapevine Video (length: 77 minutes), but the visual quality of this DVD is poor.
17. In the German version, the spy's name is Tabakowitsch—as in Bíró's novel.
18. For a brief overview of the politicized press reception of *Hotel Imperial*, see also Thomas J. Saunders, "Politics, the Cinema, and Early Revisitations of War in Weimar Germany," *Canadian Journal of History* 23, no. 1 (1988): 25–48.

19. See, for example, "Hotel Stadt Lemberg," *Berliner Börsen-Courier*, no. 8, 6 January 1927; and Dr Konrad Glück, "Hotel Stadt Lemberg," *Berliner Morgenpost*, no. 6, 7 January 1927.
20. Ernst Blass, "Hotel Stadt Lemberg," *Berliner Tageblatt*, no. 14, 9 January 1927.
21. "Nationalistische Filme: 'Hotel Stadt Lemberg'," *Rote Fahne*, no. 5, 7 January 1927. Or should the film be greeted as the product of a "pointed desire for reconciliation," asked e.b. [Erna Büsing], "Hotel Stadt Lemberg," *Vorwärts*, no. 14, 9 January 1927. Or was the film a "worthy and sublime" portrayal of the events of the war, as stated by r., "Hotel Stadt Lemberg," *Neue Preußische Zeitung*, no. 9, 7 January 1927.
22. Fritz Olimsky, "Hotel Stadt Lemberg," *Berliner Börsen-Zeitung*, no. 8, 6 January 1927.
23. Ernst Blass, "Hotel Stadt Lemberg," *Berliner Tageblatt*, no. 14, 9 January 1927. In the context of the larger controversy surrounding the genre of war films at that time, *Germania*, the journal of the Catholic Center Party, attacked the film because "all the work spent on peace scatters like so much chaff in the face of these splendidly staged scenes"; thus, for *Germania* the film was totally unfit to stabilize the will to "No More War!" J., "Hotel Stadt Lemberg," *Germania*, no. 9, 7 January 1927. According to the social-democratic *Vorwärts*, the film "glossily serves the commonplaces of the usual militaristic hype" and alienates those opposed to national military films: "[If] further cinematic illustrations of the reports of the OHL [Army High Command] should follow, then we had better prepare for the worst." e.b. [Erna Büsing], "Hotel Stadt Lemberg," *Vorwärts*, no. 14, 9 January 1927.
24. l.r., "Nationalistische Filme: 'Hotel Stadt Lemberg'," *Rote Fahne*, no. 5, 7 January 1927.
25. Willy Haas, "Hotel Stadt Lemberg," *Film-Kurier*, no. 5, 6 January 1927. Quoted from, Haas, *Der Kritiker als Mitproduzent*, 195.
26. Siegfried Kracauer, "Hotel Stadt Lemberg," *Frankfurter Zeitung* (Stadt-Blatt), 29 January 1927. Quoted from Kracauer, *Werke. Vol. 6: Kleine Schriften zum Film*, ed. Inka Mülder-Bach (Frankfurt am Main, 2004), vol. 6, part 1, 288.
27. Referring to the decision of Mayer and Schenck to end the Max Davidson series, Richard W. Bann notes: "It was important, they believed, to steer clear of anything that might provoke antisemitism. They reasoned that called for suppression of all Jewishness in their movies." Richard W. Bann, "Max Davidson—Blow by Blow," *Max Davidson Comedies*, DVD (Munich, 2011).
28. See Steven Alan Carr, *Hollywood and Anti-Semitism: A Cultural History up to World War II* (Cambridge, 2001), 60–93; on Ford's campaign, 82–93.
29. See, for example, the account of Jewish themes in Hollywood films from the 1920s in Patricia Erens, *The Jew in American Cinema* (Bloomington, 1984), 74–107; see Erens' remarks on Max Davidson, 92–95.
30. Bíró, *Hotel Stadt Lemberg*, 16.
31. Ibid., 52. The group of Jews is again divided into two groups, one with old Jews wearing black caftans, the others dressed in Western European clothes.

32. On Bíró, see Kőbányai, "Bíró, Lajos."
33. The title *Leichte Kavallerie* refers to an operetta of the same title by Franz von Suppé and Karl Costa written in 1866; it deals with love life in a provincial town in Austria that is affected by the arrival of Hungarian Hussars.
34. See F.D.-S. [Fränze Dyck-Schnitzer], "Leichte Kavallerie," *Berliner Volks-Zeitung*, no. 494, 19 October 1927.
35. See the photography of Arno as Wasserstrahl in *Illustrierter Film-Kurier*, no. 688, 1927 (Deutsche Kinemathek, Schriftgutsammlung).
36. Oly. [Fritz Olimsky], "Leichte Kavallerie," *Berliner Börsen-Zeitung*, no. 485, 16 October 1927. On the representation of Jewishness in *Light Cavalry* see Kerry Wallach, *Passing Illusions: Jewish Visibility in Weimar Germany* (Ann Arbor, 2017), 89–92.
37. Quoted from censorship card for "Leichte Kavallerie," B. 16777, 28 September 1927 (Bundesarchiv-Filmarchiv, Berlin), Act 6, Title 2.
38. Next to Arno, Albert Steinrück received critical praise as the rabbi. Steinrück was famous for impersonating Rabbi Loew in Paul Wegener's *Der Golem. Wie er in die Welt kam* (*The Golem. How He Came into the World*) in 1920. On the other hand, the casting of Elizza la Porta as Rahel and André Mattoni as Starhemberg was harshly criticized for the amount of cliché. See, for example, "Leichte Kavallerie," *B.Z. am Mittag*, no. 267, 14 October 1927 and G.H., "Leichte Kavallerie," *Berliner Morgenpost*, no. 248, 16 October 1927.
39. See censorship card for "Leichte Kavallerie," Act 3, Title 13, Act 5, Title 3 and 6, Act 7, Title 18.
40. See Georg Herzberg, "Leichte Kavallerie," *Film-Kurier*, no. 243, 14 October 1927. According to *Berliner Volks-Zeitung*, no. 494, 19 October 1927, the entry of the victorious army was accompanied by the "Radetzky-Marsch."
41. Censorship card for "Leichte Kavallerie," Act 7, Title 14.
42. Hans Sahl, "Leichte Kavallerie," *Berliner Börsen-Courier*, no. 485, 16 October 1927. See also lo., "Leichte Kavallerie," *Berliner Tageblatt*, no. 490, 16 October 1927.
43. Fedor Kaul, "Leichte Kavallerie," *Der Film (Kritiken der Woche)*, 15 October 1927. See also Georg Herzberg, "Leichte Kavallerie," *Film-Kurier*, no. 243, 14 October 1927.
44. See, for example, Dr F.K. [Fedor Kaul], "Opfer," *Der Film (Kritiken der Woche)*, 21 January 1928. Heinz Pol speaks of a "dull extraction" of *Hotel Imperial* in H.P. [Heinz Pol], "Opfer," *Vossische Zeitung*, no. 37, 22 January 1928.
45. Neither the German version of *Surrender*, released under the title *Opfer*, nor the German censorship card has survived. Therefore, what follows is based on an American DVD version released by Grapevine Video (length: 77 minutes). The length of the DVD differs greatly from the length of the German version from 1928 (2.400 m; 96 minutes at 22 frames/second), which again differed from the American original version (which, according to the catalogue of the American Film Institute, was 2.514 m long). The existing 77-minute DVD release is apparently made from a restored 16 mm copy from the National Center for Jewish Film (Brandeis University).

46. See Kevin Brownlow, *Behind the Mask of Innocence—Sex, Violence, Prejudice, Crime: Films of Social Conscience in the Silent Era* (Berkeley, 1990), 407–8. By 1927, Sloman had already directed several films set in Jewish milieus, among them *Vengeance of the Oppressed* (USA 1916), a drama about a Jewish student who emigrated from Russia to the United States to avenge the murder of his family in a pogrom by a Cossack regiment. On Sloman's work, see Brownlow, *Behind the Mask*, 406–17.
47. The name is also spelled Ivan Mozzhukhin, Ivan Mosjoukine, and Iwan Mosschuchin.
48. See the reviews by M.K. [Michael Kurd], "Hingabe oder Opfer," *Welt am Abend*, no. 15, 18 January 1928, and bon. [Werner Bonwitt], "Opfer," *B.Z. am Mittag*, no. 20, 20 January 1928.
49. r., "Opfer," *Vorwärts*, no. 37, 22 January 1928.
50. Ernst Jäger, "Opfer" ("Hingabe"), *Film-Kurier*, no. 16, 10 January 1928. Mordaunt Hall hints to another literary source next to the Bible with Esther and Judith, namely Guy de Maupassant's story *Boule de Suif* (1880) which is set on the backdrop of the Franco-German War of 1870. See "The Ingrates," *New York Times*, 11 October 1927.
51. See decision of Board of Censorship (Film-Prüfstelle), no. 17911, 16 January 1928 (Deutsches Filminstitut, Schriftgutarchiv), http://www.difarchiv.deutsches-filminstitut.de/zengut/df2tb503zb.pdf.
52. The couple of Lea and Konstantin could also be seen as "victims"—victims of circumstance and hatred. However, this understanding would rather apply to the play *Lea Lyon* in which the death of both lovers in the end seems to quote the death of Romeo and Juliet. For a hint to Shakespeare, see Elsa Stephani, "Lea Lyon," *Pester Lloyd*, 5 September 1915.
53. In 1923, Dupont had already directed another film, *Das alte Gesetz* (*The Ancient Law*), which set into dialogue the orthodox Jewish world of the Galician shtetl and the secular metropolis of Vienna. *Das alte Gesetz*, too, was a story of border crossing and transformation, in this case in the mid nineteenth century. In *Two Worlds*, Dupont collaborated with the same set designer with whom he had worked on *Das alte Gesetz*, Alfred Junge. For an analysis of *Two Worlds*, see Siegbert Salomon Prawer, *Between Two Worlds: The Jewish Presence in German and Austrian Film, 1910–1933* (New York, 2005), 141–49; on *Das alte Gesetz*, 21–28.
54. A "remarkable resemblance" between the story of *Two Worlds* on the one hand and *Hotel Imperial* and *Lea Lyon* on the other was mentioned, for example, by Eugen Szatmari, "Zwei Welten," *Berliner Tageblatt*, no. 439, 17 September 1930. *Two Worlds* was even regarded as a (rather bad) rip-off of the "unforgotten film by Mauritz Stiller" by Oly. [Fritz Olimsky], "Zwei Welten," *Berliner Börsen-Zeitung*, no. 434, 17 September 1930.
55. My analysis is based on a substantially cut, 73-minute version of *Two Worlds* from the Cineteca Nazionale (Rome); the German release version had a length of 119 minutes (3.260 m). The existing version is again based on the German version with German actors; that is, even when the title of the English version is cited in what follows, I am referring to the German version. However, most of the scenes with dialogue are missing (or dialogue

has been replaced by music). Instead of German dialogue, this version has Italian intertitles. Several songs sung in German are still included. Since a number of important scenes for the understanding of the film are missing, my summary also refers to the information given by Prawer, *Between Two Worlds*, 141 ff. Another German version of *Two Worlds* is held by the British Film Institute (BFI) in London (length: 1.512 m); at the BFI there also exists an English version (length: 2.459 m). Given this lamentable situation, all of my descriptions and deductions are obviously flawed as they relate to a copy that is far from complete.

56. The scene in which Goldscheider has to appear at the Austrian headquarters and is imprisoned is missing in the existing Roman copy.
57. See Prawer, *Between Two Worlds*, 140 ff.
58. For instance, the popular song "Rosa, wir fahr'n nach Lodz" (1915) by Fritz Löhner-Beda (lyrics) and Artur M. Werau (music) is juxtaposed later in the film with a Yiddish song.
59. E.J. [Ernst Jäger], "Zwei Welten," *Film-Kurier*, no. 220, 17 September 1930. Jäger also notes that the film's script follows the tracks of Lajos Bíró and Ladislaus Vajda who wrote the script for *Westfront 1918*.
60. See decision of the High Board of Censorship, no. 952, 16 October 1930, 3 (Bundesarchiv-Filmarchiv, Schriftgutarchiv), http://www.difarchiv.deutsches-filminstitut.de/zengut/df2tb702z.pdf.
61. M.W., "Zwei Welten," *Der Angriff*, no. 79, 2 October 1930.
62. Eugen Szatmari, "Zwei Welten," *Berliner Tageblatt*, no. 439, 17 September 1930. Mostly negative reviews can also be found in Kn. [Kurt Kersten], "Zwei Welten," *Welt am Abend*, no. 218, 18 September 1930; Armin Kessler, "Zwei Welten," *Berliner Börsen-Courier*, no. 459, 20 September 1930; F.S., "Zwei Welten," *Berliner Volks-Zeitung*, no. 450, 24 September 1930.
63. Kurt Mühsam, "Zwei Welten," *B.Z. am Mittag*, no. 254, 17 September 1930. See also Kn. [Kurt Kersten], "Zwei Welten," *Welt am Abend*, no. 218, 18 September 1930; Oly. [Fritz Olimsky], "Zwei Welten," *Berliner Börsen-Zeitung*, no. 434, 17 September 1930.
64. With regards to *Hotel Imperial* and *Surrender*, one might add that 1920s Hollywood saw European history (with the exception of the First World War) mainly as material for overtly melodramatic and often operetta-like productions. Also, Hollywood cultivated a fairly ambivalent position towards Russia, most often condemning brutalities under the Czar and demonizing the Bolshevist regime.

Bibliography

Bann, Richard W. "Max Davidson—Blow by Blow." *Max Davidson Comedies*. DVD. Munich: Edition Filmmuseum, 2011.

Bíró, Lajos (Ludwig). *Hotel Stadt Lemberg*. Translated from the Hungarian by Eduard Kadossa. Berlin: Ullstein, 1916.

——. *Hotel Imperial. Szinmü négy felvonásban*. Budapest: Légrády Testvérek, 1917.

———. *Die Juden von Bazin*. Berlin: Oesterheld, 1921.
Brownlow, Kevin. *Behind the Mask of Innocence—Sex, Violence, Prejudice, Crime: Films of Social Conscience in the Silent Era*. Berkeley: University of California Press, 1990.
———. *The Parade's Gone By...* New York: Alfred A. Knopf, 1968.
Carr, Steven Alan. *Hollywood and Anti-Semitism: A Cultural History up to World War II*. Cambridge: Cambridge University Press, 2001.
Edelman, Rob. "Hotel Imperial." In *Magill's Survey of Cinema: Silent Films*, vol. 2, edited by Frank N. Magill, 558–61. Englewood Cliffs, NJ: Salem Press, 1982.
Erens, Patricia. *The Jew in American Cinema*. Bloomington: Indiana University Press, 1984.
Haas, Willy. *Der Kritiker als Mitproduzent: Texte zum Film 1920–1933*. Edited by Wolfgang Jacobsen et al. Berlin: Ed. Hentrich, 1991.
Jacobsen, Wolfgang. *Erich Pommer: Ein Produzent macht Filmgeschichte*. Berlin: Argon, 1989.
Kőbányai, János. "Bíró, Lajos." In *The Yivo Encyclopedia of Jews in Eastern Europe*. http://www.yivoencyclopedia.org/article.aspx/Biro_Lajos.
Koszarski, Richard. *An Evening's Entertainment: The Age of the Silent Feature Picture 1915–1928*. History of the American Cinema 3. Berkeley: University of California Press, 1990.
Kracauer, Siegfried. *Werke. Vol. 6: Kleine Schriften zum Film*. Edited by Inka Mülder-Bach. Frankfurt am Main: Suhrkamp, 2004.
Lunde, Arne. "Hotel Imperial: The Border Crossings of Mauritz Stiller." In *Nordic Exposures: Scandinavian Identities in Classical Hollywood Cinema*, 63–90. Seattle: University of Washington Press, 2010.
Negra, Diane. "Immigrant Stardom in Imperial America: Pola Negri and the Problem of Typology." In *Off-White Hollywood: American Culture and Ethnic Female Stardom*, 55–83. London and New York: Routledge, 2001.
Prawer, Siegbert Salomon. *Between Two Worlds: The Jewish Presence in German and Austrian Film, 1910–1933*. New York: Berghahn Books, 2005.
Sanders, Ivan. "Bródy, Sándor." In *The Yivo Encyclopedia of Jews in Eastern Europe*. http://www.yivoencyclopedia.org/article.aspx/Brody_Sandor.
Saunders, Thomas J. "Politics, the Cinema, and Early Revisitations of War in Weimar Germany." *Canadian Journal of History* 23, no. 1 (1988): 25–48.
Schacht, Roland. "Das Problem der deutschen Filmproduktion." *Kunstwart* 40, no. 6 (March 1927): 416–419.
Schindler, John R. *Fall of the Double Eagle: The Battle for Galicia and the Demise of Austria-Hungary*. Lincoln: Potomac Books, 2015.
Schuster, Frank M. *Zwischen allen Fronten: Osteuropäische Juden während des Ersten Weltkriegs (1914–1919)*. Cologne: Böhlau, 2004.
Wallach, Kerry. *Passing Illusions: Jewish Visibility in Weimar Germany*. Ann Arbor: University of Michigan Press, 2017.
Watson, Alexander. *Ring of Steel: Germany and Austria-Hungary in World War I*. New York: Basic Books, 2014.

10

AGNON ON THE GERMAN HOME FRONT IN *IN MR LUBLIN'S STORE*
Hebrew Fiction of the First World War
Glenda Abramson

The literature of the First World War, written by soldier-authors and civilians on the home front during the war and for some years after it, often stands midway between a historical document and a subjective rendering of an ordeal that seems to have been, for the most part, unbearable. While there are hundreds of such works in various languages, very little has been written in any form about the experience of Jewish combatants and civilians in the First World War. Fiction and poetry in Hebrew on the topic is even rarer, too sparse to constitute a sub-genre. Nonetheless, there exists a modest body of such work about which little is known to this day. Many of these responses to the war experience were written some time after the events, or by Hebrew writers such as Yosef Hayim Brenner (1881–1921), Aharon Reuveni (1886–1971), Shmuel Yosef Agnon (1888–1970), and Devora Baron (1887–1956), who were not combatants but endured considerable hardship on the home fronts or in exile.

As with much war fiction in general, Hebrew war fiction was largely autobiographical. Authors wove fictional characters together with historical personalities, into real historical contexts, blurring the boundaries between history and fiction. A good example of this occurs in Agnon's "novel" *In Mr Lublin's Store*, in which the narrator offers a friend a ticket to a symphony concert given by the Leipzig Gewandhaus Orchestra conducted by Arthur Nikisch. Nikisch became the orchestra's resident conductor in 1895 and was living in Leipzig at the time of Agnon's arrival there in 1917. Much of the Hebrew war writing is neither entirely history nor entirely fiction—in the sense of untruth—but a form of fictionalized autobiography, that is, stories closely based on the author's lived experience, which involve real people, events and places, and sometimes, in Agnon's case, his own name.

The contemporary re-evaluation of the opposition of fiction and history, the challenge to our preconceptions about what is meant by fiction and non-fiction, the generic blurring, all these are significant in terms of truth. After suggesting that the distinction between history and fiction is no longer tenable, Beverley Southgate asks whether this lack of distinction matters.[1] His conclusion, with which I agree, is that it does matter. If one is considering the fictional texts as providing elements of historiography, the question of "truth" is always a concern. How is the close relationship between the historical narrative and the fictional one disentangled? If we are left only with the perceived truth of the author of the fiction as opposed to the "facts" of a war, for example, does this provide us with a reliable picture of the war? Postmodernist historians may be right in identifying the limits of historical truth, giving some leave for the claim of fiction to serve historiography, and the representation of subjective experience, while not scientifically verified, may give us at least a sense of place and atmosphere.[2] The novelist who interprets historical material "with imagination" can provide such a sense.[3]

The role of fiction in the mediating of history is particularly evident in the recounting of "horrible events,"[4] the Holocaust being the obvious one. The victims of these events, even in fiction, are our messengers, serving both memory and history, the overarching topic transcending the smallness of the story. Fiction has the power to convey the unique, human quality of these events, despite the awfulness of the memories. As Jorge Semprun writes, in a widely quoted passage relating to Holocaust fiction, "Only the artifice of masterly narrative will prove capable of conveying some of the truth of such testimony."[5] This applies as well to war literature and certainly to Agnon's writing about the First World War as a commemoration of the destruction of Galician Jewry, in successive works of fiction.

Agnon was born in Buczacz, Galicia, in 1888 to a middle-class family in which Orthodox Judaism and modern European culture coexisted. He left Buczacz in 1908, partly through fear of recruitment into the Austro-Hungarian army, and settled in Palestine. On 28 October 1912, he departed from his home in Jaffa for Berlin together with Arthur Ruppin, the director of the Zionist office in Palestine. Berlin seemed to Agnon to be the ideal environment in which to develop as a writer. During the first decade of the twentieth century, Berlin was a center of a lively Jewish émigré culture that included Hebrew and Yiddish writers, a center that was greatly extended and enriched during the Weimar Republic.

Agnon remained in Berlin for about two years before moving between Berlin, Leipzig, Bad Brückenau, and Bad Homburg. He lived in wartime Leipzig at different periods, first in February 1917, having to depart after three months, unable to extend his residency permit in the city. He returned for a short time in June of that year, again from the end of November through mid May 1918, and again from October 1918 through March 1919.

Sponsored and supported by the wealthy entrepreneur and publisher Zalman Schocken, Agnon was able to concentrate on his work, having avoided military service in the Austro-Hungarian army through ill health and never in any danger as a civilian.[6] Despite the difficulties he had endured in attempting to find lodgings, work, and sources of sustenance immediately after his arrival in Berlin in 1912, he spent the time establishing his career as a writer, editing and publishing his work and achieving a reputation among the Jewish reading public. However, none of the works written between 1914 and 1918 dealt either with the war or with his life in Germany, or his attitude to German Jewry and Germans in general. His concern during the war years was the life and culture of East European Jewry, stories that reflected Jewish life in Galicia and his home town in particular.[7] Although the Great War had provided the historical context for *Oreaḥ nata lalun* (1939; *A Guest for the Night*, 1968), he directly confronted it only several decades later in *To This Day*,[8] *In Mr Lublin's Store*,[9] and a handful of short stories, only two of which were published.

When Agnon finally turned to the war later in his life, he portrayed it as a cataclysm that brought to an end one of the most constructive periods in Jewish history. The war is foregrounded in the two novels in all its horror and chaos, a literally inescapable part of the narrator's life, overwhelming every episode and character in the novel, manipulating their lives, their livelihood, their families, even their religious observance. In *In Mr Lublin's Store*, the war appears both as a historical phenomenon and an unavoidable element of human existence: "The world is never free of war. Every nation prepares itself for war. They make war constantly. If you know of a generation that has not experienced war, you can be sure that it is preparing itself for war."[10] Entire communities in the East, predominantly the Jewish communities, are being destroyed. The war distorts the novel's society, filling it with bereaved and fragmented families. On a more specific narrative plane, the war prevents the narrator from studying the Talmud, it interferes with his study of Judaism, and it is therefore a negative force in his quest for spiritual self-realization. He sees newspapers replacing the Torah, the quotidian replacing the eternal. The war therefore undermines the foundations of faith and God's law.

One of Agnon's central preoccupations, which will be explored in greater detail below, derives from the contradictory attitudes to the war by members of the German Jewish community, attitudes he depicts in both his war novels. Through his eponymous narrator, Agnon criticizes what he considers to be their self-deluded expectations of the war. Agnon did not count himself among those German Jews who believed that "only blood spilled in the struggle for fatherland and liberty would lead to emancipation."[11] In *Mr Lublin*, his narrator supports an elderly Christian artisan who questions what came to be known as "the spirit of 1914," and who unequivocally condemns the war. Agnon also represented the views of the Jews who had enthusiastically embraced the war in 1914 but whose faith in it diminished as the conflict wore on. He was, of course, writing in hindsight. The point he was making, the fruitlessness of faith in external salvation despite Jewish sacrifice, is, in hindsight, a profoundly Zionist conclusion.

Of course, we do not know the *exact* nature of Agnon's experience in Leipzig and moreover he is representing it in a work that has been designated as fiction. His imaginative excursions, mainly created out of the personifications of circumstances or ideas, are not in the purview of strictly factual forms of writing.[12] Still, in this chapter I intend to show that in *Mr Lublin*, Agnon provides us with accurate information about the locations in which he lived during the war and some of the situations he endured. Biographical evidence bears this out.[13] His fiction serves as his personal response to a time of crisis and fills out the subjective gaps missing from the historiographical narrative. I suggest, throughout this chapter, that we have the supporting evidence of historiography to allow us to presume that Agnon is not only fabricating, but also reproducing, elements of the time and place.

In Mr Lublin's Store

The story of *Mr Lublin* is simple: the narrator, who has moved from Jerusalem to Berlin and from there to Leipzig, is caught, in a sense imprisoned, in Germany because of the war that bars him from leaving: "I can't return to the Land of Israel because all the routes are blocked by the army, I can't return to my birthplace because the Russians have destroyed it" (36). On his way one Sabbath eve to buy what he requires for his Sabbath meals, he runs into his friend Mr Lublin, wealthy entrepreneur and philanthropist, who is the proprietor of a mail order company.[14] Mr Lublin has an urgent appointment and has no-one to mind his office. Through his contacts with city officialdom he has made it possible for the narrator to remain in Leipzig, despite rights of residence being severely restricted during wartime.[15] The author himself never obtained this right.

In gratitude, the narrator agrees to mind Mr Lublin's store. There are no books or any reading material in the single room that constitutes the company's main office, the telephone has been disconnected, and in any case, it is already the Sabbath. Mr Lublin has taken the newspapers with him, leaving the narrator with nothing to do other than reflect on his life, on German Jewry, Galicia, his birthplace, and on Germany and the war.

The novel is a study in memory and reflection. Its framing story draws on Agnon's memories of his sojourns in Leipzig. His narrator defines himself as a researcher, writing a book on clothing through the ages, an enigmatic symbolic choice. Only once he modestly admits that he is "something of a writer." In fact, the narrator is as insulated from the war as Agnon was, basking in Schocken's patronage, and whose most serious problem was the fear of conscription.[16] Confined to sitting within four walls, all the narrator can do is allow his imagination to range far beyond them, without boundaries of time and space. His is, in a sense, a double confinement: first in Germany, being unable to leave, and then in Mr Lublin's store. The absence of newspapers ensures that the news of the day is not a distraction from the narrator's own chronicle of memory. Peace reigns inside Mr Lublin's store. In fact, if we are to make a temporal demarcation in the novel, the present is fictional while everything outside Mr Lublin's store is a more direct representation of history interwoven with memory and autobiography. War as a historical reality and the social responses to it are the reference points for the documentary aspects of the novel.

Many years interceded between the events and Agnon's recalling of them in fiction. We are entitled to ask whether his memory of the time is reliable enough to offer an insight into the history of the period. An example of the fallibility of historical memory is demonstrated by W. G. Sebald in *Austerlitz*, which, by the judicious use of real photographs in a fictional text, blurs the boundaries between memory and imagination. Like Sebald, Agnon mixes past and present, fact and fiction, autobiography and intertextuality, "to create a space that destabilizes the reliability of memory."[17]

We do not know whether Agnon kept notes at the time of his sojourn in Germany and the only form of non-fiction autobiography he left is *From Myself to Myself*. Yet we may assume that the detail in his description of life in Germany in *Mr Lublin*, while being largely a construction of memory, has a basis in the real, a "corrective" to memory alone.[18] Agnon himself enters the debate in *From Myself to Myself*: "During the Great War I was living in Leipzig. I wrote down in *To This Day* some of the things that happened to me."[19] He continues in the same chapter to describe events he subsequently incorporated into *Mr Lublin*. His literary representation and his autobiography are therefore often indivisible.[20]

In *Mr Lublin* the narrator remembers wartime Leipzig, a city Agnon liked and recalled with obvious affection, for at least one reason: the city's Jewish population was composed overwhelmingly of recent immigrants from Galicia and Russia. Towards the end of the nineteenth century, municipal officials introduced measures to encourage some Jewish traders to settle permanently in Leipzig. In contrast to German administrations elsewhere, the Leipzig municipality even relaxed its naturalization process so that dealers could acquire Saxonian citizenship. Those Galician Jews who had established themselves in Leipzig continued to play an active role in trade.[21] The percentage of foreigners among the Jews of Leipzig rose to about 67 percent just before the war.[22] The ratio of foreign-born to German-born Jews made Leipzig unique among medium-sized German Jewish communities.[23]

According to Robert Willingham, the essential division within the community was between "Germans," those whose families had been resident in Leipzig for generations, and "foreigners," those who had come from abroad, mainly Eastern Europe, and whose numbers were greatly increased by the wave of *Ostjuden* (Eastern European Jews).[24] In *Mr Lublin*, Mr Lublin crosses these boundaries from being a "foreigner" to becoming a "German," not only through residence, but also through new citizenship, wealth, and social acceptance.

Agnon (with some hindsight) illustrates the differences between Leipzig's Jewish community and that of Berlin:

> Berlin is also not entirely void of Jews. You'll find Jews from Galicia and from my town there, but a few of the Berlin Jews are worthless and if you were to encounter one of them his appearance might give you the wrong impression. The echo of his ancestors who deserted the people of Israel taunts you. You'll see a Galician Jew with his sidecurls tucked behind his ears, a styled beard and a short coat folded into itself so that it doesn't seem to be long, and when he speaks he shifts into "German," which is neither proper German nor Yiddish. (41)

Agnon's narrator is researching a book on clothing and he therefore identifies the Galician Jews primarily by their distinctive dress: their long coats, the hats made of black silk or velvet, the high boots with colorful flaps. The Jews who arrived in Leipzig during and after the war

> did not change their style, their clothes or their language. Even those whose ancestors had already lived here for a few generations were identifiable as being of Galician origin. Even if they exactly observe the Leipzig customs, more even than the non-Jews in Leipzig, and speak perfect Leipzigese, a hint of Galicia announces that they are Galicia's children. (42)

Yet the narrator expresses his fondness for Mr Lublin who has cast off his Galician birthplace and succeeded in making the transition to complete Germanness. In addition, throughout the novel, through characters like Mr Lublin, his father-in-law, and countless others who are businessmen, dealers, entrepreneurs, and peddlers, Agnon emphasizes the Leipzig Jewish community's devotion to trade and dealing.

The Home Front in *Mr Lublin*

The War

Agnon reports the experience of an urban civilian in Germany during wartime, with the home front as his locus and the impetus for the structure of his two novels. The war was at its height and encroached on the civilian population by daily deprivation, in addition to the mounting grief of loss. It was in Leipzig in 1918 that Agnon heard that the war had come to an end. Life in wartime Germany seems to have left so deep an impression on him that he devoted two novels to his memory of it almost half a century later. He follows the linearity of the war experience: from the early excitement at its outbreak, when the young men "rushed" into it (his judgment in the novel), to the well-documented disillusionment, and then, as the years wore on, the grief and suffering and, finally, resignation. His grasp of social involvement in the novel is impressive, drawing on his daily life and his contacts among the Jewish intelligentsia of Berlin and Leipzig. He was never a conscript. He did not experience personal loss or all the privations that afflicted the entire German home front. His biographer Dan Laor reports that while on the front the cannons roared and the civilian population was feeling the effects of the war, Agnon was in the heart of Berlin, protected on all sides from any harm, free to devote his time to meeting the great writers of the period when "at that fateful time in the world's history, they and they alone were the only things that really interested him."[25]

In one respect, Agnon suffered certain hardships, being classified as a foreigner and obliged to register with the police despite being a national of an allied country. Generally, imperial Germany made it difficult for foreigners to settle within its borders. Few of them could evade its tight residency permit system. All those, including German citizens who moved between cities, had to register. In fact, most countries kept foreigners under strict surveillance during wartime.[26] During his first visit, Agnon had been granted permission to remain in the city for eight days, after which he had to appear at the local police station, as did his narrator, in order to extend his license. Once military rule had been established in German cities, including Leipzig, the restrictions for foreigners increased and he was eventually required to leave Leipzig permanently without having been able to obtain a residence permit. It was easier, reports the exasperated narrator, to settle in Berlin.

In *Mr Lublin*, Agnon confirms the distrust with which foreigners were treated: when the narrator, himself a foreigner, welcomes Jewish guests from Russia, his distrustful neighbors regard him as a spy. This anecdote is based on fact. All Russian Jewish civilians in Germany lost their rights once the war began. As enemy aliens they were in limbo, watched by the police and since they were objects of general suspicion they tended to keep to themselves. Russian Jewish students in particular suffered from police surveillance and were forbidden from participating in local politics.[27] Agnon's narrator in *To This Day* reports sardonically that due to their unhappy situation, the Russian Jews trapped in Germany were obliged to pray for the pogrom-loving tsar's victory so that they could go home. "Their longing made Russia seem like a utopia inhabited by the world's most virtuous people."[28]

Agnon's views on the German Jews' response to the war are quite clear. The perception that German society entered the war with unqualified enthusiasm, with even the political parties united in the spirit of the *Burgfrieden* (the so-called "fortress" truce), should be modified, even though Thomas Mann, for example, confessed that he was "tired, sick and tired" of peace and saw the war as "a purification, a liberation, an enormous hope."[29] Others followed with equally hyperbolic statements. Yet in less intellectual and middle-class communities in Germany, anxiety and fear were as widespread as jubilation,[30] and the well-documented euphoria was rather more tempered. Germans experienced the outbreak of the war differently according to class, gender, and location.[31] Rather than enthusiasm, the crowds greeted news of the war with excitement, a response that led to the myth of the "spirit of

1914."[32] Propaganda and persuasion were used in the early years of the war to mobilize the population and to encourage a belief in Germany's desire for victory, although initially there was little collective opposition to the war.[33]

The collective *Jewish* response was driven in many instances by the hope that the Jewish community had more than their Christian German compatriots to gain from the war. Many Jewish individuals and communities believed that their participation would lead to an enhancement of their civil rights. Not only that, but some saw the fight against the tsarist regime as comparable to Moses' fight for liberation from the Pharaoh.[34] About 100,000 German Jewish soldiers of all denominations took up arms,[35] among them those who not only saw their participation as a mark of their patriotism and loyalty to their German homeland, but also anticipated civic improvement for the Jewish community. Echoing the Kaiser's speech,[36] a rabbi wrote with hopeful ecumenism on 12 August 1914: "In the German Fatherland there are no longer any Christians and Jews, any believers and disbelievers, there are only Germans. May God allow these great times to become a part of the consciousness of our people, and to make us a truly united people."[37]

Two days after the outbreak of the war, the Centralverein deutscher Staatsbürger jüdischen Glaubens (Central Association of German Citizens of the Jewish Faith, CV) published a declaration of support for the war, saying, "Every German Jew is ready to sacrifice property and blood as duty demands." There were other equally patriotic calls from Jewish and Zionist organizations.[38] A number of Jewish intellectuals and artists added their names to an open letter written in support of the conflict. For example, Max Reinhardt announced that the war was necessary in defense of German culture, and Ludwig Frank, who was killed in the early days of the war, marched away "joyful and sure of our victory."[39] In Agnon's *To This Day*, the narrator describes his visit to a proud Jewish couple in Leipzig the day their son volunteered for the German army: "I remember the mother scrutinizing every item that [the son] packed into his kitbag, her eyes bright with joy at the sight of her boy going off to defend the Fatherland."[40] Agnon's Mr Lublin echoes the CV's sentiment, "... There must be some change for the better because Germany sees all of us, the German Jewish citizens, sacrifice our children and our wealth for the war against the enemy. Is it possible that after this they will still deprive us of our rights?" (189). In the spirit of the *Burgfrieden*, acculturated German Jews, like Mr Lublin, as well as Zionists,[41] demonstrated both the "authenticity of their patriotism"[42] and their hope for civil and political acceptance.

Agnon was not one of them. He was not a German and he had worked hard to avoid conscription, making himself ill in the process. His narrator is a religiously observant *Ostjude*, as different from the assimilated German Jews as he is from blond, blue-eyed Mr Arno (né Aaron) Lublin, father of Heinz, Thomas, and Gerda, who could not wait to shake the dust of his East European town off his feet.

Like the mother in *To This Day*, many Jewish characters in *Mr Lublin* embrace the war in their self-deluded hope for its social benefit. The narrator in *Mr Lublin* reflects Agnon's own attitude to war as physically, socially, and morally destructive. He demonstrates, sometimes satirically, his scorn for any patriotic utterances by Jews. For example, the narrator and Mr Lublin's wife visit a Jewish merchant whose son is a soldier:

> When he saw her he rubbed his hands together with satisfaction and began to speak about the war and the obligation of every person to his fatherland, the Jews in particular. He was not from Germany but from Austria and not even from Austria but from Galicia, but after Germany had taken him in and made him a German citizen he saw himself as an absolute German in every respect. Particularly as a Jew faithful to God and His Torah he felt a double obligation to do as much as was possible for Germany. He sent his son to war and even before they demanded it from him he donated generously to the war effort. (161)

It is as if the narrator deliberately subverts the CV's statement by sneering: "They all utter a single phrase and one word, to volunteer for the war in body and pocket for the sake of truth and justice" (132). Agnon's bitterest statement is given to one of his non-Jewish characters, an old knife-sharpener:

> The sharpener held out the knife and Rabbi Jonathan examined it. He paid him and said, "It is sharp and smooth." The sharpener replied, "The war's teeth are sharper. I would be surprised if its teeth didn't grow larger through overeating." (57)

A gentile expresses these moral sentiments while the Jews throw themselves wholeheartedly into the war, according to the narrator's caustic judgment. Being a Galician and mourning the tragedy of East European Jewry, the destruction of towns like his own, the murder of entire Jewish communities, Jewish displacement and exile, the narrator abhors Jews' willingness to sacrifice themselves for their inevitably (according to the narrator) hostile host country. In his focus in the novel on the dislocated millions of Eastern European Jews, Agnon might have welcomed Germany's battle with their oppressors, but he proclaimed his antiwar sentiments throughout his life, including later, in Israel.[43]

In *Mr Lublin*, the narrator accentuates what he considered to be the misguided fervor of the young Jews going to battle for their fatherland (for which, in *To This Day*, Agnon ironically uses the ideologically loaded term *moledet*)[44] and he has a few acerbic things to say about the women who encourage the young soldiers on their way, the men "intoxicated with joy" in national service.[45] "They immediately rushed into battle as soon as war was declared. The older son was taken prisoner by the French and the young one who hadn't yet reached the age of service but volunteered as a conscript was on the Russian front or somewhere on a different front," writes Agnon in *Mr Lublin* (12). He reiterates many times throughout the novel, "This boy rushed into the war, he rushed into the war and was killed. The war stretched out its arms and grabbed him …" (31). "Through love of his fatherland he rushed into the war before his time had come to join up …" (58).

> Because he rushed into the war before his time the war rushed onto him before his time and he died without coming back. Still a fledgling he died in the war and we don't know where he died and where he is buried, and perhaps he doesn't even have a small piece of land to lie in and he has become fodder for the beasts of the field and the birds of the sky. (109)

The narrator even derides his friend and admirer, the composer Grete Hinnings, for her uplifting war songs. He deplores not only the young German women's encouragement of men in uniform, but particularly those who see their men off to the war and then take their jobs.

Mr Lublin is a monument to the young men who died. The story of Mrs Salzmann, the proprietor of the café favored by Mr Lublin, is the paradigmatic testament of parents' grief. The narrator tells at length the terrible, heartbreaking story of the Salzmanns' dead son. Mrs Salzmann represents all the parents whose sons have been killed on the battlefield and her dignified agony is among the most moving parts of the book. A beloved only son, the boy volunteered for service and became the fictional representative of the thousands of anonymous casualties of the conflict. Moreover, as Mrs Salzmann laments, she has no idea where he is buried or whether he has a grave at all. Agnon has gleaned this, too, from the real tragedies of German families. For example, after a Jewish soldier from Hamburg was killed, his grave could not be located despite his wife's and rabbi's numerous appeals to the War Ministry.[46]

In *Mr Lublin*, the soldiers are always victims. In Agnon's story "Fernheim," the ex-prisoner of war, now free, remains a victim after his family's rejection of him. In "Between Two Towns," the returned soldier is so severely disabled that he disables his family as well. In *To This Day*, the central character, an infantryman, is mentally impaired as a result of a head wound. The only heroic Jewish serviceman in *Mr Lublin* returns home to be outdone by a religious restriction.

The narrator observes bitterly that the medals on the soldiers' chests are placed there as substitutes for the limbs and the faculties the men have lost. One of the anecdotes in *Mr Lublin* concerns a slaughtered pet goose, killed with casual cruelty as a boast. It is reminiscent of a scene in *To This Day* of dead animals in a butcher's window, signifying the dead on the battlefield. There is no hint of any glory in the returning soldier.

Even Mr Lublin does not escape the effects of the war: his eldest son is a prisoner of the French, and the parents have no idea of his whereabouts or indeed whether he is alive. The other son is somewhere in the field. The Red Cross then delivers a letter.[47] Mrs Lublin is distraught while her husband is overcome almost to the point of incoherence. Agnon implies the confusion of the normally composed Mr Lublin by his repetition of phrases, which in themselves are trivial, and his breathless sentences:

> The Red Cross advised us that a letter had arrived from our son from his place of internment. They brought us the letter and we read it standing up and again while sitting down and we recognized his handwriting, his handwriting hadn't changed and there was no difference between this letter and the earlier letters he had written to us before the war when he was touring the cities of Germany with his friends. The letters and the words were the same. There was no difference between the shape of the letters or even between the words "I am well" that he wrote during peacetime and the shape of the letters of "well" written from the enemy country. (177)

Even his strong emotion does not deter Mr Lublin from somber reflection about the nature of warfare:

> It is somewhat incomprehensible that he doesn't say that his captors forced him to write this way because we read in our papers about the brutality of our enemies who are worse than wild beasts. Even if I imagine that the newspapers exaggerate they don't exaggerate to this extent. Or perhaps there is no exaggeration, for even we can't say that we treat our prisoners mercifully. (177)[48]

Among the German support organizations were churches, synagogues, and individual clergy, which provided frameworks for comfort and assistance. Yet in his novel, Agnon mocks the vainglorious attempt of one Hasidic rabbi to console a bereaved father by boasting about the value to God of his, the rabbi's, prayer. The rabbi falls asleep while comforting the father, and moreover fails to remember the correct name of the dead son. For Agnon in *Mr Lublin* there is no consolation for the loss of a child, including one who has been so infected by the idea of national glory and heroic sacrifice that he embraces death. The narrator includes everyone in his implicit condemnation—the rabbis, the parents, and Jewish society as a whole. While he has little compassion for any civilians, except perhaps the bereaved Salzmanns, his compassion for the dead and wounded soldiers is unmistakable. He mocks the award of medals in accordance with the soldier's injury as payment by the war with useless symbols. His narrator comments on the sudden appearance of men with the terrible injuries of battle, missing limbs, maimed in body and spirit. He says, "... my heart aches when I see men without an arm, without legs, blind and lame because of the war" (85).

> [The war] has already taken its share of them, whether an arm or a leg or an internal organ that we do not see, which has marked him as released from war work. He has fulfilled his obligation to the war which pays him off with symbols of bravery. The calculation is made, this one with a crutch, that one with a rubber leg, this one without an arm and that one with other infirmities—and the medals on their chests are calculated accordingly. (154)[49]

Lack of Food and Rationing

In the novel, the German civilians are affected by lack of food, by fear, by the constant anxiety about sons and husbands in battle, rather than by suffering a military onslaught, bombing, or invasion. Their greatest enemy on the home front is hunger. Mr Lublin observes, "Now that the war is at its height I doubt you'll find anything to eat here" (34). The Great War affected Leipzig's economy, leading to a catastrophic drop in the production of consumer goods. Leipzig faced a serious shortage of grains, meat, dairy products, and vegetables. In *From Myself to Myself*, Agnon explains that an acquaintance was refused the right of residence in Leipzig not because of antisemitism but due to the food shortages. "Leipzig barely manages to feed its citizens," he writes. "It wouldn't be right to take food out of their mouths to give to strangers."[50] The quality of bread deteriorated after the authorities decided to save on grain by mixing increasing amounts of filler into the dough.[51] "This bread we eat is unsatisfying, it only irritates and plagues us like a stuffed belly and the bread and all the food make us ill" (*Mr Lublin*, 155). By early summer 1916, stores had run out of sugar and clothing; shoes and all foodstuffs were rationed.[52] Only the war satisfies its greed:

> Adam Isba pours himself a cup of coffee and cuts a slice of bread, which he contemplates because during wartime one must estimate whether this piece of bread we are holding in our hands to put into our mouths

is the last of all our food because the war swallows everything: first the slice in the hand, afterwards the hand itself, afterwards the soul, afterwards it demolishes the earth beneath the body wallowing in its own blood. (99)

Agnon refers to rationing more than once. The war "allocates food coupons to everyone and inspects everyone's name" (51). Mr Lublin admonishes his assistant: "Your wife and children are hungry and waiting for you for dinner. Go, so that the potatoes and cabbage don't get cold, because they handed out cabbage and potatoes as our food rations today" (176). In *To This Day*, the narrator describes the hunger he suffered, having forgotten to bring his ration book.[53] Rationing affected people's livelihoods. A character in *Mr Lublin* sells her possessions to open a grocery store, but the narrator asks, "When food is rationed, what income can a shopkeeper expect from his shop?" (59). Vast quantities of eggs had been imported before the war, becoming scarce as communities rationed them in wartime. Between October 1916 and April 1917, Berlin citizens received a total of eleven eggs per person.[54] In *Mr Lublin*, Agnon tells the story of Mr Lublin's solution to the dearth of eggs:

> According to the city statutes, the administrators of the city's food supply confiscated the eggs from grocers and took cellars away from their owners to store eggs, and sought, but didn't find, willing hands to prevent them from going bad because most of the specialists had been conscripted and the few who remained in the city were happy to look the other way because the mice had already begun gnawing the eggs. Thousands of eggs had already been thrown into the Alster, the Pleisse and the Parthe rivers. Mr. Lublin told the City Councillors to take out the eggs and give them to the populace to eat. His advice was accepted and they distributed three eggs to each person. The councillors were satisfied with having found a solution that diverted the people's anger away from them and the people were satisfied because while Berlin sees an egg only once in three weeks, in Leipzig every person eats three eggs a week. (150–51)

The narrator describes Leipzig's workers encountering each other "with their tired legs, their exhausted limbs, their threadbare clothes, their patched shoes, their pain" (155). His comment about "the people's anger" is more than an aside. Deteriorating home front conditions began to ignite frustration and anger, which occasionally turned violent.[55] Street protests took place not only against the lack of food, but against black marketers' hoarding of it. The food riots of 1916 represented the most serious public disorder in Leipzig. Almost invariably they would break out after women in a queue complained that the shop owner was holding back goods for sale to put them on the black market.[56] The narrator observes: "Because of the war all the good merchandise has disappeared. The war has swallowed up all of it. Black marketers have hidden what was left of it…" (157). He asks, "Where does she [a greengrocer] obtain her excellent products when hoarders and black marketers proliferate…?" (117).

The unfair trading, rather than the shortages themselves, sparked the disturbances.[57] The government announced a cut in the bread ration in April 1917. Major strikes erupted in several cities, most notably Berlin and Leipzig.[58] *Mr Lublin* is peopled with petty food vendors, black marketers, housewives who return from the market and stores empty-handed, peddlers who eke out a living selling vegetables, and cooking pots that are so empty they do not require cleaning.

In the absence of food and everyday necessities, substitutes began to flood the market. Agnon's narrator informs us that the visitors to the Leipzig fair sit in the café at the main train station and in other restaurants and cafés, drinking coffee that is not coffee, eating food that is food in name only. According to Laurence Moyer, "Every facet of life, large and small, became one gigantic ersatz experience."[59] The narrator in *Mr Lublin* describes shop windows filled with *Ersatzprodukten* (substitute products), merely images of the real thing, "not even imitations of the counterfeits" (229). Ersatz products "were not infrequently substitutes for substitutes."[60]

While the narrator generally dines well and avoids the severe hunger that afflicted Leipzig's citizens, the surrounding shortages affected him to the extent that one of the main focuses of the novel is food. Almost every character, including the conductor Nikisch, is associated somehow with food. From the wealthy Lublins and their elegant table to poorer characters who earn their living by purveying food, and those who suffer near-starvation, food and eating are central themes in the novel, to the extent of debating the correct fodder to offer an elephant. The reader may assume that food was uppermost in the narrator's mind even though he himself did not go hungry. On the contrary, he remembers eating pastries, drinking good wine, and dining in a fine restaurant (179–80). Yet the novel begins with the narrator's statement, which he repeats throughout the text, that he was on his way to the market to buy food for the Sabbath. He does not reach the market or buy the food. Sitting in Mr Lublin's store in the present moment, he repeatedly reiterates that he has failed to buy his supplies for the Sabbath meals, he has no food or drink. He is as hungry as the rest of the wartime populace.

The War at Sea

The mechanics of the war were not lost on Agnon. The narrator refers in general terms to weapons of war, "all kinds of weapons able to kill from near and far, destroying many men at once" (54), but mentions only one explicitly: the German U-Boat.

> Outside rages the most vicious war of all previous wars because earlier wars stopped at nightfall but this one does not stop day or night, it kills both on and off the battlefield, in the skies above and the seas below. All the instruments of war can be found in the Bible, apart from the submarine that makes its war under the sea ... But in our time these submarines that make war under the seas are unimaginable and therefore the end of the world has come and with it the End of Days. (75)

Despite ongoing controversy, the German military command, believing that a victory against Britain would force it out of the war, decided to use submarines for an all-out offensive against the British Empire. Because the British blockade had been the source of so much suffering and deprivation on the German home front, the idea of submarine warfare became popular with the public.[61] Discussion was so widespread—leading to rallies and school projects, posters, brochures, and popular literature—that Agnon could scarcely have avoided it. The U-boat campaign destroyed not only passenger ships, the most tragic being the *Lusitania* as early as 1915, but also tons of merchant shipping, and eventually brought the USA into the war.[62] In due course, the Germans apologized for the sinking of the *Lusitania* but not before one of the newspapers, the *Kölnische Volkszeitung*, hailed it a "success of moral significance."[63]

Women

In *Mr Lublin*, women are not spared. The narrator, who tells us that he is twenty-seven years old, mentions more than once, with a certain disapproval, that women have taken over the essential work during wartime while their men are serving, and "when they take up the men's work they assume an angry expression, a mistake they make because they think that an angry face is a sign of manliness" (135). According to the narrator, "We ride a trolley car—a woman is driving it. We travel in a train driven by a woman. If the war does not end soon there will not be a man left in the country" (151). After the outbreak of the war in Germany, women who had not previously gone out to work were obliged to join the workforce once their breadwinners were on the battlefield. At the start, the women's role was supportive, keeping the home fires burning, taking care of their children. Maintaining the home front was still conceived as a woman's task.[64] Before the war, women were expected to be homemakers and find a husband to support them. Later, however, women became indispensable to the war effort and to the war economy, although in many cases they earned less than the men for the same work.[65] Women joined the labor market to an unprecedented extent. By the end of the conflict, over one-third of the industrial workforce was female. The case of Leipzig illustrates the "feminization" of the home population, where 60 percent of the population in 1917 were women.[66] All this reinforces the argument that the First World War bolstered women's emancipation in Germany, as it had in other countries, but the question remains whether the war brought long-term improvement to the status of women.[67]

Even middle-class women found that the war had created opportunities they had never had, mainly as health workers, secretaries, and in other clerical positions. Wealthy upper-class women, like the fictional Mrs Lublin, created women's and soldiers' clubs to help both the disadvantaged and the heroic. All these activities increased the anxiety about women's so-called "invasion of the workplace,"[68] which Agnon's narrator shares.

Yet despite his apparent misogyny, the narrator often commends the work women do: in the novel, almost without exception, lower-class women, both Jewish and gentile, are the breadwinners, often purveyors of foods. One of the anecdotes in the book concerns an enterprising young woman who takes over her husband's business raising chickens while he is at war. A canny greengrocer grows and sells her vegetables to the wealthy housewives. On a different social level, Mrs Lublin, an occasional playwright, has founded a soldiers' club, her daughter works in a military hospital, a young Orthodox woman keeps her father's company books, Mrs Salzmann runs a café, Lotte Lemke, the narrator's young acquaintance, is an athletics star, and Grete Hinnings is renowned for her patriotic songs that keep the civilians' spirits up. While women populate the novel in a variety of functions, the eroticism that is a feature of *To This Day* is absent. However, the narrator tells many stories of romantic love, including that of Mr Lublin's elevation from extreme poverty to financial success, thereby winning the hand of the daughter of a prominent Leipzig Jewish family.

Agnon's Return to the First World War in the 1950s and 1960s

Agnon's two-month visit to Leipzig in 1930 to supervise the printing of his collected works in Hebrew undoubtedly brought the First World War to mind. Yet it took a further two decades for him to commit his impressions to paper. The reason for his having written *To This Day* and *In Mr Lublin's Store* so long after the events they describe has never been clarified. It may be connected to the loss of his library in a fire at his home in Bad Homburg in 1924, which occasioned his return to Palestine. Agnon was too much the ironist to have interpreted the fire as divine punishment for his years in the diaspora, yet after settling in Jerusalem he did not go abroad again, except to visit Sweden for medical attention in 1951 and then again on winning the Nobel Prize in 1966.

His only significant response to Germany during the Great War occurred in his work only after the Second World War. It could be, therefore, that by focusing on the First World War Agnon was, in hindsight, foretelling the second, implying that the moral and political chaos sparked by the Great War led to Nazism. In *To This Day*, the narrator's Leipzig friend, Dr Mittel, comments, "One war leads to another."[69] According to Mittel, there is no escape from history. Hillel Weiss similarly attributes to Agnon his own view of the Second World War and the Holocaust as the continuation of the Great War.[70] By 1960, the Holocaust had rarely appeared overtly in Agnon's writing, although he had been deeply preoccupied with it since the 1940s. In his autobiographical "confession"[71] "*Ha-siman*" (The Sign), which appeared first in 1944, expanded in the 1950s, and published in 1962, shortly after the Eichmann trial in 1961, Agnon portrays, with vivid grief, the destruction of the Galician communities, including Buczacz, in the Holocaust.

In his war novels, Agnon perhaps tried to comprehend the historical continuity, the etiology of genocide in Germany in the closing of a historical era. In *Mr Lublin*, the narrator encounters a city official called Dr Paul Bötticher who enables him to remain in Leipzig when residence for foreigners was restricted. This fictional Paul Bötticher is the namesake of a real Orientalist and German nationalist, Paul de Lagarde (1827–91), born Paul Bötticher, one of the leading advocates of what was later to become National Socialism. He was a so-called "prophet" of a group who espoused racial purity, hatred of foreign nations, nationalism, antisemitism, and pan-Germanism.[72] In the novel, Dr Bötticher has fulfilled the narrator's profound wish to remain in Leipzig by placing his seal of approval on the official document. The narrator is overjoyed and expresses his gratitude to Bötticher at many junctures throughout the novel, giving the reader the impression that Bötticher is a fair-minded person. Yet underneath the cover, the prim outer clothing, of the implicitly benign Dr Bötticher lurks de Lagarde, one of the early architects of the deadly system that brought an end to the dream of the narrator and others like him of sharing their fate with Germany and its people. Agnon, writing in the 1960s, seems to reprimand the German Jews for their reliance on the metaphorical Böttichers into whose trap they willingly fell and whose sons "rushed" into battle in the well-meaning defense of Bötticher's fatherland.

Agnon says little overtly about antisemitism in the novel, apart from a few taunts about Jew-haters in general, such as those learned Germans, for example, "steeped in the Scriptures and the Holy Tongue who write evil and bitter things about us" (85). On the contrary, one of the characters in *Mr Lublin* says, in relation to the trial of Mendel Beilis in 1913, "Given dark times of slander and benighted nations, our own time and the countries in which we live, which regard the Jews as citizens, are exemplary and even if there is a country or a state that has bad laws that distinguish between the Jews and the local population, they have no fear of such contemptible lies" (112). Yet throughout the text there are small incidents that offer implicit confirmation that antisemitism "was never far below the surface in Wilhelmine Germany."[73] In one example, a lawyer refuses to act for Jews, and in another, the narrator encounters a wealthy arms manufacturer, a Mr. von Herr, while on holiday at a spa. The two men begin a pleasant conversation until von Herr says, "'I'm sick and tired of Katzenau because of the Jews one runs into on every sidewalk.' I said to him calmly, 'You surprise me, Mr. von Herr, you're sick and tired of the Jews and yet you come to visit one.' Mr. von Herr said to me, 'But you are not like the other Jews'" (10). The *Judenzählung*, the "Jewish census" of 1916, shocked the Jewish community. In the face of all the joyous fervor and patriotism, young Jewish men joining up in their thousands and serving with distinction, the *Judenzählung* emerged from unfounded and untrue accusations that Jews were shirking frontline military service and remaining safely in support roles behind the lines. In addition to this blow to German Jewish self-esteem, postwar social and political factors entrenched antisemitism throughout the country. This is perhaps Agnon's point in his strong emphasis on the war in both novels: that this war, with its consolidation of already existing antisemitism, was the first stage in bringing Jewish life in Europe to an end. He did not, however, mention the Jewish census. By the time of writing in the 1960s, he would certainly have heard about it. It had been openly debated from 1916 onwards.

A totally different perspective on Agnon's late contending with the war is proposed by Yaakov Ariel, who suggests that the novel's context of Leipzig and the Great War points to Agnon's idea of a choice between Jewish tradition and modernity, rigid Orthodoxy or assimilated Jews espousing German art and culture. These, Ariel argues, are the realities of 1960s Israel no less than in Leipzig of the early twentieth century, and although *Mr Lublin* unfolds at that time and place, it represents Agnon's opinions at the time of writing.[74] A third possibility is offered by Agnon's biographer Dan Laor, who suggests that Agnon might have been affected by the death of his mentor and patron, Zalman Schocken: "The closeness of events, between his beginning to write *Mr Lublin* — the first chapters were published in 1964 — and Schocken's death in 1959 raise the possibility that this novel, in which the narrator presents himself as Mr Lublin's protégé, is, among other things, a tribute to the character of that same successful German Jewish businessman."[75]

Conclusion

The war brought about a change in the self-perception of the Germans, a new image that excluded the Jews. Postwar Germany was the new order from which, according to *Mr Lublin*, the Jews were to be displaced. Despite his compassion for wounded soldiers and prisoners of war, the narrator in *To This Day* contemptuously refers to the brain-injured German soldier as a "golem," a man of clay. In the novel's context, this man is less a traumatized soldier than a metaphor, a blank tablet upon which anything, even Germany's future, could be written. His homecoming in the novel is unfortunate for the narrator. The injured soldier is welcomed home by his German family as if he were a prince, while the narrator, who had been occupying his room as a much-loved lodger, is relegated to a bathtub, the Jew evicted.[76]

On the other hand, wartime in Germany had unforeseen positive consequences within the German Jewish community itself. While the desired "community of the trenches"[77] did not materialize, the home front strengthened the ties of even the acculturated German Jews like Mr Lublin with the East European immigrant Jewish community. The narrator and Mr Lublin have little in common other than their origin in Galicia, but despite Mr Lublin's aversion to the hometown they share, he pursues his friendship with the narrator. Rather than rejecting the *Ostjuden*, German Jews discovered solidarity with East European Jewry during the war.[78] Their fading hopes of German Jewish accommodation led to their growing conviction that authentic Judaism was to be found only in the East.[79] This, in part, accounted for Agnon's popularity within the cultured Jewish community in Berlin.

Agnon's *Mr Lublin* provides a kind of "filling" for the historical facts, its fictionality approaching "a higher order of truth."[80] The novel, in addition, is Agnon's commemoration of the East and Central European Jews, a resurrection of the communities as he remembered them. In this sense, his war novels and stories are monuments to these Jews and the places in which they lived before and during the two world wars. In the surreal final chapter of *Mr Lublin*, the narrator is visited by a ghost, the spirit of an old friend and fellow townsman whose displacement from the Galician town of their birth is a consequence of the wartime persecution of the East European Jews. This silent, mournful figure fades away before the narrator's eyes. It is Agnon's last word on the Great War in *In Mr Lublin's Store*.

Glenda Abramson is a native of Johannesburg, South Africa, and is now Emeritus Professor of Hebrew and Jewish Studies and Emeritus Fellow of St. Cross College and of the Oxford Centre for Hebrew and Jewish Studies. Her publications include *The Writing of Yehuda Amichai* (SUNY Press, 1989); *Drama and Ideology in Modern Israel* (Cambridge University Press, 1998); *Hebrew Writing of the First World War* (Vallentine Mitchell, 2008); *Soldiers' Tales: Two Ottoman Jewish Soldiers in the First World War* (Vallentine Mitchell, 2013). Her edited books include *The Encyclopedia of Modern Jewish Culture* (Routledge, 2005) and *Religious Perspectives in Modern Muslim and Jewish Literatures* (Routledge, 2006, with Hilary Kilpatrick). She is editor-in-chief of *The Journal of Modern Jewish Studies*.

Notes

1. See Beverly Southgate, *History Meets Fiction* (London, 2009), 197.
2. For a discussion of postmodernist historians, see Patrick O'Brien, "Book Review: An Engagement with Postmodern Foes, Literary Theorists and Friends on the Borders with History," *History in Focus* 2 (Autumn 2002), Online journal (London Institute of Historical Research), https://www.history.ac.uk/ihr/Focus/Whatishistory/obrien.html.
3. See Susanna Gierds, *The Relationship between History and Fiction: Why Historical Fiction Captures Our Malleable Identities*, Booklet (Munich, n.d).
4. William VanderWolk, *Rewriting the Past: Memory, History and Narration in the Novels of Patrick Modiano* (Amsterdam, 1997), 103.
5. Ruth Franklin, *A Thousand Darknesses: Lies and Truth in Holocaust Fiction* (Oxford, 2011), 13.

6. See Dan Laor, *Agnon: A Biography* (Jerusalem and Tel Aviv, 1998), 103 [Hebrew].
7. Aharon Appelfeld credited Agnon with having taught him how it was possible to "carry the town of your birth with you anywhere and live a full life in it. Your birthplace is not a matter of fixed geography. And you can extend its border outwards or raise them to the skies." See Tamar S. Hess, *Self as Nation: Contemporary Hebrew Autobiography* (Waltham, MA, 2016), 96.
8. *Ad Hena*, originally published in two sections in 1952 and 1953. Translated by Hillel Halkin as *To This Day* (New Milford, CT, 2009).
9. *Baḥanuto shel Mr Lublin*. This work consists of eight chapters. The first four chapters and the last one were published separately in the 1960s and the book came out in its entirety in 1975, five years after Agnon's death in 1970. His daughter edited the unpublished chapters from notes and drafts. Hundreds of pages and notes constituted the manuscript which, for some reason, Agnon did not organize into a coherent whole. It is generally designated a novel because of the elements of fantasy interspersed with autobiographical sections.
10. Page 71; quotations and page numbers are from *In Mr Lublin's Store*, translated by Glenda Abramson (Jerusalem, 2016), hereafter *Mr Lublin*. See also Glenda Abramson, "The Return of the Soldier: Agnon's Novels of the First World War," in *Simon Dubnow Institute Yearbook 2014*, ed. Dan Diner (Göttingen, 2014), 263.
11. George L. Mosse, *The Jews and the German War Experience* (New York, 1977), 3.
12. See Franklin, *A Thousand Darknesses*, 13.
13. See Laor, *Agnon: A Biography*, 103–21. See also Laor, "'Their New Dreams' II: Where Was Mr Lublin's Store? A Visit to Leipzig in the Footsteps of Haim Be'er," *Oneg Shabbat* (11 July 2014): 2–21 [Hebrew]; Laor, *S. Y. Agnon, New Perspectives* (Tel Aviv, 1995), 98–126 [Hebrew]. The Israeli novelist and scholar Haim Be'er spent some months in Leipzig visiting the sites of Agnon's various dwellings there. I was privileged to have him as my guide during my own visit to these sites.
14. It is not difficult to see Zalman Schocken in the figure of Mr Lublin.
15. For Agnon's comment on an acquaintance of his who sought permission to reside in Leipzig, see *From Myself to Myself*, a series of autobiographical fragments, speeches, essays, and lectures (Jerusalem and Tel Aviv, 1976), 266–67. [Hebrew]
16. See Laor, *Agnon: A Biography*, 108. In the guise of a protagonist called Hemdat, Agnon explains that the effort to avoid conscription derives from nothing more than the fear of having to eat proscribed foods and profane the Sabbath (*From Myself to Myself*, 12).
17. See Todd Presner, "'What a Synoptic and Artificial View Reveals': Extreme History and the Modernism of W. G. Sebald's Realism," *Criticism* 46, no. 3 (Summer 2004): 349.
18. Evelyn Ender, *Architexts of Memory: Literature, Science and Autobiography* (Ann Arbor, 2005), 13.

19. "An event" (February 1952), *From Myself to Myself*, 265.
20. On the one hand, Agnon denies that his characters represent specific individuals; on the other, he writes in an essay on his narrative probity, "I won't say a word about [the Balfour Declaration] due to my respect for the Jews who made the mistake of considering it to be complete redemption. But I have expressed my opinion of it in one of my short stories." *From Myself to Myself*, 340. One of the clearest examples of Agnon's manipulation of reality appears in his presentation in honor of Martin Buber's eightieth birthday in February 1963. He writes: "In those days the late David Feldman was the head of the Beth Din of the Orthodox community there [in Leipzig]. Every day ... we used to sit together and study Talmud." One of the central themes of *Mr Lublin* concerns the nightmarish obstacles, including the war, always hindering the narrator in his attempts to study Talmud with "Rabbi Jonathan," who represents the real Feldman. This learning is never achieved. See *From Myself to Myself*, 265.
21. Jack Wertheimer, *Unwelcome Strangers: East European Jews in Imperial Germany* (Oxford, 1991), 93.
22. Ezra Mendelsohn, ed., *Studies in Contemporary Jewry XV. People of the City: Jews and the Urban Challenge* (Oxford, 2000), 86.
23. Robert Allen Willingham II, "Jews in Leipzig," PhD dissertation (University of Texas at Austin, 2005), 19.
24. Ibid.
25. Laor, *Agnon: A Biography*, 110.
26. Tobias Brinkmann, "From Green Borders to Paper Walls: Jewish Migrants from Eastern Europe in Germany before and after the Great War," *History in Focus* 11 (2006), Special Issue on Migrations/Crossing Borders, http://www.history.ac.uk/ihr/Focus/Migration/articles/brinkmann.html.
27. See Wertheimer, *Unwelcome Strangers*, 113–14.
28. Agnon, *To This Day*, 112.
29. Holder H. Herwig, *The First World War: Germany and Austria-Hungary 1914–1918* (London, 1997), 35.
30. See Roger Chickering, *Imperial Germany and the Great War 1914–1918*, 2nd rev. ed. (Cambridge, 2004), 16.
31. Jeffrey Verhey, *The Spirit of 1914: Militarism, Myth and Mobilization in Germany* (Cambridge, 2000), 234.
32. Ibid., 235.
33. Death notices in German newspapers at the beginning of the war differed markedly in tone from those that appeared later. Traditional wartime phrases such as "he gave his life for the fatherland" had almost disappeared by 1917. See David McKibbin, "The Leipzig Working Class and World War 1: A Methodology for Inferring Historical Attitudes from Behavior," *Historical Methods* 23, no. 4 (Fall 1990): 152. In *Mr Lublin*, Agnon is mocking this patriotic mantra. See also David Welch, *Germany and Propaganda in World War 1: Pacifism, Mobilization and Total War* (London, 2000), 2; John Horne, ed., *State, Society and Mobilization in Europe during the First World War: Studies in the Social and Cultural History of Modern Warfare* (Cambridge, 1997), 5, 21–38.

34. Antonello Biagini and Giovanna Motta, eds., *The First World War: Analysis and Interpretation*, vol. 2 (Newcastle, 2015), 27.
35. See Tim Grady, *German-Jewish Soldiers of the First World War in History and Memory* (Liverpool, 2011), 27; Abraham G. Duker, *Jews in the First World War: A Brief Historical Sketch* (New York, 1939), 9.
36. German text reprinted in Wolfdieter Bihl, ed., *Deutsche Quellen zur Geschichte des Ersten Weltkrieges* (Darmstadt, 1991), 49.
37. Verhey, *The Spirit of 1914*, 160.
38. Grady, *German-Jewish Soldiers*, 24, 25.
39. Amos Elon, *The Pity of It All: A Portrait of Jews in Germany 1743–1933* (New York, 2002), 294.
40. Agnon, *To This Day*, 30.
41. For Zionism and the First World War in Germany, see Jehuda Reinharz, "Consensus and Conflict between Zionists and Liberals in Germany before World War 1," in *Texts and Responses: Studies Presented to Nahum N. Glatzer on the Occasion of His Seventieth Birthday by His Students* edited by Michael A. Fishbane and Paul R. Mendes-Flohr (Leiden, 1975), 236; Hagit Lavsky, *Before Catastrophe: The Distinctive Past of German Zionism* (Detroit, 1996), 37–38; David Aberbach, *The European Jews, Patriotism and the Liberal State, 1789–1939: A Study of Literature and Social Psychology* (Abingdon, 2013). "In the early days of the war German Zionists felt committed to aid their fatherland, but this only lasted for the duration of the war." Yehuda Reinharz, in Reinharz and Anita Shapira, eds., *Essential Papers on Zionism* (New York, 1996), 281. See also Steven Aschheim, *Brothers and Strangers* (Madison, 1982), 142.
42. Chickering, *Imperial Germany*, 128.
43. "I know that people here get stirred up by a military march on Independence Day, I know that women become very emotional about it but it makes absolutely no impression on me." Agnon in *Ma`ariv*, 27 September 1964.
44. Lit. "birthplace." In the Jewish historical context it has accrued greater significance, having come to mean "homeland." The word *moledet* has a strongly Jewish nationalistic connotation, signifying the Land of Israel, interpreted as the birthplace of the Jewish people.
45. Elon, *The Pity of It All*, 304.
46. See Grady, *German-Jewish Soldiers*, 43–44.
47. Agnon does not tell us which branch of the Red Cross he is referring to. All Red Cross organizations in combatant countries were involved with prisoners of war.
48. For treatment of prisoners of war, see Heather Jones, *Violence against Prisoners of War in Britain, France and Germany 1914–1920* (Cambridge, 2011), 70–120. We do not know the source of Mr Lublin's comment, other than the instruments of German propaganda, newspapers, posters, and films, which were well distributed. See Welch, *Germany and Propaganda in World War 1: Pacifism, Mobilization and Total War*.
49. See also Agnon's little-known story, "Merutsat ha-sus" [The Galloping Horse], in which men and women work in the fields without singing, "perhaps because the war has left women without their husbands and

the young girls see nothing but old or disabled men, so there's no point in singing." A Bundle of Stories (Jerusalem, 1984), 28–34. [Hebrew]
50. *From Myself to Myself,* 266. In *To This Day,* a grocer in Grimma comments, "There's no food available. The town has barely enough for itself and no-one wants to share it with a stranger, especially if the stranger is a Jew" (42).
51. Sean Dobson, *Authority and Upheaval in Leipzig, 1910–1920: The Story of a Relationship* (New York, 2001), 139.
52. In *To This Day,* Dr Mittel tells the narrator, "Once upon a time doctors told us that saccharin is bad for our health. Now that there's no sugar in Germany they tell us how healthy it is" (146).
53. Agnon, *To This Day,* 39–42.
54. Laurence V. Moyer, *Victory Must Be Ours: Germany in the Great War 1914–1918* (New York, 1995), 160.
55. Ibid., 167.
56. Dobson, *Authority and Upheaval in Leipzig,* 146.
57. Moyer, *Victory Must Be Ours,* 146.
58. Ibid., 167.
59. Ibid., 263–64. See also Herwig, *The First World War,* 288–89.
60. Moyer, *Victory Must Be Ours,* 262.
61. One young schoolboy, evidently echoing the adults, wrote that a submarine was "the Hindenburg of the seas." Moyer, *Victory Must Be Ours,* 186. See also Chickering, *Imperial Germany,* 89–90.
62. Moyer, *Victory Must Be Ours,* 181–87.
63. Martin Gilbert, *The First World War* (London, 1995), 157.
64. Christa Hämmerle, Oswald Überegger, and Birgitta Bader-Zaar, eds., *Gender and the First World War* (Basingstoke, Hampshire/New York, 2014), 1.
65. Dobson, *Authority and Upheaval in Leipzig,* 113.
66. Horne, *State, Society and Mobilization,* 285n22.
67. Hämmerle, Überegger, and Bader-Zaar, *Gender and the First World War,* 1–5.
68. Chickering, *Imperial Germany,* 119.
69. Agnon, *To This Day,* 36.
70. Hillel Weiss, "The Presence of the Holocaust in Agnon's Writings," in *Agnon and Germany,* ed. Hans Juergen Becker and Hillel Weiss (Ramat Gan, 2010), 427–43.
71. Dan Laor, "Did Agnon Write about the Holocaust?" *Yad Vashem Studies* 22 (1992): 43.
72. Francis Ludwig Carsten, *The Rise of Fascism,* 2nd rev. ed. (Berkeley, 1992), 25–26.
73. Grady, *German-Jewish Soldiers,* 32.
74. Yaakov Ariel, "Good Germans, Confused Jews, and the Tragedy of Modernity: S. Y. Agnon Remembers Leipzig," in *Leipziger Beiträge zur jüdischen Geschichte und Kultur,* vol. 3, edited by Dan Diner (Munich, 2005), 286.
75. Laor, *S. Y. Agnon, New Perspectives,* 99.

76. Once again, Agnon is tapping into the culture of the time: many golem narratives developed around the First World War. For example, in the preface to his book *Der Prager Golem*, serialized in 1917, published in 1920, Chaim Bloch notes that the wartime world itself is a golem. See Maya Barzilai, *Golem: Modern Wars and Their Monsters* (New York, 2016).
77. See Michael Brenner and Derek Penslar, eds., *In Search of Jewish Community: Zionist Identities in Germany and Austria 1918–1933* (Bloomington, 1998), 32.
78. Ibid.
79. See, for example, ibid., 145; Maya Barzilai, "S. Y. Agnon's German Consecration and the 'Miracle' of Hebrew Letters," *Prooftexts* 33 (2013): 53; Aschheim, *Brothers and Strangers*, 184; Shachar Pinsker, *Literary Passports: The Making of Modernist Hebrew Fiction in Europe* (Palo Alto, CA, 2010), 113; Sander Gilman, "The Rediscovery of Eastern Jews," in *Jews and Germans from 1860–1933: The Problematic Symbiosis*, ed. David Bronsen (Heidelberg, 1979), 338–42.
80. Kate McLoughlin, Lara Feigel, and Nancy Martin, "Writing War, Writing Lives," *Textual Practice* 29, no. 7 (2015): 1219.

Bibliography

Aberbach, David. *The European Jews, Patriotism and the Liberal State, 1789–1939: A Study of Literature and Social Psychology*. Abingdon: Routledge, 2013.

Abramson, Glenda. *Hebrew Writing of the First World War*. London: Vallentine Mitchell, 2008.

———. "The Return of the Soldier: Agnon's Novels of the First World War." In *Simon Dubnow Institute Yearbook 2014*, edited by Dan Diner, 263–84. Göttingen: Vandenhoeck & Ruprecht, 2014.

Agnon, Shmuel Yosef. *A Bundle of Stories*. Jerusalem: Schocken, 1984. [Hebrew]

———. *A Guest for the Night*. Translated by Misha Louvish. New York: Schocken Books, 1968.

———. "Between Two Towns." In *Collected Stories of Shmuel Yosef Agnon*, vol. 6, 78-92. Jerusalem and Tel Aviv: Schocken, 1979. [Hebrew]

———. *From Myself to Myself*. Jerusalem and Tel Aviv: Schocken, 1976. [Hebrew]

———. "Fernheim." In *Collected Stories of Shmuel Yosef Agnon*, vol. 7. 320–335. Jerusalem and Tel Aviv: Schocken, 1953. [Hebrew]

———. *In Mr Lublin's Store*. Translated by Glenda Abramson. New Milford, CT: The Toby Press, 2016.

———. *To This Day*. Translated by Hillel Halkin. New Milford, CT: The Toby Press, 2009.

Ariel, Yaakov. "Good Germans, Confused Jews, and the Tragedy of Modernity: S. Y. Agnon Remembers Leipzig." In *Leipziger Beiträge zur jüdischen Geschichte und Kultur*, vol. 3, edited by Dan Diner, 275–92. Munich: K G Saur, 2005.

Aschheim, Steven. *Brothers and Strangers*. Madison: University of Wisconsin Press, 1982.

Barzilai, Maya. *Golem: Modern Wars and Their Monsters*. New York: New York University Press, 2016.
Barzilai, Maya. "S. Y. Agnon's German Consecration and the 'Miracle' of Hebrew Letters." *Prooftexts* 33 no. 1 (2013): 48–75.
Biagini, Antonello, and Giovanna Motta, eds. *The First World War: Analysis and Interpretation*, vol. 2. Newcastle: Cambridge Scholars Publishing, 2015.
Bihl, Wolfdieter, ed. *Deutsche Quellen zur Geschichte des Ersten Weltkrieges*. Darmstadt: Wissenschaftliche Buchgesellschaft, 1991.
Brenner, Michael. *The Renaissance of Jewish Culture in Weimar Germany*. New Haven, CT: Yale University Press, 1996.
Brenner, Michael, and Derek Penslar, eds. *In Search of Jewish Community: Zionist Identities in Germany and Austria 1918–1933*. Bloomington: Indiana University Press, 1998.
Brinkmann, Tobias. "From Green Borders to Paper Walls: Jewish Migrants from Eastern Europe in Germany before and after the Great War." *History in Focus* 11 (2006): Special Issue on Migrations/Crossing Borders. http://www.history.ac.uk/ihr/Focus/Migration/articles/brinkmann.html.
Carsten, F. L. [Francis Ludwig]. *Essays in German History*. London: Bloomsbury, 1985.
———. *The Rise of Fascism*. 2nd rev. ed. Berkeley: University of California Press, 1992.
Chickering, Roger. *Imperial Germany and the Great War 1914–1918*. 2nd rev. ed. Cambridge: Cambridge University Press, 2004.
Crosthwaite, Paul. "'A Secret Code of Pain and Memory': War Trauma and Narrative Organisation in the Fiction of J. G. Ballard." http://www.jgballard.ca/criticism/jgb_secretcode.html.
Dobson, Sean. *Authority and Upheaval in Leipzig, 1910–1920: The Story of a Relationship*. New York: Columbia University Press, 2001.
Duker, Abraham G. *Jews in the First World War: A Brief Historical Sketch*. New York City: American Jewish Committee, 1939.
Elon, Amos. *The Pity of It All: A Portrait of Jews in Germany 1743–1933*. New York: Picador, 2002.
Ender, Evelyn. *Architexts of Memory: Literature, Science and Autobiography*. Ann Arbor: University of Michigan Press, 2005.
Franklin, Ruth. *A Thousand Darknesses: Lies and Truth in Holocaust Fiction*. Oxford: Oxford University Press, 2011.
Gierds, Susanna. *The Relationship between History and Fiction: Why Historical Fiction Captures Our Malleable Identities*. Booklet. Munich: GRIN Verlag, n.d.
Gilbert, Martin. *The First World War*. London: HarperCollins, 1995.
Gilman, Sander. "The Rediscovery of Eastern Jews." In *Jews and Germans from 1860–1933: The Problematic Symbiosis*, edited by David Bronsen, 338–42. Heidelberg: Winter, 1979.
Grady, Tim. *German-Jewish Soldiers of the First World War in History and Memory*. Liverpool: Liverpool University Press, 2011.
Hämmerle, Christa, Oswald Überegger, and Birgitta Bader-Zaar, eds. *Gender and the First World War*. Basingstoke, Hampshire/New York: Palgrave Macmillan, 2014.

Herwig, Holder H. *The First World War: Germany and Austria-Hungary 1914–1918*. London: Arnold, 1997.
Hess, Tamar. *Self as Nation: Contemporary Hebrew Autobiography*. Waltham, MA: Brandeis University Press, 2016.
Hoffmann, Christhard. "Between Integration and Rejection of the Jewish Community in Germany 1914–1918." In *State, Society and Mobilization in Europe during the First World War: Studies in the Social and Cultural History of Modern Warfare*, edited by John Horne, 89–104. Cambridge: Cambridge University Press, 1997.
Horne, John, ed. *State, Society and Mobilization in Europe during the First World War: Studies in the Social and Cultural History of Modern Warfare*. Cambridge: Cambridge University Press, 1997.
Jones, Heather. *Violence against Prisoners of War in Britain, France and Germany 1914–1920*. Cambridge: Cambridge University Press, 2011.
Laor, Dan. *Agnon: A Biography*. Jerusalem and Tel Aviv: Shocken, 1998. [Hebrew]
———. "Did Agnon Write about the Holocaust?" *Yad Vashem Studies* 22 (1992): 17–63.
———. *S. Y. Agnon, New Perspectives*. Tel Aviv: Sifriat Po'alim, 1995. [Hebrew]
———. "'Their New Dreams' II: Where Was Mr Lublin's Store? A Visit to Leipzig in the Footsteps of Haim Be'er." *Oneg Shabbat* (11 July 2014): 2–21. [Hebrew]
Lavsky, Hagit. *Before Catastrophe: The Distinctive Past of German Zionism*. Detroit: Wayne State University Press, 1996.
McKibbin, David. "The Leipzig Working Class and World War 1: A Methodology for Inferring Historical Attitudes from Behavior." *Historical Methods* 23, no. 4 (Fall 1990): 151–57.
McLoughlin, Kate, Lara Feigel, and Nancy Martin. "Writing War, Writing Lives." *Textual Practice* 29, no. 7 (2015): 1219–23.
Mendelsohn, Ezra, ed. *Studies in Contemporary Jewry XV. People of the City: Jews and the Urban Challenge*. Oxford: Oxford University Press, 2000.
Mommsen, Wolfgang J. "German Artists, Writers and Intellectuals and the Meaning of War 1914–1918." In *State, Society and Mobilization in Europe during the First World War: Studies in the Social and Cultural History of Modern Warfare*, edited by John Horne, 21–38. Cambridge: Cambridge University Press, 1997.
Mosse, George L. *The Jews and the German War Experience 1914–1918*. New York: Leo Baeck Institute, 1977.
Moyer, Laurence V. *Victory Must Be Ours: Germany in the Great War 1914–1918*. New York: Hippocrene Books, 1995.
O'Brien, Patrick. "Book Review: An Engagement with Postmodern Foes, Literary Theorists and Friends on the Borders with History." *History in Focus* 2 (Autumn 2002). Online journal (London Institute of Historical Research). https://www.history.ac.uk/ihr/Focus/Whatishistory/obrien.html.
Pinsker, Shachar. *Literary Passports: The Making of Modernist Hebrew Fiction in Europe*. Palo Alto, CA: Stanford University Press, 2010.
Presner, Todd. "'What a Synoptic and Artificial View Reveals': Extreme History and the Modernism of W. G. Sebald's Realism." *Criticism* 46, no. 3 (Summer 2004): 341–60.

Reinharz, Jehuda. "Consensus and Conflict between Zionists and Liberals in Germany before World War 1." In *Texts and Responses: Studies Presented to Nahum N. Glatzer on the Occasion of his Seventieth Birthday by His Students*, edited by Michael A. Fishbane and Paul R. Mendes-Flohr, 226–230. Leiden: Brill, 1975.

Reinharz, Yehuda, and Anita Shapira, eds. *Essential Papers on Zionism*. New York: New York University Press, 1996.

Sebald, W. G. Austerlitz. Translated by Anthea Bell. London: Penguin, 2011.

Southgate, Beverly. *History Meets Fiction*. London: Longmans, 2009.

Stark, Gary D. "All Quiet on the Home Front: Popular Entertainment, Censorship and Civilian Morale in Germany 1914–1918." In *Authority, Identity and Social History of the Great War*, edited by Frans Coetzee and Marilyn Shevin-Coetzee, 57–80. Oxford: Berghahn Books, 1995.

VanderWolk, William. *Rewriting the Past: Memory, History and Narration in the Novels of Patrick Modiano*. Amsterdam: Rodopi, 1997.

Verhey, Jeffrey. *The Spirit of 1914: Militarism, Myth and Mobilization in Germany*. Cambridge: Cambridge University Press, 2000.

Weiss, Hillel. "The Presence of the Holocaust in Agnon's Writings." In *Agnon and Germany*, edited by Hans Juergen Becker and Hillel Weiss, 427–43. Ramat Gan: Bar Ilan University Press, 2010.

Welch, David. *Germany and Propaganda in World War 1: Pacifism, Mobilization and Total War*. London: I. B. Tauris, 2014.

Wertheimer, Jack. *Unwelcome Strangers: East European Jews in Imperial Germany*. Oxford: Oxford University Press, 1991.

Willingham, Robert Allen II. "Jews in Leipzig." PhD dissertation, University of Texas at Austin, 2005.

PART IV

CONTESTED MEMORIES

WORKING THROUGH THE LEGACIES OF WAR

11

PAPER PSYCHES
On the Psychography of the Front Soldier According to Paul Plaut

Julia Barbara Köhne

> The soldier has experienced the war in its most elementary
> and authentic form in himself.
> Therefore, from this point onwards,
> we shall try to enter the mystery,
> and where possible find a solution for him.
> —Paul Plaut, *Psychography of the Warrior*, 1920

During the First World War, research psychologists considered the encounter with "war space" to be an enormous challenge. On the whole, however, the field of psychology was strengthened ideologically, institutionally, and in terms of personnel by its interactions with war. This chapter will examine representatives of experimental psychology, including William Stern, Otto Lipmann, and in particular Paul Plaut, who not only took advantage of the war as an experimental field, but also the German army as a customer, a contracting authority. With the army's support, all three were able to construct and profile their specific survey methods, distribute their findings, and professionalize their field. Psychology gradually placed itself as an independent science in the research landscape, and the profession of the psychologist was established.[1] Stefan von Máday, from the garrison hospital in Przemyśl (Poland), even spoke in this context of a "war progress for the sciences."[2]

These developments often stemmed from nationalistic and patriotic views and ideologies that affirmed the war. Even Jewish scientists—defined according to their family origin, not necessarily their belief or religious practice—allowed themselves to be put in front of the cart of military ideology, insofar as they helped to design a psychology of war that could be instrumentalized politically. Along with other German psychologists, they partnered psychotechnics with the selection and classification of recruits. The three expert representatives discussed in this chapter—Stern, Lipmann, and Plaut—just as many other researchers who left the university lecture theatres for this purpose, focused on the theme of war in their experiments and research as a means to increase the strength of the German army.[3] Acculturated and integrated as German Jews in the Wilhelminian period, the war gave them experiential opportunities to unfold their professional potential and to position themselves strategically within their field. In the Weimar Republic, the multiplicity of research trajectories in psychology arising from the war period were canonized and institutionalized even further. Psychology gained recognition, not least through its reliance on the military field of practices—by means of psychotechnics, aptitude tests, and personnel selection—which helped its stabilization and further differentiation, and this process continued after the war. In the Second World War, the National Socialist *Wehrmacht*-psychology profession referred to and relied on the knowledge that had been accumulated decades before; once again, psychologists collaborated with the military leadership.[4]

During the First World War, Paul Plaut's study on the psychology of war represents a special case in these examples of wartime professionals. On the one hand, Plaut's thinking was critical and innovative. His study aimed at demystification and transparency. On the other hand, his investigation also contains passages filled with sacralizing vocabulary that justified war. For this reason, an evaluation of his writing turns out to be a complex undertaking. Presumably, since psychology and psychoanalysis were stigmatized and degraded not only by many of his contemporaries, but also later on as typical "Jewish sciences," Plaut remained silent regarding both his own family background and the question of whether Jewish soldiers differed from their non-Jewish comrades because of, for example, their minority status. Nor did he mention the Jewish religion, not even in the religious section of his "Psychography of the Warrior." Only in the questionnaire is a short reference made ("any special opinion of the Jew towards Russia"; PdK 111).[5] Nevertheless, Plaut's work can be analyzed in the context, first, of German Jewish relationships during and after the war, which George L. Mosse in his 1977 Leo Baeck Memorial Lecture, "The Jews and the German War Experience 1914–1918," described as, on the whole, "precarious,"[6] and, second, of the shared war experience, which Mosse characterized as an "almost irresistible temptation" for Jews as so many "were willing to pay a high price in order to complete the process of assimilation even if it meant accepting foreign and inherently hostile myths and structures of thought."[7] Unlike many German Jews who anticipated the possibility of integration and acceptance into mainstream German culture through universal psychological experiences like comradeship, patriotism, and nationalism, Plaut was much more pessimistic about the unifying or emancipative psychological effects of the war. In his eyes, the war certainly had universal psychological effects, but these tended to be negative: disillusionment, division, attrition, brutalization, and stress in the face of unprecedented violence. Thus, any wartime or postwar constructions of camaraderie, fraternization, or a more complete union of Germans and Jews actually concealed the reality of more basic instincts towards survival. Preserving the "soul life" (*Seelenleben*) of the soldier was paramount, but, based on Plaut's work, it did not explicitly open up opportunities for Jewish integration, or a (retrospectively assumed) equality between Jews and gentiles in the community of the trenches, let alone long-term ecumenical cooperation.

Background on the Psychologists: Stern and Lipmann

In 1907, Louis William Stern (1871–1938) founded the Institute for Applied Psychology and Psychological Collection Research (Institut für angewandte Psychologie und psychologische Sammelforschung) with Otto Lipmann (1880–1933) in Berlin. From 1896 he lived in Wrocław, where he achieved his habilitation at Friedrich-Wilhelms-Universität in 1897 and from 1907 held a chair in philosophy and psychology. In March 1916, he followed a call to Hamburg[8] in order to take over Ernst Meumann's former chair in philosophy, in particular psychology and pedagogy, within the Colonial Institute's "General Offerings of Public Lectures," as well as the lead for the "psychological laboratory" in the philosophy department. In 1919, he was significantly involved in the founding of the University of Hamburg and committed to extracurricular university courses for war refugees. He transformed the existing laboratory into the "University Institute of Psychology," and established psychology as an examination subject.[9] From this point onwards, he worked in the neighborhood of Ernst Cassirer, who held the chair for philosophy. During the 1920s, Stern had to fight against anti-Jewish hostilities, for example when the German *Völkisch* Offensive and Defensive Alliance[10] (Deutschvölkischer Schutz- und Trutzbund) and the Reich Hammer League (Reichshammerbund) distributed antisemitic pamphlets that warned students about lectures by Jewish professors.[11] From April 1933 onwards, Stern—who in his adult life had always emphasized his Germanness over his Jewish origins[12] —was no longer allowed to enter the institute due to reprisals by the National Socialists as they enforced the Law for the Restoration of the Professional Civil Service (*Gesetz zur Wiederherstellung des Berufsbeamtentums*). The racial laws and his non-Aryan origins foiled Stern's official teaching and research activities; he had to leave all academic offices. Shortly thereafter, he fled Germany, which he regarded, "just as many generations of Jews before him," "as his country,"[13] moved to the Netherlands, and finally became a guest professor at Duke University in Durham, North Carolina. In 1938, Stern died of heart failure in American exile.[14]

Stern undertook many diverse projects. In 1904, he participated in the founding of the German Society for Psychology (Deutsche Gesellschaft für Psychologie, DGP) and in 1931 was elected as its president. From 1907 onwards, together with Otto Lipmann, he edited the *Journal of Applied Psychology and Psychological Collection Research* (*Zeitschrift für angewandte Psychologie und psychologische Sammelforschung*). In 1909, alongside Sigmund Freud and Carl Gustav, Stern received an honorary doctorate from Clark University. In 1912, he invented the "intelligence quotient" (IQ) as a measure of intellectual abilities determined in the test and, following that, conducted further research into "special and high talent."[15] In his individualized psychology, Stern placed the single individual in his/her integrity, indivisibility, manifoldness, and purposeful progression at the center of his ideas. He wanted to study the individual experimentally—with regard to the interplay of, on the one hand, constitution and disposition, and on the other hand the current state of personality as well as environmental factors—and, subsequently, honor it in its ambiguity.[16] Stern's intelligence research achieved great popularity and contributed to the differentiation of economic and occupational psychology, as well as to vocational aptitude research and personnel selection, supported by questionnaire and reaction test analyses. As early as 1903, Stern coined the term "psychotechnics." He made a significant contribution to the formation and systematization of practice-oriented, differential, and applied psychology and excelled in the fields of forensic and child psychology. He also worked in the fields of children's speech, student selection, and teacher training.

The suicides of his former student and esteemed assistant at the Hamburg Institute, Martha Muchow (1892–1933), in early October 1933—before she had been forced out of the institute—and, some days later, his longtime employee and friend Otto Lipmann, seriously affected Stern. Lipmann was born in Wrocław in 1880 and was one of Stern's longstanding students. In 1904, he wrote his doctoral thesis for the chair of the department, Hermann Ebbinghaus. The two worked together for almost three decades on various projects from 1906 onwards. This included collaborating as leaders of the Institute for Applied Psychology and Psychological Collection Research close to Potsdam beginning in 1916. Lipmann, who supported the project with his private assets, was the sole director. Soon after, they worked together until 1933 on an edition of the *Journal of Applied Psychology* and its supplementary booklet, which made both of them widely known.[17] In the early 1920s, the institute fell into an economic crisis, and Lipmann had to ask for financial help from various organizations, among them the American Psychological Association.[18]

Although Lipmann published many writings on his own and continually acted as a coeditor, he never got academic tenure. Lipmann dealt with questions of applied psychology, with psychodiagnostics, ergonomics, psychology statements, forensics, children's language, performance of individuals, and the topos of self-inflicted stress.[19] Methodologically, he used statistics, mass surveys, and various test instruments. Within the field of occupational sciences, he was interested in a method that would allow him to find a special ability for a particular form of work or employment via in-depth observation and testing of the individual personality. Lipmann also classified, archived, and rearranged the psychological raw material that had been collected in the institute (questionnaires, tables, schemes, experimental protocols, children's drawings, and so on) with the help of other employees, and transformed it into intelligible psychological knowledge.[20] In 1932, he received a teaching assignment for the "psychology of work" in Berlin, which was revoked the following year by the Reich Ministry of Science, Education and Culture (Reichs- und Preußisches Ministerium für Wissenschaft, Erziehung und Volksbildung). The *Journal of Applied Psychology* was forbidden by the National Socialists, and the institute and Lipmann's home were demolished by the SA. On 7 October 1933, Lipmann took his own life, although the authorities declared his suicide rather obliquely as only a "sudden death."[21]

Psychotechnics in the German Army

Stern and Lipmann were widely known for collecting psychological research and mass surveys that they, in 1914/15, also applied to the field of military psychology. Their questionnaire for front soldiers—"On the Psychography of the Warrior"— pushed them into relatively new scientific territory.[22] In the latter years of the war, related studies on experimental psychology increased, as is shown below. It was not until December 1917 that the Ministry of War ordered doctors to introduce psychological suitability tests as part of the check to see if men were fit for service.[23] Overall, the connection between the military and practical psychology during the First World War flourished but it lacked structure, systematization, and consensus-building. The military's psychological individual studies, including one by Major A. Meyer from the time before the First World War and one by psychologist and psychotechnician Curt Piorkowski, strengthened psychological practice and experimental psychology.[24] On the whole, during the First World War, sensory and mass psychological as well as army-psychotechnical considerations, combined with practical examination arrangements, prevailed. In 1917, Franz Janssen and others pleaded for a military psychological pre-selection of recruits, depending on their psycho-physical constitution and "reaction type," as well as for a classification and skillful placement of soldiers in the various areas of activity of the army and in combat. The goal was to "position the right man in the right place by the judgment of the physician," whereby—in addition to "high performance"—in the end, virtues like "sense of duty, sense of responsibility, punctuality, sense of order, legitimate ambition, comradely attitude, among others, completed the soldier's personality."[25] It was about the rationalization and economization of working and fighting actions, as well as an "optimizing of each individual's performance." The increase in the military efficiency of the army collective, which should also be conveyed by measuring "intelligence levels," was believed to be predisposed in man's nature and therefore an essential human trait. Psychology was at the service of a psychotechnologization of the members of the military apparatus. Janssen wrote further about these visions of human technology:

> But when would such an opportunity reappear, like what is offered by the present chaotic time, to observe the psyche of the masses and contribute to their knowledge! It is not only for the purposes of the garrison and peace that a mass psychology would be needed to be written in the military sense. Far more urgently there are other topics that, with respect to the terrible seriousness of war, we are forced to deal with: the psychology of leadership, enthusiasm, influence of larger and smaller associations in the field, in the various living situations of the march, of rest phases, in the trenches, in the drumfire, on patrol, a psychology of the attack, of perseverance, of the return march and much more.[26]

According to Janssen, the psychology of the individual combined with the psychology of the "crowd" or the collective body, the army, ought to make it possible to initiate a military crowd psychology that should help to get all urgent problems under control, for example the problem of leadership or fear of death. Such a military psychology was supposed to, on the one hand, control the soul of the soldier, the individual psyche, and make it more strong-willed, not to mention more efficient, for example when firing during a frontline attack. On the other hand, the officers, who had been educated psychologically in advance for the purpose of better leadership, ought to be mentored.

Stern and his staff members devoted themselves to this—from an ethical point of view—*thorny* field of suitability tests and to the question of increasing the efficiency of the army, in terms of psychotechnology.[27] They took some research assignments from the German army. From autumn 1916 onwards, Stern, for example, did research on the "flight suitability" of pilot candidates, including their ability to develop their orientation skills and their ability to focus, their situational awareness (*Gestaltauffassung*), and readiness for action. These research projects developed due to the great importance of the air force (*Luftstreitkräfte*), which, in the First World War, was used extensively for the first time. At about the same time, Lipmann used experimental sensory research to test the suitability of radio-telegraphists, their learning and hearing ability, speed, as well as the accuracy of their optical perception.[28] Diverse research and application-oriented concepts were also developed—for pedagogy to help the war-disabled and for women's vocational aptitude. This included women who, for example, due to the lack of male employees, were deployed in the civil transport sector.[29] Stern and his team are considered to be the one research group that co-invented psychotechnics, the diagnosis of suitability, and the psychology of vocational aptitude in Germany. All this was done in the service of the German war effort, but also as scientists whose work benefited from the necessities and particular conditions of the First World War.

Paul Plaut's Psychography of the Warrior

What was the main goal of the research project and the questionnaire "On the Psychography of the Warrior," which will be discussed in more detail in the following section? First of all, in Breslau in March 1915, Stern was found unfit for military service (*wehrdienstuntauglich*) in the German *Landsturm*.[30] Nevertheless, in his projects he advocated for a positive, patriotic, nationalist perception of the war.³¹ Although in *Adolescent Life of the Mind and War* (*Jugendliches Seelenleben und Krieg*) Stern pointed to the destructive and traumatizing influence of war on youth, he did not continue to problematize this further.³² During this period, Stern was primarily concerned with the progress of German science and exploring the psyches of adolescents and their fortitude — in his words, with "German national education" and "patriotic human economy."³³ As mentioned above, in 1914/15, together with Lipmann, he developed an extensive questionnaire in order to systematically and in detail record the motivations, living conditions, and psychological readiness of front soldiers. However, after only a few weeks the questionnaire was forbidden. The risk of generating dissatisfaction and the possibility that psychological injuries sustained by soldiers could be made public was obviously too risky for the military leadership and the War Ministry.³⁴ In other contexts of military medical and social science, like military neuropsychiatry, psychologically wounded soldiers and officers were expected to remain concealed, according to the War Ministry. In the case of so-called "war hysterics" or "war neurotics," it was repeatedly emphasized that — in spite of the fact that cases already appeared en masse in the first months of the war — this phenomenon should remain as invisible as possible, even if their extraordinary outer appearance, the shivering and shaking, as well as other mobility disorders, forms of paralyses, tics, and disabilities in speaking, seeing, walking, sitting, or standing, made this almost impossible. Although military psychiatry was striving to do away with this "disease" via various, sometimes violent treatment methods, in numerous cases the symptoms persisted until the end of the war and beyond.³⁵ Eventually, a third researcher, who evaluated the questionnaire and published its results in an impressive way, expanded the Stern-Lipmann collaboration.

Paul Israel Plaut (1894–1960) grew up in a Jewish family with many children in Berlin (Figure 11.1). His father Hermann was a professor of oriental studies who died several years before the war. In early May 1915, as a student, Paul Plaut reported as a volunteer (Figure 11.2). His army pass (*Militärpaß*) and military travel book (*Überweisungsnationale 1915–1918*) (Figures 11.3 and 11.4)³⁶ indicate that he became a member of the *Feld-Rekruten-Depot der 4. Ersatzdivision* and, only several weeks later, fought at the front as part of the Reserve-Infanterie-Regiment 237, first battalion (Figures 11.5 and 11.6). Later on, he was stationed at the Western Front, in Belgium, at Langemarck (Figure 11.7), and at the Yser as well as in France close to Verdun, promoted several times to a higher grade, awarded various medals, among them the

Iron Cross Second Class,[37] and discharged as a non-commissioned officer (*Unteroffizier*) at the end of the war. Among his private belongings that have been archived is the *Field Prayer Book for Jewish Men* (*Feldgebetbuch für die jüdischen Mannschaften des Heeres*), edited by the

Figure 11.1 Paul Plaut as a child in sailor jacket, around 1900; Jewish Museum Berlin, donated by Claire Allen. Published with permission.

Figure 11.2 Plaut in uniform with dagger, farewell postcard to Rudi Cassierer, dated 6 July 1915; Jewish Museum Berlin, donated by Claire Allen. Published with permission.

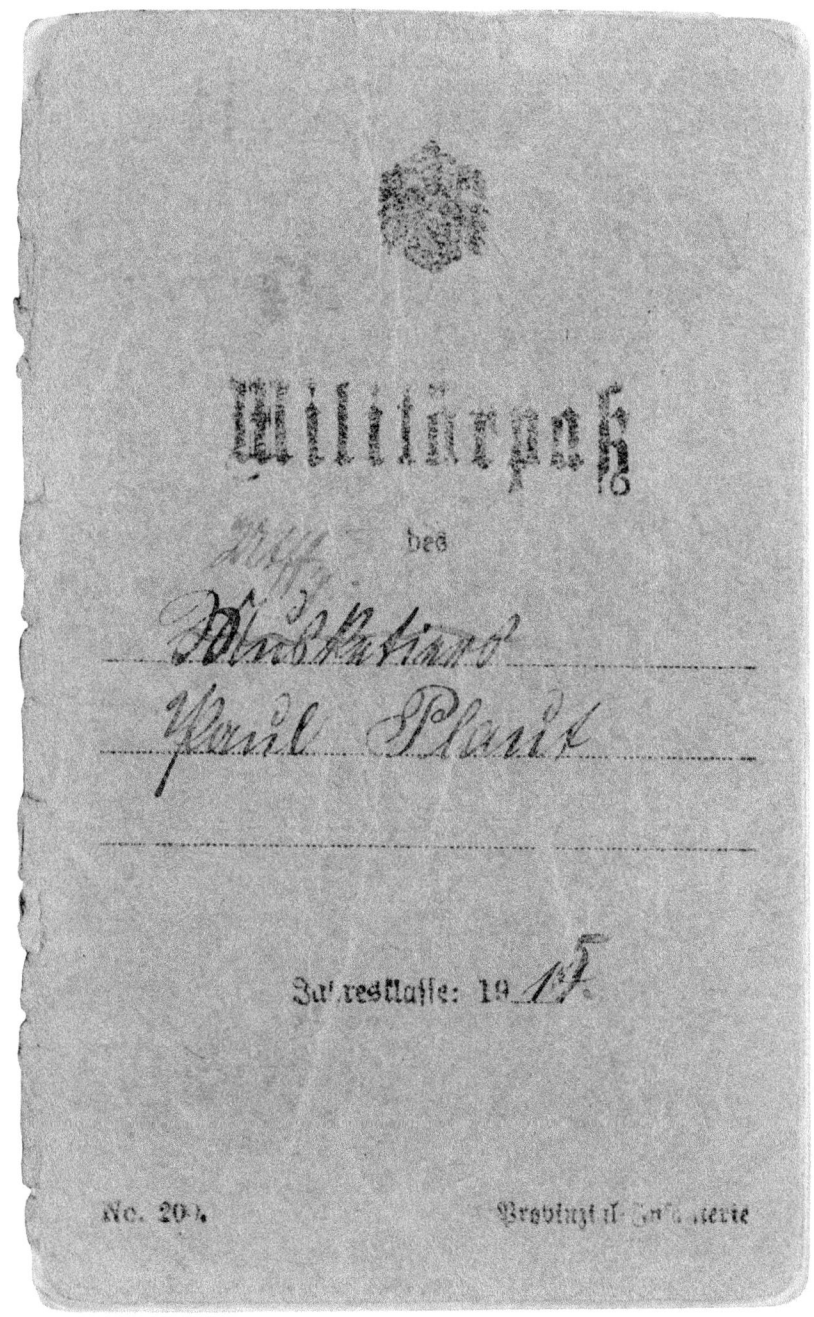

Figure 11.3 Plaut's *Militärpaß*; Jewish Museum Berlin, donated by Claire Allen. Published with permission.

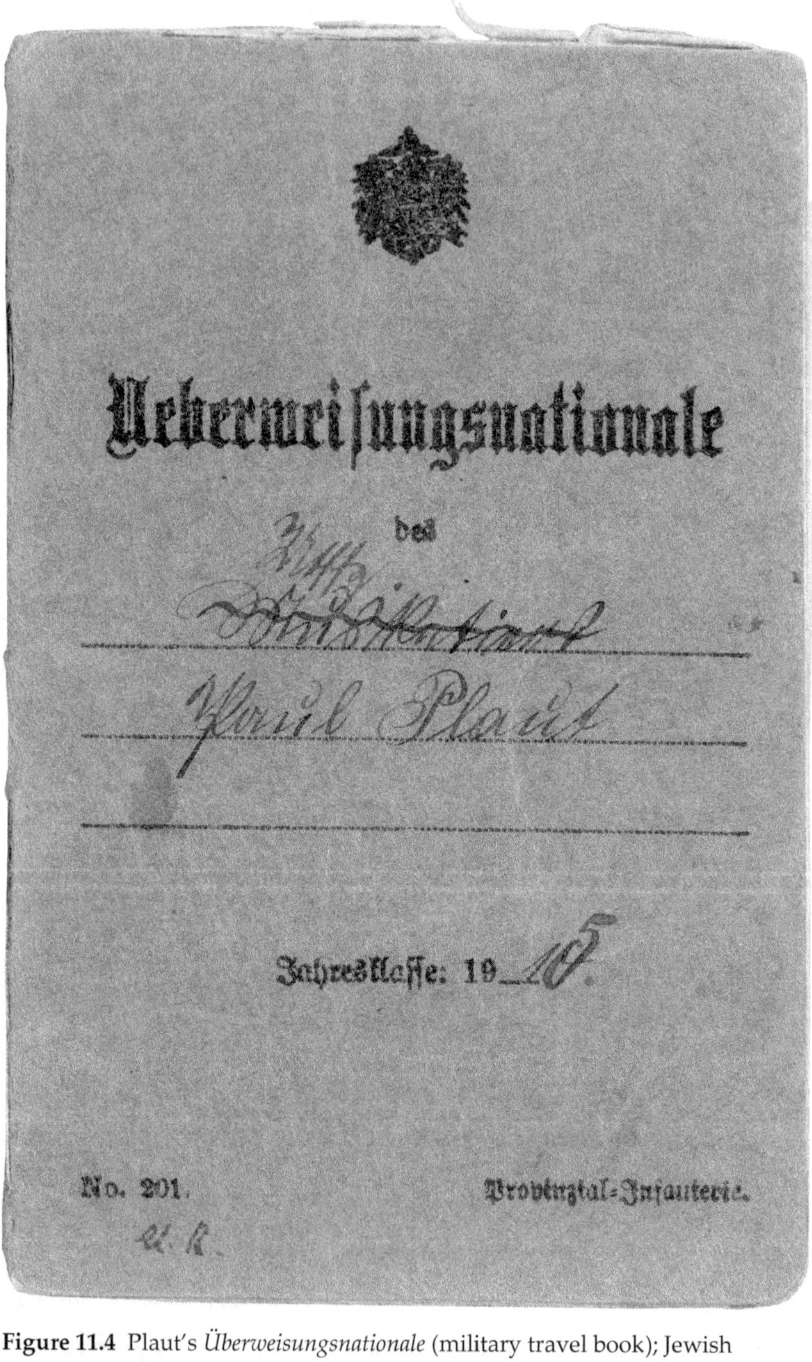

Figure 11.4 Plaut's *Überweisungsnationale* (military travel book); Jewish Museum Berlin, donated by Claire Allen. Published with permission.

Figure 11.5 Plaut in uniform with spiked helmet, dated 11 July 1916; Jewish Museum Berlin, donated by Claire Allen. Published with permission.

Figure 11.6 Group photo of Reserve-Infanterie-Regiment 237 (Plaut: top row, tenth from left), Roulers in Flanders, 1915; Jewish Museum Berlin, donated by Claire Allen. Published with permission.

Figure 11.7 Photograph of the destroyed school of Langemarck; Jewish Museum Berlin, donated by Claire Allen. Published with permission.

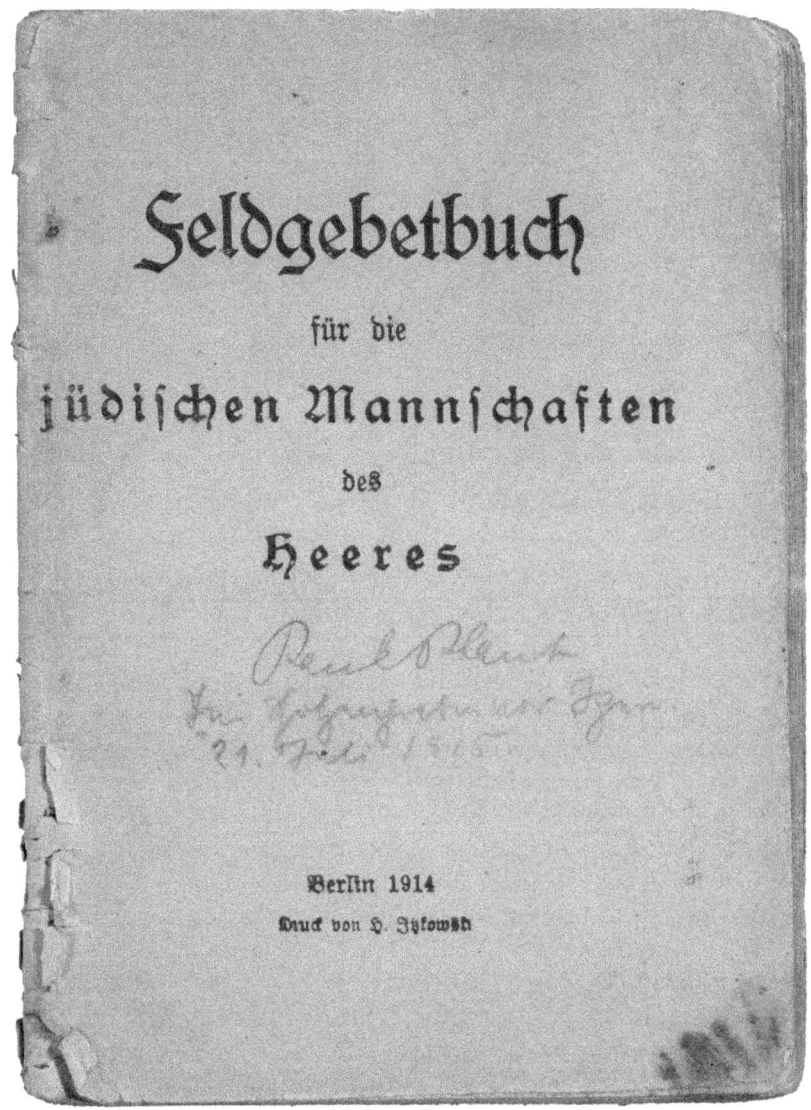

Figure 11.8 Plaut's copy of *Feldgebetbuch für die jüdischen Mannschaften des Heeres*; Jewish Museum Berlin, donated by Claire Allen. Published with permission.

Verband der Deutschen Juden and published in 1914 in Berlin, which shows traces of being used[38] (Figure 11.8). Like many Jewish veterans, with the rise of the National Socialist regime in 1933, he asked the Ministry of the Interior (Reichsamt des Innern) as well as the Austrian

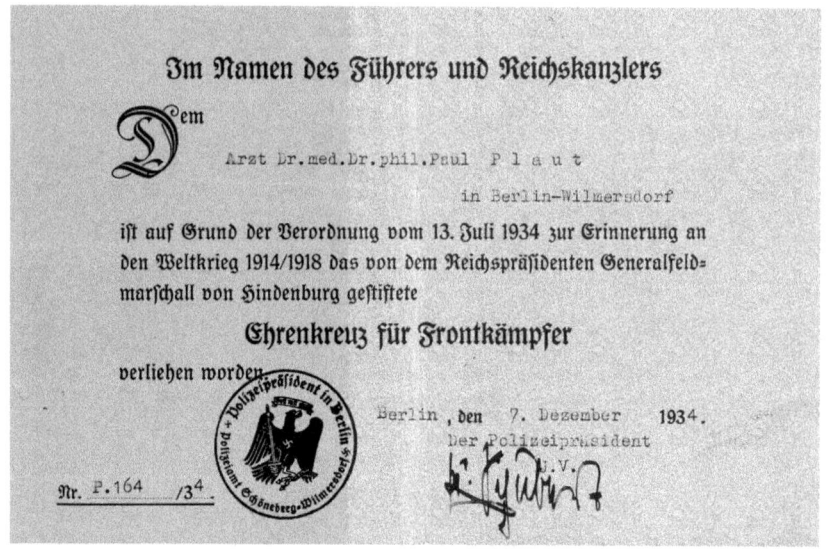

Figure 11.9 Plaut's *Ehrenkreuz für Frontkämpfer*; Jewish Museum Berlin, donated by Claire Allen. Published with permission.

Ministry of National Defense (Österreichisches Bundesministerium für Landesverteidigung) to document his active participation in the war in order to prevent his prohibition from professional practice.[39] In 1934 and 1935, they replied by sending him the Hindenburg Cross of Honor for Front Veterans (Figure 11.9) in the name of the Führer and Reichskanzler as well as the Austrian Medal to Commemorate the War, with Swords (Figure 11.10).[40]

After the end of the war, the academicus gained a dual doctorate: in 1920, a degree in philosophy from the Universität zu Greifswald[41] based on his earlier interest in philosophy and literature, as well as a degree in medicine in the late 1920s. From this point on, he committed himself to medicine, in particular forensic medicine, psychotherapy, psychology, and neuropsychiatry. After his practice opened in Berlin-Wilmersdorf in 1927, he also worked as an "unbesoldeter Hilfsassistent" (hospital assistant) at the Wittenauer sanatorium at the nerve clinic in Wiesengrund.[42] In the years after the First World War, Plaut increasingly dealt with the question of a psychological war science (*psychologische Kriegswissenschaft*), with the "suitability test for combatants" as the main focus.[43] He also explored the credibility of witnesses, the role of lying in various scientific fields,[44] and the possibility of a psychology of art and culture. Among a larger number of articles, his research resulted in his most famous book, *Psychology*

Bundesministerium für Landesverteidigung
3. _14.625_ /KEM. von 193_5_

Ausweis

Herrn
Frau _Dr. Paul Plaut_
~~Fräulein~~

in _Berlin_ wurde die

österreichische Kriegserinnerungsmedaille mit den Schwertern

verliehen.

Wien, am _12. Juni_ 193_5_

Im Namen der österreichischen Bundesregierung:

Für den Bundesminister für Landesverteidigung

[signature]

O 593/1934. — Druck der Österreichischen Staatsdruckerei in Wien. (Streng verrechenbar.)

Figure 11.10 Plaut's *Österreichische Kriegserinnerungsmedaille mit den Schwertern*; Jewish Museum Berlin, donated by Claire Allen. Published with permission.

of the Productive Personality (*Psychologie der produktiven Persönlichkeit*).⁴⁵ During the Weimar Republic, Plaut also worked as a psychological consultant specializing in criminal psychology and proceedings, sexology, and characterology sexology.⁴⁶ In 1938, he emigrated with his family to Great Britain, where he opened a small private practice. In London, Plaut, who never returned to Germany, very enthusiastically and successfully carried out research on the psychology of sex deviants, persons engaging in disturbing sexual behavior, as well as (adolescent) sex offenders and perpetrators, at the Institute for the Scientific Treatment of Delinquency (Portman Clinic), and, during the Second World War, at the East London Child Guidance Clinic (Tavistock Clinic).⁴⁷ Between July 1942 and January 1943, his mother Ernestine (née Löwenthal) was murdered by the Lager-SS in the Theresienstadt concentration camp. After retirement from the Portman Clinic and shortly before his death from a heart attack in 1960, he finalized the work on his manual *The Sexual Offender and His Personality* (*Der Sexualverbrecher und seine Persönlichkeit*).⁴⁸

After the First World War, when Plaut resumed the project "Psychography of the Warrior," the contours of military psychology and its methods, more than ever, were in motion. Max Margulies from Wittenau wrote in December 1918 that the field of psychology as it existed then would not have been able to bring about a reliable and "binding theory" that could cover "the totality of phenomena" during the war years.⁴⁹ At the time, there existed two directions in research: one of them addressed the external, anatomical, somatic character of the pathological disturbance, the other explored the patient's "subjective process of experiencing." However, it was not sufficient to merely describe the "internal experiences" and, where appropriate, reflect them in metaphors to the readership. Instead, according to Plaut, when analyzing patients' lives, "every experience" had to be translated into a general approach that would enable an "exhaustive rendering," while at the same time immediately highlight that which is essential. A distinction must be made between the pure representation of "the inner life of others"⁵⁰ and its exploitation for scientific utility. A central point was that "each experience," as James Lewin wrote shortly thereafter, is "an indivisible unity" in which the "abstract individual components," artificially separated by psychology, are merged in an "experiential unit that could not be dissolved."⁵¹ Moreover, such a psychological investigation must be carried out "according to principles that allow a scientific investigation and integration of the object."⁵² Apparently, Plaut followed parts of this self-description of psychology and the directives derived from it. According to personal statements in his

"Psychography of the Warrior," everything which is subjectively experienced ought to be made comprehensible, transparent, and objectified. Like his colleagues in experimental psychology, he strove to come closer to the scientific ideal of accuracy and objectivity. At the same time, he tried to legitimize his theses as philosophically relevant and to place himself in a good position in the expanding scientific community.[53] In addition, according to Irmingard Staeuble, his research results should be stripped of their metaphysical content and be translated into the general. If possible, they should function as societal reformers and, moreover, be connected to the level of national culture.[54]

For his "Psychography of the Warrior" (Figure 11.11), Plaut drew upon his autobiographical experiences as a front soldier and as an *Unteroffizier* as well as on material he had collected himself. Further, he included the questionnaire conceptualized by Stern and Lipmann in 1914/15 and responses to it. The list of questions included formal questions asking for age, branch of service, and service grade, and, second, fifteen detailed batteries of questions, each of them subdivided into several subquestions: Attitude towards war and the enemies, attitude towards other soldiers, danger, injuries, captives, civilians, as well as towards property of others, relatives at home, sexual life, and religious behavior (PdK 111–18). With the help of this questionnaire, the specific experiences of the soldiers due to modern warfare were to be revealed gradually and described systematically. Above all, the survey was supposed to uncover that part of the "martial soul" that was related to the sensory apparatus and the ability to react and act (*Tatbereitschaft*). The questionnaire was planned to be distributed on a larger scale among frontline soldiers, and in this way explore the individual psycho-physiological changes that occurred under extreme war conditions and, if necessary, make them controllable. However, already at the beginning of 1915, military censorship thwarted the continuation of the inquiry project, presumably because neither the questions nor the sample of answers conformed to official military ideals and self-image. Plaut had already selected and evaluated parts of the material during the war and had prepared it for publishing, but he was hindered from carrying it out because of censorship.[55] It was only with a five-year delay, in 1920, that he again examined the material, with the help of his sister Ellen Plaut, and prepared it for the essay, which will be examined in more detail below. This newly gained distance enabled him to take a partially de-mythologized and de-idealized perspective on the war.[56]

Figure 11.11 Title *Beihefte zur Zeitschrift für angewandte Psychologie*. Public domain image.

Putting the Psyche on Paper: Reconstructing and Envisioning the War

What does it mean to write a "Psychography of the Warrior"? Within differential psychology, psychography sought to record and evaluate a person's state of mind, as well as his or her talents, abilities, intelligence, attention, temperament, and physiological characteristics, in detail and as comprehensively as possible.[57] With the help of the questionnaire "On the Psychography of the Warrior," it was possible to create psychograms, which allowed conclusions to be drawn from the respondents' answers about their psyche. The secondary goal of this method of studying humans was the activation and promotion of insufficiently mobilized and underused personality areas and resources.

On the first pages of his "Psychography of the Warrior," Plaut expressed the discomfort he felt when faced with the immense amount of war literature that had been produced during the war, the reports of war correspondents, stacks of letters from the front (*Feldpostbriefe*), comprehensive diaries, and the innumerable letters to relatives and friends at home. All these genres of sources would, in most cases, be impregnated with "war enthusiasm," sensitive but less objective and critical language, a lack of analytical distance, and the primary goal of giving readers the chance to feel the emotions generated by subjective war experiences of others.[58] Plaut interpreted war fever verging on "blind faith" as an expression of a psychological crisis and not, like many of his contemporaries, as a sign of a higher development (PdK 19). The texts were more or less characterized by individual or social "pathologies," such as hero worship, credulity, an "addiction to lies" (*Lügensucht*), fantasy, exaggeration (PdK 9), exuberant gratitude to the "dear *Feldgrauen*" and people who defend their fatherland (*Vaterlandsverteidiger*, PdK 2), or self-glorification. Plaut saw the existing literary documents as "a mixture of 'poetry and truth'" (*Dichtung und Wahrheit*). Instead of immersing his psychological study into this "over-production" of problematic war literature, Plaut retrospectively tried to approach the "reality of war" through other paths that were more critical of sources (PdK 1–3).

In his "psychohistorical reconditioning of the world war experience,"[59] Plaut first of all distinguished himself from already existing psychological studies, for example Otto Binswanger's *Psychological Effects of War* (*Seelische Wirkungen des Krieges*, 1914),[60] August Messer's *On the Psychology of War* (*Zur Psychologie des Krieges*, 1915),[61] and Max Dessoir's "Reflections on the Psychology of War" ("Kriegspsychologische

Betrachtungen," 1916).⁶² These texts either lacked direct experience or they did not extend beyond the year 1916. He did not explicitly mention a series of other texts—outlined below—at this point, although he quotes from most of these studies in the course of his text, and in some cases dissociates himself from them: Otto Turmlitz's "Psychological and Pedagogical Phenomena from Austrian Battlefields" ("Psychologisches und Pädagogisches von österreichischen Schlachtfeldern," 1915), R. Zentgraf's adolescent psychological study "The Soldier, an Attempt at Military Psychology" ("Der Soldat, ein Versuch zur Militärpsychologie," 1915), Robert Sommer's *War and Life of the Mind* (*Krieg und Seelenleben*, 1916),⁶³ Wilhelm Stekel's *Our Life of the Soul in War: Psychological Observations of a Neurologist* (*Unser Seelenleben im Kriege: Psychologische Betrachtungen eines Nervenarztes*, 1916), Kurt Lewin's "War Landscape" ("Kriegslandschaft," 1917), and Ph. Stein's *The Soldier in Battles of Attrition* (*Der Soldat im Stellungskampf*, 1917).⁶⁴ Of all of these texts, Plaut only viewed Everth's *From the Soul of the Soldier in the Field* (*Von der Seele des Soldaten im Felde*) in a positive light, because of its systematic structure.⁶⁵ However, Everth's investigation period, although he had briefly been a soldier himself, ended as early as 1915. Everth's and Plaut's studies have several things in common concerning their approach and delineation. Similar to what Plaut tried to achieve just five years later, Everth sought to "fathom the truth of the facts." Comparable with Plaut, Everth distanced himself from "false idealizations," "whitewashing," "enthusiasm," and speaking in superlatives. Furthermore, he also referred to questions of health, alcohol, "changes in the consciousness of reality" of the soldier, feelings of freedom in the field, "transformations of the value awareness," "thoughts of death," as well as "religious problems." Just like Everth in 1915, Plaut endeavored to emphasize opposing or contradictory feelings that the war provoked in the soldier's psyche. This is in contrast to Everth, who wanted to speak "about the tremendous events with their wildness and horror":⁶⁶

> Nothing is as rich in contrasts as the war. In addition to all the oppressive and uplifting reality, it has some unreal moments, so many things that seem to be questionable and volatile, so that in spite of all highly conscious physicality and the reality of the events, one does not always retain the feeling one is standing "with firm, pithy bones on the well-founded permanent earth." ... Out there, destruction is constantly hovering over the people who live so intensely. Precisely because, in many respects, they feel life most vigorously, death is closest to them, and perhaps, for that very reason, they feel life, as long as it lasts, so strongly. ... And this dying often occurs in a way that is so incredibly abrupt [*etwas*

so unglaublich Plötzliches] ... that is how, for instance, a human being stops in mid-sentence while lying next to you and is dead. Insane, unlikely, but cruelly true ....[67]

For his own purpose, Plaut refocused on his psychological training and interpreted the answers to the questionnaire, as well as the military ego-documents and war reports he consulted, with great care. Longer, especially intense passages were based on notes taken by Plaut during his own actions in the war that he reworked for this context. With this collage method, he tried to distinguish his work from fiction, poetry, and other approaches to psychological research, which he, with regard to the soldier's psyche, apparently regarded as less valuable in their analytical potencies. Plaut was primarily concerned with analyzing sources in the most neutral way possible, sources that tried to "detach from the mere external experience, and, in contrast, go into themselves and pull out from there what is the most original, true and unadulterated feeling." Contemporary witnesses, evidently, "did not succeed in finding the way to themselves, to the causal epicenter of the experience [*zu dem kausalen Knotenpunkt des Erlebnisses*]" (PdK 3). He found reasons for this in the still blurred contours of war psychology, which had fuzzy concepts and definitions, and in the mass psychological character of the subject of war. To explore war required temporal and mental-emotional distance and definitely needed support from the introspective researcher.[68] Plaut wanted to intervene here with his study, which, according to its objective, was "scientific psychological" (*wissenschaftlich psychologisch*). Plaut's goal was a profound understanding and a broad attempt to interpret war experiences as well as the "life of the soul and feeling" accompanying it. The interpretation of war experiences, in his investigation, should appear as part of an even more comprehensive (cultural) history of the war:

> For it cannot be stressed enough: this war was more than a passage at arms, its experience is not only anchored in the soldier who defends himself or attacks with a rifle and a hand grenade. It was a general sacrifice, which the entire people, indeed the whole world culture, has had to line up for. Every human being has experienced the war for himself, some more and some less but nobody remained untouched. (PdK 5)

With his historicizing positivistic-psychological gaze and "objective severity" (PdK 5), Plaut tried to analyze every single emotion related to war experiences that was expressed by front soldiers and other contemporary eyewitnesses. He urged scholars to derive safe results by meticulously reconstructing interrelations between the statements and sources (PdK 6). This corresponded to the trend in the scientific community of the time, as scientists regarded regularities of experiences and psychological observations as cause-effect relationships and deduced strict psychological laws from them. Plaut's investigation, on the one hand, focused on the content of the respective descriptions, their psychological characteristics, and, on the other hand, on particular forms of narrative and ambiguous rhetorical styles (for example phenomena of German jingoism, or *Deutschtümelei*), pathos-laden terms (myths of comradeship, "mobilization psychoses," or "degeneration"; PdK 9), and (religious) metaphors (war as a "holy cause").

The Army En Masse versus Front Soldier-Individuals

Plaut merged Gustave Le Bon's reflections on mass psychology of the "collective soul," which alleged that individuals in a group would start to feel, think, and act differently as single persons, with his own interpretations of the psychological effects of the war. The soldier "did not represent a type of his own ..., but only a partial [member] of a collective [the warlike group], who only exhibits typical behavior ...." The specific state of the "warlike mass," the "life in the collectivity," depended on the particular war situation and its inherent "imperative necessities." In this, he states, "individual" statements of the soldiers were "compulsorily collectivized," that is, individuals would be subordinated to the compulsory character of the military collective.[69] In this "collective necessity" (*kollektive Notwendigkeit*), which existed only temporarily and in contrast to the "world of peace," Plaut saw the characteristic "collective law" of war psychology. It is obvious that Plaut here joined Le Bon and other mass psychologists of the nineteenth century who regarded the "crowd" as a collection of individuals with *one* collective psyche. This anthropomorphizing approach to the community compares it to a human organism. The soul, which is associated with this multitudinous *individual*, the "mass soul," allegedly let its members function in accordance with its own laws; civilians turned into soldiers who were supposed to act as a unified entity.[70]

The descriptions of the nineteenth-century phase of theories on the characteristics of the "masses" contained a variety of feminine metaphors, by which the "mass" was feminized, demonized, pathologized, and devalued.[71] The "mass," derived from the Greek word stem *mazza*, which means "bread dough," was commonly associated with nervousness, panic, and hysteria, which, in turn, were caused by a lack of will and ego-strength and overall a deficiency of stability and form. Le Bon wrote:

> Among the peculiar qualities of masses are some—such as impulsiveness, irritability, incapacity to reason, a lack of judgment and critical spirit, an exaggeration of emotions ..., which are almost always observed in beings belonging to a low stage of evolution, women, slaves and children, for example.[72]

But even during the First World War, military psychologists ascribed de-differentiating and de-individualizing elements to the "mass." Not only did the different army formations (corps, divisions, brigades, regiments, battalions, companies, and so on) form a new kind of "mass," but the psychologically wounded soldiers and officers, whose symptoms crossed the well-ordered military structure, formed a disturbing subgroup, which also manifested mass symptoms and syndromes. Since, for example, the military-psychiatric figure of the "war hysteric" embodied the danger of overthrowing the army formation into the feared state of massiveness, it itself received the typical attributions of the "mass." The military psychiatrist Karl Bonhoeffer postulated:

> One of the reasons sending psychopaths to the front was carefully avoided at the beginning of the war was to avoid bringing psychic-infectious material into the suggestible mass mood [*Massenstimmung*]. ... The psycho-physically weakened person is particularly susceptible to the suggestive effect of the mass.[73]

Plaut also saw the suggestibility of the "soldierly mass" as a central change in psychological character that was triggered by the war; according to him, it resulted in a "suggestively affected storming towards the goal: war" (PdK 10).

Another important feature of how soldiers were mentally conditioned in the First World War was, according to Plaut, contradictory experiences, or "the turmoil of changing emotions" (PdK 8): oscillating from one extreme to the other, from pacifism to irrepressible enthusiasm, from the "half-unconscious and senseless" jubilant tumult of the first days of August 1914 to the pensive, skeptical, pessimistic worldview, from feeling safe within the mass to the isolated existence on one's own, as a "single individual," from mobilization to being captured in the trench (PdK 8, 9). This, too, was one of the contortions of war, Plaut stated: "even true friends of peace at that time joyfully took up arms" (PdK 9). To be part of the "drunken intoxication" was everything they wanted, whereby "the immediate seriousness of the rushing blood [functioned] as an educator" (PdK 9, footnote 1, quoted from Gottfried Traub). At this point, Plaut makes audible the voice of a contemporary witness from the pool of soldiers who had been interviewed by the Institute for Applied Psychology and Psychological Collection Research, made anonymous by the initials:

> E. B.: Entered the first mobilization day as a war volunteer. I knew from the start that a modern war is a tragedy, and a crime against mankind. … But the sentiment of the first days, in due course, told me what I had to do. My patriotism [*Vaterlandsliebe*] had not been unrestricted until then; from now on I recognized myself as a patriot. … A strong impact of thirst for adventure was quite certainly there in this mood of the first days. … First and foremost, my sense of duty was decisive. (PdK 11 f., InstAngPs)

It is precisely these conflicting attitudes, which are united in one breast, that Plaut recognizes as individual characteristic motifs for war: "self- and victory-consciousness" and the conviction to lead a "legal battle" (PdK 13) on one side, sober disappointment over the cruel war-reality on the downside.

A further new development, which the First World War brought about as a specific experience, was a comprehensive change in the "registers of feeling"—"rooted emotional complexes" fade away, new "tumultuous feelings" arise (PdK 19 f.). After a longer passage in his text, in which Plaut reports his own war experiences, he turns to another psychological survey conducted by the Italian psychologist E. Ragazzoni:

> You want to know what you feel when you first enter the fire …? No one has any clear idea of things at all. You stumble forward, you are running, you fall to the ground, rise again and fire like in a dream. Every concept of time has disappeared. … One is only a particle, a splinter, a molecule of a shapeless mass that writhes in excitement and battles. … There is a new instinct that temporarily interrupts the activity of thought and the sensation-experience. Later, when everything is over, you feel a sort of shivering because of everything that has happened and what you have seen. … In the battle, I had the idea I was in a cage desperately struggling to free myself, … but I had the feeling I would never get out of this cage alive. (Ragazzoni, quoted after PdK 20 et seq.)

Plaut described the psychological state in the fight as "moments of the highest tension of the nerves," which cause such a constriction of consciousness that "the man with his abundance of thoughts" and "complexes of imagination" becomes the "soldier of the battle," "a mass individual, endowed with a mass consciousness, or better yet with a mass instinct" (PdK 23). Plaut's image of the bellicose "mass individual" develops further still in its outline by assigning to it—as two decades before, by the psychologists of the crowd—a tendency to fall into panic, fury, and "indescribable confusion" (PdK 40). Plaut sees a further reason for a psycho-physical shift in the impressions given by a British war correspondent:

> One could see the bright flashes from some of the hostile cannons, a deafening noise came from them, regularly rolling like thunder, interrupted by sudden disturbances which proliferated through the brain and felt like a gruesome process of dissolution in the whole body ... The sound of the flying grenade—this vast sound of an angry giant bee leaving its burning hive, ... until the sound dissolves in the booming of a deadly explosion. (Ph. Gibbs, quoted after PdK 32)

A characteristic experience of an infantryman would be a sharpening of the sensorium, which is simultaneously stimulated on all sensory channels. The "eardrum vibrates," the "light beam of a bursting bullet hits the retina," powder vapor permeates his sense of smell, the body "eats its way deeply into the ground" and receives the impulse to go to cover or seek protection (PdK 35). Furthermore, Plaut determined that in the case of being wounded, unique "moments of consciousness" take over, which initially push away the pain of the wound, which means that the shock effect only comes through with a delay. Essential for not getting wounded and surviving would be the ability to correctly interpret noise at the front. For Plaut, the "ability to distinguish armaments" implied that the soldier was able to differentiate between cannons, mortars, hand grenades, airborne missiles, bombshells, shrapnel, and gunshots and their respective distance, and, at the same time, being able to reduce this sensitivity to "a state of being consciously deaf to noise" (PdK 31).

On the whole, these psycho-physical shifts depended on the particular type of soldier, and on the type of warfare, trench or mobile. Plaut wrote that the war in the trenches, these "months of perseverance in complete defensiveness" and psychological concentration, was often described by combatants as "slow suicide," for which "iron nerves," "rock-solid, unshakeable calmness and deliberation, even stubbornness to the point of exuberance and complete insensibility" (PdK 41 et seq.) are needed. And this, even though people are "literally torn to pieces," the "man next to you is devoured, buried, or seriously injured by a grenade," and all around "the moaning, whimpering and groaning of the mutilated and dying" (PdK 44) can be heard.

In the next section of his study of war psychology, Plaut examined the sometimes confusing manifestations of soldierly sexuality, and their sexual functions under the influence of the war, a subject that was also explored by sexologists from 1914 onwards. According to his observations, the war and its exertions suppressed the libido, which is concentrated mostly on the family at home. Behind the front line, however, the "imprisoned heat" could "burst out with primordial force" — "a hot desire falls into my soul" —and urges to unload. The sex drive was often forgotten in the field, only to emerge all the more powerfully in the resting phases behind the front (PdK 55 et seq.).

A similar conceptualization of (repressed) sexuality while in the field or in another male-dominated realm can be found, for example, in historical sources that describe the widespread phenomenon of cross-dressing at the front and in the internment camps of the First World War.[74] For the temporal theatrical performances, the travesty shows, combatants who had especially "feminine" features were selected. Masquerading as male divas and *prima donnas*, they represented an important foil for other soldiers to envision eroticized and eroticizing femininity and to imagine an illusionary encounter with the female counterpart which, in fact, was a rare reality in the spheres of the trenches and camps. However, the play with gender roles, cross-dressing, or watching the performances of cross-dressers did not necessarily mean a homosexual interest or serve as socially shared foreplay for sexual encounters. In the majority of cases, it generated situations characterized by humor, relaxation, and distraction.[75] Just like Plaut described, the sexual drive was often suppressed and showed up more powerfully on other occasions.

Plaut's Heroic Warrior Ideal and Religiosity

Plaut points out that, ideally, the soldier was concerned with a "deeper heroism," beyond "reckless ambition," the striving for personal honor and the "world of weapons." A qualitatively good soldier's attitude determined by the "needs of war" would express itself in an "awareness of action" and taking "being outside" as a matter of course. The goal was to evolve further "through humanity and towards becoming a personality" without losing "a lot of words" about it (PdK 60 et seq.). Plaut saw the war as a "periodic experience," an "episode" that every soldier tries to overcome as quickly as possible in order to return to civilian life ("Whoever is in the midst of the struggle for his naked existence, learns to love it most .... They all want to go beyond the war, to only live..."; PdK 90). No soldier wanted a "heroic death," even the volunteers did not want to die: "... when the soldier himself is the most terrifying killer, he wants it least because he wants to live" (PdK 65). And yet soldiers would have resigned themselves to the death they were constantly facing, as an "unalterable necessity." At the same time, they constantly fought it with their urge for "life and victory." Only those to whom death meant a result and a goal gave their life with equanimity and serenity—in the end, it would be a question of morale and devotion, the "elation of maybe dying in the midst of wanting to live," Plaut summarizes. The death of the "true" hero created new things that the dying person would see at the moment of death. Here, death was "a component of the new-rising fatherland in its life-size and glory" in "ruthless pitilessness with oneself and with others" (PdK 66).

Here, Plaut maps out a higher form of heroism, whose bearers fully and "respectfully" acknowledge the conditions and necessities of the war and surrender to their fate. Herein lies the deeper level of the psychotechnological advisory function of his "Psychography of the Warrior." As noted in the above-mentioned motto of this text, the question of a "solution" for the soldier becomes increasingly apparent in the chapter on "The soul of the soldier." It is the surrendering into and surrender to the war, as soon as one has become part of it and acts in it as a "man of action" (*Tatenmensch*). Plaut expresses it in the words of the French soldier and writer Henri Barbusse. At the death of a close comrade, you "first feel a sharp blow in your own flesh, before you completely understand he has disappeared. It is as if you suddenly experience a little of your own dying .... They [the soldiers] all have given everything; they sacrificed their whole strength drop by drop, until they finally gave themselves completely. They have gone beyond life, and their sacrifice has something superhuman and perfect" (PdK 68, quoted from the novel *Le Feu*, 1917).

In this context, Plaut also analyzes the psychological structure of largely taboo phenomena. Objectification and disillusionment, which increased in accumulating war experiences, produced a new morality, which also manifested itself, for example, in war plundering. In addition, he observed in soldiers a lust for violence and killing, which had led to excesses in the war. Plaut approaches the ethically difficult question of murder in the field, quoting from the questionnaire again. The appropriate question and pre-defined possible answer in the questionnaire can be found in the section "II. Behavior towards danger" and it reads: "5. Behavior in shooting and in the melee (does it become clear one kills people, or is the enemy only perceived as an object, like the deer on the hunt, the target on the shooting range? ... Can something like blood rush, a tendency to cruelty be observed?)" (PdK 112). Killing is interpreted here, in the question and the answer, as a necessary matter; the enemy is killed, "in the same way that a predator standing in the way is killed." "The man in the field is by no means aware that he is murdering ...." Plaut also touches upon the question of the lust to kill in war, the "bloodlust, thirst for revenge." "Death and killing are ... stripped of the selfish moment, ennobled by the sacred cause" (PdK 69, *InstAngPs*). The above-cited example reveals how suggestive and paternalistic the questionnaire was in a specific case. In response to the comparison of the enemy with a "deer on the hunt," a soldier being questioned answered promptly that the enemy was killed "in the same way one would kill a predator." In contrast to his preface, however, Plaut does not criticize the suggestive effect of the questionnaire at this point. In addition, Plaut broadens the effects of civilian ethics to the wartime sphere, where killing is not punished as a crime but perceived as a "sacred cause." Once again, Plaut sees "not only brutal violence," but also "constantly changing and growing diversity, as a result of clashing opposites and contradictions," as the main characteristic of the "essence of war," which he describes as both "'great' and 'degrading'" (PdK 70). In this context, Plaut speaks of a personal greatness in character that was needed in order to withstand this tension and to face it.

In this and some other passages, it almost seems as if the past caught up with Plaut insofar as he, in this psychological retrospective, imagined himself as an *Unteroffizier* in the First World War again, and argued accordingly. Here, Plaut justified war and elevated the killing process on an extreme level; he declared it to be sacrosanct and quasi-sacred. Criticism here alternated with party-line loyalty, and this continued beyond the end of the war. In these moments, he wrote in the historical present tense, reawakening the war period in his imagination. One by one, Plaut combined individual stones of a mosaic into an ideal image of the soldier, which is less descriptive than instructive for future operations. With the use of self-inflicted religious metaphors, Plaut indicated that he saw Christianity as vital for the combatants in a broad spectrum of ideas about suffering and eternity. These religious beliefs would have been ubiquitous anyway because of the possibility of being wounded and the permanent closeness to death and anticipation of it. Many frontline soldiers had "cried like animals led like lambs to the slaughter; as if they were trying to drown the howling of the shells with the 'Our Father.'" Here Plaut quotes Erwin von Mattanovich, lieutenant Field Marshal, who celebrated the war as a "religious renewer" (*Neuschöpfer*), since distress teaches us to pray.[76] The then widespread perception and invocation of the emperor as "godfather," as "a kind of unattainable saint" (PdK 94), or as head of a "crusade," would fit into this picture. In Plaut's eyes, the sometimes sudden attention to religion in the field was psychologically explainable in the following way: the "instinct of self-preservation" led to an increased inner agitation and contemplation, which was "consistently denied" before the war. At this point, Plaut counts little on statistical surveys and doubts in many cases that it was "real religiosity." Rather, he assumed there was a superficial imitation of sensitivity (PdK 74). Plaut doubted there was a general revitalization of religious consciousness among combatants, which had been so asserted by theologians. Just as important as faith was superstition, which he also called "autohypnosis" (PdK 78). The latter also fulfilled the function of nurturing the hope to survive. Items such as crucifixes, lucky charms, or medals would spontaneously be seen as amulets for preservation. Plaut affirmed: "The soldier wants to live—his old life, as he lived it in peace, on his soil with his family" (PdK 94).

To summarize Plaut's reflections, the collective life of the "mass of soldiers" as an "aggregated multiplicity" arises from the unifying uniform, the idea of the fatherland, comradeship, drill, and discipline; "all moments of consciousness are under their influence, as is the whole emotional life through which it [the mass] receives its constant emphasis." The amalgamation of discipline, freedom, and commitment, at the same time, became an "inner structure" characterized by the "necessity of full power development" (PdK 91 et seq.). Unlike his colleagues in psychology, Plaut did not believe soldiers experienced a homogenous sensation, with simultaneous automatic fraternization, solidarity, and "unity" (*Verbündelung*) between individual soldiers. Instead, opposing forces and frictions were even more pronounced than in civilian life. Plaut designed a psychic image of the soldier that is fluid. He hypothesized a professional and only temporary solidarity, a superficial religiosity, no genuine, self- and boundless comradeship, but merely a "war comradeship." In his study, Plaut apparently attempted to clarify the meaning, or to shift the meaning of concepts that seemed to be used self-evidently in literary and psychological discourse about the First World War.

> There is a large sense in which psychological forces play the chief role in all wars. It is they that cause war, that carry it on, that make or wreck morale both in the army and at home, … that are or ought to be the chief heirs of all war's results.[77]

Conclusion: Paper Psyches

Regarding the present volume's aim to make visible and interpret German Jewish experiences in relation to the time of the war, it can be deduced that the nexus between biographical knowledge on Plaut, his research on psychological effects of the war, especially his work on the psyche of front soldiers, and his later remarkable career as a psychologist and neuropsychiatrist provides some interesting insights into this research question. Plaut's socialization in a Jewish family, his scholarly ambitions and double doctorate, his time as a German Jewish soldier and *Unteroffizier*, and his Jewish wedding make it look as if Plaut, on a personal-biographical level, identified with his Jewishness. In 1915, he indicated his belief in the mosaic religion in Sütterlin writing ("mos.," 3 May 1915) in the *Überweisungsnationale*, and he carried the Jewish field prayer book in the military missions in which he participated. While his 1915 decision to volunteer as a soldier in the Imperial German Army (*Deutsches Heer*) can be interpreted as a gesture of national solidarity and conformity in order to show his patriotic interest in assimilating to the German community of values, the application for retroactively earning the *Ehrenkreuz* and the *Kriegserinnerungsmedaille* in the middle of the 1930s shows his increasing concerns and feelings of disintegration and a threatened sense of integrity. The fact that he and his family were falling under the Nazi ideology's definition of "Jews" affected him; the 1933 prohibition by the Nazi government to engage in certain professions led to his emigration to Great Britain and his mother was murdered during the "Third Reich." In his case, these tendencies of a growing social insecurity could, at least to some extent, be compensated by the spontaneous help he received from his strong Jewish professional network in Great Britain, for example with letters of recommendation, which derived from his grand reputation as an internationally known neuropsychiatrist, psychologist, and psychotherapist.[78]

In contrast, his scientific writings as a war psychology researcher in the Weimar Republic, for example his "Psychography of the Warrior," explicitly address neither the notion of "Jewishness" nor particular problems of integration or exclusion that might have accompanied his own life, the life of his research colleagues, or his Jewish comrades during the time of the war. The fact that "Jewishness" as such is not featured in Plaut's analysis could be regarded as the wish to level out or strictly refuse to acknowledge the alleged differences between Germans and Jews that were often associated with antisemitic tendencies. This silencing of the tensions between different religions in combination with (pseudo-)biologistic conceptions of opposing "races" (*Rassen*) could be seen as a sign of trying to suppress or deny longstanding problems in the German-Jewish dialogue.

On the contrary, the de-thematization could be interpreted as overidentification with the symbolic position of "Germanness" and an attempt to, more or less, emancipate from his Jewish heritage. Referring to German-Jewish relations during the First World War, Mosse wrote

Figure 11.12 German soldier in the trenches of the First World War, Plaut's possession; Jewish Museum Berlin, donated by Claire Allen. Published with permission.

about the widespread adaptation of Christian symbolism and new myths about "Germanhood" that trench warfare created. In the eyes of the historian, these references and visions enabled a mental escape from the horrors of war, transcending of the devastating trench experiences and mass death—"death was so close, with bodies all around"[79] (Figures 11.12 and 11.13). For example, could this mechanism of superelevation be found in the "cult of the fallen soldier," or the analogy of death for the fatherland to the passion and resurrection of Christ. Mosse described the trans-religious fantasies of an "ecumenical cooperation" and a "*communio sanctorum*" under extreme human conditions as effects of a certain way of dealing with Christian rhetorics: "The cross became a national symbol for a war which was regarded as holy by all combatants."[80]

The argument suggesting overidentification is strengthened by the fact that, in his 1920 and 1928 studies on war psychology, he stuck overall to the dominant ideological and representational framework of German symbolism and patriotism as well as the rhetoric of the army—the psychological questionnaire had originally been designed for reasons of army psychotechnics and efficiency. But at the same time, his study pointed to another subtle direction, as it highlighted the vulnerable side of the psychological effects of the war on German

Figure 11.13 Memorial stone for the fallen soldiers of the Reserve-Infanterie-Regiment 237; Jewish Museum Berlin, donated by Claire Allen. Published with permission.

as well as German Jewish combatants without differentiating between them. Therefore, the study criticized war as such and, at the same time, celebrated the independence of (objective) scientific thinking.

How did Plaut develop his approach in his 1920 essay, "Psychography of the Warrior"? He scanned professional and fictitious war publications and analyzed their subjective and sultry language in order to make the concepts behind it potentially more objective. His method deflated attempts at mythologization and idealization by revealing contradictions and taboos. For example, he observed that the "ending of war that progressively became more obvious" had felt like an "eerie fall into some darkness" (PdK 75). Plaut also worked to combat stereotyping. For example, he believed he could prove through the use of his questionnaire for soldiers that, in contrast to a widely held view, alcohol was not used extensively to make the soldiers more aggressive fighters. His treatment of theories of crowd psychology is also distinct. He used dialectical images to tear down clichés of mass psychology. He saw the various collective army formations as "conflict under the guise of cooperation" (*Gegeneinander als Miteinander*): the huge "army block is fragmented into millions of atoms that rub against each other, depending on the question of whether they contain differences in feeling, opinion, and worldview; but by this the struggle of unity is not diminished,

Figure 11.14 Plaut's photography of a destroyed farm with Christian cemetery crosses in the background. Public domain image.

nor fragmented ...." The communal experience (*Gemeinschaftserlebnis*) is fed from a "condensation of all mental and physical forces" (PdK 92, 96). By this, Plaut distinguished himself from Ernst Jünger's vision of the army as a soldierly collective body ("In the short weeks of training, we had melted into a great, enthusiastic body"[81]) as well as from psychological representations of a crowd that merged into a "mass soul," which was believed to determine everything and suppress the individual. Plaut rather saw the "soldier mass" as

> a multiplicity of individual fighters for a single fate, for the individual personality. ... Everyone becomes a warrior, everyone a conscious fighter for his personality, everyone wants to be free or become free when the goal is achieved, because he himself is the goal. That is why everyone gathers together all his strength, pulls himself together, filters his feelings—he disciplines himself and integrates himself harmoniously into the whole disciplined formation, into which he does not seem to fit. (PdK 93)

Plaut saw the "warlike group" as a temporary work community, characterized by necessity, sense of duty, and instinct of self-preservation. Thus, the individual had to subsume himself into the "mass" in order to survive, but it was not an experience that necessarily generated long-term bonds of unity or a path of integration for men who felt they were social outsiders before the war.

At the end of his study, Plaut partly withdrew his claim to a scientifically correct objectivity, which he had still claimed at the beginning of his text. Here he expressed his opinion that, in the case of combatants, it was not a "unity of experience" that statistically and graphically could be translated into periodic patterns. For this purpose, a "strict method" and firm "conceptual definitions," which did not yet exist, would be needed. According to Plaut, the soul-life of front soldiers was dependent on the pressure of the situation and the respective rank; it was subject to strong fluctuations and at the same time adaptive. He assumed that the psychophysical adaptations of the front soldier were temporary, but the reorganization of the psychological structures also had long-term effects that survived the war. The mind would be capable of development (PdK 59) and tended towards objectification and disillusionment. It functioned as part of a "mass psyche," but was not limited to its characteristics. In Plaut's study, the soldier collective was characterized as a fluid, variable, "artificially synthesized psychic multitude," which at the end of the war dissolved due to mental and physical exhaustion (PdK 110). He depicted the experience of the war as "an aggregate of innumerable substances," a "colorful mosaic formation" (PdK 95), full of mutually interdependent aspects, such as a "sense of duty and self-awareness," unconscious and conscious ideas, full of "influential ecstasy" and, at the same time, "inner necessity and regularity" (PdK 110).

Despite his desire for final answers, hyper-precision, and high professionalism, and despite his massive attempts to put "soul material" on paper, Plaut had to admit that the soldier's "paper psyche," in the end, retrospectively, could not be deciphered. In his own writing and his analysis of the sensitively compiled writings of others, Plaut seemed to demonstrate decisively that the psyche of soldiers did not merge in its psychographization, psychotechnologization, or the increase of its efficiency. Instead, it spoke a very different language—marked by "multiplicity," "inconsistency," the "episodic" and satirical, through distortions, and "simulation" (PdK 97 et seq.). For Plaut, herein lies the "unreal reality," or "reality in its full bareness" (PdK 99 et seq.), which expressed itself in the thought and behavior, the culture, language, and soul of the soldier. Plaut's desire to grant an exclusive "insight behind the psychological backdrops of war" (PdK 16) succeeded insofar as he gave a remarkable dynamic space (of its own) to the individual dimension of the war.

Julia Barbara Köhne is a visiting professor at the Institute for the History and Theory of Culture at Humboldt-Universität zu Berlin.

Her publications include *Kriegshysteriker: Strategische Bilder und mediale Techniken militärpsychiatrischen Wissens, 1914–1920* (Matthiesen, 2009) and *Geniekult in Geisteswissenschaften und Literaturen um 1900 und seine filmischen Adaptionen* (Böhlau, 2014). Her current research project is titled "Trauma Translations: Stagings and Imaginations in Film and Theory."

Notes

A shorter German version of this chapter, "Papierne Psychen: Zur Psychographie des Frontsoldaten nach Paul Plaut," has been published in Ulrike Heikaus and Julia B. Köhne, eds., *Krieg! Juden zwischen den Fronten 1914–1918* (Berlin: Hentrich und Hentrich, 2014), 67–104.

1. On the generally disordered structure of the "field of psychology" in the run-up to the First World War, cf. an author with the initials B. C. In 1938, he described in retrospection of his time as a psychology student (in *Synthesis* 3, no. 12, 21 et seq.) that "instead of a great authority, he had found countless authorities and mini-authorities, instead of *one* science which could have been the authority, numerous sciences, whose representatives opposed and degraded each other with exasperation."
2. Paul Plaut, "Prinzipien und Methoden der Kriegspsychologie," in *Handbuch der biologischen Arbeitsmethoden*, ed. Emil Abderhalden (686. Abt. VI: Methoden der experimentellen Psychologie, part C) (Berlin, 1928).
3. Eckart Scheerer, "Kämpfer des Wortes: Die Ideologie deutscher Psychologen im Ersten Weltkrieg und ihr Einfluß auf die Psychologie der Weimarer Zeit," *Psychologie und Geschichte* 1, no. 3 (1989): 12–22, here 13 et seq. Cf. on this question also Peter Riedesser and Axel Verderber, *Aufrüstung der Seelen: Militärpsychiatrie und Militärpsychologie in Deutschland und Amerika* (Freiburg im Breisgau, 1985), 59–62.
4. For a more detailed description of these developments: Mitchell G. Ash and Ulfried Geuter, eds., *Geschichte der deutschen Psychologie im 20. Jahrhundert: Ein Überblick* (Opladen, 1985), 45–82.
5. See Paul Plaut, "Psychographie des Kriegers," in *Beihefte zur Zeitschrift für angewandte Psychologie* 21, ed. William Stern and Otto Lipmann (Leipzig, 1920), 1–123 (in the following abbreviated PdK); questionnaire "On the Psychography of the Warrior," here 111–18.
6. George L. Mosse, "The Jews and the German War Experience 1914–1918," in *The Leo Baeck Memorial Lecture* 21 (New York, 1977), 1–27, here 15.
7. Ibid., 25.
8. Stern noted in a letter of December 1915 to the Freiburg philosopher Jonas Cohn: "[Here] a Jew has never been replaced by a Jew; the Univ. Wroclaw, which when I arrived had 5 Jew. ordinaries, has since been systematically *entjudet* [being freed from Jews]." The non-religious Stern rejected the proposal of his colleagues in Wroclaw to be baptized in order to get a permanent position. See Helmut E. Lück and Dieter-Jürgen Löwisch,

eds., *Der Briefwechsel zwischen William Stern und Jonas Cohn: Dokumente einer Freundschaft zwischen zwei Wissenschaftlern* (Beiträge zur Geschichte der Psychologie, 7) (Frankfurt/Main, 1994), 95; Eva Michaelis-Stern, "Erinnerungen an meine Eltern," in *Über die verborgene Aktualität von William Stern*, ed. Werner Deutsch (Frankfurt/Main, 1991), 133–41, here 134.
 9. Gerald Bühring, *William Stern oder Streben nach Einheit* (Beiträge zur Geschichte der Psychologie, 13, ed. Helmut E. Lück) (Frankfurt/Main, 1996), 114.
10. For this translation, compare Barry A. Jackisch, *The Pan-German League and Radical Nationalist Politics in Interwar Germany, 1918–39* (London, 2016), 26, 209, 211.
11. James T. Lamiell, *William Stern (1871–1938): A Brief Introduction to His Life and Works* (Lengerich, 2010), 82.
12. Ibid., 15.
13. Quoted after Eva Michaelis-Stern, "William Stern 1871–1938: The Man and His Achievements," *Yearbook XVII of the Leo Baeck Institute* 17 (1972): 143–54, here 146.
14. Deutsch, *Über die verborgene Aktualität von William Stern*; Martin Tschechne, *William Stern* (Hamburg, 2010), 146 et seq.
15. William Stern, "Psychologische Begabungsforschung und Begabungsdiagnose," in *Aufstieg der Begabten*, ed. P. Petersen (Leipzig, 1916), 105–20; also Madison Bentley, "Individual Psychology and Psychological Varieties," *The American Journal of Psychology* 52, no. 2 (April 1939): 300–301.
16. Dirk Brietzke, "William Stern," in *Hamburgisches Biografie-Personenlexikon*, vol. 2, ed. Franklin Kopitzsch and Dirk Brietzke (Göttingen, 2003), 406–8.
17. Lothar Sprung and Rudi Brandt, "Otto Lipmann und die Anfänge der angewandten Psychologie in Berlin," in *Zur Geschichte der Psychologie in Berlin*, ed. Lothar Sprung and Wolfgang Schönpflug (Frankfurt/Main, 2003 [1992]), 347 et seq.
18. J. B. Miner, "Dr. Lipmann's Laboratory of Applied Psychology," *Science, New Series* 56, no. 1446 (15 September 1922): 310 et seq.
19. Otto Lipmann, *Leistungsfähigkeit und Selbstbeanspruchung: Eine psychologische Betrachtung* (Leipzig, 1932).
20. See the obituary by William Stern: "Otto Lipmann: 1880–1933," *The American Journal of Psychology* 46, no. 1 (January 1934): 153 et seq.
21. Although Stern wrote in a letter to Cohn as well as in public obituaries about a heart attack, it can be assumed that Lipmann committed suicide; cf. a personal announcement by Eva Michaelis-Stern, in the year 1988, Sprung an Brandt, "Otto Lipmann und die Anfänge der angewandten Psychologie," 363. Also: Stern, "Otto Lipmann: 1880–1933," 153n1.
22. Plaut, "On the Psychography of the Warrior," 111–18.
23. Ulfried Geuter, "Polemos panton pater: Militär und Psychologie im Deutschen Reich 1914–1945," in Ash and Geuter, *Geschichte der deutschen Psychologie*, 146–71, here 149 et seq.
24. Franz Janssen, "Psychologie und Militär," *Zeitschrift für pädagogische Psychologie und Jugendkunde* 18, no. 2 (1917): 97–109; see also 97n1.

25. Ibid., 103, 109.
26. Ibid., 108.
27. Gerald Bühring psychologically explains Stern's commitment as follows: "[Stern] is subject to a far higher cultural adjustment pressure due to his Jewish inferiority feelings than the average German, which he tries to compensate by overidentification, that means he 'plays' the patriot and presents himself more German than German." See Bühring, *William Stern oder Streben nach Einheit*, 111. This compensatory argument is often part of the retrospective assessment of the motivation and behavior of Jewish scholars of this period. However, it is worth discussing.
28. Otto Lipmann, *Die psychische Eignung der Funkentelegraphisten: Programm einer analytischen Prüfungsmethode und Bericht über eine Experimentaluntersuchung* (Schriften zur Psychologie der Berufseignung und des Wirtschaftslebens 9, ed. Otto Lipmann and William Stern) (Leipzig, 1919).
29. William Stern, "Notwendigkeiten und Möglichkeiten der Kriegsverletztenpädagogik," *Zeitschrift für pädagogische Psychiatrie und experimentelle Pädagogik* XVII (1916): 208–14, here 208.
30. Lück and Löwisch, *Der Briefwechsel zwischen William Stern und Jonas Cohn*, 92 et seq.
31. Bühring, *William Stern oder Streben nach Einheit*, 99.
32. William Stern, *Jugendliches Seelenleben und Krieg: Materialien und Berichte*, supplement 12 [*Beiheft*] of *Zeitschrift für angewandte Psychologie und psychologische Sammelforschung* (1915).
33. William Stern, *Die Jugendkunde als Kulturforschung: Mit besond. Berücks. d. Begabungsproblems* (Leipzig, 1916), 17.
34. The material of the survey is now regarded as missing, although some survived the censorship (in the following abbreviated *InstAngPs*). Cf. Bernd Ulrich, *Die Augenzeugen: Deutsche Feldpostbriefe in Kriegs- und Nachkriegszeit, 1914–1933* (Essen, 1997), 295n236.
35. Julia B. Köhne, *Kriegshysteriker: Strategische Bilder und mediale Techniken militärpsychiatrischen Wissens, 1914–1920* (Husum, 2009). See Hans-Georg Hofer on the traditional association of "Jews" and "nervousness," in "Juden und 'Nervosität'," in *Jüdische Identitäten: Einblicke in die Bewusstseinslandschaft des österreichischen Judentums*, ed. Klaus Hödl (Innsbruck, 2000), 95–120.
36. I would like to thank the Jewish Museum Berlin Foundation, and especially the *Sammlung Paul Plaut*, for their courtesy in giving the printing permission for the photographs and documents on Plaut included in the present chapter. See *Sammlung Paul Plaut*, convolute 217, inventory number: 2009/2/1–283, BID/–338/0, ca. 1890–1990. Here 2009/2/1–189, 190.
37. In PdK, Plaut depreciates the psychological effect of war medals which, at the beginning of the war, had been a traditional "symbol of the war experience in oneself." Due to bureaucracy and obscure ways of distributing it, in the end, it would have been no more than a "paper receipt" saying that the one awarded had been in the war (PdK 62).
38. Jewish Museum Berlin Foundation, *Sammlung Paul Plaut*, convolute 217, folder 4: "Korrespondenz; Militär," inventory number: 2009/2/188.
39. Cf. Ulrich, *Die Augenzeugen*, 294 et seq., footnote 234.

40. Jewish Museum Berlin Foundation, *Sammlung Paul Plaut*, convolute 217, folder 4: "Korrespondenz; Militär," inventory number: 2009/2/191, 192.
41. Cf. Plaut's doctor certificate, Jewish Museum Berlin Foundation, *Sammlung Paul Plaut*, convolute 217, folder 5, inventory number: 2009/2/193.
42. Cf. professional certificate, Jewish Museum Berlin Foundation, *Sammlung Paul Plaut*, convolute 217, folder 5, inventory number: 2009/2/195.
43. Plaut, "Prinzipien und Methoden der Kriegspsychologie," 684.
44. Otto Lipmann and Paul Plaut, eds., *Die Lüge in psychologischer, philosophischer, juristischer, pädagogischer etc. Betrachtung* (Leipzig, 1927).
45. Paul Plaut, *Psychologie der produktiven Persönlichkeit* (Stuttgart, 1929).
46. Among other writings, Paul Plaut, "Psychologische Gutachten in Strafprozessen: Aktenmäßig dargestellt," *Zeitschrift für angewandte Psychologie* VI, supp. 65 [*Beiheft*], ed. William Stern and Otto Lipmann (1932).
47. Cf. obituary for Paul Plaut, M.D., Ph.D. in *British Medical Journal*, 19 March 1960, 884; see Jewish Museum Berlin Foundation, *Sammlung Paul Plaut*, convolute 217, folder 7, inventory number: 2009/2/221.
48. Cf. Bernd Ulrich, "Paul Plaut: Psychologie zwischen den Kriegen," in *Die Weimarer Republik zwischen Metropole und Provinz: Intellektuellendiskurse zur politischen Kultur*, ed. Wolfgang Bialas et al. (Weimar, 1996), 97–109. And: Paul Plaut, *Der Sexualverbrecher und seine Persönlichkeit* (Stuttgart, F. Enke, 1960).
49. Max Margulies, "Zur Technik psychologischer Analyse," *Zeitschrift für die gesamte Neurologie und Psychiatrie/Originalien* 45, ed. O. Foerster, R. Gaupp, and W. Spielmeyer (1919 [1918]): 413–23.
50. Ibid., 413 et seq.
51. James Lewin, "Das Hysterie-Problem," *Monatsschrift für Psychiatrie und Neurologie* XLVIII, ed. Karl Bonhoeffer (1920): 204–26, here 207.
52. Margulies "Zur Technik psychologischer Analyse," 414.
53. Mitchell G. Ash, "Die experimentelle Psychologie an den deutschsprachigen Universitäten von der Wilhelminischen Zeit bis zum Nationalsozialismus," in Ash and Geuter, *Geschichte der deutschen Psychologie*, 45–82, here 45.
54. Irmingard Staeuble, "'Psychologie im Dienst praktischer Kulturaufgaben': Zur Realisierung von William Sterns Programm 1903–1933," in *Psychologiegeschichte heute*, ed. Angela Schorr and E. G. Wehner (Göttingen, 1990), 164–73.
55. Cf. Plaut, "Prinzipien und Methoden der Kriegspsychologie," 625n1: "This questionnaire ... was elaborated and sent. ... Only a few sheets were executed. We have edited the material at that time ...." And ibid., 631.
56. A few years later, Plaut published a further contribution on this topic: "Prinzipien und Methoden der Kriegspsychologie," 621–87.
57. In the later essay from 1928, "Prinzipien und Methoden der Kriegspsychologie," Plaut criticized this psychographical approach. Above all, he regarded the "postulated" sample responses given in the questionnaire as suggestive and, in some cases, as influencing the spontaneity and authenticity of the answers. For this reason, the interviewee would not give an insight into his own unique psyche, but rather artificially immerses

himself in the situation of being questioned (Plaut, "Prinzipien und Methoden der Kriegspsychologie," 631 et seq.).
58. Plaut considers this "enthusiasm" for the alleged monumentality and incomprehensibility of the war, not just as "acquired and officially forced on" but as a product of mass suggestibility and something that still characterized the beginning of the war in 1914, indeed "stigmatized" it (PdK 7).
59. Ulrich, *Die Augenzeugen*, 301.
60. Otto Binswanger, *Die seelischen Wirkungen des Krieges* (Der deutsche Krieg. Politische Flugschriften 12) (Stuttgart, 1914).
61. August Messer, *Zur Psychologie des Krieges* (Berlin, 1915).
62. Max Dessoir, *Kriegspsychologische Betrachtungen* (Zwischen Krieg und Frieden 37) (Leipzig, 1916).
63. Robert Sommer, *Krieg und Seelenleben* (Gießen, 1916).
64. Philipp Stein, *Der Soldat im Stellungskampf: Psychologisch-militärische Betrachtungen in Anlehnung an Erich Everths "Die Seele des Soldaten im Felde"* (Berlin, 1917).
65. Erich Everth, *Von der Seele des Soldaten im Felde: Bemerkungen eines Kriegsteilnehmers* (Tat-Flugschriften 10) (Jena, 1915).
66. Ibid., 1, 3.
67. Ibid., 34 et seq.
68. Elsewhere, Plaut speaks of the falsifying, strongly discoloring effect of temporal distance to war experiences (exaggerations, constructions, combinations). Cf. Plaut, "Prinzipien und Methoden der Kriegspsychologie," 645.
69. Plaut, "Prinzipien und Methoden der Kriegspsychologie," 683 et seq.
70. Gustave Le Bon, *Psychologie der Massen* [*Psychologie des foules*, 1895] (Leipzig, 1932), 12.
71. See the investigation on the revolution of 1848: Ute Gerhard, "Die Masse als Weib: Kollektivsymbolische Verfahren als Strategien des politischen und literarischen Diskurses im 19. Jahrhundert," in *Argument-Sonderband 172: Frauen—Literatur—Politik*, ed. Annegret Pelz et al. (Hamburg, 1988), 145–53.
72. Le Bon (1908), *Psychologie der Massen*, 55 et seq., quoted after Karen J. Kenkel, "Das Gesicht der Masse: Soziologische Visionen," in *Gesichter der Weimarer Republik: Eine physiognomische Kulturgeschichte*, ed. Claudia Schmölders and Sander Gilman (Cologne, 2000), 218.
73. Karl Bonhoeffer, "Über die Bedeutung der Kriegserfahrungen für die allgemeine Psychopathologie und Ätiologie der Geisteskrankheiten," in *Handbuch der ärztlichen Erfahrungen im Weltkriege 1914/1918*, vol. 4, *Geistes- und Nervenkrankheiten*, ed. Otto von Schjering (Leipzig, 1922), 1–44, here 10.
74. Hermann Pörzgen, *Theater ohne Frau: Das Bühnenleben der kriegsgefangenen Deutschen 1914–1920* (Königsberg, 1933); Martin Baumeister, *Kriegstheater: Großstadt, Front und Massenkultur 1914–1918* (Essen, 2005).
75. Cf. Julia B. Köhne and Britta Lange, "Mit Geschlechterrollen spielen: Die Illusionsmaschine Damenimitation in Front- und Gefangenentheatern des Ersten Weltkriegs," in *MEIN KAMERAD—DIE DIVA: Theater an der*

Front und in Gefangenenlagern des Ersten Weltkriegs, ed. Julia B. Köhne, Britta Lange, and Anke Vetter (Munich, 2014), 25–41.
76. PdK 70 et seq., quoted after Erwin von Mattanovich, Mut und Todesverachtung (Graz, 1915).
77. G. Stanley Hall, "Some Relations between the War and Psychology." *The American Journal of Psychology* 30, no. 2 (1919): 211–23.
78. Cf. Jewish Museum Berlin Foundation, *Sammlung Paul Plaut*, convolute 217, folder 5, inventory number: 2009/2/193–213; 215–17.
79. Mosse, "The Jews and the German War Experience," 5.
80. Ibid., 5–6.
81. Ernst Jünger, *In Stahlgewittern* (Stuttgart, 1990 [1929]), 5.

Bibliography

Archival Sources

Jewish Museum Berlin Foundation, *Sammlung Paul Plaut*, convolute 217, folder 4: "Korrespondenz; Militär," inventory numbers: 2009/2/188; 2009/2/1–189; 2009/2/191; 2009/2/193; 2009/2/195; 2009/2/193–213; 2009/2/221; 2009/2/1–283.

Printed Sources

Ash, Mitchell G. "Die experimentelle Psychologie an den deutschsprachigen Universitäten von der Wilhelminischen Zeit bis zum Nationalsozialismus." In *Geschichte der deutschen Psychologie im 20. Jahrhundert: Ein Überblick*, edited by Mitchell Ash and Ulfried Geuter, 45–82. Opladen: Westdeutscher Verlag, 1985.
Ash, Mitchell, and Ulfried Geuter, eds. *Geschichte der deutschen Psychologie im 20. Jahrhundert: Ein Überblick*. Opladen: Westdeutscher Verlag, 1985.
Baumeister, Martin. *Kriegstheater: Großstadt, Front und Massenkultur 1914–1918*. Essen: Klartext-Verlag, 2005.
Bentley, Madison. "Individual Psychology and Psychological Varieties." *The American Journal of Psychology* 52, no. 2 (April 1939): 300–301.
Binswanger, Otto. *Die seelischen Wirkungen des Krieges*. Der deutsche Krieg. Politische Flugschriften 12. Stuttgart: Deutsche Verl.-Anst., 1914.
Bonhoeffer, Karl. "Über die Bedeutung der Kriegserfahrungen für die allgemeine Psychopathologie und Ätiologie der Geisteskrankheiten." In *Handbuch der ärztlichen Erfahrungen im Weltkriege 1914/1918*, vol. 4, *Geistes- und Nervenkrankheiten*, edited by Otto von Schjering, 1–44. Leipzig: Barth, 1922.
Brietzke, Dirk. "William Stern." In *Hamburgisches Biografie-Personenlexikon*, vol. 2, edited by Franklin Kopitzsch and Dirk Brietzke, 406–8. Göttingen: Christians, 2003.
Bühring, Gerald. *William Stern oder Streben nach Einheit*. Beiträge zur Geschichte der Psychologie, vol. 13, edited by Helmut E. Lück. Frankfurt/Main: Lang, 1996.

Dessoir, Max. *Kriegspsychologische Betrachtungen*. Zwischen Krieg und Frieden 37. Leipzig: Hirzel, 1916.
Deutsch, Werner, ed. *Über die verborgene Aktualität von William Stern*. Frankfurt/Main: Lang, 1991.
Everth, Erich. *Von der Seele des Soldaten im Felde: Bemerkungen eines Kriegsteilnehmers*. Tat-Flugschriften 10. Jena: Diederichs, 1915.
Gerhard, Ute. "Die Masse als Weib: Kollektivsymbolische Verfahren als Strategien des politischen und literarischen Diskurses im 19. Jahrhundert." In *Argument-Sonderband 172: Frauen—Literatur—Politik*, edited by Annegret Pelz et al., 145–53. Hamburg: Argument, 1988.
Geuter, Ulfried. "Polemos panton pater: Militär und Psychologie im Deutschen Reich 1914–1945." In *Geschichte der deutschen Psychologie im 20. Jahrhundert: Ein Überblick*, edited by Mitchell Ash and Ulfried Geuter, 146–71. Opladen: Westdeutscher Verlag, 1985.
Hall, G. Stanley. "Some Relations between the War and Psychology." *The American Journal of Psychology* 30, no. 2 (1919): 211–23.
Hofer, Hans-Georg. "Juden und 'Nervosität'." In *Jüdische Identitäten: Einblicke in die Bewusstseinslandschaft des österreichischen Judentums*, edited by Klaus Hödl, 95–120. Innsbruck: Studienverlag, 2000.
Jackisch, Barry A. *The Pan-German League and Radical Nationalist Politics in Interwar Germany, 1918–39*. London: Routledge, 2016.
Janssen, Franz. "Psychologie und Militär." *Zeitschrift für pädagogische Psychologie und Jugendkunde* 18, no. 2 (1917): 97–109.
Jünger, Ernst. *In Stahlgewittern*. Stuttgart: Klett-Cotta, 1990 [1929].
Kenkel, Karen J. "Das Gesicht der Masse: Soziologische Visionen." In *Gesichter der Weimarer Republik: Eine physiognomische Kulturgeschichte*, edited by Claudia Schmölders and Sander Gilman, 206–77. Cologne: DuMont, 2000.
Köhne, Julia B. *Kriegshysteriker: Strategische Bilder und mediale Techniken militärpsychiatrischen Wissens, 1914–1920*. Husum: Matthiesen, 2009.
———. "Papierne Psychen: Zur Psychographie des Frontsoldaten nach Paul Plaut." In *Krieg! Juden zwischen den Fronten 1914–1918*, edited by Julia B. Köhne and Ulrike Heikaus, 67–104. Berlin: Hentrich und Hentrich, 2014.
Köhne, Julia B., and Britta Lange. "Mit Geschlechterrollen spielen: Die Illusionsmaschine Damenimitation in Front- und Gefangenentheatern des Ersten Weltkriegs." In *MEIN KAMERAD—DIE DIVA: Theater an der Front und in Gefangenenlagern des Ersten Weltkriegs*, edited by Julia B. Köhne, Britta Lange, and Anke Vetter, 25–41. Munich: edition text + kritik, 2014.
Lamiell, James T. *William Stern (1871–1938): A Brief Introduction to His Life and Works*. Lengerich: Pabst Science Publ., 2010.
Le Bon, Gustave. *Psychologie der Massen* [*Psychologie des foule*, 1895]. Leipzig: Kröner, 1932.
Lewin, James. "Das Hysterie-Problem." *Monatsschrift für Psychiatrie und Neurologie* XLVIII, edited by Karl Bonhoeffer (1920): 204–26.
Lipmann, Otto. *Leistungsfähigkeit und Selbstbeanspruchung: Eine psychologische Betrachtung*. Leipzig: Barth, 1932.

———. *Die psychische Eignung der Funkentelegraphisten: Programm einer analytischen Prüfungsmethode und Bericht über eine Experimentaluntersuchung.* Schriften zur Psychologie der Berufseignung und des Wirtschaftslebens 9, edited by Otto Lipmann and William Stern. Leipzig: Barth, 1919.

Lipmann, Otto, and Paul Plaut, eds. *Die Lüge in psychologischer, philosophischer, juristischer, pädagogischer etc. Betrachtung.* Leipzig: Barth, 1927.

Lück, Helmut E., and Dieter-Jürgen Löwisch, eds. *Der Briefwechsel zwischen William Stern und Jonas Cohn: Dokumente einer Freundschaft zwischen zwei Wissenschaftlern.* Beiträge zur Geschichte der Psychologie, 7. Frankfurt/Main: Lang, 1994.

Margulies, Max. "Zur Technik psychologischer Analyse." *Zeitschrift für die gesamte Neurologie und Psychiatrie/Originalien* 45, edited by O. Foerster, R. Gaupp, and W. Spielmeyer (1919 [1918]): 413–23.

Mattanovich, Erwin von. *Mut und Todesverachtung.* Graz: Selbstverlag H. Böhm, 1915.

Messer, August. *Zur Psychologie des Krieges.* Berlin: Stilke, 1915.

Michaelis-Stern, Eva. "Erinnerungen an meine Eltern." In *Über die verborgene Aktualität von William Stern,* edited by Werner Deutsch, 133–41. Frankfurt/Main: Lang, 1991.

———. "William Stern 1871–1938: The Man and His Achievements." *Yearbook XVII of the Leo Baeck Institute* 17 (1972): 143–54.

Miner, J. B. "Dr. Lipmann's Laboratory of Applied Psychology." *Science, New Series* 56, no. 1446 (15 September 1922): 310–11.

Mosse, George L. "The Jews and the German War Experience 1914–1918." In *The Leo Baeck Memorial Lecture* 21, 1–27. New York: Leo Baeck Institute, 1977.

Plaut, Paul. *Der Sexualverbrecher und seine Persönlichkeit.* Stuttgart: F. Enke, 1960.

———."Prinzipien und Methoden der Kriegspsychologie." In *Handbuch der biologischen Arbeitsmethoden,* edited by Emil Abderhalden (686. Abt. VI: Methoden der experimentellen Psychologie, part C). Berlin: Urban & Schwarzenberg, 1928.

———. "Psychographie des Kriegers." In *Beihefte zur Zeitschrift für angewandte Psychologie* 21, edited by William Stern and Otto Lipmann, 1–123. Leipzig: Johann Ambrosius Barth, 1920.

———. *Psychologie der produktiven Persönlichkeit,* Stuttgart: F. Enke, 1929.

———. "Psychologische Gutachten in Strafprozessen: Aktenmäßig dargestellt." *Zeitschrift für angewandte Psychologie* VI, supp. 65 [*Beiheft*], edited by William Stern and Otto Lipmann (1932).

Pörzgen, Hermann. *Theater ohne Frau: Das Bühnenleben der kriegsgefangenen Deutschen 1914–1920.* Königsberg: Ost-Europa-Verlag, 1933.

Riedesser, Peter, and Axel Verderber. *Aufrüstung der Seelen: Militärpsychiatrie und Militärpsychologie in Deutschland und Amerika.* Freiburg im Breisgau: Dreisam, 1985.

Scheerer, Eckart. "Kämpfer des Wortes: Die Ideologie deutscher Psychologen im Ersten Weltkrieg und ihr Einfluß auf die Psychologie der Weimarer Zeit." *Psychologie und Geschichte* 1, no. 3 (1989): 12–22.

Sommer, Robert. *Krieg und Seelenleben.* Gießen: Nemnich, 1916.

Sprung, Lothar, and Rudi Brandt. "Otto Lipmann und die Anfänge der angewandten Psychologie in Berlin." In *Zur Geschichte der Psychologie in Berlin*, edited by Lothar Sprung and Wolfgang Schönpflug, 347 et seq. Frankfurt/Main: Lang, 2003 [1992].

Staeuble, Irmingard. "'Psychologie im Dienst praktischer Kulturaufgaben': Zur Realisierung von William Sterns Programm 1903–1933." In *Psychologiegeschichte heute*, edited by Angela Schorr and E. G. Wehner, 164–73. Göttingen: Verlag für Psychologie Hogrefe, 1990.

Stein, Philipp. *Der Soldat im Stellungskampf: Psychologisch-militärische Betrachtungen in Anlehnung an Erich Everths "Die Seele des Soldaten im Felde"*. Berlin: Eisenschmidt, 1917.

Stern, William. *Die Jugendkunde als Kulturforschung: Mit besond. Berücks. d. Begabungsproblems*. Leipzig: Quelle & Meyer, 1916.

———. *Jugendliches Seelenleben und Krieg: Materialien und Berichte*, supplement 12 [*Beiheft*] of *Zeitschrift für angewandte Psychologie und psychologische Sammelforschung* (1915).

———. "Notwendigkeiten und Möglichkeiten der Kriegsverletztenpädagogik." *Zeitschrift für pädagogische Psychiatrie und experimentelle Pädagogik* XVII (1916): 208–14.

———. "Otto Lipmann: 1880–1933." *The American Journal of Psychology* 46, no. 1 (January 1934): 153–54.

———. "Psychologische Begabungsforschung und Begabungsdiagnose." In *Aufstieg der Begabten*, edited by P. Petersen, 105–20. Leipzig: Teubner, 1916.

Tschechne, Martin. *William Stern*. Hamburg: Ellert & Richter, 2010.

Ulrich, Bernd. *Die Augenzeugen: Deutsche Feldpostbriefe in Kriegs- und Nachkriegszeit, 1914–1933*. Essen: Klartext, 1997.

———. "Paul Plaut: Psychologie zwischen den Kriegen." In *Die Weimarer Republik zwischen Metropole und Provinz: Intellektuellendiskurse zur politischen Kultur*, edited by Wolfgang Bialas et al., 97–109. Weimar: Böhlau, 1996.

12

NARRATIVE NEGOTIATIONS
Interpreting the Cultural Position of Jews in National(social)ist War Narratives from 1914 to 1945

Florian Brückner

In many belligerent European nations, the battle for territorial and economic control that broke out in 1914 was not considered to be the "seminal catastrophe." Instead—as the often-used metaphor of the time suggests—it was seen as a cleansing "storm"[1] that broke out over an apparently decadent continent.[2] In Germany in particular, which imagined itself as "encircled" by the Triple Entente nations of England, Russia, and France, the outbreak of hostilities was seen as an opportunity to rally the nation together. Amid the so-called "spirit of August 1914," it was widely believed that the German Empire stood in solidarity across social classes, political affiliations, and backgrounds in order to fight the "defensive war" that was forced upon it.[3] This struggle against a "world of enemies" (Kaiser Wilhelm II) enabled religious minorities and politically marginalized groups, above all through public demonstrations of patriotism and performance of duty, to unite under the banner of the German nation.[4] Included in this cohort was the minority Catholic community, which, since the unification of the empire in 1870/71 and Bismarck's *Kulturkampf* (culture struggle) of the 1870s, had carried the stigma of being "enemies of the nation." Also included were the Social Democrats, who, although they constituted the political majority long before the First World War, had been suppressed by Bismarck's anti-socialist laws. Finally, there was the Jewish religious community, which had been socially, economically, and religiously marginalized since the Middle Ages, and whose sense of national belonging to the "German fatherland" had been under scrutiny since the nineteenth century. Like the Social Democrats, Jews were suspected of being in alliance with a nationless and classless internationalism and therefore deemed enemies of nationalist ideology.[5] At the same time, they were accused of being beholden to orthodox religious principles, both of which were in opposition to a conservative-nationalist worldview.[6] The question that therefore emerges, in the context of the socially integrative influence of the "Great War," is whether and to what degree Jews were integrated into the dominant nationalist narrative of the war, which was oriented towards the forging of a so-called "front community."

This chapter uses the conservative-nationalist war novel as a means for exploring the reconstruction of these (dis)integrative forces. War novels are crucial in this respect, as they formed one of the most important sites of memory through which German postwar society interpreted the defeat of 1918. Between 1918 and 1928, about 130 new titles appeared each year. The period from 1927 to 1928 in particular witnessed a verifiable boom, with pacifist-oriented war novels by Arnold Zweig (*The Case of Sergeant Grischa*, 1927), Ludwig Renn (*War*, 1928), and Erich Maria Remarque (*All Quiet on the Western Front*, 1928/29). Between 1929 and 1933, another 1,100 titles appeared, which amounted on average to 250 works per year, more than double the number that had been published in the previous years.[7]

The majority of war novels, like the famous works of Zweig, Renn, or Remarque, were not published by liberal, democratic, or left-leaning writers, but rather by conservative-nationalists who set out to defend Germany's honor against the pacifistic literature that "drained victims of meaning."[8] The watershed year 1933 saw works with a nationalistic bent on the war assert themselves more forcefully. There were countless new editions of these until 1939; many also became part of official school curricula, and therefore continued to reach an ever-wider audience.[9] Conservative war fiction not only offered a nationalistic narrative but did so in an aesthetic medium that reinforced traditional power relations; here it was decided who belonged to the in-group, who had earned their place in the "fatherland," and who was excluded. Thus, this chapter focuses on the perspective of the dominant conservative-nationalist narrative to put forth the question: to what extent did non-Jewish, conservative-nationalist authors include or exclude Jews in their literary interpretations of the First World War?

Further questions over the possible inclusion or absence of philo- or antisemitic narrative patterns are raised by the fact that from 1941 onwards, Jews were targeted for genocide, by which time a foundation of core myths and literary interpretations of the war had been delivered.[10] It is important to ask whether and to what extent National Socialists appropriated this narrative by means of aesthetic strategies, and modified it after 1933 for the purpose of indoctrinating the German population for war. Or did this narrative remain intact by virtue of the Nazis' consensus-building power—and the symbolic image of a "national community" (*Volksgemeinschaft*)—which included all social classes and professions who had contributed culturally and psychologically to the rise of National Socialism during the Weimar Republic? This chapter argues that during the 1920s and early 1930s the dominant conservative narrative of the First World War served numerous nationalist and militaristic narrative strands, but largely ignored the integration of racist and, above all, antisemitic elements. This master narrative, which initially emerged during the Weimar Republic, persisted into the Nazi era. It was only at the beginning of the Second World War that the National Socialists introduced the image of the "Jewish-Bolshevik" enemy, which from that point on served to establish an unambiguous link between Jews and communists.

Between Participation and Defamation: Jews during the War Years, 1914–18

Despite small efforts and progress towards Jewish integration during the liberal atmosphere of the nineteenth century, antisemitic sentiments remained an integral part of German society in the years leading up to 1914.[11] The outbreak of the First World War initially strengthened mechanisms for integration, which emerged out of the nationally minded bourgeoisie's identity-based understanding of itself, and which was only strengthened by upper-middle-class Jews who were socialized in a milieu that emphasized career competition, strategies for pursuing identities as self-made individuals, religious differences of faith, and above all economic circles that promoted class competition.[12] Especially in the years of chronic conflict during the world wars, German Jews served as an excellent propagandistic outlet for political and military elites who wanted to distract the population from their own problems and failures. The most influential *völkisch*-nationalist association, the Pan-German League (Alldeutscher Verband), for example, exercised considerable influence in the German High Command during the war years, and scapegoated Jews as either defeatist pacifists or capitalist war profiteers. This association was one of the first during the war years to spread the later infamous "stab-in-the-back" legend (*Dolchstoßlegende*) that accused Jews of being responsible for the defeat.[13]

Despite their readiness to sacrifice their lives for the nation, Jews encountered, as they had in the civilian world, a glass ceiling in their opportunities for military promotion. Only rarely (2.5 percent) did German Jews attain officers' rank.[14] In the monarchist officer corps, in particular, populated by the Prussian aristocracy, Jews were regarded as "enemies of the nation" (*Reichsfeinde*) who threatened to "undermine" fighting morale in the front lines, or as "shirkers" who avoided their military duty.[15] These tensions resulted in the infamous antisemitic measure in 1916, when a state-ordered "Jewish census" (*Judenzählung*) was carried out in the army.[16] Despite the result of this discriminatory order proving that as many German Jews as non-Jews had been conscripted for military service, the results were kept secret even after the war, and this state-initiated branding intensified public mistrust of Jews even further.[17]

A final stroke against any hope of social integration and recognition of German citizens of Jewish faith was the already mentioned "stab-in-the-back" legend used to explain Germany's defeat. It labeled social democratic and communist forces—whom the *völkisch*, Pan-German circles in particular identified as Jews—as the main culprits of military failure, as they had "stabbed" the fighting troops, who were allegedly on the brink of victory, "in the back" through strikes and demonstrations that triggered the November Revolution of 1918/19.[18] Paul von Hindenburg, field marshal (*Generalfeldmarschall*) during the war, and from 1925 president (*Reichspräsident*) of the Weimar Republic, propagated this myth, which had already been circulated by the Pan-German League during the war. In November 1919, during the parliamentary investigations into the question of responsibility for Germany's defeat, Hindenburg packaged it into the metaphorical pseudo-parable of the "stab-in-the-back," according to which the war had not been lost militarily against the Entente, but the German army had been betrayed by the November revolutionaries on the home front.[19] Those disappointed by the outcome of the war spread these claims throughout the 1920s with the aim of absolving the old political order of any responsibility, attributing it instead to backers of the detested parliamentary system, whose leaders, including prominent Jews like Walther Rathenau, were regarded by the political right as figures of hate.

Jews in the Literary-Imagined "Front Community", 1918–33

It could well be presumed that the conservative-nationalists had prepared the way during the interwar period for an antisemitic interpretation of the First World War. But what actually constituted the essential core of Great War mythology formed in hindsight from 1933? Which topoi and interpretive strategies were implemented? And to what extent was antisemitism an integral or marginal component, and perhaps even a non-existent element in the articulation of the "stab-in-the-back" myth?

In addition to the numerous motifs, narrative strategies, and arguments, the content of nationalist-conservative war literature relied on a common focus: the realization of a "national community" (*Volksgemeinschaft*), which emerged from the spirit of the alleged "front community" of 1914–18. Going against the grain of Remarque, who depicted a generation destroyed by war in his famous novel *All Quiet on the Western Front*, writers such as Ernst Jünger (*In Stahlgewittern*, 1920) and Werner Beumelburg (*Gruppe Bosemüller*, 1930) led the field in offering a cultural leitmotif that claimed the "steel bath" of the war had strengthened the soldiers and welded the nation together. This militaristic view held that the creative forces of the war needed to be deployed in the service of the nation. They derived a vision of a future political order from the "front community" of the First World War, with a military hierarchy ranging from "leader" (*Führer*) to group, from command and obedience to the societal structures of a militarized "national community." These authors heaped literary praise on the politically privileged "Führer" as the voice of all German front soldiers.[20]

In the 1920s, the social and political utopia of a "national community" was by no means propagated solely by the National Socialists. In the summer days of 1914, solidarity, "community," and cohesion were, at least in the major cities, the patriotic words of the hour that crossed class lines.[21] In the context of this and the "August experience," especially in the eyes of political elites, the utopian goal of a "national community," which had been hotly debated since the *fin de siècle*, was given new impetus. From the right-wing conservative standpoint, the "national community" as a "leading concept in the critique of modernity" had been supported with the hope of re-establishing a unified order that would bury the individualistic values of the Enlightenment and "egoistical" liberalism.[22] In essence, it was an attempt to overcome social class division and snobbery through national cohesion. With the outbreak of the First World War in 1914, these imagined goals were given new life by the "August experience," which had been conjured up by the educated bourgeoisie.[23] Confronted by a nation "surrounded" by hostile powers, Germans stood united, shoulder to shoulder, across social classes, a feeling that was expressed in the speech of Kaiser

Wilhelm II in August 1914, in which the emperor famously remarked that from now on he no longer recognized political parties, but only Germans.[24]

In the 1920s, nationalist-conservatives and National Socialists alike, including Franz Schauwecker (*Aufbruch der Nation*, 1929), Josef Magnus Wehner (*Sieben vor Verdun*, 1930), Alfred Hein (*Eine Kompanie Soldaten in der Hölle von Verdun*, 1930), and Hans Zöberlein (*Der Glaube an Deutschland*, 1931), stylized the ideal of a "national community" that was to be created in the postwar period, in which the front soldier as political "leader" would play a decisive role in the rebirth of the nation.[25] Moreover, during the Weimar years the vision of a "national community" was articulated by both right- and left-wing parties, including the NSDAP and the Communist Party (KPD) as a sociopolitical goal, albeit with different political constitutions, for the future of the nation.[26] As a politically hybrid leitmotif during the Weimar Republic, especially on the political left, the "national community" could therefore also include Jews. A prime example where left-oriented war novelists could find a home was the war novel *Year 1902* (*Jahrgang 1902*, 1929), which reflected Ernst Glaeser's oscillation between the political left and right in the interwar period. In a scene from the communist phase of Glaeser's life, this pacifistic novel refers to a Jewish protagonist, the business owner Silberstein, who characterizes the Jewish people as an important part of the German nation: "It's war—no one looks over the shoulder at us—they all recognize us ... 'the Jews are also Germans,' the district representative [*Landrat*] said this morning ...."[27]

Another scene from *Year 1902* celebrated the "August experience" with the explicit inclusion of politically excluded groups, including workers and Jews, as in this excerpt:

> "Look at the people [*Volk*]," said the professor to my mother, "how enthusiastic and united they are. Does that not justify the war?" He gestured to the waiting room, which boomed with singing and loud conversations. People shouted "brother," although few knew each other, and they joined hands. There were many workers among them. You could recognize them by their caps. They came from Switzerland, from Italy, and from France, where they had worked on assembly lines. They moved from table to table and fraternized with the citizens who came out for fresh summer air. In one corner sat a man who looked Jewish and had two anxious daughters with him; he continued to pay for the workers' beer, and when they sang, he sang. "We are all brothers," cried the workers. The gentleman nodded enthusiastically and paid. "Is that not wonderful?" said the Professor, "all the opposites stand up!"[28]

Glaeser was supposed to emigrate from Germany in 1933, but he returned to the Reich in 1939 and was utilized by National Socialist propaganda as a model example of a "converted conservative."[29] However, such philosemitic passages tended to be characteristic of leftist war literature, whose conception of comradeship aimed at building an international alliance of war victims.[30] The realization of this concept was attempted, for example, by communist and social democratic authors, especially in their pronounced break from the bourgeoisie and the aristocracy, who had, in their view, been the originators and advocates of a war that did not build compromise between different social classes, but rather used workers as "cannon fodder" for imperialist purposes.[31]

At the same time, philosemitic passages, even in leftist-oriented war novels, were marginal, rather than central points and were often not the main drivers of these narratives. For example, this can be seen in the case of Arnold Zweig, the "full-blown Jew" as Kurt Tucholsky described him.[32] Zweig was intensely concerned with the life of the Jews living in the occupied territories on the Eastern Front. One of the protagonists in his 1927 novel *The Case of Sergeant Grischa* (*Der Streit um den Sergeanten Grischa*) was the court martial counselor Posnanski.[33] He tried in vain to save the life of Sergeant Grischa, a Russian soldier in captivity who had been sentenced to death. In the end, however, Zweig did not develop in *Grischa* a decisively philosemitic discursive product.

Even minor examples of Jewish life and soldiers' culture in the literary imagination came under attack from *völkisch*, nationalist-conservative, and National Socialist circles. In the literary landscape of the 1920s, antisemitic ideology was quickly implemented through racist defamation. This can be seen in the case of the Catholic-raised Erich Maria Remarque, whose major success *All Quiet on the Western Front* did not make any references to Judaism, and yet still became the target of attacks by right-wing groups. The National Socialist *Völkische Beobachter*, for example, sustained a smear campaign against Remarque. The newspaper claimed that the name Remarque was, in reality, an anonym of the Jewish name Kramer, and that his narrative represented the pacifistic ramblings of a "November criminal."[34] The book's distribution by the Jewish-owned Ullstein publishing house, as well as the filming of the work by the Jewish director Lewis Milestone and the Jewish producer Carl Laemmle in 1930, only added more fuel to the fire of such baseless accusations.

Remarque, on the other hand, responded to such conspiracy theories in his own way. In his sequel to *All Quiet on the Western Front*, the 1931 novel *The Road Back*, he had a Jewish protagonist, Max Weil, appear as a figure of suffering and a symbol of the failed democratic hopes after 1918.[35] He described Weil using the same Jewish stereotypes so often favored by National Socialist, *völkisch*, and antisemitic authors, especially in the journalistic circles. Weil, a member of a group of front soldiers, gradually comes to support a revolution, although not a communist one following the Soviet model, but rather a vision of a democratic republic. As an intellectual, Remarque describes him as "a quiet man who always sits around and reads books."[36] He is apparently a "man of the mind" (*Kopfmensch*), who thus makes a sharp contrast to the decisive and intuitive "man of action" (*Helden der Tat*), as right-wing authors used to describe German soldiers in anti-intellectual terms.[37] Together with his left-leaning comrades, Weil swore allegiance to the revolution, formed a soldiers' council with them, and assumed a leading role in their organization during the revolutionary uprisings.[38] Thus Remarque, from the point of view of nationalist authors and believers in the "November criminals," used the classical narrative of the alleged "stab-in-the-back" led by Jews.

Weil's antagonist was his company commander, *Oberleutnant* Heel, whom the author described as the typical supporter of the imperialist-militarist worldview, which was the basis for Wilhelmian Germany entering the war. The disillusionment with Germany's defeat made him seek revenge and he saw Weil as an enemy over the course of the novel.[39] Thus, at the height of revolutionary demonstrations raging in an unnamed city, the fatal meeting of the two figures takes place. Heel had assumed command in the city after the uprisings had failed. Attempts by the revolutionaries to win the soldiers over to the democratic revolution ended when Heel ordered his troops to open fire on the insurgents, and Weil was killed. Heel had not realized that members of his old company were among the insurgents, and therefore unknowingly shot a former comrade.[40] Weil's death was symbolic: the ideal of comradeship was, according to Remarque, extinguished along with the hopes of democracy.

Because of antisemitic accusations against Remarque, it could be presumed that National Socialist and conservative circles were engaged in the sensationalism of antisemitic narrative patterns, not only in public media debates but also in fictional war literature. On the basis of widely researched examples of war novels, however, it must be noted that antisemitic elements did not really play a central theme in decidedly nationalist-conservative or even National Socialist war literature of any type before 1933.[41] The reasons for this are, on the one hand, that not every nationalist-conservative author was necessarily antisemitic. It is true that antisemitic concepts, as has been shown, were a means for members of the bourgeoisie to distinguish themselves from Jews socially, culturally, and economically and that these concepts were deeply anchored in their Protestant and Catholic middle-class milieus. Nevertheless, since the granting of the freedom of religion by Frederick II, the principle of tolerance for other religions was not a secondary virtue, but a primary one, consistent with Prussian values.

An example of this attitude can be found in the case of Walter Bloem. With his 1912 trilogy on the Franco-Prussian War, *The Iron Year, People against People*, and *The Forge of the Future* (*Das eiserne Jahr, Volk wider Volk, Die Schmiede der Zukunft*), he had already become famous. In his war novel *Fraternity* (*Brüderlichkeit*, 1922), Bloem, who had seen and criticized the discrimination of Jews by the military hierarchy during the First World War, dealt with the conflict-ridden relationship between the conservative-nationalist bourgeoisie and Jews during the Weimar Republic.[42] In this novel, the author focused on antisemitic currents that were a driving force in academia.[43] In the most detailed terms, he described antisemitic animosities between different student groups. The heroic protagonist of the novel is Hans-Joachim, a member of a flight squadron. He assists an oppressed Jewish protagonist of the novel, who is ultimately murdered in an attack by *völkisch*-nationalists. Bloem represented Hans-Joachim as a nationalist, but in no case was he racist or antisemitic. The novel describes the origins of antisemitic ideology as well as alleged "blood" purity of the German people as inaccurate historical myths: "The antisemitism of our day is a medieval fossil. We must finally deal with the problem of the Jews, and we can do this only by means of clear and logical actions, not by noise and agitation and perpetuating untenable claims ... for Jews, who are of good will, who bear so much pain—who use all means to educate the ignorant about their Germanness—then, but only then, do we have the right and the duty to fight maliciousness by all means."[44]

In addition, the novel rejects as un-German the possibilities of pogroms as well as plans for expulsion and deportation that were discussed in antisemitic circles in the Weimar Republic. One reason for this is Walter Bloem's affinity with the Catholic teachings of Carl Sonnenschein, who, in the economically precarious 1920s, was actively engaged in the social welfare of academic circles and was also highly regarded in Jewish communities. However, the novel signaled the end of the literary career of Bloem, who, because of his affinity towards Jews, lost support from nationalist readers who believed in the "stab-in-the-back" myth.[45] During the Nazi era in particular, he lost an immense amount of influence because of his philosemitic attitude.

Another example is provided by Rudolf Binding, who had not actually been socialized in Prussian Protestantism, but who represented those members of the bourgeoisie repelled by vulgar antisemitism. For this reason, Binding was "of a more humane opinion when it came to the Jewish question."[46] In 1925, he published the book *Out of the War (Aus dem Kriege)*, in which he narrated his own experiences from his time as cavalry captain (*Rittmeister*) and staff officer during the war, glorifying the heroism of front soldiers. This was followed by his 1928 autobiography *Experienced Life (Erlebtes Leben)*, which was rife with anecdotes of the war told in a heroic style. His philosemitic nature was expressed in private life when he met Elisabeth Jungmann, the secretary of Gerhart Hauptmann, supported her, and spent his life with her until his death in 1938.

After 1933, tensions over the "Jewish question" led to problems between Binding and the National Socialist regime. Binding supported Fritz Walther (Friedrich) Bischoff and Ernst Hardt after they had been removed from their posts at a radio station because of their alleged Jewish background. In the poetry division of the Prussian Academy of Arts, Binding also fought against the deposition of his Jewish colleague, Alfred Mombert.[47] His efforts were unsuccessful, however. As a result, he experienced great difficulties with the Nazi regime, personal censorship, and a prohibition on his speeches. The fact that Binding was also surrounded by numerous Jews in his professional environment—such as his publishers Neumann and Oswalt, the owners of the well-established Rütten & Loening publishing house—was also not beneficial to his livelihood.

Many of the right-wing conservative war novels did not focus on the image of Jews as an "enemy" per se, but rather concentrated on national affiliations such as the "Tommy" or the "Frenchman." German nationalists saw democracies as political systems in cultural decline, according to the cyclical models of history developed by the influential Arthur Moeller van den Bruck or Oswald Spengler.[48] If racist antagonism manifested itself at all in these novels, it was mainly directed at the African colonial troops that France and Britain had used. It should be remembered that the stationing of black French troops in the Rhineland in 1919 was considered an affront to Germany, and nationalist authors did their part to shape the "image of a bestial black man."[49]

Considering the widespread antisemitism that prevailed in nationalist circles around Ernst Jünger,[50] and among influential leaders of the nationalistic veterans' association, the "Steel Helmet" (Stahlhelm—Bund der Frontsoldaten), the absence of antisemitic imagery in conservative war literature is quite surprising.[51] This can be explained, on the one hand, by the fact that many of the novels were set primarily during the great battles on the Western Front, in particular on the central sites of memory such as Ypres, Flanders, and, most importantly, Verdun. This included a deictic focus on the period 1914–17, a narrated time that resembled a heroic military epic and only rarely alluded to Germany's impending defeat, and therefore did not require an antisemitic-infused "stab-in-the-back" legend.

Instead of concentrating on permanent ascriptions of guilt to anyone responsible for defeat, many nationalist war writers described the events and places that were regarded as the "hours of birth" of a "new military man," forged in the "steel bath of war."[52] For this reason they largely avoided any mention of the "stab-in-the-back," which was destructive for hero-making, and instead focused on the creative forces of the war that were essential for the revival of the German nation. Despite the omission of the "stab-in-the-back" legend, they used numerous stylistic means, semantic fillers, and scenes with speech that evoked stress and traumatization, but above all, the message was that of the "silent heroism" of the "stoic front soldier," whose main burden was regarded as an altruistic self-awareness of sacrifice for the national community. For example, the wartime texts of the right-wing conservative writer Werner Beumelburg convey the horrors that they experienced.[53] The death of comrades was expressed in his works through paratactic, often elliptical sentences, or in overused instances of protagonists' speechlessness. Beumelburg (1899–1963), whose first war novels emerged between 1923 and 1928, included many scenes of fragmented speech, that is, paragraphs in which protagonists showed themselves unable to put into words the daily experienced horrors of war. For example, at roll call, Beumelburg described the daily list of the fallen at the front in minimalistic speech, without much moral and emotional upheaval: "'Dead ...' one responds, 'bomb shrapnel in the forehead.'"[54] Where sadness and pain threatened to take hold, semantic mechanisms of repression were used: "For a moment there is a silence that startles even the most jaded."[55] Another example: "But the ammunition drivers are seldom used to talking. They load their inventory and then make sure they get away. It is not a forest for storytelling. What should they report? Air attacks, heavy flak fire, exploded ammunition depots ... Is that even worth a conversation?"[56] Many characters appeared speechless in such scenes in which the author avoided coping in communicative and psychological terms. In *Flandern 1917*, a helper appeared in a bunker, "quite distracted, and does not say a word."[57] In fact, the author's unarticulated fears in the literary construction of the front often sent him into feverish dream-like scenes, which offered the protagonist a short-term escape from the war in order not to suffer terrible injuries in the fictional here and now.[58]

These representational techniques and the interpretative consequences of speechlessness were in no way an explicit attempt to exclude Jews from the war experience or to invoke the "stab-in-the-back" legend and the military defeat. Most of the right-wing conservative war novels dealt with the figure of the unknown front soldier, who could be any man, and thus any Jew. This concept, developed through literary-imagined scenes of traumatization, made it possible to glorify the figure of the front soldier as "man of action"—agile and religious but unspecified heroes, with whom even Jewish front soldiers could identify.

In addition, numerous militaristic—as well as pacifist—writers put their novels into a mode of presentation that had become paradigmatic from 1920 to 1930, as exemplified by Ernst Jünger's 1920 literary war diary *Storm of Steel (In Stahlgewittern)*.[59] This book stood out stylistically with a realistic narrative technique, which over the course of four years of brutal war broke away from heroic pathos to an expressionist glorification of combat. Post-1918 and "post-Jünger," in the wake of the terrible experiences of the war, anyone who still sang the patriotic war songs of the old Wilhelmian period, which had been paradigmatic for the flood of war literature published in August 1914, risked jeopardizing the popularity and success of their works.[60] Also important was the level of authenticity in the literary representation, which made it necessary, even in pro-war narratives, not to conceal the horrors of daily life at the front. The totally new dimensions of terror experienced in industrialized violence were instead used in such narratives to portray the heroic worth of the soldiers, and to treat the stressful conditions at the front in an even more brilliant light.

In order to achieve, on a literary level, this image of the hardened front soldier, and to describe the war as a phenomenon that recurs naturally, one that had to be prepared for, Jünger consistently refused to reflect on the political causes and social consequences of the war in *Storm of Steel*. For that reason, many of the cornerstones of the "stab-in-the-back" narrative, such as the Reichstag Peace Resolution of 1917, the January strikes and sailor strikes of 1918, the military defeat and the democratic revolution in the same year, were removed from the narrative.[61] More often, in *Storm of Steel* Jünger took the autodiegetic perspective of an agile, enthusiastic-for-battle group leader who, as a "heroic individualist," defied the danger of losing his relevance amid a highly mechanized total war. For this reason, Jünger's first person narrator merely intended to reproduce the experience, to make the reader identify with the narrator, and, in the subjectivity of his life, to abstain from commentary on political and social issues and the causes of war.

Jünger had supposedly only "documented" the war in another mode, which was to be just as decisive for the literary aestheticization of the war—the processing of the struggle as an "inner experience," as he methodically reflected on in his eponymous 1922 extended essay.[62] This narrative perspective, which was exclusively focused on the experiential world of the attack troop leader (*Stoßtruppführers*) and his group, was found in almost every right- and left-wing novel appearing from 1928 onwards. It coined as well a form of timeless logic, which downplayed the political and social causes of the war and only glorified the positive and worthwhile achievements of the soldier in the war.

Even more importantly, many militaristic writers, consciously refraining from using the abstract categories of reserve lines and to some degree the "home front," leveled political accusations and assigned blame. Their ostentatious omission of soldiers who lamented the horrors of war had essentially two consequences. First, in literary terms, it was the militaristic author who had to avoid discussion of the moral dilemma of the war. Secondly, the potential for sentimentality had to remain unarticulated in order not to undermine the countless scenes of suffering and the comradeship-injected "silent heroism."

In this context, many right-wing conservative authors also seemed to adhere to another interpretation of Jünger, who served as the patron of an anti-democratic-oriented "new nationalism" that he introduced into conservative, National Socialist, and *völkisch* battles over memory during the interwar period. In 1927, Jünger wrote one of his first essays that addressed the so-called "Jewish question," "The Antinational Powers" ("Die antinationalen Mächte").[63] It dealt with the virulent question circulating in right-wing circles about whether Judaism was nation-friendly, patriotic, or internationalist, thus questioning Judaism's place and modes of action in the German Reich. Where National Socialist antisemitic concepts played a key ideological role and propagated the segregation of Judaism as a central solution to the re-establishment of Germany into a great European power, Jünger regarded the antisemitic worldview as over-emphasized in the more general ideology of "new nationalism." For this reason, Jünger rejected the reduction of nationalism to the clarification of the "Jewish question" and he called such an approach a "great darkness and narrowing of the horizon."[64] In addition, he felt that the "new nationalism" in its current form should not "hold the view that the German question is resolved by the Jewish question."[65]

In another example of programmatic writing from 1929 titled "'Nationalism' and Nationalism" ("'Nationalismus' und Nationalismus"),[66] Jünger reiterated the fundamental differences between Wilhelmian nationalism of the old school and a revolutionary nationalism of a new form, in which he once again explained the importance of antisemitism. He wrote that it was not the "main characteristic of the nationalist, that at breakfast he already ate three Jews—antisemitism is not a question of essential importance to him."[67] Finally, Jünger published a further programmatic statement, his "Closing Words to an Essay"; here he wrote, "the questions of antisemitism played themselves out on a subordinate stage."[68]

Jünger was in no way a "friend of the Jews," as right-wing circles liked to claim when he made such ideological assumptions. All of the statements cited here were quotes from sentences, which—as if to excuse their core claims—were surrounded by the most profoundly despicable antisemitic passages in which Jünger used a pseudo-biological, thoroughly racist, and conspiratorial discourse, which was in no way more subtle or cryptic than that used by the National Socialists.[69] Nevertheless, in regard to the genre of fictional war literature, it must be said that such questions were fought mainly at the level of political publications, for example non-fiction specialized journalism, but not in the fictitious worlds of pro-war writings, in which the conservative masterpiece of the First World War, *Storm of Steel*, became well-known in the Weimar Republic.

When focusing on general remarks about epoch-transforming changes in war literature that came in the midst of two contradictory political systems, it is necessary to examine at least two examples of war novels that the National Socialists produced in the 1920s, in which the integration of antisemitic narrative elements was to be expected: Richard Euringer's 1929 novel *Flight School 4: Logbook of the Unit (Fliegerschule 4: Buch der Mannschaft)*[70] and Hans Zöberlein's 1931 *Faith in Germany (Der Glaube an Deutschland)*.[71] But if anyone looks in these National Socialist works for conspiracy theories about a long-planned "Aryan genocide" in the world war carried out by "the elders of Zion," they are looking in vain. Even "old fighters," that is, party members who had already joined the Nazi Party before 1933, rejected such demagogic interpretations when writing their war novels. For example, the expressionist flying novel *Flight School 4* presented the militaristic narrative, as discussed earlier, of the comradeship-affirming novel, as evoked in typical novels about storm troops (*Stoßtrupps*) by Werner Beumelburg such as *Group Bosemüller (Gruppe Bosemüller*, 1930) or Josef Magnus Wehner's *Seven in Front of Verdun (Sieben vor Verdun*, 1930). Even in the Christianity-infused passages typical of pro-war novels, in which the sufferings of the front soldiers were juxtaposed with the Passion of Christ, Euringer did not include any antisemitic references.[72]

It is remarkable that such a deeply ideologically influenced Nazi author such as Hans Zöberlein, who believed in National Socialism so strongly that he still had deserters executed as late as April 1945, maintained that his work *Faith in Germany* (*Der Glaube an Deutschland*, 1931), signed with a foreword by Hitler, offered antisemitism only as cheap sensationalism. Even when the "stab-in-the-back" legend would have offered him excellent possibilities for distorting history, Zöberlein restrained himself in his 890-page literary "running amok" (Stefan Busch).[73] It was only at the very end of the book that a single word, "treason," blatantly articulated blame.[74] In the final chapter, "Peace," Jews first appeared as the cause of the defeat, but only in ephemeral passages on the last pages of a nearly 900-page novel. Here Zöberlein described the reception of returning front soldiers by communist revolutionaries: "Outside the platform came a group of these sloppy, filthy Red Guards, the guns with the muzzles down."[75] These "dark figures" were described by the author as Jews:

> It [the soldier's conscience] is like a mirror that always remains the same, which never dims. We can look into it, and an honest soldier's spirit looks at us. But today's gentlemen [Jews and Communists] cannot. Judas, who betrayed his master by thirty pieces of silver, grins at them, if they look into it. Yet the one whom Judas betrayed remains the master.[76]

The techniques of representation and focal points of argumentation in *Flight School 4* and *Faith in Germany* can thus be assessed as covering nearly the same ground as many other conservative war novels. For this reason, the interjection of antisemitic ideas can hardly be counted as *differentia specifica*, used to distinguish a genuinely National Socialist version of the world war from a purely nationalist one.

Jews, then, were not explicitly included in nationalist war narratives, but they were also not directly excluded. By simply ignoring this cohort, a familiar semantic image could emerge—for example the confession-less, classless, and thus political hybrid figure of the "unknown front soldier"—which Jews were also reading about, and with whom they could also identify. It was exactly the same Jewish veterans of the world war who in the wake of the "Jew Count" and the "stab-in-the-back" legend found themselves under constant pressure to re-emphasize their own efforts to defend the fatherland. Part of the reason, though not the sole purpose, for the establishment of the Reichsbund jüdischer Frontsoldaten in February 1919, was to counter the numerous accusations from the political right while also celebrating Jewish heroism and the fundamental bond between Jews and the German nation.

An example of this celebration of Jewish heroism can be found in the work of Friedrich Sternthal, who was raised as a Jew and reviewed in the liberal *Literarische Welt* (edited by Willy Haas and Ernst Rowohlt) Werner Beumelburg's 1929 literary-influenced monograph on the world war, *Barrage of Fire around Germany* (*Sperrfeuer um Deutschland*). In what he professed was a "passionate search for truth," Sternthal—and one must put this extensive praise into the right context—glorified the book as representative of soldierly nationalism.[77] Beumelburg had fought on the Western Front from 1916 to 1918.[78] In both his war novels, which came out in 1920s,[79] as well as in his right-wing conservative journalism,[80] the young author presented himself as a nationalist-militarist who advocated that Germany return to its status as a leading European great power through further war. Where Sternthal's characterization of Beumelburg's monograph in the 1920s was full of praise, in contrast Kurt Sontheimer, a social democratic-oriented historian, was far more scathing in his 1962 work, *Anti-Democratic Thinking in the Weimar Republic*. Sontheimer called the book "the most one-sided thing that has ever been written about it [i.e., the First World War]," and he criticized the fundamentally right-wing character of this work.[81]

Contemporaries saw this quite differently. According to Sternthal, for example, Beumelburg renounced the cheap sensationalism of the "stab-in-the-back"[82] legend—which the author himself said actually had happened[83]—and instead identified "mistakes"[84] of the people, the military, and the political system. Sternthal summarized *Sperrfeuer* as a book that was consistently critical of Germany. He praised the fact that, in spite of the militaristic tenor of Beumelburg's work, from critical hindsight it "did not miss anything. It's all there: the madness of the Hindenburg program, which they did not dare to carry out properly, and whose half-heartedness had disastrous results. The nonsense of rationing … The mistakes of erroneous financial regulation," which led to the devastating inflation of 1923.[85]

In his critiques of Beumelburg, Sternthal was quite perceptive and he in no way ignored Beumelburg's point, which can be regarded as "contrapuntal." That is, the "heroism of a whole people and the heroism of the individual soldier were clearly distinguished from the incompetence of German statesmen and the unimaginativeness of the Supreme Army Command." Although the glimmering image of the "professional officer" appeared only occasionally in *Sperrfeuer*, Sternthal nevertheless praised the work as a "heroic song, which tells the truth," and he recommended it to the youth, "who only know the war from hearsay"[86]—not to prepare them for war as Beumelburg intended, but to make them detest it. For contemporary readers such as

Sternthal, nationalism, which seemed to be injected with considerable subtlety in *Sperrfeuer*, was not too great a stumbling block, and the book merely gave a picture of what happened, in his eyes, over the course of four years.

The seeming absence of an explicit, nationalist agenda allowed journalists like Alfred Kantorowicz, who was raised in a liberal Jewish household, joined the Communist Party in 1931, and who had published the works of Heinrich Mann, to offer perspectives similar to Sternthal on the representation of soldier nationalism in *Sperrfeuer*. In a review of Jünger's collected volume *War and Warriors* (*Krieg und Krieger*, 1930), Kantorowicz argued that the appeal to the nation among soldier-nationalists was primarily based on "metaphysical" reasons, which obscured the "secular" intentions of the texts.[87] Never, according to Kantorowicz, are there speeches about the state or its citizens in the books, but rather it is always about the abstract idea of the nation and its constant efforts to defend itself. The more malleable or suited for the masses these nationalist conceptions were, the more effective they were in making a connection between the values and maxims of front soldiers and the indoctrinated reading public.

Moreover, there were special interest groups like the Association of National German Jews (Verband der nationaldeutschen Juden), which advocated nationalistic, anti-democratic, and militaristic interests, and who were in line with the master narrative of the First World War created by right-wing conservative authors in the 1920s. Amid the controversy that erupted over Remarque, Zweig, and Renn from 1929 onwards, the Association decisively took the side of the new nationalists grouped around Ernst Jünger. In this context, the Association's press organ, *The German National Jew* (*Der nationaldeutsche Jude*), gradually developed into a cultural magazine, which, through the discussion and evaluation of pro-war titles, pursued a semitic-nationalist cultural policy. During this period in which there was a flood of war literature, the Association gave a forum to militaristic writers like Friedrich Hielscher, Fritz Meyer-Schönbrunn, and Franz Schauwecker.[88]

Max Naumann, the founder and chairman of the Association, wrote specifically against Zweig's *Grischa*, who in his opinion denied the "lively, warm-blooded totality [*blutwarme Ganzheit*]"[89] of the German people. Zweig, with his decidedly Zionist and pacifist views, was one of the greatest adversaries of the Association, which constantly brought him into conflict with Naumann. Thus, the Association stood behind conservative representations of the war, like the new nationalists who embraced Ernst Jünger. The "pacifist-humanitarian questioning of the 'national German' legitimacy of war,"[90] whether from someone like Renn, Remarque, or Zweig, did not find any traction within the Association.

Continuities in Conservative War Literature, 1933–39

The first phase of nationalist war narratives, which stretched until the outbreak of the Second World War, was marked by two dominant strands: first, the disintegration of a pacifist interpretation of war and its philosemitic ideology; and second, the continued articulation of conservative-nationalist world war narratives. These had given the National Socialists a valuable cultural and psychological boost during the Weimar years, and would undergo numerous new editions after 1933.[91]

Although it is not possible to undertake an exhaustive review of every single new edition published, what can be confirmed is that the existing conservative paradigm continued into the Nazi years, with war narratives that for the most part rejected antisemitism.[92] Up until 1936, this trend can be attributed to the following reasons: on the one hand, National Socialism was, after only fourteen years, a relatively new political movement, which in the short period of its existence would have been unlikely to have produced literary talents who shared the Nazis' ideological worldview. Committed National Socialist war authors such as Thor Goote, Hanns Johst, Richard Euringer, and Hans Zöberlein had hardly been able to contend with the dominant conservative camp centered on Ernst Jünger. Therefore, the nationalist-conservative elites, who had been crucial for the "seizure of power," and were furthermore needed for the intellectual mobilization of the German population for a new war, and for the construction of the *Wehrmacht*, were irreplaceable in the initial phases of the NS dictatorship. For this very reason they were saturated with official titles and benefices as their literary production was brought into the state's sphere of influence. The re-establishment of numerous conservative war narratives and their canonization in classroom instruction was in this case a means of domesticizing these books, making them dependent on the state.[93]

At the same time, the regime had its own international concerns, which meant it initially tempered the radicalization of conservative war narratives. Up until 1936, the regime pursued a dual agenda: it prepared for war behind the scenes, while simultaneously maintaining a public policy of appeasement and concealment vis-à-vis the concerned European powers.[94]

In 1936, for example, the city of Berlin, the National Socialist Cultural Community, and the Reich War Victims Care Association invited several "reliable" authors to an annually held writers' week in Berlin. From 6 to 10 October, experienced authors on the First World War were to hold lectures and presentations at Berlin's schools and cultural institutions.[95] At the same time, however, several prominent Nazis articulated pseudo-pacifist demands in speeches held before the war writers at the Charlottenburg Palace. In the course of Hitler's peace overtures, Bernhard Rust, the Minister of Science, Education, and National Culture, stylized the invited war writers into banner-bearers of peace-thinking (*Friedensgedanken*). The world war, Rust claimed, had been a "mass murder of the Aryan Peoples," something that could never be allowed to repeat itself, and he actually thanked the assembled war writers for framing the war precisely in this spirit![96] In this way, war narratives were shaped by internal political consolidations as well as outward appeasement.

Interpreting the Significance of Second World War Narratives, 1939–45

How, then, was the war novel, which represented a co-mingling of narratives, sustained as a literary medium after the beginning of the Second World War? Due to the problematic availability of sources, this question can be answered only vaguely. There was actually a range of factors that brought the flood of war literature, which had continued unabated until 1939, to an end.[97] First, with the start of the war, a shortage of paper set in.[98] Second, many writers were called up for military service. And third, many battles—and in the end the entire war—resulted in defeat. As a result, many of the nascent, unfinished works simply disappeared after 1945, and were deemed politically contaminated by their writers.

Nevertheless, the few available literary sources enable us to draw the conclusion that at the beginning of the Second World War the image of the enemy was dramatically radicalized and deeply associated with communists and Jews, which in most cases were conflated. Such a linkage between communists and Jews is exemplified in Hitler's speech on the eighth anniversary of the "seizure of power" on 30 January 1939. Speaking to the Reichstag, Hitler prognosticated threateningly:

> And on this memorable day for us Germans, and perhaps for others as well, I would like now to make a pronouncement on one more matter; I

have often been a prophet in my life and have been mostly laughed at ... Today, I want once more to be a prophet: If international finance Jewry in and outside Europe succeeds in plunging the peoples into *yet another* world war, then the end result will not be the bolshevization of the earth and the consequent victory of Jewry, but the annihilation of the Jewish race in Europe.[99]

Aside from the contradiction that an alleged "finance Jewry" would support a "bolshevization of the earth," Hitler established the connection between political movements (Bolshevism) and religious confessions (Jewry); with the proverbial collocation "yet another," he placed the blame for the outbreak of the First World War squarely on the Jews. This can be considered a key change to the national conservative war narrative, which had previously never proclaimed such an argument. Hitler thereby reiterated a passage from the second edition of *Mein Kampf* from 1927, in which he had characterized Jews as instigators of the world war and had equated them with communists:

> Kaiser Wilhelm II was the first German Kaiser to offer the leaders of Marxism his hand in reconciliation without suspecting that these scoundrels have no honor. While they held the Kaiser's hand in their own, their other hand reached for the dagger. There can be no deal-making with the Jews, only an either or. That is when I decided to become a politician.[100]

Thus, Hitler gave an explicitly antisemitic parameter of meaning in his public speech before the Reichstag, shortly before the outbreak of the Second World War. He thereby established a close connection between interpretation and wartime deployment, which most likely encouraged the writers loyal to the regime to adopt this strategy.

One of the few examples that at least partially answers the question, how literary narratives of the Second World War would have played themselves out, is Edwin Erich Dwinger's 1940 book, *A Death in Poland*.[101] Written by request of the Reich Propaganda Ministry, Dwinger legitimized the invasion of Poland by describing in graphic detail over the course of the 170 pages the alleged persecution, deportation, torture, rape, and murder of ethnic Germans by Poles, thereby giving justification to Nazi Germany's attack on its eastern neighbor in 1939. Dwinger's attempt to stage a permanent rationalization served foremost to construct an image of Poland—and with it, the communists—as a "Jewish enemy." In the final sections of the novel, chapters 12, 15, and 16, Dwinger introduced antisemitic stereotypes as German civilians are deported to Warsaw. In these final chapters, the Poles are exposed as Jews who proceed to mercilessly murder their opponents:

"I often heard a soldier say," old Rausch resumes, "when a badly injured White [a member of the bourgeois, nationalist faction] fell into their [Polish] hands and the Red Jewish Commissar wanted to let him die without even a bandage: 'Wrap him up a bit anyway, for God's reward — even this man had a mother who labored to give birth to him!' Have you ever, even once, heard a Pole say something like that?"[102]

In this propaganda novel, Dwinger also appropriates the antisemitic stereotype of the greedy Jew, who is so fixated on war profiteering that he forgets who the actual "enemy" is. Dwinger portrayed the "Caftan Jews" in Warsaw's Nalewki Jewish quarter as beating the German deportees "with their umbrellas, in a rage."[103] The author thereby implements a new image of the enemy.

If we finally take a look at Hitler's political testament from 29 April 1945, one of the last documents produced by the collapsing National Socialist state, we can see that here the dictator for the last time connects his statements from 1927 and 1939 about the alleged guilt of Jews for the world wars.[104] In his last breaths, Hitler once again assigned the full burden of guilt for the outbreak of both the First and the Second World War.[105] One day before his suicide inside the "Führer-Bunker" in Berlin, the dictator reckoned this with a reference to his voluntary participation during the "forced world war" of 1914, with the much hated, and in 1945 nearly annihilated, religious community. In order to legitimize the Second World War as well as the mass murder of the European Jews, the departing chancellor invoked his statements from 1939: it is "false," claimed Hitler, "that I or anyone else in Germany had wanted the war in 1939. It was desired and instigated exclusively by those international statesmen who were either of Jewish descent or worked for Jewish interests."[106] Hitler further claimed: "Centuries will pass away, but out of the ruins of our towns and monuments the hatred against those finally responsible whom we have to thank for everything, international Jewry and its helpers, will grow."[107] Moreover, he had "made it quite plain that, if the peoples of Europe are again to be regarded as mere shares to be bought and sold by these international conspirators in money and finance, then that race, Jewry, which is the real criminal of this murderous struggle, will be saddled with the responsibility."[108] In this manner, the narrative of the First World War was channeled into that of the Holocaust, which, Hitler stated in his final proclamation, was to be perpetuated *ad infinitum*, as he called on the German people and the new leaders he named in his testament "to scrupulous observance of the laws of race and to merciless opposition to the universal poisoner of all peoples, international Jewry."[109] With Hitler's death, this narrative came to an abrupt end. Scarcely any of the "Landser novels" of the 1950s adopted this narrative, for now a new myth emerged in the literature. Numerous war novels glorified the military feats of the Wehrmacht, making it necessary, as we know today, to conceal the proven involvement of the Wehrmacht in the murder of the European Jews, and to push the blame on the members of the SA and SS. The purpose of this literature was the preservation of the myth of the "clean Wehrmacht," which left no place for a Jewish protagonist of any kind.

Conclusion

If Jews were excluded from nationalist discourse as alleged "enemies of the nation" until 1914, the beginning of the First World War opened the possibility for them to return to the nation by sacrificing their lives for the "fatherland." Having focused on war literature written after 1918, this chapter asked whether nationalist-conservative, non-Jewish authors included or excluded Jews in their official interpretations of the First World War, and how this narrative was preserved, even throughout the intensification of antisemitic discourse in 1933–45. It argued that during the Weimar Republic, the dominant narrative of the First World War served numerous nationalist and militaristic narrative strands, but generally renounced the integration of racist and, above all, antisemitic elements. In spite of the range of narrative possibilities afforded by antisemitic variants of the "stab-in-the-back" legend, there is no evidence that this pronounced antisemitic discourse made its way into nationalist-conservative narratives of the First World War. Because many nationalist writers concentrated mainly on the image of the "unknown front soldier," Jews and Jewish veterans' associations also had the opportunity to appeal to and interpret this symbolic figure in their reception of these works, providing Jewish soldiers with a means to also demonstrate their "loyalty to the fatherland." After 1933, this narrative continuity persisted, due largely to the continuity of personnel in the nationalist-conservative nomenclature of war writing, as well as because of Nazi peace propaganda. With regard to the narrative on the world war from 1939 onwards, which was also written by nationalist-conservative authors of the old school, the Nazi regime gave concrete guidelines for interpretation, which were aimed primarily towards establishing "the Jew" as the enemy of a National Socialist Germany. This radicalization took place, in particular, by creating an ideological link between communists and Jews, who in this new interpretation bore the burden of the guilt for the outbreak of both the First and Second World Wars.

Florian Brückner is a research associate at the Chair of Modern History in Stuttgart. He studied history and philosophy at the universities of Munich and Helsinki and received his Ph.D. from the University of Stuttgart in 2016. His monograph, *In der Literatur unbesiegt: Werner Beumelburg (1899–1963). Kriegsdichter in der Weimarer Republik und im Nationalsozialismus* (LIT Verlag, 2017) examined the life and work of Werner Beumelburg and how literature about the First World War was perceived by contemporaries. His current research project focuses on the political transformation of the duchy of Baden and the kingdom of Württemberg from monarchies to democratic republics in 1918/19.

Notes

1. Quoted from Heinrich Claß, the director of the Alldeutschen Verbandes, in Johannes Leicht, "Heinrich Claß," in *Handbuch des Antisemitismus: Judenfeindschaft in Geschichte und Gegenwart*, vol. 2/1, ed. Wolfgang Benz (Munich, 2009), 141–44, here 142.
2. See Christiane Barz, *Weltflucht und Lebensglaube: Aspekte der Dekadenz in der skandinavischen und deutschen Literatur der Moderne um 1900* (Leipzig, 2003).
3. Steffen Bruendel, *Volksgemeinschaft oder Volksstaat: Die "Ideen von 1914" und die Neuordnung Deutschlands im Ersten Weltkrieg* (Berlin, 2003), 67.
4. Wilhelm II, "An das deutsche Volk!" *Neue Preußische Zeitung*, 7 August 1914, morning edition.
5. Key socialist and communist thinkers like Karl Marx, Moses Hess, Ferdinand Lassalle, Rosa Luxemburg, Leo Trotzki, and Léon Blum were of Jewish origins.
6. Werner E. Mosse, "Die Krise der europäischen Bourgeoisie und das deutsche Judentum," in *Judentum in Krieg und Revolution 1916–1923*, ed. Werner E. Mosse and Arnold Paucker (Tübingen, 1971), 1–26, here 10, 13.
7. Thomas Schneider, Julia Heinemann, and Frank Hischer, eds., *Die Autoren und Bücher der deutschsprachigen Literatur zum Ersten Weltkrieg 1914–1939: Ein bio-bibliographisches Handbuch* (Göttingen, 2008), 9.
8. Karl Prümm, *Die Literatur des soldatischen Nationalismus der 20er Jahre*, 2 vols. (Kronberg, 1974).
9. See unknown author, "Sperrfeuer," *Die höhere Schule im Freistaat Sachsen* 7, no. 19/20 (1929): 327.
10. On theories of myth construction, see Jan Assmann, *Das kulturelle Gedächtnis: Schrift, Erinnerung und politische Identität in frühen Hochkulturen* (Munich, 1997), 76; Hans Blumenberg, *Arbeit am Mythos* (Frankfurt a. M., 1984), 40–67; see also Maurice Halbwachs, *Das kollektive Gedächtnis* (Frankfurt a. M., 1991).
11. Mosse, " Die Krise der europäischen Bourgeoisie," 8–14.

12. Thomas Nipperdey, *Deutsche Geschichte 1866–1918*, vol. 2, *Machstaat vor der Demokratie* (Munich, 1998), 310f.
13. Ibid.; on antisemitic agitation from 1918 to 1939, see Alfred Kruck, *Geschichte des Alldeutschen Verbandes 1890–1939* (Wiesbaden, 1954), 130–34.
14. Saul Friedländer, "Die politischen Veränderungen der Kriegszeit und ihre Auswirkungen auf die Judenfrage," in Mosse and Paucker, *Judentum in Krieg und Revolution*, 27–65, here 37–38.
15. Ibid.
16. Ibid.
17. Ibid.
18. See Rainer Sammet, *"Dolchstoss": Deutschland und die Auseinandersetzung mit der Niederlage im Ersten Weltkrieg (1918–1933)* (Berlin, 2003), 115–21; on antisemitic accusations of the "stab-in-the-back" legend during the revolution of Kurt Eisner, see Boris Barth, *Dolchstoßlegenden und politische Desintegration: Das Trauma der deutschen Niederlage im Ersten Weltkrieg 1914–1933* (Düsseldorf, 2003), 224–27; on the origins of the alleged association between Jews and communists, see Agnieszka Pufelska, "Bolschewismus," in *Handbuch des Antisemitismus: Begriffe, Theorien, Ideologien*, vol. 3, ed. Wolfgang Benz et al. (Berlin, 2010), 46–48, here 47f.
19. Such was his explanation on 18 November 1919, in Herbert Michaelis and Ernst Schraepler, eds., *Ursachen und Folgen: Vom deutschen Zusammenbruch 1918 und 1945 bis zur staatlichen Neuordnung Deutschlands in der Gegenwart. Eine Urkunden- und Dokumentensammlung zur Zeitgeschichte*, 4 vols (Berlin, 1958), 7f.
20. On the relevant representatives of "soldier nationalism," see Armin Mohler and Karlheinz Weissmann, eds., *Die Konservative Revolution in Deutschland 1918–1932: Ein Handbuch* (Graz, 2005), 497–99.
21. Bruendel, *Volksgemeinschaft oder Volksstaat*, 67.
22. Ulrich Herbert, "Echoes of the Volksgemeinschaft," in *Visions of Community in Nazi Germany: Social Engineering and Private Lives*, ed. Martina Steber and Bernhard Gotto (Oxford, 2014), 60–69, here 60.
23. Hans Ulrich Wehler, *Deutsche Gesellschaftsgeschichte*, vol. 4, *Vom Beginn des Ersten Weltkriegs bis zur Gründung der beiden deutschen Staaten 1914–1949* (Munich, 2003), 16.
24. "Verhandlungen des Reichstags, dreizehnte Legislaturperiode. Zweite Session 1914," Opening session, 4 August 1914, *Reichstagsprotokolle, 1914/18*, 1, retrieved 18 May 2015 from http://www.reichstagsprotokolle.de/Blatt_k13_bsb00003402_00012.html.
25. Mohler and Weissmann, *Die Konservative Revolution in Deutschland*, 497–99.
26. Hans Ulrich Thamer argues that the "national community" (*Volksgemeinschaft*) had already developed into a "dominant political form of interpretation" in Germany before 1933. See "Volksgemeinschaft: Mensch und Masse," in *Erfindung des Menschen: Schöpfungsträume und Körperbilder 1500–2000*, ed. Richard von Dülmen (Vienna, 1998), 367–88, here 367. On the conceptual history of the *Volksgemeinschaft*, compare Norbert Götz's observations in *Die Konstruktion von nationalsozialistischer*

Volksgemeinschaft und schwedischem Volksheim (Baden-Baden, 2001), 63–83, here 68.
27. Ernst Glaeser, *Jahrgang 1902* (Berlin, 1929), 115.
28. Ibid., 103.
29. Ernst Klee, *Das Kulturlexikon zum Dritten Reich: Wer war was vor und nach 1945* (Frankfurt a. M., 2007), 184.
30. Thomas Kühne, *Kameradschaft: Die Soldaten des nationalsozialistischen Krieges und das 20. Jahrhundert* (Göttingen, 2006), 58–67.
31. See, for example, the debates over numerous war novels in the press organ of the KPD, *Die Rote Fahne*, in Karl August Wittfogel, "Romane über den imperialistischen Krieg," *Die Rote Fahne* 13, no. 160 (26 July 1930).
32. Peter Panter (Kurt Tucholsky), "Der Streit um den Sergeanten Grischa," *Die Weltbühne* 23, no. 50 (13 December 1927): 892.
33. See the explanations on this by Gerd Koenen, *Der Russland-Komplex: Die Deutschen und der Osten, 1900–1945* (Munich, 2005), 74.
34. For an example of the National Socialists' strategies at defamation, see unknown author, "Erich Maria Remarque," in *Völkischer Beobachter/ Bayernausgabe* 4, no. 3 (16 March 1929).
35. Erich Maria Remarque, *Der Weg zurück* (Cologne, 1931), 229. See also the illuminating afterword by Thilmann Westphalen, 315f.
36. Ibid., 33.
37. People in this description were often also members of the General Staff who judged according to official manuals and regulations. See Florian Brückner, *In der Literatur unbesiegt: Werner Beumelburg (1899–1963)— Kriegsdichter in der Weimarer Republik und im Nationalsozialismus* (Berlin, 2017), 119.
38. Remarque, *Der Weg zurück*, 33.
39. Ibid.
40. Ibid., 253.
41. The basis for this statement is in the following body of sources: Ernst Jünger, *In Stahlgewittern* (Berlin, 1920) and *Der Kampf als inneres Erlebnis* (Berlin, 1922); Werner Beumelburg, *Douaumont* (Oldenburg, 1929), *Ypern 1914* (Oldenburg, 1925), *Loretto* (Oldenburg, 1927), *Flandern 1917* (Oldenburg, 1928), *Sperrfeuer um Deutschland* (Oldenburg, 1929), and *Die Gruppe Bosemüller* (Oldenburg, 1930); Richard Euringer, *Fliegerschule 4: Buch der Mannschaft* (Hamburg, 1929); Franz Schauwecker, *Aufbruch der Nation* (Berlin, 1929) and *Der feurige Weg* (Berlin, 1930); Josef Magnus Wehner, *Sieben vor Verdun* (Munich, 1930); Hans Zöberlein, *Der Glaube an Deutschland* (Munich, 1931); Walter Bloem, *Frontsoldaten* (Leipzig, 1930) and *Heiliger Frühling: Ein Roman junger Deutscher im Kriege* (Berlin, 1933); Paul Ettighoffer, *Gespenster am toten Mann* (Gütersloh, 1931); Thor Goote, *Wir fahren den Tod* (Gütersloh, 1930); Hans Henning Grote, *Die Höhle von Beauregard: Erlebnis der Westfront 1917* (Berlin, 1930). See also the work of Jörg Lehmann, which includes an extensive body of sources: Jörg Lehmann, *Imaginäre Schlachtfelder: Kriegsliteratur in der Weimarer Republik. Eine literatursoziologische Studie* (Bonn, 2003).

42. Horst Heidermann, "Auf dem Weg zum Führer: Walter Bloem," in *Geschichte im Wuppertal*, vol. 15, ed. Bergischer Geschichtsverein Wuppertal (Neustadt an der Aisch, 2006), 28–44, here 30–32, retrieved 28 February 2017 from http://www.bgv-wuppertal.de/GiW/Jg15/4Bloem.pdf.
43. See also Rodler Morris who places this novel in the center of his book: Rodler F. Morris, *From Weimar Philosemite to Nazi Apologist: The Case of Walter Bloem* (Lewiston, 1988).
44. Walter Bloem, *Brüderlichkeit* (Leipzig, 1922), 290.
45. Heidermann, "Auf dem Weg zum Führer," 33.
46. Unknown author, "Binding-Briefe: Randerscheinungen," *Der Spiegel* 11, no. 46 (13 November 1957): 56–61.
47. Ibid.
48. Arthur Moeller van den Bruck, *Das Recht der jungen Völker* (Munich, 1919); Oswald Spengler, *Der Untergang des Abendlandes*, 2 vols. (Vienna, 1918/22).
49. Lehmann, *Imaginäre Schlachtfelder*, 60.
50. Sven Olaf Berggötz, ed., *Ernst Jünger: Politische Publizistik 1919–1933* (Stuttgart, 2001), epilogue, 861–66; Jan Robert Weber, *Ästhetik der Entschleunigung: Ernst Jüngers Reisetagebücher (1934–1960)* (Berlin, 2011), 40, 392; Helmuth Kiesel, *Ernst Jünger: Die Biographie* (Munich, 2007), 309–16; Steffen Martus, *Ernst Jünger* (Stuttgart, 2001), 55–57.
51. The antisemitic tendencies in the Stahlhelm, which had actually been working together with the Reichsbund jüdischer Frontsoldaten in pragmatic political affairs, were varied. See Brian E. Crim, *Antisemitism in the German Military Community and the Jewish Response, 1914–1938* (Lanham, MD, 2014), 33–64; Volker Berghahn, *Der Stahlhelm: Bund der Frontsoldaten 1918–1935* (Düsseldorf, 1966), 64ff., 84, 239ff., 256; and Tim Grady, *The German-Jewish Soldiers of the First World War in History and Memory* (Liverpool, 2011), 63f., 91–93.
52. The majority of war novels were focused on the strategically more decisive Western Front (see note 41).
53. Olaf Simons, "Werner Beumelburg," retrieved 9 July 2015 from http://www.polunbi.de/pers/beumelburg-01.html; Beumelberg, *Douaumont* (*Schlachten des Weltkrieges*, vol. 8), *Ypern 1914* (*Schlachten des Weltkrieges*, vol. 10), *Loretto* (*Schlachten des Weltkrieges*, vol. 16), and *Flandern 1917* (*Schlachten des Weltkrieges*, vol. 27).
54. Beumelberg, *Loretto*, 81f.
55. Ibid.
56. Beumelberg, *Flandern 1917*, 67.
57. Ibid., 85.
58. See, for example, Beumelberg, *Douaumont*, 57, 83.
59. See Klaus Hammer "'Einmal die Wahrheit über den Krieg schreiben': Ludwig Renns Krieg im Urteil der Zeitgenossen," in *Kriegserlebnis und Legendenbildung: Das Bild des "modernen" Krieges in Literatur, Theater, Photographie und Film*, vol. 1, ed. Thomas Schneider (Osnabrück, 1999), 283–90, here 284; Wojciech Kunicki, "Erich Maria Remarque und Ernst

Jünger: Ein unüberbrückbarer Gegensatz?" in Schneider, *Kriegserlebnis und Legendenbildung,* 291–307.
60. See Nicolas Detering, ed., *Populäre Kriegslyrik im Ersten Weltkrieg* (Münster, 2013).
61. Compare this against Jörg Lehmann's thesis, in which he argues that the "majority of war books use ... the stab-in-the-back legend as a strong narrative moment." Lehmann bases his claim mainly on biographical memoir literature, which he also classifies as war literature. See Lehmann, *Imaginäre Schlachtfelder,* 291.
62. Jünger, *Der Kampf als inneres Erlebnis.*
63. Jünger, "Die antinationalen Mächte," in Berggötz, *Ernst Jünger,* 291–96 (quoted from Arminius, *Kampfschrift für deutsche Nationalisten* 8, no. 5 [30 January 1927]: 3–5).
64. Ibid., 295.
65. Ibid.
66. Jünger, "'Nationalismus' und Nationalismus," in Berggötz, *Ernst Jünger,* 501–9 (quoted from *Das Tagebuch,* Berlin, 10, no. 38 [21 September 1929]: 1552–58).
67. Ibid., 504.
68. Jünger, "Schlußwort zu einem Aufsatze," in Berggötz, *Ernst Jünger,* 538–46 (quoted from *Widerstand: Zeitschrift für nationalrevolutionäre Politik* 5, no. 1 [1930]: 8–13).
69. See Jünger's essay on nationalism and the "Jewish question" in the deeply antisemitic *Süddeutschen Monatsheften*: Jünger, "Über Nationalismus und Judenfrage," in Berggötz, *Ernst Jünger,* 587–92 (quoted from *Süddeutsche Monatshefte* 27, no. 12 [1930]: 843–45).
70. Euringer, *Fliegerschule 4.*
71. Zöberlein, *Der Glaube an Deutschland.*
72. For example, Euringer, *Fliegerschule 4,* 254–58.
73. Stefan Busch, *"Und gestern, da hörte uns Deutschland": NS-Autoren in der Bundesrepublik. Kontinuität und Diskontinuität bei Friedrich Griese, Werner Beumelburg, Eberhard Wolfgang Möller und Kurt Ziesel* (Würzburg, 1998), 106.
74. Zöberlein, *Der Glaube an Deutschland,* 870.
75. Ibid.
76. Ibid., 871.
77. Friedrich Sternthal, "Ein neuartiges Kriegsbuch," *Die literarische Welt* 6, no. 3 (1930): 5.
78. Brückner, *In der Literatur unbesiegt.*
79. See note 53.
80. Beumelburg worked between 1920 and 1924 for the *Deutsche Soldatenzeitung,* the *Deutsche Allgemeine Zeitung,* as well as the *Düsseldorfer Nachrichten.*
81. Kurt Sontheimer, *Antidemokratisches Denken in der Weimarer Republik: Die politischen Ideen des deutschen Nationalismus zwischen 1918 und 1933* (Munich, 1962), 136.
82. See note 77.

83. Beumelburg explicitly pointed out in his private correspondence that he had used the "stab-in-the-back" legend. Letter from Werner Beumelburg to Marie Beumelburg, 3 November 1929, Private Collection Kläre Schlarb (Meisenheim).
84. Sternthal, "Ein neuartiges Kriegsbuch."
85. Ibid.
86. Ibid.
87. Alfred Kantorowicz, "Krieg und Krieger," *Die literarische Welt* 3, no. 9 (1927): 5.
88. Matthias Hambrock, *Die Etablierung der Außenseiter: Der Verband Nationaldeutscher Juden 1921–1935* (Cologne, 2003), 318.
89. Ibid., 319, there cited after Max Naumann, "Grischa-Kunst," *Der Nationaldeutsche Jude* 5, no. 10 (October 1928): 3f., originally published 17 October 1928 in the *Berliner Börsen-Zeitung*, reprinted under the title "Ein Wort über Arnold Zweig" in the *Chemnitzer Tageblatt*, no. 337 (5 December 1930).
90. Hambrock, *Die Etablierung der Außenseiter*, 319.
91. Schneider, Heinemann, and Hischer, *Die Autoren*, 10.
92. Karl Prümm, "Das Erbe der Front: Der antidemokratische Kriegsroman der Weimarer Republik und seine nationalsozialistische Fortsetzung," in *Die deutsche Literatur im Dritten Reich: Themen—Traditionen—Wirkungen*, ed. Horst Denkler (Stuttgart, 1976), 138–64, here 139f.
93. Ulrike Vorwald, *Kriegsliteratur im Unterricht zwischen 1929 und 1939 und Werner Beumelburgs Roman "Die Gruppe Bosemüller"* (Ludwigsfelde, 2005), 39f.
94. Max Domarus, *Hitler: Reden und Proklamationen 1932–1945*, 4 vols. (Wiesbaden, 1973).
95. Unknown author, "Wer kommt zum Kriegsdichtertreffen," *Völkischer Beobachter* 49, no. 264 (20 September 1936).
96. Unknown author, "Dichtung aus völkischem Bewußtsein," *Völkischer Beobachter* 49, no. 283 (9 October 1936).
97. Schneider, Heinemann, and Hischer, *Die Autoren*, 9–11.
98. See the secret general situation report of the Sicherheitsdienst (SD) from 22 August and 28 October 1940 regarding paper shortage, in Heinz Boberach, ed., *Meldungen aus dem Reich: Die geheimen Lageberichte des Sicherheitsdienstes des SS 1938–1945*, vol. 5 (Herrsching, 1985), 1492 / no. 117, 1713 / no. 136.
99. Author's emphasis. Max Domarus, *Hitler: Reden und Proklamationen*, vol. 3, 1939–1940, part II, 1058, 1047–1073 (Leonberg, 1977). See also note 94 and bibliography.
100. Adolf Hitler, *Mein Kampf*, vol. 2 (Munich, 1927), 225.
101. Edwin Erich Dwinger, *Der Tod in Polen* (Jena, 1940).
102. Ibid., 114.
103. Ibid., 159.
104. Adolf Hitler, "Mein politisches Testament," retrieved 7 March 2018 from http://www.1000dokumente.de/index.html?c=dokument_de&dokument=0228_hte&object=facsimile&l=de.

105. Regarding Hitler's claims about the First World War, see Gerhard Hirschfeld, "Der Führer spricht vom Krieg: der 1. Weltkrieg in den Reden Adolf Hitlers," in *Nationalsozialismus und Erster Weltkrieg*, ed. Anke Hoffstadt, Arndt Weinrich, and Gerd Krummeich (Essen, 2010), 35–51.
106. Hitler, "Mein Politisches Testament," 4f.
107. Ibid., 5.
108. Ibid.
109. Ibid., 7.

Bibliography

Assmann, Jan. *Das kulturelle Gedächtnis: Schrift, Erinnerung und politische Identität in frühen Hochkulturen*. Munich: C. H. Beck, 1997.

Barth, Boris. *Dolchstoßlegenden und politische Desintegration: Das Trauma der deutschen Niederlage im Ersten Weltkrieg 1914–1933*. Düsseldorf: Droste Verlag, 2003.

Barz, Christiane. *Weltflucht und Lebensglaube: Aspekte der Dekadenz in der skandinavischen und deutschen Literatur der Moderne um 1900*. Leipzig: Kirchhof & Franke, 2003.

Berggötz, Sven Olaf, ed. *Ernst Jünger: Politische Publizistik 1919–1933*. Stuttgart: Klett-Cotta, 2001.

Berghahn, Volker. *Der Stahlhelm: Bund der Frontsoldaten 1918–1935*. Düsseldorf: Droste, 1966.

Beumelburg, Werner. *Douaumont*. Oldenburg: Stalling Verlag, 1923.

———. *Flandern 1917*. Oldenburg: Stalling Verlag, 1928.

———. *Die Gruppe Bosemüller*. Oldenburg: Gerhard Stalling, 1930.

———. *Loretto*. Oldenburg: Stalling Verlag, 1927.

———. *Sperrfeuer um Deutschland*. Oldenburg: Gerhard Stalling, 1929.

———. *Ypern 1914*. Oldenburg: Stalling Verlag, 1925.

Binding, Rudolf. *Aus dem Kriege*. Frankfurt a. M.: Rütten & Loening, 1925.

———. *Erlebtes Leben*. Frankfurt a. M.: Rütten & Loening, 1928.

Bloem, Walter. *Brüderlichkeit*. Leipzig: Grethlein & Co, 1922.

———. *Das eiserne Jahr*. Leipzig: Grethlein & Co, 1910.

———. *Frontsoldaten*. Leipzig: Grethlein, 1930.

———. *Heiliger Frühling: Ein Roman junger Deutscher im Kriege*. Berlin: Neufeld & Henius, 1933.

———. *Die Schmieder der Zukunft*. Leipzig: Grethlein & Co, 1912.

———. *Volk wider Volk*. Leipzig: Grethlein & Co, 1912.

Blumenberg, Hans. *Arbeit am Mythos*. Frankfurt a. M.: Suhrkamp Verlag, 1984.

Boberach, Heinz, ed. *Meldungen aus dem Reich: Die geheimen Lageberichte des Sicherheitsdienstes des SS 1938–1945*. 5 vols. Herrsching: Pawlak, 1985.

Brückner, Florian. *In der Literatur unbesiegt: Werner Beumelburg (1899–1963) — Kriegsdichter in der Weimarer Republik und im Nationalsozialismus*. Berlin: LIT Verlag, 2017.

Bruendel, Steffen. *Volksgemeinschaft oder Volksstaat: Die "Ideen von 1914" und die Neuordnung Deutschlands im Ersten Weltkrieg*. Berlin: De Gruyter, 2003.

Busch, Stefan. *"Und gestern, da hörte uns Deutschland": NS-Autoren in der Bundesrepublik. Kontinuität und Diskontinuität bei Friedrich Griese, Werner Beumelburg, Eberhard Wolfgang Möller und Kurt Ziesel*. Würzburg: Königshausen u. Neumann, 1998.

Crim, Brian E. *Antisemitism in the German Military Community and the Jewish Response, 1914–1938*. Lanham, MD: Lexington Books, 2014.

Detering, Nicolas, ed. *Populäre Kriegslyrik im Ersten Weltkrieg*. Münster: Waxmann, 2013.

Domarus, Max. *Hitler: Reden und Proklamationen 1932–1945*. 4 vols. Wiesbaden: Bolchazy-Carducci, 1973.

Dwinger, Edwin Erich. *Der Tod in Polen*. Jena: Diedrichs Verlag, 1940.

Ettighoffer, Paul. *Gespenster am toten Mann*. Gütersloh: C. Bertelsmann, 1931.

Euringer, Richard. *Fliegerschule 4: Buch der Mannschaft*. Hamburg: Hanseatische Verlagsanstalt, 1929.

Friedländer, Saul. "Die politischen Veränderungen der Kriegszeit und ihre Auswirkungen auf die Judenfrage." In *Deutsches Judentum in Krieg und Revolution*, edited by Werner E. Mosse and Arnold Paucker, 27–65. Tübingen: Mohr Siebeck, 1971.

Glaeser, Ernst. *Jahrgang 1902*. Berlin: Gustav Kiepenheuer, 1929.

Goote, Thor. *Wir fahren den Tod*. Gütersloh: C. Bertelsmann, 1930.

Götz, Norbert. *Die Konstruktion von nationalsozialistischer Volksgemeinschaft und schwedischem Volksheim*. Baden-Baden: Nomos Verlag, 2001.

Grady, Tim. *The German-Jewish Soldiers of the First World War in History and Memory*. Liverpool: Liverpool University Press, 2011.

Grote, Hans Henning. *Die Höhle von Beauregard: Erlebnis der Westfront 1917*. Berlin: Mittler, 1930.

Halbwachs, Maurice. *Das kollektive Gedächtnis*. Frankfurt a. M.: Suhrkamp Verlag, 1991.

Hambrock, Matthias. *Die Etablierung der Außenseiter: Der Verband Nationaldeutscher Juden 1921–1935*. Cologne: Böhlau, 2003.

Hammer, Klaus. "'Einmal die Wahrheit über den Krieg schreiben': Ludwig Renns *Krieg* im Urteil der Zeitgenossen." In *Kriegserlebnis und Legendenbildung: Das Bild des "modernen" Krieges in Literatur, Theater, Photographie und Film*, vol. 1, edited by Thomas Schneider, 283–290. Osnabrück: Universitätsverlag Rasch, 1999.

Heidermann, Horst. "Auf dem Weg zum Führer: Walter Bloem." In *Geschichte im Wuppertal*, 15 vols., edited by Bergischer Geschichtsverein Wuppertal, 28–44. Neustadt an der Aisch: Selbstverlag, 2006. Retrieved 28 February 2017 from http://www.bgv-wuppertal.de/GiW/Jg15/4Bloem.pdf.

Herbert, Ulrich. "Echoes of the Volksgemeinschaft." In *Visions of Community in Nazi Germany: Social Engineering and Private Lives*, edited by Martina Steber and Bernhard Gotto, 60–69. Oxford: Oxford University Press, 2014.

Hirschfeld, Gerhard. "Der Führer spricht vom Krieg: der 1. Weltkrieg in den Reden Adolf Hitlers." In *Nationalsozialismus und Erster Weltkrieg*, edited by Anke Hoffstadt, Arndt Weinrich, and Gerd Krummeich, 35–51. Essen: Klartext, 2010.

Hitler, Adolf. *Mein Kampf*. 2 vols. Munich: Eher Verlag, 1927.

———. "Mein politisches Testament." Retrieved 7 March 2018 from http://www.1000dokumente.de/index.html?c=dokument_de&dokument=0228_hte&object=facsimile&l=de.

Jünger, Ernst. "Die antinationalen Mächte." In *Ernst Jünger: Politische Publizistik 1919–1933*, edited by Sven Olaf Berggötz, 291–96 (quoted from *Arminius, Kampfschrift für deutsche Nationalisten* 8, no. 5 [30 January 1927]: 3–5). Stuttgart: Klett-Cotta, 2001.

———. *Der Kampf als inneres Erlebnis*. Berlin: Mittler Verlag, 1922.

———. *In Stahlgewittern*. Berlin: Mittler & Sohn, 1920.

———. *Krieg und Krieger*. Berlin: Junker und Dünnhaupt, 1930.

———. "'Nationalismus' und Nationalismus." In *Ernst Jünger: Politische Publizistik 1919–1933*, edited by Sven Olaf Berggötz, 501–9 (quoted from *Das Tagebuch*, Berlin, 10, no. 38 [21 September 1929]: 1552–58). Stuttgart: Klett-Cotta, 2001.

———. "Schlußwort zu einem Aufsatze." In *Ernst Jünger: Politische Publizistik 1919–1933*, edited by Sven Olaf Berggötz, 538–46 (quoted from *Widerstand: Zeitschrift für nationalrevolutionäre Politik* 5, no. 1 [1930]: 8–13). Stuttgart: Klett-Cotta, 2001.

———. "Über Nationalismus und Judenfrage." In *Ernst Jünger: Politische Publizistik 1919–1933*, edited by Sven Olaf Berggötz, 587–92 (quoted from *Süddeutsche Monatshefte* 27, no. 12 [1930]: 843–45). Stuttgart: Klett-Cotta, 2001.

Kantorowicz, Alfred. "Krieg und Krieger." *Die literarische Welt* 3, no. 9 (1927): 5.

Kiesel, Helmuth. *Ernst Jünger: Die Biographie*. Munich: Siedler, 2007.

Klee, Ernst. *Das Kulturlexikon zum Dritten Reich: Wer war was vor und nach 1945*. Frankfurt a. M.: Fischer Verlag, 2007.

Koenen, Gerd. *Der Russland-Komplex: Die Deutschen und der Osten, 1900–1945*. Munich: C. H. Beck, 2005.

Kruck, Alfred. *Geschichte des Alldeutschen Verbandes 1890–1939*. Wiesbaden: Franz Steiner, 1954.

Kühne, Thomas. *Kameradschaft: Die Soldaten des nationalsozialistischen Krieges und das 20. Jahrhundert*. Göttingen: Vandenhoeck & Ruprecht, 2006.

Kunicki, Wojciech. "Erich Maria Remarque und Ernst Jünger: Ein unüberbrückbarer Gegensatz?" In *Kriegserlebnis und Legendenbildung: Das Bild des "modernen" Krieges in Literatur, Theater, Photographie und Film*, vol. 1, edited by Thomas Schneider, 291–307. Osnabrück: Universitätsverlag Rasch, 1999.

Lehmann, Jörg. *Imaginäre Schlachtfelder: Kriegsliteratur in der Weimarer Republik. Eine literatursoziologische Studie*. Bonn: Freie Universität Berlin Universitätsbibliothek, 2003.

Leicht, Johannes. "Heinrich Claß." In *Handbuch des Antisemitismus: Judenfeindschaft in Geschichte und Gegenwart*, vol. 2/1, edited by Wolfgang Benz, 141–44. Munich: Saur, 2009.

Martus, Steffen. *Ernst Jünger*. Stuttgart: J. B. Metzler, 2001.

Michaelis, Herbert, and Ernst Schraepler, eds. *Ursachen und Folgen: Vom deutschen Zusammenbruch 1918 und 1945 bis zur staatlichen Neuordnung Deutschlands in der Gegenwart. Eine Urkunden- und Dokumentensammlung zur Zeitgeschichte*. 4 vols. Berlin: Wendler, 1958.

Moeller van den Bruck, Arthur. *Das Recht der jungen Völker*. Munich: Piper, 1919.
Mohler, Armin, and Karlheinz Weissmann, eds. *Die Konservative Revolution in Deutschland 1918–1932: Ein Handbuch*. Graz: Stocker Leopold, 2005.
Morris, Rodler F. *From Weimar Philosemite to Nazi Apologist: The Case of Walter Bloem*. Lewiston: Mellen, 1988.
Mosse, Werner E. "Die Krise der europäischen Bourgeoisie und das deutsche Judentum." In *Judentum in Krieg und Revolution 1916–1923*, edited by Werner E. Mosse and Arnold Paucker, 1–26. Tübingen: Mohr Siebeck, 1971.
Nipperdey, Thomas. *Deutsche Geschichte 1866–1918*, vol. 2, *Machstaat vor der Demokratie*. Munich: C. H. Beck, 1998.
Panter, Peter (Kurt Tucholsky). "Der Streit um den Sergeanten Grischa." *Die Weltbühne* 23, no. 50 (13 December 1927): 892–899.
Prümm, Karl. "Das Erbe der Front: Der antidemokratische Kriegsroman der Weimarer Republik und seine nationalsozialistische Fortsetzung." In *Die deutsche Literatur im Dritten Reich: Themen—Traditionen—Wirkungen*, edited by Horst Denkler, 138–64. Stuttgart: Reclam, 1976.
———. *Die Literatur des soldatischen Nationalismus der 20er Jahre*, 2 vols. Kronberg: Skriptor Verlag, 1974.
Pufelska, Agnieszka. "Bolschewismus." In *Handbuch des Antisemitismus: Begriffe, Theorien, Ideologien*, edited by Wolfgang Benz et al., 3 vols, 46–48. Berlin: De Gruyter, 2010.
Remarque, Erich Maria. *All Quiet on the Western Front*. Berlin: Propyläen Verlag, 1929.
———.*Der Weg zurück*. Cologne: Kiepenheuer & Witsch, 1931.
Renn, Ludwig. *War*. Frankfurt a. M.: Frankfurter Societäts-Druckerei, 1928.
Sammet, Rainer. *"Dolchstoss": Deutschland und die Auseinandersetzung mit der Niederlage im Ersten Weltkrieg (1918–1933)*. Berlin: trafo, 2003.
Schauwecker, Franz. *Aufbruch der Nation*. Berlin: Frundsberg Verlag, 1929.
———. *Der feurige Weg*. Berlin: Frundsberg Verlag, 1930.
Schneider, Thomas, Julia Heinemann, and Frank Hischer, eds. *Die Autoren und Bücher der deutschsprachigen Literatur zum Ersten Weltkrieg 1914–1939: Ein bio-bibliographisches Handbuch*. Göttingen: Vandenhoeck & Ruprecht, 2008.
Simons, Olaf. "Werner Beumelburg." Retrieved 9 July 2015 from http://www.polunbi.de/pers/beumelburg-01.html.
Sontheimer, Kurt. *Antidemokratisches Denken in der Weimarer Republik: Die politischen Ideen des deutschen Nationalismus zwischen 1918 und 1933*. Munich: Nymphenburger Verlag, 1962.
Spengler, Oswald. *Der Untergang des Abendlandes*. 2 vols. Vienna: Verlag Braumüller, 1918/22.
Sternthal, Friedrich. "Ein neuartiges Kriegsbuch." *Die literarische Welt* 6, no. 3 (1930): 5.
Thamer, Hans Ulrich. "Volksgemeinschaft: Mensch und Masse." In *Erfindung des Menschen: Schöpfungsträume und Körperbilder 1500–2000*, edited by Richard von Dülmen, 367–88. Vienna: Böhlau, 1998.
Unknown author. "Binding-Briefe: Randerscheinungen." *Der Spiegel* 11, no. 46 (13 November 1957): 56–61.

Unknown author. "Dichtung aus völkischem Bewußtsein." *Völkischer Beobachter* 49, no. 283 (9 October 1936).
Unknown author. "Erich Maria Remarque." *Völkischer Beobachter/Bayernausgabe* 4, no. 3 (16 March 1929).
Unknown author. "Sperrfeuer." *Die höhere Schule im Freistaat Sachsen* 7, no. 19/20 (1929): 327.
Unknown author. "Wer kommt zum Kriegsdichtertreffen." *Völkischer Beobachter* 49, no. 264 (20 September 1936).
Vorwald, Ulrike. *Kriegsliteratur im Unterricht zwischen 1929 und 1939 und Werner Beumelburgs Roman "Die Gruppe Bosemüller"*. Ludwigsfelde: Ludwigsfelde Verlaghaus, 2005.
Weber, Jan Robert. *Ästhetik der Entschleunigung: Ernst Jüngers Reisetagebücher (1934–1960)*. Berlin: Matthes & Seitz, 2011.
Wehler, Hans Ulrich. *Deutsche Gesellschaftsgeschichte*, vol. 4, *Vom Beginn des Ersten Weltkriegs bis zur Gründung der beiden deutschen Staaten 1914–1949*. Munich: C. H. Beck, 2003.
Wehner, Josef Magnus. *Sieben vor Verdun*. Munich: Verlag Albert Langen, 1930.
Wilhelm II. "An das deutsche Volk!" *Neue Preußische Zeitung*, 7 August 1914.
Wittfogel, Karl August. "Romane über den imperialistischen Krieg." *Die Rote Fahne* 13, no. 160 (26 July 1930).
Zöberlein, Hans. *Der Glaube an Deutschland*. Munich: Eher-Verlag, 1931.
Zweig, Arnold. *The Case of Sergeant Grischa*. Potsdam: Kiepenheuer, 1927.

Afterword

GERMAN JEWRY AND THE FIRST WORLD WAR
Beyond Polemic and Apologetic
Derek Jonathan Penslar

Polemics and apologetics are battles fought with words. The former, taken from the ancient Greek word for war (*polemos*), is a verbal attack, a biting critique, and the latter, the *apologia*, is a speech of defense. In language, as in battle, offense and defense are intermingled. Since antiquity, Jews have responded to polemics against them with attacks against their accusers and justifications of the worth of their faith and their way of life. In the Middle Ages, the verbal battle between Jews, Christians, and Muslims centered on the interpretation of Scripture. In modernity, the subject shifted to the Jews' cultural creativity, economic utility, and capacity for good citizenship. In Germany, the nineteenth-century practitioners of Judaic scholarship, known as the *Wissenschaft des Judentums*, remained engaged in the cycle of polemic and apologetic, producing works that glorified the textual fruits of Jewish civilization and denigrated the intolerance and fanaticism of the Jews' gentile oppressors.

The suitability of Jews for military service lay at the center of debates about Jewish emancipation in modern Europe. Opponents of emancipation claimed that Jews lacked honor, courage, and a spirit of sacrifice, and that they cared for no one but themselves. This was a misandrist discourse in that it targeted Jewish men, accusing them of being weak, cowardly, and prone to shirk hard work of any kind, let alone the rigors and dangers of military service. These polemics elicited a volley of apologetic Jewish responses such as rabbinical sermons protesting Jewish patriotism, historical accounts of Jewish military service throughout the ages, articles in the Jewish press glorifying the valor of Jewish soldiers, especially officers, and statistics documenting the presence of Jews in every European war, and on every side. Ironically, the fact that Jews were now armed soldiers serving in the armies of Europe and dying on its battlefields did nothing to reduce the quantity or intensity of verbal skirmishes between Jews and their opponents.

The legacy of apologetic and polemic loomed over German Jewry in the First World War. Jewish activists rushed to prepare statistical studies documenting their brethren's role in the war effort and refuting antisemitic accusations that Jews were profiteering from the war economy. After 1918, German Zionists, stung by antisemitism before and during the war, produced a new brand of polemic, denouncing the German Jewish symbiosis as illusory. Liberal and assimilationist Jews, on the other hand, cranked up the production of apologetics. Jewish periodicals repeated over and again that a full 100,000 Jews had served Germany during the war and that 12,000 had died. There was, in fact, nothing remarkable about those numbers, given that some 15 percent of mobilized Germans died during the war, and that the percentage of German Jews who were mobilized was slightly lower than that of Germans as a whole. But apologetics employ statistics for rhetorical purposes, not scholarly ones. They are no more inherently accurate than polemics. Thus, scholars must view them as primary sources, as expressions of sensibility and desire, not of historical truth, although they may lead us to that truth.

After the Second World War, apologetic and polemic, like binary planets, continued to exert a gravitational pull upon each other in the production of German Jewish historiography. Emigré scholars, transplanted from Central Europe to the United States, the United Kingdom, and Israel, continued to document both the Jewish contribution to modern Germany—a contribution that included military service for king, emperor, and fatherland in the First World War—and the betrayal of German Jewry by their Christian fellows, a betrayal epitomized in the notorious "Jew Count" ordered by the German army in 1916. In Germany, non-Jewish scholars also began to explore the subject. Confronted with the legacy of Nazism, which denied the Jews any place in the German *Volksgemeinschaft*, they implicitly maintained venerable apologetic tropes about Jewish patriotism, valor, and sacrifice.

Over the past twenty years, these frameworks have begun to crumble, with new forms of understanding rising to take their place. There has not been a radical revisionism that replaces one narrative with another—the basic story of German Jewish participation in the war remains largely intact—or that adopts an opposite political valence, and thereby a new polemical approach. But the affective base of historiographical inquiry on German Jewry during the First World War has changed. German Jewish apologetics and polemics from the *fin de siècle* through the 1930s were nourished by feelings such as hope or pride, which are associated with the imminent fulfillment of desire, or by opposed feelings such as disappointment, desperation, or anger, which are associated with desire's frustration. After 1945, literature on German Jewry in the First World War, responding to the destruction of European Jewish civilization in the Holocaust, no longer engaged in the debate about the possibilities for integration. For scholars writing in the Holocaust's aftermath, feelings elicited by anticipation or betrayal gave way to melancholy over loss and a sense of mission to bear witness, to document lives lost or interrupted.

Closer to our own day, however, scholars are approaching the subject as observers, not witnesses, and their affective base is sympathy, not empathy. As the field of modern Jewish history has been increasingly integrated into universities throughout the English-speaking world, and to a growing extent in Germany, historians have challenged the notion of a separate German Jewish war experience. While acknowledging the distinctiveness of groups, they are aware of the fluid nature of collective identifications. At a distance of three generations from the Holocaust, they reconstruct the rhetorical battles of previous generations without internalizing them.

This volume employs the case of the First World War to make important contributions to what may be called a unified field of modern German and Jewish history. Several of the chapters homogenize "Jews and other Germans,"[1] showing us that the wartime experiences of German Jews, be they men in the armed forces or women on the home front, and their Christian counterparts did not necessarily differ substantively. At the same time, there is an openness to deconstructing "German" as an analytical category, making possible the study of "Jews and other Others," such as Alsatians who came under German rule in 1871. These approaches complicate, but do not deny, German Jews' feelings of solidarity with Jews in other countries during the war, or the value of comparisons between "Jews and other Jews" (for example the experiences of German and Austrian Jewry during the war), or between "present and past Jews," that is, the German Jews in the First World War and their grandfathers who fought against Austria or France in 1866 and 1870–71.

Among these innovative forms of lumping and splitting, perhaps the most promising is that which separates German Jews by class, levels of religiosity, and political orientation. Doing so provides a new approach to understanding why German Jews offered startlingly different accounts of the presence or absence of antisemitism among their wartime communities. Let us take into account insights from the study of emotions, which, it is claimed, are inseparable from their verbal articulation.[2] In turn, "experience" does not exist apart from its interpretation and representation, both of which are shaped by cognitive structures that, in the case of the subjects of this book, were well established before they took part in the war.[3]

No less diverse, we learn from this book, were Christian Germans' wartime perceptions of Jews, which ran along a spectrum from antipathy to sympathy. It is an error to group together all forms of negative feelings about Jews under the word "antisemitism," as doing so conceals the changing salience of those feelings from one person to another and the differing circumstances under which those feelings were expressed. Just as the term "situational ethnicity" has been applied to German Jews, who identified as "Jewish" or "German" depending on the circumstances, so may we speak of a "situational hostility" directed against them.[4] The relationship between these two concepts deserves further study.

Another subject for future research is the formation of communicative patterns among German Jews and the relationship between written and verbal discourse about the war. I argued earlier that varying forms of interpretation can account for whether a Jewish participant in an encounter or event involving German Christians framed it as antisemitic and whether it assumed lasting or ephemeral significance. Varying forms of representation, however, open up a different set of questions about the sources and degree of external censorship and self-censorship in wartime and postwar life writings such as letters, diaries, and memoirs. Often, war-related life writings deal with the horrors of war tersely and indirectly, yet there are spectacular exceptions. Accounting for the uneven communication of war experience, which is often repressed, sanitized, or cryptic, yet at times is vivid, detailed, and emotionally raw, presents a challenge for all social historians of modern warfare.[5] Moreover, during the First World War, on the Western Front there were channels of verbal as well as written communication of the war experience during furloughs as well as after discharge from active duty.[6]

As in much contemporary scholarship in the humanities and social sciences, so in this volume the emphasis is on fluidity, hybridity, and entanglement in human relations rather than homogeneity, essentialism, and separation. This conceptual framework rejects the zero-sum and Manichean thinking that brought on the catastrophic wars of the twentieth century and that threatens to cause even greater calamities in our own. It rejects the underlying principles of polemic and apologetic which, each in its own way, asserts consistent, all-consuming alterity. The editors' and authors' intents are admirable, their methodology is sophisticated, and their findings are valuable. The challenge they, like all future scholars of the subject, will face is that however motile and protean Difference may be, Difference still remains; that however much German Jews were truly part of their environment, they often imagined profound links with Jews elsewhere, even in remote lands, and that however contingent "situational hostility" against the Jews in wartime Germany may have been, after 1933 a new situation irrevocably recast the memory of that experience and cloaked it in shadow.

Derek Jonathan Penslar is the William Lee Frost Professor of Modern Jewish History at Harvard University. His books include *Shylock's Children: Economics and Jewish Identity in Modern Europe* (University of California Press, 2001); *Orientalism and the Jews* (with Ivan Kalmar, University Press of New England, 2005), *Israel in History: The Jewish State in Comparative Perspective* (Routledge, 2006), *The Origins of Israel, 1882–1948: A Documentary History* (with Eran Kaplan, University of Wisconsin Press, 2011), and *Jews and the Military: A History* (Princeton University Press, 2013).

Notes

1. Till van Rahden, *Jews and Other Germans: Civil Society, Religious Diversity, and Urban Politics in Breslau, 1860–1925* (Madison, 2008).
2. William Reddy, *The Navigation of Feeling: A Framework for the History of Emotions* (Cambridge, 2001).
3. On the salience of prewar cultural frameworks for the interpretation and legacy of war experience, see Benjamin Ziemann, *War Experiences in Rural Germany, 1914–1923* (London, 2007).
4. For the application of J. Y. Okamura's concept of situational ethnicity to German Jewry, see van Rahden, *Jews and Other Germans*, and Jacob Borut, "'Verjudung des Judentums': Was There a Zionist Subculture in Weimar Germany?" in *In Search of Jewish Community: Jewish Identities in Germany and Austria, 1918–1933*, ed. Michael Brenner and Derek J. Penslar (Bloomington, 1998), 92–114.
5. For a lucid statement of the problem, see William G. Rosenberg, "Reading Soldiers' Moods: Russian Military Censorship and the Configuration of Feeling in World War I," *American Historical Review* 119, no. 3 (June 2014): 714–40.

6. On this point, see Adrian Gregory, *The Last Great War: British Society and the First World War* (Oxford, 2008).

Bibliography

Borut, Jacob. "'Verjudung des Judentums': Was There a Zionist Subculture in Weimar Germany?" In *In Search of Jewish Community: Jewish Identities in Germany and Austria, 1918–1933*, edited by Michael Brenner and Derek J. Penslar, 92–114. Bloomington: Indiana University Press, 1998.

Gregory, Adrian. *The Last Great War: British Society and the First World War.* Oxford: Oxford University Press, 2008.

Rahden, Till van. *Jews and Other Germans: Civil Society, Religious Diversity, and Urban Politics in Breslau, 1860–1925.* Madison: University of Wisconsin Press, 2008.

Reddy, William. *The Navigation of Feeling: A Framework for the History of Emotions.* Cambridge: Cambridge University Press, 2001.

Rosenberg, William G. "Reading Soldiers' Moods: Russian Military Censorship and the Configuration of Feeling in World War I." *American Historical Review* 119, no. 3 (June 2014): 714–40.

Ziemann, Benjamin. *War Experiences in Rural Germany, 1914–1923.* London: Berg, 2007.

Index

Abteilung Frauen- und Jugendfürsorge (Department of Women's and Youth Welfare), 207–208
acculturation, Jewish. *See* assimilated Jewry
Adler, Victor, 55
Agnon, Shmuel Yosef, 286 ff
  and *A Guest for the Night*, 288
  "Between Two Towns", 296
  "Fernheim," 296
  From Myself to Myself, 291, 298
  The Galloping Horse, 309
  In Mr Lublin's Store, 286 ff
  To This Day, 288, 293, 294, 295, 296, 297, 299, 302, 303
  "Sign, The," 303
Alldeutscher Verband (Pan-German League), 130
Allgemeine Zeitung des Judenthums, newspaper, 36–39, 211
Alliance Israélite Universelle (Universal Jewish Alliance), 211
Allgemeiner Deutscher Frauenverein (General German Women's Association), 173, 180, 195
Alfieri, Emauel, 269
Alsace-Lorraine
  and annexation of, 35–36, 38
  casualties in the First World War, 85–86
  discrimination against, 89, 91, 92, 93, 96, 97, 100–101, 102
  Franco-Prussian War, 101
  French nationalist narrative, 82–83
  (Alsatian) Jewish soldiers 35, 37
  Ministry of, 97
  as nationally suspect, 81, 88, 90, 91, 93, 94, 95
  participants in the First World War, 85
  pensions and support for war disabled, 98–100
  pensions and support, 98–100
  treatment of under German occupation, 80–81
American Hebrew, newspaper, 150
American Jewish Committee, 153
Antisemitism
  and American society, 266
  in diaries and memoirs, 3, 61, 113–114, 181–184, 232–234, 236–238, 241
  on the combat front, 3–4, 7, 113, 116–118, 122–123, 126, 232–234, 236–239
  the Dreyfus Affair, 33, 42, 45
  in fiction, 303–304, 368–371, 375, 379, 381–382
  in film, 259, 266, 273
  in France, 41–42
  gender specific, 185
  in the Habsburg Empire, 56, 62
  on the home front, 10, 154, 171–173, 176, 298, 319–320
  the *Judenzählung* (*see* "Jew Count")
  the memory of the 1870/71 war, 42–43
  the "stab-in-the-back" (*see* "stab-in-the-back" legend)
  the psychiatric profession, 318–320, 348
  refugees, 158
  in Russia, 148, 176, 257
  stereotypes, 6, 9, 32, 125–126, 174, 237, 243–244, 381–382, 396
  in the supply lines, 64–65
  Weimar Germany, 5

Antisemitism (*cont.*)
  women's responses to, 181,
    185–187, 203, 207
Appelfeld, Aharon, 307n7
Arbeitsvermittlung (Work Placement
  Agency), Berlin, 208
Argentina, 207
Ariel, Yaakov, 305
Armenkommission (Commission for
  the Poor), 206
Aron, "Hermann", 215
Aron, Sara, 215
assimilated Jewry, 112, 113, 114, 115,
  120–123, 126–129, 133, 154–156,
  175, 305, 318, 396
assimilation. *See* assimilated Jewry
Archives israélites, newspaper, 45
Arno, Siegfried, 268
Austro-Hungarian Empire, 145–47,
  151–52, 154, 157–61, 257–258,
  262–263, 266–267, 273
  and Compromise of 1867, 56
  dissolution of, 55
  ethnic divisions, 3, 56–57
  Jewish soldiers and officers, 2, 55,
    58, 60–65, 67–70, 268 (*see also*
    Galician Jews)

Balfour Declaration, 157, 308
Baron, Devora, 286
Bauer, Max, 130
Bauer, Otto, 55
Bäumer, Gertrud, 173
Barsqueaux, Hermann Berel, 126
Ber, Ilja, 211
Berliner Jüdisches Gemeindeblatt, 211
Berliner Tageblatt, 264, 276
Berrel, August, 99
Berthold-Auerbach Lodge, Berlin,
  217
Bettannier, Albert, 82–83
Bethmann-Hollweg, Theobold von,
  79
Beutler, Joachim, 116, 124
Bing, Bernhard, 126–128
Bíró, Lajos (Ludwig), 258–262,
  265–266, 269
B'nai B'rith, 203–204, 211, 216–220
Börsen-Zeitung, 264

bourgeois, 120, 173, 179, 184, 207–208,
  364, 366, 369, 371
Brandeis, Louis, 150
Brenner, Yosef Hayim, 286
Brenon, Herbert, 261
Brest-Litovsk, Treaty of, 95
Bródy, Sándor (Alexander), 257, 260,
  267
Brulier, Nigel de, 270
Buber, Martin, 308n20
Buczacz, Galicia, 287
Bund Deutscher Frauenvereine
  (Union of German Women's
  Organizations), 173
Burgfrieden ("civil truce"), 3, 171–171,
  175, 177, 179, 240, 293, 294

Carré, Albert, 87, 104
Catholic Church and Catholics, 32,
  37, 39, 59, 60
Cassirer, Ernst, 319
Cemetery, Jewish, Berlin-Weißensee,
  214
Centralverein deutscher Staatsbürger
  jüdischen Glaubens (Central
  Association of German
  Citizenship), 146, 149, 152, 155,
  156, 160, 162, 172, 175, 218, 294
Citizens of Jewish Faith), 120, 131,
  155, 156
Christian Churches. *See also* Catholic
  Church and Protestants
  worship services, 233
Cohen, Hermann, 156
Columbia University, 151
comradeship
  and combat, 115–117, 118–120
  ideals of, 9–10, 111, 228–231, 319
  and identity, 120–124, 132–133
  conversion to Christianity, Jewish,
    122, 181
Coogan, Jackie, 265
Crémieux, Adolphe, 36
Crosland, Alan, 266

Dallwitz, Hans von, 85, 98
Damblans, Eugène, 88
Davidson, Max, 263, 265
Deimling, Berthold von, 80, 88

Degelow, Carl, 245
Delmont, Joseph, 259
De-Nazification, 246
Der Israelit, newspaper, 31–32, 43
Deutsch-Evangelischer Frauenbund (League of Protestant Women), 173
Deutsch, Gotthard, 152-153
Dienemann, Mally, 181-183
Dienemann, Max, 182
Dreyer, Carl Theodor, 259
Drückeberger. *See* shirking
Dupont, E. A., 260, 273

Eastern European Jews, 145–146, 148, 152–155, 157–161, 204, 211–212, 214–215, 257–278. *See also* Galician Jews *and* Polish Jews
Eichmann trial, 303
Ehrenberg, Albert, 217, 220
Ehrenberg, Hedwig, 217, 220
emancipation of Jews, 31, 33–38, 42–45, 122, 151, 172, 206, 289, 395
Eschmann, Eugen, 93, 94
Ersatzprodukt, 300
Etappe (rear area), 115, 125, 131
Everth, Erich, 338
Evidence of the Participation of Jewish Conscripts in the Army (*Nachweisung der beim Heere befindlichen wehrpflichtigen Juden*) questionnaire, 3, 137

Federation of American Zionists, 151
Feilchenfeld, Wilhelm, 206
Feldgebetbuch für die jüdischen Mannschaften des Heeres (Field Prayer Book for Jewish Men), 325, 331,
Film-Kurier, 264, 272
Final solution. *See* Holocaust
Ford, Henry, 266
Franco-Prussian War 1870/71
  French defeat, 36, 43
  Memory of, 31, 41, 370
Frank, Fritz, 118
Frank, Ludwig, 176, 294
Franz Joseph (Emperor), 157

Frauenkomitee der Allgemeinen Kriegshilfe, Hamburg (Women's Committee of War Relief, Hamburg), 175
French Foreign Legion, 45
French Jews
  Officer corps, 36
  self-definition, 32–34, 38–40, 45
French Revolution, 35
Freud, Sigmund, 11, 190, 197, 320
Frick, Wilhelm, 275
Fries, Otto, 263
Furthman, Jules, 265

Galician Jews, 58–60, 66–58, 145, 147–159, 160, 176, 218, 243, 257–258, 260–261, 265–275, 277, 287–288, 292, 295
Gay, Peter, 247
gender roles. *See also* masculinity
  First World War, 9–10, 120
  ideals of, 9–10, 230–232
German air force (*Luftstreitkräfte*), 228, 244–246, 323
Germanness, 112–113, 120–121, 127, 133, 145–47, 149, 154–57, 159, 160–61, 220–21, 292, 320, 348, 397
Germany
  home front, 171, 177, 182, 184, 203–221
  revolution, November 1918, 179, 185
Gibson, Vivian, 268
Goldberg, Fritz, 126
Goldmann, Felix, 156
Göring, Hermann, 228, 245–246
Gorlice-Tarnów, Battle of, 257–258, 262
Gottheil, Gustave, 151
Gottheil, Richard, 150–151
Great Britain, 217, 273
Greenberg, Leopold, 144, 148
Grenzsperre (border barrier), 171, 177

Haas, Willy, 264
Habsburg Empire. *See* Austro-Hungarian Empire
Halle, Edwin, 115–117, 119
Hall, James, 262

Halm, Alfred, 259
Harvard University, 132
Hebrew Standard, newspaper, 153
Hebrew Union College, 152–153
Heine, Heinrich, 234
Heinsheimer, Edward, 153
Hertling, Georg von, 176
Herzfeld, Levi, 38
Hilfsverein der Deutschen Juden (German Association for Assistance of German Jews), 211
Hindenburg, Paul von, 310, 332, 365, 377
Hirsch, Jenny, 178, 183
Hirschfeld, Magnus, 11
Hitler, Adolf, 132, 245, 376, 380–382
Holocaust, 5, 8, 73, 181, 185–186, 207, 229, 247, 287, 303, 382, 397
Hospitals, 208, 212–213, 216–217

Illés, Eugen, 259
immigration, 45, 145–46, 151–52, 154, 156, 161, 171, 175–177, 181, 241, 246, 291
Institut für angewandte Psychologie und psychologische Sammelforschung (Institute for Applied Psychology and Psychological Collection Research), 319, 321, 342
Israelitisch-humanitärer Frauenverein (Jewish Humanitarian Women's Association), 174
Israelitische Wochenschrift, 37
Israelitischer Frauenverein (Jewish Women's Association), 207
Italy
    and Caporetto, battle of, 72
    in the First World War, 67, 70

Jacobs, Samuel, 131
Jäger, Ernst, 275
Janovics, Jenő, 259
Janson, Victor, 259
Jeschurun, newspaper
"Jew Count" or "Jewish Census" (*Judenzählung*), 3–5, 7–8, 12, 15, 113, 114, 128–131, 154, 171, 175, 177, 184–185, 187, 229, 235, 237–238, 241, 247, 304, 365, 376, 396
Jewish Chronicle, newspaper, 144
Jewishness, 112–113, 121–123, 132–133, 145–47, 149, 154–61, 396
Jewish Theological Seminary (Breslau), 152
Jewish Soldiers' Home (*Jüdisches Soldatenheim*), 240
Jewish World, newspaper, 148, 153
Judenzählung. See "Jew Count" or "Jew Census"
Jüdische Zeitung, newspaper, 158
Jüdischer Frauenbund (League of Jewish Women), 173–174, 203, 207, 218, 220
Jüdischer Volksverein (Jewish People's Association), 204, 211–216, 219–220
Jüdisches Archiv, journal, 67
Jünger, Ernst, 351, 366, 371, 373–379, 386–388
Julian, Rupert, 272

Kallen, Horace, 151
Kampers, Fritz, 268
Katholischer Frauenbund (Catholic Women's League), 173
Kayßler, Friedrich, 273
Kirschstein, Paula, 214, 220
Kirschstein, Salli, 211, 214, 220
Klugmann, Hermann, 111–112
Koch, Alfred, 116, 118–119, 121–123, 124, 125–128
Kohner, Paul, 271
Kölnische Volkszeitung, 301
Kommunistische Partei Deutschlands (Communist Party of Germany), 183
Korda, Sándor (Alexander), 258–259
Kracauer, Siegfried, 265
Kriegserlebnis (war experience), 111–113, 114–124, 132–133, 177
Kriegshilfskommission (War Relief Commission), 204, 207, 214, 220
Krleža, Miroslav, 69–70

Lagarde, Paul de, 303–304
Laemmle, Carl, 271
Laor, Dan, 292, 305
Lasky, Jesse, 265
League of American Citizenship, 152
Lechner, Jean, 80, 82, 91, 95, 101
Leipzig Gewandhaus Orchestra, 286
Lemberg, Battle of, 258
Le Pèlerin, 87–88
Levy, Benas, 208
Levy, Henri, 81
Lewin, Adolf, 42
Lewin, Reinhold, 112
Liebknecht, Karl, 183
Lilienthal, Rosa, 211
Lipmann, Otto, 317–324, 335–355
Lissauer, Ernst, 44
Logan, James A., 102
London Times, newspaper, 144
Löwenberg, Ernst, 124–125
Lubitsch, Ernst, 261
Ludendorff, Erich, 89, 92–93, 95 130
Lusitania, 301
Luxemburg, Rosa, 183

Maccabaean, newspaper, 151
Magnes, Judah, 150
Mann, Thomas, 293
Marcuse, Harry and Mimi, 1–2
Marx, Julius, 6, 122–124, 237–239
Marshall, Louis, 150–151, 153
masculinity
   crisis of, 9, 124–126, 323–361
   ideals of, 9, 116–117, 120, 230–232, 263
   male association (Männerbund), 231
Matieson, Otto, 270
Mattoni, André, 268
Mayer, Louis, 265
Meyer, Helene, 205–208, 211, 220–221
Meyer, Otto, 117–118, 119
Meyer, Samuel, 207, 220
Milestone, Lewis, 269
military censorship
   (Militärzensurkommissionen), 7, 335
Moses, 270, 294
Moses, Hugo, 133

Mosse, George L., 318–319, 348–349, 353, 358, 360
Mosjukin, Ivan, 270–272
Moyer, Laurence, 300
Muchow, Martha, 320
Mugdan, Albrecht, 120–121
Mühsam, Hans, 211
Muslims, 59, 62, 395
Mylong-Münz, Jack, 268

Napoleon I, 31, 42
Napoleon III, 36
National Socialism, or Nazism,
   and authors, 376
   censorship, 275–276, 371
   comradeship, 231
   concentration camps, 77, 181, 241, 334
   ideology, 348, 320, 348, 383
   film, 275–276
   front community, 10, 17, 231, 236
   literature, 363–394, 376–380
   national community
      (Volksgemeinschaft), 17, 231, 236, 364, 396
   Nazi Party, 273, 331, 375
   Novemberpogrom, 111, 122, 132, 237
   Propaganda, 383
   rise of, 182, 273, 275, 303
Nationaler Frauendienst (National Women's Service), 173, 182, 220
Negri, Pola, 261–262, 264, 267
Nicholas II (Tsar), 293
Nikisch, Arthur, 286, 300
Nobel Prize, 303
Nuremberg Laws, 181, 237, 245

Oppenheim, Hermann, 11, 23
Oppenheimer, Franz, 138, 176
Oppenheimer, Moritz, 42, 50
orthodox Judaism, 58–60, 68, 112, 113, 115, 121–122, 126, 131, 153, 154, 158–159, 186, 204, 258, 268, 287, 305, 363

Palestine (Eretz Israel), 287
Pabst, Georg Wilhelm, 275
Pappenheim, Bertha, 173
Palestine, 31, 156, 181–182, 287, 303

Philbin, Mary, 270–272
Plaut, Paul Israel, 317–361
pogroms, 72, 176, 211, 257, 260, 370
Polish Jews, 58, 64, 66, 69, 175, 176, 259
Polke, Max Moses, 132
Pommer, Erich, 261, 265
Porta, Elizza la, 268
Protestants, France, 32, 37, 39
Prussia,
    government, 171–172, 175–177, 183, 185
    High Command, 171, 175, 177
    War Ministry, 3, 126, 128–129, 175
Psychiatry/Psychology
    (experimental)
    mass psychology, 340–342, 351
    Psychography of the front soldier, 317–361
    Psychological effects of war, 11–12, 317–361
    Psychotechnics, 318, 320–323, 345, 349, 352
    Zeitschrift für angewandte Psychologie und psychologische Sammelforschung (Journal of Applied Psychology and Psychological Collection Research), 320

Randolf, Rolf, 260
Rathenau, Walther, 2, 365
Reform Judaism, 112, 182, 186. See *also* assimilated Jewry
refugees, 2, 68, 111, 158, 160, 183, 218
Reichsland Elsass-Lothringen (Reichsland), 79, 82, 84, 86, 87, 88, 89, 91, 92, 95, 96, 100, 102. See *also* Alsace-Lorraine
Reichsbund jüdischer Frontsoldaten (RjF), 5, 8, 112, 130, 131, 236
Reichspogromnacht, 132, 236–237. See *also* National Socialism, *Novemberpogrom*
Reichsrat (Austrian Imperial Assembly), 159
Reinert, Robert, 11
    Nerven, film, 11
Reinhardt, Max, 294

Remarque, Erich Maria, 130, 363, 366, 368–369, 378–379
Reuveni, Aharon, 286
Ribeauvillé, 99–100
Richert, Dominik, 80, 90, 91, 93, 95, 105
Roach, Hal, 265
Road Back, The (novel), 130
Rosenau, William, 149
Rosh Hashanah, 234
Romanian front, 232–233
Rosenstein, Willy, 228, 244–246
Rosenzweig, Franz, 121, 124, 128, 189
Rothziegel, Leo, 55
Ruppin, Arthur, 287
Russian empire, 44, 115, 144, 147–149, 151, 157, 176, 258
Russian revolution, 151, 235

Schenck, Nicholas, 265
Schiff, Jacob, 150
Schocken, Zalman, 288, 290, 305, 307n14
Scholem, Gershom, 43
Schwabacher, Adolf, 153
Schwarz, Meyer, 217
Schwarz, Minna, 216–218, 220
Sebald, W.G., 290, 307, 314
Semprun, Jorge, 287
Shoah, 5. See *also* Holocaust
Shirking, 124–126, 128, 131, 365
Sieburg, Helene, 274
Siegmann, George, 262
Simmel, Georg, 115
Simon, Ernst, 112
Sloman, Edward, 260, 269, 271–272
Social Democratic Party, 55, 204
Socialism, 43–44, 55, 80
Somme, Battle of the, 38, 116, 238, 243
South Africa, 245–248
Southgate, Beverley, 287
Spartacist League, 183
Spirit of August 1914 (*Augusterlebnis*), 3, 122, 129, 172–173, 293–294
"stab-in-the-back" legend (*Dolchstoßlegende*), 3, 44, 130, 185, 229, 236, 364, 372
Stahlhelm – Bund der Frontsoldaten, 130, 371

Steinitz, Elsa, 182-183
Steinrück, Albert, 268
Stern, William, 318–324, 335, 353–361
Stiller, Mauritz, 260–261, 265, 269, 271
Stoecker, Adolf, 230
Synagogue services, 121, 123, 204–205, 233, 242–243

Tauber, Majer, 159

Überweisungsnationale (military travel book), 324, 328, 348
Univers israélite, newspaper, 38
Upper Silesia, 182

Valentino, Rudolph, 272
Vallentin, Hermann, 274
Várkonyi, Mihály, 259
Vavitch, Michael, 262
Verband der deutschen Juden, 175, 192, 223, 331
Verdun, Battle of, 116, 120
Vereinigung jüdischer Organizationen Deutschlands zur Wahrung der Rechte der Juden des Ostens (Union of German Jewish Organizations for Protecting the Rights of the Jews in the East), 176
Vidor, King, 269
Vorarlberger Wacht, newspaper, 55
Voß, Peter, 274

Wandel, Franz von, 85, 88
Wandervogel, 231
Wendel, Hermann, 80
Warburg, Felix, 152
Warburg, Max, 175
War fiction, 17, 363
  Hebrew, 286
War Press Office (*Kriegspressequartier*) in Austria-Hungary, 69
War Raw Materials Department (*Kriegsrohstoffabteilung des preußischen Kriegsministeriums*), 2

War Surveillance Office (Kriegsüberwachungsamt) in Austria-Hungary, 68
Weil, Alexandre, 41
Weimar Republic,
  and cinema, 277
  literature, 364
  Jewish culture, 288
  political divisions, 367–368, 383
  psychiatric medicine, 318
Weininger, Otto, 230
Weiss, Hillel, 303
Welfare
  charities, 203–204, 206–219
  and food supplies, 208–209, 214, 216, 219
  and fundraising, 209–211
  and refugees, 211–213, 218
  and training, 208, 219
Wendell, Hermann, 80
Widows, 204, 207
Wieruszowski, Alfred Ludwig, 180
Wieruszowski, Jenny, 179–180, 183
Wieruszowski, Ruth, 180–181
Wilder, Billy, 261
Wilhelm II (Kaiser), 115, 120, 172, 362, 367, 381, 383
Willingham Robert, 291
Wittlin, Joseph, 63, 65
women
  and feminism, 173–174, 179
  gender roles, 10, 263, 277, 301–302
  under occupation, 260, 263, 268, 271
  work on the home front, 2, 61, 171, 182, 184, 203–209, 213–221, 301

Zionism, 33, 43–44, 112–115, 121–123, 126–128, 132–133, 154–157, 186, 309, 396
Zionistische Vereinigung für Deutschland (Zionist Federation of Germany), 172
Zukor, Adolph, 265

CPSIA information can be obtained
at www.ICGtesting.com
Printed in the USA
LVHW081140071221
R170573000001B/R170573PG704918LVX00001B/1